Nāgārjuna's Treatise
On the Ten Bodhisattva Grounds

Volume Two

To refrain from doing any manner of evil,
to respectfully perform all varieties of good,
and to purify one's own mind—
This is the teaching of all buddhas.

> The Ekottara Āgama Sūtra
> (T02 n.125 p.551a 13–14)

A Note on the Proper Care of Dharma Materials

Traditional Buddhist cultures treat books on Dharma as sacred. Hence it is considered disrespectful to place them in a low position, to read them when lying down, or to place them where they might be damaged by food or drink.

Nāgārjuna's Treatise on the Ten Grounds

The Daśabhūmika Vibhāṣā

VOLUME TWO

As Translated into Chinese
By Tripiṭaka Master Kumārajīva
(c 410 CE)

Annotated Chinese-to-English Translation by Bhikshu Dharmamitra

Kalavinka Press
Seattle, Washington
www.kalavinkapress.org

KALAVINKA PRESS
8603 39TH AVE SW
SEATTLE, WA 98136 USA
(WWW.KALAVINKAPRESS.ORG)

Kalavinka Press is associated with the Kalavinka Dharma Association, a non-profit organized exclusively for religious educational purposes as allowed within the meaning of section 501(c)3 of the Internal RevenueCode. Kalavinka Dharma Association was founded in 1990 and gained formal approval in 2004 by the United States Internal Revenue Service as a 501(c)3 non-profit organization to which all donations are tax deductible.

Donations to KDA are accepted by mail and on the Kalavinka website where numerous free Dharma translations and excerpts from Kalavinka publications are available in digital format.

Edition: SZPPS-SA-Vol. 2-1019-1.0-Bilingual
Kalavinka Buddhist Classics Book 13a
Copyright © 2019 by Bhikshu Dharmamitra
All Rights Reserved
Two-Volume Set ISBN: 978-1-935413-19-6
Library of Congress Control Number: 2019432028
(Volume Two ISBN: 978-1-935413-18-9)

Kalavinka Press books are printed on acid-free paper.
Cover and interior designed by Bhikshu Dharmamitra.
Printed in the United States of America

General Table of Contents
Volume Two

Volume Two Directory to Chapter Subsections	699
Ch. 21 - Forty Dharmas Exclusive to Buddhas (Part 1)	709
Ch. 22 - Forty Dharmas Exclusive to Buddhas (Part 2)	733
Ch. 23 - Forty Dharmas Exclusive to Buddhas (Part 3)	789
Ch. 24 - Verses Offered in Praise	847
Ch. 25 - Teachings to Aid Mindfulness-of-the-Buddha Samādhi	867
Ch. 26 - The Analogy Chapter	901
Ch. 27 - A Summarizing Discussion of the Bodhisattva Practices	933
Ch. 28 - Distinctions in the 2nd Ground's Courses of Karmic Action	961
Ch. 29 - Distinctions Pertaining to Śrāvakas and Pratyekabuddhas	1031
Ch. 30 - Distinctions Pertaining to the Great Vehicle	1057
Ch. 31 - Guarding the Moral Precepts	1121
Ch. 32 - An Explanation of the Dhūta Austerities	1167
Ch. 33 - Aids to Gaining the Fruits of Śīla	1223
Ch. 34 - In Praise of the Moral Precepts	1263
Ch. 35 - The Karmic Rewards of the Moral Precepts	1277
Volume Two Endnotes	1291
Variant Readings from Other Chinese Editions	1321
Bibliography	1353
Glossary	1355
About the Translator	1367
Kalavinka Buddhist Classics' Fall, 2019 Title List	1369

Directory to Chapter Subsections
Volume Two

I.	**Chapter 21: Forty Dharmas Exclusive to Buddhas (Part 1)**	709
	A. Introduction to the Forty Dharmas Exclusive to Buddhas	709
	B. 1) Sovereign Mastery of the Ability to Fly	711
	C. 2) [The Ability to Manifest] Countless Transformations	715
	D. 3) Boundless Psychic Powers of the Sort Possessed by Āryas	717
	E. 4) Sovereign Mastery of the Ability to Hear Sounds	721
	F. 5) Immeasurable Power of Knowledge to Know Others' Thoughts	723
	G. 6) Sovereign Mastery in [Training and Subduing] the Mind	723
	H. 7) Constant Abiding in Stable Wisdom	725
	I. 8) Never Forgetting	727
	J. 9) Possession of the Powers of the Vajra Samādhi	727
II.	**Chapter 22: Forty Dharmas Exclusive to Buddhas (Part 2)**	733
	A. Q: Your Claim That Omniscience Exists Is False for these Reasons	733
	B. A: Wrong. As I Shall Now Explain, The Buddha Truly Is Omniscient	749
III.	**Chapter 23: Forty Dharmas Exclusive to Buddhas (Part 3)**	789
	A. 10) Thorough Knowing of Matters That Are Unfixed	789
	B. 11) Thorough Knowing of Formless Absorption Phenomena	795
	C. 12) The Knowledge of All Matters Related to Eternal Cessation	801
	D. 13) Thorough Knowing of Non-Form Dharmas Unrelated to Mind	803
	E. 14) The Great Powers Pāramitā	805
	F. 15) The Four Unimpeded Knowledges Pāramitā	805
	G. 16) The Pāramitā of Perfectly Complete Replies and Predictions	807
	H. 17) Invulnerability to Harm by Anyone	813
	I. 18) Their Words Are Never Spoken without a Purpose	815
	J. 19) Their Speech Is Free of Error	819
	K. 20) Complete Use of the Three Turnings in Speaking Dharma	821
	L. 21) They Are the Great Generals among All Āryas	821
	M. 22–25) They Are Able to Remain Unguarded in Four Ways	823
	N. 26–29) They Possess the Four Types of Fearlessnesses	825
	O. 30–39) They Possess the Ten Powers	829
	1. The First Power	829
	2. The Second Power	831
	3. The Third Power	833
	4. The Fourth Power	835
	5. The Fifth Power	835
	6. The Sixth Power	837
	7. The Seventh Power	837
	8. The Eighth Power	837
	9. The Ninth Power	839
	10. The Tenth Power	839

	P. 40) They Have Achieved Unimpeded Liberation	839
	Q. Summary Discussion of the Dharmas Exclusive to the Buddha	841
IV.	**Chapter 24: Verses Offered in Praise**	**847**
	A. The Importance of Praises to Mindfulness-of-the-Buddha Practice	847
	B. The Praise Verses	847
	1. Verses in Praise of the Forty Dharmas Exclusive to the Buddhas	847
	2. Verses Praising the Four Bases of Meritorious Qualities	853
	a. Verses Praising the Truth Basis of Meritorious Qualities	855
	b. Verses Praising the Relinquishment Basis of Meritorious Qualities	855
	c. Verses Praising the Quiescence Basis of Meritorious Qualities	859
	d. Verses Praising the Wisdom Basis of Meritorious Qualities	861
	3. Concluding Praise Verses	865
V.	**Chapter 25: Teachings Aiding Mindfulness-of-the Buddha Samādhi**	**867**
	A. Initial Instructions on the Mindfulness-of-the Buddha Samādhi	867
	B. Four Dharmas Capable of Bringing Forth This Samādhi	871
	C. Four More Dharmas Capable of Bringing Forth This Samādhi	873
	D. Four More Dharmas Capable of Bringing Forth This Samādhi	873
	E. Four More Dharmas Capable of Bringing Forth This Samādhi	873
	F. Four More Dharmas Capable of Bringing Forth This Samādhi	875
	G. Four More Dharmas Capable of Bringing Forth This Samādhi	875
	H. Five More Dharmas Capable of Bringing Forth This Samādhi	875
	I. Five More Dharmas Capable of Bringing Forth This Samādhi	877
	J. The Guidelines for Lay and Monastic Cultivation of This Samādhi	877
	1. Twenty Guidelines for Lay Cultivators of This Samādhi	879
	2. Sixty Guidelines for Monastic Cultivators of This Samādhi	879
	3. Fifty Dharmas Supporting Cultivation of This Samādhi	885
	K. The Benefits of Cultivating This Pratyutpanna Samādhi	889
	L. This Samādhi's Various Stations and Levels of Cultivation	895
	M. Various Qualitative Variations in How This Samādhi Manifests	895
	N. Various Abhidharmic Classifications of This Samādhi	897
	O. The Practitioner's Offerings, Roots of Goodness, and Teaching	897
	P. The Practitioner's Use of the Four Means of Attraction	899
	Q. The Practitioner's Dedication of Roots of Goodness	899
VI.	**Chapter 26: The Analogy Chapter**	**901**
	A. The Bodhisattva Should Study, Cultivate, and Reach the Grounds	901
	B. Seven Practices Characteristic of the First Ground Bodhisattva	901
	C. Eight Accomplishments Associated with Entering the First Ground	903
	D. The Essential Aspects of the Bodhisattva's First Ground Cultivation	905
	E. Additional Factors That the Bodhisattva Must Learn	907
	F. The Benefit of Knowing These Dharmas and Their Skillful Means	913
	G. An Analogy for a Bodhisattva's Knowledge of the 10 Grounds Path	913
VII.	**Chapter 27: A Summarizing Discussion of Bodhisattva Practices**	**933**
	A. A Brief Presentation Intended to Finish the First Ground Discussion	933
	B. Q: Before Finishing, Please Summarize the Bodhisattva Path	935

Directory to Chapter Subsections   701

C. A: A Series of Statements Summarizing the Bodhisattva Practices	935
1. Practice All Bodhisattva Dharmas & Abandon All Transgressions	935
2. Be Single-Minded and Non-Neglectful in Practicing Good Dharmas	937
3. Two Dharmas That Subsume the Path to Buddhahood	937
4. Three Dharmas That Subsume the Path to Buddhahood	937
5. Four Dharmas That Subsume the Path to Buddhahood	939
6. Five Dharmas That Subsume the Path to Buddhahood	939
7. Six Dharmas That Subsume the Path to Buddhahood	939
8. Seven Dharmas That Subsume the Path to Buddhahood	941
9. Eight Dharmas That Subsume the Path to Buddhahood	941
10. Nine Dharmas That Subsume the Path to Buddhahood	943
11. Ten Dharmas That Subsume the Path to Buddhahood	943
12. Faults to Be Urgently Abandoned on the Path to Buddhahood	945
a. One Fault That Must Be Urgently Abandoned on the Buddha Path	945
b. Two Faults That Must Be Urgently Abandoned on the Buddha Path	945
c. Three Faults to Be Urgently Abandoned on the Buddha Path	947
d. Four Faults to Be Urgently Abandoned on the Buddha Path	947
e. Five Faults to Be Urgently Abandoned on the Buddha Path	949
f. Six Faults to Be Urgently Abandoned on the Buddha Path	949
g. Seven Faults to Be Urgently Abandoned on the Buddha Path	951
h. Eight Dharmas to Be Urgently Abandoned on the Buddha Path	951
i. Nine Dharmas to Be Urgently Abandoned on the Buddha Path	953
j. Ten Dharmas to Be Urgently Abandoned on the Buddha Path	953
13. The 32 Dharmas of Genuine Bodhisattvas	955
14. Seven Additional Dharmas of Genuine Bodhisattvas	959
VIII. Ch. 28: Distinctions in the 2nd Ground's Karmic Actions	961
A. The Ten Resolute Intentions Necessary for Entering the 2nd Ground	961
1. The Straight Mind and the Pliant Mind	963
2. The Capable Mind	963
3. The Restrained Mind	963
4. The Quiescent Mind	963
5. The Truly Sublime Mind	963
6. The Unmixed Mind	963
7. The Unattached Mind	965
a. Q: Doesn't an Unattached Mind Contradict the Bodhisattva Vow?	965
b. A: No, One Must Accord with the Mind of Equanimity	967
c. Q: Why Must the Bodhisattva Again Develop the Straight Mind, etc.?	969
d. A: Now, on the 2nd Ground, These Minds Become Solidly Established	969
e. Q: What Is the Result of Deep Delight and Solid Establishment?	969
f. A: These Types of Mind Will Forever After Be Effortlessly Invoked	969
g. Q: What Are the Fruits of Acquiring These Ten Types of Mind?	971
h. A: He Will Attain the Second Ground and a Threefold Stainlessness	971
B. The 2nd Ground Bodhisattva's Ten Courses of Good Karmic Action	971
1. Q: How Many Are Physical, How Many Verbal & How Many Mental?	971
2. A: Physical and Mental Are Threefold and Verbal Are Fourfold	973

C.	Definitions of Each of the Ten Courses of Good & Bad Karmic Action	973
	1. Killing	973
	2. Stealing	973
	3. Sexual Misconduct	975
	4. False Speech	975
	5. Divisive Speech	977
	6. Harsh Speech	977
	7. Scattered or Inappropriate Speech	977
	8. Covetousness	977
	9. Ill Will	979
	10. Wrong Views	979
	11. Right View	979
D.	Abhidharma Categories Analyzing the 10 Courses of Karmic Action	981
	1. Twenty Factors Used in Abhidharmic Analysis of Actions	981
	2. The Twelvefold Discussion of Origins and Such	1001
	3. The Seven Types of Bad Actions, Their Origins, and Four Distinctions	1007
	4. More Subsidiary Distinctions Related to the Good and Bad Actions	1011
	5. Distinguishing "Karmic Deeds" versus "Courses of Karmic Action"	1013
	6. Four Distinctions: "Karmic Deeds" and "Courses of Karmic Action"	1015
	7. Three Kinds of Purity Used to Move Beyond the First Ground	1017
	8. The 10 Courses of Good and Bad Karma As Arbiters of One's Destiny	1019
	9. Resolving to Abide in the 10 Good Actions & Teach This to Others	1021
	10. One Should Learn the Rebirth Results of the 10 Good & Bad Actions	1023

IX. **Chapter 29: Distinctions Pertaining to the Two Vehicles** — 1031
    1. Q: Which Beings Can Use the 10 Courses to Fulfill the Śrāvaka Path? — 1031
        a. Stanza #1 Commentary — 1033
        b. Stanza #2 Commentary — 1037
        c. Stanza #3 Commentary — 1037
        d. Stanza #4 Commentary — 1039
        e. Stanza #5–6 Commentary — 1041
        f. Stanza #7 Commentary — 1041
    2. Q: Who Can Use the Ten Courses to Become a Pratyekabuddha? — 1043
        a. Stanza#1 Commentary — 1045
        b. Stanza#2 Commentary — 1045
        c. Stanza #3 Commentary — 1047
        d. Stanza #4 Commentary — 1049
        e. Stanza #5 Commentary — 1051
        f. Stanza #6–7 Commentary — 1053

X. **Chapter 30: [Distinctions Pertaining to] the Great Vehicle** — 1057
    A. Q: Which Beings Can Use the Ten Courses to Become Buddhas? — 1057
    B. A: The Ten Courses Enable Buddhahood for Beings of This Sort (Verse) — 1057
    C. An Extensive Line-by-Line Explanation of the Verse's Deep Meaning — 1059
        1. "Superiority of the Bodhisattva's Cultivation of the Ten Courses" — 1059
            a. Five Ways in Which the Bodhisattva's Practice is Superior — 1061
                1) Superiority of Vows — 1063

Directory to Chapter Subsections

2) Superiority of Solid Resolve		1063
3) Superiority of Resolute Intentions		1065
4) Superiority of Thoroughgoing Purity		1065
5) Superiority in the Use of Skillful Means		1067
2. The Bodhisattva's "Measureless Cultivation"		1067
a. Immeasurability of Time		1067
b. Immeasurability of Roots of Goodness		1067
c. Immeasurability of Objective Conditions		1069
d. Immeasurability of Ultimate Ends		1069
e. Immeasurability of Dedication of Merit		1071
3. The Bodhisattva's "Extraordinary Cultivation"		1071
a. His Extraordinary Capacity to Endure		1071
b. His Extraordinary Vigor		1071
c. His Solidity of Resolve		1073
d. His Extraordinary Wisdom		1073
e. His Extraordinary Karmic Fruits		1073
4. The Bodhisattva's Vows		1075
a. The "Solidity" of His Vows		1075
b. The "Goodness" of His Vows		1075
5. The Bodhisattva's "Great Compassion"		1077
6. The "Unimpeded" Nature of the Bodhisattva's Compassion		1077
7. The Bodhisattva's "Thorough Practice of Skillful Means"		1079
a. His Knowledge of "the Correct Place and Time"		1079
b. His Knowledge of "What Delights the Minds of Others"		1081
c. His Knowledge of "What Causes Others to Turn & Enter the Path"		1081
d. His Knowledge of "What Constitutes the Correct Sequence"		1081
e. His Knowledge of "How to Lead and Guide Beings"		1087
8. The Bodhisattva's "Patient Endurance of Pain and Anguish"		1089
9. The Bodhisattva's "Never Abandoning Any Being"		1091
10. The Bodhisattva's "Deep Delight in the Buddhas' Wisdom"		1093
11. "Delight in Those Who Practice the Buddhas' Powers & Masteries"		1095
12. The Buddhas' "Practice of the Powers"		1095
13. The Buddhas' "Practice of the Sovereign Masteries"		1097
14. The Bodhisattva's "Ability to Refute All Wrong Views"		1099
15. The Bodhisattva's "Preservation and Protection of Right Dharma"		1099
16. The Bodhisattva's "Valor"		1103
17. The Bodhisattva's "Ability to Endure"		1105
18. The Bodhisattva's "Vigor"		1107
19. The Bodhisattva's "Solid Resolve in Teaching Beings"		1109
20. The Bodhisattva's "Not Coveting His Own Happiness"		1109
21. The Bodhisattva's "Not Coveting a Measurelessly Long Life"		1111
22. The Bodhisattva's "Supremacy in All Endeavors"		1113
23. The Bodhisattva's "Freedom from Fault in All the Works They Do"		1115
24. The Bodhisattva's "Complete Purity" & "Success in Supreme Bases"		1115
25. How the Ten Courses Enable the Attainment of Buddhahood		1117

XI. Chapter 31: Guarding the Moral Precepts — 1121
A. General and Specific Results of the Ten Courses of Karmic Action — 1121
1. The Ten Courses of Good Karmic Action — 1121
   a. General Karmic Results of the Ten Courses of Good Karmic Action — 1121
   b. Specific Karmic Results of the Ten Courses of Good Karmic Action — 1121
2. The Ten Courses of Bad Karmic Action — 1123
   a. General Karmic Results of the Ten Courses of Bad Karmic Action — 1123
   b. Specific Karmic Results of the Ten Courses of Bad Karmic Action — 1123
B. The Bodhisattva's Implementation of Moral Virtue on the Path — 1125
1. Cherishing the Dharma and Increasing Kindness and Compassion — 1125
2. The Motivation to Teach Beings and Cause Them to Enter the Path — 1127
3. The Genesis of a Bodhisattva's Wish to Rescue Beings from Suffering — 1127
4. The Vow to Cause 2 Vehicles Practitioners to Enter the Mahāyāna — 1131
5. The Power of the Precepts and Deep Entry into the Second Ground — 1135
6. Reaching the 2nd Ground, the Bodhisattva May See a 1000 Buddhas — 1137
7. One Makes Offerings to the Buddhas & Receives the 10 Courses Again — 1139
8. Having Received Them Again, One Forever Upholds the Precepts — 1139
9. One Abandons Miserliness, Practices Giving, & Delights in Precepts — 1139
C. Śīla Pāramitā's Aspects, Arising, Powers, Purification & Distinctions — 1141
1. The Sixty-Five Aspects of the Perfection of Moral Virtue — 1141
2. The Arising of the Moral Precepts — 1147
3. The Powers of the Moral Precepts — 1151
4. The Purification of the Moral Precepts — 1151
5. Distinctions in the Moral Precepts — 1153
D. The Essential Constituents of Śīla (Moral Virtue) — 1155
1. Q: Does Moral Virtue Consist Only of Good Actions of Body & Speech? — 1155
2. A: No, There Are Other Factors Integral to Moral Virtue — 1155
3. The Supreme Cultivation of Moral Virtue — 1157
   a. Q: Please Explain the Bases of Supreme Cultivation of Moral Virtue — 1157
   b. A: No "I," No "Mine," No Elaboration, and Inapprehensibility — 1157
   c. Scriptural Descriptions of Supreme Cultivation of Moral Virtue — 1157
   d. The Inexhaustibility of the Bodhisattvas' Moral Virtue — 1161
4. A Clarification Regarding Aspects versus Essence of Moral Virtue — 1163

XII. Chapter 32: An Explanation of the Dhūta Austerities — 1167
A. Having Seen 10 Benefits, Wear Correct Robes and Go on Alms Round — 1167
1. The Ten Benefits of the Appropriate Robes — 1167
2. The Ten Benefits of Obtaining One's Food from the Alms Round — 1169
B. Dwelling in a Forest Hermitage — 1169
1. To Derive the Benefits of Dhūta Practice, Do Not Accept Invitations — 1169
2. Having Observed Ten Benefits, Remain in Solitude with 3 Exceptions — 1171
3. The Ten Benefits of Dwelling in Solitude in Forest Hermitage — 1171
4. When Leaving, One Should Maintain the Perception of Emptiness — 1171
5. Ten Reasons a Forest Dweller Might Come to a Temple or Stupa — 1173
6. The Forest Dweller's Vigorous Cultivation of Right Dharma — 1173
7. Scriptural Citation on the Correct Purposes of a Forest Dweller — 1175

8. The Appropriate Dharmas of a Forest Dweller	1179
9. The Means for Extinguishing Fear	1179
10. Four Cases in Which a Forest Dweller May Gather with Others	1187
11. The Aspects Defining Hermitage Dwelling Approved by the Buddhas	1189
12. Hermitage Dwelling as a Means to Fulfill the Six Perfections	1193
13. The Buddha's Four Prerequisite Dharmas for Hermitage Dwelling	1193
14. Other Bodhisattvas for Whom Hermitage Dwelling Is Beneficial	1195
15. Four Fourfold Dharmas for the Forest Dweller	1195
16. The Bad Results of Forest Dwelling without Wisdom and Vigor	1197
C. Additional Discussions of the Dhūta Austerities	1199
1. A Listing and Brief Discussion of The Other Ten Dhūta Austerities	1201
2. The Benefits of the Other Ten Dhūta Austerities	1203
a. The Ten Benefits of Wearing Cast-Off Robes	1203
b. The Ten Benefits of Taking One's Single Meal in a Single Sitting	1203
c. The Ten Benefits of Always Sitting and Never Lying Down	1205
d. The Ten Benefits of Not Accepting Food at the Wrong Time	1205
e. The Ten Benefits of Possessing Only One Three-Part Set of Robes	1205
f. The Ten Benefits of Accepting Robes Woven from Animal Hair	1207
g. The Ten Benefits of Laying out One's Sitting Mat Wherever One Is	1207
h. The Ten Benefits of Dwelling beneath a Tree	1207
i. The Ten Benefits of Dwelling in a Charnel Field	1209
j. The Ten Benefits of Dwelling out in the Open	1209
3. Additional Discussion of Matters Related to Hermitage Dwelling	1211
a. Five Types of Monks Who Dwell in a Forest Hermitage	1211
b. Additional Discussion of When One May Leave a Hermitage	1211
1) Proper Motivation When Leaving the Forest Hermitage	1213
2) Generating the Motivation to Benefit Both Self and Others	1213
c. On the Importance of Revering One's Spiritual Teacher	1215
1) On the Difficulty of Repaying the Kindness of One's Teacher	1215
2) On Maintaining the Proper Attitude toward One's Teacher	1217
3) On Taking Direction from One's Teacher	1217
4) On Not Seeking Praise or Benefit in Relating to a Teacher	1217
5) On Making the Teacher's Good Qualities Well Known	1217
6) On the Need to Become a Good Lineage-Preserving Disciple	1217
XIII. Chapter 33: Aids to Gaining the Fruits of Śīla	1223
A. On the Purification of Śīla, Moral Virtue	1223
1. Four Dharmas Enabling Purification of Moral Virtue	1223
2. Four More Dharmas Enabling Purification of Moral Virtue	1225
3. Four More Dharmas Enabling Purification of Moral Virtue	1225
4. Four More Dharmas Enabling Purification of Moral Virtue	1227
5. Four More Dharmas Enabling Purification of Moral Virtue	1235
6. Four More Dharmas Enabling Purification of Moral Virtue	1241
7. Four Kinds of Monks Who Break the Moral Precepts	1247
8. Four Kinds of Monks of Which One Should Become the Fourth	1247
a. He Who Is a Monk Only in Form and Appearance	1249

	b.	He Who Merely Feigns Extraordinary Deportment	1249
	c.	He Who Is a Monk Only for Fame and Self-Benefit	1251
	d.	The Monk Who Genuinely Carries on Right Practice	1251
	9.	Wrong Motivations for Upholding the Practice of Moral Virtue	1253
	10.	Right Motivations for Upholding the Practice of Moral Virtue	1255
	11.	The Benefits of Perfecting the Practice of Moral Virtue	1257
XIV.	**Chapter 34: In Praise of the Moral Precepts**		1263
XV.	**Chapter 35: The Karmic Rewards of the Moral Precepts**		1277
	A.	The Second Ground Bodhisattva as a Wheel-Turning King	1277
	B.	The Wheel-Turning King's Treasures	1277
	1.	His Gold Wheel Treasure	1277
	2.	His Elephant Treasure	1279
	3.	His Horse Treasure	1279
	4.	His Prime Minister of Military Affairs Treasure	1279
	5.	His Treasury Minister Treasure	1279
	6.	His Jewel Treasure	1281
	7.	His Jade Maiden Treasure	1281
	C.	Four Qualities of the Wheel Turning King	1285
	D.	A Description of a Wheel-Turning King's Domain, Rule & Qualities	1285

正體字

十住毘婆沙論卷第[11]十
　　[*]聖者龍樹造
　　[*]後秦龜茲國三藏鳩摩羅什譯
　　四十不共法品第二十一
菩薩如是以三十二相八十種好念佛生
身已。今應念佛諸功德法。所謂。
　又應以四十　　不共法念佛
　諸佛是法身　　非但肉身故
諸佛雖有無量諸法不與餘人共者有
四十法。若人念者則得歡喜。何以故。諸佛
非是色身。是法身故。如經說。汝不應但以
色身觀佛。當以法觀。四十不共法者一者
飛行自在。二者變化無量。三者聖如意無邊。
四[12]聞聲自在。五無量智力知他心。六心得
自在。七常在安慧處。八常不妄誤。九得金
剛三昧力。十善知不定事。十一善知無色定
事。十二具足通達諸永滅事。

简体字

四十不共法品第二十一

　　菩萨如是以三十二相八十种好念佛生身已。今应念佛诸功德法。所谓。

　　又应以四十　　不共法念佛
　　诸佛是法身　　非但肉身故

　　诸佛虽有无量诸法不与余人共者有四十法。若人念者则得欢喜。何以故。诸佛非是色身。是法身故。如经说。汝不应但以色身观佛。当以法观。四十不共法者一者飞行自在。二者变化无量。三者圣如意无边。四闻声自在。五无量智力知他心。六心得自在。七常在安慧处。八常不妄误。九得金刚三昧力。十善知不定事。十一善知无色定事。十二具足通达诸永灭事。

Chapter 21
Forty Dharmas Exclusive to Buddhas (Part 1)

I. Chapter 21: Forty Dharmas Exclusive to Buddhas (Part 1)
   A. Introduction to the Forty Dharmas Exclusive to Buddhas

It is in the above-discussed manner that the bodhisattva uses the thirty-two major marks and eighty secondary characteristics in his contemplative mindfulness of the Buddha's physical body. Now one should proceed to mindfulness of the dharmas exemplifying the Buddha's meritorious qualities, namely:

> One should also use the forty exclusive dharmas
> in one's contemplation of the Buddhas,
> for the Buddhas are their Dharma body
> and are not merely associated with their physical bodies.

Although the Buddhas possess countless dharmas not held in common with any other persons, there are forty dharmas that, if borne in mind, will cause one to experience joyful happiness. And why [should one bear them in mind]? It is not the case that the Buddhas are their form bodies, for they are rather to be identified with the Dharma body. This accords with this scriptural testimony: "You should not contemplate the Buddha merely in terms of his form body, for it is on the basis of Dharma that one should carry on such contemplation."

As for the forty dharmas exclusive to the Buddhas, they are as follows:[1]

  1) Sovereign mastery of the ability to fly;
  2) [The ability to manifest] countless transformations;
  3) Boundless psychic powers of the sort possessed by *āryas*;
  4) Sovereign mastery of the ability to hear sounds;
  5) Immeasurable power of knowledge to know others' thoughts;
  6) Sovereign mastery in [training and subduing] the mind;
  7) Constant abiding in stable wisdom;
  8) Never forgetting;
  9) Possession of the powers of the vajra samādhi;
  10) Thorough knowing of matters that are unfixed;
  11) Thorough knowing of matters pertaining to the formless realm's meditative absorptions;
  12) The completely penetrating knowledge of all matters associated with eternal cessation;

正體字	十三善知心不 071c25 ‖ 相應無色法。十四大勢波羅蜜。十五無礙波 071c26 ‖ 羅蜜。十六一切問答及[13]記具足答波羅蜜。 071c27 ‖ 十七具足三[14]轉說法。十八所說不空。十九 071c28 ‖ 所說無謬失。二十無能害者。二十一諸賢聖 071c29 ‖ 中大將。二十五四不守護。二十九四無所畏。 072a01 ‖ 三十九佛十種力。四十無礙解脫。是為四十 072a02 ‖ 不共之法。今當廣說。飛行自在者。諸佛飛行 072a03 ‖ 如意自在。如意滿足速疾[1]無量無礙。所以者 072a04 ‖ 何。佛若欲於虛空先舉一足次舉一足。即 072a05 ‖ 能如意。若欲舉足躡虛空[2]而去。若欲住 072a06 ‖ 立不動而去。即能得去。若結跏趺安坐而去 072a07 ‖ 亦能得去。若欲安臥而去亦復能去。若欲 072a08 ‖ 於青琉璃莖真珊瑚葉黃金為鬚如意珠臺 072a09 ‖ 無量圍繞如日初出是寶蓮花遍於空中蹈 072a10 ‖ 上而去。若欲如日月宮殿帝釋勝殿夜摩天 072a11 ‖ 兜率陀天化樂天
简体字	十三善知心不相应无色法。十四大势波罗蜜。十五无碍波罗蜜。十六一切问答及记具足答波罗蜜。十七具足三转说法。十八所说不空。十九所说无谬失。二十无能害者。二十一诸贤圣中大将。二十五四不守护。二十九四无所畏。三十九佛十种力。四十无碍解脱。是为四十不共之法。今当广说。飞行自在者。诸佛飞行如意自在。如意满足速疾无量无碍。所以者何。佛若欲于虚空先举一足次举一足。即能如意。若欲举足躡虚空而去。若欲住立不动而去。即能得去。若结跏趺安坐而去亦能得去。若欲安卧而去亦复能去。若欲于青琉璃茎真珊瑚叶黄金为须如意珠台无量围绕如日初出是宝莲花遍于空中蹈上而去。若欲如日月宫殿帝释胜殿夜摩天兜率陀天化乐天

13) Thorough knowing of the non-form dharmas unassociated with the mind;[2]
14) The great powers *pāramitā*;
15) The [four] unimpeded [knowledges] *pāramitā*;
16) The *pāramitā* of perfectly complete replies and predictions in response to questions;
17) Invulnerability to harm by anyone;
18) Their words are never spoken without a purpose;[3]
19) Their speech is free of errors and mistakes;
20) Complete implementation of the three turnings [of the Dharma wheel] in speaking Dharma;
21) They are the great generals among all *āryas*;
22–25) They are able to remain unguarded in four ways;[4]
26–29) They possess the four types of fearlessness;
30–39) They possess the ten powers;
40) They have achieved unimpeded liberation.

These are the forty dharmas exclusive to the Buddhas. We shall now discuss them more extensively, as below:

B. 1) Sovereign Mastery of the Ability to Fly

As for "sovereign mastery of the ability to fly" all buddhas fly with sovereign mastery, entirely as they wish, and with a manner and speed that are limitless and unimpeded. How is this so? If the Buddha wishes to raise one foot and then the other, walking through space in just such a fashion, then he is immediately able to do so. If he wishes to simply step into space and depart in this manner or if he wishes to simply stand motionlessly in space and depart in this way, he is immediately able to do so.

If he prefers to just sit there peacefully in the full lotus posture and depart like that, then he is also able to leave that way. If he wishes instead to lie down peacefully and then depart, he is able to leave in that way as well.

If he decides to stand upon a precious lotus blossom extending to the very boundaries of empty space, one with a blue *vaiḍūrya* stem, real coral petals, pistils of yellow gold, wish-fulfilling pearls for its pedestal, and countless sorts of surrounding phenomena, one that appears like the sun on first rising—departing in just such a fashion—then he does just that.

Or if, alternatively, he wishes to create through spontaneous psychic transformation a palace like the palaces of the sun or moon, like the supremely marvelous palace of Indra, or like those of the Yāma Heaven devas, the Tuṣita Heaven devas, the Nirmāṇarati Heaven

正體字

```
            他化自在天諸梵王等宮
072a12 ‖ 殿。隨意化作如彼宮殿坐中而去即能成
072a13 ‖ 辦。若更以餘種種因緣隨意能去。是故說
072a14 ‖ 言。隨諸所願皆能滿足。是故諸佛能以一
072a15 ‖ 步。過恒河沙等三千大千世界。有人言。佛
072a16 ‖ 能一念頃過若干[3]百千國土。有人言。若知
072a17 ‖ 佛一步一念能如是去即可得量。經中說
072a18 ‖ 諸佛力無量。是故當知。諸佛虛空飛行自在
072a19 ‖ 無量無邊。何以故。若大聲聞弟子神通自在
072a20 ‖ 以一念頃。能過百億閻浮提瞿陀尼弗婆提
072a21 ‖ 欝多羅越四大[4]王天忉利天夜摩天兜率陀
072a22 ‖ 天化樂天他化自在天梵天。一瞬中過若干
072a23 ‖ 念。積此諸念以成一日七日一月一歲。乃
072a24 ‖ 至百歲。一日過五十三億二百九十六萬六
072a25 ‖ 千三千大千世界。如是聲聞人百歲所過。佛
072a26 ‖ 一念能過。復次假令恒河中沙一沙為一[5]劫。
072a27 ‖ 有大聲聞神通第一壽命如是諸恒河沙大
072a28 ‖ 劫。於一念中過若干世界。
```

简体字

他化自在天诸梵王等宫殿。随意化作如彼宫殿坐中而去即能成办。若更以余种种因缘随意能去。是故说言。随诸所愿皆能满足。是故诸佛能以一步。过恒河沙等三千大千世界。有人言。佛能一念顷过若干百千国土。有人言。若知佛一步一念能如是去即可得量。经中说诸佛力无量。是故当知。诸佛虚空飞行自在无量无边。何以故。若大声闻弟子神通自在以一念顷。能过百亿阎浮提瞿陀尼弗婆提郁多罗越四大王天忉利天夜摩天兜率陀天化乐天他化自在天梵天。一瞬中过若干念。积此诸念以成一日七日一月一岁。乃至百岁。一日过五十三亿二百九十六万六千三千大千世界。如是声闻人百岁所过。佛一念能过。复次假令恒河中沙一沙为一劫。有大声闻神通第一寿命如是诸恒河沙大劫。于一念中过若干世界。

Chapter 21 — *Forty Dharmas Exclusive to Buddhas (Part 1)*

devas, the Paranirmita Vaśavartin Heaven devas, the Brahma Heaven kings, or like the palaces of any of the other devas, and if he then wishes to create any such palaces, sit down within them, and then depart in that fashion [in one of those flying palaces], then he is immediately able to do precisely that.

Then again, if he prefers to use any of the many other means [for flying from one place to another], then he is freely able to depart however he chooses. Hence it is said, "He is able to completely fulfill whatever wishes he makes." Consequently, with but a single step, the Buddhas can pass beyond great trichiliocosms as numerous as the sands of the Ganges.

There are those who claim that the Buddha is able to move beyond some particular number of hundreds of thousands of lands in but a single mind-moment, whereas there are yet others who claim that, if anyone [supposed he could] know that the Buddha could depart such a distance with but a single step and in but a single mind-moment, then that would be [to infer that the Buddha's abilities] could be limited. But the sutras declare that the powers of the Buddhas surpass all limits. One should therefore realize that the sovereign power of the Buddhas to freely fly through empty space is limitless and boundless.

So how is this the case? Given that one of the great *śrāvaka* disciples using his sovereign mastery of the psychic powers is able in a single mind-moment to pass beyond a hundred *koṭis* of Jambudvīpas, Avara-godānīyas, Pūrva-videhas, Uttara-kurus, Four Heavenly Kings Heavens, Trāyastriṃśa Heavens, Yāma Heavens, Tuṣita Heavens, Nirmāṇarati Heavens, Paranirmita Vaśavartin Heavens, and Brahma Heavens—and given that there are a particular number of mind-moments in the wink of an eye and given that one might aggregate enough of these mind-moments to comprise a whole day, seven whole days, a whole month, a whole year, and so forth, on up to a full hundred years, and if in only a single day, such a *śrāvaka* disciple might pass through fifty-three *koṭis* plus two million, nine hundred and sixty-six thousand, that large a number of great trichiliosms, any Buddha would still be able in a mere mind-moment to exceed that number of great trichiliocosms passed through by such a *śrāvaka* disciple in the course of a full hundred years.

Then again, if one were to allow the passage of a single kalpa for each and every grain of sand in the Ganges—and if there was a great *śrāvaka* disciple foremost in psychic powers who, across the course of a life span of kalpas as numerous as the Ganges' sands, passed through in each successive mind-moment just such a number of world systems [as described above]—and if he were to do this for a number of

正體字

```
         積如是念以為
072a29 ‖ 日月歲數以自在力盡是諸大劫數所過
072b01 ‖ 國土。佛能一念中過。諸佛飛行自在如是速
072b02 ‖ 疾。於一切鐵圍山十寶山四天[6]王處忉利
072b03 ‖ 天處夜摩兜率陀化樂他化自在梵世梵眾大
072b04 ‖ 梵少光無量光光音少淨無量淨遍淨廣果無
072b05 ‖ [7]相不廣不惱喜見妙見阿迦尼吒天如是諸
072b06 ‖ 處。大風大水劫盡火等。及諸天龍夜叉乾闥
072b07 ‖ 婆阿修[8]羅緊那羅摩睺羅伽諸天魔及梵沙
072b08 ‖ 門婆羅門及得諸神通者不能為礙。是故
072b09 ‖ 說飛行無礙。又飛行自在如意所作出沒於
072b10 ‖ 地能過石壁諸山障礙等。佛於此事勝諸
072b11 ‖ 聖人。又佛能以常身立至梵天。聲聞人所
072b12 ‖ 不能及。有如是等差別。變化自在者。變化
072b13 ‖ 事中有無量力。餘聖變化有量有邊。諸佛變
072b14 ‖ 化無量無邊。餘聖於一念中變化一身。佛
072b15 ‖ 以一念隨意變化有無量事。
```

简体字

积如是念以为日月岁数以自在力尽是诸大劫数所过国土。佛能一念中过。诸佛飞行自在如是速疾。于一切铁围山十宝山四天王处忉利天处夜摩兜率陀化乐他化自在梵世梵众大梵少光无量光光音少净无量净遍净广果无相不广不恼喜见妙见阿迦尼吒天如是诸处。大风大水劫尽火等。及诸天龙夜叉乾闼婆阿修罗紧那罗摩睺罗伽诸天魔及梵沙门婆罗门及得诸神通者不能为碍。是故说飞行无碍。又飞行自在如意所作出没于地能过石壁诸山障碍等。佛于此事胜诸圣人。又佛能以常身立至梵天。声闻人所不能及。有如是等差别。变化自在者。变化事中有无量力。余圣变化有量有边。诸佛变化无量无边。余圣于一念中变化一身。佛以一念随意变化有无量事。

mind-moments equivalent to a day, month, or year, doing so with the free exercise of all of his powers even to the exhaustion of such a number of great kalpas—all of those lands passed through by that great śrāvaka disciple during that entire time could still be passed through by a buddha in but a single mind-moment. The Buddhas may freely fly from one place to another with just such a speed as this.

In this, they cannot be obstructed by the iron-ring mountains, the ten jeweled mountains, the stations of the Four Heavenly Kings, the stations of the Trāyastriṃśa Heavens, the stations of the Yāma Heavens, Tuṣita Heavens, Nirmāṇarati Heavens, Paranirmita Vaśavartin Heavens, Brahma World Heavens, Brahma Assembly Heavens, Great Brahma Heavens, Lesser Light Heavens, Limitless Light Heavens, Light-and-Sound Heavens, Lesser Purity Heavens, Measureless Purity Heavens, Universal Purity Heavens, Vast Fruition Heavens, Non-Perception Heavens, Not Vast Heavens, No Heat Heavens, Delightful Vision Heavens, Sublime Vision Heavens, or the Akaniṣṭha Heaven.

[Nor can their flight be obstructed by] the great winds, by the great floods, or by the fires that occur at the end of the kalpa. Nor can it be obstructed by any heavenly dragon, *yakṣa, gandharva, asura, kinnara, mahoraga,* deva, Māra, Brahmā, *śramaṇa,* brahman, or anyone possessed of all the psychic powers. It is therefore said of the Buddhas that they are unimpeded in their ability to fly.

Additionally, by virtue of the sovereign mastery of their flight, they are able to exercise that ability in any manner they wish, by sinking into or emerging from the earth, or by passing through the obstructions presented by stone cliffs, mountains, and such. The Buddha is superior in this ability to any of the other *āryas.* Also, the Buddha is able to make his normal standing body reach in its height on up to the Brahma Heavens. *Śravaka* disciples are unable to match this. There are all manner of differences of this sort.

C. 2) [The Ability to Manifest] Countless Transformations

As for the Buddhas' sovereign mastery in "the ability to manifest transformations," in the matter of manifesting phenomena, they have immeasurable power to do this. The capacity to manifest transformations as possessed by the other classes of *āryas* is both measurable and bounded whereas the Buddhas' capacity to manifest transformations is measureless and unbounded.

The other *āryas* are able, in but a single mind-moment, to manifest a single transformation body whereas the Buddhas are able, in but a single mind-moment, to manifest countless phenomena in whatever way they wish.

正體字

如大神通經
072b16 ‖ 中說。佛從臍中出蓮花。上有化佛次第遍
072b17 ‖ 滿上至阿迦尼吒天。諸佛變化所作眾事。種
072b18 ‖ 種色種種形皆以一念。又聲聞人能於千國
072b19 ‖ 土內變化。諸佛能於無量無邊國土變化自
072b20 ‖ 在。又能倍是諸佛得堅固變化三昧。又諸佛
072b21 ‖ 變化。能過恒沙世界。皆從一身出。復次佛
072b22 ‖ 能普於十方無量無邊世界現生受身墮地
072b23 ‖ 行七步。出家學道破魔軍眾。得道轉法輪。
072b24 ‖ 如是等事皆以一念作之。是諸化佛皆亦復
072b25 ‖ 能施作佛事。如是等諸佛所變化事無量無
072b26 ‖ 邊。又於聖如意中有無量力。聖如意者。所
072b27 ‖ 謂從身放光[9]猶如猛火又出諸雨。變化壽
072b28 ‖ 命隨意長短。於一念頃能至梵天能變諸
072b29 ‖ 物。隨意自在能動大地。光明能照無量世
072c01 ‖ 界而不斷絕。聖如意者。不與凡夫等故。
072c02 ‖ 無有量故。過諸量故。諸凡夫等雖變化諸
072c03 ‖ 物少不足言。聲聞人能裂千國土。還使令
072c04 ‖ 合。

简体字

如大神通经中说。佛从脐中出莲花。上有化佛次第遍满上至阿迦尼吒天。诸佛变化所作众事。种种色种种形皆以一念。又声闻人能于千国土内变化。诸佛能于无量无边国土变化自在。又能倍是诸佛得坚固变化三昧。又诸佛变化。能过恒沙世界。皆从一身出。复次佛能普于十方无量无边世界现生受身堕地行七步。出家学道破魔军众。得道转法轮。如是等事皆以一念作之。是诸化佛皆亦复能施作佛事。如是等诸佛所变化事无量无边。又于圣如意中有无量力。圣如意者。所谓从身放光犹如猛火又出诸雨。变化寿命随意长短。于一念顷能至梵天能变诸物。随意自在能动大地。光明能照无量世界而不断绝。圣如意者。不与凡夫等故。无有量故。过诸量故。诸凡夫等虽变化诸物少不足言。声闻人能裂千国土。还使令合。

Chapter 21 — Forty Dharmas Exclusive to Buddhas (Part 1)

This is as described in the *Sutra on the Great Spiritual Powers*: "The Buddha may send forth from his navel a lotus blossom with transformation buddhas sitting atop it that then, in an orderly fashion, fill up all of space on up to the Akaniṣṭha Heaven. The many sorts of transformations created by the Buddhas take all sorts of different forms and all sorts of different shapes and are all created in but a single mind-moment."

Also, *śrāvaka* disciples are able to perform transformations within a thousand lands whereas the Buddhas are able to freely perform transformations within a countless and boundless number of lands and are additionally able to do much more than this, for the Buddhas have gained the solid transformation samādhi. Also, the transformations performed by but one of the Buddhas' bodies are able to occur in worlds as numerous as the sands of the Ganges.

Additionally, a buddha is able in a countless and boundless number of worlds of the ten directions to manifest a buddha being born, taking on a body, dropping to the earth, taking seven steps, leaving the home life, studying the path, defeating Māra's armies, achieving enlightenment, and turning the Dharma wheel. All of these phenomena are created in but a single mind-moment. All of these transformation buddhas are themselves also able to carry out the work of the Buddhas. And the transformation-generated phenomena created by all of those buddhas are themselves countless and boundless.

D. 3) Boundless Psychic Powers of the Sort Possessed by Āryas

Also, the Buddhas have "boundless psychic powers of the sort possessed by *āryas*." As for "the psychic powers possessed by *āryas*," this refers to phenomena such as: radiating light from their bodies that may manifest as raging fire and also pouring forth rains; transforming their length of life however they wish, either lengthening it or shortening it; being able in a single thought to go to the Brahma Heaven; being able to perform transformations of various phenomena, being able to shake the great earth whenever they wish; or being able to ceaselessly radiate light capable of illuminating countless worlds.

Also, "psychic powers possessed by *āryas*" are referred to as such because they are incomparably different from those possessed by common people, because of their being boundless, and because of their going beyond all limits. Although common people may possess some ability to perform transformations of various phenomena, their power to do so is so minor as to be beneath mention here.

A *śrāvaka* disciple may be able to split a thousand lands and then cause them to join back together again, may be able to lengthen his life

正體字

072c05	能令壽命若至一劫若減一劫。還能令短。短已[10]不能令長。於一念中能至千國
072c06	土梵世界。能於千國土隨意變化。能動千
072c07	國土。能身出光明相續不絕照千國土。設
072c08	使身滅能留神力變化如本於千國土。小
072c09	辟支佛能於萬國土萬種變化。中辟支佛能
072c10	於百萬國土百萬種變化。大辟支佛能於三
072c11	千大千國土變化如上。諸佛世尊能過諸恒
072c12	河沙世界算數變化身出水火能[11]末恒河
072c13	沙等世界令如微塵。又能還合能住。壽命無
072c14	量劫數還能令少。少已還能令長。能於無量
072c15	時住。變化隨意。能以一念至無量無邊恒
072c16	河沙等世界。能以常身立至梵世。又能變
072c17	化無量無邊阿僧祇世界皆令作金。或令
072c18	作銀瑠璃珊瑚[12]車璖馬瑙。取要言之。能令
072c19	作無量寶物。隨意所作。又復能變恒河沙
072c20	等世界大海水。皆使為乳酥油酪蜜隨意
072c21	而成。又能以一念變[13]化諸山皆是真金。
072c22	過諸算數不可稱計。又能震動無量無邊
072c23	世界一切欲界色界諸天宮殿。又以一念能
072c24	令若干金色光明遍照如是無量世界。

简体字

能令寿命若至一劫若减一劫。还能令短。短已不能令长。于一念中能至千国土梵世界。能于千国土随意变化。能动千国土。能身出光明相续不绝照千国土。设使身灭能留神力变化如本于千国土。小辟支佛能于万国土万种变化。中辟支佛能于百万国土百万种变化。大辟支佛能于三千大千国土变化如上。诸佛世尊能过诸恒河沙世界算数变化身出水火能末恒河沙等世界令如微尘。又能还合能住。寿命无量劫数还能令少。少已还能令长。能于无量时住。变化随意。能以一念至无量无边恒河沙等世界。能以常身立至梵世。又能变化无量无边阿僧祇世界皆令作金。或令作银琉璃珊瑚车碟马瑙。取要言之。能令作无量宝物。随意所作。又复能变恒河沙等世界大海水。皆使为乳酥油酪蜜随意而成。又能以一念变化诸山皆是真金。过诸算数不可称计。又能震动无量无边世界一切欲界色界诸天宫殿。又以一念能令若干金色光明遍照如是无量世界。

Chapter 21 — *Forty Dharmas Exclusive to Buddhas (Part 1)*

span to a kalpa or somewhat less than a kalpa in duration and then be able to shorten it, but after having shortened it, he will be unable to make it long again. He may be able in a single mind-moment to go to the brahma worlds of a thousand lands, may be able to freely perform transformations in a thousand lands, may be able to shake the earth in a thousand lands, may be able to ceaselessly radiate light from his body that can illuminate a thousand lands, and, even if his body is destroyed, he may retain the presence of his spiritual powers and their ability to perform transformations just as before, doing so in a thousand lands.

The lesser *pratyekabuddha* is able to perform a myriad transformations in a myriad lands. The middling *pratyekabuddha* is able to perform a million transformations in a million lands. A great *pratyekabuddha* is able to perform the sorts of transformations cited above, doing so throughout all lands in a great trichiliocosm.

The Buddhas, the Bhagavats, are able to perform transformations in worlds more numerous than the Ganges' sands wherein they send forth fire and water from their bodies. They are even able to grind to fine dust worlds as numerous as the Ganges' sands and then cause them to be restored. They are able to abide for a life span of countless kalpas, are able to shorten that life span, and having shortened it, they are then able to lengthen it again. They are able to abide for an immeasurably long period of time. They are able to freely perform transformations such that, in the space of but a single mind-moment, they are able to go to countless and boundless worlds as numerous as the sands in the River Ganges.

They are able to cause their usual body, when standing, to reach all the way up to the Brahma Worlds. They are also able to perform a transformation whereby countless and boundless *asaṃkhyeyas* of worlds are all caused to be transformed into gold, or into silver, or into *vaiḍūrya*, coral, mother-of-pearl, or carnelian. To sum up the essential point, they are freely able in accordance with their wishes to cause them to be transformed into a countless number of precious things.

They are also able in accordance with their wishes to transform the waters of the great oceans in worlds as numerous as the Ganges' sands into milk, ghee, yogurt, or honey. They are also able in but a single mind-moment to transform incalculably many mountains into real gold.

They are also able to shake the heavenly palaces of the desire realm and form realm heavens of countless and boundless worlds. They are also able in but a single mind-moment to cause gold-colored radiance to so universally illuminate an immeasurably great number of worlds

正體字	日月 072c25 ‖光明及欲色界諸天宮殿光明皆令不現。雖 072c26 ‖滅度後能於如是諸世界中隨意久近。流 072c27 ‖布神力常不斷絕。聞聲自在者。諸佛所聞聲 072c28 ‖中隨意自在。若無量百千萬億[14]技樂同時俱 072c29 ‖作。若無量百千萬億眾生一時發言。若遠若 073a01 ‖近隨意[1]所聞。假令恒河沙等三千大千世界 073a02 ‖所有眾生。同時俱作若干百千萬種伎樂遍 073a03 ‖滿世界。復有恒河沙等世界眾生。同時以梵 073a04 ‖音。遍滿一切世界。諸佛若欲於中聞一音 073a05 ‖聲隨意得聞。餘者不聞。聲聞所應聞者。 073a06 ‖若有大神力障者不能得聞。諸佛所聞音 073a07 ‖聲雖有大神力障亦能得聞。聲聞能聞千 073a08 ‖國土內音聲。諸佛世尊所聞音聲過無量無 073a09 ‖邊世界最細音聲皆亦得聞。大神力聲聞住 073a10 ‖梵世界。發大音聲能滿千國土內。諸佛世 073a11 ‖尊若住於此若住梵世若住餘處。音聲能 073a12 ‖滿無量無邊世界。若欲令眾生聞過無量 073a13 ‖無邊世界最細音聲能令得聞。欲令不聞 073a14 ‖即便不聞。
简体字	日月光明及欲色界诸天宫殿光明皆令不现。虽灭度后能于如是诸世界中随意久近。流布神力常不断绝。闻声自在者。诸佛所闻声中随意自在。若无量百千万亿技乐同时俱作。若无量百千万亿众生一时发言。若远若近随意所闻。假令恒河沙等三千大千世界所有众生。同时俱作若干百千万种伎乐遍满世界。复有恒河沙等世界众生。同时以梵音。遍满一切世界。诸佛若欲于中闻一音声随意得闻。余者不闻。声闻所应闻者。若有大神力障者不能得闻。诸佛所闻音声虽有大神力障亦能得闻。声闻能闻千国土内音声。诸佛世尊所闻音声过无量无边世界最细音声皆亦得闻。大神力声闻住梵世界。发大音声能满千国土内。诸佛世尊若住于此若住梵世若住余处。音声能满无量无边世界。若欲令众生闻过无量无边世界最细音声能令得闻。欲令不闻即便不闻。

that the light from all those suns and moons and heavenly palaces of the desire-realm and the form-realm no longer appear at all.

Although a buddha may have already passed into nirvāṇa, afterward, he is still freely ever able in all those worlds to remain for however long he wishes, ceaselessly implementing his spiritual powers.

E. 4) SOVEREIGN MASTERY OF THE ABILITY TO HEAR SOUNDS

As for "sovereign mastery in the ability to hear sounds," the Buddhas have sovereign mastery in their ability to hear sounds however they please. Even if there were countless hundreds of thousands of myriads of *koṭis* of musical sounds being simultaneously played and hundreds of thousands of myriads of *koṭis* of beings simultaneously speaking— whether those sounds are far or near, the Buddhas are freely able to hear whichever sounds they please.[5]

If one were to cause all beings in great trichiliocosms as numerous as the Ganges' sands to simultaneously create any given number of hundreds of thousands of myriads of *koṭis* of kinds of music that filled up all those worlds, and if at the same time all beings in worlds as numerous as the Ganges' sands were to fill up all those worlds with the voice of Brahmā, if any buddha wished to hear only one single sound from among all those sounds, then that buddha would be freely able to hear that single sound while not hearing any other sound.

In the case of the sounds heard by *śrāvaka* disciples, if someone possessed of great spiritual powers were to block any given sound, then they would not be able to hear it. In the case of sounds heard by buddhas, even though there might be someone possessed of great spiritual powers seeking to block their hearing some sound, the Buddhas are nonetheless able to hear it.

A *śrāvaka* disciple may be able to hear any sound within a thousand lands. The Buddhas, the Bhagavats, are able to hear even the most subtle sounds even from a distance spanning countlessly and boundlessly many world systems.

A *śrāvaka* disciple possessed of great spiritual powers and abiding in the Brahma World Heavens is able to issue such a great sound that it is capable of pervasively filling a thousand lands. As for the Buddhas, the Bhagavats, it matters not whether they are abiding here or in the Brahma World Heaven, or are instead in yet some other place—their voices are still able to fill up countlessly and boundlessly many world systems. If they wish to cause a particular being to hear the most subtle sound across a distance of countlessly and boundlessly many worlds, they can cause him to hear it and if they wish to prevent someone from hearing a sound, then that person will indeed be unable to hear it at

正體字

是故但有諸佛於[2]聞聲中得
073a15 ‖ 自在力。知他心無量自在力者。諸佛世尊
073a16 ‖ 於無量無邊世界現在眾生悉知其心。餘人
073a17 ‖ 但隨名相故知。諸佛以名相義故知。又餘
073a18 ‖ 人不能知無色界眾生諸心。諸佛能知。餘
073a19 ‖ 人雖有知他心智。大[3]力者障則不能知。假
073a20 ‖ 使一切眾生成就心通。皆如舍利弗目[4]犍
073a21 ‖ 連辟支佛等。以其神力障一人心。不令他
073a22 ‖ 知。而佛能壞彼神力得知其心。復次佛以
073a23 ‖ 神力悉知眾生上中下心垢心淨心。又知諸
073a24 ‖ 心各有所緣從是緣至是緣次第。遍知一
073a25 ‖ 切諸緣。又以實相知眾生心。是故諸佛以
073a26 ‖ 無[5]量力悉知他心。第一調伏心波羅蜜者。
073a27 ‖ 善知諸禪定三昧解脫住入起時。諸佛若入
073a28 ‖ 定若不入定。欲繫心一緣中。隨意久近
073a29 ‖ 如意能住。

简体字

是故但有诸佛于闻声中得自在力。知他心无量自在力者。诸佛世尊于无量无边世界现在众生悉知其心。余人但随名相故知。诸佛以名相义故知。又余人不能知无色界众生诸心。诸佛能知。余人虽有知他心智。大力者障则不能知。假使一切众生成就心通。皆如舍利弗目犍连辟支佛等。以其神力障一人心。不令他知。而佛能坏彼神力得知其心。复次佛以神力悉知众生上中下心垢心净心。又知诸心各有所缘从是缘至是缘次第。遍知一切诸缘。又以实相知众生心。是故诸佛以无量力悉知他心。第一调伏心波罗蜜者。善知诸禅定三昧解脱住入起时。诸佛若入定若不入定。欲系心一缘中。随意久近如意能住。

Chapter 21 — Forty Dharmas Exclusive to Buddhas (Part 1)

all. Consequently, it is only the Buddhas who have gained sovereign mastery with regard to the hearing of sounds.

F. 5) Immeasurable Power of Knowledge to Know Others' Thoughts

As for "measureless power of sovereign mastery in the ability to know others' thoughts," the Buddhas, the Bhagavats, are completely aware of all the thoughts of all beings of the present existing throughout countlessly and boundlessly many worlds. Others may develop the ability to know someone else's thoughts, but only as represented by the words [contained in others' thoughts]. The Buddhas, however, know others' thoughts in terms of the associated meanings of the words [contained in others' thoughts].

Moreover, others remain unable to know the thoughts of beings in the formless realm, but the Buddhas are able to know them. Although others may possess the ability to know someone else's thoughts, if anyone possessed of great powers wishes to block that ability, then they will no longer be able to know others' thoughts.

Supposing that all beings had developed psychic powers to the same degree as Śāriputra, Maudgalyāyana, or a *pratyekabuddha*. Now suppose that they used all of their collective spiritual powers to block anyone from knowing someone's thoughts. In such a case, a buddha would still be able to break their spiritual powers and would still succeed in knowing that person's thoughts.

Additionally, a buddha is able to use his spiritual powers to completely know any being's superior, middling, and inferior thoughts, his defiled thoughts, and his pure thoughts. Moreover, he is able to know with regard to each thought, the condition taken as the object of that thought, is able to know also the sequential progression of each thought as it moves from one objective condition to another, and is able to comprehensively know all of the conditions associated with any given thought. Also, he is able to know any being's thoughts in accordance with their true character.

It is on these bases that the Buddhas are acknowledged to have immeasurable powers to completely know the thoughts of others.

G. 6) Sovereign Mastery in [Training and Subduing] the Mind

As for the Buddhas' "*pāramitā* of being foremost in training and subduing the mind," they well know all of the *dhyānas*, samādhis, and liberations and well understand entry into them, abiding in them, and emerging from them. Whether a buddha is immersed in meditative absorption or not, should he wish to focus his mind on a single object, then he is freely able to focus upon it for however long he wishes and

正體字

從此緣中更住餘緣隨意能住。
073b01 ‖ 若佛住常心欲令人不知則不能知。假使
073b02 ‖ 一切眾生。知他心智如大梵王如大聲聞
073b03 ‖ 辟支佛。成就智慧知他人心。以此[6]諸智
073b04 ‖ 令一人得。是人欲知佛常心。若佛不聽則
073b05 ‖ 不能知。如七方便經中說。行者善知定相。
073b06 ‖ 善知住定相。善知起定相。善知安隱定相。
073b07 ‖ 善知定行處相。善知定生相。善知宜諸
073b08 ‖ 定法不宜諸定法。是名諸佛第一調伏心
073b09 ‖ 波羅蜜。諸佛常安慧者。諸佛安慧常不動
073b10 ‖ 念常在心。何以故。先知而後[7]行。隨意所緣
073b11 ‖ 中住無疑行故。斷一切煩惱故。出過動
073b12 ‖ 性故。如佛告阿難。佛於此夜得阿耨多羅
073b13 ‖ 三藐三菩提。一切世間若天魔梵沙門婆羅
073b14 ‖ 門。以盡苦道教化周畢入無餘涅槃。於其
073b15 ‖ 中間佛於諸受知起知住

简体字

从此缘中更住余缘随意能住。若佛住常心欲令人不知则不能知。假使一切众生。知他心智如大梵王如大声闻辟支佛。成就智慧知他人心。以此诸智令一人得。是人欲知佛常心。若佛不听则不能知。如七方便经中说。行者善知定相。善知住定相。善知起定相。善知安隐定相。善知定行处相。善知定生相。善知宜诸定法不宜诸定法。是名诸佛第一调伏心波罗蜜。诸佛常安慧者。诸佛安慧常不动念常在心。何以故。先知而后行。随意所缘中住无疑行故。断一切烦恼故。出过动性故。如佛告阿难。佛于此夜得阿耨多罗三藐三菩提。一切世间若天魔梵沙门婆罗门。以尽苦道教化周毕入无余涅槃。于其中间佛于诸受知起知住

Chapter 21 — *Forty Dharmas Exclusive to Buddhas (Part 1)*

then is able to change from this object to focusing on some other condition, freely abiding in that focus for however long he wishes.

If the Buddha, abiding in his normal thoughts, wishes to cause others to remain unaware of his thoughts, then they would be unable to know them. Even if all beings had perfected the ability to know others' minds to a degree comparable to the ability to know others' thoughts as possessed by a king of the Great Brahma Heaven, a great *śrāvaka* disciple, or a *pratyekabuddha*, and they all then caused a single person to acquire their collective abilities in this, and this person then wished to know the normal thought of a buddha, so long as that buddha did not permit it, that person would still be unable to acquire that knowledge.

This is as described in the *Sutra on the Seven Expedients*: "The practitioner:

Well knows the signs of meditative absorption;
Well knows the signs of abiding in meditative absorption;
Well knows the signs of emerging from meditative absorption;
Well knows the signs of stable and secure meditative absorption;
Well knows the signs of the stations of practice in meditative absorption;
Well knows the signs of the development of meditative absorption;
And well knows what is and is not appropriate to the dharmas of meditative absorption."[6]

This is what is meant by the Buddhas' "*pāramitā* of being foremost in training and subduing the mind."

H. 7) Constant Abiding in Stable Wisdom

As for the Buddhas' "constant abiding in stable wisdom," the Buddhas' stable wisdom is constant and unshakable and their mindfulness is always maintained in their minds. And why is this the case? It is because they first know and then act, because they freely dwell on whichever object they choose while having no doubt in their actions, because they have cut off all afflictions, and because they have gone utterly beyond the realm[7] of movement itself.

This is as the Buddha told Ānanda:

The Buddha, in this one evening, gains *anuttarasamyaksaṃbodhi* and proceeds then to teach the path to the ending of suffering to everyone in the world, whether they be a deva, Māra, Brahmā, a *śramaṇa*, or a brahman, and then, in the end, finally enters the nirvāṇa without residue.

During the interim, the Buddha, with respect to every feeling, is aware of its arising, is aware of its abiding, is aware of its birth and

正體字

```
             知生知滅。諸相
073b16 ||  諸觸諸覺諸念亦知起知住知生知滅。惡
073b17 ||  魔七年晝夜不息常隨逐佛不得佛短。不
073b18 ||  見佛念不在念安慧。是名諸佛常住安慧
073b19 ||  行中。不忘失法者。諸佛得不退法故。通達
073b20 ||  五藏法故。得無上法故。諸佛常不忘失。諸
073b21 ||  佛菩提樹下所得。乃至入無餘涅槃。若天魔
073b22 ||  梵沙門婆羅門。及餘聖人。無能令佛有所
073b23 ||  忘失。如法印經中說。道場所得是名實得
073b24 ||  更無勝法。如衣毛竪經說。舍利弗。若人實
073b25 ||  語。有能於法不忘失者。應說我是。何以
073b26 ||  故。唯我一人無所忘失。是名諸佛於法無
073b27 ||  忘失。金剛三昧者。諸佛世尊金剛三昧。是不
073b28 ||  共法。無能壞故。於一切處無有障礙故。
073b29 ||  得正遍知故。壞一切法障礙故。等貫穿故。
073c01 ||  得諸功德利益力故。諸禪定中最上故。
```

简体字

知生知灭。诸相诸触诸觉诸念亦知起知住知生知灭。恶魔七年昼夜不息常随逐佛不得佛短。不见佛念不在念安慧。是名诸佛常住安慧行中。不忘失法者。诸佛得不退法故。通达五藏法故。得无上法故。诸佛常不忘失。诸佛菩提树下所得。乃至入无余涅槃。若天魔梵沙门婆罗门。及余圣人。无能令佛有所忘失。如法印经中说。道场所得是名实得更无胜法。如衣毛竪经说。舍利弗。若人实语。有能于法不忘失者。应说我是。何以故。唯我一人无所忘失。是名诸佛于法无忘失。金刚三昧者。诸佛世尊金刚三昧。是不共法。无能坏故。于一切处无有障碍故。得正遍知故。坏一切法障碍故。等贯穿故。得诸功德利益力故。诸禅定中最上故。

is aware of its cessation. With respect to all perceptions,[8] all tactile contact, all ideation, and all mental discursion, he is aware of their arising, aware of their abiding, aware of their birth, and aware of their cessation.

Māra the Evil One,[9] constantly and without resting, followed along after the Buddha both day and night for seven years yet was never in all that time able to come upon any shortcomings of the Buddha and was never able to observe an instance of the Buddha's mindfulness not abiding in a state of stable wisdom. This is what is meant by the Buddha's constant abiding in the practice of stable wisdom.

I. 8) Never Forgetting

As for the dharma of "never forgetting," because the Buddhas have gained the dharma of irreversibility, have reached a penetrating understanding of the five categorical repositories of dharmas,[10] and have acquired the unsurpassable Dharma, the Buddhas never forget.

With respect to all that the Buddhas have realized beneath the bodhi tree and have then subsequently acquired up to the time when they enter the nirvāṇa without residue, no matter whether it be a deva, Māra, Brahmā, a śramaṇa, a brahman, or some other ārya, there is no one who is able to cause the Buddhas to forget anything at all.

This is as described in the *Sutra on the Seal of Dharma*: "As for that which is realized at the *bodhimaṇḍa*, this is known as the genuine realization and there is no dharma superior to it."

This is also as described in the *Horripilation Sutra*: "Śāriputra. If anyone could claim truthfully that they do not have any aspect of Dharma that they forget, I would be the one who could make that claim. How is this so? I alone do not forget anything whatsoever."

This is what is intended when it is said that the Buddhas never forget Dharma.

J. 9) Possession of the Powers of the Vajra Samādhi

As for "the vajra samādhi," the vajra samādhi of all the Buddhas, the Bhagavats, is one of the exclusive dharmas, [so named]:

Because it cannot be destroyed by anything;
Because there is no place where it can be obstructed;
Because it is associated with right and universal knowledge;
Because it destroys all hindrances to Dharma;
Because it is able to equally penetrate [all dharmas];
Because it brings about the power to acquire the benefit of all meritorious qualities;
And because it is the most supreme of all *dhyāna* samādhis.

正體字	無能 073c02 ‖壞者。是故名為金剛三昧。如金剛寶無物 073c03 ‖能破者。是三昧亦如是。無[8]有法可以壞 073c04 ‖者。是故名金剛三昧。問曰。何故不可壞。答 073c05 ‖曰。一切處無有[9]閡故。如帝釋金剛無有 073c06 ‖閡處。是三昧亦如是。問曰。是三昧。何故 073c07 ‖名一切處不閡。答曰。正通達一切法故。諸 073c08 ‖佛住是三昧。悉能通達過去現在未來。過 073c09 ‖[10]出三世不可說五藏所攝法。是故名一切 073c10 ‖處不閡。若諸佛住是三昧。諸所有法若不通 073c11 ‖達名為有礙。而實不爾。是故名無礙。問曰。 073c12 ‖何以故。是三昧通達一切法。答曰。是三昧能 073c13 ‖開一切障礙法故。所謂煩惱障閡定障閡智 073c14 ‖障閡能開故。是名能通達一切法。問曰。是 073c15 ‖三昧。何故能開一切障。餘三昧不能。答曰。 073c16 ‖是三昧善等貫穿[11]二法。能壞諸煩惱山令 073c17 ‖無餘故。正遍通達一切法故。善得不壞心 073c18 ‖解脫故。是故此三昧能開一切障閡。
简体字	无能坏者。是故名为金刚三昧。如金刚宝无物能破者。是三昧亦如是。无有法可以坏者。是故名金刚三昧。问曰。何故不可坏。答曰。一切处无有阂故。如帝释金刚无有阂处。是三昧亦如是。问曰。是三昧。何故名一切处不阂。答曰。正通达一切法故。诸佛住是三昧。悉能通达过去现在未来。过出三世不可说五藏所摄法。是故名一切处不阂。若诸佛住是三昧。诸所有法若不通达名为有碍。而实不尔。是故名无碍。问曰。何以故。是三昧通达一切法。答曰。是三昧能开一切障碍法故。所谓烦恼障阂定障阂智障阂能开故。是名能通达一切法。问曰。是三昧。何故能开一切障。余三昧不能。答曰。是三昧善等贯穿二法。能坏诸烦恼山令无余故。正遍通达一切法故。善得不坏心解脱故。是故此三昧能开一切障阂。

Chapter 21 — Forty Dharmas Exclusive to Buddhas (Part 1)

As for its being called "the vajra samādhi" because there is nothing that can destroy it, it is like the precious vajra gem that cannot be crushed by anything at all. This samādhi is just like this. There is no dharma capable of destroying it. It is therefore known as "the vajra samādhi."

Question: Why is it that it cannot be destroyed?

Response: This is because there is nothing anywhere that obstructs it. It is just as with Indra's vajra that meets no obstruction anywhere. This samādhi is just like that.

Question: Why is this samādhi said to have nothing anywhere that obstructs it?

Response: Because it possesses a right and utterly penetrating comprehension of all dharmas. All buddhas, abiding in this samādhi, are able to utterly penetrate all of the dharmas subsumed within the five categorical repositories of dharmas: all dharmas of the past, of the present, of the future, those that transcend the three periods of time, and those that are ineffable dharmas. It is for this reason that it is said to meet with no obstruction anywhere.

If it were the case that, while abiding in this samādhi, all buddhas still did not have an utterly penetrating comprehension of all dharmas, then that would be a case of still having obstructions. But, in truth, this is not the case. It is therefore said to not be obstructed by anything whatsoever.

Question: How is it that this samādhi brings about a penetrating comprehension of all dharmas?

Response: It is because this samādhi is able to open up all obstructive dharmas, namely the obstacle of the afflictions, the obstacles to meditative absorption, and the obstacles to knowledge. Because it is able to open up all obstructions, it is therefore said to bring about an utterly penetrating comprehension of all dharmas.

Question: How is it that this samādhi is able to open up all obstructions whereas other samādhis remain unable to do so?

Response: This samādhi is well able to penetrate three[11] dharmas:

- Because it is able to destroy the mountain of afflictions so that nothing remains of them;
- Because it brings about the right and universal comprehension of all dharmas;
- And because it brings about the thoroughgoing attainment of the liberation of the indestructible resolve.

It is for these reasons that this samādhi is said to be able to open up all obstructions.

正體字

問曰。
073c19 ‖ 是三昧何故等貫穿[*]二法。答曰。住是三昧
073c20 ‖ 得力故。能得一切諸功德。餘三昧無如是
073c21 ‖ 力。是故是三昧能等貫穿。問曰。何故住是
073c22 ‖ 三昧得力故能得一切諸功德。答曰。是三
073c23 ‖ 昧於諸定中最為第一。是故住是三昧能
073c24 ‖ 得諸功德。問曰。何故是三昧於諸定中最
073c25 ‖ 為第一。答曰。是三昧無量無邊善根所成
073c26 ‖ 故。於諸定中最為第一。問曰。是三昧何故
073c27 ‖ 無量無邊善根所成。答曰。是三昧唯一切智
073c28 ‖ 人有餘人所無。是故名為金剛三昧。

简体字

问曰。是三昧何故等贯穿二法。答曰。住是三昧得力故。能得一切诸功德。余三昧无如是力。是故是三昧能等贯穿。问曰。何故住是三昧得力故能得一切诸功德。答曰。是三昧于诸定中最为第一。是故住是三昧能得诸功德。问曰。何故是三昧于诸定中最为第一。答曰。是三昧无量无边善根所成故。于诸定中最为第一。问曰。是三昧何故无量无边善根所成。答曰。是三昧唯一切智人有余人所无。是故名为金刚三昧。

Chapter 21 — Forty Dharmas Exclusive to Buddhas (Part 1)

Question: How is it that this samādhi is able to equally penetrate these three dharmas?[12]

Response: This is because, when one abides in this samādhi, one gains the power by which one is then able to acquire every sort of meritorious quality. None of the other samādhis possess this sort of power. It is for this reason that this samādhi is able to "equally penetrate" [all dharmas].

Question: How is it that, abiding in this samādhi, one gains the power by which one is then able to acquire every sort of meritorious quality?

Response: This samādhi is the foremost among all meditative absorptions. It is because of this that, abiding in this samādhi, one is able to gain every sort of meritorious quality.

Question: How is it that this samādhi is foremost among all samādhis?

Response: This samādhi is foremost among all meditative absorptions because it is produced through the possession of measurelessly and boundlessly many roots of goodness.

Question: How is it that this samādhi is produced through the possession of measurelessly and boundlessly many roots of goodness?

Response: This samādhi is possessed only by those who are equipped with all-knowledge. It has not been acquired by anyone else. Hence it is known as "the vajra samādhi."

The End of Chapter Twenty-One

四十不共法中難一切智人品第二十二

問曰。汝說金剛三昧。唯一切智人有。餘人所無。若是三昧但一切智人有。餘人無者。即無是三昧。何以故。無一切智人故。何以故。所知法無量無邊。而智慧有量有邊。以此有量有邊智慧。不應知無量事。如今現閻浮提水陸眾生過諸算數。是眾生三品。若男若女非男非女在胎孩童少壯衰老苦樂等法。過去未來現在諸心心數法。及諸善惡業。已集今集當集。已受報今受報未受報。萬物生滅及閻浮提中山河泉池草木叢林根莖枝葉花果。所可知者無有邊際。餘三天下亦如是[1]如四天下三千大千世界物亦如是。[*]如三千大千世界物一切世界所可知物亦如是。但世間數尚無量無邊難可得知。何況諸閻浮提諸世間中。眾生非眾生諸物[2]分。

Chapter 22
Forty Dharmas Exclusive to Buddhas (Part 2)

Challenges to the Reality of Omniscience

II. Chapter 22: Forty Dharmas Exclusive to Buddhas (Part 2)
  A. Q: Your Claim That Omniscience Exists Is False for these Reasons

Question: You claim that only those possessed of all-knowledge possess the vajra samādhi and no one else has it. If this samādhi was only possessed by someone who has all-knowledge and no one else possessed it, then this samādhi does not even exist. Why? Because there is no one who possesses all-knowledge.

And why is this? It is because the dharmas that might be known are measureless and boundless whereas the knowledge that might know them is measurable and bounded. It should not be the case that this measurable and bounded knowledge could know measurelessly many phenomena.

For instance, on the present-day continent of Jambudvīpa, the number of beings dwelling in its waters and on its lands are beyond count. Also, consider the three categories of beings, whether male, female, or neither male nor female, those still in the womb, the children, the young and strong, the frail and old, and also the dharmas associated with their suffering, happiness, and so forth. Also, consider all of the mind and mental dharmas of the past, future, and present, as well as all good and bad karmic actions accumulated in the past, present, and future, all the karmic retributions undergone in the past, present, and future, all the births and deaths of the myriad creatures, and also all of Jambudvīpa's mountains, rivers, springs, ponds, grasses, trees, dense forests, roots, stems, branches, leaves, blossoms, and fruit. The things that can be known are limitlessly many.

The same is true for the other three continents. And just as this is the case with these four continents, it is also the case throughout all of the worlds of the great trichiliocosm. And just as this is the case with all of the worlds of the great trichiliocosm, so too is it also the case for all things that can be known in all other worlds.

As for the number of the worlds, that matter alone is measureless, boundless, and difficult to know. How much the more so is this the case for all of the sentient and insentient beings and all other categories of things on the Jambudvīpa continents in all those worlds.

| 正體字 | 074a16 ‖ 以是因緣當知。所可知物無量無邊故。無
074a17 ‖ 一切智者。若謂智慧有大力於所知法中
074a18 ‖ 無障閡故遍知一切可知。法如虛空遍
074a19 ‖ 在一切法中。是故應有一切智人者。是事
074a20 ‖ 不然。智大力可爾。[3]大智不能自知。如指
074a21 ‖ 端不自觸。是故無一切智。若謂更有智能
074a22 ‖ 知是智。是亦不然。何以故。有無窮過故。[4]智
074a23 ‖ 若自知若以他知。二俱不然。若是[*]智有
074a24 ‖ 無量力。以不自知故。不得言有無量力。
074a25 ‖ 是故無有能知一切法[5]智。無知一切法
074a26 ‖ 智故。則無一切智者。何以故。一切智者。以
074a27 ‖ 智知一切法[6]故。復次所知法無量無邊。若
074a28 ‖ 和合百千萬億智人尚不能盡知。何況一
074a29 ‖ 人。是故無有一人能知一切法。無有一切
074b01 ‖ 智。若謂不以遍知一切山河眾生非眾生
074b02 ‖ 故名一切智人。但以盡知一切經書故名 |

简体字: 以是因缘当知。所可知物无量无边故。无一切智者。若谓智慧有大力于所知法中无障阂故遍知一切可知。法如虚空遍在一切法中。是故应有一切智人者。是事不然。智大力可尔。大智不能自知。如指端不自触。是故无一切智。若谓更有智能知是智。是亦不然。何以故。有无穷过故。智若自知若以他知。二俱不然。若是智有无量力。以不自知故。不得言有无量力。是故无有能知一切法智。无知一切法智故。则无一切智者。何以故。一切智者。以智知一切法故。复次所知法无量无边。若和合百千万亿智人尚不能尽知。何况一人。是故无有一人能知一切法。无有一切智。若谓不以遍知一切山河众生非众生故名一切智人。但以尽知一切经书故名

Chapter 22 — Forty Dharmas Exclusive to Buddhas (Part 2)

For these reasons, one should realize that the things that can be known are countless and limitless and, because of that, it cannot be that there is anyone at all who is possessed of all-knowledge.

Suppose that one were to claim that the knowledge [of someone who is omniscient] is possessed of such great power that, because it is unimpeded with respect to those dharmas it cognizes, it is able to pervasively know all those dharmas in just the same manner as empty space is able to reach everywhere in its universal pervasion of all things. Suppose too that one were to claim that, because of this, it ought to be the case that there truly is such a thing as an omniscient person. If one were to make such a claim, this still could not be so, for even if knowledge could possess such a great power as this, even such great knowledge as this would still remain unable to know itself in just the same way that one's fingertip remains unable to touch itself. Therefore, there is no such thing as all-knowledge.

If, [in response to this], one were to claim that there is yet some other knowledge possessed of the capacity to know this knowledge, this could not be the case, either. And why not? That is because this proposition would then fall into the fallacy of infinite regression. Knowledge either knows itself or is known by something other. They cannot both be true.

If, as you say, this knowledge is somehow possessed of measureless power, because of the fact that it still remains unable to know itself, one really cannot claim that it is possessed of measureless power. Therefore there is no such thing as some knowledge possessed of the ability to know all dharmas.

If there is no such thing as some knowledge possessed of the ability to know all dharmas, then there could not be anyone possessed of all-knowledge. And why is this the case? It is because anyone possessed of all-knowledge [could only be so by] availing himself of just such a [nonexistent] knowledge that knows all dharmas.

Furthermore, the dharmas that can be known are measureless and boundless. Even if one were to employ the combined knowing capacity of a hundred thousand myriads of *koṭis* of wise men, they would still be unable to exhaustively know them all. How much the less could a single person do so. Therefore there is no such thing as any single person who is able to know all dharmas and there is no such thing as "all-knowledge."

If one were to claim that it is not on the basis of comprehensively knowing every mountain, river, being, or non-being that we speak of someone possessed of all-knowledge, but rather it is simply on the basis of exhaustively knowing all scriptures that one speaks of

正體字

074b03 ｜｜ 一切智人者。是亦不然。何以故。佛法中不
074b04 ｜｜ 說韋陀等經書義。若佛是一切智[7]人者。應
074b05 ｜｜ 用韋陀等經書而實不用是故。佛非一切
074b06 ｜｜ 智人。又四韋陀羅經有量有限。今世尚無盡
074b07 ｜｜ 能知者。況有盡知一切經書。是故無有一
074b08 ｜｜ 切智人。復次有經書能增長貪欲。歌舞音樂
074b09 ｜｜ 等。若一切智人知是事者即有貪欲。是經
074b10 ｜｜ 書[8]者是貪欲因緣。若有因必有果。若一切
074b11 ｜｜ 智人不知此事則不名一切智人。復次有
074b12 ｜｜ 諸經書能助瞋恚喜誂於人。所謂治世經書
074b13 ｜｜ 等。若知是事則有瞋恚。何以故。有因必有
074b14 ｜｜ 果故。若不知則不名一切智人。是故知無
074b15 ｜｜ 一切智人。復次佛不必盡知未來世事。譬
074b16 ｜｜ 如我今難一切智人。佛無經書[9]豫記是人
074b17 ｜｜ 如是姓如是家在某處以如是事難一切
074b18 ｜｜ 智人。若謂佛盡知何以故不說是事。

简体字

一切智人者。是亦不然。何以故。佛法中不说韦陀等经书义。若佛是一切智人者。应用韦陀等经书而实不用是故。佛非一切智人。又四韦陀罗经有量有限。今世尚无尽能知者。况有尽知一切经书。是故无有一切智人。复次有经书能增长贪欲。歌舞音乐等。若一切智人知是事者即有贪欲。是经书者是贪欲因缘。若有因必有果。若一切智人不知此事则不名一切智人。复次有诸经书能助嗔恚喜诳于人。所谓治世经书等。若知是事则有嗔恚。何以故。有因必有果故。若不知则不名一切智人。是故知无一切智人。复次佛不必尽知未来世事。譬如我今难一切智人。佛无经书豫记是人如是姓如是家在某处以如是事难一切智人。若谓佛尽知何以故不说是事。

Chapter 22 – Forty Dharmas Exclusive to Buddhas (Part 2)   737

someone possessed of all-knowledge, this is also wrong. How so? It is because, within the sphere of the Buddha's Dharma, one does not speak of the concepts treated in the Vedas and other such scriptures. If the Buddha really were, [in this sense of the term], a man possessed of all-knowledge, then he should make use of the Vedas and other such scriptures, but in truth, he does not use these, and so, because of this, the Buddha is not an all-knowing man.

Moreover, the scriptures comprising the four Vedas are themselves measurable and limited in their scope and, even so, there is not even anyone capable of exhaustively knowing those scriptures, how much the less could there be anyone who exhaustively knows all the scriptures in existence. Therefore there is no such thing as a person possessed of "all-knowledge" [even in this limited sense of the term].

Moreover, there are scriptures that are able to cause the proliferation of desire and that devote themselves to such things as dance and music and such. If a person possessed of all-knowledge were to become knowledgeable with respect to these matters, then he would be subjected to the arising of desire. Scriptures of these sorts constitute the causes and conditions for the arising of desire. Where there is a given cause, there must necessarily be the corresponding result [ensuing from it]. If a person possessed of all-knowledge does not know these matters, then he could not be validly referred to as someone possessed of all-knowledge.

Furthermore, there are scriptures that are able to influence a person to become full of hate and to take delight in deceiving others, specifically such works as those classics concerned with ruling the world. Were one to become knowledgeable about such matters, then one would come to be possessed of hatred. How is the case? It is because, where there is such a given cause, then there must necessarily be the corresponding result ensuing from it. And were one to not know such matters, then one could not be validly referred to as possessed of all-knowledge. One should therefore realize that there really is no such thing as a person who is possessed of all-knowledge.

Additionally, it is not necessarily the case that a buddha could exhaustively know matters pertaining to the future. Take for instance my present challenge to the plausibility of there being anyone who is omniscient. The Buddha has no scriptural record of having predicted that in the future there would be this particular man of this particular caste from this particular clan in this particular place who would on these particular grounds challenge the plausibility of there being anyone who might be omniscient. If one were to claim that the Buddha exhaustively knows such things, why did he not speak of this matter? If

正體字

若說
經者經中應有不說是事。是故知非一切
智人。復次佛若盡知未來世事。應當[*]豫知
調達出家已破僧。若知者不應聽出家。復
次佛不知木機激石。佛若[*]豫知者則不應
於中經行。復次佛不知旃遮婆羅門女以
婬欲謗。若佛先知。應告諸比丘未來當
有是事。復次有梵志嫉佛故於餘處殺
梵志女孫陀羅於祇洹塹中埋。佛不知是
事。若知是者。應於諸梵志所救此女命。
至調達所推石下。不說婆羅門女梵志女
事。以不知故。當知佛不盡知未來世。是故
非一切智人。復次佛入婆羅門聚落乞食
空鉢而出。不能豫知魔時轉諸人心。乃至
不得一食。佛若知者則不應入婆羅門聚
落。是[10]故知佛不盡知未來事。復次阿闍世
王欲害佛故放守財醉象。佛不知故入王
舍城乞食。若[*]豫知者則不應入[11]城。是[12]故

简体字

若说经者经中应有不说是事。是故知非一切智人。复次佛若尽知未来世事。应当豫知调达出家已破僧。若知者不应听出家。复次佛不知木机激石。佛若豫知者则不应于中经行。复次佛不知旃遮婆罗门女以淫欲谤。若佛先知。应告诸比丘未来当有是事。复次有梵志嫉佛故于余处杀梵志女孙陀罗于祇洹堑中埋。佛不知是事。若知是者。应于诸梵志所救此女命。至调达所推石下。不说婆罗门女梵志女事。以不知故。当知佛不尽知未来世。是故非一切智人。复次佛入婆罗门聚落乞食空钵而出。不能豫知魔时转诸人心。乃至不得一食。佛若知者则不应入婆罗门聚落。是故知佛不尽知未来事。复次阿闍世王欲害佛故放守财醉象。佛不知故入王舍城乞食。若豫知者则不应入城。是故

Chapter 22 — *Forty Dharmas Exclusive to Buddhas (Part 2)*

he is the one who spoke these scriptures, then those scriptures should have a record of such matters, but he did not speak of these matters. Therefore one knows that he was not omniscient.

Moreover, if the Buddha exhaustively knew future matters, then he should have known in advance that, after Devadatta left home to become a monk, he would then create a schism in the Sangha. If he had knowledge of that, then he should not have allowed Devadatta to become a monk. Also, the Buddha did not know that Devadatta would use a stick to pry loose a boulder [that would roll down and draw blood from the Buddha's foot]. If the Buddha had known of this matter in advance, then he should not have been walking in that place.

Additionally, the Buddha failed to know in advance that Ciñca, the brahman woman, would slander him by accusing him of having had sexual relations with her. If the Buddha had known of this in advance, then he should have told the bhikshus that, in the future, there would be just such an occurrence.

Also, there was the case of the *brahmacārin* who, because he was jealous of the Buddha, killed a *brahmacārin* woman named Sundarī in another place and then buried her in a trench in the vicinity of the Jeta Grove. The Buddha did not know of this matter. If he had known of this, then he should have sought among the brahmans to [find a way to] see that her life would be saved.

The Buddha went to that place beneath which Devadatta was about to set loose the falling boulder and he also failed to announce in advance the incidents having to do with the brahman woman and the *brahmacārin* woman. Because he did not know of these matters, one should realize that the Buddha did not exhaustively know the future. Therefore he could not possibly have been omniscient.

Furthermore, the Buddha once entered a brahman village seeking food on the alms round but then had to leave with an empty bowl. He was unable then to know in advance that Māra would so turn the minds of the villagers against him that he would be unable to obtain anything to eat. If the Buddha had known of this matter, then he should not have entered that brahman village. Therefore one knows that the Buddha did not exhaustively know how matters would transpire in the future.

Moreover, because King Ajātaśatru wished to harm the Buddha, he released a drunken elephant used to guard the treasury.[13] Because the Buddha did not know of this matter, he entered the city of Rājagṛha on his alms round. If he had known of this matter in advance, then he should not have gone into the city. Therefore he did not have

074c07 ‖ 不知未來事。不知未來事故則非一切智
074c08 ‖ 人。復次佛不知惡涅達多請佛因緣。即受
074c09 ‖ 其請將諸比丘詣韋羅闍國。是婆羅門忘
074c10 ‖ 先請故。使佛食馬麥。若佛豫[13]知則不應
074c11 ‖ 受請三月食馬麥。是故知佛不知未來事。
074c12 ‖ 不知未來事故則非一切智人。復次佛受
074c13 ‖ 須涅叉多羅為弟子故則不知未來事。是
074c14 ‖ 人惡心堅牢難化不信佛語。佛若知者云何
074c15 ‖ 受為弟子。受為弟子故則不知未來事。不
074c16 ‖ 知未來事故則非一切智人。復次若佛是
074c17 ‖ 一切智人則應防護未有犯罪者當為結
074c18 ‖ 戒。以先不知結戒因緣有作罪已方乃結
074c19 ‖ 戒則不知未來事。不知未來事故則非一
074c20 ‖ 切智人。復次佛法但以出家受戒[14]歲數處
074c21 ‖ 在上座恭敬禮拜。不以耆年貴族諸家功德
074c22 ‖ 智慧多聞禪定果斷神通為大。若是一切智
074c23 ‖ 者。

不知未来事。不知未来事故则非一切智人。复次佛不知恶涅达多请佛因缘。即受其请将诸比丘诣韦罗阇国。是婆罗门忘先请故。使佛食马麦。若佛豫知则不应受请三月食马麦。是故知佛不知未来事。不知未来事故则非一切智人。复次佛受须涅叉多罗为弟子故则不知未来事。是人恶心坚牢难化不信佛语。佛若知者云何受为弟子。受为弟子故则不知未来事。不知未来事故则非一切智人。复次若佛是一切智人则应防护未有犯罪者当为结戒。以先不知结戒因缘有作罪已方乃结戒则不知未来事。不知未来事故则非一切智人。复次佛法但以出家受戒岁数处在上座恭敬礼拜。不以耆年贵族诸家功德智慧多闻禅定果断神通为大。若是一切智者。

Chapter 22 — *Forty Dharmas Exclusive to Buddhas (Part 2)*

knowledge of future matters. Because he did not have knowledge of future matters, he therefore could not have been omniscient.

Additionally, the Buddha did not know of the causal circumstances involved in Agnidatta's invitation to the Buddha. Consequently he immediately accepted that invitation and then led the bhikshus to the state of Verañjā. Because this brahman had forgotten his prior issuance of that invitation, he caused the Buddha to eat only horse fodder. If the Buddha had known of this matter in advance, then he should not have accepted that invitation on account of which he spent the entire three months [of the rains retreat] surviving only on horse fodder. We know therefore that the Buddha did not have knowledge of future matters. Because he did not have knowledge of future matters, he therefore could not have been omniscient.

Also, because the Buddha accepted Sunakṣatra as a disciple, he could not have had knowledge of future matters. This man possessed an obdurately evil mind, made himself difficult to teach, and did not believe the words of the Buddha. If the Buddha had known of this, how could he have accepted him as a disciple? Because he accepted him as a disciple, then he could not have known future matters. Because he did not have knowledge of future matters, he therefore could not have been omniscient.

Furthermore, if the Buddha had been omniscient, then, in order to prevent inevitable future instances of moral transgressions, he would have formulated his moral precepts in advance. Because he had no prior knowledge of the causal circumstances that eventually led to the formulation of each particular moral precept, it was only after someone had committed such a transgression that he then subsequently laid down these moral regulations. This being the case, he could not have known of future matters. Because he did not have knowledge of future matters, he therefore could not have been omniscient.

Moreover, in the Dharma set forth by the Buddha, it is solely on the basis of seniority in years of monastic ordination that, within the community, one sits more toward the front and is accorded reverence and obeisance [by those of fewer years of seniority]. One is not acknowledged as of greater eminence merely on the basis of one's venerable age, one's noble birth, the stature of one's clan, one's meritorious qualities, the level of wisdom one has developed, the degree of learning one has achieved, the particular *dhyāna* absorptions one has entered, the fruits of the path one has gained, the fetters one has cut off, or the spiritual powers one has acquired.

If the Buddha had really been someone possessed of all-knowledge, then he would have accorded eminence, higher priority in the receipt

正體字

應以耆年貴族諸家功德智慧多聞禪定
074c24 ‖ 果斷神通為大供養恭敬。若如是者名為
074c25 ‖ 善制。歲數者受戒年數。如五歲道人禮六
074c26 ‖ 歲者。貴族者世間有四品眾生。婆羅門剎利
074c27 ‖ [15]韋舍首陀羅。首陀羅應恭敬韋舍剎利婆
074c28 ‖ 羅門。韋舍應恭敬剎利婆羅門。剎利應恭
074c29 ‖ 敬婆羅門。諸家者。工巧家商[16]估家居士家長
075a01 ‖ 者家大臣家王家等。於諸家中。其小家應
075a02 ‖ 恭敬大家。如是於貧賤中出家者。應恭
075a03 ‖ 敬富貴中出家者。功德者毀戒人應恭敬禮
075a04 ‖ 拜持戒[1]者。持戒者不應禮毀戒者。不行
075a05 ‖ 十二頭陀者。應禮行十二頭陀者。不具足
075a06 ‖ 行頭陀者。應禮具足行頭陀者。智慧者。
075a07 ‖ 無智慧人應禮敬有智慧者。多聞者。少聞
075a08 ‖ 人應禮多聞者。不多誦者應禮敬多誦者。
075a09 ‖ 果者。須陀洹應禮敬斯陀含。如是展轉應

简体字

应以耆年贵族诸家功德智慧多闻禅定果断神通为大供养恭敬。若如是者名为善制。岁数者受戒年数。如五岁道人礼六岁者。贵族者世间有四品众生。婆罗门刹利韦舍首陀罗。首陀罗应恭敬韦舍刹利婆罗门。韦舍应恭敬刹利婆罗门。刹利应恭敬婆罗门。诸家者。工巧家商估家居士家长者家大臣家王家等。于诸家中。其小家应恭敬大家。如是于贫贱中出家者。应恭敬富贵中出家者。功德者毁戒人应恭敬礼拜持戒者。持戒者不应礼毁戒者。不行十二头陀者。应礼行十二头陀者。不具足行头陀者。应礼具足行头陀者。智慧者。无智慧人应礼敬有智慧者。多闻者。少闻人应礼多闻者。不多诵者应礼敬多诵者。果者。须陀洹应礼敬斯陀含。如是展转应

Chapter 22 – *Forty Dharmas Exclusive to Buddhas (Part 2)*

of offerings, and stature in receipt of reverential obeisance on the basis of one's venerable age, one's noble birth, the stature of one's clan, one's meritorious qualities, the level of wisdom one has developed, the degree of learning one has achieved, the particular *dhyāna* absorptions one has entered, the fruits of the path one has gained, the fetters one has cut off, and the spiritual powers one has acquired. If the Buddha had made stipulations of this sort, then that would qualify as having established a well-regulated community.

Regarding the matter of years of monastic ordination seniority, this is the principle by which a practitioner of the path ordained for only five years is enjoined to accord reverential obeisance to a monk ordained for six years.

As for the issue of nobility of birth caste, the world has four classes of beings: *brahmans, kṣatriyas, vaiśyas,* and *śūdras*. *Śūdras* are enjoined to revere *vaiśyas, kṣatriyas,* and *brahmans*. *Vaiśyas* ought to pay obeisance to *kṣatriyas* and *brahmans*. *Kṣatriyas* are supposed to pay reverential obeisance to *brahmans*.

As for the status of clans, there are the artisan clans, the business-and-trade clans, the merchant clans, the clans led by those of senior status, the clans of great officials, royal clans, and so forth. Among them, the members of lesser-status clans are supposed to revere members of the eminent clans. This being the case, when those from poor and base clans leave the home life to become monks, they should be enjoined to pay reverence to monks from wealthy and noble clans.

With respect to meritorious qualities, whoever has broken moral precepts should be enjoined to revere and bow in formal obeisance to those who uphold the moral precepts. Those who strictly observe the moral precepts should not be bowing in reverence to anyone who has broken the moral precepts.

Those who do not practice the twelve *dhūta* austerities[14] should bow in reverence to those who are practitioners of the twelve *dhūta* austerities. Those who are not perfectly complete in their practice of the *dhūta* practices should bow in reverence to those who are perfect in their practice of the *dhūta* austerities.

As for the matter of wisdom, people devoid of wisdom should bow in reverence to those possessed of wisdom. With regard to learning, those of shallow learning should bow in reverence to those who have achieved a high level of learning. Those who do not recite many scriptures should bow in reverence to those who are able to recite many sutras from memory.

As for the fruits of the path, the stream enterer should bow in reverence to the *sakṛdāgāmin* and it should proceed in this fashion on up to

正體字

075a10 ‖ 禮阿羅漢。一切凡夫應禮得果者。斷者。少
075a11 ‖ 斷結使及未斷者應禮多斷者。神通者。若
075a12 ‖ 未具神通者應禮[2]具神通者。佛若如是
075a13 ‖ 次第善說供養恭敬法者。是為上說。而實
075a14 ‖ 不爾。是故知非一切智人。復次佛尚不能
075a15 ‖ 知現在事。汝若謂我云何知佛不知現在
075a16 ‖ 事者。今當說之。有眾生結使薄者。無業
075a17 ‖ 障者。離八難者。堪行深法者。能成正法
075a18 ‖ 者。而佛不知。佛成道已初欲說法。生如是
075a19 ‖ 疑。我所得法甚深玄遠微妙寂滅難知難解。
075a20 ‖ 唯有智者可以內知。世間眾生貪著世事。
075a21 ‖ 此中除斷一切煩惱滅愛厭離第一難見。若
075a22 ‖ 我說法眾生不解。徒自疲苦。生如是疑。而
075a23 ‖ 實眾生有薄結使無業障者。有離八難
075a24 ‖ 者。堪行深法者。能成正法者。佛不能知
075a25 ‖ 如是眾生。是故當知不知現在事。

简体字

礼阿罗汉。一切凡夫应礼得果者。断者。少断结使及未断者应礼多断者。神通者。若未具神通者应礼具神通者。佛若如是次第善说供养恭敬法者。是为上说。而实不尔。是故知非一切智人。复次佛尚不能知现在事。汝若谓我云何知佛不知现在事者。今当说之。有众生结使薄者。无业障者。离八难者。堪行深法者。能成正法者。而佛不知。佛成道已初欲说法。生如是疑。我所得法甚深玄远微妙寂灭难知难解。唯有智者可以内知。世间众生贪着世事。此中除断一切烦恼灭爱厌离第一难见。若我说法众生不解。徒自疲苦。生如是疑。而实众生有薄结使无业障者。有离八难者。堪行深法者。能成正法者。佛不能知如是众生。是故当知不知现在事。

Chapter 22 – *Forty Dharmas Exclusive to Buddhas (Part 2)*

[the circumstance where realizers of the first three fruits of the path are enjoined to] bow in reverence to the arhat. As for all of the common people, they should bow in reverence to anyone who has gained any of the fruits of the path.

Those who have severed fewer of the fetters as well as those who have not yet severed any of the fetters should all bow in reverence to those who have severed many of the fetters.

Regarding the matter of spiritual powers, if one has not yet acquired any of the spiritual powers, he should then be bowing in obeisance to whomever has already acquired spiritual powers.

If the Buddha had skillfully set forth such sequentially ranked protocols regarding the making of offerings and the according of reverence, then his proclamations on these matters would be of a superior order. But, in truth, he did not do so. One can therefore know that the Buddha was not omniscient.

Furthermore, the Buddha was not even able to know all matters having to do with the present. If you were to ask me how I know that the Buddha did not have knowledge of present-era matters, then I would now inform you as follows:

There were beings whose fetters were but slight, who had no karmic obstacles, who were free of the eight difficulties, who were capable of practicing deep dharmas, and who were able to be successful in the cultivation of right Dharma, and yet the Buddha did not realize this. After the Buddha had attained enlightenment and was first on the verge of proclaiming the Dharma, he gave rise to the following doubt:

> The Dharma that I have gained is extremely profound, recondite, far-reaching, sublime, quiescent, difficult to know, difficult to comprehend, and such as only the wise might be able to realize inwardly. The beings in this world are attached by their desires to worldly matters. That there might be any among them who might be able to cut off their afflictions, extinguish craving, and develop renunciation—this would be the rarest of possibilities. If I were to expound the Dharma, beings would fail to comprehend it. Such an endeavor would be but a useless experiencing of wearisome hardship.

And so the Buddha generated just such a doubt even though there were in fact beings whose fetters were but slight, who had no karmic obstacles, who were free of the eight difficulties, who were capable of practicing deep dharmas, and who were able to be successful in the cultivation of right Dharma. Because the Buddha was unable to know of the existence of such beings, one should therefore know that the Buddha failed to know matters having to do with the present time.

| 正體字 | 又作是 075a26 ‖念。昔我苦行。五比丘供養執侍應先利益。今
075a27 ‖ 在何處。作是念已時有天告。今在波羅捺
075a28 ‖ 鹿野苑中。是故當知佛不知現在事。不知
075a29 ‖ 現在事故。則非一切智人。復次佛得道已
075b01 ‖ 受請說法而作是念。我今說法誰應先聞。
075b02 ‖ 即復念言。欝頭藍弗。此人利[3]智易可開悟。
075b03 ‖ 爾時此人先[4]已命終。而佛[5]訪求。時天告言。
075b04 ‖ 昨夜命終。佛又思惟迴心欲度阿羅[6]邏。天
075b05 ‖ 復白言。是人亡來七日。若佛是一切智者先
075b06 ‖ 應知此諸人命終。而實不知。不知過去事
075b07 ‖ 故則不名一切智人。一切智人法應度可度
075b08 ‖ 者。不可則置。復次佛處處有疑語。如巴
075b09 ‖ [7]蓮弗城。是事當以三因緣壞。若水若火若
075b10 ‖ 內人與外人謀。若佛是一切智人者則不
075b11 ‖ 應有疑惑語。是故知非一切智人。復次佛
075b12 ‖ 問比丘。汝等聚會為說何事。如是等問。若
075b13 ‖ 一切智人者則不應問如是等事。以問他
075b14 ‖ 故非一切智人。 |

简体字

又作是念。昔我苦行。五比丘供养执侍应先利益。今在何处。作是念已时有天告。今在波罗捺鹿野苑中。是故当知佛不知现在事。不知现在事故。则非一切智人。复次佛得道已受请说法而作是念。我今说法谁应先闻。即复念言。郁头蓝弗。此人利智易可开悟。尔时此人先已命终。而佛访求。时天告言。昨夜命终。佛又思惟回心欲度阿罗逻。天复白言。是人亡来七日。若佛是一切智者先应知此诸人命终。而实不知。不知过去事故则不名一切智人。一切智人法应度可度者。不可则置。复次佛处处有疑语。如巴莲弗城。是事当以三因缘坏。若水若火若内人与外人谋。若佛是一切智人者则不应有疑惑语。是故知非一切智人。复次佛问比丘。汝等聚会为说何事。如是等问。若一切智人者则不应问如是等事。以问他故非一切智人。

Chapter 22 — *Forty Dharmas Exclusive to Buddhas (Part 2)*

The Buddha also thought as follows: "Previously, when I was practicing ascetic austerities, the five bhikshus made offerings to me and supported me. It is only appropriate that I first benefit them. Where are they now?" After he had this thought, a deva informed him, "They are now in Benares, in the place known as 'Deer Park.'"

Because of this, one knows that the Buddha did not even know of matters having to do with the present. If he failed to know of matters having to do with the present, then we can know from this that the Buddha could not have been omniscient.

Furthermore, after he had attained enlightenment, the Buddha accepted the invitation to expound on Dharma and then had this thought, "As I now proceed to proclaim the Dharma, who is it that ought to be the first to hear it?" He then had another thought, "Udraka Rāmaputra—this is a man of sharp wisdom, one who might easily become enlightened."

By this time, that man had already died and yet the Buddha nonetheless went in search of him. A deva then informed him, "His life came to an end just last night." The Buddha thought again and, having reflected, he decided he wanted to liberate Ārāda Kālāma. A deva then told him, "This man died seven days ago."

If the Buddha had been omniscient, he should have known beforehand that these men had already died, but in truth he did not know these events had happened. Because the Buddha did not know about past matters, he could not have been omniscient.

The methods employed by an omniscient man would be such that he should strive to bring about the liberation of those capable of achieving liberation while also setting aside those incapable of success in this.

Moreover, in place after place, the Buddha spoke in terms revealing the presence of doubts on his part. Take for example the city of Pāṭaliputra that he said was bound to be destroyed by one of three causes: by flood, by fire, or by a conspiracy between insiders and outsiders. If the Buddha had really been omniscient, then he should not have had instances where his speech was marked by the presence of doubts. One knows therefore that he could not have been omniscient.

Additionally, the Buddha inquired of the bhikshus, "What matter have you all come together to discuss?" He asked questions of this sort. If he were omniscient, then he should not have asked about matters of this sort. Because he was compelled to ask others [in order to know of these matters], then he could not have been omniscient.

正體字

復次佛自稱讚身毀[8]訾他
人。如經中說。佛告阿難。唯我一人第一無
比無與等者。告諸比丘尼[*]犍子等是弊惡
人成就五邪法。諸尼[*]犍子等無信無慚無愧
寡聞懈怠少念薄智。又說梵志尼[*]犍諸外道
弟子等諸不可事。若自稱讚毀[*]訾他人。世
人尚愧。何況一切智人。有此事故非一切
智人。復次佛經始終相違如經中說。諸比丘
我新得道。又言我得往古諸佛所得道。世
間有智尚離終始相違。何況出家一切智人
而有相違。以終始相違故。當知非一切智
人。是故汝說金剛三昧唯一切智人得。是事
不然。無一切智人故。一切智三昧亦不成。
答曰。汝莫說此。佛實是一切智人。何以故。
凡一切法有五法藏。所謂過去法。未來法。現
在法。出三世法。不可說法。唯佛如實遍知
是法。如汝先難所知法無量無邊故無一切
智人者。我今當答。

简体字

复次佛自称赞身毁訾他人。如经中说。佛告阿难。唯我一人第一无比无与等者。告诸比丘尼犍子等是弊恶人成就五邪法。诸尼犍子等无信无惭无愧寡闻懈怠少念薄智。又说梵志尼犍诸外道弟子等诸不可事。若自称赞毁訾他人。世人尚愧。何况一切智人。有此事故非一切智人。复次佛经始终相违如经中说。诸比丘我新得道。又言我得往古诸佛所得道。世间有智尚离终始相违。何况出家一切智人而有相违。以终始相违故。当知非一切智人。是故汝说金刚三昧唯一切智人得。是事不然。无一切智人故。一切智三昧亦不成。答曰。汝莫说此。佛实是一切智人。何以故。凡一切法有五法藏。所谓过去法。未来法。现在法。出三世法。不可说法。唯佛如实遍知是法。如汝先难所知法无量无边故无一切智人者。我今当答。

Chapter 22 — *Forty Dharmas Exclusive to Buddhas (Part 2)*

Also, the Buddha engaged in self-praise while deprecating others. This is as described in the sutras, "The Buddha told Ānanda, 'I alone am foremost, without a peer, unequaled by anyone.'"[15]

He told the bhikshus, "The Nirgranthas and others of that sort are base and evil people who have perfected the five types of deviant dharmas. The Nirgranthas and such have no faith, have no sense of shame, have no dread of blame, and are people of but little learning who are indolent and possessed of only scant mindfulness and shallow wisdom."

He also discussed all manner of impermissible endeavors engaged in by *brahmacārins*, by Nirgranthas, and by the disciples and other followers of the non-Buddhist traditions.

Self-praise and deprecation of others is a behavior of which even common people of the world are ashamed. How much the more so should this be the case for someone who is omniscient. Because the Buddha engaged in behaviors of this sort, he could not have been omniscient.

Furthermore, comparing beginnings and endings, one finds that the Buddhist scriptures are self-contradictory. Take for instance the statements in the sutras in which, on the one hand, the Buddha claims, "Bhikshus, I am one who has newly discovered the path." Then, on the other hand, he claims, "I have attained that path which has previously been attained by all buddhas of antiquity."

Even wise worldly people abandon any tendency to contradict themselves through chronological inconsistencies. How much the less should it be that a monastic possessed of all-knowledge could stumble into such chronological self-contradictions. Because the Buddha fell into chronological inconsistencies, one should realize that he could not possibly have been omniscient. Therefore your claim that the vajra samādhi is only acquired by omniscient men is wrong, this because there is no such thing as an omniscient person. Nor can one establish any case for the existence of some sort of omniscience samādhi.

B. A: Wrong. As I Shall Now Explain, The Buddha Truly Is Omniscient

Response: You should not speak this way. The Buddha truly is omniscient. And how is this so? In general, all dharmas are comprised of five categorical repositories of dharmas, namely: past dharmas, future dharmas, present dharmas, dharmas that transcend the three periods of time, and ineffable dharmas. It is only a buddha who completely knows all these dharmas in accordance with reality.

I shall now respond to your earlier challenge that asserts, because knowable dharmas are measureless and boundless, there are no

正體字

若所知法無量無邊。智
亦無量無邊。以無量無邊智知無量無邊法
無咎。若謂是知亦應以智知是則無窮者。
今當答。[9]法應以智知。[10]智如世間人言。我
是智者我是無智者。我是麁智者。我是細智
者。以是因緣以智知[*]智故。則無無窮過。
如以現在[*]智知過去智則盡知一切法
無有遺餘。復次如人數他通身為十知亦
如是。自知亦[11]知他則無有咎。如燈自照
亦照他。如汝所說和合百千萬億智人尚
不能盡知一切法。何況一人知者。是事不
然。何以故。一[12]切智慧人能知眾事。雖復眾
多無有智慧不能有所知。如百千盲人
不[13]任作導。一人有眼任為導師。是故汝
以一人為難。雖復多智於佛則無智。是
事不然。

简体字

若所知法无量无边。智亦无量无边。以无量无边智知无量无边法无咎。若谓是知亦应以智知是则无穷者。今当答。法应以智知。智如世间人言。我是智者我是无智者。我是粗智者。我是细智者。以是因缘以智知智故。则无无穷过。如以现在智知过去智则尽知一切法无有遗余。复次如人数他通身为十知亦如是。自知亦知他则无有咎。如灯自照亦照他。如汝所说和合百千万亿智人尚不能尽知一切法。何况一人知者。是事不然。何以故。一切智慧人能知众事。虽复众多无有智慧不能有所知。如百千盲人不任作导。一人有眼任为导师。是故汝以一人为难。虽复多智于佛则无智。是事不然。

Chapter 22 — *Forty Dharmas Exclusive to Buddhas (Part 2)*

omniscient people. Insofar as knowable dharmas might be measureless and boundless, the corresponding knowledge is also measureless and boundless. There is no fault in claiming that it is by means of measureless and boundless knowledge that one may know measureless and boundless dharmas.

As for your earlier assertion that knowing should somehow also involve a knowledge that knows [itself] and that this would entail the fallacy of infinite regress, I shall now respond, as follows:

It should be the case that dharmas are known by one's cognition. This cognition is similar to what is referenced when the world's common people describe themselves in this way: "I am a knowledgeable person," "I am someone with no knowledge," "I am someone possessed of only a coarse type of knowledge," or "I am someone who possesses subtle knowledge."

One should realize from these circumstances that it is with one's own cognitive ability that one knows [the character of one's own] knowledge. This being the case, there is no fallacy of infinite regress involved here. This is just a case of using one's own present cognitive ability to know one's past knowledge. It is in this way that one can exhaustively know all dharmas without any omissions.

Also, this is just like when someone counts others [in addition to oneself], thus reaching [for instance a total of] ten [people in all]. The capacity to know is just like that. For knowing to thereby know both itself and others is thus a concept free of any fault. This is also analogous to when a lamp is able to illuminate both itself and other things as well.

As for your contention that even the aggregated knowing capacity of a hundred thousand myriads of *koṭis* of wise people could not exhaustively know all dharmas, how much the less might a single person be able to know them—this is wrong. How is this so? An omniscient person is able to know the many things. Although there may be some additional multitude of people, if they have no cognitive ability, they won't know much of anything.

This is comparable to a situation in which there was a group of a hundred thousand blind men. [Even together], they still could not get hired as guides, but just one single person with good eyes might well be able to serve as a guide. Consequently, as regards your challenge to [the plausibility of omniscience on the part of] a single person, even in a situation where many knowers might be involved, they would still have no knowledge at all compared to the Buddha's capacities in this regard. Therefore your position as stated is erroneous.

正體字

汝謂佛不說[14]韋陀等外經故非
075c18 ‖ 一切智人者。今當答。韋陀中無善寂滅法。
075c19 ‖ 但有種種諸戲論事。諸佛所說皆為善寂滅
075c20 ‖ 故。佛雖知韋陀等經。不能令人得善寂
075c21 ‖ 滅。是故不說。問[15]曰。韋陀中亦有善寂滅解
075c22 ‖ 脫說。世間先皆幽闇都無所有。初有大人出
075c23 ‖ 現如日。若有見者得度死難。更有餘[16]導。
075c24 ‖ 又說。人身小則神小。人大則神大。身為神
075c25 ‖ 宅常處其中。若以智慧開解神縛則得解
075c26 ‖ 脫。是故當知韋陀中有寂滅解脫。答曰。無
075c27 ‖ 是事也。何以[17]故。韋陀[18]經中有四顛倒。世間
075c28 ‖ 無常而別有常世間。如說一作天祠墮落
075c29 ‖ 再亦墮落三作則不墮。是為無常中常顛倒。
076a01 ‖ 世間苦而說有常樂處。是為苦中樂顛倒。
076a02 ‖ 又說我神轉為子願使壽百歲。子是他身云
076a03 ‖ 何為我。是為無我中我顛倒。

简体字

汝谓佛不说韦陀等外经故非一切智人者。今当答。韦陀中无善寂灭法。但有种种诸戏论事。诸佛所说皆为善寂灭故。佛虽知韦陀等经。不能令人得善寂灭。是故不说。问曰。韦陀中亦有善寂灭解脱说。世间先皆幽闇都无所有。初有大人出现如日。若有见者得度死难。更有余导。又说。人身小则神小。人大则神大。身为神宅常处其中。若以智慧开解神缚则得解脱。是故当知韦陀中有寂灭解脱。答曰。无是事也。何以故。韦陀经中有四颠倒。世间无常而别有常世间。如说一作天祠堕落再亦堕落三作则不堕。是为无常中常颠倒。世间苦而说有常乐处。是为苦中乐颠倒。又说我神转为子愿使寿百岁。子是他身云何为我。是为无我中我颠倒。

Chapter 22 — Forty Dharmas Exclusive to Buddhas (Part 2)

As for your contention that, because the Buddha does not discuss the Vedas and other such non-Buddhist scriptures, he must therefore not be omniscient—I shall now respond to that as follows:

The Vedas are entirely lacking in the dharma of [liberation achieved through] skillful realization of nirvāṇa.[16] They contain only all manner of conceptual elaboration. Since what the Buddhas proclaim is all entirely devoted to the skillful realization of nirvāṇa, even though the Buddha is already well aware of the contents of the Vedas and other such scriptures, the Buddha does not discuss such things because those [Vedic] teachings have no capacity to lead anyone to the skillful realization of nirvāṇa.

Question: The Vedas *do* contain discussions of the skillful realization of nirvāṇa. Before the arising of this world, all was darkness and nothing whatsoever existed. In the beginning there existed a great man who appeared like the rising of the sun. If one was able to see him, then one could be liberated from the difficulty of being subject to dying.

[The Vedas] contain yet more guidance on these matters. They state that, because one's person is but small, then one's spiritual soul is correspondingly small. However, if one's person is great, then one's spiritual soul will be correspondingly great in scope, for the body is the home of the spiritual soul that always abides within it. If one uses wisdom to untie the bonds restraining one's spiritual soul, one will then gain liberation. Therefore one should realize from this that the Vedas *do* contain teachings leading to liberation through attainment of nirvāṇa.

Response: This is simply not so. Why not? The Vedic scriptures are tied up with the four inverted views. The world is impermanent and yet they posit the existence of a separate and permanent world. They claim that only one or two sacrifices to their deva [is insufficient and] conduces to falling away from it, but with a third sacrifice, one will not be subject to falling away from it. This scenario involves the inverted view that falsely ascribes permanence to what is itself impermanent.

The world is a place of suffering and yet the Vedas claim the existence of a sphere of eternal bliss. This is just an instance of the inverted view that falsely ascribes bliss to what is inherently bound up with suffering.

The Vedas also claim that one's soul may transform into one's son and be subject through prayer to an extended lifetime of a hundred years. But a "son" is another person, so how could it constitute a self? This is just an instance of the inverted view that falsely ascribes selfhood to what is not actually a self.

說身清淨

076a04 ‖ 第一無比。金銀珍寶無及身者。是名[1]無淨
076a05 ‖ 中淨顛倒。顛倒則無實。無實云何有寂滅。
076a06 ‖ 是故韋陀中無善寂滅法。問曰。韋陀中說。能
076a07 ‖ 知韋陀者清淨安隱。云何言無善寂滅法。
076a08 ‖ 答曰。知韋陀者雖說安隱非畢竟解脫。
076a09 ‖ 於異身中生解脫想。是說因長壽天。說為
076a10 ‖ 解脫。是故韋陀中實無解脫。復次韋陀中。略
076a11 ‖ 說有三義。一者呪願。二者稱讚。三者法則。
076a12 ‖ 呪願名為令我得妻子牛馬金銀珍寶。稱讚
076a13 ‖ 名為汝火神頭黑頸赤體黃常在眾生五大
076a14 ‖ 中。法則名為是事應作是不應作。如從昴
076a15 ‖ 星初受火法而實呪願稱讚法。則無有寂
076a16 ‖ 滅解脫。何以故。貪著世樂然蘇呪願無真
076a17 ‖ 智慧。不斷煩惱何有解脫。問曰。韋陀法自
076a18 ‖ 古有之第一可信。汝言無善寂滅故不可
076a19 ‖ 信者。是事不然。何以故。

说身清净第一无比。金银珍宝无及身者。是名无净中净颠倒。颠倒则无实。无实云何有寂灭。是故韦陀中无善寂灭法。问曰。韦陀中说。能知韦陀者清净安隐。云何言无善寂灭法。答曰。知韦陀者虽说安隐非毕竟解脱。于异身中生解脱想。是说因长寿天。说为解脱。是故韦陀中实无解脱。复次韦陀中。略说有三义。一者咒愿。二者称赞。三者法则。咒愿名为令我得妻子牛马金银珍宝。称赞名为汝火神头黑颈赤体黄常在众生五大中。法则名为是事应作是不应作。如从昴星初受火法而实咒愿称赞法。则无有寂灭解脱。何以故。贪着世乐然苏咒愿无真智慧。不断烦恼何有解脱。问曰。韦陀法自古有之第一可信。汝言无善寂灭故不可信者。是事不然。何以故。

Chapter 22 — *Forty Dharmas Exclusive to Buddhas (Part 2)*

They also claim that one's body is possessed of the foremost level of purity and so incomparable in this respect that not even the purity of gold, silver, or precious gems can approach the purity of the body. This is just an instance of the inverted view that falsely ascribes purity to what is devoid of purity.

If one holds inverted views, then [one's views] are devoid of reality. [If such teachings] are devoid of reality, how could they possess [a path to] nirvāṇa? Therefore the Vedas are devoid of any good methods for attaining nirvāṇa.

Question: The Vedas assert that whoever is able to know the Vedas becomes purified and possessed of peace and security. How then can you state that they have no good methods for attaining nirvāṇa?

Response: Although the Vedas assert that whoever knows the Vedas will gain peace and security, this is not ultimate liberation. Rather, this is but an envisioning of liberation projected onto another body. This claim bases itself on the idea that existence in the long-life heavens constitutes liberation. Therefore the Vedas truly contain no means to achieve liberation.

Furthermore, the teachings in the Vedas generally embody three types of concepts: The first involves chants and prayers. The second involves the utterance of praises. The third involves the principles of their dharma.

"Chants and prayers" refers to praying, "May I be caused to obtain a wife and sons, cows, horses, gold, silver, and precious jewels."

"Utterance of praises" refers to statements such as, "Oh, you, the spirit of fire with your black head, your red neck, and your yellow body—you abide eternally in the five great elements of living beings."

"Principles of their dharma" refers to teachings stating that one should do this and abstain from doing that.

Just as with their [erroneous teaching that] fire was first received from the Pleiades, so too, in truth, their methods of using chants and prayers and utterances of praises are all devoid of [any means to achieve] nirvāṇa's liberation. How is this so? Covetous attachment to worldly pleasures, [offerings of] burning ghee, spells, and incantations—these are all devoid of genuine wisdom. Since these do not cut off the afflictions, how could [the Vedas] have [the means to achieve] liberation?

Question: The dharmas in the Vedas have come forth from antiquity and are deserving of the foremost degree of faith. As for your contention that they have no good methods by which one might reach nirvāṇa, they are therefore not fit to be believed, this is wrong. Why?

正體字	
	佛法近乃出世。韋
076a20 ‖	陀自古久遠常在世間。是故古法可信近法
076a21 ‖	不可信。汝言韋陀中無善寂滅法。是事不
076a22 ‖	然。答曰。時不可信。[2]無明先出正智後出。邪
076a23 ‖	見先出正見後出。不可以無明邪見先出故
076a24 ‖	可信。正智正見後出不可信。如先有污泥
076a25 ‖	後有蓮花。先有[3]病後有藥。如是不可以
076a26 ‖	在先出者為貴。是故韋陀先出。佛法後出。
076a27 ‖	謂不可信者。是事不然。復次過去[4]錠光等
076a28 ‖	諸佛皆先出世。其法則古出。韋陀是後出。若
076a29 ‖	汝以先久為貴者。此諸佛及法則應是貴。
076b01 ‖	問曰。韋陀不能作善寂滅。是故佛法中不
076b02 ‖	說。若佛知不能作寂滅。何用知為。若不知
076b03 ‖	則非一切智人。二俱有過。答曰。汝語非也。
076b04 ‖	佛先知韋陀不能善寂滅故不說亦不修
076b05 ‖	行。問曰。若佛知韋陀無有利益故而說不
076b06 ‖	修習者何用知為。答曰。大智之人應悉分別
076b07 ‖	是正道是邪道。欲令無量人眾度險惡道故
076b08 ‖	行於正道。

簡體字

佛法近乃出世。韦陀自古久远常在世间。是故古法可信近法不可信。汝言韦陀中无善寂灭法。是事不然。答曰。时不可信。无明先出正智后出。邪见先出正见后出。不可以无明邪见先出故可信。正智正见后出不可信。如先有污泥后有莲花。先有病后有药。如是不可以在先出者为贵。是故韦陀先出。佛法后出。谓不可信者。是事不然。复次过去锭光等诸佛皆先出世。其法则古出。韦陀是后出。若汝以先久为贵者。此诸佛及法则应是贵。问曰。韦陀不能作善寂灭。是故佛法中不说。若佛知不能作寂灭。何用知为。若不知则非一切智人。二俱有过。答曰。汝语非也。佛先知韦陀不能善寂灭故不说亦不修行。问曰。若佛知韦陀无有利益故而说不修习者何用知为。答曰。大智之人应悉分别是正道是邪道。欲令无量人众度险恶道故行于正道。

Chapter 22 – Forty Dharmas Exclusive to Buddhas (Part 2)

Whereas the Buddha's Dharma has only recently emerged into the world, the Vedas have come down from long distant antiquity and have always prevailed in the world. Therefore, given that ancient dharmas are deserving of belief and newly arisen dharmas are not deserving of belief, your claim that the Vedas are devoid of any good methods by which one might realize nirvāṇa—this is wrong.

Response: Their relative antiquity is no justification for faith. Ignorance tends to come first whereas right knowledge comes only later. Erroneous views emerge first whereas right views emerge later. One cannot have faith in ignorance and erroneous views simply because they happened to emerge first nor can one deem right knowledge and right views to be unbelievable simply because they emerged later. This is analogous to there first being mud and only later lotuses, first being disease and only later a cure. Matters of these sorts are not worthy of being valued simply because they happened to appear first. Therefore, as for your contention that, because the Vedas came first and the Buddha's Dharma came later, the latter is unworthy of belief, this is a fallacy.

Furthermore, Dīpaṃkara Buddha and the other buddhas of the past all came into the world earlier. Their Dharma principles emerged in antiquity whereas the Vedas actually came forth only later. If you insist on relying on chronological primacy and long history as your bases for according esteem, then the Buddhas and their Dharma should be most highly valued.

Question: You claim it is because the Vedas have no good methods for reaching nirvāṇa that they are therefore not discussed in the Buddha's Dharma. But if the Buddha had really already known they are unable to lead to nirvāṇa, why did he bother to become knowledgeable about them? If in fact he was not *already* knowledgeable about them, he could not have been omniscient. Both stances are faulty.

Response: Your claim is wrong. The Buddha knew from early on that the Vedas have no good methods for reaching nirvāṇa. It is for this reason that he neither discussed them nor practiced what they teach.

Question: If it really was because the Buddha already knew there is no benefit to be had through the Vedas that he therefore instructed others not to cultivate their teaching, what was the point in his acquiring knowledge about them?

Response: People possessed of great knowledge should thoroughly distinguish between the correct path and the erroneous path. It is because one wishes to cause countless beings to go beyond dangerous and bad paths that one takes up the practice of the right path. This

正體字

```
         譬如導師善分別邪道正道。佛亦
076b09 ‖ 如是。既自得出生[5]老死險道。亦復欲令
076b10 ‖ 眾生出故。善知八[6]真聖道。亦知韋陀等邪
076b11 ‖ 險惡道。為離邪惡道故。行於正道[7]故。但
076b12 ‖ 知而不說。猶如農夫為穀種植至秋收穫
076b13 ‖ 亦得草[麩-夫+戈]。佛亦如是。為無上道故勤行精
076b14 ‖ 進得菩提[8]道。亦知韋陀等諸邪道。是故無
076b15 ‖ 咎。如汝先說無人能有具知四韋陀者。
076b16 ‖ 此難不然。世間人各有念力。有人一日能
076b17 ‖ 誦五偈。有誦百偈。有誦二百偈。若人一日
076b18 ‖ 不誦十偈則謂無能誦百偈出百偈者。
076b19 ‖ 此非實語。汝等不能盡知故。便言都無智
076b20 ‖ 者。若人見一人不能度河便言無能度
076b21 ‖ 者。是人不名正說。何以故。自有餘大力者
076b22 ‖ 能度。此亦如是。設使餘人不能盡知。一切
076b23 ‖ 智者知之何咎。復次脾娑仙人。皆讀韋陀亦
076b24 ‖ 應成一切智。若有盡讀韋陀。何以言無一
076b25 ‖ 切智。
```

简体字

譬如导师善分别邪道正道。佛亦如是。既自得出生老死险道。亦复欲令众生出故。善知八真圣道。亦知韦陀等邪险恶道。为离邪恶道故。行于正道故。但知而不说。犹如农夫为谷种植至秋收获亦得草[麩-夫+戈]。佛亦如是。为无上道故勤行精进得菩提道。亦知韦陀等诸邪道。是故无咎。如汝先说无人能有具知四韦陀者。此难不然。世间人各有念力。有人一日能诵五偈。有诵百偈。有诵二百偈。若人一日不诵十偈则谓无能诵百偈出百偈者。此非实语。汝等不能尽知故。便言都无智者。若人见一人不能度河便言无能度者。是人不名正说。何以故。自有余大力者能度。此亦如是。设使余人不能尽知。一切智者知之何咎。复次脾娑仙人。皆读韦陀亦应成一切智。若有尽读韦陀。何以言无一切智。

is analogous to a guide who skillfully distinguishes between errant paths and the right path.

The Buddha is just the same in this respect. Since he himself had already succeeded in escaping the dangerous path of birth, aging, and death and also wished to cause other beings to escape from it as well, he knew well the genuine eightfold path of the Āryas and also knew the dangerous and bad paths of the Vedas and other such teachings. It was in order to facilitate others' abandonment of deviant and bad paths and in order to encourage their practice of the correct path that, [with regard to the Vedas], he merely became knowledgeable about them, but did not discuss them.

This is analogous to the situation with farmers who plant their fields and then, with the arrival of autumn, reap a harvest that may also happen to include a few useless weeds. The Buddha is like this as well. For the sake of achieving success in the unsurpassable path, he cultivates assiduously and vigorously and consequently gains the path of bodhi while incidentally gaining knowledge of the Vedas and other such erroneous paths. Hence there is no fault on his part in any of this.

As for your previous statement claiming that no single person can completely know the four Vedas, this challenge of yours is false. People of the world each have the power of memory. There are those who, in a single day, can only recite five verses from memory, whereas others can recite one or two hundred verses from memory. If a particular person who cannot even recite ten verses from memory then holds the opinion that nobody could be able to recite from memory a hundred or more than a hundred verses, this would be an untruthful claim. It is because people such as yourself are unable to completely know the Vedas that you then claim nobody knows them.

If someone observes that some other person was unable to ford a particular river and then claims that nobody can cross that river, this person's statement on the matter does not qualify as correct speech. Why not? It is because there will naturally be some other person possessed of great strength who can indeed cross that river. This case is just like that. Even if one supposes that other [ordinary people] would be unable to entirely know [the Vedas], what fault is there in stipulating that someone possessed of all-knowledge would know them?

Furthermore, the *pisuo*[17] rishis all study the Vedas and ought themselves to be able to reach all-knowledge. Thus if there are these persons who have completely studied the Vedas, how can you say that nobody can have all-knowledge?

正體字	若汝言有經書能生貪欲瞋恚者。我 076b26 ‖ 今當答。若人欲長壽。應離死因緣。佛亦如 076b27 ‖ 是欲斷一切眾生貪欲瞋恚。應知貪欲[9]瞋 076b28 ‖ 恚因緣。復次如汝[10]說能知生貪欲瞋恚 076b29 ‖ 經書則有貪欲瞋恚者。無有是[11]處也。佛 076c01 ‖ 雖知是不用不行故無過咎。如人知死因 076c02 ‖ 緣則不死。若行死因緣則死。是事亦爾。若 076c03 ‖ 汝說不知未來事故不名一切智者。我今 076c04 ‖ 當答。此則非難。我等亦知有難一切智者 076c05 ‖ 如經中說。佛告諸比丘。凡夫無[12]智有三相。 076c06 ‖ 不應思而思。不應說而說。不應作而作。 076c07 ‖ 是故皆已總說。汝等未來世凡夫皆在其中 076c08 ‖ 無利益故。何用分別說其名字等。若謂佛 076c09 ‖ 知有難不[*]豫答者亦不須此。今現四眾 076c10 ‖ 中亦有善斷疑難者。今亦有能破諸難問 076c11 ‖ 者。何用先答。如汝今日現見比丘之中能 076c12 ‖ 破婆羅門者。是故不須先答。
简体字	若汝言有经书能生贪欲嗔恚者。我今当答。若人欲长寿。应离死因缘。佛亦如是欲断一切众生贪欲嗔恚。应知贪欲嗔恚因缘。复次如汝说能知生贪欲嗔恚经书则有贪欲嗔恚者。无有是处也。佛虽知是不用不行故无过咎。如人知死因缘则不死。若行死因缘则死。是事亦尔。若汝说不知未来事故不名一切智者。我今当答。此则非难。我等亦知有难一切智者如经中说。佛告诸比丘。凡夫无智有三相。不应思而思。不应说而说。不应作而作。是故皆已总说。汝等未来世凡夫皆在其中无利益故。何用分别说其名字等。若谓佛知有难不豫答者亦不须此。今现四众中亦有善断疑难者。今亦有能破诸难问者。何用先答。如汝今日现见比丘之中能破婆罗门者。是故不须先答。

Chapter 22 — *Forty Dharmas Exclusive to Buddhas (Part 2)*

I shall now respond to your [above-stated] claim that there are scriptures which [by their explication of the causes and conditions conducing to desire] are capable of causing one to feel desire or hatred. If one wishes to have a long life, he should abandon causes and conditions conducive to death. The Buddha, too, in this same way, wished to influence beings to cut off their desires and hatreds. This required that he know the causes and conditions that initiate the arising of desire and hatred.

Additionally, as for your contention that, if one is able to know the classical texts concerned with generating desire or hatred, one will then become afflicted with desire and hatred—this is a baseless claim. Although the Buddha had knowledge of these texts, because he did not use them or implement their practices, he was without fault in this respect. So too, if a person merely knows the causes and conditions that precipitate death, this does not entail his dying [as a result]. Only if he were to implement the causes and conditions that precipitate death would he then die as a result. This case is just the same as that one.

I shall now address your contention that, if one does not know future matters, then one does not qualify as omniscient. This does not constitute as a valid challenge. We already know of instances involving challenges to the plausibility of omniscience. As stated in the sutras: "The Buddha told the bhikshus, 'The common person bereft of wisdom has three characteristics: He contemplates what he should not contemplate, discusses what he should not discuss, and does what he should not do.'"[18]

Everything of relevance is already comprehensively mentioned in that statement. You common people of this future time are all included in it. As it would have no particular benefit, what would be the point in his having distinguished and mentioned names and such [related to future events]?

If one were to claim [that there is a contradiction] if the Buddha knew there would be these challenges, yet failed to reply to them in advance, there would really have been no need for this, for, in this presently existing fourfold assembly there are already those well able to cut off doubts in their responses to challenges [such as this]. We now already have those well able to refute challenging inquiries. What then would be the point in [the Buddha himself] responding in advance to such things? Right now, among the bhikshus you encounter in the present day, there are already those well able to refute the tenets posited by brahmans. Therefore there is no need [for the Buddha] to have responded in advance to such challenges.

正體字

```
              又先時亦有
076c13 ||  答。散在眾經。人不能具知佛法故。不知
076c14 ||  處所。若言受調達出家事。我今當答。謂
076c15 ||  受調達出家則非一切智人者。是[13]語不然。
076c16 ||  調達出家非佛所度。問曰。若餘人度者佛何
076c17 ||  以聽。答曰。善惡各有時。不必出家便惡。調
076c18 ||  達出家之後有持戒諸功德。是故出家無
076c19 ||  過。復次調達於十二年清淨持戒誦六萬
076c20 ||  法藏。此果報者當來不空必有利益。汝說調
076c21 ||  達機關激石[14]者。我今當說。諸佛成就無殺
076c22 ||  法故。一切世間無能奪命者。問曰。若成就
076c23 ||  不殺法者。何故迸石而來。答曰。佛於先世
076c24 ||  種壞身業定報應受。示眾生業報不可捨故
076c25 ||  現受。是故自來。汝言旃遮女佛不先說者。
076c26 ||  我今當答。以旃遮女故譏佛者。不能壞
076c27 ||  一切智人因緣。若佛先說旃遮女當來
```

简体字

又先时亦有答。散在众经。人不能具知佛法故。不知处所。若言受调达出家事。我今当答。谓受调达出家则非一切智人者。是语不然。调达出家非佛所度。问曰。若余人度者佛何以听。答曰。善恶各有时。不必出家便恶。调达出家之后有持戒诸功德。是故出家无过。复次调达于十二年清净持戒诵六万法藏。此果报者当来不空必有利益。汝说调达机关激石者。我今当说。诸佛成就无杀法故。一切世间无能夺命者。问曰。若成就不杀法者。何故迸石而来。答曰。佛于先世种坏身业定报应受。示众生业报不可舍故现受。是故自来。汝言旃遮女佛不先说者。我今当答。以旃遮女故讥佛者。不能坏一切智人因缘。若佛先说旃遮女当来

Chapter 22 — *Forty Dharmas Exclusive to Buddhas (Part 2)* 763

Furthermore, there have already been prior responses to such challenges that are scattered in various places throughout the many sutras. Because people are unable to completely know the Dharma of the Buddha, they do not know where those passages are located.

I shall now address your challenge on the matter of the Buddha's having allowed Devadatta to leave the home life and become a monk. As for your opinion that, if the Buddha allowed Devadatta to leave the home life, he could not have been omniscient, this statement is wrong. When Devadatta left the home life to become a monk, it was not the Buddha who was involved in allowing him to become a monastic.

Question: Even if it was someone else who allowed him to become a monastic, why did the Buddha allow this to happen?

Response: The doing of good and the doing of evil each have the season in which they occur. It was not necessarily the case that, having left home, he would immediately embark on doing evil. After Devadatta left home to become a monk, he had all of the meritorious qualities that are associated with upholding the moral precepts. Therefore there was no fault in [permitting] his leaving the home life.

Additionally, for twelve years, Devadatta was pure in his observance of the moral precepts and also became able then to recite from memory sixty-thousand lines from the treasury of Dharma. The karmic reward from this is such that, in the future, [such cultivation] will not have been in vain. In fact, it will definitely benefit him later on.

I will now reply to your statement regarding Devadatta's prying loose of a boulder [in an attempt to murder the Buddha]. Because all buddhas have already perfected the dharma of not killing, nobody in any world can ever rob them of life.

Question: If the Buddha had actually perfected the dharma of not killing, why did the boulder shatter and [allow a piece of it] to come down [and strike him in the foot]?

Response: The Buddha had planted karmic causes associated with damage to the body for which he was bound to undergo this fixed retribution. He manifested the appearance of having to undergo it in order to demonstrate to beings that karmic retributions cannot be escaped. It was for this reason that he voluntarily came to that place.

I shall now respond to your contention that there was some problem in the Buddha's not having spoken in advance about the incident involving that woman, Ciñcā. There is nothing in that woman, Ciñcā's, disparaging of the Buddha that can serve as a causal basis for impugning his qualification as omniscient. If the Buddha had announced in advance, "In the future, that woman, Ciñca, will come forth and

謗我者。旃遮女則不來。復次佛先世謗人罪業因緣。今必應受。汝說佛何以不遮孫陀利入祇洹事。我今當答。此事不能壞一切智人因緣。佛無有力令一切眾生盡作樂人。又諸佛離一切諍訟不自高身不著持戒。是故不遮。復次佛先世業熟故。必應受七日謗。又眾生見佛聞謗不憂。[1]雪明不喜故。發無上道心。作是願言。我等亦當得如是清淨心。是故無咎。汝先說佛入婆羅門聚落空鉢而出非一切智人者。今當答。佛不以[2]飲食先觀人心入聚落已魔轉其意。問曰。是事佛應先知。我入聚落魔當轉人心。答曰。佛亦先知此事。為大利益眾生。諸佛非但以受人食故。以為利益度脫眾生。有以清淨心迎逆敬禮和顏瞻視。此皆大利何必飲食。以種種門利益眾生。非空入聚落。

slander me," then that woman, Ciñca, would not in fact have come forth as she did. Furthermore, it was due to the karmic causes and conditions associated with the Buddha's having slandered others in a previous lifetime that he was now definitely bound to undergo [the corresponding retribution]. [19]

I shall now address your challenge as to how it could have been that the Buddha failed to prevent the incident that occurred when Sundarī entered the Jeta Grove.[20] This incident does not constitute a reason for impugning the Buddha's qualification as omniscient. The Buddha does not have some power by which he is able to cause every being's life to be an entirely happy one. Also, the Buddhas have all left behind disputation, do not elevate themselves, and are not attached to [making others] uphold moral precepts, consequently he did not act to prevent this incident.

Additionally, it was because of the ripening of karma from a previous life that he was definitely bound to undergo that seven days of slander. Moreover, when beings observed that the Buddha was neither perturbed over hearing himself slandered nor joyful when his innocence was made clear, they brought forth the resolve to follow the unsurpassable path, uttering this vow, "We too shall acquire just such a pure mind as this." Therefore there was no fault [in the Buddha's having acted as he did].

I shall now respond to your contention that, because the Buddha entered a brahman village and then left with an empty bowl, he was therefore not omniscient.[21] The Buddha [did not go to that village] for the sake of food and drink, [but rather because] he had contemplated the minds of the people there. It was only after he entered the village that Māra changed the villagers' minds.

Question: This is a matter about which the Buddha should have become aware in advance, thinking, "If I go into this village, Māra will change these peoples' minds."

Response: The Buddha in fact *did* know about this matter in advance [and entered that village anyway] in order to bring great benefit to those beings. It is not solely on the basis of receiving alms food from them that the Buddhas benefit beings and facilitate their liberation. There were those who welcomed him there with pure minds, bowed in reverence to him, and looked up to him with congenial gazes. All of these things already served great benefit. Why should it be an essential requirement that he be given food and drink? There are many different sorts of methods by which he was able to be of benefit to beings. Thus it was not in vain that he entered that village.

正體字

汝說佛逆趣醉象者。今當答。佛雖知
此事。以因緣故往以此醉象必應得度。又
能障其害佛罪業。復次此象身如黑山。眾
人見此低頭禮佛皆起恭敬。以是因緣故
[3]佛故往趣。復次佛趣此象無有過失。若
有惡事可作此難。汝難至隨蘭若者。為
受先世業果報故。汝說畜須[4]洹叉多羅
為弟子者。今當說。佛身口意命不須守護。
無所畏故聽為弟子。復次是人常近佛故
得見種種大神力。見諸天龍夜叉乾闥婆阿
修羅等諸王來供養佛請問種種甚深要法
心得清淨。心清淨故得利益因緣。是故雖
惡聽為弟子。問曰。此人於佛多生惡心。是
故不應聽為弟子。答曰。若不聽為弟子亦
有惡心。是故聽為弟子無咎。汝說先未作
罪時何以不制戒。今當答。

简体字

汝说佛逆趣醉象者。今当答。佛虽知此事。以因缘故往以此醉象必应得度。又能障其害佛罪业。复次此象身如黑山。众人见此低头礼佛皆起恭敬。以是因缘故佛故往趣。复次佛趣此象无有过失。若有恶事可作此难。汝难至随兰若者。为受先世业果报故。汝说畜须洹叉多罗为弟子者。今当说。佛身口意命不须守护。无所畏故听为弟子。复次是人常近佛故得见种种大神力。见诸天龙夜叉乾闼婆阿修罗等诸王来供养佛请问种种甚深要法心得清净。心清净故得利益因缘。是故虽恶听为弟子。问曰。此人于佛多生恶心。是故不应听为弟子。答曰。若不听为弟子亦有恶心。是故听为弟子无咎。汝说先未作罪时何以不制戒。今当答。

I shall now respond to your statement about the Buddha's having gone up the road on which there was a drunken elephant.[22] Although the Buddha already knew of this matter, there was a reason he deliberately went there. It was because this drunken elephant was definitely at a point where he could be brought across to liberation. The Buddha was also intent on preventing his falling into the karmic offense of harming a buddha.

Additionally, this elephant's body had the appearance of a black mountain. When the population there saw this elephant bow down its head in reverence to the Buddha, they all brought forth thoughts of reverence. It was for these reasons that the Buddha deliberately went up that road. Also, there was no error involved in the Buddha's having entered that road to encounter that elephant. Only if some unfortunate incident had transpired would you have a basis for bringing up this challenge.

As for your challenge regarding the Buddha's having gone to Verañjā, that was simply a case of having to undergo retribution for karmic deeds committed in a previous life.[23]

I shall now address your statement on the issue of the Buddha's having accepted Sunakṣatra as a disciple.[24] The Buddha has no need to guard against errors in actions of body, speech, mind, or livelihood.[25] It was because he is utterly without fear that he permitted Sunakṣatra to become a disciple.

Also, because this man always dwelt in close proximity to the Buddha, he was thus able to observe the display of all manner of spiritual powers and also saw the arrival of devas, dragons, *yakṣas*, *gandharvas*, *asuras*, kings, and others, all coming to make offerings to the Buddha and to pose respectful questions to him on all manner of extremely profound and essential dharmas. Hence his mind was thereby able to become purified. Because he was able to achieve purification of mind, this was a causal basis for his [eventual] benefit. Therefore, even though he was an evil man, the Buddha nonetheless accepted him as a disciple.

Question: This man had many evil thoughts about the Buddha. Therefore the Buddha should not have permitted him to become a disciple.

Response: Even if the Buddha had not accepted him as a disciple, the man still would have had those evil thoughts. Therefore there was no fault in the Buddha's permitting him to become a disciple.

I shall now respond to your challenge as to why the Buddha did not formulate the moral precepts in advance of [his disciples'] commission

正體字

佛先結戒。說八聖道正見正思惟正語正業正命正精進正念正定。說是至涅槃道故。已說一切諸戒。復次佛說三學。善學戒善學心善學慧。當知已說一切諸戒。復次佛告諸比丘。一切惡決定不應作。是不名先結戒耶。復次佛說十善道。離殺盜婬兩舌惡罵妄言綺語貪嫉瞋恚邪見。不名先結戒耶。佛先十二年中說一偈為布薩法。所謂一切惡莫作。一切善當行。自淨其志意。是則諸佛教。是故當知先已結戒。復次佛說諸小惡因緣皆應當離。如說。

　　離身諸惡行　　亦離口諸惡
　　離意諸惡行　　餘惡悉遠離

如是說者當知先[5]已結戒。復次佛先已說諸守護法。如說。

　　護身為善哉　　能護口亦善
　　護意為善哉　　護一切亦善

简体字

佛先结戒。说八圣道正见正思惟正语正业正命正精进正念正定。说是至涅槃道故。已说一切诸戒。复次佛说三学。善学戒善学心善学慧。当知已说一切诸戒。复次佛告诸比丘。一切恶决定不应作。是不名先结戒耶。复次佛说十善道。离杀盗淫两舌恶骂妄言绮语贪嫉瞋恚邪见。不名先结戒耶。佛先十二年中说一偈为布萨法。所谓一切恶莫作。一切善当行。自净其志意。是则诸佛教。是故当知先已结戒。复次佛说诸小恶因缘皆应当离。如说。

　　离身诸恶行　　亦离口诸恶
　　离意诸恶行　　余恶悉远离

如是说者当知先已结戒。复次佛先已说诸守护法。如说。

　　护身为善哉　　能护口亦善
　　护意为善哉　　护一切亦善

of the corresponding transgressions. The Buddha did in fact formulate moral precepts in advance. He set forth the eightfold path of the Āryas that consist of right views, right thought, right speech, right action, right livelihood, right effort, right mindfulness, and right meditative concentration. Because he did describe this path leading to the attainment of nirvāṇa, he in fact had already formulated all of the precepts.

Furthermore, the Buddha described the three trainings wherein one thoroughly trains in moral virtue, thoroughly trains in [focusing] the mind, and thoroughly trains in wisdom. One should then realize from this that he had in fact already set forth all of the moral precepts.

Additionally, the Buddha told the bhikshus that they should definitely not do any sort of evil. Does this not constitute prior formulation of moral precepts?

Also, the Buddha spoke of the path of the ten courses of good karmic action, namely abandoning killing, stealing, sexual misconduct, divisive speech, harsh speech, false speech, frivolous speech, covetousness, ill will, and wrong views. Does this not constitute prior formulation of moral precepts?

Twelve years earlier, the Buddha described in a single verse the *upoṣadha* dharma,[26] namely:

To refrain from doing any sort of evil deed,
to respectfully engage in every sort of good deed,
and to purify one's own mind—
This is the teaching of all Buddhas.[27]

One should therefore realize that the Buddha in fact *did* formulate the moral precepts in advance.

Also, the Buddha stated that one should abandon even all of the most minor causes and conditions associated with evil, as stated in these lines:

Abandon all evil actions of the body.
Also abandon all evil speech,
abandon all evil actions of the mind,
and utterly abandon all other forms of evil.

On the basis of statements such as these, one should realize that the Buddha had already formulated the moral precepts in advance. Additionally, the Buddha had already described in advance the dharmas through which one guards against transgressions, as stated in these lines:

To guard the body is good indeed.
To be able to guard one's speech is also good.

正體字

077b19 ‖　　比丘護一切　　　得遠離諸[6]惡
077b20 ‖ 如是說者當知先已結戒。復次佛先說善
077b21 ‖ 相。如說。
077b22 ‖　　手足勿妄犯　　　節言慎所行
077b23 ‖　　當樂守定意　　　是名真比丘
077b24 ‖ 如是說者當知先已結戒。復次說沙門法
077b25 ‖ 故。當知先已結戒。沙門有四法。一於瞋不
077b26 ‖ 報。二於罵默然。三杖捶能受。四害者忍之。
077b27 ‖ 復次佛說四念處。觀身觀受觀心觀法。是
077b28 ‖ 涅槃道住處故。當知先[7]已結戒。若微小惡
077b29 ‖ 尚不聽。何況身口惡業。如是等因緣當知
077c01 ‖ 先已結戒。如王者立制。不應作惡。後有
077c02 ‖ 犯者隨事輕重作如是罪如是治之。佛
077c03 ‖ 亦如是。先總說戒。後有犯者說其罪相。如
077c04 ‖ 有作惡者教令懺悔。作如是罪

简体字

　　比丘护一切　　　得远离诸恶
如是说者当知先已结戒。复次佛先说善相。如说。
　　手足勿妄犯　　　节言慎所行
　　当乐守定意　　　是名真比丘
　　如是说者当知先已结戒。复次说沙门法故。当知先已结戒。沙门有四法。一于瞋不报。二于骂默然。三杖捶能受。四害者忍之。复次佛说四念处。观身观受观心观法。是涅槃道住处故。当知先已结戒。若微小恶尚不听。何况身口恶业。如是等因缘当知先已结戒。如王者立制。不应作恶。后有犯者随事轻重作如是罪如是治之。佛亦如是。先总说戒。后有犯者说其罪相。如有作恶者教令忏悔。作如是罪

Chapter 22 — Forty Dharmas Exclusive to Buddhas (Part 2)

> To guard one's mind is good indeed,
> and to guard against all errors is good as well.[28]
> The bhikshu guards against all errors
> and thereby succeeds in abandoning all evil.

One should realize on the basis of these statements that the Buddha in fact *did* formulate the moral precepts in advance. Moreover, the Buddha also described in advance the characteristics of goodness, as stated in these lines:

> Do not allow hands or feet to carelessly commit transgressions.
> Restrain your words and take care in actions done.
> One should take pleasure in guarding and focusing the mind.
> It is on these bases that one is rightfully called a bhikshu.[29]

One should realize on the basis of statements such as this that the Buddha in fact *did* formulate the moral precepts in advance.

Furthermore, because the Buddha described the dharmas by which one is a *śramaṇa*, one should realize he did in fact formulate the moral precepts in advance. There are four dharmas by which one is a *śramaṇa*: First, one does not respond in kind to hate-filled actions. Second, one remains silent in the face of scolding. Third, one is able to endure even being beaten with staves. And fourth, one maintains patience with those who have dealt one harm.

Moreover, the Buddha taught the four stations of mindfulness, namely the contemplation of the body, the contemplation of feelings, the contemplation of thoughts, and the contemplation of dharmas, doing so because they constitute the abode of the path to nirvāṇa. Hence one should realize that he *did* formulate the moral precepts in advance.

The Buddha would not even permit the most subtle form of evil, how much the less would he condone any sort of evil karma in one's physical actions or speech. For reasons such as these, one should realize that he did indeed formulate the moral precepts in advance.

This is analogous to a king's establishment of laws in which one is forbidden to do evil deeds. When, later on, there are transgressions against those laws, it is according to the relative gravity of the crime that corresponding punishments are imposed. The Buddha is just the same in this respect. He first made general statements describing the moral precepts. Later on, when offenses occurred, he described the specific characteristic factors by which the given action constituted an offense.

Where there were those who committed evil deeds, they were instructed and caused to repent. He instructed that, for a given offense,

正體字

應如是
懺。不見擯滅擯不共住等。成如是事故。後
乃結戒。[8]
十住毘婆沙論卷第十　　十住毘婆沙論卷第十一
　　　　聖者龍樹造
　　　後秦龜茲國三藏鳩摩羅什譯
　　　四十不共法中難一切智人品之餘
[9]汝說耆年貴族家等應為上座。今當答。道
法中耆年貴族家等於道無益。何以故。生
佛法中名為貴族好家中生。從受大戒數
其年數名為耆年。汝謂耆年應供養者。先
出家受戒非是大耶。[10]又從受戒以後無
有諸姓等差別。諸比丘受大戒。名為生在
佛家。是則失先大小家名皆為一家。汝說
持戒者。出家在先持戒日久長夜護持。年歲
多故應為上座。如結戒中說。汝說持戒之
人不應禮破戒者。今當答。破戒人尚不
應共住。何況禮拜供養。以其自言是比丘
故。隨其大小而為作禮。如禮泥木天像。以
念真天故。

简体字

应如是忏。不见摈灭摈不共住等。成如是事故。后乃结戒。

　　汝说耆年贵族家等应为上座。今当答。道法中耆年贵族家等于道无益。何以故。生佛法中名为贵族好家中生。从受大戒数其年数名为耆年。汝谓耆年应供养者。先出家受戒非是大耶。又从受戒以后无有诸姓等差别。诸比丘受大戒。名为生在佛家。是则失先大小家名皆为一家。汝说持戒者。出家在先持戒日久长夜护持。年岁多故应为上座。如结戒中说。汝说持戒之人不应礼破戒者。今当答。破戒人尚不应共住。何况礼拜供养。以其自言是比丘故。随其大小而为作礼。如礼泥木天像。以念真天故。

Chapter 22 – *Forty Dharmas Exclusive to Buddhas (Part 2)*

a given corresponding form of penance was to be performed or that either temporary expulsion or complete expulsion was stipulated so that the miscreant could not dwell together with the community, and so forth. It was only with the establishment of these sorts of cases that we came to have the subsequent formulation of moral precepts.

I shall now address your contention that superior position in the monastic community should be accorded on the basis of age, nobility of birth caste, status of one's clan, and so forth. In the dharmas of the path, issues of age, nobility of birth caste, status of one's clan, and so forth afford no benefit. How is this so? It is on the basis of being born into the Dharma of the Buddha that one qualifies as being born into nobility and into a fine clan. Seniority is determined on the basis of the number of years one has received the higher ordination and this is the rationale for being referred to as an elder.

As for your opinion that those who are merely older in years should be given priority in the receipt of offerings, is it not the case that those who first left the home life and received the ordination precepts are better regarded as of greater eminence?

Furthermore, from the time one receives the ordination precepts onward, there are no longer any distinctions on the basis of one's caste and such. It is only when bhikshus receive the precepts of the higher ordination that they then qualify as having been born into the family of the Buddhas. It is at this point that one loses any name associated with prior birth into a greater or lesser clan and everyone then belongs to this one single family.

As for your statements on upholding the precepts—those who first left the home life to become monastics and who have observed the moral precepts for the longest time and then proceed to uphold those moral precepts for a long time—it is because of their years of seniority in this that they should be accorded a superior position within the monastic community. This is as set forth in the original formulation of the moral precept code.

I shall now address your contention that those who are most strictly observant in their upholding of the moral precepts should not bow in reverence to those who have broken the moral precepts. Those who truly have broken the moral precepts should not even be allowed to dwell together with the community, how much the less should they receive reverential obeisance or offerings.

It is on the basis of their claim to be a bhikshu that one pays reverence to them according to their order of seniority. This is similar to when one bows in reverence before a deity's image made of clay or wood, doing so as a means of bearing in mind that actual deity.

正體字

佛勅年少應禮上座。順佛教
077c28 ‖ 故則便得福。汝說以頭陀故應敬禮者。今
077c29 ‖ 當答。若頭陀[11]人有五種故難得分別。一者
078a01 ‖ 愚癡無所知故貪受難法。二者鈍根悕望
078a02 ‖ 得利。三者惡意欺誑於人。四者狂亂。五者
078a03 ‖ 作念。頭陀法者。諸佛賢聖所共稱讚。以其
078a04 ‖ 隨順涅槃道故。是五種人。行頭陀法真偽
078a05 ‖ 難別。多聞者。多聞之人亦如頭陀難可分
078a06 ‖ 別。何以故。或以樂道故多聞。或以利養故
078a07 ‖ 多聞。如是等亦難分別。又佛法貴如說行。
078a08 ‖ 不貴多讀多誦。又如佛說行一法句能自
078a09 ‖ [1]利益名為多聞。智慧亦如是。若不能如
078a10 ‖ 所說行何用智慧為。是故不以智慧故說
078a11 ‖ 為上座。

简体字

佛敕年少应礼上座。顺佛教故则便得福。汝说以头陀故应敬礼者。今当答。若头陀人有五种故难得分别。一者愚痴无所知故贪受难法。二者钝根悕望得利。三者恶意欺诳于人。四者狂乱。五者作念。头陀法者。诸佛贤圣所共称赞。以其随顺涅槃道故。是五种人。行头陀法真伪难别。多闻者。多闻之人亦如头陀难可分别。何以故。或以乐道故多闻。或以利养故多闻。如是等亦难分别。又佛法贵如说行。不贵多读多诵。又如佛说行一法句能自利益名为多闻。智慧亦如是。若不能如所说行何用智慧为。是故不以智慧故说为上座。

Chapter 22 — *Forty Dharmas Exclusive to Buddhas (Part 2)*

The Buddha decreed that those of fewer years seniority should revere those who are seated in a superior position within the monastic order. It is through according with the Buddha's instructions in this that one acquires karmic merit.

I shall now respond to your statement that the according of reverence should be based on one's practice of the *dhūta* austerities. In this matter of those who take up the *dhūta* practices, there are five general types of practitioners among which it is difficult to make clear distinctions:[30]

- First, there are those who are deluded and who, due to an absence of right knowledge, are driven by desire to practice these difficult dharmas;
- Second, there are those possessed of only dull faculties who wish to acquire benefits as a result;
- Third, there are those with evil intentions focused on deceiving others;
- Fourth, there are those who are mentally ill;
- And fifth, there are those who [take them up], thinking, "The dharmas of the *dhūta* austerities are praised by all buddhas, worthies, and *āryas* because they accord with the path to nirvāṇa."

Among these five classes of practitioners of the *dhūta* austerities, it is difficult to distinguish which are genuine and which are false.

Now, as for this matter of one's level of learning, just as with the *dhūta* austerities, it is difficult to distinguish clearly among those who have acquired abundant learning. How is this so? It could be that it is on the basis of delighting in the path that one has accrued much learning. Or perhaps it is only for the sake of receiving offerings that one has accrued much learning. It is difficult to make clear distinctions in matters such as these.

Additionally, in the Dharma of the Buddha, it is practice in accordance with one's words that is accorded esteem. One does not accord esteem merely on the basis of having engaged in much study or having become able to recite many scriptures. Also, according to the statements of the Buddha himself, if one practices but a single sentence of Dharma and is thereby able to derive self-benefit from that, this itself qualifies as abundant learning.

So too it is with this matter of wisdom. If one remains unable to implement a level of practice consistent with one's level of discourse, of what use is this wisdom? Consequently, it is not on the basis of one's degree of wisdom that one determines who is accorded a superior position in the monastic order.

正體字

譬如世間現事弟雖多聞多智而
兄不為作禮。是故不以智慧故先受供養
禮拜如是。雖多聞智慧應禮先受戒者。若
先供養多聞智慧者則為鬪亂。餘[2]得沙門
果斷結。得神通最難知。是人得果是不
得果。是多[3]斷結是少[*]斷結。是得神通是
不得神通。不可以此為上座。若同得道
果斷結神通誰為上座。是故隨佛教行最
為第一。汝說佛於說法生疑。今當答。佛
於深法尚不有疑。何況應說不應說中而
有疑乎。佛不言我都不說法。但云心樂閑
靜不務[4]興事。而後於說法中無咎。復次
諸外道言。佛為大聖寂默無戲論。何用畜
眾而教化為。設使教化亦不可盡。似如分
別何用說法畜養弟子是貪著相。是故佛自
思惟。我法甚深智慧方便

简体字

譬如世间现事弟虽多闻多智而兄不为作礼。是故不以智慧故先受供养礼拜如是。虽多闻智慧应礼先受戒者。若先供养多闻智慧者则为斗乱。余得沙门果断结。得神通最难知。是人得果是不得果。是多断结是少断结。是得神通是不得神通。不可以此为上座。若同得道果断结神通谁为上座。是故随佛教行最为第一。汝说佛于说法生疑。今当答。佛于深法尚不有疑。何况应说不应说中而有疑乎。佛不言我都不说法。但云心乐闲静不务兴事。而后于说法中无咎。复次诸外道言。佛为大圣寂默无戏论。何用畜众而教化为。设使教化亦不可尽。似如分别何用说法畜养弟子是贪着相。是故佛自思惟。我法甚深智慧方便

This is analogous to the current way of doing things in the world. Although a younger brother may indeed be more learned or more wise, the elder brother is still not enjoined to pay him reverence. Therefore, after this same fashion, it is not on the basis of one's level of wisdom that one gains priority in the receipt of offerings or reverence. So it is then that, even though one may indeed have accrued much learning or wisdom, one should still accord reverence on the basis of who first received the ordination precepts. Were one to accord priority in the receipt of offerings to those of greater learning or a higher level of wisdom, this would inevitably result in discord within the community.

As for the other [criteria you propose for priority in according reverence], namely realization of the śramaṇa's fruits of the path, severance of fetters, and acquisition of spiritual powers, those are the most difficult matters to know. Whether or not this person has attained a fruit of the path, whether he has cut off more fetters or fewer fetters [than this other person], and whether or not he has acquired spiritual powers—one cannot use such matters as the basis for superior position in the monastic order. Consider for instance those who have realized the same fruits of the path, cut off the same fetters, and acquired the same spiritual powers. Who among them should be accorded superior position in the monastic order? Consequently, it is by far the best to simply accord with the Buddha's instructions on these matters.

I shall now address your contention that the Buddha himself was beset by doubt about whether he should expound the Dharma.[31] The Buddha had no doubts at all even with regard to the most profound sorts of dharmas, how much the less might he have had doubts with regard to whether or not he should expound the Dharma. The Buddha never said that he would entirely forego his teaching of the Dharma. He merely indicated a preference for continuing to abide in serenity, refraining from becoming involved in numerous endeavors. There was no fault in his having simply waited till later to begin expounding the Dharma.

Also, the non-Buddhist partisans would say, "If the Buddha is such a great ārya that he remains silent and declines to involve himself in conceptual elaboration, what use could he have for assembling a following and offering to give teachings?" Then again, once he started teaching, this would inevitably turn into an endless endeavor. It was as if he was weighing the utility of proceeding to teach the Dharma and assemble a group of disciples when this could appear outwardly as if it were a mark of covetous attachment.

Due to these factors, the Buddha reflected, "Though my Dharma is extremely deep, the wisdom and skillful means that might be

正體字

```
           無量無邊。而可度
078a27 ||  者少。是故自言不如默然。又防外道所譏
078a28 ||  呵故。令梵天王求請說法。即時梵天王等
078a29 ||  白佛言。眾生可愍。中有利根結使薄者易
078b01 ||  可化度。是故受諸梵王等請。如人得大寶
078b02 ||  藏應示餘人。如是諸聖自得法利亦應利
078b03 ||  人。如汝所說佛不知阿蘭迦蘭等先已命
078b04 ||  終欲為說法者。今當答。佛不念其死與
078b05 ||  不死。但念此人結使微薄[5]堪任化度。隨所
078b06 ||  念處則有智生。是故佛先自說。而後天告理
078b07 ||  故宜然。又佛先出家。就此二人曾經宿止。
078b08 ||  諸天人民[6]儻能疑佛受其妙法餘處得道。
078b09 ||  佛欲斷彼疑故。即時唱言彼人長衰如此。妙
078b10 ||  法如何不聞。推如是義。五比丘事亦復可
078b11 ||  知。但念其可度因緣。不念其住止所在。後
078b12 ||  念住處即便得知。
```

简体字

无量无边。而可度者少。是故自言不如默然。又防外道所讥呵故。令梵天王求请说法。即时梵天王等白佛言。众生可愍。中有利根结使薄者易可化度。是故受诸梵王等请。如人得大宝藏应示余人。如是诸圣自得法利亦应利人。如汝所说佛不知阿兰迦兰等先已命终欲为说法者。今当答。佛不念其死与不死。但念此人结使微薄堪任化度。随所念处则有智生。是故佛先自说。而后天告理故宜然。又佛先出家。就此二人曾经宿止。诸天人民傥能疑佛受其妙法余处得道。佛欲断彼疑故。即时唱言彼人长衰如此。妙法如何不闻。推如是义。五比丘事亦复可知。但念其可度因缘。不念其住止所在。后念住处即便得知。

Chapter 22 — *Forty Dharmas Exclusive to Buddhas (Part 2)*

employed in teaching it would be measureless and boundless. Still, those who are actually amenable to gaining liberation are but few." Consequently, he thought to himself, "It would be better to remain silent." It was also to defend against the potential for mocking deprecation by non-Buddhist partisans that he instead influenced the Brahma Heaven King to [first] request the proclamation of Dharma. The Brahma Heaven King and others then immediately addressed the Buddha, saying, "Beings are surely worthy of pity. There are among them those of sharp faculties and but few fetters who would be easy to teach and bring across to liberation."

Because of this, the Buddha acceded to the request of the Brahma Heaven King and others. It was as if someone who had just found a great treasury of jewels felt he should reveal their presence to others. In this same way, when *āryas* themselves gain the benefits of the Dharma, they feel they should also use it to benefit others.

I shall now address your contention that, because the Buddha expressed a wish to speak the Dharma for Ārāḍa Kālāma and others and therefore had not realized they had already died, [this contradicts the plausibility of his being omniscient]. The Buddha had not brought to mind the issue of whether or not they had already died, but rather was only considering the fact that, because these men's fetters were but scant, they would be capable of being instructed and brought across to liberation. It is in correspondence with the point upon which one's thought is focused that a corresponding knowledge arises. It was as a consequence of this that the Buddha first said this to himself and a deva then appropriately informed him.[32]

Also, since earlier on, when the Buddha had just abandoned the home life, he had gone to those men, [Ārāḍa Kālāma and Udraka Rāmaputra], and had spent time with them, the devas and other people could have entertained doubts in which they thought the Buddha had perhaps received the sublime Dharma from them and had then become enlightened in another location. Because the Buddha wished to cut off any doubts that they might have had, he immediately exclaimed, "Oh, those men—they have for so long suffered such misfortune as this. How can it be that they have still not heard this sublime Dharma?"

By inferring the implications of this idea, one can deduce the nature of the matter of the five bhikshus. It was because the Buddha had only brought to mind the causes and conditions associated with their capacity to gain liberation that he had not yet considered precisely where they were currently dwelling. Afterward, once he had thought about where they were dwelling, he then knew where they were.

正體字

是故不應破一切智人。
汝言疑說巴連弗城壞者。今當答。是城破因
緣不定。不定因緣而定說者是則為過。又我
先說四十不共法中諸佛善知不定。答者則
不受此難。汝說佛問諸比丘。汝等聚會為
何所說。今當答。佛將欲說法門故。作如是
問。或欲結戒故。[7]命其自說如是種種說
法故。問而無咎。世間亦有知而復問。如見
人食問言食耶。如天寒時問言寒耶。佛亦
如是知而復問隨俗無咎。汝言自讚毀他
非一切智人者。今當答。佛不貪身不貪
供養。不患他人不增上慢。所以自說我
於世間最第一者。有信眾生諸根猛利捨
惡知識。以我為師是人長夜當得安隱。是
故佛自讚身。復次有人求第一樂道。而有
懈怠不能精進。

简体字

是故不应破一切智人。汝言疑说巴连弗城坏者。今当答。是城破因缘不定。不定因缘而定说者是则为过。又我先说四十不共法中诸佛善知不定。答者则不受此难。汝说佛问诸比丘。汝等聚会为何所说。今当答。佛将欲说法门故。作如是问。或欲结戒故。命其自说如是种种说法故。问而无咎。世间亦有知而复问。如见人食问言食耶。如天寒时问言寒耶。佛亦如是知而复问随俗无咎。汝言自赞毁他非一切智人者。今当答。佛不贪身不贪供养。不患他人不增上慢。所以自说我于世间最第一者。有信众生诸根猛利舍恶知识。以我为师是人长夜当得安隐。是故佛自赞身。复次有人求第一乐道。而有懈怠不能精进。

Chapter 22 – Forty Dharmas Exclusive to Buddhas (Part 2)

Therefore one should not look upon these issues as refuting the plausibility of there being an omniscient person.

I shall now address your stated doubt with regard to the causes for the destruction of the city of Pāṭaliputra. The precise causes and conditions by which this city would meet its destruction were still unfixed. To make a fixed pronouncement on the unfolding of unfixed causes and conditions would itself be a fault.

Also among the forty exclusive dharmas listed earlier, I stated that all buddhas are thoroughly cognizant of dharmas that are unfixed. In response then, I do not accept this challenge as valid.

I shall now address your contention about the Buddha's querying the bhikshus as to the contents of their conversation by asking, "So, what are you all gathered together to discuss?" It was because the Buddha was about to hold forth on some aspect of Dharma that he initiated the discussion by asking a question of this sort. It could have been that, because he wished to formulate another of the moral prohibitions, he directed them to talk about what they were discussing. Because he took all sorts of such instances as occasions for speaking Dharma, the Buddha's posing a question was free of any fault [in relation to the issue of his omniscience].

Furthermore it is a commonplace in the world, even when one is already well aware of what is happening, for one to go ahead and ask a question. For instance, on observing someone eating, one may ask, "Oh, so you're eating, are you?" Or, for instance, on a particularly cold day, one may ask, "Isn't it cold?"

In this same way, even though he already knew, the Buddha would nonetheless pose a question. Being but a means of conforming to convention, this is entirely free of fault.

I shall now address your judgment that anyone who praises himself and criticizes others could not possibly be an omniscient person. The Buddha entertained no desires with respect to himself and so was not the least bit covetous of receiving offerings. He did not hate other men and was not possessed of overweening pride. As for the reason for his having declared himself to be foremost among everyone in the world, it was because there were beings who were amenable to faith and possessed of acutely sharp faculties who, if they cast aside bad spiritual guides and took the Buddha as their teacher, they could then gain that peace and security that would see them through the long night [of subsequent rebirths]. It was for this reason that the Buddha did in fact praise his own personal qualities.

Additionally, there were those who, although they sought the path to the supreme bliss, were still indolent and unable to bring forth

正體字

是故佛言無上利中不應
懈怠。我於世間第一導師善說正法。宜勤
精進可得道果。如是等因緣自讚其身。非
為自貴輕賤他人。呵惡人者欲令除滅
惡法。非為憎恚眾生。有人求如法利。其心
清淨質直。而與惡知識和合。欲令遠離此
故而呵罵之。未得佛時尚以髓腦施人。何
況成佛而當呵罵。汝說佛法初後相違。今當
答。佛法中無有始終相違事。汝等不知佛
法義故以為相違。是涅槃道者。從迦葉佛
滅已來。無復人說。亦無人得。是故言我新
得道。餘處復說我得故道。是道錠光等諸佛
所得。所謂八聖道能至涅槃。一道一因緣故名
為故道。是故當知佛成一切智。問曰。所言
一切智者。云何名為一切智。為知一切故
名為一切智耶。答曰。一切智者知可知。可
知者五法藏。

简体字

是故佛言无上利中不应懈怠。我于世间第一导师善说正法。宜勤精进可得道果。如是等因缘自赞其身。非为自贵轻贱他人。呵恶人者欲令除灭恶法。非为憎恚众生。有人求如法利。其心清净质直。而与恶知识和合。欲令远离此故而呵骂之。未得佛时尚以髓脑施人。何况成佛而当呵骂。汝说佛法初后相违。今当答。佛法中无有始终相违事。汝等不知佛法义故以为相违。是涅槃道者。从迦叶佛灭已来。无复人说。亦无人得。是故言我新得道。余处复说我得故道。是道锭光等诸佛所得。所谓八圣道能至涅槃。一道一因缘故名为故道。是故当知佛成一切智。问曰。所言一切智者。云何名为一切智。为知一切故名为一切智耶。答曰。一切智者知可知。可知者五法藏。

vigorous effort. Consequently the Buddha declared, "In this matter of gaining the most supreme benefit, one must not be indolent. I am the supreme spiritual guide in this world, the one who well proclaims right Dharma. It is only fitting then that you become assiduous and vigorous, for it is only then that you may gain the fruits of the path." And so it was that, for reasons such as these, the Buddha did indeed praise his own personal qualities. It was not out of a wish to be accorded esteem, nor was it out of a wish to slight and deprecate others.

In cases where the Buddha rebuked evil men, it was for the sake of inducing them to get rid of evil dharmas. It was not because he detested other beings. In some cases, there were those seeking to achieve benefit through Dharma, people whose minds were pure and of straightforward character, but who were locked in relationships with bad spiritual guides. In order to induce them to abandon these bad teachers, the Buddha would sometimes criticize and rebuke them. Even before he had achieved buddhahood, [in earlier lifetimes] he even sacrificed his own brain and the very marrow of his bones as gifts to others. How much the less could it be that, once he had already attained buddhahood, he would be inclined to berate and scold others?

I shall now respond to your contention that there were chronologically contradictory tenets in the Buddha's Dharma. There are no contradictions present in the Dharma of the Buddha between what came at the beginning and what followed later on. It is only because you and your cohorts do not understand the concepts involved in the Buddha's Dharma that you have the opinion that it is inherently contradictory.

This path leading to the realization of nirvāṇa had not been either proclaimed or realized by anyone during the entire time between Kāśyapa Buddha's nirvāṇa on forward to the present. It was for this reason that the Buddha declared, "I am he who has newly attained the path." In other places, he also said, "I have attained the ancient path." The path is that which was previously realized by Dīpaṃkara Buddha and the other buddhas of the past, namely the eightfold path of the Āryas that is able to lead one to nirvāṇa. It is because, in all these cases, it is but a single path relying on but a single set of causes and conditions that it is referred to it as "the ancient path." One should realize from this that the Buddha did obtain all-knowledge.

Question: As for the so-called "all-knowledge," precisely what is it that constitutes all-knowledge? Is it really on the basis of knowing absolutely everything that it is referred to as "all-knowledge"?

Response: "All-knowledge" refers to knowing all that can be known. "What can be known" refers to the five categorical repositories of

| 正體字 | 過去未來現在出三世不可說
所用。知此五藏者名為知。是故知及所知
名為一切。問曰。知可知[8]名一切者。是事不
然。何以故。是法但是一。可知知亦是可知
故。如世間言是人知利是人知鈍。答曰。若
一切是一者則寒熱相違皆應是一。明闇苦
樂諸相違事亦應是一。但是事不然。是故不
得言一切皆是一。問曰。汝所執亦同此過。
若可知是一者。苦樂等亦應是一而實不
一。答曰。我不言一切可知是一。汝所執一
切皆是一。是故不與汝同過。復次汝說同有
過故。汝自執中有過。若人自受所執中過
即墮負處。汝知所執有過。不應復說他過。
是故汝說同有過者。是事不然。復次若謂
知可知二法為一者。應用可知法知瓶衣
等物而實用知知一切物。|

简体字：过去未来现在出三世不可说所用。知此五藏者名为知。是故知及所知名为一切。问曰。知可知名一切者。是事不然。何以故。是法但是一。可知知亦是可知故。如世间言是人知利是人知钝。答曰。若一切是一者则寒热相违皆应是一。明闇苦乐诸相违事亦应是一。但是事不然。是故不得言一切皆是一。问曰。汝所执亦同此过。若可知是一者。苦乐等亦应是一而实不一。答曰。我不言一切可知是一。汝所执一切皆是一。是故不与汝同过。复次汝说同有过故。汝自执中有过。若人自受所执中过即堕负处。汝知所执有过。不应复说他过。是故汝说同有过者。是事不然。复次若谓知可知二法为一者。应用可知法知瓶衣等物而实用知知一切物。

Chapter 22 — *Forty Dharmas Exclusive to Buddhas (Part 2)*

dharmas, namely all past, future, and present dharmas, the dharmas that transcend the three periods of time, and the ineffable dharmas. That which is used in knowing these five categories of dharmas is cognition. Hence it is both cognition and those things that it knows that are referred to as the "all" [in the term "all-knowledge."]

Question: As for this contention that it is both the faculty of cognition and those things it knows that together comprise the "all" [of all-knowledge], this is wrong. How so? This is but a singular dharma, this because that cognition that is capable of knowing is itself knowable as when people of the world speak of this person's cognitive ability as sharp whereas that person's cognitive ability is dull.

Response: Well, if as you state that "all" is itself just a singular entity, then it should be that those polar opposites such as "hot" and "cold" are but one thing. And so too it should be that "bright" and "dark," "suffering" and "happiness," and all polar opposites should in each case be but a single thing. But this is not the case. Therefore, one cannot claim that "all" is but a singular entity.

Question: That idea to which you are clinging is itself possessed of this same fault. If the faculty of cognition is one thing, then [that which it knows, namely] "suffering," "happiness," and so forth—those should all also be but singular entities, but in truth, they are not.

Response: I never claimed that everything that can be known is, [in aggregate], but one single thing. Now that idea to which *you* are clinging is indeed that everything [that can be known] *is* somehow, [in its collective aggregate], but a single thing. Therefore, [what I am saying] is not the same as that faulty concept you are proposing.

Furthermore, since you claim that [both of] these positions are equally at fault, that idea to which you are clinging is faulty. In a case where someone accepts that the idea he is proposing is faulty, his position is thereby refuted. Now, when you understand that the idea to which you have been clinging is faulty, you should not continue to claim that someone else is the party whose position is faulty. Hence, as for your contention that what I have set forth here is somehow possessed of the same fault that characterizes your position—this is wrong.

Moreover, if you claim that the two dharmas consisting of the faculty of cognition on the one hand and that which is known on the other are somehow but a single entity, then one should be able to use any particular knowable dharma to know phenomena like vases and robes and such, but in truth it is solely the faculty of cognition that can be used in the knowing of all things.

若謂瓶衣等於
079a01 ‖ 知無異者。今瓶衣等不能知物。即應有
079a02 ‖ 異而實用知知一切物。如是處處有過故
079a03 ‖ 不得言一切[1]皆是一。復次知所知是二名
079a04 ‖ 為一切知。是一切法故。名如來名一切
079a05 ‖ 智者。是一切智人因金剛三昧。是故金剛
079a06 ‖ 三昧成。汝先言金剛三昧不成一切智不成
079a07 ‖ 者。是事不然。[2]

若谓瓶衣等于知无异者。今瓶衣等不能知物。即应有异而实用知知一切物。如是处处有过故不得言一切皆是一。复次知所知是二名为一切知。是一切法故。名如来名一切智者。是一切智人因金刚三昧。是故金刚三昧成。汝先言金刚三昧不成一切智不成者。是事不然。

Chapter 22 – *Forty Dharmas Exclusive to Buddhas (Part 2)*

If you are going to claim that phenomena like vases and robes and such are no different from the faculty of cognition—this vase and robe and so forth—they are entirely unable to know any phenomenon at all. It immediately follows that it ought to be the case that they are different [from the faculty of cognition] and it is truly the case that one uses the faculty of cognition to know everything.

Because your position is faulty in these ways in place after place, you cannot thus claim that the constituent phenomena forming the "all" of all-knowledge are all collectively but a single thing.

So, again, the faculty of cognition and that which is known, these two things—they are what constitute the "all" of "all-knowledge," this because they together constitute all dharmas. It is because of the Buddha's knowing of all of these dharmas that he is known as the Tathāgata and is renowned as one who is possessed of all-knowledge. This omniscient man became possessed of all-knowledge because of the *vajra* samādhi. Therefore the *vajra* samādhi is indeed something that can be established. As for your initial contentions that the *vajra* samādhi cannot be established and that "all-knowledge" is also not something that can be established, these contentions are both wrong.

The End of Chapter Twenty-Two

[3]四十不共法中善知不定品第二十三

善知不定法者。諸法未生未出未成未定未分別。是中如來智慧得力。如佛分別業經中說。佛告阿難。有人身行善業。口行善業。意行善業。是人命終而墮地獄。有人身行惡業。口行惡業。意行惡業。是人命終而生天上。阿難白佛言。何故如是。佛言。是人或先世罪福因緣已熟。今世罪福因緣未熟。或臨命終生正見邪見善惡心。垂終之心其力大故。又[4]首迦經中說。叔迦婆羅門子白佛言。瞿曇。諸婆羅門在家白衣。能修福德善根勝出家者。是事云何。佛言。我於此中不定答。出家或有不修善則不如在家。

十住毗婆沙论卷第十
四十不共法中善知不定品第二十三

善知不定法者。诸法未生未出未成未定未分别。是中如来智慧得力。如佛分别业经中说。佛告阿难。有人身行善业。口行善业。意行善业。是人命终而堕地狱。有人身行恶业。口行恶业。意行恶业。是人命终而生天上。阿难白佛言。何故如是。佛言。是人或先世罪福因缘已熟。今世罪福因缘未熟。或临命终生正见邪见善恶心。垂终之心其力大故。又首迦经中说。叔迦婆罗门子白佛言。瞿昙。诸婆罗门在家白衣。能修福德善根胜出家者。是事云何。佛言。我于此中不定答。出家或有不修善则不如在家。

Chapter 23[33]
Forty Dharmas Exclusive to Buddhas (Part 3)

III. Chapter 23: Forty Dharmas Exclusive to Buddhas (Part 3)
A. 10) Thorough Knowing of Matters That Are Unfixed

As for knowing well the unfixed dharmas, the Tathāgata's wisdom has achieved power within the sphere of all dharmas even at that point when they have not yet arisen, have not yet come forth, have not yet reached completion, have not become definitively fixed, and have not yet become clearly distinguishable. This is as stated in the *Sutra on the Buddha's Distinguishing of Karma* wherein it states:

> The Buddha told Ānanda, "There are people who practice good deeds with the body, who practice good deeds through speech, and who practice good deeds with the mind, and yet, when their lives come to an end, they then fall into the hells. There are yet other people who practice evil deeds with the body, who practice evil deeds through speech, and who practice evil deeds with the mind, and yet, when their lives come to an end, they are nonetheless reborn in the heavens."
>
> Ānanda addressed the Buddha and asked, "Why do events occur in this way?"
>
> The Buddha replied, "It may have been that the causes and conditions associated with previous life karmic offenses or meritorious deeds had already ripened, whereas the karmic offenses or meritorious deeds of the present life had not yet ripened. Or, alternatively, when approaching the end of life, they gave rise to either right views or erroneous views that precipitated either wholesome or evil thoughts, this because the power of the thoughts produced as one approaches the moment of death—their power is immense."[34]

Additionally, in the *Śuka Sutra*, it states:

> Śuka, son of a brahman, addressed the Buddha and asked, "Gotama, why is it that the brahman laity are in some cases able to cultivate meritorious deeds and roots of goodness in a manner superior to that of some of those who have left the home life and become monastics?"
>
> The Buddha replied, "For these sorts of matters, I do not present a fixed reply. There may be cases in which someone who has left behind the home life does not cultivate goodness and, as a consequence, in this endeavor, he does not equal the efforts of a given

正體字	在 079a21 ‖ 家能修善則勝出家。又大涅槃經中說。巴 079a22 ‖ 連弗城當以三事壞。或[5]水或火或內人與 079a23 ‖ 外人謀。又因波梨末梵志說。是裸形波梨末 079a24 ‖ 梵志。若不捨是語。若是心若是邪見。到我 079a25 ‖ 目前無有是處。若皮繩斷。若身斷。終不來 079a26 ‖ 到佛前。又筏喻經中說。我此法甚深。以方 079a27 ‖ 便說令淺易解。若有直心如教行者得二 079a28 ‖ 種利。若今世盡漏。若不盡漏當得不還道。 079a29 ‖ 又增一阿含舍迦梨經中。佛告阿難。若人故 079b01 ‖ 起業。無有不受報而得道者。若現受報 079b02 ‖ 若生受若後受。又增一阿浮羅經中說。佛告 079b03 ‖ 諸比丘。諸惡人死若作畜生若墮地獄。善 079b04 ‖ 人生處若天若人。又無畏王子經中說。無畏 079b05 ‖ 白佛言。佛有所說能令他瞋不。佛言。王子 079b06 ‖ 是事不定。佛或憐愍心故。令他人瞋
简体字	在家能修善则胜出家。又大涅槃经中说。巴连弗城当以三事坏。或水或火或内人与外人谋。又因波梨末梵志说。是裸形波梨末梵志。若不舍是语。若是心若是邪见。到我目前无有是处。若皮绳断。若身断。终不来到佛前。又筏喻经中说。我此法甚深。以方便说令浅易解。若有直心如教行者得二种利。若今世尽漏。若不尽漏当得不还道。又增一阿含舍迦梨经中。佛告阿难。若人故起业。无有不受报而得道者。若现受报若生受若后受。又增一阿浮罗经中说。佛告诸比丘。诸恶人死若作畜生若堕地狱。善人生处若天若人。又无畏王子经中说。无畏白佛言。佛有所说能令他嗔不。佛言。王子是事不定。佛或怜愍心故。令他人嗔

Chapter 23 — *Forty Dharmas Exclusive to Buddhas (Part 3)*

householder. This is a case in which a householder is able to cultivate goodness in a manner superior to that of a particular monastic."

Furthermore, the *Great Nirvāṇa Sutra* states that the city of Pāṭaliputra is bound to be destroyed by one of three circumstances: by flood, by fire, or by a conspiracy between insiders and outsiders.

Also, [another example of an unfixed statement] arose because of a *brahmacārin* named Patikaputra about which the Buddha said:

> As for this naked ascetic, the *brahmacārin* named Paṭikaputra, if he fails to relinquish this statement, these thoughts, and these wrong views, then it will be impossible for him to come and appear before me. He will either be trapped by a broken rope or prevented from leaving by a broken body. In any case, he will never be able to arrive here in the presence of the Buddha.

Additionally, in the *Sutra on the Analogy of the Raft*, the Buddha said:

> This Dharma of mine is extremely deep. It is by resort to expedients that I enable even those who are shallow to easily reach an understanding of it. If there be anyone possessed of a straightforward mind who is willing to practice in accordance with the teachings, he will gain one of two kinds of benefit from this, either the cessation of the contaminants in this present lifetime or, in the event that he doesn't achieve the cessation of the contaminants, he will still succeed in attaining the path of the non-returner (*anāgāmin*).[35]

Also, in the *Ekottara Āgama's Shejiali Sutra*,[36] the Buddha told Ānanda:

> As for whosoever deliberately undertakes the requisite karmic actions, none among them will fail to gain the karmic rewards and thus achieve success in the path, whether that be through receiving the results of present-life karma in this present life, whether that be through receiving them in the next birth, or whether that be through receiving them in subsequent lives.[37]

In addition, we also have this statement in the *Ekottara Āgama's Afuluo Sutra*:[38] "The Buddha told the bhikshus, 'When evil people die, they may become animals or they may fall into the hells. Good people will be reborn either in the heavens or among humans.'"

Also, in the *Prince Fearless Sutra*, it states:

> Prince Fearless addressed the Buddha, saying, "Does the Buddha not have instances in which what he proclaims is able to cause others to become angry?"
>
> The Buddha replied, "Prince, this is an unfixed matter. It may happen that the Buddha, motivated by pity, will influence someone to become angry with the intended result that they will thereby

正體字

```
            得種
079b07 ‖ 善因緣。如乳母以曲指鉤出小兒口中惡
079b08 ‖ 物雖傷無患。又阿毘曇中說。眾生三品。從
079b09 ‖ 不定聚或墮邪定。或墮正定。如是等四法
079b10 ‖ 藏中無定事。數千萬種。問曰。若人智慧不定
079b11 ‖ 無決定心。於事中或爾或不爾則不名一
079b12 ‖ 切智人。一切智人者不二語者。決定語者。明
079b13 ‖ 了語者。是故善知不定。不得[6]名為佛不共
079b14 ‖ 法。答曰。不定事。若爾若不爾。隨屬眾因緣
079b15 ‖ 故。是中不應定說。[7]又若不定事而作定
079b16 ‖ [8]答不名一切智人。是故於不定事中必
079b17 ‖ 應用不定智。是故有不定智不共法。復次
079b18 ‖ 若人於一切法中決定知。是人即墮必定
079b19 ‖ 邪論中。若一切法必定則諸所[9]作為則不
079b20 ‖ 須人功方便而得。如說。
079b21 ‖    若好醜已定      人功則應定
079b22 ‖    不須諸因緣      方便而修習
079b23 ‖ 復次現見不自守護身則有眾苦。若自防
079b24 ‖ 護身則安利。
```

简体字

得种善因缘。如乳母以曲指钩出小儿口中恶物虽伤无患。又阿毗昙中说。众生三品。从不定聚或堕邪定。或堕正定。如是等四法藏中无定事。数千万种。问曰。若人智慧不定无决定心。于事中或尔或不尔则不名一切智人。一切智人者不二语者。决定语者。明了语者。是故善知不定。不得名为佛不共法。答曰。不定事。若尔若不尔。随属众因缘故。是中不应定说。又若不定事而作定答不名一切智人。是故于不定事中必应用不定智。是故有不定智不共法。复次若人于一切法中决定知。是人即堕必定邪论中。若一切法必定则诸所作为则不须人功方便而得。如说。

　　若好丑已定　　人功则应定
　　不须诸因缘　　方便而修习

复次现见不自守护身则有众苦。若自防护身则安利。

Chapter 23 – Forty Dharmas Exclusive to Buddhas (Part 3)

plant the causes and conditions for goodness. This is analogous to a wet-nurse having to use a crooked finger to clear an infant's mouth of some dangerous object. Although it may inflict injury, it is done in order to prevent a calamity."[39]

There is also the statement recorded in the Abhidharma: "Beings fall into three groups. From the [karmically] indefinite group, they may fall into the definitely deviant group or the definitely righteous group."[40]

There are several thousand or even myriads of similar such types of unfixed phenomena that are cited within the four repositories of the Dharma.[41]

Question: If a person's wisdom is unfixed and characterized by indefinite thought that takes a given circumstance to perhaps be this way or perhaps not be this way, then this is not someone who is omniscient. One who is omniscient would not make two different statements [with regard to a single matter], but rather would instead be able to make definitive pronouncements, pronouncements that are utterly clear. Because of this, "thoroughly knowing unfixed matters" cannot be referred to as a dharma exclusive to the Buddha.

Response: Unfixed matters are such that they may either be this way or not this way. It is because they develop in accordance with a multiplicity of causes and conditions that one should not make definite pronouncements about them.

Moreover, were one to offer definite answers regarding indefinite phenomena, then that itself would indicate that one is *not* omniscient. Consequently, in assessing unfixed phenomena, it is essential to employ the knowledge of unfixed matters. Hence there is this exclusive dharma referred to as "the knowledge of unfixed matters."

Additionally, if one were to claim definitive knowledge with respect to all dharmas, then one would fall into the erroneous determinist fallacy. If all dharmas really were already definitely fixed, then all that one does would not require any human effort and skillful means to bring it about. This idea is as set forth here:

If good or bad experiences were already definitely determined,
then the character of a person's efforts should be fixed as well.
There would be no need for any of the causal factors
involved in the skillful means that one uses in one's cultivation.

Moreover, it is already manifestly clear that if one fails to take care with regard to one's personal behavior, then one will bring about manifold sufferings, whereas, if one is guarded with respect to one's personal behavior, then one will enjoy peace and benefit as a result of doing so.

正體字

又如種種作業事中受諸疲
079b25 ‖ 苦後得種種富樂果報。或復有人今世靜默
079b26 ‖ 都無所作而得果報。是故有是不定事。為
079b27 ‖ 知是不定事故。知有不定智。問曰。汝守護
079b28 ‖ 不守護。施功不施功。而亦有不定事成者。
079b29 ‖ 有人好自防護而得苦惱。不自防護不
079c01 ‖ 得苦惱。又勤自疲苦不得功果。不勤施
079c02 ‖ 功而得功果。是事不定。答曰。汝所說則成
079c03 ‖ 我不定義。若有不定事應有不定智。我不
079c04 ‖ 言若人不自防護悉皆受苦。又不言離
079c05 ‖ 功業有果報。有人雖作功夫先世罪障故
079c06 ‖ 不得受樂。不言一切皆爾。是故汝難非也。
079c07 ‖ 是名諸佛於不定事中獨有不定智具足。
079c08 ‖ 知無色處者。聲聞辟支佛。知生無色處眾
079c09 ‖ 生及法少分。諸佛世尊

简体字

又如种种作业事中受诸疲苦后得种种富乐果报。或复有人今世静默都无所作而得果报。是故有是不定事。为知是不定事故。知有不定智。问曰。汝守护不守护。施功不施功。而亦有不定事成者。有人好自防护而得苦恼。不自防护不得苦恼。又勤自疲苦不得功果。不勤施功而得功果。是事不定。答曰。汝所说则成我不定义。若有不定事应有不定智。我不言若人不自防护悉皆受苦。又不言离功业有果报。有人虽作功夫先世罪障故不得受乐。不言一切皆尔。是故汝难非也。是名诸佛于不定事中独有不定智具足。知无色处者。声闻辟支佛。知生无色处众生及法少分。诸佛世尊

Chapter 23 — Forty Dharmas Exclusive to Buddhas (Part 3)

Also, this is just as in all sorts of endeavors involved in carrying on one's livelihood wherein, on the one hand, one is required to endure a good deal of weariness and suffering to later acquire a reward in the form of all manner of wealth and happiness, whereas, on the other hand, someone else is able to simply remain still and silent in this present life, doing nothing whatsoever, only to then reap karmic rewards. So it is that there are these unfixed circumstances. It is because they are cognizant of these unfixed circumstances that we can know that the Buddhas possess the knowledge of what is unfixed.

Question: Whether or not you personally take care and whether or not you make a direct personal effort, these unfixed circumstances will still occur. On the one hand there are those who skillfully defend against untoward developments and yet still end up being subjected to intense anguish while on the other hand there are those who do not defend against such exigencies at all and yet do not encounter any intense anguish at all. Also, there are those who, in their diligence, undergo much weariness and pain, but still do not obtain the fruits of their efforts, whereas there are others who are not the least bit diligent and make no particular effort and, even so, they still manage to gain fruits [otherwise] associated with making an effort. These matters are all unfixed.

Response: Your statement simply serves to cooperate in the establishment of my position regarding unfixed matters. If these unfixed matters do indeed exist, then this wisdom that is cognizant of whatsoever is unfixed should exist. I never claimed that if someone failed to guard against untoward events they would always be subjected to suffering. Nor did I ever claim that, without the expenditure of effortful action, one would necessarily be able to enjoy fruitful results. There are those people who, despite making an effort, are still blocked from the enjoyment of happiness by karmic obstacles originating in earlier lifetimes. I never claimed that all cases were necessarily this way. Therefore the challenges that you have posed on this topic are wrong.

This is what is meant [when it is said] with regard to unfixed circumstances that it is the Buddhas alone who possess complete knowledge of what is unfixed.

B. 11) Thorough Knowing of Formless Absorption Phenomena

As for knowing the formless realm stations, *śrāvaka* disciples and *pratyekabuddhas* know a lesser portion of the beings and dharmas associated with the formless realm stations of existence whereas the Buddhas, the Bhagavats, have a perfectly complete knowledge of the

於無色處眾生及法
具足悉知。是無色處有若干眾生生此處。
若干眾生生彼處。若干眾生生初無色定處。
若干眾生生第二處。若干眾生生第三處。
若干眾生生第四處。若干眾生生來爾所
時。若干眾生經爾所時當退沒。若干眾
生極壽爾所時。若干眾生畢定壽命。若干
眾生不畢定壽命。若干眾生從欲界命終
來生此中。若干眾生從色界命終來生此
中。若干眾生從無色界命終還生此中。若
干眾生人中命終即來生此。若干眾生天中
命終即來生此。是諸眾生於此命終。若生
欲界若生色界若生無色界。是諸眾生此
中命終。若生天道若生人道若生阿修羅
道。若生地獄[10]畜生餓鬼道中。是諸眾生
於彼處入涅槃。

于无色处众生及法具足悉知。是无色处有若干众生生此处。若干众生生彼处。若干众生生初无色定处。若干众生生第二处。若干众生生第三处。若干众生生第四处。若干众生生来尔所时。若干众生经尔所时当退没。若干众生极寿尔所时。若干众生毕定寿命。若干众生不毕定寿命。若干众生从欲界命终来生此中。若干众生从色界命终来生此中。若干众生从无色界命终还生此中。若干众生人中命终即来生此。若干众生天中命终即来生此。是诸众生于此命终。若生欲界若生色界若生无色界。是诸众生此中命终。若生天道若生人道若生阿修罗道。若生地狱畜生饿鬼道中。是诸众生于彼处入涅槃。

Chapter 23 — Forty Dharmas Exclusive to Buddhas (Part 3)

beings and dharmas associated with the formless realm stations of existence.

Regarding these formless realm stations of existence, the Buddhas know:

That a certain number of beings are born into this station;

That a certain number of beings are born into that station;

That a certain number of beings are born into the station associated with the first formless absorption;

That a certain number of beings are born into the second station;

That a certain number of beings are born into the third station;

That a certain number of beings are born into the fourth station;

That a certain number of beings have dwelt there for a particular amount of time since they were born there;

That a certain number of beings, after a particular period of time, will fall away from that realm;

That a certain number of beings will enjoy a maximum life span of a particular amount of time;

That a certain number of beings will have a definitely fixed life span;

That a certain number of beings will enjoy a life span the length of which is not definitely fixed;

That a certain number of beings will be born here after their lifetimes in the desire realm have come to an end;

That a certain number of beings will be born here after their lifetimes in the form realm have come to an end;

That a certain number of beings will return to be reborn here after their lifetimes in this formless realm have come to an end;

That a certain number of beings will be born here directly after their lives in the human realm come to an end;

That a certain number of beings will be reborn here directly after their lives in the heavens have come to an end;

That, when the lives of these particular beings end here, they will then take birth in the desire realm, that they will then take birth in the form realm, or that they will then take birth in the formless realm;

That, when the lives of these particular beings end here, they will then take birth in the celestial realm rebirth destiny, that they will then take birth in the human realm rebirth destiny, that they will then take birth in the *asura* realm rebirth destiny, or that they will then take birth in the rebirth destinies of the hell realms, the animal realms, or the hungry ghost realms;

That these particular beings will enter nirvāṇa in that particular place;

正體字

079c25 ‖ 若干眾生皆是凡夫。若
079c25 ‖ 干眾生是佛賢聖弟子。若干眾生凡夫弟子。
079c26 ‖ 若干眾生成聲聞乘。若干眾生成辟支佛
079c27 ‖ 乘。若干眾生皆成大乘。若干眾生不成
079c28 ‖ 聲聞乘。若干眾生不成辟支佛乘。不成大
079c29 ‖ 乘。若干眾生行滅者。若干眾生不行滅者。若
080a01 ‖ 干眾生上行。若干眾生某佛弟子。諸佛又知
080a02 ‖ 是定受味。是定不受味。是善是無記。是定
080a03 ‖ 中斷若干結。是定上中下。略說無色諸定。
080a04 ‖ 唯有諸佛以一切種智悉能分別大小深
080a05 ‖ 淺心相[1]應不相應果報非果報等。是名

简体字

若干众生皆是凡夫。若干众生是佛贤圣弟子。若干众生凡夫弟子。若干众生成声闻乘。若干众生成辟支佛乘。若干众生皆成大乘。若干众生不成声闻乘。若干众生不成辟支佛乘。不成大乘。若干众生行灭者。若干众生不行灭者。若干众生上行。若干众生某佛弟子。诸佛又知是定受味。是定不受味。是善是无记。是定中断若干结。是定上中下。略说无色诸定。唯有诸佛以一切种智悉能分别大小深浅心相应不相应果报非果报等。是名

Chapter 23 — *Forty Dharmas Exclusive to Buddhas (Part 3)*

That a particular group of beings are all merely common people;

That a particular group of beings are *ārya* disciples of buddhas;

That a particular group of beings are [buddhas'] disciples who are common people [that have not yet become *āryas*];

That a particular group of beings will achieve success in the Śrāvaka Disciple Vehicle;

That a particular group of beings will achieve success in the Pratyekabuddha Vehicle;

That a particular group of beings will all achieve success in the Great Vehicle;

That a particular group of beings will fail to achieve success in the Śrāvaka Disciple Vehicle;

That a particular group of beings will fail to achieve success in the Pratyekabuddha Vehicle and will also fail to achieve success in the Great Vehicle;

That a particular group of beings will develop their practice to the point of reaching nirvāṇa;

That a particular group of beings will fail to develop their practice to the point where they reach nirvāṇa;

That a particular group of beings will pursue a superior level of practice;

And that a particular group of beings are all disciples of a particular buddha.

The Buddhas also know:

That this particular meditative absorption is one in which one is exposed to delectably blissful experiences;[42]

That in this particular meditative absorption there will be no exposure to delectably blissful experiences;

[That this particular meditative absorption] is wholesome or is merely neutral;

That in this particular meditative absorption one may successfully sever a certain number of fetters;

And that this particular meditative absorption is superior, is middling, or is inferior.

To summarize, only the Buddhas, by employing their knowledge of all modes are able to clearly distinguish which of these formless-realm meditative absorptions are greater or lesser, which are deeper or shallower, which involve mental dharmas, which involve dharmas not associated with the mind, which are acquired as resultant effects [of previous karma], which are not acquired as resultant effects [of previous karma], and so forth. This is what is meant when it is said that the

正體字

諸佛
具足悉知無色定處通達。滅法者。諸辟支佛
諸阿羅漢。過去現在滅度者。諸佛通達如經
中說。諸比丘是賢劫前九十一劫。毘婆尸佛
出至三十一劫。有二佛出。一名尸棄。二名
毘式婆。此賢劫中鳩樓孫迦那含牟尼迦葉佛
出。如是過去諸佛大知見。[2]經此中應說。及
諸聲聞弟子滅度入無餘涅槃。及辟支佛。號
曰成。號曰華相。號曰見法。號曰法篋。號
曰喜見。號曰無垢。號曰無得。如是等諸辟
支佛。入無餘涅槃佛悉通達。復次未滅度
在有餘涅槃。生緣都盡通達是事。亦名通
達知滅。如經說。佛告阿難。我於此人悉知
無有微闇。是人畢定盡是內法。是人命終
當入涅槃。亦名知滅。又於餘人通達四
諦能知其事。亦名知滅。如經說。我何不
方便。令此人即於此處漏盡解脫。

简体字

诸佛具足悉知无色定处通达。灭法者。诸辟支佛诸阿罗汉。过去现在灭度者。诸佛通达如经中说。诸比丘是贤劫前九十一劫。毗婆尸佛出至三十一劫。有二佛出。一名尸弃。二名毗式婆。此贤劫中鸠楼孙迦那含牟尼迦葉佛出。如是过去诸佛大知见。经此中应说。及诸声闻弟子灭度入无余涅槃。及辟支佛。号曰成。号曰华相。号曰见法。号曰法篋。号曰喜见。号曰无垢。号曰无得。如是等诸辟支佛。入无余涅槃佛悉通达。复次未灭度在有余涅槃。生缘都尽通达是事。亦名通达知灭。如经说。佛告阿难。我于此人悉知无有微闇。是人毕定尽是内法。是人命终当入涅槃。亦名知灭。又于余人通达四谛能知其事。亦名知灭。如经说。我何不方便。令此人即于此处漏尽解脱。

Buddhas thoroughly know the stations of existence corresponding to the formless meditative absorptions.

C. 12) The Knowledge of All Matters Related to Eternal Cessation

As for [the completely penetrating knowledge of all] dharmas pertaining to cessation, the Buddhas possess a penetrating knowledge of the *pratyekabuddhas* and arhats who have entered nirvāṇa either in the past or present eras. This is as recorded in the sutras where it states:

> Bhikshus, ninety-one kalpas prior to this "Worthy Kalpa" (*bhadrakalpa*), Vipaśyin Buddha appeared. After thirty-one kalpas, there followed two more buddhas, the first of whom was Śikhin and the second of whom was Viśvabhū. Then, in this Worthy Kalpa, Krakucchanda, Kanakamuni, and Kāśyapa Buddha emerged.[43]

Just such great knowledge and vision regarding all buddhas of the past should be discussed [more extensively] herein in relation to this sutra.[44] It also reaches to those *śrāvaka* disciples who have entered the nirvāṇa without residue and extends also to the *pratyekabuddha* named "Success," to the one named "Floral Insignia," to the one named "Seer of Dharma," to the one named "Dharma Basket," to the one named "Delightful Vision," to the one named "Stainless," to the one named "Free of Gain," and to the other such *pratyekabuddhas* as well. So it is that the Buddhas possess a completely penetrating knowledge of those who have entered the nirvāṇa without residue.[45]

Additionally, in cases where they have not yet entered final nirvāṇa, but rather still abide in the nirvāṇa with residue, the Buddhas possess a penetratingly comprehensive knowledge with regard to the utter ending of all conditions associated with taking birth. [These matters] also pertain to their penetrating knowledge of [the phenomena associated with] cessation.

This is as recorded in the sutras wherein it states, "The Buddha told Ānanda, 'I entirely know with respect to this person that he no longer has even the slightest darkness. This person has definitely put an end to these particular inward dharmas. When this person reaches the end of this life, he will enter nirvāṇa.'" This too is included in what is meant by "having knowledge of cessation."[46]

Also, regarding other people's penetrating comprehension of the four truths, he is able to know their circumstances. This too is included in what is meant by "having knowledge of cessation."

As it is said in the sutras, "Why should I not simply resort to expedients to cause this person in this very place to gain the liberation associated with ending the contaminants?"

正體字

如佛告
080a22 ‖ 阿難。汝樂禪定樂斷結使。亦名通達知
080a23 ‖ 滅。如佛告舍利弗。我知涅槃知至涅槃
080a24 ‖ 道。知至涅槃眾生。如是等諸經。此中應
080a25 ‖ 說。是名諸佛通達知滅。善知心不相應非
080a26 ‖ 色法者。戒善根使善律儀不善律儀等諸心
080a27 ‖ 不相應非色法。聲聞辟支佛不能通達。諸佛
080a28 ‖ 善能通達如現目前。於心不相應諸法中。
080a29 ‖ 成就第一智慧力故。問曰。戒善律儀不善律
080b01 ‖ 儀是色法。何以言非色法。答曰。戒善律儀
080b02 ‖ 不善律儀有二種。有作有無作。作是色。無作
080b03 ‖ 非色。無作非[3]色。佛以不共力故現前能知。
080b04 ‖ 餘人以比智知。問曰。諸佛但善知心不相
080b05 ‖ 應非色法。不善知相應法耶。答曰。若通達
080b06 ‖ 不相應法。相應法無所復論。如人能

简体字

如佛告阿难。汝乐禅定乐断结使。亦名通达知灭。如佛告舍利弗。我知涅槃知至涅槃道。知至涅槃众生。如是等诸经。此中应说。是名诸佛通达知灭。善知心不相应非色法者。戒善根使善律仪不善律仪等诸心不相应非色法。声闻辟支佛不能通达。诸佛善能通达如现目前。于心不相应诸法中。成就第一智慧力故。问曰。戒善律仪不善律仪是色法。何以言非色法。答曰。戒善律仪不善律仪有二种。有作有无作。作是色。无作非色。无作非色。佛以不共力故现前能知。余人以比智知。问曰。诸佛但善知心不相应非色法。不善知相应法耶。答曰。若通达不相应法。相应法无所复论。如人能

And as the Buddha told Ānanda, "You delight in *dhyāna* concentration and delight in cutting off the fetters." These circumstances too are associated with what is meant by having a completely penetrating knowledge of cessation.

This is also as illustrated in the Buddha's statement to Śāriputra, "I know nirvāṇa, know the path leading to the realization of nirvāṇa, and know those beings who will arrive at the realization of nirvāṇa."[47]

Such sutras as we have cited herein should all be discussed at greater length. The ideas cited above are indicative of what is meant by all buddhas possessing the penetrating comprehension of all matters having to do with cessation.

D. 13) Thorough Knowing of Non-Form Dharmas Unrelated to Mind

As for thorough knowing of the non-form dharmas unassociated with the mind, roots of goodness associated with the moral precepts influence all of those non-form dharmas unassociated with the mind such as the moral regulations requiring wholesome actions and the moral regulations prohibiting bad actions. *Śrāvaka* disciples and *pratyekabuddhas* are unable to possess a completely penetrating comprehension of such matters. The Buddhas, however, are so well able to penetratingly comprehend them that these become as manifestly clear to them as if they were right before their very eyes. This is because they have perfected the foremost power of wisdom with respect to dharmas unassociated with the mind.

Question: Moral regulations requiring wholesome actions and moral regulations prohibiting bad actions are form dharmas. Why do you refer to them as "non-form" dharmas?

Response: Moral regulations requiring wholesome actions and moral regulations prohibiting bad actions are of two kinds, namely those involving actions and those not involving actions. Those involving actions are within the sphere of form dharmas whereas those not involving actions are "non-form" dharmas. As for those non-form dharmas not involving actions, employing his exclusive power of knowing, the Buddha is able to have a clear and present knowledge of them whereas others are compelled to rely upon inferential knowledge to understand them.

Question: Are the Buddhas only able to thoroughly know the non-form dharmas unassociated with the mind while not being able to thoroughly know the dharmas associated with the mind?

Response: If one already possesses a penetrating comprehension of the unassociated dharmas, then there is no need even to bring up the associated dharmas. It is as if we were speaking of an archer able to

正體字	射毫 080b07 ‖毛。麁物則不論。復次七百不相應法中。聲聞 080b08 ‖ 辟支佛以第六識能知七法。一名二相三 080b09 ‖ 義四無常五生六不生七度。佛以第六識皆 080b10 ‖ 悉能知。佛知四諦相及知世俗法。是故言 080b11 ‖ 諸佛善知心不相應無色法。勢力波羅蜜者。 080b12 ‖ 於一切所知法無餘中得一切種智勢力十 080b13 ‖ 力四無所畏四功德處助成故。又善得[4]十 080b14 ‖ 力故。是故佛能成就勢力波羅蜜。是勢力 080b15 ‖ 在第十六心中得增益。一切智常在佛身。 080b16 ‖ 乃至無餘涅槃。因是事故。於一切法中得 080b17 ‖ 無礙智。無礙智波羅蜜者。法義辭樂說。於此 080b18 ‖ 四法勢力無量通達無礙。如經中說。佛告 080b19 ‖ 諸比丘。如來四[5]弟子成就第一念力智慧 080b20 ‖ 力堪受力。如善射射樹葉即過無難。是諸 080b21 ‖ 弟子以四念處來問難。我常不休息。除飲 080b22 ‖ 食便利睡眠。於百年中如來常答。樂說智慧 080b23 ‖ 無有窮盡。
简体字	射毫毛。粗物则不论。复次七百不相应法中。声闻辟支佛以第六识能知七法。一名二相三义四无常五生六不生七度。佛以第六识皆悉能知。佛知四谛相及知世俗法。是故言诸佛善知心不相应无色法。势力波罗蜜者。于一切所知法无余中得一切种智势力十力四无所畏四功德处助成故。又善得十力故。是故佛能成就势力波罗蜜。是势力在第十六心中得增益。一切智常在佛身。乃至无余涅槃。因是事故。于一切法中得无碍智。无碍智波罗蜜者。法义辞乐说。于此四法势力无量通达无碍。如经中说。佛告诸比丘。如来四第子成就第一念力智慧力堪受力。如善射射树叶即过无难。是诸弟子以四念处来问难。我常不休息。除饮食便利睡眠。于百年中如来常答。乐说智慧无有穷尽。

Chapter 23 — Forty Dharmas Exclusive to Buddhas (Part 3)

pierce a single fine feather [floating through the air]. One would have no need in such a case to inquire if his arrow might be able to hit something large.

Furthermore, *śrāvaka* disciples and *pratyekabuddhas* are able to employ their sixth consciousness to know but seven among the seven hundred unassociated dharmas, namely: first, names; second, characteristic marks; third, meanings; fourth, impermanence; fifth, production; sixth, nonproduction; and seventh, crossing on beyond. The Buddhas, however, are able to employ their sixth consciousness to know every one of them. The Buddhas also know the marks of the four truths as well as the mundane dharmas. It is for these reasons that it is said that the Buddhas thoroughly know the non-form dharmas unassociated with the mind.

E. 14) The Great Powers Pāramitā

As for the powers *pāramitā*, [the Buddhas] gain the power of the knowledge of all modes with respect to all knowable dharmas without exception and are assisted in this by the ten powers, the four fearlessnesses, and the four bases of meritorious qualities. Also, it is due to having gained the ten powers that the Buddhas are therefore able to perfect the powers *pāramitā*. This power is increased in the sixteenth mind-moment [involved in achieving the direct seeing of the path]. All-knowledge is always present in the person of the Buddha until he attains the nirvāṇa without residue. It is because of this that he gains the unimpeded knowledge of all dharmas.

F. 15) The Four Unimpeded Knowledges Pāramitā

As for the *pāramitā* of the [four] unimpeded knowledges (*pratisaṃvid*), they are unimpeded knowledge with respect to: dharmas (*dharma-pratisaṃvid*), meaning (*artha-pratisaṃvid*), language (*nirukti-pratisaṃvid*), and eloquence (*pratibhāna-pratisaṃvid*). [The Buddhas] possess an unlimited penetrating comprehension of these four dharmas that is unimpeded in its implementation. As described in the sutras:[48]

> The Buddha told the bhikshus, "There are four of the Tathāgata's disciples who have perfected the foremost power of mindfulness, power of wisdom, and power of endurance so consummately that they are like a skilled archer who can shoot any single tree leaf without difficulty. Even if these disciples were to all come forth and pose challenging questions on the four stations of mindfulness, setting aside the time required for drink, food, toilet, and sleep, I could always and incessantly respond to their questions for a hundred years during which the Tathāgata would always reply with inexhaustible eloquence and wisdom."

正體字

佛於此中以少欲相自論智
080b24 ‖ 慧。若三千大千世界所有四天下滿中微塵。
080b25 ‖ 隨爾所塵數作爾所三千大千世界。滿中
080b26 ‖ 眾生皆如舍利弗如辟支佛。皆悉成就智
080b27 ‖ 慧樂說。壽命如上塵數大劫。是諸人等因
080b28 ‖ 四念處盡其形壽問難如來。如來還以四
080b29 ‖ 念處義答其所問。言義不重樂說無盡。法
080c01 ‖ 無礙智者。善能分別諸法名字通達無礙。
080c02 ‖ 義無礙者。於諸法義通達無礙。辭無礙者。
080c03 ‖ 隨眾生類以諸言辭令其解義通達無礙。
080c04 ‖ 樂說無礙者。問答時善巧說法無有窮盡。
080c05 ‖ [6]餘賢聖不能究盡。唯有諸佛能盡其邊。是
080c06 ‖ 故名無礙智波羅蜜。具足答波羅蜜者。一切
080c07 ‖ 問難中。佛善能具足答。何以故。於四種問答
080c08 ‖ 中無有錯亂。善知義故。具足不壞義波羅
080c09 ‖ 蜜故。樂欲深知

简体字

佛于此中以少欲相自论智慧。若三千大千世界所有四天下满中微尘。随尔所尘数作尔所三千大千世界。满中众生皆如舍利弗如辟支佛。皆悉成就智慧乐说。寿命如上尘数大劫。是诸人等因四念处尽其形寿问难如来。如来还以四念处义答其所问。言义不重乐说无尽。法无碍智者。善能分别诸法名字通达无碍。义无碍者。于诸法义通达无碍。辞无碍者。随众生类以诸言辞令其解义通达无碍。乐说无碍者。问答时善巧说法无有穷尽。余贤圣不能究尽。唯有诸佛能尽其边。是故名无碍智波罗蜜。具足答波罗蜜者。一切问难中。佛善能具足答。何以故。于四种问答中无有错乱。善知义故。具足不坏义波罗蜜故。乐欲深知

Chapter 23 — Forty Dharmas Exclusive to Buddhas (Part 3)

Here the Buddha, with his characteristically scant wish to do so, discussed his own implementation of these knowledges. Supposing that there were a number of great trichiliocosms as numerous as all the atoms in all four continents of all worlds in a great trichiliocosm, supposing also that all those world systems were filled with beings all of whom were the likes of Śāriputra and the *pratyekabuddhas*, and suppose too that all these beings employed their perfected knowledges and eloquence to pose difficult questions to the Tathāgata on the four stations of mindfulness, doing so to the exhaustion of lifetimes extending to a number of kalpas as numerous as all the aforementioned atoms—the Tathāgata would still be able to reply to their questions on the meanings involved in the four stations of mindfulness, expounding on their meaning without redundancy and with inexhaustible eloquence.[49]

Now, as for the unimpeded knowledge with respect to dharmas, [the Buddhas] are well able to distinguish all details involved in the designations of dharmas with an unimpededly penetrating comprehension.

As for the unimpeded knowledge with respect to meaning, they are able to bring to bear an unimpededly penetrating comprehension of the meanings associated with those dharmas.

In the case of their unimpeded knowledge with respect to language, the Buddhas are able to accord with the languages and phrases through which the various sorts of beings are caused to understand those meanings, doing so with an unimpededly penetrating comprehension.

Regarding their unimpeded knowledge as it applies to eloquence, during that entire time in which they are answering questions, they are skillful and clever in speaking on Dharma and they are able to carry on in this fashion endlessly. Whatever topic all other worthies and *āryas* are unable to treat exhaustively, it is only the Buddhas who can reach the limits of that topic.

It is on these bases that we speak of the *pāramitā* of the unimpeded knowledges.

G. 16) The Pāramitā of Perfectly Complete Replies and Predictions

Regarding the *pāramitā* of perfection in the answering of questions, the Buddha is well able to answer in all situations involving the posing of difficult questions. And why is this so? It is because, in the four types of responses, he remains utterly free of erroneous or disordered presentations, because he well knows the conceptual meanings, because he has perfected the *pāramitā* of preserving the undamaged meaning, and because he delights in a profound knowing of the natures of

正體字

一切眾生性所行所樂故。
080c10 ‖ 如舍利弗白佛言。世尊。佛為人說善法。而
080c11 ‖ 是中多有眾生得證。證已心無渴[7]愛。無
080c12 ‖ 渴愛故於世間無所受。無所受已心則
080c13 ‖ 內滅。佛於善法中無上事盡知無餘。更無
080c14 ‖ 勝者。問曰。汝言四種問答。[8]何謂為四。答曰。
080c15 ‖ 一定答。二分別答。三反問答。四置答。定答
080c16 ‖ 者。如一比丘問佛。世尊。頗有色常不變異
080c17 ‖ 不。世尊。受想行識常不變異不。佛答言。比
080c18 ‖ 丘無有色常[9]而不變。無有受想行識常而
080c19 ‖ 不[10]變。如是等名為定答。分別答者。如布
080c20 ‖ 多梨子梵志問[11]娑摩提。有人故作身口意
080c21 ‖ 業。受何等果報。娑摩提定答。有人以身口
080c22 ‖ 意故作業受苦惱報。是問應分別答。是梵
080c23 ‖ 志後來問佛是事。佛答言。布多梨子。

简体字

一切众生性所行所乐故。如舍利弗白佛言。世尊。佛为人说善法。而是中多有众生得证。证已心无渴爱。无渴爱故于世间无所受。无所受已心则内灭。佛于善法中无上事尽知无余。更无胜者。问曰。汝言四种问答。何谓为四。答曰。一定答。二分别答。三反问答。四置答。定答者。如一比丘问佛。世尊。颇有色常不变异不。世尊。受想行识常不变异不。佛答言。比丘无有色常而不变。无有受想行识常而不变。如是等名为定答。分别答者。如布多梨子梵志问娑摩提。有人故作身口意业。受何等果报。娑摩提定答。有人以身口意故作业受苦恼报。是问应分别答。是梵志后来问佛是事。佛答言。布多梨子。

all beings, what they themselves practice, and what they themselves find pleasing. This is illustrated by the instance in which Śāriputra addressed the Buddha, saying:

> Bhagavat, when the Buddha discourses on the good Dharma, many are the beings who, upon hearing this, then gain realizations. Having gained such realizations, their minds become free of all craving. And because they become free of all craving, they no longer have anything in the world that they indulge. And once they no longer have anything at all that they indulge, their minds achieve a state of inward cessation.

The Buddha exhaustively knows, without exceptions, the unsurpassable aspects of the good Dharma. There is no one who is superior to him in this regard.

Question: You spoke of the four types of replies. What are those four?

Response:

> First, the definitive reply.
> Second, the distinguishing reply.
> Third, the counter-questioning reply.
> And, fourth, the reply that sets aside the question.

In the case of the definitive reply, this is illustrated by the instance where a bhikshu asked the Buddha, "Bhagavat, is it or is it not the case that there could be some form that is eternal and unchanging? Bhagavat, is it or is it not the case that there could be any feelings, perceptions, formative factors, or consciousnesses that are permanent and unchanging?"

The Buddha replied, saying, "Bhikshu, there is no form that is permanent and unchanging. There are no feelings, perceptions, formative factors, or consciousnesses that are permanent and unchanging."

Cases such as these illustrate the "definitive reply."

The distinguishing reply is illustrated by the instance where Potaliputta,[50] the Brahmacārin, inquired of Samiddhi,[51] asking: [52] "In instances where a person deliberately performs actions of body, speech, or mind, what sorts of karmic retributions ensue therefrom?"

Samiddhi responded with a definitive reply, saying, "In instances where persons deliberately perform actions of body, speech, or mind, they are bound to undergo retributions involving suffering and anguish."

But this should have involved a distinguishing reply. This *brahmacārin* later came and asked the Buddha about this matter, to which the Buddha replied, saying, "Potaliputta, in instances where

正體字

有人
080c24 ‖ 若身口意故作業。是業或受苦報。或受樂
080c25 ‖ 報。或受不苦不樂[12]報。苦業受苦報。樂業受
080c26 ‖ 樂報。不苦不樂業受不苦不樂報。如是等諸
080c27 ‖ 經皆分別答。反問答者。如先尼梵志問佛。
080c28 ‖ [13]佛言。我還問汝。隨汝意答。先尼於汝意
080c29 ‖ 云何。色是如來不。受想行識是如來不。答言。
081a01 ‖ 非也世尊。離[1]色受想行識是如來不。答言。
081a02 ‖ 非也世尊。如是等經應廣說。是名反問答。
081a03 ‖ 置答者。十四種邪見是。所謂世間常世間無
081a04 ‖ 常。世間常無常。世間非常非無常。世間有邊。
081a05 ‖ 世間無邊。世間亦有邊[2]亦無邊。世間非有邊
081a06 ‖ 非無邊。如來滅後有。如來滅後無。如來滅後
081a07 ‖ 亦有亦無。如來滅後非有非無。[3]身即是神。
081a08 ‖ 身異[4]神異。

简体字

有人若身口意故作业。是业或受苦报。或受乐报。或受不苦不乐报。苦业受苦报。乐业受乐报。不苦不乐业受不苦不乐报。如是等诸经皆分别答。反问答者。如先尼梵志问佛。佛言。我还问汝。随汝意答。先尼于汝意云何。色是如来不。受想行识是如来不。答言。非也世尊。离色受想行识是如来不。答言。非也世尊。如是等经应广说。是名反问答。置答者。十四种邪见是。所谓世间常世间无常。世间常无常。世间非常非无常。世间有边。世间无边。世间亦有边亦无边。世间非有边非无边。如来灭后有。如来灭后无。如来灭后亦有亦无。如来灭后非有非无。身即是神。身异神异。

Chapter 23 — Forty Dharmas Exclusive to Buddhas (Part 3)

someone deliberately performs actions of body, speech, or mind, this karma may result in undergoing painful retributions, in undergoing pleasurable retributions, or in undergoing retributions that are neither painful nor pleasurable. Pain-inducing actions result in undergoing painful retributions. Pleasure-inducing actions result in undergoing pleasurable retributions. Actions that are neither pain-inducing nor pleasure-inducing result in undergoing karmic retributions that are neither painful nor pleasurable."

Scriptural passages such as these illustrate instances of the distinguishing reply.

The counter-questioning reply is illustrated by that instance in which the *brahmacārin* named Śreṇika inquired of the Buddha and the Buddha replied, "I shall now return the question to you whereupon you may reply in accordance with your own idea on this matter. Śreṇika, what do you think? Do physical forms constitute the Tathāgata, or not? Or is it that feelings, perceptions, formative factors, or consciousnesses constitute the Tathāgata?"

He replied, "No, Bhagavat. They do not."

[The Buddha then asked him], "Is the Tathāgata apart from form, feelings, perceptions, formative factors, or consciousnesses, or not?"

He replied, "No, Bhagavat. He is not."

These types of passages from scripture should be more extensively discussed. They illustrate what is meant by the counter-questioning reply.

As for the reply that sets aside the question, this applies to the response to questions regarding the fourteen classic erroneous views, namely:

Is the world eternal?
Is the world non-eternal?
Is the world both eternal and non-eternal?
Is the world neither eternal nor non-eternal?
Is the world bounded?
Is the world unbounded?
Is the world both bounded and unbounded?
Is the world neither bounded nor unbounded?
Does the Tathāgata exist after his nirvāṇa?
Does the Tathāgata not exist after his nirvāṇa?
Does the Tathāgata both exist and not exist after his nirvāṇa?
Does the Tathāgata neither exist nor not exist after his nirvāṇa?
Is the body identical with a spiritual soul (*jīva*)?
Is the body different from a spiritual soul?

正體字

　　　如上一切眾生如大辟支佛智
081a09 ‖ 慧樂說以如是四種問佛。佛皆隨順答其
081a10 ‖ 所問。不多不少。是故說佛具足答波羅蜜。
081a11 ‖ 無有能害。佛者得不可殺法故。無能斷佛
081a12 ‖ 身分支節存亡自在。如經說。若人欲方便
081a13 ‖ 害佛者。無有是處。問曰。佛壽命為定為不
081a14 ‖ 定。答曰。有人言不定。若佛壽命有定者。於
081a15 ‖ 餘定壽命者有何差別。而實佛壽命不定。無
081a16 ‖ 能害者。乃為希有。有人言。佛壽命有定。餘
081a17 ‖ 人壽命雖定。而手足耳鼻可斷。佛無是事。
081a18 ‖ 問曰。云何佛不可害。是不共法。答曰。諸佛
081a19 ‖ 不可思議。假喻可知。假使一切十方世界眾
081a20 ‖ 生皆有勢力。設有一魔有爾所勢力。復令
081a21 ‖ 十方一一眾生力如惡魔。欲共害佛。尚不
081a22 ‖ 能動佛一毛。況有害者。問曰。若爾者調達
081a23 ‖ 云何得傷佛。答曰。此事先已答。佛欲示眾
081a24 ‖ 生三毒相。

简体字

如上一切众生如大辟支佛智慧乐说以如是四种问佛。佛皆随顺答其所问。不多不少。是故说佛具足答波罗蜜。无有能害。佛者得不可杀法故。无能断佛身分支节存亡自在。如经说。若人欲方便害佛者。无有是处。问曰。佛寿命为定为不定。答曰。有人言不定。若佛寿命有定者。于余定寿命者有何差别。而实佛寿命不定。无能害者。乃为希有。有人言。佛寿命有定。余人寿命虽定。而手足耳鼻可断。佛无是事。问曰。云何佛不可害。是不共法。答曰。诸佛不可思议。假喻可知。假使一切十方世界众生皆有势力。设有一魔有尔所势力。复令十方一一众生力如恶魔。欲共害佛。尚不能动佛一毛。况有害者。问曰。若尔者调达云何得伤佛。答曰。此事先已答。佛欲示众生三毒相。

Chapter 23 — *Forty Dharmas Exclusive to Buddhas (Part 3)*

As stated above, even in an instance where all beings possessed the wisdom and eloquence of the *pratyekabuddha* and they inquired of the Buddha on these four matters, the Buddha would in all cases adapt to their needs in answering their questions, offering replies that are neither excessive nor deficient. It is for these reasons that the Buddhas are said to possess the *pāramitā* of perfection in the answering of questions.

H. 17) Invulnerability to Harm by Anyone

There is no one whatsoever who can harm the Buddha. This is because he has gained that dharma by which one cannot be killed. There is no one who can cut off any part of the Buddha's body. He has sovereign mastery over whether he will live or die. This is as stated in scripture, wherein it states: "Were one to seek some method by which to inflict harm on the Buddha—there simply is no such possibility at all."

Question: Is the life span of a buddha fixed or is it unfixed?

Response: There are those who claim that it is unfixed. But if a buddha's life span were actually fixed, what difference then would there be between his case and that of all others who have fixed life spans? Still, in truth, the life span of a buddha is not fixed. That there is no one who can harm a buddha—now *that* is extraordinary. There are those who say that the life span of a buddha is fixed. However, whereas others whose life spans are fixed are indeed subject to having hands, feet, ears, and nose sliced off, the Buddha [is unique in that he] is entirely free of any such vulnerability.

Question: How is it that the Buddhas have this exclusive dharma of being invulnerable to being harmed?

Response: The inconceivability of the Buddhas can be understood by resort to analogy. Suppose for instance that all beings throughout the worlds of the ten directions were to have a given amount of power. Now, if a single *māra* could possess a certain amount of power, also suppose that each and every one of those beings throughout the ten directions was caused to possess powers like those of Māra, the Evil One. Even if all of those beings then joined in wishing to inflict harm on the Buddha, they would still be unable to move even a single hair on the Buddha's body. How much the less might they actually succeed in harming the Buddha.

Question: Well, if that is the case, how then could Devadatta have succeeded in injuring the Buddha?

Response: This question was already answered earlier. The Buddha wished to show beings the character of the three poisons. Even though

正體字

調達雖持戒修善貪著利養而
081a25 ‖ 作大惡。又令知佛於諸人天心無有異。
081a26 ‖ 加以慈愍視調達羅睺羅如左右眼。佛常
081a27 ‖ 說等心。是時現其平等。天人見此起希有
081a28 ‖ 心益更信樂。又長壽[5]天見佛先世有惡業
081a29 ‖ 行。若今不受謂惡行無報。佛欲斷其邪見
081b01 ‖ 故現受此報。復次佛於苦樂心無有異。無
081b02 ‖ 吾我心。畢竟空故。諸根調柔不可變故。不
081b03 ‖ 須作方便離苦受樂。如菩薩藏中說。佛
081b04 ‖ 以方便故現受此事。應當廣知。是名佛不
081b05 ‖ 可殺害不共法。說法不[6]空者。諸佛所有言說
081b06 ‖ 皆有果報。是故諸佛說法不空。何以故。諸
081b07 ‖ 佛未說法時。先觀眾生本末心在何處結
081b08 ‖ 使厚薄。知其先世所從功德。見其根性勢
081b09 ‖ 力多少。知其障礙方處時節。[7]應軟法可度

简体字

调达虽持戒修善贪着利养而作大恶。又令知佛于诸人天心无有异。加以慈愍视调达罗睺罗如左右眼。佛常说等心。是时现其平等。天人见此起希有心益更信乐。又长寿天见佛先世有恶业行。若今不受谓恶行无报。佛欲断其邪见故现受此报。复次佛于苦乐心无有异。无吾我心。毕竟空故。诸根调柔不可变故。不须作方便离苦受乐。如菩萨藏中说。佛以方便故现受此事。应当广知。是名佛不可杀害不共法。说法不空者。诸佛所有言说皆有果报。是故诸佛说法不空。何以故。诸佛未说法时。先观众生本末心在何处结使厚薄。知其先世所从功德。见其根性势力多少。知其障碍方处时节。应软法可度

Devadatta had previously upheld the moral precepts and cultivated goodness, because he was attached to receiving offerings, he then committed immensely evil deeds.

[The Buddha] also allowed this to happen to enable [beings] to realize that the mind of the Buddha does not vary in the way it regards any human or deva. His having compassion and pity for Devadatta on the one hand and Rāhula[53] on the other was the same as his equal regard for his own left and right eyes.

The Buddha always spoke of the mind of uniformly equal regard for everyone. He revealed his equality of regard at this time. When the devas and people observed this, they were struck by the extraordinary nature of this and thus felt even stronger resolute faith.

In addition, because of this, the devas of the long-life heavens could see that the Buddha was still bound to undergo retribution for bad karmic actions done in previous lives. Had he not undergone it now, they might have thought that bad actions could be free of corresponding karmic retributions. Because the Buddha wished to cut off their wrong views, he thereby revealed his own undergoing of this karmic retribution.

Furthermore, the Buddha's mind is no different in the presence of pain or pleasure. His mind is free of any concept of a self. This is because it is ultimately empty. Because his sense faculties have all been made pliant and imperturbable by change, he has no need to use expedients to separate from pain and enjoy pleasures. This is as described in the Bodhisattva canon where it states: "It was merely as an expedient that the Buddha manifested as subject to this experience." One should infer the broader implications of this.

The above points illustrate what is meant by the Buddha's exclusive dharma of being invulnerable to being killed or harmed.

I. 18) Their Words Are Never Spoken without a Purpose

In speaking on the Dharma, their words are never empty. All words spoken by the Buddhas have a corresponding intended effect. Therefore, when the Buddhas speak on Dharma, their words are never empty. And how is this so? Before the Buddhas begin to speak on Dharma, they first contemplate from root to branch where beings' minds abide and whether their fetters are thick or only scant. Thus they know the origins of their meritorious qualities in previous lives, observe the nature and strength of their karmic roots, and know:

Where and when beings [will encounter] obstacles;
Whether they are susceptible to liberation through gentle teaching methods;

正體字

081b10 ‖ 苦事可度。或復應以軟苦事度。或[8]須小發
081b11 ‖ 度。或廣分別度。有以陰入界十二因緣而
081b12 ‖ 得度者。或以信門或以慧門而得入者。是
081b13 ‖ 人應從佛度。是人應從聲聞度。是人應
081b14 ‖ 以餘緣得度。是人應成聲聞乘。是人應成
081b15 ‖ 辟支佛乘。是人應成大乘。是人久習貪欲
081b16 ‖ 習瞋恚習愚癡。是人習貪欲瞋恚。是人習
081b17 ‖ 貪欲愚癡。如是各各分別。是人墮斷見。是
081b18 ‖ 人墮常見。是人多[9]著身見。是人多習邊見。
081b19 ‖ 是人多習戒取見取。是人多習憍慢。是人多
081b20 ‖ 習自卑諂曲。是人心多疑悔。

简体字

苦事可度。或复应以软苦事度。或须小发度。或广分别度。有以阴入界十二因缘而得度者。或以信门或以慧门而得入者。是人应从佛度。是人应从声闻度。是人应以余缘得度。是人应成声闻乘。是人应成辟支佛乘。是人应成大乘。是人久习贪欲习瞋恚习愚痴。是人习贪欲瞋恚。是人习贪欲愚痴。如是各各分别。是人堕断见。是人堕常见。是人多着身见。是人多习边见。是人多习戒取见取。是人多习憍慢。是人多习自卑谄曲。是人心多疑悔。

Whether they are susceptible to liberation through harsh teaching methods;

Whether they are susceptible to liberation through a combination of gentle and harsh teaching methods.[54]

Whether they need only a little bit of instigation to gain liberation;

Whether they require extensive distinguishing instructions to gain liberation;

That there are those who gain liberation through [teachings on] the aggregates, the sense bases, the sense realms, or the twelve links of conditioned co-production;

Whether they may gain access [to liberation] through the gateway of faith or through the gateway of wisdom;

That this person should gain liberation through the teaching of a buddha;

That this person should gain liberation through the teaching of a *śrāvaka* disciple;

That this person should gain liberation through some other set of conditions;

That this person should be able to gain success in the Śrāvaka Disciple Vehicle;

That this person should be able to gain success in the Pratyekabuddha Vehicle;

That this person should be able to gain success in the Great Vehicle;

That this person has long practiced habitual greed, habitual hatred, and habitual delusion;

That this person has practiced habitual greed and hatred;

And that this person has practiced habitual greed and delusion.

In this way, they distinguish and determine with regard to each and every situation:

That this person has fallen into an annihilationist view;

That this person has fallen into an eternalist view;

That this person is for the most part attached to the view that seizes on the existence of a real self in association with the body [or any of the other four aggregates];[55]

That this person is most often habitually attached to extreme views;

That this person is most often habitually attached to the views that seize upon either prohibitions or on opinionated views;

That this person is for the most part habitually arrogant;

That this person is for the most part habitually inclined toward feelings of inferiority and the tendency to flattery and deviousness;

That this person's mind is mostly inclined toward doubt and regret.

正體字	是人好樂言 081b21 ‖ 辭。有貴義理有樂深義有樂淺事。是人 081b22 ‖ 先世集助道法。是人今世集助道法。是人但 081b23 ‖ 集福報善根。是人但集貫穿善根。是人應 081b24 ‖ 疾得道。是人久乃得道。佛先觀察籌量隨 081b25 ‖ 應得度。而為說法而度脫之。是故一切說 081b26 ‖ 法皆悉不空。如經說。世尊先知見而說法。 081b27 ‖ 非不知見說法。無謬無失者。諸佛說法無 081b28 ‖ 謬無失。無謬者。語義不乖違故。無失者。 081b29 ‖ 不失義故。不失道因緣故名不失。不謬 081c01 ‖ 道果因緣故名不謬。不少故名不失。不過 081c02 ‖ 故名不謬。
简体字	是人好乐言辞。有贵义理有乐深义有乐浅事。是人先世集助道法。是人今世集助道法。是人但集福报善根。是人但集贯穿善根。是人应疾得道。是人久乃得道。佛先观察筹量随应得度。而为说法而度脱之。是故一切说法皆悉不空。如经说。世尊先知见而说法。非不知见说法。无谬无失者。诸佛说法无谬无失。无谬者。语义不乖违故。无失者。不失义故。不失道因缘故名不失。不谬道果因缘故名不谬。不少故名不失。不过故名不谬。

That this person has developed a fondness for refined literary expressiveness;

That there are those who prize refinement in meanings and principles;

That there are those who delight in profundities;

That there are those who enjoy topics that are merely superficial;

That, in previous lifetimes, this person has accumulated the Dharma provisions requisite to success in the path;

That this person is accumulating the Dharma provisions for the path in this present lifetime;

That this person has only accumulated roots of goodness conducive to enjoying karmic rewards [from previous meritorious actions];

That this person has only accumulated roots of goodness associated with thorough understanding;

That this person should be able to rapidly become enlightened;

And that this person will require a long time before he can become enlightened.[56]

The Buddha first engages in investigative contemplation and assessment of individual circumstances and then, according with whichever approach is appropriate to instigate someone's liberation, he then speaks Dharma for them and thereby brings about their liberation.

It is as a consequence of this that every instance of the Buddha's speaking of Dharma is free of any merely empty discourse. This is as described in a sutra: "The Bhagavat first knows and sees and only then speaks Dharma. It is not the case that he speaks Dharma without first knowing and seeing."

J. 19) Their Speech Is Free of Error

Regarding the absence of errors and mistakes [in their speech], when the Buddhas speak Dharma, they do not commit any errors or make any mistakes. "Absence of errors" refers to there being no instances in which the meaning of what they say is contradictory. "Absence of mistakes" means they make no mistakes with regard to meanings.

It is because they do not make mistakes with regard to causes and conditions as they relate to the path that they are said to not make mistakes. It is because they do not commit errors with regard to causes and conditions as they relate to the fruits of the path that they are said to not commit any error.

It is because they are not deficient that they are said to not make mistakes and it is because they are not excessive that they are said to not commit any error.

正體字	以通達四無礙智故。念安慧常 081c03 ‖ 調和故。遠離斷常無因邪因等諸見故。所說 081c04 ‖ 法中不使人有迷悶。所言初後無相違過。 081c05 ‖ 隨此義經。應此中廣說。如經說。諸比丘為 081c06 ‖ 汝說法。初善中善後善。語善義善淳一無雜 081c07 ‖ 具說梵行。以希有事說法者。隨所教化即 081c08 ‖ 得道果。是名希有。若有所答若所受記皆 081c09 ‖ 實不[10]異。是亦希有。佛有所說道。此道不 081c10 ‖ 雜煩惱能斷煩惱。是亦希有。佛有所說皆 081c11 ‖ 有利益終不空言是亦希有。若人於佛法 081c12 ‖ 中勤心精進。能斷不善法增益善法。是亦 081c13 ‖ 希有。復次有三希有。現神通希有。逆說彼 081c14 ‖ 心希有。[11]有教化希有。以是三希有說法。名 081c15 ‖ 為以希有說法。諸眾聖中最上導師者。諸佛 081c16 ‖ 知一切眾生心所行所樂。結使
简体字	以通达四无碍智故。念安慧常调和故。远离断常无因邪因等诸见故。所说法中不使人有迷闷。所言初后无相违过。随此义经。应此中广说。如经说。诸比丘为汝说法。初善中善后善。语善义善淳一无杂具说梵行。以希有事说法者。随所教化即得道果。是名希有。若有所答若所受记皆实不异。是亦希有。佛有所说道。此道不杂烦恼能断烦恼。是亦希有。佛有所说皆有利益终不空言是亦希有。若人于佛法中勤心精进。能断不善法增益善法。是亦希有。复次有三希有。现神通希有。逆说彼心希有。有教化希有。以是三希有说法。名为以希有说法。诸众圣中最上导师者。诸佛知一切众生心所行所乐。结使

Chapter 23 — *Forty Dharmas Exclusive to Buddhas (Part 3)*

This is accomplished through their possession of a penetrating comprehension of the four unimpeded knowledges, through their constant harmonization of mindfulness and stable wisdom, and through their utter abandonment of views associated with annihilationism, eternalism, acausality, erroneous causality, or other such wrong views.

In the Dharma that they speak, there is no cause by which people become perplexed. In whatsoever they say, there are no faults involving inconsistencies between what is set forth in the beginning and in the end.

Scriptures accordant with these concepts should be discussed more extensively herein. As it says in one of the sutras: "Bhikshus. When I speak Dharma for you, it is good in the beginning, good in the middle, and good in the end. The phrasings are good and the meanings are good. It possesses a singular purity free of any debasing admixture and it is perfectly complete in its proclamation of *brahmacarya*."[57]

K. 20) Complete Use of the Three Turnings in Speaking Dharma

As regards the matter of [the Buddha's] speaking of Dharma involving rarities, whomever they undertake to teach is immediately enabled to realize the fruits of the path. This is a rarity.

Whenever they provide a reply or offer a prediction, their statements are always genuine and do not differ [from actual circumstances]. This too is a rarity.

The Buddha has the path as the subject of his discourse. This path as it is proclaimed by the Buddha is not admixed with afflictions and is able to bring about the severance of the afflictions. This too is a rarity.

Whenever the Buddha speaks, benefit ensues from it and it never involves mere empty words. This too is a rarity.

Whenever a person applies mental diligence and vigor to the cultivation of the Buddha's Dharma, he can cut off the unwholesome dharmas and bring about increase in the good dharmas. This too is a rarity.

There are three additional rarities: the rarity of displaying spiritual powers, the rarity of foretelling the content of others' thoughts, and the rarity of being able to accomplish the transformational teaching of others. It is on the basis of these three sorts of rarities in the proclaiming of Dharma that the Buddha's discourse on Dharma is said to be characterized by rarities.[58]

L. 21) They Are the Great Generals Among All Āryas

Regarding [the Buddha's] eminence as the most superior spiritual guide among all the Āryas, buddhas know what the minds of beings course in, know what they delight in, know whether their fetters are

	深淺諸根利
081c17 ‖	鈍。上中下智慧。善知通達故。於眾聖中最
081c18 ‖	上導師。又能善知四諦相。善知諸法總相別
081c19 ‖	相。又以說法不空因緣不謬不失法故。於
081c20 ‖	眾聖中最上導師。問曰。四眾亦能說法破外
081c21 ‖	道令入佛法。何以但稱佛為最上導師。答
081c22 ‖	曰。當以假喻說。若一切眾生智慧勢力皆如
081c23 ‖	辟支佛。是諸眾生若不承佛意。欲度一人
081c24 ‖	無有是處。若是諸人說法時。乃至不[12]能
081c25 ‖	斷無色界結使毫釐[13]分。若佛欲度眾生有
081c26 ‖	所言說。乃至外道邪見諸龍夜叉等及餘不
081c27 ‖	解佛語者皆悉令解。是等亦能轉化無量
081c28 ‖	眾生。乃至今日聲聞眾令眾生住四果中。
081c29 ‖	皆是如來最上導師相。是故佛名最上導師。
082a01 ‖	於眾聖中不共之法。四不守護法者。諸佛
082a02 ‖	不守護身業。不[1]護口業。不[*]護意業。不
082a03 ‖	[*]護

深浅诸根利钝。上中下智慧。善知通达故。于众圣中最上导师。又能善知四谛相。善知诸法总相别相。又以说法不空因缘不谬不失法故。于众圣中最上导师。问曰。四众亦能说法破外道令入佛法。何以但称佛为最上导师。答曰。当以假喻说。若一切众生智慧势力皆如辟支佛。是诸众生若不承佛意。欲度一人无有是处。若是诸人说法时。乃至不能断无色界结使毫厘分。若佛欲度众生有所言说。乃至外道邪见诸龙夜叉等及余不解佛语者皆悉令解。是等亦能转化无量众生。乃至今日声闻众令众生住四果中。皆是如来最上导师相。是故佛名最上导师。于众圣中不共之法。四不守护法者。诸佛不守护身业。不护口业。不护意业。不护

Chapter 23 — *Forty Dharmas Exclusive to Buddhas (Part 3)*

deep or shallow, know whether their faculties are sharp or dull, and know whether their wisdom is superior, middling, or inferior. It is because they know these matters well and know them with penetrating comprehension that they are the most superior spiritual guides among all the Āryas.

They are also able to well know the characteristics of the four truths, and to well know all the general and specific characteristics of all dharmas.

It is also because, when they speak on the Dharma, their words are not empty and because, when they speak on the Dharma, they commit no errors and make no mistakes that they are therefore the most superior spiritual guides among all the Āryas.

Question: But the other four groups are also able to speak on the Dharma and thus refute the teachings of the non-Buddhists and thereby cause them to enter into the Dharma of the Buddha. Why then does one only speak of the Buddha as the most superior spiritual guide?

Response: This should be explained by an analogy. Suppose all beings possessed the wisdom powers of a *pratyekabuddha*. If all of these beings did not receive the intentional assistance of the Buddha and yet wished somehow to bring about the liberation of but a single person, this would be a complete impossibility. When all of these persons spoke Dharma, they would still be unable to cause the severance of a tiny fraction of even one of the formless realm fetters.

If, on the other hand, the Buddha wished to bring about the liberation of some being and then proceeded to say something, even those burdened with the erroneous views of the non-Buddhists, the dragons, the *yakṣas*, and the various other sorts of beings who do not understand the language of the Buddha—these would all still be caused to understand. Then all of these would in turn be able to teach countless other beings. And so this proceeds even to the point that, today, whenever those within the community of *śrāvaka* disciples cause beings to abide in the four fruits of the path, they are all emblematically representative of the Tathāgata as the most superior of all spiritual guides.

It is for these reasons that the Buddha is known as the most superior spiritual guide, and it is for these reasons that this is regarded as an exclusive dharma not held in common with the other *āryas*.

M. 22–25) They Are Able to Remain Unguarded in Four Ways

As for the four unguarded dharmas, the Buddhas are unguarded in their physical actions, are unguarded in their verbal actions, are unguarded in their mental actions, and are unguarded with respect to

正體字

```
          資生。何以故。是四事於他不護。不作
082a04 ‖ 是念。我身口意命恐他人知。何以故。長夜
082a05 ‖ 修習種種清淨業故。皆善見知斷一切煩惱
082a06 ‖ 法故。成就一切無比善根故。善行可行法
082a07 ‖ 無可呵故。具足行捨波羅蜜故。捨者。眼見
082a08 ‖ 色捨憂喜心。乃至意法亦如是。婆[2]呵提欝
082a09 ‖ 多羅等諸經應此中說。四無所畏者。問曰。一
082a10 ‖ 法名為無畏。何以故有四。答曰。於四事中
082a11 ‖ 無有疑畏[3]故有四。一者如佛告諸比丘。
082a12 ‖ 我自發誠言。是一切智人。此中若有沙門婆
082a13 ‖ 羅門諸天魔梵及餘世間智人。如法難[4]言。
082a14 ‖ 不知此法。我於此中乃至不見有[5]微畏
082a15 ‖ 相。不見是相故。得安隱無畏。是初無畏。如
082a16 ‖ 實盡知一切法故。二者自發誠言。我一切
082a17 ‖ 諸漏盡。若沙門婆羅門諸天魔梵。言是漏不
082a18 ‖ [6]盡。
```

简体字

资生。何以故。是四事于他不护。不作是念。我身口意命恐他人知。何以故。长夜修习种种清净业故。皆善见知断一切烦恼法故。成就一切无比善根故。善行可行法无可呵故。具足行舍波罗蜜故。舍者。眼见色舍忧喜心。乃至意法亦如是。婆呵提郁多罗等诸经应此中说。四无所畏者。问曰。一法名为无畏。何以故有四。答曰。于四事中无有疑畏故有四。一者如佛告诸比丘。我自发诚言。是一切智人。此中若有沙门婆罗门诸天魔梵及余世间智人。如法难言。不知此法。我于此中乃至不见有微畏相。不见是相故。得安隐无畏。是初无畏。如实尽知一切法故。二者自发诚言。我一切诸漏尽。若沙门婆罗门诸天魔梵。言是漏不尽。

Chapter 23 — Forty Dharmas Exclusive to Buddhas (Part 3)

the means for sustaining life. And why is this? These four matters are not protected from others' [knowledge]. They do not think, "Regarding my [actions of] body, speech, and mind, and my [means of sustaining] life—I fear that others might come to know about them."

And why is this? This is because, during the long night [of previous lifetimes], they have cultivated every sort of pure karmic deed and have always well seen, well known, and well severed every one of the dharmas associated with the afflictions. And this is because they have perfected every sort of peerless root of goodness, because they have so well practiced whatever dharma is amenable to practice, because they have reached the point where there is nothing about them the least bit worthy of criticism, and because they have utterly perfected the *pāramitā* of equanimity.

Now, on this matter of their "equanimity," when their eyes view form, they relinquish any thoughts of either distress or delight. And so it goes [with the other sense faculties and objects] up to and including the mind faculty's engagement with dharmas [as objects of mind]. In this connection, one would ideally also discuss here citations from such scriptures as the *Poheti* and *Uttara* sutras.[59]

N. 26–29) They Possess the Four Types of Fearlessnesses

Now, as for the four types of fearlessness….

Question: There is a single dharma known as "fearlessness." How is it that we here have four of them?

Response: It is because there are four matters in which there is an absence of doubt or fear that we therefore speak of four of them, as follows:[60]

First, as the Buddha told the bhikshus, "I myself here utter these truthful words: 'I am a man possessed of all-knowledge.' If anyone here, whether he be a *śramaṇa*, brahman, deva, Māra, Brahmā, or other person possessed of worldly knowledge were to challenge this statement in a manner consistent with Dharma, claiming that I do not indeed possess a direct knowledge of this Dharma, I would not then experience in this challenge even the slightest sign of fearfulness, and it is because of not experiencing any such sign that I have become established in security and fearlessness in this regard." This is the first type of fearlessness. It is a result of exhaustively knowing all dharmas in accordance with reality.

As for the second type of fearlessness, the Buddha said, "I myself here utter these truthful words: 'I have brought all of the contaminants to an end.' If any *śramaṇa*, brahman, deva, Māra, or Brahmā were to claim that these contaminants have not indeed been brought to an end,

正體字		乃至不見有[7]是相。不見是相故安 082a19 ‖ 隱無畏。是二無畏。善斷諸煩惱及斷煩惱 082a20 ‖ 習氣故。三者我說障道法。此中若有沙門 082a21 ‖ 婆羅門諸天魔梵及餘世間智人。如法難言。 082a22 ‖ 是法雖用不能障道。我於此中不見有 082a23 ‖ 微畏相。不見是相故得安隱無有疑畏。 082a24 ‖ 是三無畏。善知障解脫法故。四者我所說 082a25 ‖ 道如法說行者。得至苦盡。若有沙門婆羅 082a26 ‖ 門諸天魔梵及餘世間智人。如法難言。[8]如 082a27 ‖ 是法雖如說行不能至盡苦道。我於此 082a28 ‖ 中無有微畏相。不見是相故得安隱無 082a29 ‖ 有疑畏。是四無畏。善知至苦盡道故。是四 082b01 ‖ 無畏皆過怖畏心驚毛竪等相故。名為無 082b02 ‖ 畏。又在大眾威德殊勝故。名為無畏。又善 082b03 ‖ 知一切問答故。名為無畏。諸天會經此中 082b04 ‖ 應廣說。
简体字		乃至不见有是相。不见是相故安隐无畏。是二无畏。善断诸烦恼及断烦恼习气故。三者我说障道法。此中若有沙门婆罗门诸天魔梵及余世间智人。如法难言。是法虽用不能障道。我于此中不见有微畏相。不见是相故得安隐无有疑畏。是三无畏。善知障解脱法故。四者我所说道如法说行者。得至苦尽。若有沙门婆罗门诸天魔梵及余世间智人。如法难言。如是法虽如说行不能至尽苦道。我于此中无有微畏相。不见是相故得安隐无有疑畏。是四无畏。善知至苦尽道故。是四无畏皆过怖畏心惊毛竖等相故。名为无畏。又在大众威德殊胜故。名为无畏。又善知一切问答故。名为无畏。诸天会经此中应广说。

Chapter 23 — Forty Dharmas Exclusive to Buddhas (Part 3)

I would not then experience in this challenge even the slightest sign of fearfulness.[61] It is because of not experiencing any such sign that I have become established in security and fearlessness in this regard." This is the second type of fearlessness. It is a result of having thoroughly cut off all afflictions and having also cut off the habitual propensities associated with past afflictions.

As for the third [type of fearlessness], [the Buddha said], "I have proclaimed which dharmas constitute obstacles to realization of the path. If anyone herein, whether he be a śramaṇa, brahman, deva, Māra, Brahmā, or other person possessed of worldly knowledge were to challenge this statement in a manner consistent with Dharma, claiming that, even though one might avail oneself of these dharmas, they would not be able to cause an obstacle to the path, I would not then experience in this challenge even the slightest sign of fearfulness. It is because of not experiencing any such sign that I have become established in security and fearlessness in this regard." This is the third type of the fearlessness. It is a result of having thoroughly known those dharmas that constitute obstacles to the achievement of liberation.

As for the fourth [type of fearlessness, the Buddha said], "Whoever practices the path I have proclaimed, practicing it in accordance with the way I have explained the Dharma, will succeed in reaching the end of suffering. If any śramaṇa, brahman, deva, Māra, Brahmā, or other person possessed of worldly knowledge were to challenge this statement in a manner accordant with Dharma, claiming that, although one might practice a dharma such as this in a manner consistent with the way it has been explained, one would be unable to reach the path that brings about the end of suffering, I would not then experience in this challenge even the slightest sign of fearfulness. It is because of not experiencing any such sign that I have become established in security and fearlessness in this regard." This is the fourth type of fearlessness. It is a result of thoroughly knowing the path leading to the extinguishing of suffering.

All four of these types of fearlessness are referred to as "fearlessnesses" because they all involve leaving behind such characteristic signs as fearfulness, terror, or horripilation. They are also termed "fearlessnesses" because they are able to maintain within the Great Assembly an awe-inspiring power of virtue extraordinary in its excellence. They are also called "fearlessnesses" because they so well know how to respond to all sorts of questions. Here, one should extensively discuss citations from *The Sutra on the Convocation of the Devas*.[62]

問曰。若佛是一切智人。應於一切法盡無畏。何以[9]但說四。答曰。略舉大要以開事端。餘亦如是。佛十力者。力名扶助。氣勢不可窮盡。無能沮壞。雖有十名而實一智。緣十事故名為十力。佛智緣一切事故。應有無量力。以此十力足度眾生故。[10]但說十力。但開此十力。餘皆可知。初力者。一切法因非因。決定通達智。名為初力。如佛說。若是狂人不捨是語不捨邪見不捨是心。來在佛前無有是處。如佛告阿難。世間二佛一時出世無有是處。一佛出世則有是處。是事為一佛世界故說。而實十方無量無邊諸世界中。百千萬億無數諸佛一時出世。又經說身口意惡業有妙愛果報無有是處。若身口意善業有妙愛果報則有是處。如是等五藏諸經應此中廣說。

问曰。若佛是一切智人。应于一切法尽无畏。何以但说四。答曰。略举大要以开事端。余亦如是。佛十力者。力名扶助。气势不可穷尽。无能沮坏。虽有十名而实一智。缘十事故名为十力。佛智缘一切事故。应有无量力。以此十力足度众生故。但说十力。但开此十力。余皆可知。初力者。一切法因非因。决定通达智。名为初力。如佛说。若是狂人不舍是语不舍邪见不舍是心。来在佛前无有是处。如佛告阿难。世间二佛一时出世无有是处。一佛出世则有是处。是事为一佛世界故说。而实十方无量无边诸世界中。百千万亿无数诸佛一时出世。又经说身口意恶业有妙爱果报无有是处。若身口意善业有妙爱果报则有是处。如是等五藏诸经应此中广说。

Chapter 23 — *Forty Dharmas Exclusive to Buddhas (Part 3)*

Question: If the Buddhas are indeed possessed of all-knowledge, then they should be fearless in relation to all dharmas. Why is it then that we speak only of these four types [of fearlessness]?

Response: These serve to raise the major essential topics in order to introduce the most important instances. All other instances are similar to these.

O. 30–39) They Possess the Ten Powers

As for the ten powers of the Buddha, "power" refers to the inexhaustible energetic strength that assists them and makes them invulnerable to interference by anyone. Although there are ten designations in this regard, in truth, this involves a single type of knowledge that, because it takes ten different circumstances as objective conditions, [these ten exemplary manifestations] are known as "the ten powers."

Because the knowledge of the Buddha takes all things as its objective conditions, it should be that there are countless powers. But it is because these ten powers are adequate to bring about the liberation of beings that we only speak of "the ten powers." Through merely introducing these ten powers, one can then know the others by inference.

1. The First Power

The first power is [the Buddha's] definite and completely penetrating knowledge with respect to all dharmas of what does and does not constitute the cause. This is the first power. [This was the basis for, as cited earlier], the Buddha's having said [in reference to the *brahmacārin* named Patikaputra], "If this crazy person does not relinquish these claims, does not relinquish these perverse views, and does not relinquish these thoughts, then, as for his being able to arrive here in the presence of the Buddha—this is an utter impossibility."

[This is also the basis for] the Buddha's having said to Ānanda:

> It is utterly impossible that two buddhas might arise in the world at the same time. However, it is indeed possible for a single buddha to come forth into the world."[63] This was said solely with respect to the circumstance of a single buddha emerging in a single world. In truth, in all of the countless and limitless worlds throughout the ten directions, there are countless hundreds of thousands of myriads of *koṭis* of buddhas simultaneously emerging throughout those worlds.
>
> Additionally, the sutras state: "It is impossible that bad physical, verbal, and mental karmic actions might have excellent and desirable results. However, it is indeed possible that good physical, verbal, and mental karmic actions may have excellent and desirable results."[64]

Here one should extensively discuss related scriptural citations from among the five categorical repositories of Dharma.

|正體字|

第二力者。於過去未來現在諸業諸[11]法
082b21 ‖ 受佛如實分別知處所知事知果報。佛若
082b22 ‖ 欲知一切眾生過去諸業過去業報[12]即能
082b23 ‖ 知。或業過去報在現在。或業過去報在未
082b24 ‖ 來。或業過去報在過去。或業過去報在過去
082b25 ‖ 未來。或業過去報在過去現在。或業過去報
082b26 ‖ 在未來現在。或業過去報在過去未來現在。
082b27 ‖ 或業現在報在現在。或業現在報在未來。或
082b28 ‖ 業現在報在現在未來。或業未來報在未來。
082b29 ‖ 有如是等分別受法者。四受法。現受樂後
082c01 ‖ 世受苦。現受苦後世受樂。現受樂後受
082c02 ‖ 樂。現受苦後受苦。處者。隨業時方所在。又
082c03 ‖ 知是業受報處。

|简体字|

第二力者。于过去未来现在诸业诸法受佛如实分别知处所知事知果报。佛若欲知一切众生过去诸业过去业报即能知。或业过去报在现在。或业过去报在未来。或业过去报在过去。或业过去报在过去未来。或业过去报在过去现在。或业过去报在未来现在。或业过去报在过去未来现在。或业现在报在现在。或业现在报在未来。或业现在报在现在未来。或业未来报在未来。有如是等分别受法者。四受法。现受乐后世受苦。现受苦后世受乐。现受乐后受乐。现受苦后受苦。处者。随业时方所在。又知是业受报处。

Chapter 23 — Forty Dharmas Exclusive to Buddhas (Part 3)

2. THE SECOND POWER

The second power is [the Buddha's] knowing in accordance with reality and with distinguishing clarity the place, the circumstances, and the karmic retributions associated with all past, future, and present karmic deeds along with all the dharmas that are involved in experiencing [those retributions].

If the Buddha wishes to know with regard to any being their past karmic deeds and their past karmic retributions, he is able to immediately know them. So too, he is immediately able to know:

With respect to past karmic deeds, their retribution in the present;
With respect to past karmic deeds, their retribution in the future;
With respect to past karmic deeds, their retribution in the past;
With respect to past karmic deeds, their retribution in both the past and the future;
With respect to past karmic deeds, their retribution in both the past and the present;
With respect to past karmic deeds, their retribution in both the future and the present;
With respect to past karmic deeds, their retribution in the past, the future, and the present;
With respect to present karmic deeds, their retribution in the present;
With respect to present karmic deeds, their retribution in the future;
With respect to present karmic deeds, their retribution in both the present and the future;
And with respect to future karmic deeds, their retribution in the future.

There are all manner of such distinctions regarding the dharmas involved in undergoing karmic retributions. There are four dharmas categorizing such karmic retributions, namely:

Undergoing blissful experiences in the present followed by undergoing suffering in future lifetimes;
Undergoing suffering in the present followed by undergoing blissful experiences in future lifetimes;
Undergoing blissful experiences in the present followed by blissful experiences in the future;
And undergoing suffering in the present followed by undergoing suffering in the future as well.[65]

As regards [the Buddha's knowing] "the place," this refers to his knowing for any karmic deed the time and place [of its occurrence] as well as the precise place in which this retribution will be undergone.

| 正體字 | 事者。或隨因緣。或隨三不
082c04 ‖ 善根。或多自作。或多因他。如是等善惡業
082c05 ‖ 因緣佛盡知。報者。知諸業各各有報。善業
082c06 ‖ 或善處生或得涅槃。惡業諸惡處生。佛悉知
082c07 ‖ 是諸業本末因緣自身及他。是中智力不退
082c08 ‖ 故名為力。三力者。佛於禪定解脫三昧垢淨
082c09 ‖ 相如實知。禪者四禪。定者四無色定四無量
082c10 ‖ 心等皆名為定。解脫者八解脫。三昧者除
082c11 ‖ 諸禪解脫餘定盡名三昧。有人言。三解脫門
082c12 ‖ 及有覺有觀定。無覺有觀定。無覺無觀定。名
082c13 ‖ 為三昧。有人言。定小三昧大。是故一切諸佛
082c14 ‖ 菩薩所得定。皆名三昧。是四處皆攝在一切
082c15 ‖ 禪波羅蜜。 |

| 简体字 | 事者。或随因缘。或随三不善根。或多自作。或多因他。如是等善恶业因缘佛尽知。报者。知诸业各各有报。善业或善处生或得涅槃。恶业诸恶处生。佛悉知是诸业本末因缘自身及他。是中智力不退故名为力。三力者。佛于禅定解脱三昧垢净相如实知。禅者四禅。定者四无色定四无量心等皆名为定。解脱者八解脱。三昧者除诸禅解脱余定尽名三昧。有人言。三解脱门及有觉有观定。无觉有观定。无觉无观定。名为三昧。有人言。定小三昧大。是故一切诸佛菩萨所得定。皆名三昧。是四处皆摄在一切禅波罗蜜。 |

Chapter 23 — *Forty Dharmas Exclusive to Buddhas (Part 3)*

As regards [the Buddha's] knowing "the circumstances," this refers to knowing the corresponding causes and conditions, knowing the three corresponding types of bad karmic roots, knowing whether the deed was primarily performed by oneself, or knowing whether the deed occurred for the most part through the instigation of someone else. The Buddha entirely knows all such causes and conditions associated with good and bad karmic deeds.

As regards [the Buddha's knowing] "the karmic retributions," he knows that all karmic deeds have their corresponding karmic retributions. For instance, good karmic deeds may result in being reborn in a good place or in attaining nirvāṇa, whereas bad karmic deeds may result in being reborn in any of the wretched destinies.

The Buddha knows entirely with respect to all these karmic deeds their roots, their branches, their associated causes and conditions, and whether they were done at one's own behest or at the behest of others. It is because this power of knowledge does not diminish that it is referred to as a "power."

3. THE THIRD POWER

The third power is the Buddha's knowing in accordance with reality the *dhyānas*, the meditative concentrations, the liberations, and the samādhis, together with their corresponding marks of defilement and purity.

"*Dhyānas*" refers to the four *dhyānas*. "Meditative concentrations" refers to the four formless-realm meditative concentrations, the four immeasurable minds, and other such states, all of which are referred to as "meditative concentrations." "Liberations" refers to the eight liberations. As for "samādhis" all of the other meditative concentrations aside from the *dhyānas* and the liberations are referred to as "samādhis."

There are others who claim that the three gates to liberation, meditative concentrations still characterized by initial ideation (*vitarka*) and discursive thought (*vicāra*), meditative concentrations characterized by the absence of initial ideation and the presence of discursive thought, and meditative concentrations devoid of both initial ideation and discursive thought—these may all be referred to as "samādhis."

There are yet others who claim that "meditative concentrations" are relatively minor [meditative states] whereas "samādhis" are relatively major. Therefore, one may refer to all meditative concentrations realized by any buddha or bodhisattva as constituting a "samādhi."

All four of these constituent categories are subsumed within all explanations of *"dhyāna pāramitā."*

正體字	垢名[13]受味。淨名不[*]受味。復次 082c16 ‖ 垢名有漏定。淨名無漏[14]定。三昧解脫等分 082c17 ‖ 別者。[15]如是禪分別知他眾生他人上下諸 082c18 ‖ 根。如實知名第四力。他眾生者凡夫是。他 082c19 ‖ 人者須陀洹等諸賢聖是。或有人言。眾生名 082c20 ‖ 為凡夫。及諸學人煩惱未盡故。他人者阿羅 082c21 ‖ 漢等煩惱盡故。或有人言。眾生與人一種名 082c22 ‖ 有差別。諸根者。信精進念定慧非眼等根。上 082c23 ‖ 名猛利堪任得道。下名闇鈍不堪受道。 082c24 ‖ 佛於此二根上下如實知不錯謬。他眾生 082c25 ‖ 他人心各有所樂如實知。是第五力。所樂 082c26 ‖ 名為貴所向事。
简体字	垢名受味。净名不受味。复次垢名有漏定。净名无漏定。三昧解脱等分别者。如是禅分别知他众生他人上下诸根。如实知名第四力。他众生者凡夫是。他人者须陀洹等诸贤圣是。或有人言。众生名为凡夫。及诸学人烦恼未尽故。他人者阿罗汉等烦恼尽故。或有人言。众生与人一种名有差别。诸根者。信精进念定慧非眼等根。上名猛利堪任得道。下名闇钝不堪受道。佛于此二根上下如实知不错谬。他众生他人心各有所乐如实知。是第五力。所乐名为贵所向事。

Chapter 23 — Forty Dharmas Exclusive to Buddhas (Part 3)

As for "defilement," this refers to [meditative states characterized by] the experience of delectably pleasurable (*āsvādana*) sensations whereas "purity" refers here to not indulging delectably pleasurable sensations.

Then again, "defilement" may refer to any meditative concentration still characterized by the contaminants (*āsrava*) whereas "purity" may refer to any meditative concentration characterized by the absence of the contaminants.

As for the distinctions among the samādhis, liberations, and so forth, [the Buddha] knows with distinguishing clarity these sorts of *dhyāna* meditation states.

4. The Fourth Power

The fourth power is [the Buddha's] knowing in accordance with reality the relative superiority or inferiority of the faculties of other beings and other personages.

"Other beings" refers to common persons. "Other personages" refers here to the stream enterer and the other classes of worthies and *āryas*. There may be others who interpret "beings" as a reference not only to common persons, but also even to those practitioners still involved in the learning stages, this because all of these have still not succeeded in putting an end to all of the contaminants. For them, "other personages" is a reference reserved for arhats and such, this because they have utterly ended all afflictions.

Yet others point out that both "beings" and "other personages" are but a single category and it is only the designations themselves that differ.

As for their "faculties," in this context they refer to faith, vigor, mindfulness, concentration, and wisdom and *not* to the sense faculties such as the eye and so forth [as the word might otherwise signify].

"Superior," as it applies to these faculties, refers to faculties that are fiercely sharp and which have the capacity to enable the attainment of enlightenment. "Inferior," on the other hand, refers to [faculties] that are dim, dull, and inadequate to enable one to take up [the practice of] the path.

The Buddha knows the relative superiority and inferiority of these two types of faculties and knows these matters in accordance with reality and in a manner free of any sort of error.

5. The Fifth Power

The fifth power is [the Buddha's] knowing in accordance with reality that in which the minds of other beings and other personages delight. "That in which they delight" refers to whatever endeavors they esteem

正體字

```
          如有人貴財物世樂或
082c27 ‖  有貴重福德善法。是事佛如實知。世間種
082c28 ‖  種性無量性。佛如實知。是第六力。種種性者
082c29 ‖  雜性萬端。無量性者。於一一性有無量種
083a01 ‖  分別。性者從先世來心常習用常所樂行修
083a02 ‖  習故成性。是二善惡性佛如實知。至一切
083a03 ‖  處道如實知。是第七力。至一切處道者。能
083a04 ‖  得一切功德。是道名為至一切處道。所謂五
083a05 ‖  分三昧。若五[1]知三昧。若八聖道分是。或聖
083a06 ‖  道所攝諸法。或四如意足。如經說。比丘善
083a07 ‖  修習四如意足無利不得。有人言四禪是。
083a08 ‖  如經說。比丘得四禪。心安住一處清淨。除
083a09 ‖  諸煩惱滅諸障礙。調和堪用不復動轉。若
083a10 ‖  迴向知宿命事。即能知宿命事。是第八力。
083a11 ‖  佛若欲念自身及一切眾生無量無邊宿命。
```

简体字

如有人贵财物世乐或有贵重福德善法。是事佛如实知。世间种种性无量性。佛如实知。是第六力。种种性者杂性万端。无量性者。于一一性有无量种分别。性者从先世来心常习用常所乐行修习故成性。是二善恶性佛如实知。至一切处道如实知。是第七力。至一切处道者。能得一切功德。是道名为至一切处道。所谓五分三昧。若五知三昧。若八圣道分是。或圣道所摄诸法。或四如意足。如经说。比丘善修习四如意足无利不得。有人言四禅是。如经说。比丘得四禅。心安住一处清净。除诸烦恼灭诸障碍。调和堪用不复动转。若回向知宿命事。即能知宿命事。是第八力。佛若欲念自身及一切众生无量无边宿命。

Chapter 23 — Forty Dharmas Exclusive to Buddhas (Part 3)

and are inclined to engage in. For instance, there are those people who esteem wealth and worldly pleasures, whereas there are others who deeply esteem karmic merit and the practice of good dharmas. The Buddha knows all of these matters in accordance with reality.

6. THE SIXTH POWER

The sixth power is the Buddha's knowing in accordance with reality the different types of natures of beings in the world as well as the countless [distinctions among those] natures. "Different types of natures" refers to the myriad variations in these natures. "Countless natures" is a reference to the countless distinctions in each and every one of these types of natures. As for the term "nature," it is because one's mind has always habitually practiced [particular sorts of endeavors] and has always delighted in practicing and cultivating them throughout one's past lives right up until the very present—it is for this reason that they therefore form the basis of one's "nature." The Buddha knows in accordance with reality these two categories of natures, the good and the bad.

7. THE SEVENTH POWER

The seventh power is [the Buddha's] knowing in accordance with reality the paths leading to all destinations. As for "the paths leading to all destinations," those are the means by which one may succeed in acquiring all meritorious qualities. These paths are referred to as "the paths leading to all destinations."

These include, for instance, the five-factor samādhi,[66] the fivefold awareness samādhi,[67] the eightfold path of the Āryas, all dharmas subsumed by the path of the Āryas, or the four bases of psychic power, the latter as cited in a sutra that says: "If a bhikshu cultivates the four bases of psychic power, there is no benefit that he will not acquire."

There are others who claim that this may also refer to the four *dhyānas*, as cited in a sutra that says: "When a bhikshu gains the four *dhyānas*, his mind comes to abide with stability and purity in a single place in which he then succeeds in ridding himself of all afflictions and in destroying all obstacles. It then becomes well-regulated so that it becomes serviceable and no longer subject to movement or distraction."

8. THE EIGHTH POWER

The eighth power is the [Buddha's] immediate ability to know past-life matters whenever he chooses to direct his awareness to events from previous lives. If the Buddha wishes to recall any of the countless and limitless lifetimes of either himself or all other beings, he then

正體字

083a12 ‖ 一切事皆悉知。無有不知過恒河沙等劫
083a13 ‖ 事。是人何處生。姓名貴賤飲食資生苦樂所
083a14 ‖ 作事業所受果報。心何所行本從何來。如
083a15 ‖ 是等事。以天眼清淨過於人眼。見六道眾
083a16 ‖ 生隨業受身。是第九力。大力聲聞以天眼
083a17 ‖ 見小千國土。亦見中眾生生時死時。[2]小辟
083a18 ‖ 支佛見千小千國土。見中眾生生時死時。
083a19 ‖ 中力辟支佛見百萬小千國土。見中眾生生
083a20 ‖ 時死時。大力辟支佛見三千大千國土。見
083a21 ‖ 中眾生生死所趣。諸佛世尊見無量無邊不
083a22 ‖ 可思議世間。亦見是中眾生生時死時。第十
083a23 ‖ 力者。欲漏有漏無明漏一切漏盡。諸煩惱及
083a24 ‖ 氣都盡。是名第十力。無礙解脫者。解脫有三
083a25 ‖ 種。一者於煩惱障礙解脫。二者於定障礙
083a26 ‖ 解脫。三者於一切法障礙解脫。是中得慧
083a27 ‖ 解脫阿羅漢。得離煩惱障礙解脫。

简体字

一切事皆悉知。无有不知过恒河沙等劫事。是人何处生。姓名贵贱饮食资生苦乐所作事业所受果报。心何所行本从何来。如是等事。以天眼清净过于人眼。见六道众生随业受身。是第九力。大力声闻以天眼见小千国土。亦见中众生生时死时。小辟支佛见千小千国土。见中众生生时死时。中力辟支佛见百万小千国土。见中众生生时死时。大力辟支佛见三千大千国土。见中众生生死所趣。诸佛世尊见无量无边不可思议世间。亦见是中众生生时死时。第十力者。欲漏有漏无明漏一切漏尽。诸烦恼及气都尽。是名第十力。无碍解脱者。解脱有三种。一者于烦恼障碍解脱。二者于定障碍解脱。三者于一切法障碍解脱。是中得慧解脱阿罗汉。得离烦恼障碍解脱。

knows all of these matters entirely. There are no instances in which he is unable to know some particular matter even beyond a number of kalpas equal to the number of sands in the Ganges River.

He knows where this person was born, what his name was, whether he was of noble or lowly caste, what he drank and ate, how he sustained his life, whether he experienced suffering or happiness, the types of endeavors in which he engaged, the karmic retributions that he underwent, what his mind engaged in, and from whence he originally came. He knows all such matters.

9. THE NINTH POWER

The ninth power is the [Buddha's] ability to see with the heavenly eye purified beyond the power of man's eyes the beings of the six destinies taking on bodies in accordance with their karmic deeds.

A *śrāvaka* disciple possessed of great powers uses the heavenly eye to see the lands contained within a small chiliocosm and also sees when the beings therein are born and when they die.

A lesser *pratyekabuddha* sees the lands of a thousand small chiliocosms and sees when the beings therein are born and when they die.

A *pratyekabuddha* possessed of middling powers sees the lands contained in a hundred myriads of small chiliocosms and sees when the beings therein are born and when they die.

A *pratyekabuddha* possessed of great powers sees the lands contained in a great trichiliocosm and sees the destinies to which they proceed when they die and are reborn.

The Buddhas, the Bhagavats, see a countless, boundless, and inconceivable number of worlds and also see when the beings therein are born and when they die.

10. THE TENTH POWER

As for the tenth power, it is the [Buddha's] ending of all contaminants, including the contaminant of sensual desire, the contaminant of [craving for] existence, and the contaminant of ignorance, these together with the utter ending of all afflictions or affliction-associated energetic propensities. This is the tenth power.

P. 40) THEY HAVE ACHIEVED UNIMPEDED LIBERATION

As for unimpeded liberation, there are three types of liberations. The first is the liberation from the obstacles of the afflictions. The second is the liberation from the obstacles to meditative concentration. The third is the liberation from the obstacles to [the knowledge of] all dharmas. Among these, an arhat who has achieved liberation through wisdom gains liberation from the obstacles of the afflictions. Both the

正體字

共解脫
083a28 ‖ 阿羅漢及辟支佛。得離煩惱障礙解脫。得
083a29 ‖ 離諸禪定障礙解脫。唯有諸佛具三解脫。
083b01 ‖ 所謂煩惱障礙解脫。諸禪定障礙解脫。一切
083b02 ‖ 法障礙解脫。總是三種解脫故。佛名無礙解
083b03 ‖ 脫。常隨心共生。乃至無餘涅槃則止。是四十
083b04 ‖ 不共法。略開佛法門令眾生[3]解故說。所
083b05 ‖ 不說者無量無邊。所謂一常不離慧。二知
083b06 ‖ 時不失。三滅一切習氣。四得定波羅蜜。五
083b07 ‖ 一切功德殊勝。六隨所宜行波羅蜜。七無
083b08 ‖ 能見頂者。八無與等者。九無能勝者。十世
083b09 ‖ 間中上。十一不從他聞得道。十二不轉法
083b10 ‖ 者。十三自言是佛終不能到佛前。十四不
083b11 ‖ 退法者。十五得大[4]悲者。十六得大慈者。十
083b12 ‖ 七第一可信受者。

简体字

共解脱阿罗汉及辟支佛。得离烦恼障碍解脱。得离诸禅定障碍解脱。唯有诸佛具三解脱。所谓烦恼障碍解脱。诸禅定障碍解脱。一切法障碍解脱。总是三种解脱故。佛名无碍解脱。常随心共生。乃至无余涅槃则止。是四十不共法。略开佛法门令众生解故说。所不说者无量无边。所谓一常不离慧。二知时不失。三灭一切习气。四得定波罗蜜。五一切功德殊胜。六随所宜行波罗蜜。七无能见顶者。八无与等者。九无能胜者。十世间中上。十一不从他闻得道。十二不转法者。十三自言是佛终不能到佛前。十四不退法者。十五得大悲者。十六得大慈者。十七第一可信受者。

doubly-liberated arhat and the *pratyekabuddha* succeed in achieving both the liberation from the obstacles of the afflictions and the liberation from the obstacles to the *dhyāna* concentrations.

It is only the Buddhas who have completely achieved all three of these liberations, namely liberation from the obstacles of the afflictions, liberation from the obstacles to acquisition of the *dhyāna* concentrations, and the liberation from the obstacles to [the knowledge of] all dharmas. It is because he brings together all three of the liberations that the Buddha is designated as having achieved unimpeded liberation. This [unimpeded liberation] always accompanies the mind all the way up to the point of entry into the nirvāṇa without residue.

Q. SUMMARY DISCUSSION OF THE DHARMAS EXCLUSIVE TO THE BUDDHA

These forty dharmas exclusive to the Buddhas provide a general introduction to an entryway into the dharmas of the Buddha. They are discussed here because this allows beings to thereby acquire an understanding of them. However, those [exclusive dharmas] that remain undiscussed herein are innumerable and boundless. Specifically, these include the following:

1) [The Buddha] never departs from wisdom.
2) He never errs in knowing the right time.
3) He has extinguished all habitual karmic propensities.
4) He has gained the meditative concentration *pāramitā*.
5) All of his meritorious qualities are possessed of extraordinary supremacy.
6) He has perfected the *pāramitā* of always according in his actions with what is appropriate to the circumstances.
7) No one is able to view the very top of [the light rays radiating from] the crown of his head.
8) No one is his equal.
9) No one is able to surpass him.
10) He is superior to all beings in the world.
11) His attainment of the path is not learned from anyone else.
12) He never turns away from the Dharma.
13) Whoever else might claim to be a buddha is forever unable to enter the presence of the Buddha.
14) He has perfected the dharma of never retreating.
15) He has acquired the great compassion.
16) He has acquired the great kindness.
17) He is the foremost among all whose teachings one may accept in faith.

正體字	十八第一名聞利養。十九 083b13 ‖ 與佛同止。諸師無與佛等者。二十諸師無 083b14 ‖ 有得[*]弟子眾如佛者。二十一端正第一見 083b15 ‖ 者歡悅。二十二佛所使人無能害者。二十三 083b16 ‖ 佛欲度者無有傷害。二十四心初生時能 083b17 ‖ 斷思惟結。二十五可度眾生終不失時。二 083b18 ‖ 十六第十六[5]智得阿耨多羅三藐三菩提。二 083b19 ‖ 十七世間第一福田。二十八放無量光明。二 083b20 ‖ 十九所行不同餘人。三十百福[6]德相。三十 083b21 ‖ 一無量無邊善根。三十二入胎時。三十三生 083b22 ‖ 時。三十四得佛道時。三十五轉法輪時。三 083b23 ‖ 十六捨長壽命時。三十七入涅槃時能動三 083b24 ‖ 千大千世界。三十八擾動無量無邊諸魔宮 083b25 ‖ 殿令無威德皆使驚畏。三十九諸護世天 083b26 ‖ 王釋提桓因夜[7]摩天王兜率陀天王化樂天 083b27 ‖ 王自在天王梵天王淨居諸天等。一時來集 083b28 ‖ 請轉法輪。四十佛身堅固如那羅延。
简体字	十八第一名闻利养。十九与佛同止。诸师无与佛等者。二十诸师无有得第子众如佛者。二十一端正第一见者欢悦。二十二佛所使人无能害者。二十三佛欲度者无有伤害。二十四心初生时能断思惟结。二十五可度众生终不失时。二十六第十六智得阿耨多罗三藐三菩提。二十七世间第一福田。二十八放无量光明。二十九所行不同余人。三十百福德相。三十一无量无边善根。三十二入胎时。三十三生时。三十四得佛道时。三十五转法轮时。三十六舍长寿命时。三十七入涅槃时能动三千大千世界。三十八扰动无量无边诸魔宫殿令无威德皆使惊畏。三十九诸护世天王释提桓因夜摩天王兜率陀天王化乐天王自在天王梵天王净居诸天等。一时来集请转法轮。四十佛身坚固如那罗延。

Chapter 23 — Forty Dharmas Exclusive to Buddhas (Part 3)

18) He is the foremost among those [who are worthy of] fame and offerings.
19) No guru who is a contemporary of the Buddha is equal to the Buddha.
20) No guru gains a community of disciples equal to that of the Buddha.
21) The supreme refinement of his appearance causes all who see him to be delighted.
22) Whoever is sent forth as an emissary of a Buddha cannot be harmed by anyone.
23) No one is able to injure anyone whom the Buddha has set out to liberate.
24) From the very moment he first brings forth a thought, he is able to sever all thought-related fetters.
25) He never misses the right time [to provide appropriate instruction to] beings who are capable of achieving liberation.
26) In the sixteenth [mind-moment involved in the acquisition of] wisdom, a buddha attains *anuttarasamyaksaṃbodhi*.
27) He is the foremost among the world's fields of merit.
28) He emanates measureless radiant light.
29) His actions differ from those of anyone else.
30) He possesses the [physical] marks that are associated with a hundredfold generation of merit.[68]
31) He has measureless and boundless roots of goodness.
32) When he enters the womb—
33) When he is born—
34) When he achieves buddhahood—
35) When he turns the wheel of the Dharma—
36) When he relinquishes the possibility of the long life span—
37) And when he enters nirvāṇa—[on all these occasions], he is able to cause all the worlds throughout the great trichiliocosm to shake.
38) [On all of the above occasions], he sets quaking the countless palaces of the *māras*, causing them to lose their awesome power and be struck with terror.
39) [When he achieves buddhahood], the world-protecting heavenly kings, Śakra, ruler of the devas, the Yāma Heaven King, the Tuṣita Heaven King, the Nirmāṇarati Heaven King, the Paranirmita Vaśavartin Heaven King, the Brahma Heaven King, the devas of the Pure Abodes, and the other devas—they all simultaneously assemble and request the turning of the Dharma wheel.
40) The Buddha's body is as solid as the body of Nārāyaṇa.[69]

正體字

四十一　083b29 ‖ 未有結戒而初結戒。四十二有所施作勢
083c01 ‖ 力勝人。四十三菩薩處胎母於一切男子
083c02 ‖ 無染著心。四十四力能救度一切眾生。佛
083c03 ‖ 不共法有如是等無量無數。妨餘事故不
083c04 ‖ 須廣說。聲聞法雖[8]似佛法。優劣不同則
083c05 ‖ 有差別。復次總說諸佛一切諸法無量無邊
083c06 ‖ 不可思議第一希有。一切眾生所不能共。
083c07 ‖ 假使十方諸三千大千世界過諸算數是中
083c08 ‖ 所有眾生智慧皆如大梵天王。皆如大辟支
083c09 ‖ 佛。皆如舍利弗。合集是諸智慧令一人得。
083c10 ‖ 欲及於佛四十不共法中微少分者。無有
083c11 ‖ 是處。若於一法百千萬億分中不及其一。
083c12 ‖ 諸佛有如是無量無邊功德之力。何以故。無
083c13 ‖ 數大劫安住四功德處。深行六波羅蜜。善能
083c14 ‖ 具足菩薩一切所行諸法。不共一切眾生
083c15 ‖ 故。果報亦不共。[9]
083c16 ‖ 十住毘婆沙論卷第十一

简体字

四十一未有结戒而初结戒。四十二有所施作势力胜人。四十三菩萨处胎母于一切男子无染着心。四十四力能救度一切众生。佛不共法有如是等无量无数。妨余事故不须广说。声闻法虽似佛法。优劣不同则有差别。复次总说诸佛一切诸法无量无边不可思议第一希有。一切众生所不能共。假使十方诸三千大千世界过诸算数是中所有众生智慧皆如大梵天王。皆如大辟支佛。皆如舍利弗。合集是诸智慧令一人得。欲及于佛四十不共法中微少分者。无有是处。若于一法百千万亿分中不及其一。诸佛有如是无量无边功德之力。何以故。无数大劫安住四功德处。深行六波罗蜜。善能具足菩萨一切所行诸法。不共一切众生故。果报亦不共。

Chapter 23 — Forty Dharmas Exclusive to Buddhas (Part 3)

41) When the moral precepts have not yet been formulated, he is the one who first formulates the moral precepts.
42) Whenever he takes up any endeavor, his power in accomplishing this is superior to that of any man.
43) During the entire time the Bodhisattva is residing in his mother's womb, she loses all thoughts of defiling attachment for men.
44) His power is such that he is able to bring about the rescue and liberation of all beings.

There are measurelessly and innumerably many dharmas such as these that are exclusive to the Buddha. Because it would interfere with the explanation of other matters, there is no need to present an extensive discussion of them here. Although these dharmas as found in the Dharma of the Śrāvaka Disciples do resemble dharmas of the Buddha, due to dissimilarities in the degree of superiority or inferiority, there are distinct differences [in how they are described].

Moreover, to summarize, all of the dharmas of the Buddhas are measureless, limitless, inconceivable, of the foremost degree of rarity, and such that no other being is able to have them in common [with any buddha]. Even if all the countless beings in the worlds of all the great trichiliocosms throughout the ten directions possessed wisdom comparable to the king of the Great Brahma Heaven, comparable to a great *pratyekabuddha*, or comparable to Śāriputra, and one were somehow able to collect all this wisdom together in a single person—even if that one person then wished to approach the most minutely small fraction of these forty dharmas exclusive to the Buddhas—this would still be an utter impossibility. He could not even measure up to but one part in a hundred thousand myriads of *koṭis* of parts of just a single one of those dharmas.

The Buddhas possess the power of just such an immeasurable and limitless number of meritorious qualities. And why is this so? It is because they have securely established themselves in the four bases of meritorious qualities for a countless number of great kalpas during which they have deeply practiced the six *pāramitās* and have become well able to completely equip themselves with all dharmas practiced by the bodhisattva. Because [these dharmas] are not held in common with any other beings, so too, the fruits resulting [from their practice] are not held in common with any beings, either.

The End of Chapter Twenty-Three

|正體字|

083c19 ‖ 十住毘婆沙論卷第十二 083c20 ‖
083c21 ‖ 　　聖者龍樹造
083c22 ‖ 　　後秦龜茲國三藏鳩摩羅什譯
083c23 ‖ [10]讚偈品第二十四
083c24 ‖ 已如是解四十不共法竟。應取是四十不
083c25 ‖ 共法相念佛。又應以諸偈讚佛。如現在
083c26 ‖ 前對面共語。如是則成念佛三昧。如偈說。
083c27 ‖ 　聖主大精進　四十獨有法
083c28 ‖ 　我今於佛前　敬心以稱讚
083c29 ‖ 　如意及飛行　其力無邊限
084a01 ‖ 　於聖如意中　無有與等者
084a02 ‖ 　聲聞中自在　他心智無量
084a03 ‖ 　善能調伏心　隨意而應適
084a04 ‖ 　其念如大海　湛然在安隱
084a05 ‖ 　世間無有法　而能擾亂者
084a06 ‖ 　諸佛所稱歎　金剛三昧寶
084a07 ‖ 　得之在胸中　如賢懷直心
084a08 ‖ 　善知不定法　四無色定事
084a09 ‖ 　微細難分別　盡知無有餘

|简体字|

赞偈品第二十四
　已如是解四十不共法竟。应取是四十不共法相念佛。又应以诸偈赞佛。如现在前对面共语。如是则成念佛三昧。如偈说。
　　圣主大精进　四十独有法
　　我今于佛前　敬心以称赞
　　如意及飞行　其力无边限
　　于圣如意中　无有与等者
　　声闻中自在　他心智无量
　　善能调伏心　随意而应适
　　其念如大海　湛然在安隐
　　世间无有法　而能扰乱者
　　诸佛所称叹　金刚三昧宝
　　得之在胸中　如贤怀直心
　　善知不定法　四无色定事
　　微细难分别　尽知无有余

Chapter 24
Verses Offered in Praise

IV. CHAPTER 24: VERSES OFFERED IN PRAISE
  A. THE IMPORTANCE OF PRAISES TO MINDFULNESS-OF-THE-BUDDHA PRACTICE

Now that, in this way, we have reached the end of this explanation of the forty dharmas exclusive to the Buddhas, one should take the aspects emblematic of these forty exclusive dharmas and use them in one's own practice of mindfulness of the Buddha. One should also use verses to praise the Buddha, doing so as if one were standing directly before him, speaking to him. If one proceeds in this manner, then one may succeed in entering the mindfulness-of-the-Buddha samādhi. Accordingly, there are verses, as follows:

  B. THE PRAISE VERSES
    1. VERSES IN PRAISE OF THE FORTY DHARMAS EXCLUSIVE TO THE BUDDHAS

Oh, greatly vigorous lord of the Āryas—
Now, in the presence of the Buddha,
I shall praise with reverential mind
these forty dharmas possessed only [by buddhas].[70]

As for his supernatural powers and travel through flight,
their power when enacted is utterly limitless.
Among the psychic powers of the other *āryas*,
there are none at all that can equal these.

Among the *śrāvaka* disciples, he holds sway with sovereign mastery,
using his measureless knowledge of others' thoughts.
Thus he is well able to train their thoughts
by according with their minds as he appropriately responds to them.

His mindfulness is as expansive as the great ocean
while also being tranquil and calmly secure.
In all the world, there is no dharma
able to cause him to become perturbed.

The jewel of the vajra samādhi
that is praised by all buddhas—
he has acquired it and it resides within in his heart
just as the Worthies embrace the straightforward mind.

He thoroughly knows the unfixed dharmas
and the matters associated with the four formless absorptions
that are so subtle they are difficult to distinguish.
He exhaustively knows them all without exception.

084a10 ‖	眾生若已滅	今滅及當滅
084a11 ‖	[1]唯獨有世尊	智慧能通達
084a12 ‖	善知不相應	非色法中事
084a13 ‖	一切諸世間	悉皆不能知
084a14 ‖	世尊大威力	功德不可量
084a15 ‖	智慧無邊際	皆無與等者
084a16 ‖	於四問答中	超絕無倫匹
084a17 ‖	眾生諸問難	一切皆易答
084a18 ‖	若諸世間中	欲有害佛者
084a19 ‖	是事皆不成	以成不殺法
084a20 ‖	若於三時中	諸有所說者
084a21 ‖	言必不虛[2]設	常有大果報
084a22 ‖	凡有所說法	無非是希有
084a23 ‖	義趣尚不謬	何況於言辭
084a24 ‖	於三聖弟子	上中下差別
084a25 ‖	四雙八輩等	第一大導師
084a26 ‖	身口意業命	畢竟常清淨
084a27 ‖	是故於此中	不復須防護
084a28 ‖	自說一切智	心無有疑畏
084a29 ‖	若人來難我	恐有所不知

众生若已灭　　今灭及当灭
唯独有世尊　　智慧能通达
善知不相应　　非色法中事
一切诸世间　　悉皆不能知
世尊大威力　　功德不可量
智慧无边际　　皆无与等者
于四问答中　　超绝无伦匹
众生诸问难　　一切皆易答
若诸世间中　　欲有害佛者
是事皆不成　　以成不杀法
若于三时中　　诸有所说者
言必不虚设　　常有大果报
凡有所说法　　无非是希有
义趣尚不谬　　何况于言辞
于三圣弟子　　上中下差别
四双八辈等　　第一大导师
身口意业命　　毕竟常清净
是故于此中　　不复须防护
自说一切智　　心无有疑畏
若人来难我　　恐有所不知

Chapter 24 — *Verses Offered in Praise*

Regarding whether a being has already died in the past,
dies now in the present, or will die at some point later in the future,
it is solely the Bhagavat, and he alone,
whose wisdom is able to fully comprehend such things.

He knows well all matters related
to the formless dharmas unassociated with the mind
that everyone else throughout all worlds
remains entirely unable to know.

The Bhagavat's great awesome powers,
his measureless meritorious qualities,
and his boundless wisdom
are all unmatched by anyone at all.

In the four types of responses to questions,
he is so preeminent that he has no peer.
As for all the challenging questions that beings present,
he replies to them all with utter ease.

If anywhere in any world
there is someone wishing to harm the Buddha,
this circumstance never comes to pass,
for he has gained the dharma by which he cannot be slain.

If at any point throughout the three periods of time
there is anything that he says,
those words are definitely not set forth in vain,
but rather always bring great fruits as a result.

Of all the dharmas that he proclaims,
none of them are not especially rare.
He is never in error as regards their significance,
how much the less might he ever err in words and phrases.

For the three types of *ārya* disciples
that differ as either superior, middling, or inferior,
and include the eight classes in four pairs,[71] and the others,
he is the foremost great spiritual guide.

In actions of body, speech, and mind, and in sustaining his life,
he is ultimately and always pure
and hence, in all of these,
he never again needs to act in a guarded way.

When he himself proclaims his possession of all-knowledge,
his mind remains utterly free of any doubt or fear
such that he might think, "If someone comes and challenges me,
I fear there may be something I do not know."

正體字		
084b01 ‖	自說漏盡相	盡到無漏邊
084b02 ‖	心無有疑畏	餘漏有不盡
084b03 ‖	自說障礙法	於中無疑難
084b04 ‖	雖有用此法	不能為障礙
084b05 ‖	所說八聖道	心無有疑畏
084b06 ‖	有言是八道	不能至解脫
084b07 ‖	如實知是因	是果及與非
084b08 ‖	故號一切智	名聞流無量
084b09 ‖	三世所有業	是諸業定報
084b10 ‖	及非定果報	種種皆悉知
084b11 ‖	諸禪三昧中	麁細深淺事
084b12 ‖	皆悉能了知	禪中無等者
084b13 ‖	先知眾生根	上中下差別
084b14 ‖	種種樂及性	隨宜而說法
084b15 ‖	行道得諸利	兼以化導人
084b16 ‖	是以弟子眾	如實得[3]善利
084b17 ‖	宿命知無量	天眼見無邊
084b18 ‖	一切人[4]天中	無能知其限
084b19 ‖	住金剛三昧	滅煩惱及氣
084b20 ‖	又知人漏盡	故名漏盡力

简体字

自说漏尽相　　尽到无漏边
心无有疑畏　　余漏有不尽
自说障碍法　　于中无疑难
虽有用此法　　不能为障碍
所说八圣道　　心无有疑畏
有言是八道　　不能至解脱
如实知是因　　是果及与非
故号一切智　　名闻流无量
三世所有业　　是诸业定报
及非定果报　　种种皆悉知
诸禅三昧中　　粗细深浅事
皆悉能了知　　禅中无等者
先知众生根　　上中下差别
种种乐及性　　随宜而说法
行道得诸利　　兼以化导人
是以弟子众　　如实得善利
宿命知无量　　天眼见无边
一切人天中　　无能知其限
住金刚三昧　　灭烦恼及气
又知人漏尽　　故名漏尽力

Chapter 24 — *Verses Offered in Praise*

When declaring his characteristic of having ended the contaminants,
thus reaching the utmost elimination of the contaminants,
his mind remains utterly free of any doubt or fear
that there might be residual contaminants that are not yet ended.

When proclaiming his knowledge of the obstructive dharmas,
he has no doubt at the prospect of being challenged
that, though one might indulge in these dharmas,
they might not actually then constitute an obstacle.

As for the eightfold path of the Āryas that he has proclaimed,
his mind is free of any doubt or fear
that someone might rightly claim of this eightfold path
that it is unable to lead one to reach liberation.

He knows in accordance with reality that this is a cause,
this is its result, and this other factor does not constitute [a cause].
It is for these reasons that he is said to be omniscient
and that his fame spreads immeasurably far.

All actions carried out throughout the three periods of time,
the fixed retribution associated with these actions,
and their unfixed karmic results—
He thoroughly knows all of these different matters.

As for all coarse, subtle, deep, and shallow phenomena
within all of the *dhyāna* absorptions and samādhis,
he is able to entirely know them all.
In the realm of *dhyāna* absorptions, no one is his equal.

He first knows with regard to the faculties of beings,
their distinctions as either superior, middling, or inferior,
knows what they delight in, and knows their individual natures,
whereupon, adapting to what is fitting, he teaches them the Dharma.

He cultivated the path and gained its benefits
while also teaching and guiding others.
It is in this manner that the community of disciples
gains the wholesome benefit that accords with reality.

His knowledge of past lives is measurelessly vast
and the vision of his heavenly eye has no bounds.
Among all humans and devas,
no one is able to know their limits.

He abides in the vajra samādhi,
having extinguished the afflictions and karmic propensities,
and also knows the utter ending of the human contaminants.
Hence this is known as the power of having ended the contaminants.

084b21 ‖	煩惱諸禪障	一切法障礙
084b22 ‖	三礙得解脫	號無礙解脫
084b23 ‖	四十不共法	功德不可量
084b24 ‖	無能廣說者	我已略說竟
084b25 ‖	世尊若一劫	稱說此佛法
084b26 ‖	猶尚不[5]可盡	況我無此智
084b27 ‖	世尊大慈[6]蔭	無量業善集
084b28 ‖	四功德處故	得佛無量法
084b29 ‖	世尊所稱說	四功德勝處
084c01 ‖	我今還以此	稱讚於如來
084c02 ‖	三十二相具	相有百福德
084c03 ‖	八十種妙好	三界誰能有
084c04 ‖	三千大千界	眾生所有福
084c05 ‖	果報為百倍	相有如是德
084c06 ‖	如此諸福德	并及其果報
084c07 ‖	復以為百倍	成一白毫相
084c08 ‖	三十相一一	福德及果報
084c09 ‖	復以為千倍	成一肉髻相
084c10 ‖	世尊諸功德	不可得度量
084c11 ‖	如人以尺寸	量空不可盡

(正體字)

烦恼诸禅障　一切法障碍
三碍得解脱　号无碍解脱
四十不共法　功德不可量
无能广说者　我已略说竟
世尊若一劫　称说此佛法
犹尚不可尽　况我无此智
世尊大慈荫　无量业善集
四功德处故　得佛无量法
世尊所称说　四功德胜处
我今还以此　称赞于如来
三十二相具　相有百福德
八十种妙好　三界谁能有
三千大千界　众生所有福
果报为百倍　相有如是德
如此诸福德　并及其果报
复以为百倍　成一白毫相
三十相一一　福德及果报
复以为千倍　成一肉髻相
世尊诸功德　不可得度量
如人以尺寸　量空不可尽

(简体字)

The obstacle of afflictions, the obstacles to *dhyāna* absorptions,
and the obstacles to the knowledge of all dharmas—
he has gained liberation from all three obstacles
and hence is known as one who has gained unimpeded liberation.

The forty exclusive dharmas
have measureless meritorious qualities
of which no one could present an expansive explanation.
I have hereby now concluded this general explanation.

Even if, for an entire kalpa, the Bhagavat
spoke in praise of these dharmas of the Buddhas,
he would still be unable to completely describe them.
How much the less might I do so in the absence of such wisdom.

2. Verses Praising the Four Bases of Meritorious Qualities

The shade of the Bhagavat's great kindness
has been thoroughly gathered together through countless deeds.
It is because of the four bases of meritorious qualities
that he has gained the Buddha's measureless Dharma.

As for these four supreme bases of meritorious qualities
of which the Bhagavat has spoken with praise—
I shall now return to these
in setting forth praises of the Tathāgata.

He is completely endowed with the thirty-two marks,
each mark of which requires a hundredfold generation of merit.
As for the eighty marvelous secondary characteristics,
who residing in the three realms could possibly possess them?

Were one to multiply by a hundred all the karmic rewards
produced by the merit created by all the beings
residing within a great trichiliocosm,
each of the marks has just such a quantity of merit [as its cause].

It would require just such a quantity of merit
as well as its associated karmic rewards,
multiplied yet another hundred times
to produce a buddha's mid-brow white hair mark.

It would require for each and every one of thirty marks
all of their corresponding merit and karmic rewards,
multiplied yet again a thousand more times,
to produce the fleshy *uṣṇīṣa* sign atop a buddha's crown.

The meritorious qualities of the Bhagavat
are such that they could never be measured.
Any attempt to do so would be like someone using a ruler
to measure the endless expanse of empty space.

正體字	084c12 ‖	從初發大心	為度眾生故
	084c13 ‖	堅心無量劫	是故成佛道
	084c14 ‖	精勤欲成滿	如此之大願
	084c15 ‖	無量劫數中	行諸難苦行
	084c16 ‖	如諸往古佛	說四功德處
	084c17 ‖	無量劫乃成	今得安住中
	084c18 ‖	本為護實諦	捨身及親愛
	084c19 ‖	財寶諸富樂	是故得具足
	084c20 ‖	無量劫數中	見聞覺知法
	084c21 ‖	每先善思惟	而後為人說
	084c22 ‖	若於不見等	及於中有疑
	084c23 ‖	而能如實說	所益無有量
	084c24 ‖	不說他匿事	[7]嫌譏而拒逆
	084c25 ‖	念常在安慧	順化令安隱
	084c26 ‖	第一真妙諦	涅槃實為最
	084c27 ‖	餘者皆虛妄	世尊[8]德具足
	084c28 ‖	飲食臥具等	堂閣妙樓觀
	084c29 ‖	名好象馬車	端嚴諸婇女
	085a01 ‖	金銀珍寶等	聚落諸城邑
简体字		从初发大心	为度众生故
		坚心无量劫	是故成佛道
		精勤欲成满	如此之大愿
		无量劫数中	行诸难苦行
		如诸往古佛	说四功德处
		无量劫乃成	今得安住中
		本为护实谛	舍身及亲爱
		财宝诸富乐	是故得具足
		无量劫数中	见闻觉知法
		每先善思惟	而后为人说
		若于不见等	及于中有疑
		而能如实说	所益无有量
		不说他匿事	嫌讥而拒逆
		念常在安慧	顺化令安隐
		第一真妙谛	涅槃实为最
		余者皆虚妄	世尊德具足
		饮食卧具等	堂阁妙楼观
		名好象马车	端严诸婇女
		金银珍宝等	聚落诸城邑

Chapter 24 — *Verses Offered in Praise*

From the moment he brought forth the great resolve
for the sake of bringing about the liberation of all beings,
he persevered for countless kalpas with solid resolve.
It was because of this that he then achieved buddhahood.

Intensely diligent in his zeal to achieve the fulfillment
of such a magnanimous vow,
throughout an immeasurably great number of kalpas,
he has cultivated all the difficult ascetic practices.

Just as with all buddhas of the ancient past
who taught these four bases of meritorious qualities,
only after countless kalpas were they then perfected
so that now he has succeeded in securely abiding within them.

a. Verses Praising the Truth Basis of Meritorious Qualities

Their foundation lies in preservation of the actual truth,
for which he relinquished even his own body and loved ones,
his riches, treasures, and the happiness associated with wealth.
It is through this that he achieved its complete fulfillment.

Throughout measurelessly many kalpas,
in every instance, he has first thoroughly contemplated
the dharmas that are seen, heard, sensed, and known,[72]
and then, afterward, has explained them for the sake of others.

Where others had not observed (some aspect of Dharma) and such,
as well as in situations where they were beset by doubts,
he was then able to explain these matters in accordance with reality.
Those whom he benefited in this way were measurelessly many.

He would not discuss the confidential matters of others.
Even if resented or ridiculed for this, he still refused to betray them.
His thoughts always dwelt in a state of stable wisdom
as he adapted his teachings to lead others to peace and security.

As for the foremost and most genuinely sublime truth,
nirvāṇa is truly supreme,
for all else, in every case, is false.
The Bhagavat has achieved[73] its complete fulfillment.

b. Verses Praising the Relinquishment Basis of Meritorious Qualities

[He made gifts of] beverages, food, bedding, and such,
halls, buildings, marvelous residences, viewing terraces,
highly prized elephants, horses, and vehicles, and also
relinquished female companions of especially fine appearance.

[He gave away] gold, silver, pearls, jewels, and such,
villages, cities, and towns,

正體字	085a02 ‖ 國土及榮位	并以四天下
	085a03 ‖ 愛子[1]所親婦	支節及頭目
	085a04 ‖ 割肉出[2]骨髓	及以舉身施
	085a05 ‖ 憐愍諸眾生	悉施無所惜
	085a06 ‖ 為求出生死	不以求自樂
	085a07 ‖ 虛空諸星宿	地上所有沙
	085a08 ‖ 世尊菩薩時	布施數過是
	085a09 ‖ 終不以非法	求財而布施
	085a10 ‖ 無有不知施	無侵惱人施
	085a11 ‖ 不貪惜好物	而以惡者施
	085a12 ‖ 無諂曲心施	無惜而強施
	085a13 ‖ 無恚無疑心	無邪無輕笑
	085a14 ‖ 無厭無不信	[卑*頁]面等布施
	085a15 ‖ 無有分別心	此應彼不應
	085a16 ‖ 但以悲心故	平等而行施
	085a17 ‖ 不輕於眾生	以為非福田
	085a18 ‖ 見聖心恭敬	破戒者憐愍
	085a19 ‖ 不自高其身	卑下於他人
	085a20 ‖ 亦不為稱讚	不求報等施
	085a21 ‖ 無悔無憂愁	無惡賤心施
简体字	国土及荣位	并以四天下
	爱子所亲妇	支节及头目
	割肉出骨髓	及以举身施
	怜愍诸众生	悉施无所惜
	为求出生死	不以求自乐
	虚空诸星宿	地上所有沙
	世尊菩萨时	布施数过是
	终不以非法	求财而布施
	无有不知施	无侵恼人施
	不贪惜好物	而以恶者施
	无谄曲心施	无惜而强施
	无恚无疑心	无邪无轻笑
	无厌无不信	[卑*頁]面等布施
	无有分别心	此应彼不应
	但以悲心故	平等而行施
	不轻于众生	以为非福田
	见圣心恭敬	破戒者怜愍
	不自高其身	卑下于他人
	亦不为称赞	不求报等施
	无悔无忧愁	无恶贱心施

Chapter 24 — *Verses Offered in Praise*

entire states, and exalted official positions,
and gave away [his dominion over] the four continents as well.

[He relinquished] cherished sons, beloved wives,
his limbs, his head, and his eyes,
and made gifts by slicing off his flesh, removing bones and marrow,
or even giving away his entire body.

Doing so out of pity for beings,
he gave them all, having none that he continued to cherish.
He did so aspiring to go beyond *saṃsāra*
and not out of some quest to secure his own bliss.

All of the stars and constellations throughout empty space,
and all the grains of sand in this entire earth—
when the Tathāgata was still a bodhisattva,
the number of times he gave in such ways exceeded even these.

He never resorted to actions contrary to Dharma
as he sought out wealth to be used in giving.
He never engaged in giving unaccompanied by knowledge and
never engaged in giving that was invasive or distressing to others.

He never gave bad things as gifts
because he coveted some other fine thing [in return].
He never gave with an ingratiating deviousness
and never engaged in forceful giving because of coveting something.

He never gave with a hate-filled or doubting mind,
never did so with perverse intent or with derisive laughter,
never did so out of disgust or disbelief,
and never gave with the face turned away, or in other such ways.

He had no discriminating mind [by which he judged],
"This one is worthy and that one is unworthy."
Because he only relied on the mind of compassion,
it was with equal regard for everyone that he practiced giving.

He did not slight other beings,
considering them to not qualify as fields of merit.
On seeing *āryas*, his mind was reverential.
On seeing those who have broken the precepts, he felt pity for them.

He did not elevate himself above others,
treat others as mere inferiors,
engage in giving for the sake of praise,
give in expectation of rewards, or give in other such ways.

He never gave with regrets or with worry-filled misgivings
and never gave with thoughts of disdain or disrespect.

正體字	085a22 ‖	無待急恨心	無法應當施
	085a23 ‖	無不敬心施	無棄著地施
	085a24 ‖	[3]無[4]求惱者施	無[5]垢競勝施
	085a25 ‖	無戲弄求者	無不自手施
	085a26 ‖	不輕於少物	以多自高施
	085a27 ‖	不以聲聞乘	辟支佛乘施
	085a28 ‖	不限一世施	無有非時施
	085a29 ‖	世尊無數劫	行諸希有施
	085b01 ‖	皆為無上道	不為求自樂
	085b02 ‖	於諸佛法中	出家行遠離
	085b03 ‖	修習諸佛法	為諸人天說
	085b04 ‖	說如是施法	於諸施中上
	085b05 ‖	猶如日光明	星月中殊勝
	085b06 ‖	如是勝捨處	超越諸天人
	085b07 ‖	猶亦如世尊	一切世間上
	085b08 ‖	是故能具足	如是勝捨處
	085b09 ‖	名聞無量劫	流布無窮已
	085b10 ‖	世尊無量劫	護持清淨戒
	085b11 ‖	開諸禪定門	為得深寂處
简体字		无待急恨心	无法应当施
		无不敬心施	无弃着地施
		无求恼者施	无垢竞胜施
		无戏弄求者	无不自手施
		不轻于少物	以多自高施
		不以声闻乘	辟支佛乘施
		不限一世施	无有非时施
		世尊无数劫	行诸希有施
		皆为无上道	不为求自乐
		于诸佛法中	出家行远离
		修习诸佛法	为诸人天说
		说如是施法	于诸施中上
		犹如日光明	星月中殊胜
		如是胜舍处	超越诸天人
		犹亦如世尊	一切世间上
		是故能具足	如是胜舍处
		名闻无量劫	流布无穷已
		世尊无量劫	护持清净戒
		开诸禅定门	为得深寂处

He never gave with a mind affected by irritability or hostility
and never gave simply as a protocol-dictated formality.

He never gave with a disrespectful mind,
never gave by simply tossing the gift on the ground,
never gave deliberately seeking to cause distress,
and never gave out of a jealousy-driven struggle for supremacy.

He would never tease a supplicant,
never failed to present a gift with his own hands,
did not slight the recipient with a merely paltry gift,
and did not give excessively in order to enhance his own esteem.

His giving was never motivated by intentions associated with
either the Śrāvaka Disciple Vehicle or the Pratyekabuddha Vehicle.
His giving was never limited to concern for only a single lifetime
and he never engaged in giving done at the wrong time.

For countless kalpas, the Bhagavat
practiced every form of rare giving,
always doing so for the sake of the unsurpassable path
and not merely in order to seek his own happiness.

Throughout the duration of all buddhas' Dharma,
he became a monastic, practiced renunciation,
cultivated the Dharma of all buddhas,
and proclaimed the Dharma for the sake of all humans and devas.

He taught just such a dharma of giving as this
that is supreme among all types of giving,
just as, among all the stars and the moon,
it is the light of the sun that is supreme.

Such supremacy in the relinquishment basis [of meritorious qualities]
surpasses that of any deva or human,
just as it is the Bhagavat
who is superior to everyone in the world.

He was therefore able to perfect
such supreme practice of the relinquishment basis.
His fame shall endure for countless kalpas,
flowing on and spreading ceaselessly.

c. Verses Praising the Quiescence Basis of Meritorious Qualities

For countless kalpas, the Bhagavat
preserved and upheld the precepts of moral purity
and opened the gates of the *dhyāna* absorptions
for the sake of acquiring the deep quiescence basis.

正體字	085b12 ‖	先離於五相	後行八解脫
	085b13 ‖	入淨三三昧	亦[6]住三解脫
	085b14 ‖	世尊善分別	六十五種禪
	085b15 ‖	無有一禪定	先來不生者
	085b16 ‖	於此諸定中	亦不受其味
	085b17 ‖	世尊因諸[7]定	得三種神通
	085b18 ‖	以此度眾生	是故一切勝
	085b19 ‖	世尊無量劫	等心弘慈化
	085b20 ‖	阿僧祇眾生	令住於梵世
	085b21 ‖	能以巧方便	善說禪定故
	085b22 ‖	世尊菩薩時	常於無量世
	085b23 ‖	無貪煩惱纏	而往來世間
	085b24 ‖	過去得值者	無量生天上
	085b25 ‖	過去諸菩薩	所可行寂滅
	085b26 ‖	世尊菩薩時	亦等無有異
	085b27 ‖	是故於寂滅	勝處悉充滿
	085b28 ‖	世尊菩薩時	所有諸智慧
	085b29 ‖	以慧求菩提	今成是慧報
	085c01 ‖	一切所資食	如人依地生
	085c02 ‖	世尊於世世	捨十闇惡道

简体字	先离于五相	后行八解脱
	入净三三昧	亦住三解脱
	世尊善分别	六十五种禅
	无有一禅定	先来不生者
	于此诸定中	亦不受其味
	世尊因诸定	得三种神通
	以此度众生	是故一切胜
	世尊无量劫	等心弘慈化
	阿僧祇众生	令住于梵世
	能以巧方便	善说禅定故
	世尊菩萨时	常于无量世
	无贪烦恼缠	而往来世间
	过去得值者	无量生天上
	过去诸菩萨	所可行寂灭
	世尊菩萨时	亦等无有异
	是故于寂灭	胜处悉充满
	世尊菩萨时	所有诸智慧
	以慧求菩提	今成是慧报
	一切所资食	如人依地生
	世尊于世世	舍十闇恶道

He began by abandoning five characteristics[74]
and later practiced the eight liberations.
He entered and purified the three samādhis,
and also dwelt in the three liberations.

The Bhagavat well distinguishes
the sixty-five kinds of *dhyānas*.
There is no *dhyāna* whatsoever
that he has not formerly produced.

Even when abiding in these meditative absorptions,
he did not indulge in their delectably pleasurable states.
Due to the various meditative absorptions,
the Bhagavat gained three types of spiritual superknowledges.

He used these in the liberation of beings
and so became supreme in all things.
For countless kalpas, with a mind of equal regard,
the Bhagavat widely spread his kindly transformative teaching.

An *asaṃkhyeya* of beings
was thereby caused to abide in the Brahma World Heavens
because he was able to use skillful means
in thoroughly teaching the *dhyāna* absorptions.

While still a bodhisattva, the Bhagavat
for incalculably many lifetimes, always
remained free of any entanglement in the affliction of covetousness.
Thus he was able to come and go in the world.

Of those who succeeded in encountering him in the past,
countless such beings thereby achieved rebirth in the heavens.
As for that quiescence that
all bodhisattvas of the past were able to practice,

when still a bodhisattva, the Bhagavat
also practiced, doing so in a manner no different from theirs.
Thus, as regards the realization of quiescence,
that supreme basis [of meritorious qualities], it was entirely fulfilled.

d. Verses Praising the Wisdom Basis of Meritorious Qualities

All those forms of wisdom
possessed by the Bhagavat while he was still a bodhisattva—
He relied on such wisdom in his quest for bodhi
so that, as a karmic result, he has now developed this wisdom.

Just as people rely on the earth for the production
of all the food that it supplies,
[so, too], as in life after life, the Bhagavat
relinquished the ten courses of dark and bad actions

正體字	085c03 ‖	常行十善道	斯由慧氣[8]分
	085c04 ‖	捨五欲五蓋	得種種禪定
	085c05 ‖	無量劫數世	不從他人受
	085c06 ‖	善哉大聖尊	悉是慧[9]勢力
	085c07 ‖	眾生因世尊	無量生六天
	085c08 ‖	亦令至梵世	斯皆由慧力
	085c09 ‖	世尊於生死	苦樂所迷悶
	085c10 ‖	不失菩提心	斯皆是慧力
	085c11 ‖	世尊於生死	不樂而常在
	085c12 ‖	樂涅槃不取	斯皆是慧力
	085c13 ‖	安坐道場時	降魔及軍眾
	085c14 ‖	度脫諸群生	斯皆是慧力
	085c15 ‖	本求菩提時	集無量助法
	085c16 ‖	聞者常迷悶	何況能受行
	085c17 ‖	世尊能堪忍	斯皆是慧力
	085c18 ‖	經書諸技術	世世生自知
	085c19 ‖	亦能兼教人	斯皆是慧力
	085c20 ‖	親近無量佛	悉飲甘露教
	085c21 ‖	種種諮請問	亦隨而分別
	085c22 ‖	經法智慧中	未曾有悋惜

简体字	常行十善道	斯由慧气分
	舍五欲五盖	得种种禅定
	无量劫数世	不从他人受
	善哉大圣尊	悉是慧势力
	众生因世尊	无量生六天
	亦令至梵世	斯皆由慧力
	世尊于生死	苦乐所迷闷
	不失菩提心	斯皆是慧力
	世尊于生死	不乐而常在
	乐涅槃不取	斯皆是慧力
	安坐道场时	降魔及军众
	度脱诸群生	斯皆是慧力
	本求菩提时	集无量助法
	闻者常迷闷	何况能受行
	世尊能堪忍	斯皆是慧力
	经书诸技术	世世生自知
	亦能兼教人	斯皆是慧力
	亲近无量佛	悉饮甘露教
	种种咨请问	亦随而分别
	经法智慧中	未曾有吝惜

and always practiced the path of the ten good actions,
these [deeds] were all due to the power of wisdom.[75]

He renounced the five desires and the five hindrances
and thus acquired all the various *dhyāna* absorptions.
He accomplished this for the number of lifetimes in countless kalpas
and did not acquire this from others.
This is excellent indeed, O Great Honored One of the Āryas.
All of this was due to the power of wisdom.

It is because of the Bhagavat that beings,
countless in number, have taken rebirth in the six heavens.
So too has he enabled them to reach the Brahma World.
All of this was due to the power of wisdom.

Throughout the course of his births and deaths, the Bhagavat,
even when confused and perturbed by sufferings and pleasures,
never lost the resolve to attain bodhi.
All of this was due to the power of wisdom.

Throughout the course of *saṃsāra*, the Bhagavat
did not delight [in worldly existence] and yet still always remained.
He delighted in nirvāṇa, yet did not seize on its [final] realization.
All of this was due to the power of wisdom.

When sitting peacefully there in the *bodhimaṇḍa*,
he overcame Māra and his armies
and proceeded to liberate all the classes of beings.
All of this was due to the power of wisdom.

When he originally strove in quest of bodhi,
he accumulated countless provisions for the path.
If merely hearing of them causes one to be confused and perturbed,
how much the less might one be able to take on their practice.
That the Bhagavat was able to patiently endure such things
was in every case due to the power of wisdom.

That, in lifetime after lifetime, he was able to naturally know
the classic texts as well as all the arts and skills
while also being able to teach them to others
was in every case due to the power of wisdom.

He drew close to countless buddhas
and from them all drank the sweet-dew nectar of their teachings,
He consulted them and inquired about the many different topics
and then also pursued additional distinguishing [clarifications].

He was never the least bit miserly
with the wisdom of the sutras' Dharma,

正體字	085c23 ‖ 乃至僕僮奴　　亦諮受善語	
	085c24 ‖ 世尊以是故　　慧勝處流布	
	085c25 ‖ 世尊於前世　　求是菩提時	
	085c26 ‖ 於[10]一切眾生　　行大慈悲心	
	085c27 ‖ 以第一智慧　　常出大勢力	
	085c28 ‖ 悉作無量種　　希有諸難事	
	085c29 ‖ 一切諸世間　　盡共無量劫	
	086a01 ‖ 說之不可盡　　亦非算數及	
	086a02 ‖ 如是等諸事　　超越於人天	
	086a03 ‖ 一切世間中　　奇特無有比	
	086a04 ‖ 大業所獲果　　具足一切智	
	086a05 ‖ 能破生死王　　安住法王處[1]	

简体字

乃至仆僮奴　　亦咨受善语
世尊以是故　　慧胜处流布
世尊于前世　　求是菩提时
于一切众生　　行大慈悲心
以第一智慧　　常出大势力
悉作无量种　　希有诸难事
一切诸世间　　尽共无量劫
说之不可尽　　亦非算数及
如是等诸事　　超越于人天
一切世间中　　奇特无有比
大业所获果　　具足一切智
能破生死王　　安住法王处

but rather offered it even to servants, youths, and menials,
allowing them to freely receive his fine explanations.
Because of this, [the fame of] the Bhagavat's
supreme wisdom basis [of meritorious qualities] spreads on afar.

Throughout his former lifetimes, as the Bhagavat
pursued his quest for the realization of bodhi,
he practiced the great kindness and compassion
toward all beings.

Relying on the foremost wisdom,
he always marshaled his great strength
to take up and do all the countless kinds
of rare and difficult endeavors.

3. Concluding Praise Verses

In all of the many worlds,
he exhaustively contributed all his efforts for countless kalpas.
One could never come to the end of them through verbal description,
nor could one even reach it through mathematical calculation.

All of his endeavors of such sorts
surpass those done by any human or deva.
Even in all the many worlds,
there is nothing comparable to his extraordinary marvels.

The fruits reaped through such great deeds
reach complete fulfillment in the realization of all-knowledge.
He is the king of those able to destroy *saṃsāra*
and dwells securely in the place of the Dharma king.

The End of Chapter Twenty-Four

正體字

086a06 ||　　　[2]助念佛三昧品第二十五
086a07 ||　　菩薩應以此　　四十不共法
086a08 ||　　念諸佛法身　　佛非色身故
086a09 || 是偈次第略解四十不共法六品中義。是故
086a10 || 行者先念色身佛。次念法身佛。何以故。新
086a11 || 發意菩薩。應以三十二相八十種好念佛。
086a12 || 如先說。轉深入得中勢力。應以法身念佛
086a13 || 心轉深入得上勢力。應以實相念佛而不
086a14 || 貪著。
086a15 ||　　不[3]染著色身　　法身亦不著
086a16 ||　　善知一切法　　永寂如虛空
086a17 || 是菩薩得上勢力。不以色身法身深貪著
086a18 || 佛。何以故。信樂空法故。知諸法如虛空。虛
086a19 || 空者無障礙故。障礙因緣者。

简体字

十住毗婆沙论卷第十一
助念佛三昧品第二十五
　　菩萨应以此　　四十不共法
　　念诸佛法身　　佛非色身故
　是偈次第略解四十不共法六品中义。是故行者先念色身佛。次念法身佛。何以故。新发意菩萨。应以三十二相八十种好念佛。如先说。转深入得中势力。应以法身念佛心转深入得上势力。应以实相念佛而不贪着。
　　不染着色身　　法身亦不着
　　善知一切法　　永寂如虚空
　是菩萨得上势力。不以色身法身深贪着佛。何以故。信乐空法故。知诸法如虚空。虚空者无障碍故。障碍因缘者。

Chapter 25
Teachings to Aid the Mindfulness-of-the-Buddha Samādhi

V. Chapter 25: Teachings Aiding Mindfulness-of-the Buddha Samādhi
  A. Initial Instructions on the Mindfulness-of-the Buddha Samādhi

The bodhisattva should rely on these
forty exclusive dharmas
in his mindfulness of the Buddhas' Dharma body,
for the Buddhas are not their form bodies.

These [preceding] verses have sequentially and summarily explained six categories of meanings associated with the forty exclusive dharmas.[76] In doing so, the practitioner therefore first takes up the mindfulness of the Buddha's form body and then takes up the mindfulness of the Buddha's Dharma body.

Why is this the case? The bodhisattva who has only recently brought forth the resolve [to attain buddhahood] should first take up the practice of mindfulness of the Buddha in reliance on the thirty-two marks and eighty secondary characteristics [of the Buddha's form body], doing so in the manner described earlier.

Then, as one's practice progressively penetrates more deeply, one will develop a middling degree of strength in that practice. One should then rely on the Dharma body in his mindfulness of the Buddha.

Then, as one's mind progressively penetrates yet more deeply, one will then achieve a supreme degree of power in the development of this practice. At that point, one should then take up mindfulness of the Buddha in accordance with the true character of [all dharmas][77] and remain free of any sort of attachment in doing so.

One must not become deeply attached to the form body.[78]
One also refrains from becoming attached to the Dharma body.
One should thoroughly realize that all dharmas
are as eternally quiescent as empty space.

As this bodhisattva develops a superior degree of power [in this practice], he refrains from developing a deep attachment to the Buddha on the basis of either the form body or the Dharma body. Why not? Through one's resolute belief in the dharma of emptiness, one understands that all dharmas are like empty space.

Empty space is defined by the absence of obstruction. The causal circumstances associated with obstruction include phenomena like

|正體字|

諸須彌山由乾
086a20 ‖ 陀等十寶山。鐵圍山黑山石山等。如是無量
086a21 ‖ 障礙因緣。何以故。是人未得天眼故。念他
086a22 ‖ 方世界佛。則有諸山障礙。是故新發意菩薩。
086a23 ‖ 應以十號妙相念佛。如說。
086a24 ‖ 　　新發意菩薩　　以十號妙相
086a25 ‖ 　　念佛無毀失　　猶如鏡中像
086a26 ‖ 十號妙相者。所謂如來應[4]供正遍知明行足
086a27 ‖ 善逝世間解無上士調御丈夫天人師佛世
086a28 ‖ 尊。無毀失者。所觀事空如虛空。於法無
086a29 ‖ 所失。何以故。諸法本來無生寂滅故。如是一
086b01 ‖ 切諸法皆亦如是。是人以緣名號增長禪
086b02 ‖ 法則能緣相。是人爾時[5]即於禪法得相。所
086b03 ‖ 謂身得殊異

|简体字|

诸须弥山由乾陀等十宝山。铁围山黑山石山等。如是无量障碍因缘。何以故。是人未得天眼故。念他方世界佛。则有诸山障碍。是故新发意菩萨。应以十号妙相念佛。如说。

　　新发意菩萨　　以十号妙相
　　念佛无毁失　　犹如镜中像

　　十号妙相者。所谓如来应供正遍知明行足善逝世间解无上士调御丈夫天人师佛世尊。无毁失者。所观事空如虚空。于法无所失。何以故。诸法本来无生寂灭故。如是一切诸法皆亦如是。是人以缘名号增长禅法则能缘相。是人尔时即于禅法得相。所谓身得殊异

Chapter 25 — *Teachings to Aid the Mindfulness-of-the-Buddha Samādhi*

Mount Sumeru, Yugaṃdhara Mountain, the rest of the ten jeweled mountains, the Iron Ring Mountains, Black Mountain, Stone Mountain, and the others. There are all sorts of other such causal bases for the existence of obstructions.

Why is this [a point at issue]? Because this person has still not yet gained the heavenly eye, if he brings to mind buddhas abiding in the worlds off in the other directions, the various mountains will block them from his view. Consequently, The bodhisattva who has only recently brought forth the resolve [to attain buddhahood] should use the sublime characteristics described by the ten names as bases for his mindfulness of the Buddha. This is as described in these lines:

> The bodhisattva who has only recently brought forth the resolve
> uses the sublime features described by the ten names
> in practicing mindfulness of the Buddhas that is free of fault,
> seeing them just as if they were images in a mirror.

As for "the sublime features described in the ten names," those ten names are:

Tathāgata;[79]
Worthy of Offerings;
The Right and Universally Enlightened One;
Perfect in the Clear Knowledges and Conduct;
Well Gone One;
Knower of the Worlds;
Unsurpassable Trainer of Those to Be Tamed;
Teacher of Devas and Humans;
Buddha;
Bhagavat.

As for "free of fault," the phenomena that one contemplates are beheld as empty and like space itself. Thus [one's contemplation] is free of any fault with regard to the Dharma. And how is this so? It is because all dharmas, from their very origin on forward to the present, have been unproduced and quiescent. Just as this is true [with respect to these dharmas], so too is this also true of all other dharmas.

By taking these names as the object [of his contemplation], this person develops his practice of the dharma of *dhyāna* meditation. Having done so, he is then able to take these characteristic signs themselves as the object of his contemplation.

At this time, this person then immediately acquires these signs in his practice of the dharma of *dhyāna* meditation and experiences what is referred to as the direct personal experience of an especially

正體字

086b04 ‖ 快樂。當知得成般舟三昧。三
086b04 ‖ 昧成故得見諸佛。如鏡中像者。若菩薩成
086b05 ‖ 此三昧已。如淨明鏡自見面像。如清澄水
086b06 ‖ 中見其身相。初時隨先所念佛見其色像。
086b07 ‖ 見是像已後。若欲見他方諸佛隨所念方
086b08 ‖ 得見諸佛無所障礙。是故此人。
086b09 ‖ 　雖未有神通　　飛行到[6]于彼
086b10 ‖ 　而能見諸佛　　聞法無障礙
086b11 ‖ 是新發意菩薩於諸須彌山等諸山無能為
086b12 ‖ 作障礙。亦未得神通天眼天耳。未能飛行
086b13 ‖ 從此國至彼國。以是三昧力故。住此國
086b14 ‖ 土得見他方諸佛世尊。聞所說法常修習
086b15 ‖ 是三昧故。得見十方真實諸佛。問曰。如是
086b16 ‖ [7]定以何法能生。云何可得。答曰。
086b17 ‖ 　親近善知識　　精進無懈退
086b18 ‖ 　智慧甚堅牢　　信力不妄動
086b19 ‖ 以是四法能生三昧。親近善知識者。能
086b20 ‖ 以是三昧教誨人者名為善知識。應加
086b21 ‖ 恭敬

简体字

快乐。当知得成般舟三昧。三昧成故得见诸佛。如镜中像者。若菩萨成此三昧已。如净明镜自见面像。如清澄水中见其身相。初时随先所念佛见其色像。见是像已后。若欲见他方诸佛随所念方得见诸佛无所障碍。是故此人。

　虽未有神通　　飞行到于彼
　而能见诸佛　　闻法无障碍

是新发意菩萨于诸须弥山等诸山无能为作障碍。亦未得神通天眼天耳。未能飞行从此国至彼国。以是三昧力故。住此国土得见他方诸佛世尊。闻所说法常修习是三昧故。得见十方真实诸佛。问曰。如是定以何法能生。云何可得。答曰。

　亲近善知识　　精进无懈退
　智慧甚坚牢　　信力不妄动

以是四法能生是三昧。亲近善知识者。能以是三昧教诲人者名为善知识。应加恭敬

Chapter 25 – *Teachings to Aid the Mindfulness-of-the-Buddha Samādhi*

extraordinary bliss. One should realize that when this occurs, one has acquired the *pratyutpanna* samādhi. Because of developing this samādhi, one is then able to see the Buddhas.

As for "as if they were images in a mirror," once the bodhisattva has developed this samādhi, it is as if one is seeing one's own face in a clean, brightly-lit mirror or like seeing the image of one's own body in a clear, still pool of water.

Initially, whichever buddha one first brings to mind, it is that very image that one sees. After one has seen this image, if one wishes to see buddhas in other regions, then, in accordance with whichever region one brings to mind, one obtains an unimpeded vision of those very buddhas. Hence, regarding this person:

> Although he does not yet possess the spiritual superknowledges
> by which he could fly to visit them,
> he is nonetheless able to see those buddhas
> and has an unimpeded ability to listen to their Dharma.

For this bodhisattva who has only recently brought forth the resolve [to attain buddhahood], neither Mount Sumeru nor any other mountain can present an obstacle and, even though he has not yet acquired any of the spiritual superknowledges, the heavenly eye, or the heavenly ear, and even though he has not yet developed the ability to fly from this country to that country, through the power of this samādhi, even while still abiding in this country, he is able to see the Buddhas, the Bhagavats, abiding in the other regions and is able to hear the Dharma as they are speaking it. Through always cultivating this samādhi, he becomes able to see all of the buddhas throughout the ten directions just as they really are.

B. Four Dharmas Capable of Bringing Forth This Samādhi

Question: Through which dharmas is one able to bring forth this meditative absorption and how can one acquire it?

Response:

> One draws close to the good spiritual guide,
> brings forth nonretreating vigor,
> develops extremely solid and durable wisdom,
> and develops the power of unshakable faith.

It is through utilizing these four dharmas that one is able to bring forth this samādhi.

As for "drawing close to the good spiritual guide," someone able to instruct a person in the acquisition of this samādhi qualifies here as "the good spiritual guide." One should bring forth reverential respect

|正體字|

勤心親近莫有懈怠廢退捨離則得
聞是深三昧義利智通達智不失智。名為堅
牢信根深固。若沙門婆羅門若天魔梵及餘
世人無能傾動。名為信力不可動。如是四
法。能生三昧。復次。
　　慚愧愛恭敬　　供養說法者
　　猶如諸世尊　　能生是三昧
慚愧愛恭敬者。於說法者深生慚愧。恭[8]恪
愛樂供養如佛。如是四法能生是三昧。復
次初四法者。一於三月未[9]嘗睡眠。唯除便
利飲食坐起。二於三月乃至彈指不生我
心。三於三月經行不息。四於三月兼以法
施不求利養。是為四。復有四法。一能見
佛。

|简体字|

勤心亲近莫有懈怠废退舍离则得闻是深三昧义利智通达智不失
智。名为坚牢信根深固。若沙门婆罗门若天魔梵及余世人无能倾
动。名为信力不可动。如是四法。能生三昧。复次。
　　惭愧爱恭敬　　供养说法者
　　犹如诸世尊　　能生是三昧
　　惭愧爱恭敬者。于说法者深生惭愧。恭恪爱乐供养如佛。如
是四法能生是三昧。复次初四法者。一于三月未尝睡眠。唯除便
利饮食坐起。二于三月乃至弹指不生我心。三于三月经行不息。
四于三月兼以法施不求利养。是为四。复有四法。一能见佛。

Chapter 25 — Teachings to Aid the Mindfulness-of-the-Buddha Samādhi

and assiduous diligence and, in drawing close [to the good spiritual guide], one must not allow any indolence, diminishment in motivation, or relinquishing of effort to take place. If one acts accordingly, one will then be able to hear the teaching of the deep meaning of this samādhi.

Sharp wisdom, wisdom characterized by penetrating comprehension, and undiminishing wisdom are what qualify as "solid and durable" [wisdom]. One's faculty of faith is deeply and firmly established, so much so that, no matter whether it be a śramaṇa or a brahman or a celestial māra or Brahmā or anyone else in the world—none of them could cause it to quaver even slightly. This is what is meant by an unshakable power of faith. It is these very four dharmas described here that are able to bring forth this samādhi.

C. FOUR MORE DHARMAS CAPABLE OF BRINGING FORTH THIS SAMĀDHI

Furthermore:

> With a sense of shame, dread of blame, cherishing reverence,
> and offerings to those who proclaim the Dharma
> presented as if they were given to the Bhagavats themselves,
> one thereby becomes able to bring forth this samādhi.

As for "with a sense of shame, dread of blame, and cherishing reverence," one brings forth a profound sense of shame and dread of blame in relation to those who teach the Dharma. With sincere reverence and affectionate delight, one makes offerings to them as if they were the Buddhas themselves. In this way, these four dharmas are able to produce this samādhi.

D. FOUR MORE DHARMAS CAPABLE OF BRINGING FORTH THIS SAMĀDHI

Another preliminary set of fourfold dharmas is as follows:

> First, for a period of three months, one strives to refrain from sleeping and, with the exception of using the toilet and eating and drinking, one refrains from sitting down;
> Second, for that period of three months, one avoids, even for the duration of a finger snap, indulgence in any thought seizing on the existence of a self;
> Third, for that entire three months, one strives to always walk and never rest;
> Fourth, for that entire three months, when also engaged in the giving of Dharma, one refrains from seeking offerings from others.

These are the four. There are four more such dharmas, as follows:

E. FOUR MORE DHARMAS CAPABLE OF BRINGING FORTH THIS SAMĀDHI

> First, one becomes able to see the Buddhas;

正體字

```
              二安慰勸人聽是三昧。三常不貪嫉行
086c06 ||  菩提心者。四能集菩薩所行道法。是為四。
086c07 ||  復有四法。一造作佛像乃至畫像。二當善
086c08 ||  書寫是三昧經。令信樂者得[10]已誦讀。三教
086c09 ||  增上慢人令離[11]憎上慢法。使得阿耨多羅
086c10 ||  三藐三菩提。四當護持諸佛正法。是為四。
086c11 ||  [12]復有四法。一少語言。二在家出家不與共
086c12 ||  住。三常繫心取所緣相。四樂遠離空閑靜
086c13 ||  處。是為四。初五法者。一無生[13]忍法。厭離一
086c14 ||  切諸有為法。不樂一切諸所生處。不受一
086c15 ||  切諸外道法。惡厭一切世間諸欲乃至不念
086c16 ||  何況身近。二心常修習無量諸法定在一
086c17 ||  處。
```

简体字

二安慰劝人听是三昧。三常不贪嫉行菩提心者。四能集菩萨所行道法。是为四。复有四法。一造作佛像乃至画像。二当善书写是三昧经。令信乐者得已诵读。三教增上慢人令离憎上慢法。使得阿耨多罗三藐三菩提。四当护持诸佛正法。是为四。复有四法。一少语言。二在家出家不与共住。三常系心取所缘相。四乐远离空闲静处。是为四。初五法者。一无生忍法。厌离一切诸有为法。不乐一切诸所生处。不受一切诸外道法。恶厌一切世间诸欲乃至不念何况身近。二心常修习无量诸法定在一处。

Chapter 25 – *Teachings to Aid the Mindfulness-of-the-Buddha Samādhi*

Second, one reassures and encourages others to listen to the teaching of this samādhi;

Third, one is never envious or jealous of anyone who is putting the resolve to attain bodhi into practice;

Fourth, one is able to accumulate the dharmas of the bodhisattva path.

These are the four. There are four more such dharmas, as follows:

F. FOUR MORE DHARMAS CAPABLE OF BRINGING FORTH THIS SAMĀDHI

First, one makes buddha images that may also include painted images;

Second, one should carefully write out copies of the sutra that discusses this samādhi and then encourage others who have a resolute faith in it to study and recite it aloud once they have obtained it;[80]

Third, teach those of overweening pride[81] to abandon their overweening pride[82] and then influence them to pursue the attainment of *anuttarasamyaksaṃbodhi*;

Fourth, one should devote oneself to the protection and preservation of the right Dharma of all buddhas.

These are the four. There are four more such dharmas, as follows:

G. FOUR MORE DHARMAS CAPABLE OF BRINGING FORTH THIS SAMĀDHI

First, one avoids speaking;

Second, both lay and monastic practitioners are to refrain from dwelling together with others;

Third, one always anchors one's mind on the characteristic sign that has been chosen as the object of one's mental focus;[83]

Fourth, one delights in dwelling far apart from others, in a location that is vacant, serene, and silent.

These are the four. The first of the fivefold sets of associated dharmas is as follows:

H. FIVE MORE DHARMAS CAPABLE OF BRINGING FORTH THIS SAMĀDHI

First, abiding in the unproduced-dharmas patience (*anutpattika-dharma-kṣānti*), one renounces all conditioned dharmas, does not delight in any of the destinies of rebirth, refuses to accept any of the non-Buddhist dharmas, and remains so disgusted with all worldly desires that one does not even bring them to mind, how much the less might one draw physically close to them;

Second, even as one's mind always cultivates and practices countless dharmas, it remains in a state of one-pointed concentration;

於諸眾生無有瞋礙。心常隨順行四攝
法。三能成就慈悲喜捨不[14]出他過。四能多
集佛所說法如所說行。五清淨身口意業
及見。是為五。復有五法。一樂如經所讚布
施無有慳心。樂說深法無所悋惜亦能
自住。二忍辱柔和同住歡喜。惡口罵詈鞭捶
縛等。但推業緣不恚他人。三常樂聽是三
昧讀誦通利為人解說令流布增廣勤行修
習。四心無妬嫉。不自高身不下他人。除
[15]眠睡蓋。五於佛法僧寶信心清淨。於上中
下坐深心供奉。他有小恩常憶不忘。常住
真實語中。是為五復次。

　　出家諸菩薩　　所學三昧法
　　在家菩薩者　　是法應當知

于诸众生无有嗔碍。心常随顺行四摄法。三能成就慈悲喜舍不出他过。四能多集佛所说法如所说行。五清净身口意业及见。是为五。复有五法。一乐如经所赞布施无有悭心。乐说深法无所吝惜亦能自住。二忍辱柔和同住欢喜。恶口骂詈鞭捶缚等。但推业缘不恚他人。三常乐听是三昧读诵通利为人解说令流布增广勤行修习。四心无妒嫉。不自高身不下他人。除眠睡盖。五于佛法僧宝信心清净。于上中下坐深心供奉。他有小恩常忆不忘。常住真实语中。是为五复次。

　　出家诸菩萨　　所学三昧法
　　在家菩萨者　　是法应当知

One remains free of the obstacle of hatred toward any being and one's mind always accords with the practice of the four means of attraction;

Third, one becomes able to perfect kindness, compassion, sympathetic joy, and equanimity while also refraining from exposing others' transgressions;

Fourth, one becomes able to accumulate a multitude of dharmas proclaimed by the Buddha while also being able to carry them out in accordance with the way they were taught;

Fifth, one purifies one's physical, verbal, and mental actions as well as one's views.

These are the five. There are five more associated dharmas, as follows:

I. FIVE MORE DHARMAS CAPABLE OF BRINGING FORTH THIS SAMĀDHI

First, one delights in according with the practice of giving as praised in the sutras, doing so without miserly thoughts. One delights in speaking on profound dharmas, withholds nothing due to stinginess, and also remains able to dwell in those very dharmas oneself;

Second, one abides in patience, mental pliancy, and delight when abiding in close proximity to others and, if subjected to harsh speech, scolding and cursing, whippings, beatings, being tied up, or other such experiences, one simply attributes it to one's own karmic conditions and does not hate others for doing this;

Third, one always delights in listening to teachings that explain this samādhi, in reading and reciting them, in thoroughly understanding them, in explaining them for others, and in causing them to circulate and spread ever more widely even as one diligently practices and cultivates [this samādhi];

Fourth, one's mind remains free of any jealous feelings toward others, one refrains from elevating oneself and looking down on others, and one strives to rid oneself of the hindrance of drowsiness;

Fifth, one maintains a mind of pure faith in the Buddha Jewel, the Dharma Jewel, and the Sangha Jewel, offers up deeply sincere service to those of senior, middling, and lower station, always remembers and never forgets even the smallest kindnesses of others, and always abides in truthful speech.

These are the five. In addition, there are the following lines:

J. THE GUIDELINES FOR LAY AND MONASTIC CULTIVATION OF THIS SAMĀDHI

As for those samādhi dharmas
in which monastic bodhisattvas train,
householder bodhisattvas
should also know these dharmas.

正體字

087a02 ‖ 若在家菩薩欲修習是三昧一當深以信
087a03 ‖ 心。二不求業果報。三當捨一切內外物。四
087a04 ‖ 歸命三寶。五淨持五戒無有毀缺。六具足
087a05 ‖ 行十善道。亦令餘人住此法中。七斷除婬
087a06 ‖ 欲。八毀[1]呰五欲。九不嫉妬。十於妻子中
087a07 ‖ 不生愛著。十一心常願出家。十二常受[2]齊
087a08 ‖ 戒。十三心樂住寺廟。十四具足慚愧。十五
087a09 ‖ 於淨戒比丘起恭敬心。十六不慳悋法。十
087a10 ‖ 七於說法者深愛敬心。十八於說法者生
087a11 ‖ 父母大師想。十九於說法者以諸樂具敬
087a12 ‖ 心供養。二十知恩報恩。如是在家菩薩。住
087a13 ‖ 如是等功德者。則能學是三昧。出家菩薩
087a14 ‖ 修習是三昧法者。所謂

简体字

若在家菩萨欲修习是三昧一当深以信心。二不求业果报。三当舍一切内外物。四归命三宝。五净持五戒无有毁缺。六具足行十善道。亦令余人住此法中。七断除淫欲。八毁呰五欲。九不嫉妒。十于妻子中不生爱着。十一心常愿出家。十二常受齐戒。十三心乐住寺庙。十四具足惭愧。十五于净戒比丘起恭敬心。十六不悭吝法。十七于说法者深爱敬心。十八于说法者生父母大师想。十九于说法者以诸乐具敬心供养。二十知恩报恩。如是在家菩萨。住如是等功德者。则能学是三昧。出家菩萨修习是三昧法者。所谓

Chapter 25 — Teachings to Aid the Mindfulness-of-the-Buddha Samādhi

1. Twenty Guidelines for Lay Cultivators of This Samādhi

If a householder bodhisattva wishes to cultivate this samādhi, [he should observe the following twenty guidelines]:

1) One should proceed with a mind of deep faith;
2) One should not seek any sort of karmic reward;
3) One should give up all personal and extra-personal things;
4) One should take refuge in the Three Jewels;
5) One should uphold the five moral precepts purely and in a manner free of any transgression or deficiency;
6) One should perfect the practice of the ten courses of good karmic action while also influencing others to abide in these dharmas;
7) One should cut off all sexual desire;
8) One should repudiate the five types of desire;
9) One should refrain from any feelings of jealousy toward others;
10) One should not nurture an affectionate attachment for either one's spouse or one's children;
11) One should always maintain an aspiration to leave the householder's life to become a monastic;
12) One should always take on and observe the layperson's precepts of abstinence;[84]
13) One's mind should delight in the opportunity to abide within the precincts of a temple;[85]
14) One should be well possessed of a sense of shame and a dread of blame;
15) One should bring forth thoughts of reverential respect toward bhikshus who are pure in upholding the moral precepts;
16) One should not act in a miserly way with the Dharma;
17) One should maintain a mind of deep affection and reverence toward those who teach the Dharma;
18) One should think of teachers of Dharma as if they were one's father, mother, or great teaching master;
19) One should respectfully present all manner of delightful gifts as offerings to the Dharma teaching masters;
20) One should feel gratitude for the kindnesses that have been bestowed upon one and one should repay those kindnesses accordingly.

If a householder bodhisattva abides in meritorious qualities such as these, he will then be able to learn this samādhi.

2. Sixty Guidelines for Monastic Cultivators of This Samādhi

As for [the guidelines appropriate to] a monastic bodhisattva's cultivation of dharmas pertaining to this samādhi, they are as follows:

正體字

| 087a15 ‖ | 一於戒無[3]毀疵。二
持戒不雜污。三持戒不濁。四清淨戒。五無
| 087a16 ‖ | 損戒。六不取戒。七不依戒。八不得戒。九
| 087a17 ‖ | 不退戒。十持聖所讚戒。十一持智所稱
| 087a18 ‖ | 戒。十二隨波羅提木叉戒。十三具足威儀行
| 087a19 ‖ | 處。十四乃至微小罪心大怖畏。十五淨身口
| 087a20 ‖ | 意業。十六淨命。十七所有戒盡受持。十八
| 087a21 ‖ | 信樂甚深法。十九於無所得法心能忍。空
| 087a22 ‖ | 無相無願法中心不驚。二十勤發精進。二十
| 087a23 ‖ | 一念常在前。二十二信心堅固。二十三具足
| 087a24 ‖ | 慚愧。二十四不貪利養。二十五無嫉妬。二
| 087a25 ‖ | 十六住頭陀功德。二十七住細行法中。二十
| 087a26 ‖ | 八不樂說世間俗語。

简体字

一于戒无毁疵。二持戒不杂污。三持戒不浊。四清净戒。五无损戒。六不取戒。七不依戒。八不得戒。九不退戒。十持圣所赞戒。十一持智所称戒。十二随波罗提木叉戒。十三具足威仪行处。十四乃至微小罪心大怖畏。十五净身口意业。十六净命。十七所有戒尽受持。十八信乐甚深法。十九于无所得法心能忍。空无相无愿法中心不惊。二十勤发精进。二十一念常在前。二十二信心坚固。二十三具足惭愧。二十四不贪利养。二十五无嫉妒。二十六住头陀功德。二十七住细行法中。二十八不乐说世间俗语。

1) One remains free of any defect as regards observance of the moral precepts;
2) One maintains uncorrupted observance of the moral precepts;
3) One maintains unsullied observance of the moral precepts;
4) One maintains pure observance of the moral precepts;
5) One maintains undiminished observance of the moral precepts;
6) One does not seize on the moral precepts themselves [as constituting the very essence of moral virtue];
7) One does not rely on the moral precepts [alone as the sole component of one's practice];
8) One realizes that the moral precepts cannot finally be apprehended at all [as inherently existent entities];
9) One never retreats from one's observance of the moral precepts;
10) One upholds the moral precepts in the manner that is praised by the Āryas;
11) One upholds the moral precepts in the manner that is extolled by the wise;
12) One accords with the *prātimokṣa* precepts;
13) One perfects the bases for the awe-inspiring deportment;
14) One remains immensely fearful of committing even the most minor transgression of the precepts;
15) One purifies the actions of body, speech, and mind;
16) One maintains purity in right livelihood;
17) One completely upholds all of the moral precepts;
18) One maintains resolute belief in the extremely profound dharmas;
19) One is able to patiently acquiesce in the dharma of the non-apprehension [of any dharma whatsoever] and is able to not be frightened even by the dharmas of emptiness, signlessness, and wishlessness;
20) One remains diligent in bringing forth vigor [in one's practice];
21) One always maintains ever-present mindfulness;
22) One maintains a mind of solid faith;
23) One is well possessed of a sense of shame and a dread of blame;
24) One does not covet offerings;
25) One remains free of jealousy toward others;
26) One abides in the meritorious qualities associated with practicing the *dhūta* austerities;
27) One abides in the subtleties of Dharma practice;
28) One takes no delight in speaking the coarse language of the world;

正體字

二十九遠離聚語。三
087a27 ‖ 十知報恩。三十一知作恩報恩[4]者。三十二
087a28 ‖ 於和[5]上阿闍梨所[6]生恭敬忌難心。三十三
087a29 ‖ 破除憍慢。三十四降伏我心。三十五善知識
087b01 ‖ 難遇故勤心供給。三十六所從聞是法處。
087b02 ‖ 若得經卷若口誦處。於此人所生父母想
087b03 ‖ 善知識想大師想大慚愧愛敬想。三十七常
087b04 ‖ 樂阿練若。三十八不樂住城邑聚落。三十
087b05 ‖ 九不貪著檀越善知識家。四十不惜身命。
087b06 ‖ 四十一心常念死。四十二不存利養。四十
087b07 ‖ 三於諸物中心不染著。四十四無所渴愛。
087b08 ‖ 四十五守護正法。四十六不著衣鉢。四十
087b09 ‖ 七不畜遺餘。四十八但欲乞食。四十九次
087b10 ‖ 第乞食。五十常知慚愧心常有悔。五十一
087b11 ‖ 不畜金銀珍寶錢財。離諸不善悔。五十二
087b12 ‖ 心無纏垢。五十三常行慈心。

简体字

二十九远离聚语。三十知报恩。三十一知作恩报恩者。三十二于和上阿闍梨所生恭敬忌难心。三十三破除憍慢。三十四降伏我心。三十五善知识难遇故勤心供给。三十六所从闻是法处。若得经卷若口诵处。于此人所生父母想善知识想大师想大惭愧爱敬想。三十七常乐阿练若。三十八不乐住城邑聚落。三十九不贪着檀越善知识家。四十不惜身命。四十一心常念死。四十二不存利养。四十三于诸物中心不染着。四十四无所渴爱。四十五守护正法。四十六不着衣钵。四十七不畜遗余。四十八但欲乞食。四十九次第乞食。五十常知惭愧心常有悔。五十一不畜金银珍宝钱财。离诸不善悔。五十二心无缠垢。五十三常行慈心。

Chapter 25 — *Teachings to Aid the Mindfulness-of-the-Buddha Samādhi*

29) One avoids gathering in groups for [idle] conversation;
30) One knows to repay kindnesses one has received;
31) One acknowledges those who bestow kindnesses and those who repay kindnesses;
32) Toward one's monastic preceptors and monastic Dharma teachers, one brings forth thoughts of sincere reverence and appreciation for the rarity of being able to encounter them;[86]
33) One does away with any arrogance one might be harboring;
34) One overcomes the self-cherishing mind;
35) Because a good spiritual guide can only rarely be encountered, one strives with diligence to look after his needs;
36) With regard to the source from which one first learned about this Dharma, whether by obtaining a sutra text from someone or by hearing someone recite it, one thinks of them with the same regard as one would maintain for one's own father or mother, one's good spiritual guide, or a great teaching master, and with regard to them, one also feels a sense of shame, dread of blame, affection, and reverence;
37) One always delights in dwelling in a forest hermitage;
38) One does not delight in dwelling in a city or village;
39) One does not covet the opportunity to frequent the homes of benefactors[87] and good spiritual friends;
40) One does not maintain a stinting covetousness for one's own physical survival;
41) One remains ever mindful of death;
42) One does not hoard offerings;
43) One does not indulge any defiling attachment for possessions;
44) One remains free of cravings;
45) One guards and preserves right Dharma;
46) One is not attached to one's robes or bowl;
47) One does not hoard leftover things;
48) One prefers to eat only food that has been obtained on the alms round;
49) On the alms round, one moves along seeking alms according to the proper sequence;[88]
50) One always maintains a sense of shame and dread of blame and always feels remorse [for one's past transgressions];
51) One refrains from hoarding gold, silver, precious jewels, or money and also avoids indulging in unwholesome remorsefulness;[89]
52) One's mind remains free of entangling defilements;
53) One always puts the mind of kindness into practice;

五十四除斷
瞋恚。五十五常行悲心。五十六除斷愛著。
五十七常求利安一切世間。五十八常憐愍
一切眾生。五十九常樂經行。六十除却睡
眠。出家菩薩住如是等法中。應修習是三
昧。復次。

　　餘修三昧法　　亦應如是學

能生是般舟三昧。餘助法亦應修習。何等
是。一緣佛恩常[7]念在前。二不令心散亂。
三繫心在前。四守護根門。五飲食知止足。
六初夜後夜常修三昧。七離諸煩惱障。八
生諸禪定。九禪中不[8]受味。十散壞色相。
十一得不淨相。十二不貪五陰。十三不著
十八界。十四不染十二入。十五不恃族姓。
十六破憍慢。十七於一切法心常空寂。

五十四除斷嗔恚。五十五常行悲心。五十六除斷爱着。五十七常求利安一切世間。五十八常怜愍一切众生。五十九常乐经行。六十除却睡眠。出家菩萨住如是等法中。应修习是三昧。复次。

　　余修三昧法　　亦应如是学

　　能生是般舟三昧。余助法亦应修习。何等是。一缘佛恩常念在前。二不令心散乱。三系心在前。四守护根门。五饮食知止足。六初夜后夜常修三昧。七离诸烦恼障。八生诸禅定。九禅中不受味。十散坏色相。十一得不净相。十二不贪五阴。十三不着十八界。十四不染十二入。十五不恃族姓。十六破憍慢。十七于一切法心常空寂。

Chapter 25 — *Teachings to Aid the Mindfulness-of-the-Buddha Samādhi*　885

54) One cuts off all feelings of anger;
55) One always puts the mind of compassion into practice;
56) One cuts off affectionate attachments;
57) One always seeks ways to benefit and bring peace to the entire world;
58) One always feels pity for all beings;
59) One always delights in [meditative] walking;
60) One does away with lethargy and sleepiness.

The monastic bodhisattva who abides in dharmas such as these should cultivate and practice this samādhi. Additionally:

3. Fifty Dharmas Supporting Cultivation of This Samādhi

One should also train in this same manner
in the other dharmas pertaining to the cultivation of samādhi.

In order to be able to bring forth this *pratyutpanna* samādhi, one should also cultivate the other supportive dharmas. And what are these? They are:

1) One takes the Buddha's kindness as one's objective focus and always mindfully contemplates him as if he were directly before one;
2) One does not allow one's mind to become scattered;
3) One anchors one's attention directly before one;
4) One guards the gates of the sense faculties;
5) With respect to food and drink, one is easily satisfied;
6) One always cultivates samādhi in both the first and last watches of the night;
7) One abandons the obstacle of the afflictions;
8) One brings forth all of the *dhyāna* absorptions;
9) In one's practice of *dhyāna* meditation, one does not indulge in the delectably pleasurable meditation states;
10) One demolishes through separation the appearance of attractive forms;[90]
11) One acquires the sign of unloveliness;[91]
12) One does not desire the five aggregates;
13) One does not become attached to the eighteen sense realms;
14) One does not indulge any defilement in relation to the twelve sense bases;
15) One does not presumptuously rely on one's [superior] caste origins;
16) One destroys any arrogance;
17) One's mind always remains empty and quiescent in relation to all dharmas that one encounters;

正體字

087b27 ‖ 十
八於諸眾生生親族想。十九不取戒。二十
087b28 ‖ 不分別定。二十一應勤多學。二十二以是
087b29 ‖ 多學而不憍慢。二十三於諸法無疑。二十
087c01 ‖ 四不違諸佛。二十五不逆法。二十六不壞
087c02 ‖ 僧。二十七常詣諸賢聖。二十八遠離凡夫。
087c03 ‖ 二十九樂出世間論。三十修六和敬法。三十
087c04 ‖ 一常修習五解脫處。三十二除九瞋惱事。三
087c05 ‖ 十三斷八懈怠法。三十四修八精進。三十五
087c06 ‖ 常觀九[9]相。三十六得大人八覺。三十七具
087c07 ‖ 足諸禪定三昧。三十八於此禪定無所貪
087c08 ‖ 無所得。三十九聽法專心。四十壞五陰
087c09 ‖ [*]相。四十一不住事[*]相。四十二深怖畏生
087c10 ‖ 死。四十三於五陰生怨賊想。四十四於諸
087c11 ‖ 入中。生空聚想。四十五於四大中生毒蛇
087c12 ‖ 想。四十六於涅槃中生寂滅想安隱樂想。
087c13 ‖ 四十七於五欲中生涎唾想。心樂出離。

简体字

十八于诸众生生亲族想。十九不取戒。二十不分别定。二十一应勤多学。二十二以是多学而不憍慢。二十三于诸法无疑。二十四不违诸佛。二十五不逆法。二十六不坏僧。二十七常诣诸贤圣。二十八远离凡夫。二十九乐出世间论。三十修六和敬法。三十一常修习五解脱处。三十二除九瞋恼事。三十三断八懈怠法。三十四修八精进。三十五常观九相。三十六得大人八觉。三十七具足诸禅定三昧。三十八于此禅定无所贪无所得。三十九听法专心。四十坏五阴相。四十一不住事相。四十二深怖畏生死。四十三于五阴生怨贼想。四十四于诸入中。生空聚想。四十五于四大中生毒蛇想。四十六于涅槃中生寂灭想安隐乐想。四十七于五欲中生涎唾想。心乐出离。

Chapter 25 — Teachings to Aid the Mindfulness-of-the-Buddha Samādhi

18) One imagines all beings as one's close relatives;
19) One does not seize on the moral precepts themselves [as constituting the very essence of moral virtue];
20) One does not make discriminating distinctions regarding the meditative absorptions;
21) One should diligently pursue abundant learning;
22) One does not become arrogant because of this abundant learning;
23) One remains free of doubts with respect to any of the dharmas;
24) One does not oppose the Buddhas;
25) One does not act in a manner that is contrary to the Dharma;
26) One does not do anything that contributes to the destruction of the Sangha;
27) One always goes to pay one's respects to worthies and *āryas*;
28) One distances oneself from foolish common people;
29) One delights in discussion of world-transcending topics;
30) One cultivates the six dharmas of mutual harmony;[92]
31) One always cultivates the five bases of liberation;[93]
32) One rids himself of the nine bases for generating the affliction of anger;[94]
33) One cuts off the eight dharmas associated with indolence;[95]
34) One cultivates the eight types of vigor;[96]
35) One always contemplates the nine signs [of the deterioration of the corpse];[97]
36) One has realized for himself the eight realizations of great men;[98]
37) One perfects all of the *dhyāna* concentrations and samādhis;
38) One has no covetous attachment to these *dhyāna* concentrations and realizes they have no apprehensible reality;[99]
39) When listening to Dharma, one does so with a focused mind;
40) One demolishes the perception of the five aggregates [as inherently existent phenomena];
41) One does not abide in the perception of phenomena [as inherently existent];
42) One is deeply fearful of *saṃsāra*'s births and deaths;
43) One contemplates the five aggregates as like enemies;[100]
44) One contemplates the sense bases as like an empty village;
45) One contemplates the four great elements as like venomous serpents;
46) One brings forth the contemplation of nirvāṇa as quiescent, secure, and happy;[101]
47) One contemplates the five desires as worthy of being spat upon and one's mind delights in escaping from them;

正體字

　　　　四
087c14 ‖ 十八不違佛教。四十九於一切眾生無所
087c15 ‖ 諍訟。五十教化眾生令安住一切功德。復
087c16 ‖ 次。
087c17 ‖ 　　如是三昧報　　菩薩應當知
087c18 ‖ 菩薩行是般舟三昧。果報亦應知。問曰。修
087c19 ‖ 習是三昧得何果報。答曰。於無上道得不
087c20 ‖ 退轉報。復次如經所說果報。佛語[10]颰陀婆
087c21 ‖ 羅菩薩。譬如有人能摧[11]碎三千世界地皆
087c22 ‖ 如微塵。又三千大千世界中所有草木花葉
087c23 ‖ 一切諸物皆為微塵。颰陀婆羅。以一微塵
087c24 ‖ 為一佛世界。有爾所世界皆滿中上妙珍
087c25 ‖ 寶以用布施。跋陀婆羅於意云何。是人以
087c26 ‖ 是布施因緣得福多不。甚多世尊。佛言。颰
087c27 ‖ 陀婆羅。我今實語汝。若有善男子。得聞諸
087c28 ‖ 佛現前三昧。不驚不畏其福無量。何況信受
087c29 ‖ 持讀[12]諷誦為人解說。何況定心修習。如一
088a01 ‖ [1]搆牛乳頃。颰陀婆羅。我說此人福德尚無
088a02 ‖ 有量。何況能得成是三昧者。

简体字

四十八不违佛教。四十九于一切众生无所诤讼。五十教化众生令安住一切功德。复次。

　　如是三昧报　　菩萨应当知

菩萨行是般舟三昧。果报亦应知。问曰。修习是三昧得何果报。答曰。于无上道得不退转报。复次如经所说果报。佛语颰陀婆罗菩萨。譬如有人能摧碎三千世界地皆如微尘。又三千大千世界中所有草木花叶一切诸物皆为微尘。颰陀婆罗。以一微尘为一佛世界。有尔所世界皆满中上妙珍宝以用布施。跋陀婆罗于意云何。是人以是布施因缘得福多不。甚多世尊。佛言。颰陀婆罗。我今实语汝。若有善男子。得闻诸佛现前三昧。不惊不畏其福无量。何况信受持读讽诵为人解说。何况定心修习。如一构牛乳顷。颰陀婆罗。我说此人福德尚无有量。何况能得成是三昧者。

Chapter 25 — *Teachings to Aid the Mindfulness-of-the-Buddha Samādhi*

48) One never opposes the teachings of the Buddha;
49) One has no disputes or quarrels with any other being;
50) In teaching beings, one influences them to dwell securely in all of the meritorious qualities.

K. The Benefits of Cultivating This Pratyutpanna Samādhi

In addition:

> The bodhisattva should understand
> the benefits that result from such a samādhi.

The bodhisattva should also understand the benefits that result from practicing this *pratyutpanna* samādhi.

Question: What are the resulting benefits gained by cultivating this samādhi?

Response: One obtains the resulting benefit of becoming irreversible with respect to the unsurpassable path. Additionally, as for what the sutra says about these resulting benefits, we have the following:[102]

> The Buddha told Bhadrapāla Bodhisattva, "By way of analogy, suppose there was a person who was able to crush to dust all the earth in all worlds in a trichiliocosm and was also able also to crush to dust all the grasses, trees, flowers, leaves, and everything else throughout all of the worlds in a great trichiliocosm.
>
> "Bhadrapala, let us consider now that each and every one of those motes of dust were to constitute one world in which a single buddha dwells and suppose then that one filled to overflowing just such a number of worlds with sublimely marvelous precious jewels and presented all of these jewels as an offering to them.
>
> "Bhadrapāla, what do you think? By performing such an act of giving, would this person gain a great deal of merit or not?"
>
> "Indeed, O Bhagavat, he would reap a great deal."
>
> The Buddha said, "Bhadrapāla, I will now tell you truthfully that if there was a son of good family who heard of this samādhi in which all buddhas appear before one and he were then to be neither startled nor frightened by hearing of it, the merit he would reap from that alone would be immeasurably vast. How much the more so would this be the case if he were to have faith in it, accept it, uphold it, read [teachings in which it is explained], recite them, and explain them for others. How much the more so yet would this be the case if he were to actually cultivate it with concentrated mind even for the time it takes to tug a single squirt of milk from the udder of a cow.
>
> "Bhadrapāla, let me tell you: Even this person's merit would surpass one's ability to measure it. How much the more so would this be so in the case of someone who was actually able to succeed in acquiring this samādhi."

正體字

　　　佛又告颰陀
婆羅。若有善男子善女人。受持讀誦為他
人說。若劫盡時設墮此火火即尋滅。颰陀
婆羅。持是三昧者。若有官事。若遇怨賊師
子虎狼惡獸惡龍諸毒虫等。若夜叉羅剎鳩
槃[2]茶毘舍闍等。若人非人等。若害身若害
命若毀戒。無有是處。若讀誦為人說時亦
無衰惱。唯除業報必應受者。復次颰陀婆
羅。菩薩受持讀誦是三昧時。若得眼耳鼻
舌口齒病風寒冷病如是等種種餘病。以是
病故而失壽命無有是處唯除業報必應
受者。復次颰陀婆羅。若人受持讀誦是三
昧者。諸天守護諸龍夜叉摩睺羅伽人非人
四天王帝釋梵天王諸佛世尊皆共護念。復
次是人皆為諸天所共愛念乃至諸佛皆共
愛念。復次是人皆為諸天所共稱讚乃至諸
佛皆共稱讚。復次諸天皆欲見是菩薩來
至其所。乃至諸佛皆欲見是菩薩來至其
所。

简体字

佛又告颰陀婆罗。若有善男子善女人。受持读诵为他人说。若劫尽时设堕此火火即寻灭。颰陀婆罗。持是三昧者。若有官事。若遇怨贼师子虎狼恶兽恶龙诸毒虫等。若夜叉罗剎鸠槃茶毗舍闍等。若人非人等。若害身若害命若毁戒。无有是处。若读诵为人说时亦无衰恼。唯除业报必应受者。复次颰陀婆罗。菩萨受持读诵是三昧时。若得眼耳鼻舌口齿病风寒冷病如是等种种余病。以是病故而失寿命无有是处唯除业报必应受者。复次颰陀婆罗。若人受持读诵是三昧者。诸天守护诸龙夜叉摩睺罗伽人非人四天王帝释梵天王诸佛世尊皆共护念。复次是人皆为诸天所共爱念乃至诸佛皆共爱念。复次是人皆为诸天所共称赞乃至诸佛皆共称赞。复次诸天皆欲见是菩萨来至其所。乃至诸佛皆欲见是菩萨来至其所。

Chapter 25 — Teachings to Aid the Mindfulness-of-the-Buddha Samādhi

The Buddha continued, telling Bhadrapāla, "If a son or daughter of good family who receives, upholds, reads, recites, and explains [teachings on this samādhi] for others were on the verge of falling into the fires arising at the end of the kalpa, those fires would immediately become extinguished.

"Bhadrapāla, whosoever sustains this samādhi—supposing that he were to encounter some difficulty with officialdom, or supposing that he were to encounter hostile thieves, lions, tigers, wolves, fearsome beasts, fearsome dragons, any of the venomous serpents, or any other such threat, whether from *yakṣas, rākṣasas, kumbhāṇḍas, piśācis*, and such, or from humans, nonhumans, or any other sort of entity—that any of those entities might succeed in physically harming him, taking his life, or causing him to break the precepts—this would be an utter impossibility.

So too would this also be the case with respect to those who might be reading, reciting, or teaching this to others. In those cases too they would remain free of any destructive affliction, with the sole exception of instances where they were already bound to undergo compulsory karmic retributions.[103]

"Furthermore, Bhadrapala, when a bodhisattva accepts, upholds, reads, or recites the sutra on this samādhi, if he happens to contract some sickness of the eye, ear, nose, tongue, mouth, or teeth, some disease instigated by wind or cold, or any other such disease, that he might then lose his life because of any of these diseases would be an utter impossibility with the sole exception of instances where he was already bound to undergo compulsory karmic retributions.

"Also, Bhadrapāla, if a person were to accept, uphold, read, or recite the sutra on this samādhi, the devas themselves would protect him. So too would he be protected by the dragons, *yakṣas, mahoragas*, humans, nonhumans, the Four Heavenly Kings, Śakra, ruler of the devas, the Brahma Heaven King, and the Buddhas, the Bhagavats. They would all join in remaining protectively mindful of this practitioner.

"Furthermore, this person would be one of whom the devas would all be affectionately mindful, and so too would this be so for other such beings up to and including the Buddhas themselves who would also remain affectionately mindful of this practitioner.

"Additionally, this person would be one whom the devas praise, and so too, he would be one whom other beings up to and including all buddhas would praise as well.

"Also, this bodhisattva would be one whom the devas would all wish to see coming to visit them, and so too with the others on up to the Buddhas themselves who would all wish to see him coming to visit them.

正體字

	復次是菩薩受持是三昧者。所未聞經
088a21 ‖	自然得[3]聞。復次是菩薩得是三昧者。乃至
088a22 ‖	夢中皆得如是諸利益事。颰陀婆羅。菩薩若
088a23 ‖	我一劫若減一劫。說受持讀誦是三昧者
088a24 ‖	功德不可得盡。何況得成就者。颰陀婆羅。
088a25 ‖	如人於百歲中身力輕健其疾如風。是人百
088a26 ‖	歲行不休息。常至東方南西北方四維上下。
088a27 ‖	於汝意云何。是人所詣十方有人能數知
088a28 ‖	里數不。颰陀婆羅言。不可數[4]也。唯除
088a29 ‖	如來舍利弗阿惟越致餘不能知。颰陀婆
088b01 ‖	羅。若有善男子善女人以是人所行處滿中
088b02 ‖	真金布施。若有人但聞是三昧。以四種隨
088b03 ‖	喜迴向阿耨多羅三藐三菩提。常求多聞。
088b04 ‖	如過去諸佛行菩[5]薩道時隨喜是三昧。我
088b05 ‖	亦如是。如今現在菩薩隨喜是三昧。我亦
088b06 ‖	如是。如未來諸佛行菩薩道時隨喜是三
088b07 ‖	昧。我亦如是。如過去未來現在菩薩所行
088b08 ‖	三昧。我亦隨喜皆為得多聞。我亦如是求
088b09 ‖	多聞故。隨喜是三昧。颰陀婆羅。是[6]隨喜
088b10 ‖	福德。於上福德百分不及一。百千萬億分
088b11 ‖	不及一。

简体字

复次是菩萨受持是三昧者。所未闻经自然得闻。复次是菩萨得是三昧者。乃至梦中皆得如是诸利益事。颰陀婆罗。菩萨若我一劫若减一劫。说受持读诵是三昧者功德不可得尽。何况得成就者。颰陀婆罗。如人于百岁中身力轻健其疾如风。是人百岁行不休息。常至东方南西北方四维上下。于汝意云何。是人所诣十方有人能数知里数不。颰陀婆罗言。不可数也。唯除如来舍利弗阿惟越致余不能知。颰陀婆罗。若有善男子善女人以是人所行处满中真金布施。若有人但闻是三昧。以四种随喜回向阿耨多罗三藐三菩提。常求多闻。如过去诸佛行菩萨道时随喜是三昧。我亦如是。如今现在菩萨随喜是三昧。我亦如是。如未来诸佛行菩萨道时随喜是三昧。我亦如是。如过去未来现在菩萨所行三昧。我亦随喜皆为得多闻。我亦如是求多闻故。随喜是三昧。颰陀婆罗。是随喜福德。于上福德百分不及一。百千万亿分不及一。

"Furthermore, the bodhisattva who accepts and upholds the sutra on this samādhi will naturally become able to hear whichever other sutras he has not yet heard.

"Additionally, this bodhisattva who gains this samādhi will become able to acquire all of these beneficial experiences even in his dreams.

"Bhadrapāla, were I to attempt to describe the merit of this bodhisattva who accepts, uphold, reads, and recites the sutra on this samādhi, doing so even for an entire kalpa or somewhat less than a kalpa, I would still be unable to come to the end of it. How much the less would this be possible in the case of someone who actually succeeds in perfecting this samādhi.

"Bhadrapāla, if some man with strong body and speed like the wind ran for a hundred years without resting, always proceeding to the east, south, west, north, the four midpoints, above, and below, what do you think? Would anyone be able to know the number of miles he traveled in all those regions throughout the ten directions?"

Bhadrapāla replied, "That would be an incalculable number. Except for the Tathāgata, someone like Śāriputra, or an *avaivartika* [bodhisattva], nobody would be able to know such a number."

"Bhadrapāla, suppose that, on the one hand, there was a son or daughter of good family who filled up with real gold all the area traveled by that man and then give it all away as gifts. Suppose too that, on the other hand, there was someone who merely heard of this samādhi and then engaged in four types of rejoicing and dedication of merit to *anuttarasamyaksaṃbodhi* and the constant pursuit of abundant learning, [doing so by reflecting as follows]:

> Just as all buddhas of the past when practicing the bodhisattva path rejoiced in this samādhi, so too do I now rejoice in it;
>
> Just as the bodhisattvas of the present now rejoice in this samādhi, so too do I now rejoice in it;
>
> Just as all future buddhas during their practice of the bodhisattva path shall rejoice in this samādhi, so too do I now rejoice in it;
>
> And in just that fashion as this samādhi was practiced by all past, future, and present bodhisattvas, so too do I now also rejoice in all of that, and just as they all did so for the sake of pursuing abundant learning [essential to the path], so too do I now rejoice in this samādhi for the sake of the quest for such abundant learning.

"Bhadrapāla, if one were to attempt to compare the previously described merit with the merit from this rejoicing, it could not approach a hundredth part or even one part in a hundred thousand

正體字

乃至算數譬喻所不能及。是三昧
088b12 ‖ 得如是無量無邊果報。復次。
088b13 ‖ 是三昧住處　少中多差別
088b14 ‖ 如是種種相　皆當須論[7]義
088b15 ‖ 是三昧所住處。少相中相多相。如是等應分
088b16 ‖ 別。知是事應當解釋。住處者。是三昧或於
088b17 ‖ 初禪可得。或第二禪或第三禪或第四禪可
088b18 ‖ 得。或初禪中間得勢力。能生是三昧。或少
088b19 ‖ 者人勢力少故名為少。又少時住故名為
088b20 ‖ 少。又見少佛世界故。名為少。中多亦如
088b21 ‖ 是。說是三昧或說有覺有觀。或無覺有
088b22 ‖ 觀。或無覺無觀。或喜相應。或樂相應。或不
088b23 ‖ 苦不樂相應。或有入出息。或無入出息。或
088b24 ‖ 定是善性。或有漏。或無漏。

简体字

乃至算数譬喻所不能及。是三昧得如是无量无边果报。复次。

是三昧住处　少中多差别
如是种种相　皆当须论义

是三昧所住处。少相中相多相。如是等应分别。知是事应当解释。住处者。是三昧或于初禅可得。或第二禅或第三禅或第四禅可得。或初禅中间得势力。能生是三昧。或少者人势力少故名为少。又少时住故名为少。又见少佛世界故。名为少。中多亦如是。说是三昧或说有觉有观。或无觉有观。或无觉无观。或喜相应。或乐相应。或不苦不乐相应。或有入出息。或无入出息。或定是善性。或有漏。或无漏。

myriads of *koṭis* of parts. The futility of this comparison simply could not be adequately described through any form of calculation or analogy. The benefits resulting from this samādhi are just so immeasurable and boundless as this."

L. THIS SAMĀDHI'S VARIOUS STATIONS AND LEVELS OF CULTIVATION

In addition:

> As for the stations in which one may abide in this samādhi
> as well as the distinctions pertaining to lesser, middling, and greater,
> the many different characteristics such as these
> should all be taken up for a discussion of their meaning.

The stations in which one may abide in this samādhi as well as its lesser, middling, and greater characteristics—all such things should be distinguished and known and these matters should then be explained.

Regarding "the stations in which one may abide in it," this samādhi may be acquired in the first *dhyāna*, the second *dhyāna*, the third *dhyāna*, or the fourth *dhyāna* and one may acquire strength in it while in the first *dhyāna*.

It may be that someone who is "lesser" is able to bring forth this samādhi. Here, "lesser" may refer to the fact that a person is possessed of only a lesser degree of strength [in this practice]. "Lesser" may also refer to abiding [in the samādhi] for a shorter period of time. "Lesser" may also refer to the practitioner's seeing a relatively smaller number of buddha worlds. Distinctions regarding "middling" and "greater" may be made in just the same way.

M. VARIOUS QUALITATIVE VARIATIONS IN HOW THIS SAMĀDHI MANIFESTS

In discussing this samādhi, one may speak of it as:

> Sometimes involving the presence of ideation (*vitarka*) and the presence of discursion (*vicāra*);
> Sometimes involving the absence of ideation and the presence of discursion;
> Sometimes involving the absence of ideation and the absence of discursion;
> Sometimes involving the presence of joy (*prīti*);
> Sometimes involving the presence of bliss (*sukha*);
> Sometimes involving neither suffering nor bliss;
> Sometimes involving the presence of breathing;
> Sometimes involving the absence of breathing;
> Sometimes definitely being of a wholesome nature;
> Sometimes involving the presence of the contaminants;
> Sometimes involving the absence of the contaminants;

正體字

	或欲界繫。或色界
088b25	繫。或無色界繫。或非欲界。或非色界。或非無
088b26	色界繫。是三昧是心數法。心相應。隨心行法。
088b27	共心生法。非色。非現。能緣。非業。業相應。隨
088b28	業行。非先世業果報。除因報。可修可知可證。
088b29	亦以身證亦以慧證。或可斷或不可斷。有
088c01	漏應斷。無漏不可斷。知見亦如是。不與
088c02	七覺合。如是一切諸分別三昧義。皆應此
088c03	中說。復次修習是三昧得見諸佛。如說。
088c04	得見諸佛已　　勤心而供養
088c05	善根得增長　　能疾化眾生
088c06	供養名心意清淨。恭敬歡喜念佛有無量功
088c07	德。以種種讚歎名[8]口供養。

简体字

或欲界系。或色界系。或无色界系。或非欲界。或非色界。或非无色界系。是三昧是心数法。心相应。随心行法。共心生法。非色。非现。能缘。非业。业相应。随业行。非先世业果报。除因报。可修可知可证。亦以身证亦以慧证。或可断或不可断。有漏应断。无漏不可断。知见亦如是。不与七觉合。如是一切诸分别三昧义。皆应此中说。复次修习是三昧得见诸佛。如说。

　　得见诸佛已　　勤心而供养
　　善根得增长　　能疾化众生

供养名心意清净。恭敬欢喜念佛有无量功德。以种种赞叹名口供养。

Sometimes connected with the desire realm;
Sometimes connected with the form realm;
Sometimes connected with the formless realm;
Sometimes not connected with the desire realm;
Sometimes not connected with the form realm;
And sometimes not connected with the formless realm.

N. Various Abhidharmic Classifications of This Samādhi

This samādhi;

Is a mental dharma;
Is [a dharma] associated with the mind;
Is a dharma that occurs along with the mind;
Is a non-form [dharma];
Is a non-manifest [dharma];
Is able to take an object;
Is not karma [*per se*];
Is associated with karmic activity;
Is coexistent with karmic activity;
Is not the result of karmic actions from a previous life except when it is the result of a particular cause;[104]
Can be cultivated, can be known, and can be realized;
Can be realized both with the body and by means of wisdom;
Can be subject to severance or may be invulnerable to severance;
Should be severed when contaminants are present;
And is invulnerable to severance when free of the contaminants.

Similar distinctions of this sort may also made with respect to the knowledge and vision associated with this samādhi. Also, it is not necessarily conjoined with the seven limbs of enlightenment.[105] Ideally, all of these distinctions should be discussed herein.

O. The Practitioner's Offerings, Roots of Goodness, and Teaching

Furthermore, it is through the cultivation of this samādhi that one may succeed in seeing the Buddhas. Accordingly, it is said that:

After one has succeeded in seeing the Buddhas,
one proceeds with diligent resolve to present offerings [to them].
As one's roots of goodness are thus able to grow,
one becomes able to rapidly teach beings.

"Making offerings" refers to having a pure mind imbued with reverence and delight as one brings to mind the countless meritorious qualities of the Buddha. When one praises him in various ways, this constitutes the making of verbal offerings. When one makes formal

正體字	敬禮華香等 088c08 ‖ 名身供養。是故福德轉更增長。如穀子在 088c09 ‖ 地雨潤生長。疾教化者令眾生住三乘中。 088c10 ‖ 如是菩薩增長善根。 088c11 ‖ 　　以初二攝法　　攝取諸眾生 088c12 ‖ 　　後餘二攝法　　未盡能信受 088c13 ‖ 初二者布施愛語。利益同事名為後二。是 088c14 ‖ 菩薩在初地。不能具解故。但能信受。 088c15 ‖ 　　爾時諸善根　　迴向於佛道 088c16 ‖ 　　如彼成[9]煉金　　調熟則堪用 088c17 ‖ 智慧火所[*]煉故。於菩薩所行事中。善根成 088c18 ‖ 熟則堪任用。
简体字	敬礼华香等名身供养。是故福德转更增长。如谷子在地雨润生长。疾教化者令众生住三乘中。如是菩萨增长善根。 　　以初二摄法　　摄取诸众生 　　后余二摄法　　未尽能信受 　　初二者布施爱语。利益同事名为后二。是菩萨在初地。不能具解故。但能信受。 　　尔时诸善根　　回向于佛道 　　如彼成炼金　　调熟则堪用 　　智慧火所炼故。于菩萨所行事中。善根成熟则堪任用。

Chapter 25 — *Teachings to Aid the Mindfulness-of-the-Buddha Samādhi*

reverential bows and presents flowers, incenses, and other such things, this constitutes the making of physical offerings.

Because of these actions, one's karmic merit grows ever greater just as a seed starts to grow when it is planted in earth and receives moisture from the rain. "Rapidly teaching" refers to influencing beings to abide in the Three Vehicles. It is in this way that the bodhisattva brings about the growth of his roots of goodness.

P. The Practitioner's Use of the Four Means of Attraction

Through availing oneself of the first two dharmas of attraction,
one is able to attract beings [to the Dharma].
One resorts to the latter two dharmas of attraction
for those not yet fully able to believe and accept [Dharma teachings].

"The first two" refers to "giving" and to "pleasing words" whereas "beneficial actions" and "joint endeavors" constitute "the latter two dharmas" [of the four means of attraction]. Because this bodhisattva who abides on the first ground is as yet unable to completely comprehend everything, [there may be certain aspects of the teaching] that he can only accept on faith.

Q. The Practitioner's Dedication of Roots of Goodness

He then takes all of his roots of goodness
and dedicates them to the realization of buddhahood.
This is comparable to when others smelt gold
and then refine it, whereupon it thereby becomes amenable to use.

It is through being smelted by the fire of wisdom that, in all the endeavors undertaken by the bodhisattva, his roots of goodness ripen and then finally become amenable to use.

The End of Chapter Twenty-Five

正體字

088c19 ‖　　　　譬喻品第二十六
088c20 ‖　　是菩薩應[10]聞　　地相得修果
088c21 ‖　　[11]為得諸地分　　故勤行精進
088c22 ‖　相者是相貌。因以得知。得者成就。以是法
088c23 ‖　故名成就是法。修名得修行修。常念果
088c24 ‖　者。從因有事成名為果。是菩薩欲得十地
088c25 ‖　行。應善[12]聞相得修果。聞者從諸佛菩薩
088c26 ‖　所聞。及勝己者。為得諸地分者。為得是
088c27 ‖　地分故勤行精進。此中初地相者。如先說。
088c28 ‖　　菩薩在初地　　多所能堪受
088c29 ‖　　不好於諍訟　　其心多喜悅
089a01 ‖　　常樂於清淨　　悲心愍眾生
089a02 ‖　　無有瞋恚心　　多行是七事
089a03 ‖　是故堪受不諍喜悅清淨悲

简体字

譬喻品第二十六
　　是菩萨应闻　　地相得修果
　　为得诸地分　　故勤行精进
相者是相貌。因以得知。得者成就。以是法故名成就是法。修名得修行修。常念果者。从因有事成名为果。是菩萨欲得十地行。应善闻相得修果。闻者从诸佛菩萨所闻。及胜己者。为得诸地分者。为得是地分故勤行精进。此中初地相者。如先说。
　　菩萨在初地　　多所能堪受
　　不好于诤讼　　其心多喜悦
　　常乐于清净　　悲心愍众生
　　无有嗔恚心　　多行是七事
　是故堪受不诤喜悦清净悲

Chapter 26
The Analogy Chapter

VI. Chapter 26: The Analogy Chapter
  A. The Bodhisattva Should Study, Cultivate, and Reach the Grounds

> This bodhisattva should learn of the characteristic features
> of the grounds and then attain the fruits of their cultivation.
> It is in order to attain all aspects of the grounds
> that he is therefore diligent in the practice of vigor.

"Characteristic features" refers here to their appearances. It is due to [learning about them] that one is then able to know them. "Attain" refers here to bringing them to a state of complete development. It is because of this dharma [of "complete development"] that one refers to completely developing this dharma.

"Cultivation" refers to [the two types of cultivation, namely] cultivation associated with acquisition and cultivation associated with practice. As for always bearing in mind "the fruits," it is from the cause that one achieves the accomplishment of an endeavor that is referred to as its "fruits."

This bodhisattva who aspires to acquire the practices specific to the ten grounds should learn well to their characteristic features and then acquire the fruits of their cultivation. "Learning" refers to hearing [these teachings] from buddhas, bodhisattvas, and one's superiors.

"It is in order to gain all aspects of the grounds," means that it is for the sake of successful acquisition of the aspects of these grounds that one diligently practices vigor. The characteristic aspects of the first ground that are of concern here are as described earlier in this text:

  B. Seven Practices Characteristic of the First Ground Bodhisattva

> The bodhisattva who abides on the first ground
> has much that he is able to endure.
> He is not fond of struggle or disputation,
> and, for the most part, his mind is joyous and pleased.
>
> He always delights in purity.
> He has a compassionate mind and feels pity for beings.
> He has no thoughts of hatred or anger,
> and, for the most part, practices these seven things.[106]

Thus, the seven dharmas consisting of the capacity for endurance, non-disputation, being joyous and pleased, purity, compassion, an absence

正體字

> 心無瞋等七法。
> 089a04 ‖ 是初地相。成就此堪受等七法名為得。復
> 089a05 ‖ 次堪受等七法相。即是初地得。如偈說。
> 089a06 ‖ 　若厚種善根　　善行於諸行
> 089a07 ‖ 　善集諸資[1]生　善供養諸佛
> 089a08 ‖ 　善知識所護　　具足於深心
> 089a09 ‖ 　悲心念眾生　　信解無上法
> 089a10 ‖ 　具此八法已　　當自發願言
> 089a11 ‖ 　我已得自度　　當復度眾生
> 089a12 ‖ 　為得十力故　　入於必定聚
> 089a13 ‖ 　則生如來家　　無有諸過咎
> 089a14 ‖ 　即轉世間道　　入出世上道
> 089a15 ‖ 　以是得初地　　此地名歡喜
> 089a16 ‖ 是故當知。為菩提故所得決定心。名為初
> 089a17 ‖ 地得修名。從初發心乃至成諸佛現前三
> 089a18 ‖ 昧。於其中間[2]具說諸地功德。能生是諸功
> 089a19 ‖ 德。生已修集增長。名為初地。修果者。先已
> 089a20 ‖ 處處說得若干福德。不迴向聲聞辟支佛地。

简体字

心无瞋等七法。是初地相。成就此堪受等七法名为得。复次堪受等七法相。即是初地得。如偈说。

　若厚种善根　　善行于诸行
　善集诸资生　　善供养诸佛
　善知识所护　　具足于深心
　悲心念众生　　信解无上法
　具此八法已　　当自发愿言
　我已得自度　　当复度众生
　为得十力故　　入于必定聚
　则生如来家　　无有诸过咎
　即转世间道　　入出世上道
　以是得初地　　此地名欢喜

是故当知。为菩提故所得决定心。名为初地得修名。从初发心乃至成诸佛现前三昧。于其中间具说诸地功德。能生是诸功德。生已修集增长。名为初地。修果者。先已处处说得若干福德。不回向声闻辟支佛地。

of hatred in the mind, and such—these are all characteristic features of the first ground. It is the complete development of these seven dharmas consisting of the "capacity for endurance" and so forth that define their "acquisition." Furthermore, these seven dharmas comprising the characteristics of "capacity for endurance" and so forth—they are all acquired on the first ground. This is as described in verse, as follows:

C. Eight Accomplishments Associated with Entering the First Ground

Having densely planted one's roots of goodness,
having thoroughly practiced the practices,
having well accumulated all the provisions,
having made offerings to all buddhas,

having become protected by the good spiritual guide,
having completely developed the resolute intentions,
having become compassionately mindful of beings,
and having resolute belief in the unsurpassable Dharma—[107]

Once one has become completely equipped with these eight dharmas,
at one's own behest, one should bring forth a vow, saying,
"After I have accomplished my own liberation,
I shall return and liberate other beings."

For the sake of gaining the ten powers,
one enters the congregation of those at the stage of certainty.[108]
Then one is born into the family of the Tathāgatas
that is free of any transgressions.

One immediately turns away from the worldly path
and enters the supreme path that goes beyond the world.
It is because of this that one gains the first ground.
This ground is referred to as "the Ground of Joyfulness."[109]

Therefore, one should understand that the definite resolve one has developed for the sake of attaining bodhi is what constitutes the essence of one's cultivation in gaining the first ground. From that initial bringing forth of the resolve all the way to one's attainment of the samādhi in which all buddhas manifest before one—all of the meritorious qualities thoroughly described as pertaining to that intervening period are what are able to bring forth all of these meritorious qualities. And after they have arisen, their cultivation, accumulation, and growth are what define the first ground.

As for "the fruits of their cultivation," we have previously already emphasized in place after place that, when one acquires however much merit, one is not to dedicate that merit for the sake of reaching the grounds of either *śrāvaka* disciples or *pratyekabuddhas*. Now we

正體字	089a21 ‖ 今當更說。菩薩得初地果。能得菩薩數百 089a22 ‖ 定等。初地分者。所有諸法合成初地。名為 089a23 ‖ 諸分。如麴米等合能成酒故。名酒因緣。所 089a24 ‖ 有諸法能成初地。名為初地分。所謂。 089a25 ‖ 　　信力轉增上　　成就大悲[3]心 089a26 ‖ 　　慈愍眾生類　　修善心無惓 089a27 ‖ 　　喜樂於妙法　　常近善知識 089a28 ‖ 　　慚愧及恭敬　　柔軟和其心 089a29 ‖ 　　樂觀法無著　　一心求多聞 089b01 ‖ 　　不貪於利養　　離奸欺諂誑 089b02 ‖ 　　不污諸佛家　　不毀戒欺佛 089b03 ‖ 　　深樂薩婆若　　不動如[4]大山 089b04 ‖ 　　常樂修習行　　轉上之妙法 089b05 ‖ 　　樂出世間法　　不樂世間法 089b06 ‖ 　　即治歡喜地　　難治而能治 089b07 ‖ 　　是故常一心　　勤行此諸法 089b08 ‖ 　　菩薩能成就　　如是上妙法 089b09 ‖ 　　是則為安住　　菩薩初地中	
简体字	今当更说。菩萨得初地果。能得菩萨数百定等。初地分者。所有诸法合成初地。名为诸分。如麴米等合能成酒故。名酒因缘。所有诸法能成初地。名为初地分。所谓。 　　信力转增上　　成就大悲心 　　慈愍众生类　　修善心无惓 　　喜乐于妙法　　常近善知识 　　惭愧及恭敬　　柔软和其心 　　乐观法无著　　一心求多闻 　　不贪于利养　　离奸欺谄诳 　　不污诸佛家　　不毁戒欺佛 　　深乐萨婆若　　不动如大山 　　常乐修习行　　转上之妙法 　　乐出世间法　　不乐世间法 　　即治欢喜地　　难治而能治 　　是故常一心　　勤行此诸法 　　菩萨能成就　　如是上妙法 　　是则为安住　　菩萨初地中	

should state this yet again. When the bodhisattva acquires the fruition of the first ground, he is able to acquire several hundreds of meditative concentrations and other such results.

As for the "aspects" of the first ground, this refers to all the many dharmas that jointly establish the first ground. This is what is meant here by "all aspects." This is analogous to the yeast, rice, and other ingredients that, when mixed together, are able to make wine. These are what constitute the causes and conditions for the making of wine. So too it is with all the dharmas that are able to contribute to the establishment of the first ground. These are what constitute the "aspects" of the first ground. These are as follows:

D. The Essential Aspects of the Bodhisattva's First Ground Cultivation

The power of faith becomes ever more superior
as one perfects the mind of great compassion.
One feels kindness and pity for all types of beings
and tirelessly cultivates the mind of goodness.

One finds joyous delight in sublime dharmas,
always draws close to the good spiritual guide,
maintains a sense of shame, dread of blame, and reverence,
and makes one's mind gentle and harmonious.

One delights in contemplating dharmas and stays free of attachment,
single-mindedly strives to acquire abundant learning,
and refrains from coveting offerings of benefits and support,
while staying far from base cheating, flattery, and deception.

One does not defile the family of the Buddhas
and does not damage moral precepts or cheat the Buddhas.
One deeply delights in all-knowledge[110]
and remains as unmoving as an immense mountain.

One always delights in cultivating the practice
of ever more superior sublime dharmas.
One delights in the world-transcending dharmas
and does not delight in worldly dharmas.

Even as one cultivates the Ground of Joyfulness,
one is able to cultivate what is difficult to cultivate.
Therefore one is always single-minded
in the diligent practice of these dharmas.

The bodhisattva is able to perfect
such supremely sublime dharmas as these.
It is this then that constitutes secure abiding
on the bodhisattva's first ground.[111]

正體字

089b10 ‖ 問曰。菩薩何用[*]聞是初地相等為。答曰。是
089b11 ‖ 菩薩初地相等法中。應善知方便。是故應
089b12 ‖ [5]聞。問曰。菩薩但應於此法中。善知方便。
089b13 ‖ 更於餘法中善知方便。答曰。是諸法中應
089b14 ‖ 善知方便。亦於餘法善知方便。問曰。若爾
089b15 ‖ 者可略說。答曰。
089b16 ‖ 　有法能助地　　有法違於地
089b17 ‖ 　有法能生地　　有法能壞[6]地
089b18 ‖ 　有諸地相果　　有諸地中得
089b19 ‖ 　諸地清淨分　　從地至一地
089b20 ‖ 　住地轉增益　　無能令退者
089b21 ‖ 　從菩薩淨地　　至無量佛地
089b22 ‖ 　於此諸事中　　應善知方便
089b23 ‖ 　請問諸善[7]人　　除破於憍慢
089b24 ‖ 助初地法者。所謂信戒聞捨精進念慧等。如
089b25 ‖ 是等及餘諸法隨順初地者。是名助法。相
089b26 ‖ 違法者。不信破戒少聞慳[8]貪懈怠亂念無慧
089b27 ‖ 等

简体字

问曰。菩萨何用闻是初地相等为。答曰。是菩萨初地相等法中。应善知方便。是故应闻。问曰。菩萨但应于此法中。善知方便。更于余法中善知方便。答曰。是诸法中应善知方便。亦于余法善知方便。问曰。若尔者可略说。答曰。

　有法能助地　　有法违于地
　有法能生地　　有法能坏地
　有诸地相果　　有诸地中得
　诸地清净分　　从地至一地
　住地转增益　　无能令退者
　从菩萨净地　　至无量佛地
　于此诸事中　　应善知方便
　请问诸善人　　除破于憍慢

助初地法者。所谓信戒闻舍精进念慧等。如是等及余诸法随顺初地者。是名助法。相违法者。不信破戒少闻悭贪懈怠乱念无慧等

Chapter 26 — *The Analogy Chapter*

Question: What use is there for the bodhisattva in learning of these characteristic features of the first ground and other related matters?

Response: This bodhisattva should thoroughly know the skillful means associated with the characteristic features of the first ground and the other associated dharmas. Therefore he should learn about them.

Question: Should the bodhisattva come to thoroughly know only the skillful means associated with these dharmas or should he also thoroughly know other associated skillful means as well?

Response: He should not only thoroughly know the skillful means associated with all of these dharmas but should also thoroughly know the skillful means associated with other dharmas.

Question: If that is the case, then could you perhaps set forth a summary discussion [of these additional topics]?

Response:

E. Additional Factors That the Bodhisattva Must Learn

There are dharmas able to assist [in acquisition of] the ground.
There are dharmas running counter to [acquisition of] the ground.
There are dharmas able to give rise to the ground.
There are dharmas able to destroy the ground.

There are the characteristic features and fruits of each ground.
There are those things gained as one abides on each ground.
There are aspects of each ground that facilitate its purification.
There are things gained in advancing from one ground to another.

There are things that increase as one abides on each ground.
There are factors through which no one can cause one's retreat.
From the point where the bodhisattva [begins to] purify the grounds to the point he reaches the ground of the countlessly many buddhas,

when engaged in all these endeavors,
he should thoroughly know the associated skillful means,
should inquire of those who are skilled in such matters,
and should rid himself of arrogance.

As for "dharmas assisting acquisition of the first ground," these include such factors as faith, moral virtue, learning, relinquishing, vigor, mindfulness, and wisdom. It is dharmas of this sort along with the other dharmas that accord with the first ground that constitute what is meant here by "assisting dharmas."

"Dharmas running counter [to acquisition of the ground]" include disbelief, breaking of precepts, having but little learning, covetousness, indolence, chaotic thoughts, absence of wisdom, and any other

正體字

	及餘不隨順不能助初地者是。滅地法
089b28 ‖	者。能令此地退失障礙不現。如劫盡時萬
089b29 ‖	物都滅。何者是所謂能偷奪菩提心法。是先
089c01 ‖	已說。生地法者。能生能成初地。所謂不偷
089c02 ‖	奪菩提心法。是先已說。地相得果地分上已
089c03 ‖	說。清淨法者。用是法能淨初地。所謂如先
089c04 ‖	說。
089c05 ‖	初地中七法。
089c06 ‖	菩薩在初地　　多所能堪受
089c07 ‖	不好於諍訟　　其心多喜悅
089c08 ‖	常樂於清淨　　悲心愍眾[9]生
089c09 ‖	無有瞋恚心　　多[10]行是七事
089c10 ‖	如是七法能淨治初地。從[11]一地至一地
089c11 ‖	者。如從初地至二地從二地至三地。餘
089c12 ‖	亦如是。從初地至二地得不諂曲等十心
089c13 ‖	故。從二地至三地得信樂等十心故。得
089c14 ‖	如是等種種心種種法故。能從一地至一
089c15 ‖	地。

简体字

及余不随顺不能助初地者是。灭地法者。能令此地退失障碍不现。如劫尽时万物都灭。何者是所谓能偷夺菩提心法。是先已说。生地法者。能生能成初地。所谓不偷夺菩提心法。是先已说。地相得果地分上已说。清净法者。用是法能净初地。所谓如先说。

　初地中七法。
　菩萨在初地　　多所能堪受
　不好于诤讼　　其心多喜悦
　常乐于清净　　悲心愍众生
　无有嗔恚心　　多行是七事

如是七法能净治初地。从一地至一地者。如从初地至二地从二地至三地。余亦如是。从初地至二地得不谄曲等十心故。从二地至三地得信乐等十心故。得如是等种种心种种法故。能从一地至一地。

dharmas that fail to accord with the first ground and do not assist its acquisition.

As for "dharmas able to destroy the ground," these include any that might cause one to retreat from and abandon cultivation of this ground, any that might obstruct it, and any that might cause it to not manifest. These would be comparable in their effect to the utter destruction of the myriad things that occurs at the very end of the kalpa.

What are the dharmas said to have the ability to rob one of the resolve to attain bodhi? This is a matter that has already been explained [earlier in this text].

As for "dharmas able to give rise to the ground," this refers to those that are able to bring forth the first ground and those that are able to bring about successful establishment in the first ground. These are the dharmas preventing one from being robbed of the resolve to realize bodhi. These were explained earlier as well.

The meanings of "characteristic features," "acquisition of fruition," and "the aspects of the ground" were explained above.

As for "dharmas facilitating purification," if one uses these dharmas, one will be able to purify the first ground. As previously explained,[112] they are as follows:

The bodhisattva who abides on the first ground
has much that he is able to endure.
He is not fond of struggle or disputation,
and, for the most part, his mind is joyous and pleased.

He always delights in purity.
He has a compassionate mind and feels pity for beings.
He has no thoughts of hatred or anger,
and, for the most part, practices these seven things.

It is by resort to dharmas such as these seven that one is able to purify the first ground.

"Advancing from one ground to another," refers for example to when one advances from the first ground to the second ground, and from the second ground to the third ground. So too it is with the rest [of the grounds]. [That one is able to proceed] from the first ground to the second ground is due to acquiring ten types of mind including refraining from deviousness, and so forth. [And that one is able to proceed] from the second ground to the third ground is due to acquiring the ten types of mind through which one acquires resolute faith, and so forth. It is due to acquiring just such various sorts of mind and various types of dharmas that one is then able to advance from one ground to the next ground.

正體字

住地轉增益[12]者。如初地中檀波羅蜜多
第二地中尸波羅蜜多又信等諸法轉得勢
力。第三地中多聞多又布施持戒信等轉得
勢力。餘地中亦如是。無能令退者。住是地
中。若沙門婆羅門若天魔梵及餘世間無能
轉者。何以故。得大功德力故。深入法性底
故。大信解故。從菩薩淨地至無量佛地者。
若菩薩具足清淨一切地已則得佛地。於
此諸事中皆應善知方便。請問諸善人者。
成就正法故名為善人。正法者。略說一信。
二精進。三念。四定。五慧。六身口意律儀。七
無貪無恚無癡。除捨於憍慢者。自謂我於
勝人中勝。名為大慢。於與己等中勝而心
自高。名為憍慢。

简体字

住地转增益者。如初地中檀波罗蜜多第二地中尸波罗蜜多又信等诸法转得势力。第三地中多闻多又布施持戒信等转得势力。余地中亦如是。无能令退者。住是地中。若沙门婆罗门若天魔梵及余世间无能转者。何以故。得大功德力故。深入法性底故。大信解故。从菩萨净地至无量佛地者。若菩萨具足清净一切地已则得佛地。于此诸事中皆应善知方便。请问诸善人者。成就正法故名为善人。正法者。略说一信。二精进。三念。四定。五慧。六身口意律仪。七无贪无恚无痴。除舍于憍慢者。自谓我于胜人中胜。名为大慢。于与己等中胜而心自高。名为憍慢。

As for "things that increase as one abides on each ground," this includes for example the fact that the first ground is characterized by much cultivation of the perfection of giving (lit. *dāna pāramitā*), the second ground is characterized by much cultivation of the perfection of moral virtue (lit. *śīla pāramitā*) and an increase in the strength of faith and other such dharmas, and the third ground is characterized by much cultivation of abundant learning and increasing strength in giving, moral virtue, faith, and other such dharmas. The same process occurs on each of the other grounds as well.

Regarding "factors through which no one can cause one's retreat," this refers to the capacity that develops as one dwells on this ground through which no *śramaṇa* or brahman, and no celestial *māra*, Brahmā, or anyone else in the world can possibly cause one to turn back from it. Why [can't they cause one to turn back]? It is because one has gained the power of great meritorious qualities, because one has deeply penetrated to the very bottom of the nature of all dharmas, and because one has developed great resolute faith.

As for "from the point where the bodhisattva [begins to] purify the grounds to the point he reaches the ground of the countlessly many buddhas," refers to the fact that, if the bodhisattva finishes the complete purification of all the grounds, he will then succeed in reaching the Buddha Ground.

"When engaged in all of these endeavors," in every case, "he should thoroughly know the associated skillful means."

Regarding "inquiring of those who are skilled in such matters" it is on the basis of having completely perfected one's cultivation of right Dharma that one qualifies as "one who is skilled in such matters."

As for what is meant here by "right Dharma," in summary, this refers to:

First, faith;
Second, vigor;
Third, mindfulness;
Fourth, meditative concentration;
Fifth, wisdom;
Sixth, moral virtue in body, speech, and mind; and
Seventh, freedom from desire, hatred, and delusion.

Regarding "ridding himself of arrogance," when one regards oneself as superior to those who truly *are* superior, this is known as "great arrogance." When one regards oneself as superior to those who are one's equals and thus elevates oneself in one's own mind, this is what is known as "arrogance." When, with regard to those compared to

大不如他言小不如。名
為小慢。問曰。汝說於是諸法中應善知方
便。得是方便何用為。答曰。
　　菩薩若善知　　諸地中相得
　　不得成佛道　　終不轉初地
相名助諸地等[1]七法。得名相違法有八
種。滅等八法不應行。若菩薩善知是法不
得佛道終不退轉。[2]

十住毘婆沙論卷第十二　十住毘婆沙論卷第十三

聖者龍樹造　後秦龜茲國三藏鳩摩羅什譯

　　譬喻品餘

[3]問曰。菩薩善知是諸法。未得[4]佛道終不
退者。其喻云何。答曰。
　　如大力導師　　善知好道相
　　此處與彼處　　轉道之所宜
　　資糧及行具　　皆悉令備足
　　於彼險道中　　令眾得安隱
　　得至大城邑　　能令眾無患
　　由是大導師　　善能知道故
　　善知諸地轉　　具足助道法
　　菩薩善知道　　好惡此彼處

whom one is in fact vastly inferior one instead regards oneself as being only slightly inferior, this is what is known as "arrogance even in inferiority."

F. THE BENEFIT OF KNOWING THESE DHARMAS AND THEIR SKILLFUL MEANS

Question: You have stated that one should come to thoroughly know the skillful means associated with all of these dharmas. Assuming that one does gain all of these skillful means, of what use are they?

Response:
> If the bodhisattva thoroughly knows with regard to all the grounds
> their characteristic features and their acquisition,
> so long as he has not yet attained buddhahood,
> he will never turn back from the first ground.

"Characteristic features" refers to the seven [above-listed] dharmas that assist advancement through the grounds. "Acquisition" refers to [avoidance of] the eight [above-listed] dharmas that run counter to acquisition of the grounds.[113] The eight dharmas that destroy cultivation are those one should not practice. If the bodhisattva thoroughly knows these dharmas, so long as he has not yet attained buddhahood, he will never turn back.

G. AN ANALOGY FOR A BODHISATTVA'S KNOWLEDGE OF THE 10 GROUNDS PATH

Question: As for this bodhisattva who well knows all of these dharmas but will never retreat so long as he has not yet attained buddhahood, what sort of analogy would serve to describe his circumstance?

Response:
> It is as if there was a guide possessed of immense powers
> who knew well the characteristics of the good road
> and knew how best to get from this place to that place,
> knew what was appropriate when encountering a turn in the path,
>
> knew the provisions and implements to be taken on the trip,
> knew how they were all to be adequately prepared,
> knew how in the midst of that dangerous road
> one ensures that the group can remain safe and secure
>
> and succeed in reaching the great city,
> being able all the while to cause everyone to escape calamities.
> [Success in this] would be because of this great guide,
> because of his being well able to know the path,
>
> because of his knowing well the changes in the terrain,
> and due to having completely prepared the provisions for the path.
> The bodhisattva thoroughly knows the path,
> the good and bad aspects in this place and that place

正體字

090a25 ‖	自度生死險　　兼導多眾生
090a26 ‖	令至安隱處　　無為涅槃城
090a27 ‖	悉令於惡道　　不遇眾苦患
090a28 ‖	菩薩方便力　　善能知道故

090a29 ‖ [5]好道相者。多有薪草水。無有寇賊師子[6]狼
090b01 ‖ 虎及諸惡獸毒虫之屬。不寒不熱。無有惡山
090b02 ‖ 溝坑絕澗險隘深榛叢林限障。亦無高下平
090b03 ‖ 直夷通少於[7]岐道。寬博多容多人行處。行
090b04 ‖ 無厭惓多有華果可食之物。如是等事名
090b05 ‖ 為好道相。與此相違名為惡道相。此處名
090b06 ‖ 人眾止宿食息之處。彼處名從是處至異
090b07 ‖ 處。若二宿中間亦名異處。轉道名見有岐
090b08 ‖ 道。至大城者。是道應行餘者應捨。資糧名
090b09 ‖ 麨蜜[8]摶等道路所食。大力名大勢力多有
090b10 ‖ 財物善解治法。備足名多有飲食無所乏
090b11 ‖ 少。安名無有賊寇恐怖之事。

简体字

　　自度生死险　　兼导多众生
　　令至安隐处　　无为涅槃城
　　悉令于恶道　　不遇众苦患
　　菩萨方便力　　善能知道故

好道相者。多有薪草水。无有寇贼师子狼虎及诸恶兽毒虫之属。不寒不热。无有恶山沟坑绝涧险隘深榛丛林限障。亦无高下平直夷通少于岐道。宽博多容多人行处。行无厌惓多有华果可食之物。如是等事名为好道相。与此相违名为恶道相。此处名人众止宿食息之处。彼处名从是处至异处。若二宿中间亦名异处。转道名见有岐道。至大城者。是道应行余者应舍。资粮名麨蜜抟等道路所食。大力名大势力多有财物善解治法。备足名多有饮食无所乏少。安名无有贼寇恐怖之事。

so that he can himself cross beyond the dangers of *saṃsāra*
while also leading many other beings across,
thereby causing them to arrive at a safe and secure place
in the city of unconditioned nirvāṇa,

enabling them all to avoid the many anguishing calamities
encountered within the wretched destinies.
The power of a bodhisattva's skillful means
is the result of his ability to thoroughly know the path.

As for "the characteristics of the good road," this refers to knowing where there is abundant firewood, forage grasses, and water, knowing where there are no bandits, lions, wolves, tigers or any other sorts of fearsome beasts or venomous insects, knowing where it is neither too cold nor too hot, knowing where there are no fearsome mountains, crevasses, abysses, precipitous river gorges, hazardous ravines, deep thorny underbrush, jungles, or deep coves blocking the path, knowing where there are no steep ascents and plummeting descents, knowing where the path is level, straight, flat, direct in its connections, and having but few forks in the road, and knowing where it is wide, able to accommodate many people, and frequented by many travelers. It refers as well to knowing where traveling is not inordinately wearisome or exhausting, and to knowing where there is an abundance of flowers, fruit, and things one can eat. It is just such circumstances as these that define what is meant by "the characteristics of the best road." Whatever features are opposite to these characteristics are signs of a bad road.

"This place" refers to a location where the band of travelers stops, eats, and rests. "That place" refers to a different place that is reached after departing from this place, or it may also refer to the different places passed through between two overnight stops. "Turn in the path" refers to where one sees that there is a fork in the path. As for [the path that] "reaches the great city," it is this path that should be traveled, whereas all other paths must be avoided.

"Provisions" refers to supplies that are eaten along the road such as balls made of wheat and honey.

The "immense powers" [as possessed by this guide] refers to great strength, the possession of abundant resources in wealth, and a thorough understanding of the methods required to maintain order.

"Adequate preparation" refers to gathering together an abundance of food and drink so that they will encounter no shortages.

"Safety" refers to ensuring that there will be no frightful experiences involving encounters with bandits.

正體字

```
         隱名無有疾
090b12 ‖ 病苦痛衰患。[9]大城名多容人眾能令多人
090b13 ‖ 眾得至大城。導師善解道相自無患難。亦
090b14 ‖ 令人眾無有患難。善諳道故。無有寒熱飢
090b15 ‖ 渴怨賊惡獸毒虫惡山惡水深坑坎等如是
090b16 ‖ 過患。何以故。善知道路好惡相故。以此喻
090b17 ‖ 歡喜等十地。如人行路去不休息能至大
090b18 ‖ 城。菩薩如是行是十地。得至佛法入涅槃
090b19 ‖ 大城。如彼好道多有薪草水等。行者無乏。
090b20 ‖ 草名如人乘馬路多好草馬力強盛。十地
090b21 ‖ 道功德亦如是。諦捨滅慧四勝處。助諸功
090b22 ‖ 德故名為草。何以故。若人貴於實事樂隨
090b23 ‖ 諦語。當親近實語者。見實有利樂隨實事。
090b24 ‖ 深惡妄語遠離妄語。見妄語過不[10]欲樂
090b25 ‖ 聞。如是等因緣得諦勝處。捨等三處亦應
090b26 ‖ 如是[11]知。
```

简体字

隐名无有疾病苦痛衰患。大城名多容人众能令多人众得至大城。导师善解道相自无患难。亦令人众无有患难。善谙道故。无有寒热饥渴怨贼恶兽毒虫恶山恶水深坑坎等如是过患。何以故。善知道路好恶相故。以此喻欢喜等十地。如人行路去不休息能至大城。菩萨如是行是十地。得至佛法入涅槃大城。如彼好道多有薪草水等。行者无乏。草名如人乘马路多好草马力强盛。十地道功德亦如是。谛舍灭慧四胜处。助诸功德故名为草。何以故。若人贵于实事乐随谛语。当亲近实语者。见实有利乐随实事。深恶妄语远离妄语。见妄语过不欲乐闻。如是等因缘得谛胜处。舍等三处亦应如是知。

Chapter 26 — The Analogy Chapter

"Security" refers to ensuring that there will be no sickness, intensely painful incidents, or ruinous calamities.

"Great city" refers here to being able to reach a great city accommodating a large population.

This great guide thoroughly understands all of the signs along the road and is himself personally free of any troublesome difficulties while also being well able to prevent the entire group from encountering any troublesome difficulties. This is a result of his thorough familiarity with the path. There are no encounters with intense cold or heat, hunger or thirst, bandits, fearsome beasts, poisonous insects, fearsome mountainous terrain, treacherous rivers, deep chasms or other such calamities. And why is this? This is because he thoroughly knows all of the good and bad signs along the entire road.

This comparison is used as an analogy for one's progression through the Ground of Joyfulness and the rest of the ten grounds, for it is comparable to when someone who has embarked on a path refrains from resting and thereby becomes able to reach a great city. So too, the bodhisattva travels in this way through the ten grounds and thus succeeds in arriving at the Buddha Dharma's entry into the great city of nirvāṇa.

This route is comparable to that good road along which there is an abundance of firewood, forage grasses, water, and such. As a consequence, the traveler does not encounter shortages in those things. "Forage grasses" refers to that situation wherein someone traveling by horse does so on a road where, because there are excellent fields of grass along the way, the horse's strength remains robust. The meritorious qualities associated with the path of the ten grounds are just like this.

Because the four supreme bases [of meritorious qualities] consisting of truth, relinquishment, quiescence, and wisdom facilitate the arising of all the meritorious qualities, they are analogous here to those forage grasses. How is this so? If a person esteems truthfulness in his endeavors, then he delights in speaking in a manner that accords with the truth. One should draw close to those who speak the truth. One sees that truthfulness is beneficial and thus delights in according with truth in his endeavors. Hence he deeply abhors false speech, renounces false speech, sees the faults inherent in false speech, and does not wish to even hear it. Due to causes and conditions such as these, one acquires the supreme basis of truthfulness. The other three supreme bases [of meritorious qualities] consisting of relinquishment and the rest should be similarly understood.

正體字

	如彼好道須諸象馬牛驢等得
090b27 ‖	至大城草助成其力。如是諦捨滅慧處。能
090b28 ‖	令至佛法入涅槃大城。薪名多聞思修慧
090b29 ‖	能至大智慧業。如薪能[12]令火然亦令猛
090c01 ‖	[13]盛。如是聞思修慧能生大慧能令增長。
090c02 ‖	如火能燒能煮能照智慧火亦如是。燒諸
090c03 ‖	煩惱成熟諸善根照四聖諦。如火是智慧
090c04 ‖	薪是能生智慧[14]等諸法。多水名多有諸流
090c05 ‖	河渠隨意取用充足大眾。泉井及池所不
090c06 ‖	能爾。
090c07 ‖	復次多水者。如人乘船隨水至大城。井泉
090c08 ‖	陂池水則不能得爾。如經說。信為大河福
090c09 ‖	德為岸。如河除熱除渴除垢能生勢力。善
090c10 ‖	法中信亦如是。能滅三毒熱。除三惡行垢。
090c11 ‖	除三有渴。為涅槃故。於善法中得勢力。
090c12 ‖	如彼好道多有諸根藥草則行者無乏。十
090c13 ‖	地道亦如是。根名深心所愛。如有根故則
090c14 ‖	生[15]芽莖[16]枝葉等及諸果實。深心愛道。生
090c15 ‖	正憶念大願等諸功德。

简体字

如彼好道须诸象马牛驴等得至大城草助成其力。如是谛舍灭慧处。能令至佛法入涅槃大城。薪名多闻思修慧能至大智慧业。如薪能令火然亦令猛盛。如是闻思修慧能生大慧能令增长。如火能烧能煮能照智慧火亦如是。烧诸烦恼成熟诸善根照四圣谛。如火是智慧薪是能生智慧等诸法。多水名多有诸流河渠随意取用充足大众。泉井及池所不能尔。

复次多水者。如人乘船随水至大城。井泉陂池水则不能得尔。如经说。信为大河福德为岸。如河除热除渴除垢能生势力。善法中信亦如是。能灭三毒热。除三恶行垢。除三有渴。为涅槃故。于善法中得势力。如彼好道多有诸根药草则行者无乏。十地道亦如是。根名深心所爱。如有根故则生芽茎枝叶等及诸果实。深心爱道。生正忆念大愿等诸功德。

Just as, in traveling that good road, in order to reach the great city, it is essential that the elephants, horses, cattle, donkeys, and such obtain foraging grass through which they are provided with strength, so too it is that the bases of truthfulness, relinquishment, quiescence, and wisdom enable one to reach the Buddha Dharma's entry into the great city of nirvāṇa.

"Firewood" is analogous here to the wisdom associated with extensive learning, [the wisdom associated with] contemplation, and [the wisdom associated with] cultivation by which one is able to perfect the works of great wisdom. Just as firewood is able to cause a fire to burn and also cause it to become fiercely intense, so too is the wisdom of learning, contemplation, and cultivation able to produce the great wisdom that one is then able to cause to grow. In just the same manner as fire is able to burn, is able to cook, and is able to provide illumination, so too is the fire of wisdom able to burn up the afflictions, ripen one's roots of goodness, and illuminate the four truths of the Āryas. Just as fire is analogous to wisdom, firewood is analogous to the various dharmas that are capable of generating wisdom.

"Abundant water" refers to there being numerous flowing rivers and canals one can freely use to satisfy everyone's needs in a way that mere springs, wells, and ponds could not sufficiently serve.

Then again "abundant water" is analogous to when people board boats and then follow the current until they reach a great city. The water contained in wells, springs, reservoirs, and ponds is simply unable to serve in this capacity. As stated in the sutras:

> Faith serves as the great river and merit serves as its banks. Just as a river is able to relieve heat, quench thirst, rinse away filth, and produce power [for waterwheels and such], faith in good dharmas is similarly able to extinguish the fire of the three poisons, rinse away the filth of the three types of bad actions, quench the thirst associated with the three realms of existence, and contribute power to good dharmas undertaken for the sake of nirvāṇa.

Just as that good road has an abundance of roots and medicinal herbs along its course by which the traveler will not encounter shortages of those things, so too it is with the path of the ten grounds.

In this case, "roots" signifies whatever is cherished by [virtue of] one's resolute intentions. Just as when roots are established, sprouts, a trunk, branches, leaves, and an abundance of fruit grow forth, so too, when one's resolute intentions cherish the path, they then bring about the growth of right recollective mindfulness, great vows, and the other meritorious qualities.

正體字

090c15 ‖ 藥草名諸波羅蜜。如
090c16 ‖ 藥草能滅諸毒諸波羅蜜藥草滅貪恚癡毒
090c17 ‖ 諸煩惱病亦復如是。如彼好道不失韋婆
090c18 ‖ 陀。則行道安隱。[17]韋陀秦言無對義。是符檄。
090c19 ‖ 如行者不失符檄則在所欲至無有障
090c20 ‖ 礙。十地道亦如是。不失韋婆陀則[18]在所
090c21 ‖ 過諸地所集善根則能隨意助成。增長現
090c22 ‖ 在善根。彼又能教化聲聞道辟支佛道欲[19]界
090c23 ‖ 色界諸天道眾生。令住佛道。若魔若外道不
090c24 ‖ 能干亂。是名不失韋婆陀。如彼好道無有
090c25 ‖ 蚖虺毒虫之屬。十地道亦如是無有憂愁
090c26 ‖ 啼哭之聲。如彼好道無有賊難。十地道亦
090c27 ‖ 如是無有五蓋諸惡賊眾。如佛告比丘。聚
090c28 ‖ 落賊者。所謂五蓋。如賊先奪人物後乃害
090c29 ‖ 命。五蓋賊亦如是。先奪善根後斷慧命。則
091a01 ‖ 墮放逸而死。如道中無師子虎狼諸惡獸
091a02 ‖ 等。十地道亦如是無有瞋恚鬪諍。如師子
091a03 ‖ 等惡獸好惱害他瞋恚等為惱他故生亦
091a04 ‖ 復如是。如惡獸等噉肉飲血。瞋恨等食多
091a05 ‖ 聞慧肉飲修慧等血亦復如是。如彼好道
091a06 ‖ 無有寒熱過惡。十地道亦如是不墮

简体字

药草名诸波罗蜜。如药草能灭诸毒诸波罗蜜药草灭贪恚痴毒诸烦恼病亦复如是。如彼好道不失韦婆陀。则行道安隐。韦陀秦言无对义。是符檄。如行者不失符檄则在所欲至无有障碍。十地道亦如是。不失韦婆陀则在所过诸地所集善根则能随意助成。增长现在善根。彼又能教化声闻道辟支佛道欲界色界诸天道众生。令住佛道。若魔若外道不能干乱。是名不失韦婆陀。如彼好道无有蚖虺毒虫之属。十地道亦如是无有忧愁啼哭之声。如彼好道无有贼难。十地道亦如是无有五盖诸恶贼众。如佛告比丘。聚落贼者。所谓五盖。如贼先夺人物后乃害命。五盖贼亦如是。先夺善根后断慧命。则堕放逸而死。如道中无师子虎狼诸恶兽等。十地道亦如是无有嗔恚斗诤。如师子等恶兽好恼害他嗔恚等为恼他故生亦复如是。如恶兽等啖肉饮血。嗔恨等食多闻慧肉饮修慧等血亦复如是。如彼好道无有寒热过恶。十地道亦如是不堕

Chapter 26 — The Analogy Chapter

"Medicinal herbs" here signifies the *pāramitās*. Just as the medicinal herbs are able to extinguish all manner of toxins, the medicinal herbs of the *pāramitās* are able in this same manner to extinguish the poisons of greed, hatred, and delusion and do away with the sickness associated with the afflictions.

[When one possesses these *pāramitās*] it is analogous to when one travels a good road and makes sure not to lose his passport.[114] He is then able to travel safely along the road.[115] Just as when a traveler who has not lost his passport is able to go wherever he wishes without being obstructed by anyone, so too, on the path of the ten grounds, so long as one does not lose his passport, the roots of goodness gathered while ascending through the grounds are able to freely assist the increase and growth of the roots of goodness that one currently possesses.

One is then also able to teach those beings who presently abide in the paths of *śrāvaka* disciples, *pratyekabuddhas*, and devas of the desire realm and form realm, thereby influencing them to abide in the path to buddhahood. Then, no matter whether it be Māra or some proponent of a non-Buddhist tradition, one cannot be interfered with or disturbed by anyone. This is what is meant by "not losing one's passport."

Just as that good road is free of mosquitoes, horseflies, and the various sorts of poisonous insects, the path of the ten grounds is free of the sounds of sorrow, worry, weeping, and crying. Just as that good road is free of difficulties wrought by bandits, so too is the path of the ten grounds free of the five hindrances' gang of evil thieves. This is just as described by the Buddha when he told the bhikshus, "The thieves in this village are the so-called "five hindrances."[116] Just as thieves start by stealing peoples' possessions, but then later move on to murder, so too it is with the thieves of the five hindrances. They start by stealing one's roots of goodness, but then later cut off the life of one's wisdom with the result that one falls into negligence and finally dies.

Just as that road is free of lions, tigers, wolves, and the various other sorts of fearsome beasts, so too is the path of the ten grounds free of hatred, anger, fighting, and disputation. Just as lions and the other sorts of fearsome beasts enjoy tormenting and harming other beings, so too do hatred, anger, and such arise in order to afflict others in this same way. Just as those fearsome beasts eat flesh and drink blood, so too do hatred, hostility and such consume the flesh of the wisdom that arises from abundant learning. And so too do they drink the blood of the wisdom that arises from cultivation and the other [forms of wisdom][117] in this same manner.

And just as that good road is free of terribly extreme cold and heat, so too, because on the path of the ten grounds one does not fall into the

	寒冰
091a07 ‖	地獄故無有寒過惡。不墮熱地獄故無
091a08 ‖	有熱過惡。如彼好道無深坑等諸難。十地
091a09 ‖	道亦如是無有外道苦行等諸難。所謂[1]灰
091a10 ‖	身入[2]冰拔髮日三洗翹一足。日一食二日
091a11 ‖	一食。乃至一月一食默然至死。常舉一臂
091a12 ‖	常行忍辱。五熱炙身臥刺棘上。入火入水
091a13 ‖	自投高巖。深爐中立牛屎燒身。直趣一方
091a14 ‖	不避諸難。常著[3]濕衣[4]裳。水中臥[5]等。身苦
091a15 ‖	心苦不至正智。無如是等故名為無難。
091a16 ‖	如道無邪徑。十地道亦如是無身口意惡
091a17 ‖	業故名[6]為無邪徑。如道無刺棘者。十地
091a18 ‖	道亦如是無諸業障刺棘故名為無刺棘。
091a19 ‖	如刺刺脚則廢行路。業障刺棘障行佛
091a20 ‖	法入[7]涅槃。

寒冰地狱故无有寒过恶。不堕热地狱故无有热过恶。如彼好道无深坑等诸难。十地道亦如是无有外道苦行等诸难。所谓灰身入冰拔发日三洗翘一足。日一食二日一食。乃至一月一食默然至死。常举一臂常行忍辱。五热炙身卧刺棘上。入火入水自投高岩。深炉中立牛屎烧身。直趣一方不避诸难。常着湿衣裳。水中卧等。身苦心苦不至正智。无如是等故名为无难。如道无邪径。十地道亦如是无身口意恶业故名为无邪径。如道无刺棘者。十地道亦如是无诸业障刺棘故名为无刺棘。如刺刺脚则废行路。业障刺棘障行佛法入涅槃。

hells of cold and ice, it is free of terribly extreme cold. And because one does not fall into the hot hells, it is free of terribly extreme heat.

Just as that good road is free of deep chasms and other such difficulties, so too is the path of the ten grounds free of the difficulties inherent in the ascetic practices of the non-Buddhist traditions such as:

Coating the body with ashes;
Plunging into ice;
Pulling out one's hair;
Bathing three times each day;
Standing on one foot;
Eating one meal the first day, then one meal every two days, and so forth until one goes a month on only one meal;
Taking a life-long vow of silence;
Always holding up one arm;
Always practicing endurance by subjecting one's body to the five kinds of fire;
Lying down on beds of nails:
Plunging into fire;
Plunging into water;
Throwing oneself off of high cliffs;
Burning one's body by standing in a deep cauldron of cattle excrement;
Going straight off in one direction without avoiding any difficulties one might encounter;
Always wearing wet clothes;
Lying down in water;
Or subjecting oneself to any of the other sorts of physical or mental sufferings.

None of these lead to right wisdom. Because [the path of the ten grounds] is free of such things, it is said to be free of difficulties.

Just as that road is free of deviating pathways, so too it is with the path of the ten grounds. It is because it is free of evil actions of body, mouth, or mind that it is said to be free of deviating pathways.

Just as that road is free of thorny underbrush, so too it is with the path of the ten grounds. It is because it is free of the thorny underbrush of karmic obstacles that it is said to be free of thorny underbrush. Just as when thorns pierce one's feet, one is then prevented from traveling along that road, so too, the thorny underbrush of karmic obstacles impede one's ability to practice the Dharma of the Buddha and thus reach nirvāṇa.

正體字

```
              如道正直。十地道亦如是無
091a21 ‖ 一切諂曲欺誑故名為正直。如道少岐道。
091a22 ‖ 十地道亦如是少於異道。何以故。發大乘
091a23 ‖ 者少行聲聞辟支佛道。是故少於異道。或
091a24 ‖ 有菩薩行二乘道者。當知未到菩薩地。
091a25 ‖ 未入正位。行於邊行故。如彼好道無諸叢
091a26 ‖ 林妨礙。十住道亦如是無有五欲諸惡叢
091a27 ‖ 林。問曰。何故不言都無五欲叢林但言無
091a28 ‖ 惡林耶。答曰。發大乘者。福德因緣有第一
091a29 ‖ 五欲。是故不得言無。但無惡耳。復次如深
091b01 ‖ 叢林。難入難過多諸[8]難礙。菩薩五欲則不
091b02 ‖ 然。不如凡夫於五欲生諸過惡。如是故
091b03 ‖ 但說無叢林。[9]如道寬博多容不相妨礙。十
091b04 ‖ 住道亦如是多所容受。無量百千萬億眾
091b05 ‖ 生共發無上道心而不相妨[10]礙。是百千萬
091b06 ‖ 億眾生[11]若一切眾生[12]俱發阿耨多羅三藐
091b07 ‖ 三菩提心。同行此道不相妨礙。如道多人
091b08 ‖ 所行。十住道亦如是恒河沙等過去現在諸
091b09 ‖ 佛。行菩薩道時皆行此道。
```

简体字

如道正直。十地道亦如是无一切谄曲欺诳故名为正直。如道少岐道。十地道亦如是少于异道。何以故。发大乘者少行声闻辟支佛道。是故少于异道。或有菩萨行二乘道者。当知未到菩萨地。未入正位。行于边行故。如彼好道无诸丛林妨碍。十住道亦如是无有五欲诸恶丛林。问曰。何故不言都无五欲丛林但言无恶林耶。答曰。发大乘者。福德因缘有第一五欲。是故不得言无。但无恶耳。复次如深丛林。难入难过多诸难碍。菩萨五欲则不然。不如凡夫于五欲生诸过恶。如是故但说无丛林。如道宽博多容不相妨碍。十住道亦如是多所容受。无量百千万亿众生共发无上道心而不相妨碍。是百千万亿众生若一切众生俱发阿耨多罗三藐三菩提心。同行此道不相妨碍。如道多人所行。十住道亦如是恒河沙等过去现在诸佛。行菩萨道时皆行此道。

Chapter 26 — *The Analogy Chapter*

Just as that road is straight and direct, so too it is with the path of the ten grounds. It is because it is free of any ingratiating flattery, deviousness, cheating, or deception that it is said to be straight and direct.

Just as that road has but few forks in it, so too it is with the path of the ten grounds, for it has but few variant paths. How is this so? Those who have set out along the path of the Great Vehicle travel but little on the pathways of *śrāvaka* disciples and *pratyekabuddhas*. Hence there is but little involvement with variant paths. Where there may be cases in which a bodhisattva travels along in the path of those two vehicles, one should realize that he has not yet established himself on the grounds of a bodhisattva. Because he has not yet entered the right and fixed position,[118] he engages in those peripheral practices.

Just as that good path is free of jungles that obstruct the way, so too it is with the path of the ten grounds. It is free of the jungles of evils associated with the five objects of desire.

Question: Why did you not just state that it is free of *all* jungles associated with the five objects of desire, but instead only stated that it is free of the jungles of "evils" [associated with the five objects of desire]?

Response: For one who has set out in the Great Vehicle, the causes and conditions of one's merit conduce to possession of the foremost objects of the five desires. Consequently one cannot say that they are utterly nonexistent. It is just that those associated with evil are nonexistent.

Moreover, in the case of a deep jungle, it is difficult to enter, difficult to pass through, and possessed of a multitude of difficult obstructions. The objects of the five desires as encountered by the bodhisattva are not of this sort. He is not like the foolish common person who creates all manner of transgressions in association with the objects of the five desires. Because this is the case, it was only stated here that [the path of the ten grounds] is free of [such evil] jungles.

Just as that road is wide, accommodating of many people, and not conducive to mutual interference, so too is the path of the ten grounds able to accommodate many people, for the countless hundreds of thousands of myriads of *koṭis* of beings could all bring forth the resolve to embark upon this unsurpassable path and there would still be no mutual interference among these hundreds of thousands of myriads of *koṭis* of beings. In fact, all beings could bring forth the resolve to attain *anuttarasamyaksaṃbodhi* and they could all still travel together along this path and there would still be no mutual interference.

Just as that road is one along which many people travel, so too it is with the path of the ten grounds. When they were still cultivating the bodhisattva path, past and present buddhas as numerous as the sands of the Ganges all traveled along this path.

正體字

```
        如彼好道行不
091b10 ‖ 疲厭。十住道亦如是多有因果諸樂。所謂
091b11 ‖ 多生人天中受果報。樂離欲故受歡喜樂
091b12 ‖ 禪定樂無喜樂現在樂。得是諸樂故無有
091b13 ‖ 疲厭。[13]如道多有華果根。十住道亦如是多
091b14 ‖ 根華果。根者三善根。華者七覺華是。如經說。
091b15 ‖ 七華者七覺意是。果者四沙門果[14]是。無如
091b16 ‖ 是等違好道功德過故。名為離惡。如導師
091b17 ‖ 知道中是中應食是應宿彼處亦應宿。菩
091b18 ‖ 薩行十地亦如是知何處可宿何處可食。
091b19 ‖ [15]可宿名有諸現在佛處。可食名可得修
091b20 ‖ 習善法處。如食能利益諸根亦助壽命。
091b21 ‖ 諸善法亦如是。能益信等諸根助成慧命。
091b22 ‖ 異處宿名從彼佛所至餘佛所。復次此佛
091b23 ‖ 國土彼佛國土中間亦名異處。善知道轉
091b24 ‖ 者。如彼導師知道不安隱則[16]轉。菩薩亦如
091b25 ‖ 是。善知是道至聲聞。是道至辟支佛。是道
091b26 ‖ 至佛。
```

简体字

如彼好道行不疲厌。十住道亦如是多有因果诸乐。所谓多生人天中受果报。乐离欲故受欢喜乐禅定乐无喜乐现在乐。得是诸乐故无有疲厌。如道多有华果根。十住道亦如是多根华果。根者三善根。华者七觉华是。如经说。七华者七觉意是。果者四沙门果是。无如是等违好道功德过故。名为离恶。如导师知道中是中应食是应宿彼处亦应宿。菩萨行十地亦如是知何处可宿何处可食。可宿名有诸现在佛处。可食名可得修习善法处。如食能利益诸根亦助寿命。诸善法亦如是。能益信等诸根助成慧命。异处宿名从彼佛所至余佛所。复次此佛国土彼佛国土中间亦名异处。善知道转者。如彼导师知道不安隐则转。菩萨亦如是。善知是道至声闻。是道至辟支佛。是道至佛。

Just as that good road admits of travel without weariness or exhaustion, so too it is with the path of the ten grounds, for this path is associated with abundant bliss produced through cause and effect. For instance, bliss is enjoyed when one is often born into the realms of humans and devas and then enjoys one's karmic rewards there. Because [the practitioner] delights in the abandonment of desire, he then experiences joy and bliss, the bliss of *dhyāna* concentration, the bliss that is free of joy, and the bliss experienced in abiding in this present moment. Because one acquires these various sorts of bliss, one is free of weariness or exhaustion.

Just as that path has along its course an abundance of flowers, fruit, and roots, so too does the path of the ten grounds also possess an abundance of roots, flowers, and fruit. "Roots" refers here to the three types of good roots. "Flowers" refers to the flowers of the seven limbs of bodhi. This is as stated in the sutras where it says, "The seven types of flowers are the seven limbs of bodhi." "Fruit" refers to the four fruits of the *śramaṇa*.

Because one is free of any of these faults that would obstruct the attainment of meritorious qualities as one courses along this good path, one is said to have abandoned evil.

Just as that guide knows with respect to that road that one should stop and eat here, that one should spend the night here, and that one should then stop for the night there, so too it is with a bodhisattva as he travels through the ten grounds wherein he knows in which place one may stop for the night and knows in which place one may eat.

"Where one may stop for the night" refers to those places where buddhas of the present now dwell. "Where one may eat" refers to where one can cultivate the practice of good dharmas.

Just as eating is able to benefit all of one's faculties and also assists the fulfillment of one's life span, so too it is with good dharmas. They are able to increase faith and the rest of those faculties[119] while also assisting the fulfillment of one's wisdom life.

"Spending the night in another place" is a reference to going from the dwelling place of that buddha to the dwelling place of yet another buddha. Also, one may interpret "another place" as signifying the places in between this buddha's land and that buddha's land.

"Knowing well where to make a turn in the road" refers for example to when a guide recognizes that a road has become unsafe and so then takes a turn. So too it is with a bodhisattva. He knows that this particular path takes one into the realm of the *śrāvaka* disciples, that this other path takes one into the realm of the *pratyekabuddhas,* and that this other path takes one to the realization of buddhahood. Having

正體字

```
          如是知已。捨聲聞道辟支佛道。但行
091b27 ‖  至佛道。如彼好道多有飲食。十住道亦如
091b28 ‖  是多行布施持戒修禪。如彼導師以多財
091b29 ‖  物善能治法有大勢力。菩薩亦如是有財
091c01 ‖  物治法故有大勢力。財者七財。所謂信戒
091c02 ‖  慚愧捨聞慧。治法者。一切[17]魔種種沙門婆羅
091c03 ‖  門外道論師悉能摧伏。是為威勢。如彼大城
091c04 ‖  無有怨賊疫病暴死種種衰惱故。名為安
091c05 ‖  隱。涅槃大城亦如是。無有諸魔外道諸流
091c06 ‖  貪欲瞋恚放逸死憂悲苦惱啼哭故。名為安
091c07 ‖  隱。如彼大城多有飲食故名為豐饒。涅槃
091c08 ‖  城亦如是。多有諸深禪定解脫三昧故。名
091c09 ‖  為豐饒。如彼大城多所容受故名為大
091c10 ‖  城。涅槃城亦如是。多受眾生故名為大。假
091c11 ‖  令一切眾生不受諸法故。皆入無餘涅槃。
091c12 ‖  而涅槃性無增無減。如彼導師能將多眾
091c13 ‖  [18]安隱示好道故。名為導師。菩薩亦如是。
091c14 ‖  善將眾生示佛[19]法示[20]涅槃。從生死險道
091c15 ‖  得至涅槃故。名為大導師。如彼導師善知
091c16 ‖  道相故。身及餘人皆無有惡。菩薩亦如是。
```

简体字

如是知已。舍声闻道辟支佛道。但行至佛道。如彼好道多有饮食。十住道亦如是多行布施持戒修禅。如彼导师以多财物善能治法有大势力。菩萨亦如是有财物治法故有大势力。财者七财。所谓信戒惭愧舍闻慧。治法者。一切魔种种沙门婆罗门外道论师悉能摧伏。是为威势。如彼大城无有怨贼疫病暴死种种衰恼故。名为安隐。涅槃大城亦如是。无有诸魔外道诸流贪欲嗔恚放逸死忧悲苦恼啼哭故。名为安隐。如彼大城多有饮食故名为丰饶。涅槃城亦如是。多有诸深禅定解脱三昧故。名为丰饶。如彼大城多所容受故名为大城。涅槃城亦如是。多受众生故名为大。假令一切众生不受诸法故。皆入无余涅槃。而涅槃性无增无减。如彼导师能将多众安隐示好道故。名为导师。菩萨亦如是。善将众生示佛法示涅槃。从生死险道得至涅槃故。名为大导师。如彼导师善知道相故。身及余人皆无有恶。菩萨亦如是。

realized this, he relinquishes the paths of *śrāvaka* disciples and *pratyekabuddhas* and thenceforth travels solely along the path to buddhahood.

Just as that good road has much to eat and drink along the way, so too the path of the ten grounds provides sustenance through the abundant practice of giving, moral virtue, and cultivation of the *dhyāna* concentrations.

Just as that guide has great power because he has abundant wealth and is well able to use the means for maintaining order, so too does the bodhisattva also have great power because he has wealth and the means for maintaining order.

"Wealth" here refers to the seven kinds of wealth, namely: faith, [adherence to] moral precepts, a sense of shame, a dread of blame, relinquishing, learning, and wisdom.

"Means for maintaining order" refers to the ability to defeat all challenges from any *māra* or from any of the various sorts of *śramaṇas*, brahmans, or non-Buddhist treatise masters. This is what is meant by "awesome strength."

Just as that great city is deemed to be safe and secure because it is free of bandits, pestilence, the causes of violent death, and the many different sorts of distress, so too is the great city of nirvāṇa deemed to be safe and secure, this because it is free of *māras*, non-Buddhists, the contaminants, greed, hatred, neglectfulness, death, sorrow, grief, suffering, anguish, and lamentation.

Just as that great city, because it has an abundance of food and drink, is deemed to be bountiful, so too is the city of nirvāṇa deemed to be bountiful because it has an abundance of deep *dhyāna* absorptions, liberations, and samādhis.

Just as that great city, because it is able to accommodate many people, is said therefore to be a great city, so too is the city of nirvāṇa deemed to be great because it is able to accommodate many beings. If one could cause all beings to enter the nirvāṇa without residue through their nonacceptance of any dharmas [as inherently existent], the nature of nirvāṇa would still neither increase nor decrease.

Just as that guide is deemed to be a guide because he is able to lead many groups of people to safety and security by showing them the good road, so too is a bodhisattva also deemed to be a great guide, for he is able to lead forth beings, showing them the Dharma of the Buddha, showing them nirvāṇa, and guiding them out from the hazardous road of *saṃsāra* so that they successfully reach nirvāṇa.

And just as that guide, because he so well knows the signs all along that road, is able to ensure that he himself as well as the rest of his group do not encounter any calamities, so too it is with the bodhisattva.

| 正體字 | 091c17 ‖ 自不行貪瞋恚等諸蓋諸惡苦行老死深坑。
091c18 ‖ 亦不墮寒熱地獄餓鬼故。名為自不得惡
091c19 ‖ 所隨從者亦不得惡。是故偈中說善知道
091c20 ‖ 相故。自不得惡餘不得惡。[21] |

| 简体字 | 自不行贪嗔恚等诸盖诸恶苦行老死深坑。亦不堕寒热地狱饿鬼故。名为自不得恶所随从者亦不得恶。是故偈中说善知道相故。自不得恶余不得恶。|

Because he himself does not course in desire, ill will, or the other hindrances, because he does not practice bad ascetic practices, because he does not fall into the deep pit of aging and death, and because he also does not fall into the hot hells, the cold hells or the realms of the hungry ghosts, he is deemed to be one who does not encounter calamities himself while ensuring that his followers do not encounter calamities, either.

It is for these reasons that the verse says that it is due to knowing well the signs along the path that [the guide] does not encounter any calamities himself, nor do any of the others encounter calamities, either.

The End of Chapter Twenty-Six

正體字

091c21 ‖	**[22]**略行品第二十七
091c22 ‖	菩薩歡喜地　　今已略說竟
091c23 ‖	菩薩住是中　　多作閻浮王
091c24 ‖	常離慳貪垢　　不失三寶念
091c25 ‖	心常願作佛　　救護諸眾生
091c26 ‖	初地名歡喜。已略說竟。諸佛法無量無邊是
091c27 ‖	地為本。若廣說亦無量無邊。是故言略說。
091c28 ‖	菩薩住是地中。多作閻浮提勢力轉輪王。先
091c29 ‖	世修習是地因緣故。信樂布施無慳貪垢。
092a01 ‖	常施三寶故不失三寶念。常念作佛救諸
092a02 ‖	眾生。如是等善念常在心中。復次。
092a03 ‖	若欲得出家　　勤心行精進
092a04 ‖	能得數百定　　得見數百佛
092a05 ‖	能動百世界　　飛行亦如是
092a06 ‖	若欲放光明　　能照百世界
092a07 ‖	化數百種人　　能住壽百劫
092a08 ‖	能[1]擇數百法　　能變作百身

简体字

十住毗婆沙论卷第十二
略行品第二十七

　　菩萨欢喜地　　今已略说竟
　　菩萨住是中　　多作阎浮王
　　常离悭贪垢　　不失三宝念
　　心常愿作佛　　救护诸众生

初地名欢喜。已略说竟。诸佛法无量无边是地为本。若广说亦无量无边。是故言略说。菩萨住是地中。多作阎浮提势力转轮王。先世修习是地因缘故。信乐布施无悭贪垢。常施三宝故不失三宝念。常念作佛救诸众生。如是等善念常在心中。复次。

　　若欲得出家　　勤心行精进
　　能得数百定　　得见数百佛
　　能动百世界　　飞行亦如是
　　若欲放光明　　能照百世界
　　化数百种人　　能住寿百劫
　　能择数百法　　能变作百身
　　能化百菩萨　　示现为眷属

Chapter 27
A Summarizing Discussion of the Bodhisattva Practices

VII. Chapter 27: A Summarizing Discussion of Bodhisattva Practices
  A. A Brief Presentation Intended to Finish the First Ground Discussion

> We have now come to the end of the general explanation
> of the bodhisattva's Ground of Joyfulness
> The bodhisattva who abides herein
> often becomes a monarch who rules over Jambudvīpa.
>
> He is ever distant from the defilements of greed and desire,
> and never fails in his recollection of the Three Jewels.
> His mind always aspires to become a buddha
> and to rescue and protect all beings.

The first ground is known as the Ground of Joyfulness. We have come to the end of its general explanation. All of the measureless and boundless dharmas of all buddhas take this very ground as their foundation. Were one to take up an expansive discussion of it, that too would become measureless and boundless. Hence we speak here of a "summarizing" explanation.

The bodhisattva who abides on this ground will often serve as a powerful wheel-turning monarch reigning over the entire continent of Jambudvīpa. Due to having cultivated the causes and conditions for this ground in previous lives, he has a resolute belief in the practice of giving and is free of the defilement of miserliness. Because he is always gives to the Three Jewels, he never fails in his recollection of the Three Jewels. He always bears in mind his resolve to become a buddha and to rescue and protect all beings. Good thoughts such as these are always in his mind.

Additionally:

> If he aspires to leave behind the home life
> and then diligently practices vigor,
> he is able to acquire several hundred meditative concentrations,
> and is able to see several hundred buddhas.
>
> He is able to shake a hundred worlds,
> and his ability to travel [to other worlds] is also of this sort.
> If he wishes to emanate radiant light,
> he is able to illuminate a hundred worlds.

正體字

```
092a09 ‖    能化百菩薩      示現為眷屬
092a10 ‖    利根過是數      [2]依佛神力故
092a11 ‖    已說初地相      果力淨治法
092a12 ‖    今當復更說      第二無垢地
092a13 ‖ 果名得數百定見數百佛等。勢力名能化
092a14 ‖ 數百眾生。餘偈義[3]先已說。不復解餘偈。今
092a15 ‖ 當復說第二無垢地。問曰。汝欲廣說菩薩
092a16 ‖ 所行法。初地義尚多。諸學者恐轉增廣則懈
092a17 ‖ 怠心生不能讀誦。是故汝今應為不能多
092a18 ‖ 讀誦者。略解菩薩所行諸法。答曰。
092a19 ‖    菩薩所有法      是法皆應行
092a20 ‖    一切惡應捨      是則名略說
092a21 ‖ 如上來諸[4]品所說。能生能增長諸地法。如
092a22 ‖ 上諸品中說。若於餘處說者。
```

简体字

　　利根过是数　　依佛神力故
　　已说初地相　　果力净治法
　　今当复更说　　第二无垢地

　果名得数百定见数百佛等。势力名能化数百众生。余偈义先已说。不复解余偈。今当复说第二无垢地。问曰。汝欲广说菩萨所行法。初地义尚多。诸学者恐转增广则懈怠心生不能读诵。是故汝今应为不能多读诵者。略解菩萨所行诸法。答曰。

　　菩萨所有法　　是法皆应行
　　一切恶应舍　　是则名略说

　如上来诸品所说。能生能增长诸地法。如上诸品中说。若于余处说者。

Chapter 27 — A Summarizing Discussion of the Bodhisattva Practices

> He creates transformation bodies of several hundred kinds of people
> and can remain for a life span of a hundred kalpas.
> He is able to selectively investigate several hundred dharmas
> and is able to manifest a hundred transformation bodies,
>
> He is able to transformationally create a hundred bodhisattvas
> that manifest as his retinue.
> Those of sharp faculties can exceed these numbers
> through relying on the Buddha's spiritual powers.
>
> Having already explained the first ground's characteristic features,
> its fruits, its powers, and the dharmas used in its purification,
> We shall now also present an explanation
> of the second ground, the Ground of Stainlessness.

"Fruits" refers to the acquisition of several hundred meditative absorptions, the ability to see several hundred buddhas, and so forth. "Powers" refers to the ability to manifest as several hundred [kinds of] beings, and so forth. The meanings implicit in the rest of the verse have already been explained. Hence we shall not proceed with an explanation of the rest of the verse but rather shall now discuss the second ground, the Ground of Stainlessness.

B. Q: Before Finishing, Please Summarize the Bodhisattva Path

Question: You wish to present an expansive discussion of the dharmas practiced by the bodhisattva. There are still many [additional] meanings pertaining to the first ground. It is to be feared that, if the discussion becomes ever more expansive, those attempting to study this will become prone to indolent thoughts that could impair their ability to study and recite this. Therefore, for the sake of those unable to [memorize and] recite a more [extensive explanation], you should now [instead] present a summarizing explanation of the dharmas practiced by the bodhisattva.

C. A: A Series of Statements Summarizing the Bodhisattva Practices
1. Practice All Bodhisattva Dharmas & Abandon All Transgressions

Response:
> All dharmas of the bodhisattva—
> these dharmas should all be practiced.
> All forms of evil should be relinquished.
> This is what constitutes the summarizing explanation.

Dharmas such as those explained in preceding chapters are able to produce and are able to instigate growth in the dharmas pertaining to the [bodhisattva] grounds. Also, if dharmas such as those explained in previous chapters have been explained elsewhere, one should cause

正體字	
	皆應令生菩
092a23‖	薩過惡事皆應遠離。是名略說菩薩所應
092a24‖	行。如法句中說。諸惡莫作諸善奉行自淨
092a25‖	其意是諸佛教。有一法攝佛道。菩薩應行。
092a26‖	云何為一。所謂於善法中一心不放逸。如
092a27‖	佛告阿難。我不放逸故。得阿耨多羅三藐
092a28‖	三菩提。如說。
092a29‖	不放逸成佛　　世間無與等
092b01‖	若能不放逸　　何事而不成
092b02‖	復有二法能攝佛道。一不放逸。二智慧。如
092b03‖	說。
092b04‖	不放逸智慧　　佛說是利門
092b05‖	不見不放逸　　而事不成者
092b06‖	復有三法能攝佛道。一學勝戒。二學勝心。
092b07‖	三學勝慧。如說。
092b08‖	戒生上三昧　　三昧生智慧
092b09‖	智散諸煩惱　　如風吹浮雲

简体字

皆应令生菩萨过恶事皆应远离。是名略说菩萨所应行。如法句中说。诸恶莫作诸善奉行自净其意是诸佛教。有一法摄佛道。菩萨应行。云何为一。所谓于善法中一心不放逸。如佛告阿难。我不放逸故。得阿耨多罗三藐三菩提。如说。

　不放逸成佛　　世间无与等
　若能不放逸　　何事而不成

复有二法能摄佛道。一不放逸。二智慧。如说。

　不放逸智慧　　佛说是利门
　不见不放逸　　而事不成者

复有三法能摄佛道。一学胜戒。二学胜心。三学胜慧。如说。

　戒生上三昧　　三昧生智慧
　智散诸烦恼　　如风吹浮云

Chapter 27 — A Summarizing Discussion of the Bodhisattva Practices

all of those dharmas to arise as well. One should abandon all endeavors involving bodhisattva transgressions. This is what constitutes the summarizing explanation of what the bodhisattva should practice. This is as taught in the *Dharmapada*:

> To refrain from doing any manner of evil,
> to respectfully perform all varieties of good,
> and to carry out the purification of one's own mind—
> This is the teaching of all Buddhas.

2. Be Single-Minded and Non-Neglectful in Practicing Good Dharmas

There is one dharma that subsumes the path to buddhahood and that is what the bodhisattva should practice. And what is that singular teaching? It is what is referred to as being single-minded and non-neglectful in the cultivation of good dharmas. As the Buddha told Ānanda: "It is due to not being neglectful that I attained *anuttarasamyaksaṃbodhi*." This is as described here:

> It is through non-neglectfulness that one becomes a buddha,
> one who is unmatched by anyone anywhere in the world.
> If one is simply able to refrain from neglectfulness,
> what endeavor could one fail to achieve?

3. Two Dharmas That Subsume the Path to Buddhahood

There are also two dharmas that are able to subsume the path to buddhahood, namely:

First, non-neglectfulness;
And second, wisdom.

These are as described below:

> Non-neglectfulness and wisdom—
> The Buddha spoke of these as gateways to benefit.
> One does not see instances wherein one avoids neglectfulness,
> and yet those endeavors still fail to succeed.

4. Three Dharmas That Subsume the Path to Buddhahood

There are also three dharmas that are able to subsume the path to buddhahood, namely:

First, training in the supreme moral virtue;
Second, training in the supreme mind;
And third, training in the supreme wisdom.

These are as described below:

> Moral virtue produces superior samādhi,
> samādhi produces wisdom,
> and wisdom scatters the afflictions
> just as wind blows away floating clouds.

正體字

092b10 ‖ 復有四法能攝佛道。一諦處。二捨處。三滅
092b11 ‖ 處。四慧處。如說。
092b12 ‖ 　諦捨定具足　　得慧利清淨
092b13 ‖ 　精進求佛道　　當集此四法
092b14 ‖ 復有五法能攝佛道。一信根。二精進根。三
092b15 ‖ [5]念根。四定根。五慧根。如說。
092b16 ‖ 　信根精進根　　念定慧堅牢
092b17 ‖ 　是法大悲合　　終不退佛道
092b18 ‖ 　如人得五根　　能通達五塵
092b19 ‖ 　如得信等根　　能通諸法相
092b20 ‖ 復有六法能攝佛道。所謂布施持戒忍辱精
092b21 ‖ 進禪定智慧波羅蜜。

简体字

复有四法能摄佛道。一谛处。二舍处。三灭处。四慧处。如说。
　谛舍定具足　　得慧利清净
　精进求佛道　　当集此四法
复有五法能摄佛道。一信根。二精进根。三念根。四定根。五慧根。如说。
　信根精进根　　念定慧坚牢
　是法大悲合　　终不退佛道
　如人得五根　　能通达五尘
　如得信等根　　能通诸法相
复有六法能摄佛道。所谓布施持戒忍辱精进禅定智慧波罗蜜。

Chapter 27 — *A Summarizing Discussion of the Bodhisattva Practices* 939

5. FOUR DHARMAS THAT SUBSUME THE PATH TO BUDDHAHOOD

There are also four dharmas that are able to subsume the path to buddhahood, namely [the four bases of meritorious qualities]:

First, the truth basis;
Second, the relinquishment basis;
Third, the quiescence basis;
And fourth, the wisdom basis.

These are as described below:

By perfecting truth, relinquishment, and meditative concentration,
one acquires the pure benefits of wisdom.
One who vigorously pursues the path to buddhahood
should gather together these four dharmas.

6. FIVE DHARMAS THAT SUBSUME THE PATH TO BUDDHAHOOD

There are also five dharmas that are able to subsume the path to buddhahood, namely:

First, the faculty of faith;
Second, the faculty of vigor;
Third, the faculty of mindfulness;
Fourth, the faculty of meditative concentration;
And fifth, the faculty of wisdom.

These are as described below:

Through the faculty of faith and the faculty of vigor,
mindfulness, concentration, and wisdom are solid and durable.
Once these dharmas are joined with the great compassion,
one will never retreat from the path to buddhahood.

Just as a person who acquires the five sense faculties
is then able to completely comprehend the five sense objects,
similarly, if one acquires faith and the rest of the [five] faculties,
he is then able to know the [true] character of all dharmas.

7. SIX DHARMAS THAT SUBSUME THE PATH TO BUDDHAHOOD

There are also six dharmas that are able to subsume the path to buddhahood, namely the *pāramitās*:

Giving;
Moral virtue;
Patience;
Vigor;
Dhyāna concentration;
And wisdom.

正體字	
	如說。
092b22 ‖	如所說六度　　降伏諸煩惱
092b23 ‖	常增長善根　　不久當得佛
092b24 ‖	復有七法能攝佛道。所謂七正法。信慚愧
092b25 ‖	聞精進念慧。如說。
092b26 ‖	欲得七正法　　當樂定精進
092b27 ‖	除去七邪法　　能知諸功德
092b28 ‖	是人能疾得　　無上佛菩提
092b29 ‖	拔沒生死者　　令在安隱處
092c01 ‖	復有八法能攝佛道。所謂八大人覺。少欲
092c02 ‖	知足遠離精進念定慧樂不戲論。如說。
092c03 ‖	若人決定心　　住八大人覺
092c04 ‖	為求佛道故　　除諸惡覺觀

简体字

如说。
　　如所说六度　　降伏诸烦恼
　　常增长善根　　不久当得佛
　　复有七法能摄佛道。所谓七正法。信惭愧闻精进念慧。如说。
　　欲得七正法　　当乐定精进
　　除去七邪法　　能知诸功德
　　是人能疾得　　无上佛菩提
　　拔没生死者　　令在安隐处
　　复有八法能摄佛道。所谓八大人觉。少欲知足远离精进念定慧乐不戏论。如说。
　　若人决定心　　住八大人觉
　　为求佛道故　　除诸恶觉观

Chapter 27 — A Summarizing Discussion of the Bodhisattva Practices

These are as described below:

> If [one practices] the six perfections as explained,
> one will overcome the afflictions,
> will always bring about the growth of the roots of goodness,
> and, before long, will succeed in attaining buddhahood.

8. Seven Dharmas That Subsume the Path to Buddhahood

There are also seven dharmas that are able to subsume the path to buddhahood, namely the so-called "seven right dharmas":

Faith;
A sense of shame;
A dread of blame;
Extensive learning;
Vigor;
Mindfulness;
And wisdom.

These are as described below:

> One who aspires to acquire the seven right dharmas
> should delight in meditative concentration pursued with vigor.
> If one rids himself of the seven wrong dharmas,
> he will be able to know all the meritorious qualities.

> Such a person will be able to rapidly acquire
> the unsurpassable bodhi of the Buddha,
> extricate those sunken in *saṃsāra*,
> and cause them then to reside in the safe and secure abode.

9. Eight Dharmas That Subsume the Path to Buddhahood

There are also eight dharmas that are able to subsume the path to buddhahood, namely the so-called "eight types of thought of great men," namely:

Having but few desires;
Being easily satisfied;
Renunciation;
Vigor;
Mindfulness;
Meditative concentration;
Wisdom;
And delighting in the avoidance of mere conceptual elaboration.

These are as described below:

> If someone forms the definite resolve
> to abide in the eight types of thought of great men, and then,
> in order to pursue the path to buddhahood,
> rids himself of the bad forms of ideation and reflection,

正體字

092c05 ‖　　如是則不久　　疾[6]得無上道
092c06 ‖　　如人行善者　　必當得妙果
092c07 ‖　復有九法能攝佛道。所謂大忍大慈大悲慧
092c08 ‖　念堅心不貪不恚不癡。如說。
092c09 ‖　　具足於大忍　　大慈及大悲
092c10 ‖　　又能住於慧　　念及堅心中
092c11 ‖　　深心入無貪　　無恚癡善根
092c12 ‖　　若能如是者　　佛道則在手
092c13 ‖　復有十法能攝佛道。所謂十善道。自不殺
092c14 ‖　生不教他殺見殺心不稱讚見殺心不
092c15 ‖　喜。乃至邪見亦如是。以是福德迴向阿耨
092c16 ‖　多羅三藐三菩提。如說。
092c17 ‖　　不惱害眾生　　亦不行劫盜
092c18 ‖　　不婬犯他婦　　是三為身業

简体字

　　如是则不久　　疾得无上道
　　如人行善者　　必当得妙果
　复有九法能摄佛道。所谓大忍大慈大悲慧念坚心不贪不恚不痴。如说。
　　具足于大忍　　大慈及大悲
　　又能住于慧　　念及坚心中
　　深心入无贪　　无恚痴善根
　　若能如是者　　佛道则在手
　复有十法能摄佛道。所谓十善道。自不杀生不教他杀见杀心不称赞见杀心不喜。乃至邪见亦如是。以是福德回向阿耨多罗三藐三菩提。如说。
　　不恼害众生　　亦不行劫盗
　　不淫犯他妇　　是三为身业

Chapter 27 — *A Summarizing Discussion of the Bodhisattva Practices*   943

> by proceeding in this manner, before long,
> he will swiftly gain the unsurpassable path.
> This is just as when someone practices goodness:
> He is certainly bound to gain the sublime fruits [of the path].

10. NINE DHARMAS THAT SUBSUME THE PATH TO BUDDHAHOOD

There are also nine dharmas that are able to subsume the path to buddhahood, namely:

> Great patience;
> Great kindness;
> Great compassion;
> Wisdom;
> Mindfulness;
> Solid resolve;
> Non-greed;
> Non-hatred;
> And non-delusion.

These are as described below:

> If one is well equipped with great patience,
> great kindness, and great compassion,
> and is also able to abide in wisdom,
> mindfulness, and solid resolve—
>
> If with resolute intentions one enters the good roots
> of non-greed, non-hatred, and non-delusion—
> If one is able to act in this manner,
> the path to buddhahood will then be in the palm of one's hand.

11. TEN DHARMAS THAT SUBSUME THE PATH TO BUDDHAHOOD

There are also ten dharmas that are able to subsume the path to buddhahood, namely the ten courses of good karmic action. [In the case of the first of them, these include]: not killing any being oneself, not instructing others to kill, not praising any killing that one observes, and not delighting in any killing [carried out by others]. And so the list continues similarly until we come to [the tenth], not holding wrong views. One then dedicates the merit [of adhering to these ten courses of good karmic action] to the attainment of *anuttarasamyaksaṃbodhi*. These are as described below:

> One does not harass or harm any living being,
> nor does one engage in any robbery or theft,
> nor does one indulge in any sexual transgressions with another's wife.
> These are the three concerned with the karmic actions of the body.

正體字	
092c19 ‖ 不妄語兩舌	不惡口綺語
092c20 ‖ 不貪惱邪見	是七口意行
092c21 ‖ 如是則能開	無上佛道門
092c22 ‖ 若欲得佛者	當行是初門

092c23 ‖ 如是等法菩薩應生。生已應守護。守護已
092c24 ‖ 應增長。於一[7]善事從一轉增。亦應當知。
092c25 ‖ 求佛道者。於一惡法應疾遠離。所謂遠
092c26 ‖ 離[8]不放逸。如說。

092c27 ‖ 若人不能度	生死險惡道
092c28 ‖ 是為可呵責	最是罪惡事
092c29 ‖ 雖樂於富樂	而生貧賤家
093a01 ‖ 不能種善[1]根	為人作奴僕
093a02 ‖ 皆由於放逸	因緣之所致
093a03 ‖ 是故有智者	疾遠如惡毒
093a04 ‖ 若未成大悲	無生忍不退
093a05 ‖ 而行放逸者	是則名為死

093a06 ‖ 復有二過應疾遠離。一貪聲聞地。二貪辟
093a07 ‖ 支地。如佛說。

简体字

不妄语两舌　　不恶口绮语
不贪恼邪见　　是七口意行
如是则能开　　无上佛道门
若欲得佛者　　当行是初门

如是等法菩萨应生。生已应守护。守护已应增长。于一善事从一转增。亦应当知。求佛道者。于一恶法应疾远离。所谓远离不放逸。如说。

若人不能度　　生死险恶道
是为可呵责　　最是罪恶事
虽乐于富乐　　而生贫贱家
不能种善根　　为人作奴仆
皆由于放逸　　因缘之所致
是故有智者　　疾远如恶毒
若未成大悲　　无生忍不退
而行放逸者　　是则名为死

复有二过应疾远离。一贪声闻地。二贪辟支地。如佛说。

One does not engage in false speech, divisive speech,
harsh speech, or frivolous speech,
nor does one indulge covetousness, ill will, or wrong views.
These are the seven actions of the mouth and the mind.

If one acts in this manner, then one is able to open
the gate to the unsurpassable path to buddhahood.
If one wishes to attain buddhahood,
one should practice in accordance with this initial gateway.

The bodhisattva should bring forth dharmas such as these, and then, having brought them forth, he should guard them. Having guarded them, he should then increase them so that every single good endeavor subsequently brings about an ever-increasing devotion to that form of goodness.

12. Faults to Be Urgently Abandoned on the Path to Buddhahood
a. One Fault That Must Be Urgently Abandoned on the Buddha Path

One should also realize that there is one bad dharma that one who pursues the path to buddhahood should urgently abandon. We refer here to the need to abandon neglectfulness.[120] This is as described here:

If one is unable to cross beyond
saṃsāra's dangerous wretched destinies,[121]
this is something worthy of rebuke
and is the worst of all offenses.

Although one delights in wealth's pleasures,
one may still be reborn into a poor and lowly family
in which one is unable to plant any roots of goodness
and in which one becomes a slave or a servant of others.

This is all brought about by the causes and conditions
associated with neglectfulness.
Therefore one who is wise
urgently leaves it behind as if it were a lethal poison.

If one has not yet developed the great compassion
and gained the unproduced-dharmas patience and irreversibility
and yet still indulges in neglectfulness,
this is synonymous with bring on one's own death.[122]

b. Two Faults That Must Be Urgently Abandoned on the Buddha Path

There are also two faults that one should urgently abandon, namely:

First, longing for the grounds of *śrāvaka* disciples.
And second, longing for the ground of *pratyekabuddha*s.

As the Buddha said:

正體字	
093a08 ‖	若墮聲聞地　　及辟支佛地
093a09 ‖	是名菩薩死　　亦名一切失
093a10 ‖	雖墮於地獄　　不應生怖畏
093a11 ‖	若墮於二乘　　菩薩應大畏
093a12 ‖	雖墮於地獄　　不永遮佛道
093a13 ‖	若墮於二乘　　畢竟遮佛道
093a14 ‖	佛說愛命者　　斬首則大畏
093a15 ‖	如是欲作佛　　二乘應大畏
093a16 ‖	復有三過應疾遠離。一憎諸菩薩。二憎菩
093a17 ‖	薩所行。三憎甚深大乘經。如說。
093a18 ‖	小智以小緣　　憎恚諸菩薩
093a19 ‖	亦憎菩薩道　　亦憎大乘經
093a20 ‖	不解故不信　　墮在大地獄
093a21 ‖	怖畏大驚喚　　是事應遠離
093a22 ‖	復有四過應疾遠離。一諂。二曲。三急性。四
093a23 ‖	無慈愍。如說。
093a24 ‖	自言是菩薩　　其心多諂曲

简体字

　若堕声闻地　　及辟支佛地
　是名菩萨死　　亦名一切失
　虽堕于地狱　　不应生怖畏
　若堕于二乘　　菩萨应大畏
　虽堕于地狱　　不永遮佛道
　若堕于二乘　　毕竟遮佛道
　佛说爱命者　　斩首则大畏
　如是欲作佛　　二乘应大畏

复有三过应疾远离。一憎诸菩萨。二憎菩萨所行。三憎甚深大乘经。如说。

　小智以小缘　　憎恚诸菩萨
　亦憎菩萨道　　亦憎大乘经
　不解故不信　　堕在大地狱
　怖畏大惊唤　　是事应远离

复有四过应疾远离。一谄。二曲。三急性。四无慈愍。如说。

　自言是菩萨　　其心多谄曲

> If one falls down onto the grounds of the *śrāvaka* disciples
> or onto the ground of the *pratyekabuddhas*,
> for the bodhisattva, this is synonymous with dying
> and is also synonymous with complete failure.
>
> Even though one might fall into the hells,
> one should still not feel any terror.
> However, if he were to fall into the Two Vehicles,
> the bodhisattva should then feel immensely fearful.
>
> Although one might fall into the hells,
> this would not forever block one's path to buddhahood.
> However, if one were to fall into the Two Vehicles,
> this would forever block one's path to buddhahood.
>
> The Buddha has stated that one who loves his life,
> would feel immensely fearful if faced with decapitation.
> In this very same way, one who wishes to become a buddha
> should feel immensely fearful of entering the Two Vehicles.[123]

c. Three Faults to Be Urgently Abandoned on the Buddha Path

There are also three faults that one should urgently abandon, namely:

> First, hating bodhisattvas;
> Second, hating the bodhisattva practices;
> Third, hating any extremely profound Great Vehicle scripture.

These are as described below:

> Those of lesser wisdom may, over but minor conditions,
> come to hate Bodhisattvas,
> hate the bodhisattva path,
> or hate the sutras of the Great Vehicle.
>
> Because they do not understand them, they have no faith in them
> and then fall down into the great hells.
> There, struck with fear, they scream in terror.
> This is a situation that one should abandon.

d. Four Faults to Be Urgently Abandoned on the Buddha Path

There are also four faults that one should urgently abandon, namely:

> First, flattery;
> Second, deviousness;
> Third, being quick-tempered;
> And fourth, being bereft of kindness or pity.

These are as described below:

> One who describes himself as a bodhisattva
> who has a mind much given over to flattery and deviousness,

正體字	093a25 ‖　　急性無所容　　不行慈愍心 093a26 ‖　　是近阿鼻獄　　離佛道甚遠 093a27 ‖ 復有五過應疾遠離。一貪欲。二瞋恚。三睡 093a28 ‖ 眠。四調戲。五疑。是名五蓋覆心。如說。 093a29 ‖　　若人放逸者　　諸蓋則覆心 093b01 ‖　　生天猶尚難　　何況於得果 093b02 ‖　　若勤行精進　　則能裂諸蓋 093b03 ‖　　若能裂諸蓋　　隨願悉皆得 093b04 ‖ 復有六過與六波羅蜜相違。應疾遠離。一 093b05 ‖ 慳貪。二破戒。三瞋恚。四懈怠。五調戲。六愚 093b06 ‖ 癡。如說。 093b07 ‖　　慳貪垢污心　　破戒而懈怠 093b08 ‖　　無知如牛羊　　好瞋如毒蛇 093b09 ‖　　心亂如獼猴　　[2]不遠離諸蓋 093b10 ‖　　生天為甚難　　何況得佛道
简体字	急性无所容　　不行慈愍心 　　是近阿鼻狱　　离佛道甚远 复有五过应疾远离。一贪欲。二嗔恚。三睡眠。四调戏。五疑。是名五盖覆心。如说。 　　若人放逸者　　诸盖则覆心 　　生天犹尚难　　何况于得果 　　若勤行精进　　则能裂诸盖 　　若能裂诸盖　　随愿悉皆得 复有六过与六波罗蜜相违。应疾远离。一悭贪。二破戒。三嗔恚。四懈怠。五调戏。六愚痴。如说。 　　悭贪垢污心　　破戒而懈怠 　　无知如牛羊　　好嗔如毒蛇 　　心乱如猕猴　　不远离诸盖 　　生天为甚难　　何况得佛道

who is quick-tempered and intolerant,
and who does not act with a mind of kindness and pity—
This is to draw near to the Avīci Hells
and depart far from the path to buddhahood.

e. FIVE FAULTS TO BE URGENTLY ABANDONED ON THE BUDDHA PATH

There are also five faults that one should urgently abandon, namely:

First, desire;
Second, ill will;
Third, lethargy-and-sleepiness;
Fourth, excitedness-and-regretfulness;[124]
And fifth, doubtfulness.

These are the five hindrances that may cover over a person's mind which are as described below:

If a person falls into neglectfulness,
the hindrances will cover his mind,
making even birth in the heavens difficult to achieve.
how much the less might one then attain the fruits of the path?

If one is diligent in the practice of vigor,
one can then tear through the hindrances.
If one is able to tear through the hindrances,
then, whatever one wishes for, it will all be obtained.

f. SIX FAULTS TO BE URGENTLY ABANDONED ON THE BUDDHA PATH

There are also six faults that are opposite to the six *pāramitās* and that one should urgently abandon:

First, miserliness;
Second, breaking the moral precepts;
Third, anger;
Fourth, indolence;
Fifth, excited agitation;
And sixth, delusion.

These are as described below:

Having the stain of miserliness defiling one's mind,
breaking the moral precepts, indulging in indolence,
being as ignorant as a cow or sheep,
being as fond of hatred as a venomous serpent,

or having a mind as scattered as that of a monkey—
If one fails to abandon the hindrances,
then, even gaining a celestial rebirth would be extremely difficult,
how much the less could one succeed in attaining buddhahood?

正體字

```
093b11 ‖ 復有七過應疾遠離。一樂多事務。二樂多
093b12 ‖ 讀誦。三樂睡眠。四樂語說。五貪利養。六常
093b13 ‖ 欲令人喜。七迷悶於道心隨愛行。如說。
093b14 ‖   弊人樂事務    樂多誦外經
093b15 ‖   癡人樂睡眠    樂共聚眾語
093b16 ‖   雖願欲作佛    而深著利養
093b17 ‖   是恩愛奴僕    迷悶於佛道
093b18 ‖   如是諸惡人    自言是菩薩
093b19 ‖ 復有八法應疾遠離。一邪見。二邪思惟。三
093b20 ‖ 邪語。四邪業。五邪命。六邪方便。七邪念。八
093b21 ‖ 邪定。如說。
093b22 ‖   若有[3]人愚癡    行於八邪道
093b23 ‖   學邪諸經法    好隨逐邪師
093b24 ‖   遠離八聖道    深妙諸功德
093b25 ‖   堅[4]深著煩惱    而或願菩提
```

简体字

复有七过应疾远离。一乐多事务。二乐多读诵。三乐睡眠。四乐语说。五贪利养。六常欲令人喜。七迷闷于道心随爱行。如说。

　　弊人乐事务　　乐多诵外经
　　痴人乐睡眠　　乐共聚众语
　　虽愿欲作佛　　而深着利养
　　是恩爱奴仆　　迷闷于佛道
　　如是诸恶人　　自言是菩萨

复有八法应疾远离。一邪见。二邪思惟。三邪语。四邪业。五邪命。六邪方便。七邪念。八邪定。如说。

　　若有人愚痴　　行于八邪道
　　学邪诸经法　　好随逐邪师
　　远离八圣道　　深妙诸功德
　　坚深着烦恼　　而或愿菩提

Chapter 27 — A Summarizing Discussion of the Bodhisattva Practices

g. Seven Faults to Be Urgently Abandoned on the Buddha Path

There are also seven faults that one should urgently abandon:

First, delighting in pursuing many different endeavors;
Second, delighting in excessive study and recitation;
Third, delighting in sleep;
Fourth, delighting in talking;
Fifth, coveting offerings;
Sixth, always wanting to make people laugh;
And seventh, being so confused and befuddled in cultivating the path that one's mind follows the influence of craving.

These are as described below:

Inferior persons may delight in activities
or delight in much recitation of non-Buddhist scriptures.
Ignorant people may delight in sleeping
or delight in much talking amidst groups of people.

Although they aspire to become a buddha,
they are deeply attached to receiving offerings.
These slaves to craving have become confused
with regard to the path to buddhahood.

All such people as these who engage in what is bad
nonetheless claim to be bodhisattvas.

h. Eight Dharmas to Be Urgently Abandoned on the Buddha Path

There are also eight dharmas that one should urgently abandon, namely:

First, wrong views;
Second, wrong intentional thought;
Third, wrong speech;
Fourth wrong [physical] actions;
Fifth, wrong livelihood;
Sixth, wrong effort;
Seventh, wrong mindfulness;
And eighth, wrong meditative concentration.

These are as described below:

Wherever there are people who are so foolish
that they practice the eightfold wrong path,
pursue the study of deviant scriptures,
become fond of chasing after deviant spiritual guides,

and abandon the profound and sublime qualities
of the Āryas' eightfold path,
[these are people who] are solidly and deeply attached to afflictions,
and yet still may wish to succeed in realizing bodhi—

正體字

093b26 ‖	如是愚癡人　　欲度於大海
093b27 ‖	捨好堅牢船　　抱石欲求[5]渡
093b28 ‖	復有九法應疾遠離。一不聞阿耨多羅[6]三
093b29 ‖	藐三菩提。二聞已不信。三若信不受。四若
093c01 ‖	受不誦持。五若[7]又誦持不知義趣。六若知
093c02 ‖	不說。七若說不如說行。八若如說行不能
093c03 ‖	常行。九若能常行不能善行。如說。
093c04 ‖	癡人不欲聞　　無上正真道
093c05 ‖	聞已不能信　　又不能誦持
093c06 ‖	不知義不說　　不如所說行
093c07 ‖	不能常善行　　[8]又無念安慧
093c08 ‖	如是愚癡人　　不堪得道果
093c09 ‖	猶如罪惡人　　不得生天上
093c10 ‖	復有十過應疾遠離。所謂十不善道。如說。

简体字

　　如是愚痴人　　欲度于大海
　　舍好坚牢船　　抱石欲求渡

复有九法应疾远离。一不闻阿耨多罗三藐三菩提。二闻已不信。三若信不受。四若受不诵持。五若又诵持不知义趣。六若知不说。七若说不如说行。八若如说行不能常行。九若能常行不能善行。如说。

　　痴人不欲闻　　无上正真道
　　闻已不能信　　又不能诵持
　　不知义不说　　不如所说行
　　不能常善行　　又无念安慧
　　如是愚痴人　　不堪得道果
　　犹如罪恶人　　不得生天上

复有十过应疾远离。所谓十不善道。如说。

Chapter 27 — A Summarizing Discussion of the Bodhisattva Practices

People who are so deluded as this
are like those who would wish to cross over a great ocean
by abandoning a fine, solid, and durable ship,
seeking instead to make the crossing by carrying stones.

i. NINE DHARMAS TO BE URGENTLY ABANDONED ON THE BUDDHA PATH

There are also nine dharmas that one should urgently abandon, namely:

First, failing to hear [the teachings on the attainment of] *anuttarasamyaksaṃbodhi*;

Second, having heard them, failing to have faith in them;

Third, having acquired faith in them, failing to take them on;

Fourth, having taken them on, nonetheless still failing to retain them through recitation;

Fifth, though one has also begun to retain them through recitation, one nonetheless still does not understand their meaning;

Sixth, having understood their meaning and significance, one nonetheless fails to explain them [for others];

Seventh, having explained them [for others], one nonetheless fails to accord with their explanation in one's own practice;

Eighth, having begun to practice in accordance with their explanation, one is still unable to always put them into practice;

And ninth, having become able to always put them into practice, one is unable to thoroughly practice them.

These are as described below:

Foolish people do not wish to even hear
[teachings on] the unsurpassable, right, and true path,
or, having heard them, they are unable to have faith in them,
or they are unable to retain them through recitation,

or they do not understand their meaning or explain them for others,
or they do not cultivate in accordance with how they were taught,
or they are unable to always or thoroughly put them into practice.
Moreover, they have no mindfulness or stable wisdom.

Such foolish people as these
cannot obtain the fruits of the path.
In this, they are like people who, having committed karmic offenses,
cannot succeed in gaining rebirth in the heavens.

j. TEN DHARMAS TO BE URGENTLY ABANDONED ON THE BUDDHA PATH

There are also ten dharmas that one should urgently abandon, namely those comprising the ten courses of bad karmic actions. These are as described below:

癡人於少時　　貪愛弊五欲
捨離十善道　　行十不善道
諸天樂在手　　而復自捨棄
如貪小錢利　　而捨大寶藏

問曰。汝說無上道相時。種種因緣訶罵空發願菩薩自言菩薩但名字菩薩。若是三不名為菩薩者。成就何法名為真菩薩。答曰。

非但發空願　　自言是菩薩
名字為菩薩　　略說能成就
三十二法者　　乃名為菩薩

若人發心欲求佛道。自言是菩薩。空受名號不行功德慈悲心諸波羅蜜等。是不名為菩薩。如土城名寶城。但自誑身亦誑諸佛。亦誑世間眾生。若人有三十二妙法亦能發願是名真實菩薩。何等三十二。一深心為一切眾生求諸安樂。二能入諸佛智中。三自審知堪任作佛不作佛。四不憎惡他。五道心堅固。

Chapter 27 — A Summarizing Discussion of the Bodhisattva Practices

> Foolish people, when still young,
> begin to crave descending into the five desires,
> abandoning the ten courses of good karmic action,
> and engaging in the ten courses of bad karmic action.
>
> Although the bliss of the heavens is in their own hands,
> they still cast it aside and reject it,
> just as, due to greedily pursuing the benefit of but little money,
> one might somehow abandon a great treasury of jewels.

13. The 32 Dharmas of Genuine Bodhisattvas

Question: When you were explaining the characteristic aspects of the unsurpassable path, for many different reasons, you criticized and scolded empty-vow bodhisattvas, self-proclaimed bodhisattvas, and those who are bodhisattvas in name only. If those three types of individuals do not qualify as bodhisattvas, then, through the perfection of which dharmas does one qualify as a genuine bodhisattva?

Response:

> It is not merely by making empty vows
> by proclaiming oneself to be a bodhisattva,
> or by being a bodhisattva only in name.
> To state it briefly, it is those who are able to perfect
> thirty-two dharmas
> who then truly qualify as bodhisattvas.

If one brings forth the resolve by which he seeks to pursue the path to buddhahood and then claims himself to be a bodhisattva, merely emptily assuming the name but not cultivating the meritorious qualities, the mind of kindness and compassion, the *pāramitās*, and the other practices, this sort of person does not actually qualify as a bodhisattva, for he is comparable to some model city made of mud being referred to as "the jeweled city." In this, he only deceives himself, cheats all buddhas, and cheats all of the world's beings as well.

If a person comes to possess thirty-two sublime dharmas while also being able to bring forth the [bodhisattva's] vow, this is someone who qualifies as a genuine bodhisattva. What then are these thirty-two dharmas? They are:

1) He strives with resolute intentions to bring about every form of peace and happiness for all beings;
2) He is able to enter into the wisdom of all buddhas;
3) He knows through his own self-examination whether or not he is capable of becoming a buddha;
4) He does not hate or loathe anyone;
5) His resolve to succeed in the path is solid;

正體字

094a01 ‖ 　　　六不假偽結託親愛。七乃至未
094a02 ‖ 入涅槃常為眾生作親友。八親疏同心。九
094a03 ‖ 已許善事心不退轉。十於一切眾生不斷
094a04 ‖ 大慈。十一於一切眾生不斷大悲。十二常
094a05 ‖ 求正法心無疲懈。十三勤發精進心無厭
094a06 ‖ 足。十四多聞而解義。十五常省己過。十六
094a07 ‖ 不譏彼闕。十七於一切見聞事中常修菩
094a08 ‖ 提心。十八施不求報。十九持戒不求一切
094a09 ‖ 生處。二十於一切眾生忍辱無瞋礙。二十
094a10 ‖ 一能勤精進修習一切善根。二十[1]二不隨
094a11 ‖ 無色定生。二十三方便所攝智慧。二十四四
094a12 ‖ 攝法所攝方便。二十五持戒毀戒慈愍無二。
094a13 ‖ 二十六一心聽法。二十七一心阿練若處住。
094a14 ‖ 二十八不樂世間種種雜事。二十九不貪
094a15 ‖ 著小乘。三十見大乘利益為大。

简体字

六不假伪结托亲爱。七乃至未入涅槃常为众生作亲友。八亲疏同心。九已许善事心不退转。十于一切众生不断大慈。十一于一切众生不断大悲。十二常求正法心无疲懈。十三勤发精进心无厌足。十四多闻而解义。十五常省己过。十六不讥彼阙。十七于一切见闻事中常修菩提心。十八施不求报。十九持戒不求一切生处。二十于一切众生忍辱无瞋碍。二十一能勤精进修习一切善根。二十二不随无色定生。二十三方便所摄智慧。二十四四摄法所摄方便。二十五持戒毁戒慈愍无二。二十六一心听法。二十七一心阿练若处住。二十八不乐世间种种杂事。二十九不贪着小乘。三十见大乘利益为大。

Chapter 27 — A Summarizing Discussion of the Bodhisattva Practices   957

6) He does not form friendships or trusting relationships on false pretenses;
7) He always serves as a close friend to beings even up to the point of his entry into nirvāṇa;
8) Whether others are personally close or distant from him, his mind remains the same [in the way he treats them];
9) He does not retreat from good endeavors to which he has assented;
10) He never cuts off his great kindness for all beings;
11) He never cuts off his great compassion for all beings;
12) He always pursues right Dharma and his mind never becomes weary or prone to laziness;
13) He is diligent in bringing forth vigor and he has insatiable resolve;
14) He is possessed of extensive learning and comprehension of its meanings;
15) He always reflects upon his own faults;
16) He does not deride others for their shortcomings;
17) In all matters he observes or hears, he always cultivates the resolve to attain bodhi;
18) In giving, he seeks no reward;
19) His observance of the moral precepts is not motivated by the desire to take rebirth in any particular place;[125]
20) He exercises patience in his interactions with all beings and thus remains free of any hatred or obstructiveness toward them;
21) He is able to diligently and vigorously cultivate all roots of goodness;
22) He does not take on rebirths corresponding to the formless realm meditative absorptions;[126]
23) His wisdom is inclusive of appropriate expedient teaching methods;
24) His skillful means are those that lie within the four means of attraction;[127]
25) His kindness and pity for others do not differ with respect to those who observe the moral precepts versus those who break the moral precepts;
26) He is single-mindedly attentive when listening to the Dharma;
27) He remains single-mindedly focused when dwelling in a forest hermitage;
28) He does not delight in any of the many different sorts of endeavors that are admixed with worldly priorities;
29) He does not covet or retain any attachment for the Small Vehicle;
30) He perceives that the benefit brought about by the Great Vehicle is immense;

正體字

```
       三十一遠
094a15 ‖ 離惡知識。三十二親近善知識。菩薩住是三
094a16 ‖ 十二法。能成[2]七法。所謂四無量心。能遊戲
094a17 ‖ 五神通。常依於智。常不捨善惡眾生。所言
094a18 ‖ 決定[3]言必皆實。集一切善法心無厭足。是
094a19 ‖ 為三十二法。為七[4]法。菩薩成就此者。名
094a20 ‖ 為真實菩薩。
```

简体字

三十一远离恶知识。三十二亲近善知识。菩萨住是三十二法。能成七法。所谓四无量心。能游戏五神通。常依于智。常不舍善恶众生。所言决定言必皆实。集一切善法心无厌足。是为三十二法。为七法。菩萨成就此者。名为真实菩萨。

31) He stays away from bad spiritual guides;
32) He draws close to good spiritual guides.

14. SEVEN ADDITIONAL DHARMAS OF GENUINE BODHISATTVAS

As the bodhisattva abides in these thirty-two dharmas, he is able to perfect seven additional dharmas. Specifically, they are:

The four immeasurable minds;[128]
The ability to roam about, delighting in the use of the five spiritual superknowledges;
Constant reliance on wisdom;
Never forsaking either good or evil beings;
Decisiveness in all pronouncements;
Definite truthfulness in all statements;
Insatiability in the accumulation of all good dharmas.

These constitute the thirty-two dharmas with their seven additional dharmas. Any bodhisattva who perfects these dharmas qualifies as a genuine bodhisattva.

The End of Chapter Twenty-Seven

正體字

094a21 ‖ 　　　分別二地業道品第[5]一
094a22 ‖ 　諸菩薩已得　　具足於初地
094a23 ‖ 　欲得第二地　　當生十種心
094a24 ‖ 諸菩薩已得歡喜初地。為得二地故生十
094a25 ‖ 種心。因是十心能得第二地。如人欲上樓
094a26 ‖ 觀要因梯而上。問曰。何等是十心得第二
094a27 ‖ 地方便。答曰。
094a28 ‖ 　直心堪用心　　軟伏寂滅心
094a29 ‖ 　真妙不雜貪　　快大心為十
094b01 ‖ 諸菩薩已具足於初地。欲得第二地。生是
094b02 ‖ 十方便心。一直心。二堪用心。三柔軟心。四
094b03 ‖ 降伏心。五寂滅心。六真妙心。七不雜心。八
094b04 ‖ 不貪。九廣快心。十大心。

简体字

　　　分别二地业道品第二十八
　诸菩萨已得　　具足于初地
　欲得第二地　　当生十种心
　诸菩萨已得欢喜初地。为得二地故生十种心。因是十心能得第二地。如人欲上楼观要因梯而上。问曰。何等是十心得第二地方便。答曰。
　直心堪用心　　软伏寂灭心
　真妙不杂贪　　快大心为十
　诸菩萨已具足于初地。欲得第二地。生是十方便心。一直心。二堪用心。三柔软心。四降伏心。五寂灭心。六真妙心。七不杂心。八不贪心。九广快心。十大心。

Chapter 28
Distinctions in the 2nd Ground's Courses of Karmic Action

VIII. Ch. 28: Distinctions in the 2nd Ground's Karmic Actions
  A. The Ten Resolute Intentions Necessary for Entering the 2nd Ground

> The bodhisattva who has already succeeded
> in the complete fulfillment of the first ground
> and then wishes to reach the second ground
> should bring forth ten types of resolute intentions.[129]

Those bodhisattvas who have already reached the first ground, the Ground of Joyfulness, next bring forth ten types of resolute intentions for the sake of reaching the second ground. It is because of these ten kinds of resolute intentions that one is able to reach the second ground. This is comparable to when someone wishes to go up to an upper-story balcony and must rely on the stairs to do so.

Question: What then are these ten kinds of resolute intentions that serve as means for reaching the second ground?

Response:

> The straight mind, the capable mind,
> the pliant, the restrained, and the quiescent minds,
> the truly sublime, the unmixed, and the non-covetous minds,
> the happy mind, and magnanimous mind make ten in all.

The bodhisattva who has already completely fulfilled the practices of the first ground and now wishes to reach the second ground proceeds to develop these ten kinds of resolute intentions as the appropriate means, namely:[130]

1) The straight mind;
2) The capable mind;
3) The pliant mind;
4) The restrained mind;
5) The quiescent mind;
6) The truly sublime mind;
7) The unmixed mind;
8) The unattached mind;
9) The expansively happy mind;
10) The magnanimous mind.

正體字

```
           直心者。離諂
094b05 ‖ 曲。離諂曲故心轉柔軟。柔軟者。不剛強麁
094b06 ‖ 惡。菩薩得是柔軟心。生種種禪定。亦修[6]習
094b07 ‖ 諸善法。觀諸法實相。心則堪用。心堪用故
094b08 ‖ 生伏心。伏心者。善能降伏眼等諸根。如經
094b09 ‖ 中說。何等是善道。所謂比丘降伏眼根乃至
094b10 ‖ 意根。以降伏六根故。名為伏心。心已降伏
094b11 ‖ 則易生寂滅心。寂滅心者。能滅貪欲瞋恚
094b12 ‖ 愚癡等諸煩惱。先伏心已遮令寂滅。復有人
094b13 ‖ 言。得諸禪定是名寂滅心。如經說。若人善
094b14 ‖ 知禪定相不貪其味。是名寂滅心。得寂滅
094b15 ‖ 心已。必生真妙心。真妙心者。於諸禪定神
094b16 ‖ 通所願事中如意得用。譬如真金隨意所
094b17 ‖ 用。行者既得直心乃至真妙心已。為守護
```

简体字

直心者。离谄曲。离谄曲故心转柔软。柔软者。不刚强粗恶。菩萨得是柔软心。生种种禅定。亦修习诸善法。观诸法实相。心则堪用。心堪用故生伏心。伏心者。善能降伏眼等诸根。如经中说。何等是善道。所谓比丘降伏眼根乃至意根。以降伏六根故。名为伏心。心已降伏则易生寂灭心。寂灭心者。能灭贪欲嗔恚愚痴等诸烦恼。先伏心已遮令寂灭。复有人言。得诸禅定是名寂灭心。如经说。若人善知禅定相不贪其味。是名寂灭心。得寂灭心已。必生真妙心。真妙心者。于诸禅定神通所愿事中如意得用。譬如真金随意所用。行者既得直心乃至真妙心已。为守护

Chapter 28 – Distinctions in the 2nd Ground's Courses of Karmic Action

1. THE STRAIGHT MIND AND THE PLIANT MIND

Now, as for the straight mind, this is one that has abandoned flattery and deviousness. Because the mind has abandoned flattery and deviousness, it becomes characterized by pliancy. Pliancy refers to not being unyielding or gruff and ill-mannered. The bodhisattva who acquires this pliant mind develops many different *dhyāna* absorptions and also cultivates all good dharmas.

2. THE CAPABLE MIND

Once one has contemplated the true character of all dharmas, his mind then becomes capable. Because the mind has become capable, one develops the restrained mind.

3. THE RESTRAINED MIND

The restrained mind is one that is well able to restrain the eye and the other sense faculties. This is as stated in the sutras: "What is it that comprises the path of goodness? It is one wherein the bhikshu restrains his eye sense faculty and so forth until we come to his restraining of the mind faculty." It is due to restraint of the six sense faculties that we refer to "the restrained mind."

4. THE QUIESCENT MIND

Once the mind has become restrained, it is then easy to bring forth the quiescent mind. Now, as for the quiescent mind, this refers to being able to extinguish greed, hatred, delusion, and the other afflictions. Having first restrained the mind, one is able to block [the arising of those afflictions] and bring about a state of quiescence.

There are others who claim that acquisition of the *dhyāna* absorptions that itself constitutes the quiescent mind. This is as described in the sutras where it says, "If a person thoroughly knows the characteristic features of the *dhyāna* absorptions, then he will not desire the delectability [of their pleasurable meditative states]. This then is what is meant by the quiescent mind."

5. THE TRULY SUBLIME MIND

Once one has acquired the quiescent mind, he will then definitely bring forth the truly sublime mind. "The truly sublime mind" is a state in which, whatever one wishes to accomplish in the *dhyāna* absorptions and spiritual powers, one will be able to put them to use in a manner that conforms to one's wishes. This is like having real gold that one is able to use however one wishes.

6. THE UNMIXED MIND

Once the practitioner has acquired these types of mind from the straight mind on through to the truly sublime mind, in order to preserve and

正體字	094b18 ‖ 是心故。樂生不雜心。不雜心者。不與在家 094b19 ‖ 出家從事。是人作是念。我得如是等心。皆 094b20 ‖ 由禪定力故。以是諸心當得第二地等無 094b21 ‖ 量利益。若與眾人雜者則失此利。何以故。 094b22 ‖ 若人與眾人雜行。則眼等六根或時還發諸 094b23 ‖ 不善法。何以故。親近可染可瞋可癡法故。 094b24 ‖ 諸根發動煩惱火然。煩惱火然故則失此利。 094b25 ‖ 見此等過故生不雜心。不應與在家出家 094b26 ‖ 者雜行。是人得是不雜心已。次生不貪心。 094b27 ‖ 不貪心者。於在家出家人中所謂父母兄弟 094b28 ‖ 和[7]上師長等不生貪著。作是念。若我於 094b29 ‖ 在家出家生貪著者。必當來往問訊。我則 094c01 ‖ 何有不雜心耶。是故我欲令諸禪定等利 094c02 ‖ 住不雜心者。當於在家出家捨貪著心。問 094c03 ‖ 曰。菩薩法不應捨眾生。不應生捨心。如 094c04 ‖ 助菩提中說。
简体字	是心故。乐生不杂心。不杂心者。不与在家出家从事。是人作是念。我得如是等心。皆由禅定力故。以是诸心当得第二地等无量利益。若与众人杂者则失此利。何以故。若人与众人杂行。则眼等六根或时还发诸不善法。何以故。亲近可染可嗔可痴法故。诸根发动烦恼火然。烦恼火然故则失此利。见此等过故生不杂心。不应与在家出家者杂行。是人得是不杂心已。次生不贪心。不贪心者。于在家出家人中所谓父母兄弟和上师长等不生贪着。作是念。若我于在家出家生贪著者。必当来往问讯。我则何有不杂心耶。是故我欲令诸禅定等利住不杂心者。当于在家出家舍贪着心。问曰。菩萨法不应舍众生。不应生舍心。如助菩提中说。

Chapter 28 — *Distinctions in the 2nd Ground's Courses of Karmic Action*

protect these kinds of mind, he delights in bringing forth the unmixed mind. The unmixed mind is one in which one abstains from getting involved with either householders or monastics. This practitioner has this thought:

> Acquiring these types of mind depends entirely on the power of the *dhyāna* absorptions. It is by means of these types of mind that one acquires the measureless benefits of the second ground. If I allow [these types of mind] to become admixed with the affairs of these many other people, then I will lose these benefits.
>
> And why would this be so? If one allows his practice to become admixed with the affairs of other people, then, because of the eye faculty and the rest of the six sense faculties, one may sometimes then revert to the production of unwholesome dharmas. Why? Because, when one draws close to dharmas able to provoke lust, hatred, or delusion, [the sensations experienced through] the sense faculties may stir up the fires of the afflictions. It would be due to having ignited the fires of the afflictions that one would then lose these benefits.

It is because of having perceived these sorts of faults that one then develops the unmixed mind and realizes that he should not allow his practice to become admixed with the affairs of householders or other monastics.

7. The Unattached Mind

Having already developed this unmixed mind, this practitioner next develops the unattached mind. The unattached mind is that through which one does not become attached to any householders or monastics, including even one's father, one's mother, one's older or younger brother, one's preceptors, one's teachers, or one's elders. One reflects thus:

> If I become attached to householders or monastics, then this will surely involve the interactions involved with going thither and exchanging mutual greetings. In such circumstances, how could I possibly avoid the arising of mixed mind states? Therefore, if I wish to ensure that the benefits of the *dhyāna* absorptions continue to abide, doing so through preservation of the unmixed mind, then I should relinquish any thoughts of attachment for either householders or monastics.

a. Q: Doesn't an Unattached Mind Contradict the Bodhisattva Vow?

Question: The dharma of the bodhisattva prescribes that one should not forsake beings and should not entertain any thought of forsaking them. This is as stated in the *Bodhisaṃbhāra* [*Treatise*]:

正體字	094c05 ‖ 　菩薩初精進　　所有方便力 094c06 ‖ 　應[8]令諸眾生　　住於大乘中 094c07 ‖ 　若人教恒沙　　眾生住羅漢 094c08 ‖ 　不如教一人　　住大乘為勝 094c09 ‖ 　若人少勢力　　不堪發大乘 094c10 ‖ 　次當教令住　　辟支聲聞乘 094c11 ‖ 　若人不堪住　　辟支聲聞乘 094c12 ‖ 　應教此眾生　　令行福因緣 094c13 ‖ 　不任住三乘　　不堪人天樂 094c14 ‖ 　常以今世事　　隨而利益之 094c15 ‖ 　若有諸眾生　　不受菩薩利 094c16 ‖ 　於此不應捨　　應生大慈悲 094c17 ‖ 汝云何言菩薩得不雜心生不貪心。若菩 094c18 ‖ 薩不貪眾生則為捨離。何能度耶。答曰。應 094c19 ‖ 隨順菩薩道行捨心。何以故。是人因捨心 094c20 ‖ 生廣快心。作是念。我若捨是眾鬧。當得禪 094c21 ‖ 定因禪定生妙廣快法。得是法已其後則 094c22 ‖ 能利益眾生。勝今千萬倍。是故為多利益 094c23 ‖ 眾生少時捨心	
简体字	菩萨初精进　　所有方便力 　应令诸众生　　住于大乘中 　若人教恒沙　　众生住罗汉 　不如教一人　　住大乘为胜 　若人少势力　　不堪发大乘 　次当教令住　　辟支声闻乘 　若人不堪住　　辟支声闻乘 　应教此众生　　令行福因缘 　不任住三乘　　不堪人天乐 　常以今世事　　随而利益之 　若有诸众生　　不受菩萨利 　于此不应舍　　应生大慈悲 汝云何言菩萨得不杂心生不贪心。若菩萨不贪众生则为舍离。何能度耶。答曰。应随顺菩萨道行舍心。何以故。是人因舍心生广快心。作是念。我若舍是众闹。当得禅定因禅定生妙广快法。得是法已其后则能利益众生。胜今千万倍。是故为多利益众生少时舍心	

Chapter 28 — *Distinctions in the 2nd Ground's Courses of Karmic Action*

> From the very beginning, the bodhisattva exerts vigor
> in the power of every form of skillful means
> through which he should influence all beings
> to abide in the Great Vehicle.
>
> Even were one to teach beings as numerous as
> the sands of the Ganges to abide in arhatship,
> that would not equal [the merit of] instructing even one person
> to abide in the Great Vehicle, for this would be the superior deed.
>
> If one encounters someone possessed of only lesser strength
> who is thus incapable of bringing forth Great Vehicle resolve,
> one should, as a secondary priority, teach them to abide instead
> in the *śrāvaka* disciple or *pratyekabuddha* vehicles.
>
> If they find themselves incapable of abiding
> in either *śrāvaka* disciple or *pratyekabuddha* vehicles,
> then one should instruct such beings
> in a way that causes them to cultivate the causal bases of merit.
>
> If, however, they cannot take on any of the Three Vehicles
> and cannot take on [causal bases] for human or celestial bliss, either,
> then one should always resort to present-world endeavors
> to benefit them in a manner corresponding to the situation.
>
> If, even then, there happen to be those beings who
> cannot accept benefit as offered by the bodhisattva,
> one must still refrain from forsaking these beings,
> but should bring forth great kindness and compassion for them.[131]

Also, why is it that you claim that the bodhisattva takes on the unmixed mind and brings forth the unattached mind? If the bodhisattva has no attachment to other beings, then that just amounts to abandoning them. How then could he liberate them?

b. A: No, One Must Accord with the Mind of Equanimity

Response: One should accord with the practice of the mind of equanimity as prescribed by the bodhisattva path. And why? It is because of the mind of equanimity that this person then develops the expansively happy mind. Thus, one reflects:

> If I relinquish these many sorts of disturbances, then I will be able to acquire the *dhyāna* absorptions and it is because of the *dhyāna* absorptions that I will bring forth that sublime dharma of expansive happiness. Once I have acquired this dharma, I will then be able to benefit beings in ways that are ten million times more beneficial than what I can do right now.

Consequently, in order to bring about far greater benefit for other beings, one temporarily uses the mind of equanimity to provisionally

正體字

權捨眾鬧。當得禪定五神
094c24 ‖ 通等利益眾生。菩薩何故作如是方便。菩
094c25 ‖ 薩為得大心而作是念。大人樂大利益故
094c26 ‖ 不存小利。是故我今當求大人之法隨而
094c27 ‖ 修學。應如是勤加精進為大利益。所謂諸
094c28 ‖ 禪定神通滅苦解脫等。是故汝說非也。問曰。
094c29 ‖ 初地中已有直心等法。何故復說菩薩欲
095a01 ‖ 得二地生於十心。答曰。初地雖有此法
095a02 ‖ 未得深樂。未有堅固。在此地中心常憙樂
095a03 ‖ 轉深堅固堪任施用。是故汝難非也。問曰。若
095a04 ‖ 深樂堅固此法者得何[1]異事。答曰。
095a05 ‖ 　若其一時得　　深樂堅固心
095a06 ‖ 　更不復用功　　如使常隨逐
095a07 ‖ 如使一時生常隨逐人。菩薩如是一時得

简体字

权舍众闹。当得禅定五神通等利益众生。菩萨何故作如是方便。菩萨为得大心而作是念。大人乐大利益故不存小利。是故我今当求大人之法随而修学。应如是勤加精进为大利益。所谓诸禅定神通灭苦解脱等。是故汝说非也。问曰。初地中已有直心等法。何故复说菩萨欲得二地生于十心。答曰。初地虽有此法未得深乐。未有坚固。在此地中心常喜乐转深坚固堪任施用。是故汝难非也。问曰。若深乐坚固此法者得何异事。答曰。

　若其一时得　　深乐坚固心
　更不复用功　　如使常随逐
如使一时生常随逐人。菩萨如是一时得

Chapter 28 — *Distinctions in the 2nd Ground's Courses of Karmic Action*

abandon the many disturbances so that one can then acquire the *dhyāna* absorptions, the five spiritual powers, and the associated qualities with which one can benefit beings.

So, why is it that the bodhisattva engages in these sorts of skillful means? In order to acquire the magnanimous mind, the bodhisattva reflects:

> Because the great man delights in providing great benefit, he does not settle for providing merely minor benefit. Therefore I should now seek to acquire the dharmas of great men and then cultivate the corresponding course of training. I should then pursue just such a diligent application of vigor for the sake of being able to provide such great benefit, namely by acquiring the *dhyāna* absorptions, the spiritual powers, the extinguishing of the sufferings, the liberations, and so forth.

Given the above, the challenge that you have presented here is wrongly conceived.

c. Q: Why Must the Bodhisattva Again Develop the Straight Mind, etc.?

Question: One already possesses the straight mind and other such dharmas on the first ground. Why then do you yet again state that the bodhisattva wishing to gain the second ground must develop these ten types of mind?

d. A: Now, on the 2nd Ground, These Minds Become Solidly Established

Response: Although one has already come into possession of these dharmas on the first ground, one still does not deeply delight in them and still has not yet solidly established them. One's mind is always joyous on this ground. One then becomes ever more solidly established [in these dharmas] and then develops the capacity to put them to use. Therefore, this challenge of yours is wrong.

e. Q: What Is the Result of Deep Delight and Solid Establishment?

Question: In the case of those who deeply delight in these dharmas and become ever more solidly established in them, what sorts of circumstances result from this?[132]

f. A: These Types of Mind Will Forever After Be Effortlessly Invoked

Response:
> If this person succeeds even one time in acquiring
> deep delight and solid establishment in these types of mind,
> then he will never again have to apply further effort in this,
> for they will then become like servants who always follow after him.

They will become like a servant that, from the time of his birth, then always follows along after his master. So too, once the bodhisattva has

正體字

095a08 ‖ 深樂堅固心已即常隨逐。更不須用功而
095a09 ‖ 生若以少因緣便生。何以故。根深入故莖
095a10 ‖ 節相續。問曰。若菩薩得是十種心得何等
095a11 ‖ 果。答曰。
095a12 ‖ 　若得是諸心　　正住第二地
095a13 ‖ 　具三種離垢　　惡業及煩惱
095a14 ‖ 若菩薩得是直等十心。即名住第二菩薩地。
095a15 ‖ 一離垢者。地名也。二離垢者。於此地中離
095a16 ‖ 十不善道罪業之垢。三離垢者。離貪欲瞋恚
095a17 ‖ 等諸煩惱垢故。名為離垢。復次離垢義者。[2]
095a18 ‖ 十住毘婆沙論卷第十三
095a21 ‖ 十住毘婆沙論卷第十四　095a22 ‖
095a23 ‖ 　　聖者龍樹造
095a24 ‖ 　　後秦龜茲國三藏鳩摩羅什譯
095a25 ‖ 　　分別二地業道品之餘
095a26 ‖ [3]菩薩住此地　　自然不行惡
095a27 ‖ 深樂善法故　　自然行善道
095a28 ‖ 問曰。十[4]不善道自然不作。自然行十善道。
095a29 ‖ 此二種道。幾是身行。幾是口行。幾是意行。

简体字

深乐坚固心已即常随逐。更不须用功而生若以少因缘便生。何以故。根深入故茎节相续。问曰。若菩萨得是十种心得何等果。答曰。

　若得是诸心　　正住第二地
　具三种离垢　　恶业及烦恼

若菩萨得是直等十心。即名住第二菩萨地。一离垢者。地名也。二离垢者。于此地中离十不善道罪业之垢。三离垢者。离贪欲瞋恚等诸烦恼垢故。名为离垢。复次离垢义者。

　菩萨住此地　　自然不行恶
　深乐善法故　　自然行善道

问曰。十不善道自然不作。自然行十善道。此二种道。几是身行。几是口行。几是意行。

Chapter 28 — *Distinctions in the 2nd Ground's Courses of Karmic Action*

acquired deep delight in and solid establishment of these [ten types of] minds, they will immediately and always accompany him and never again require the application of special effort to cause them to arise. Thereafter, it requires only the most minor sort of causal circumstance for them to come forth yet again. Why is this so? It is because the roots [of goodness associated with these types of mind] have penetrated down so deeply that stems and branches continuously push forth [forever after].

g. Q: WHAT ARE THE FRUITS OF ACQUIRING THESE TEN TYPES OF MIND?

Question: If the bodhisattva succeeds in acquiring these ten types of mind, what sorts of fruits will he gain?

h. A: HE WILL ATTAIN THE SECOND GROUND AND A THREEFOLD STAINLESSNESS

Response:
If one acquires these types of mind,
then one will abide directly on the second ground
and will become completely equipped with a threefold stainlessness:
[Nominal]; in terms of bad karma; and in terms of the afflictions.

If the bodhisattva succeeds in acquiring these ten types of mind consisting of the straight mind as well as the others, he will then immediately qualify as abiding on the second bodhisattva ground.

The first type of stainlessness is the name of this ground, [i.e. the "stainlessness" ground]. The second type of stainlessness refers to the abandonment on this ground of the defilements associated with the karmic transgressions occurring in the ten courses of bad karmic action. The third type of stainlessness refers to abandonment of the defilements associated with greed, hatred, and the other sorts of afflictions.

It is for these reasons that this is called "the Ground of Stainlessness." Furthermore, regarding the meaning of "stainlessness":

B. THE 2ND GROUND BODHISATTVA'S TEN COURSES OF GOOD KARMIC ACTION

The bodhisattva abiding on this ground
naturally abstains from engaging in bad actions.
Because he deeply delights in good dharmas,
he naturally practices the courses of good karmic action.

1. Q: HOW MANY ARE PHYSICAL, HOW MANY VERBAL & HOW MANY MENTAL?

Question: Given that [this bodhisattva] naturally abstains from the ten courses of bad karmic action and naturally engages in the ten courses of good karmic action, how many of the actions comprising these two classes of courses of karmic action are physical, how many are verbal, and how many are mental?

正體字

答
095b01 ｜｜ 曰。
095b02 ｜｜ 　　[5]身意[6]二三種　　口四善亦爾
095b03 ｜｜ 　　略說則如是　　此應當分別
095b04 ｜｜ 不善身行有三種。所謂奪他命劫盜邪婬。
095b05 ｜｜ 不善口行四種妄語兩舌惡口散亂語。不善
095b06 ｜｜ 意行三種。貪取瞋惱邪見。善身行亦有三種。
095b07 ｜｜ 離奪命劫盜邪婬。善口行亦四種。離妄語兩
095b08 ｜｜ 舌惡口散亂語。善意行有三種。不貪取不瞋
095b09 ｜｜ 惱正見。身口意業道。是善不善應須論議
095b10 ｜｜ 令人得解。初奪命不善道者。所謂有他眾
095b11 ｜｜ 生知是[7]眾生故行惱害。因是惱害則失
095b12 ｜｜ 壽命。起此身業是名初奪命不善道。離此
095b13 ｜｜ 事故。名為離奪命善行。劫盜者。所謂屬他
095b14 ｜｜ 之物。知是物屬他生劫盜心。手捉此物舉
095b15 ｜｜ 離[8]此處。若劫若盜計是我物生我所心。

简体字

答曰。
　　身意二三种　　口四善亦尔
　　略说则如是　　此应当分别
　不善身行有三种。所谓夺他命劫盗邪淫。不善口行四种妄语两舌恶口散乱语。不善意行三种。贪取嗔恼邪见。善身行亦有三种。离夺命劫盗邪淫。善口行亦四种。离妄语两舌恶口散乱语。善意行有三种。不贪取不嗔恼正见。身口意业道。是善不善应须论议令人得解。初夺命不善道者。所谓有他众生知是众生故行恼害。因是恼害则失寿命。起此身业是名初夺命不善道。离此事故。名为离夺命善行。劫盗者。所谓属他之物。知是物属他生劫盗心。手捉此物举离此处。若劫若盗计是我物生我所心。

Chapter 28 — *Distinctions in the 2nd Ground's Courses of Karmic Action*

2. A: Physical and Mental Are Threefold and Verbal Are Fourfold

Response:

The [bad] physical and mental actions are each of three types and the [bad] verbal actions are fourfold. So too with good actions. The brief explanation then is of this sort.
This is a subject that should be distinguished [further].

There are three types of bad physical karmic actions, namely killing, stealing, and sexual misconduct. There are four types of bad verbal karmic actions, namely false speech, divisive speech, harsh speech, and scattered or inappropriate speech. There are three types of bad mental karmic actions, namely covetousness, ill will, and wrong views.

There are also three types of good physical karmic actions, namely abandoning killing, stealing, and sexual misconduct. The good verbal karmic actions are also fourfold, namely abandoning false speech, divisive speech, harsh speech, and scattered or inappropriate speech. There are three types of good mental karmic actions, namely non-covetousness, refraining from ill will, and right views.

Whether the physical, verbal, or mental courses of karmic action are good or bad is a topic requiring further discussion so as to cause people to clearly understand such matters.

C. Definitions of Each of the Ten Courses of Good & Bad Karmic Action

1. Killing

First, "killing" as a course of bad karmic action involves the following factors:
The existence of another being;
The knowledge that there is this being;
The deliberate infliction of physical injury;
The loss of life due to this infliction of physical injury.

If one brings forth these physical karmic actions, this is what is known as "killing," the first of the courses of bad karmic action. It is the abandoning of these factors that defines the good karmic action of refraining from killing.

2. Stealing

As for "stealing," it involves the following factors:
There is something belonging to someone else;
One knows that this thing belongs to someone else;
One produces a thought intent on stealing it;
One's hand grasps this thing, picks it up, and then moves it away from its current location;
Whether one openly robs or surreptitiously steals the object, one then reckons, "This is my possession" and thinks, "This is mine."

正體字

	是
095b16 ‖	名劫盜行。離此事者名為離劫盜善行。邪
095b17 ‖	婬者。所有女人。若為父母所護。親族所護。
095b18 ‖	為姓所護。世法所護。戒法所護。若他[9]人婦
095b19 ‖	知有鞭杖惱害等障礙。於此事中生貪欲
095b20 ‖	心起於身業。或於自所有妻妾。若受戒若
095b21 ‖	懷妊若乳兒若非道。是名邪婬。遠離此事
095b22 ‖	名為善身行。妄語者。覆相覆心覆見覆忍覆
095b23 ‖	欲知如是相而更異說。是名妄語。遠離此
095b24 ‖	事名為遠離妄語善行。

简体字

是名劫盗行。离此事者名为离劫盗善行。邪淫者。所有女人。若为父母所护。亲族所护。为姓所护。世法所护。戒法所护。若他人妇知有鞭杖恼害等障碍。于此事中生贪欲心起于身业。或于自所有妻妾。若受戒若怀妊若乳儿若非道。是名邪淫。远离此事名为善身行。妄语者。覆相覆心覆见覆忍覆欲知如是相而更异说。是名妄语。远离此事名为远离妄语善行。

These are the factors defining the act of stealing. It is the abandoning of these factors that defines the good karmic action of refraining from stealing.

3. Sexual Misconduct

As for "sexual misconduct," [it involves the following factors]:

There is some woman;[133]

She is under the protection of parents, under the protection of her clan, under the protection of her caste, under the protection of worldly convention or law, or under the protection of the moral precepts;

In the case of another man's wife, one may even know of the potential for such obstacles as being whipped, beaten with clubs, tormented, or afflicted with bodily injury;

Even in the midst of any of these circumstances, one nonetheless produces thoughts of lust and then actually commits one of the types of offending physical karmic actions.

In circumstances involving one's own wife, [the following factors constitute transgressions of this precept]:

She may have formally taken a [temporarily restricting] moral precept;

She may be pregnant;

She may still be nursing an infant;

The act may involve a restricted orifice.[134]

These are the factors defining the act of sexual misconduct. It is the abandonment of these factors that defines the good karmic action [of refraining from sexual misconduct].

4. False Speech

As for "false speech," [it involves the following factors]:

There is some deceptive sign;

There is the mental intent to deceive;

There is the perception that this action would constitute a deceptive falsehood;

There is the acquiescence in some circumstance constituting a deceptive falsehood;

There is the desire to deceive;

There is the knowledge that the circumstances are of this sort and yet one describes them as being otherwise.

These are the factors defining the action of false speech. It is the abandonment of these factors that defines the good karmic action of abstaining from false speech.

正體字

	兩舌者。欲離別他。
095b25 ‖	以此事向彼說。以彼事向此說。為離別
095b26 ‖	他故。和合者令別離。別離者則隨順樂為
095b27 ‖	別離。意別離好別離。是名兩舌。離如此
095b28 ‖	事名為遠離兩舌善行。惡口者。世間所有惡
095b29 ‖	語害語苦語麁語弊語令[10]他瞋惱是名惡
095c01 ‖	口。遠離此事名為離惡口善行。散亂語者。
095c02 ‖	非時語無利益語非法語無本末語無因緣
095c03 ‖	語。是名散亂語。遠離此事名為離散亂善
095c04 ‖	行。貪取者。屬他之物他所欲。他田塢他財
095c05 ‖	物。

简体字

两舌者。欲离别他。以此事向彼说。以彼事向此说。为离别他故。和合者令别离。别离者则随顺乐为别离。喜别离好别离。是名两舌。离如此事名为远离两舌善行。恶口者。世间所有恶语害语苦语粗语弊语令他嗔恼是名恶口。远离此事名为离恶口善行。散乱语者。非时语无利益语非法语无本末语无因缘语。是名散乱语。远离此事名为离散乱善行。贪取者。属他之物他所欲。他田坞他财物。

Chapter 28 — *Distinctions in the 2nd Ground's Courses of Karmic Action*

5. Divisive Speech

As for "divisive speech," [it involves the following factors]:

One wishes to cause others to separate;

One says something about this person to that person or says something about that person to this person in order to cause them to separate;

Those who previously were close are then caused to separate;

If they become separated, one is subsequently happy that they have separated, rejoices that they have separated, or is pleased that they have separated.

Factors such as these define an act of divisive speech. It is the abandonment of these factors that defines the good karmic action of abstaining from divisive speech.

6. Harsh Speech

As for "harsh speech," this is inclusive of all of the types of worldly speech that are inclined to cause anger or torment in others such as:

Harsh speech;

Injurious speech;

Bitter speech;

Coarse speech;

Abusive speech.

Factors such as these define an act of harsh speech. It is the abandonment of these factors that defines the good karmic action of abstaining from harsh speech.

7. Scattered or Inappropriate Speech

As for "scattered or inappropriate speech,"[135] [it may involve the following factors]:

Speaking [of particular topics] at an inappropriate time;

Non-beneficial speech;

Speech contrary to Dharma;

[Rambling] speech having neither beginning nor end;

Unreasonable speech.

Factors such as these define the action of scattered or inappropriate speech. It is the abandonment of these factors that defines the good karmic action of "abstaining from scattered or inappropriate speech."

8. Covetousness

As for "covetousness," [it involves the following factors]:

There are things belonging to someone else which that person wishes to keep such as his fields, lands, or wealth;

正體字

```
          心貪取願欲得。於此事中不貪不妬不
095c06 ‖ 願欲得是名不貪善行。瞋惱者。於他眾生
095c07 ‖ 瞋恨心礙心發瞋恚。作是念。何不打縛殺
095c08 ‖ 害是名瞋惱離如此事名為無瞋惱善行。
095c09 ‖ 邪見者。言無布施無有恩報。善惡業無果
095c10 ‖ 報。無今世無後世。無父母無沙門[11]無婆
095c11 ‖ 羅門。能知此世[12]後世。了了通達自身作證。
095c12 ‖ 是名邪見。正見者。為有施[13]者有恩報。有
095c13 ‖ 善惡業報有今世後世。世間有沙門婆羅
095c14 ‖ 門。知此世後世了了通達自身作證。
```

简体字

心贪取愿欲得。于此事中不贪不妒不愿欲得是名不贪善行。嗔恼者。于他众生嗔恨心碍心发嗔恚。作是念。何不打缚杀害是名嗔恼离如此事名为无嗔恼善行。邪见者。言无布施无有恩报。善恶业无果报。无今世无后世。无父母无沙门无婆罗门。能知此世后世。了了通达自身作证。是名邪见。正见者。为有施者有恩报。有善恶业报有今世后世。世间有沙门婆罗门。知此世后世了了通达自身作证。

Chapter 28 — *Distinctions in the 2nd Ground's Courses of Karmic Action*

One's mind is influenced by covetousness;
One wishes to obtain that thing.

In whichever circumstance of this sort one refrains from coveting, refrains from envy, and refrains from wishing to obtain such an object, these factors constitute the good karmic action of "non-covetousness."

9. Ill Will

As for "ill will," [it may involve the following factors] directed toward some other being:

One produces thoughts of hatred;
Or one produces thoughts inclined toward obstructiveness;
Or one becomes angry;
Or one thinks, "Why not beat him up, tie him up, or murder him?"

Factors such as these define what is meant by "ill will." It is the abandoning of these factors that defines the good karmic action of "refraining from ill will."

10. Wrong Views

As for "wrong views," this refers to claims such as these:

There is no point in practicing giving;
There is no point in repaying others for kindnesses they have bestowed;
There are no corresponding karmic effects of good or bad karmic actions;
There is no [rebirth into] the present life and no [rebirth] into future lives;
There is no need to respect one's parents;
There are no *śramaṇas* or brahmans who are able to know of [rebirth into] this life or into future lives or who personally gain utterly clear and penetrating comprehension and realizations.

Factors such as these define what is meant by "wrong views."

11. Right View

As for right view, this is reflected in such views as:

There is giving [that should be done];
It is right to repay others for kindnesses they have bestowed;
There are corresponding karmic effects resulting from good and bad actions;
There is [rebirth into] the present life and into future lives;
The world does indeed have *śramaṇas* and brahmans who know [of rebirth into] this life and into future lives and who personally gain utterly clear and penetrating comprehension and realizations.

正體字

```
                是名
095c15 ‖  正見善行。是菩薩如是入正見道。
095c16 ‖     善道不善道    各二十分別
095c17 ‖     知何處起等    十二種分別
095c18 ‖  菩薩於十不善道十善道等種種別相知二
095c19 ‖  十種分別。又於是二十種分別善知從何
095c20 ‖  處起等十二種分別。於此十不善道中有
095c21 ‖  二十種分別。所謂不離奪他命罪。一是不善。
095c22 ‖  二欲界繫。三有漏。四非心數法。五心不相應。
095c23 ‖  六不隨心行。七或共心生或不共心生。何等
095c24 ‖  共心生。實有眾生知是眾生。以身業故奪
095c25 ‖  其命。是名共心生。云何名不共心生。若人
095c26 ‖  欲殺眾生捉持牽挽撲著地已然後能死。
095c27 ‖  是名不共心生。又身不動口不言。但生心
095c28 ‖  我從今日
```

简体字

是名正见善行。是菩萨如是入正见道。

　　善道不善道　　各二十分别
　　知何处起等　　十二种分别

　　菩萨于十不善道十善道等种种别相知二十种分别。又于是二十种分别善知从何处起等十二种分别。于此十不善道中有二十种分别。所谓不离夺他命罪。一是不善。二欲界系。三有漏。四非心数法。五心不相应。六不随心行。七或共心生或不共心生。何等共心生。实有众生知是众生。以身业故夺其命。是名共心生。云何名不共心生。若人欲杀众生捉持牵挽扑着地已然后能死。是名不共心生。又身不动口不言。但生心我从今日

Chapter 28 — *Distinctions in the 2nd Ground's Courses of Karmic Action*

Factors such as these define the good karmic action of right view. It is in this manner that this bodhisattva enters the right view course [of good karmic action].

> The courses of good karmic actions and of bad karmic actions each involve twenty specific types of distinctions.
> Knowledge of factors such as point of origin and such each involve twelve different types of distinctions.

D. Abhidharma Categories Analyzing the 10 Courses of Karmic Action

With respect to the ten courses of bad karmic action and the ten courses of good karmic action, the bodhisattva knows twenty distinctions pertaining to their many different distinguishing aspects. He also thoroughly knows twelve kinds of distinctions pertaining to each of these twenty distinctions that include their point of origin and so forth.

1. Twenty Factors Used in Abhidharmic Analysis of Actions

For each of these component actions within the path of the ten bad karmic actions there are twenty distinguishing factors. For instance, in not abandoning the karmic offense of taking some other being's life, we have these factors:

> First, it is an action that is not good.
> Second, it is connected with the desire realm's planes of existence.
> Third, it involves the contaminants.
> Fourth, it is not a mental dharma.
> Fifth, it is not associated with the mind.
> Sixth, it does not follow the actions of the mind.
> Seventh, it may or may not arise in conjunction with the mind.

What all is implied by "arising in conjunction with the mind"? [This involves the following]:

> There is a truly existent being;
> One knows it is a being;
> One uses some physical action to take its life.

These factors define what is meant by "arising in conjunction with the mind."

What is meant by "not arising in conjunction with the mind"? In an instance where a person [merely] wished to kill a being, grab him, pull him forth, throw him down, and pin him to the ground, but only later was able to bring about his death, this would be a case of "[killing] not arising [directly] in conjunction with the mind."

Also, it might be that the body does not move and the mouth does not speak and one only brings forth the thought, "From this day on, I

正體字

當作殺眾生者。如是奪他命
095c29 ‖ 罪。是名不共心生。又是不離奪他命者。若睡
096a01 ‖ 若覺常積習增長。亦名不共心生。八或色或
096a02 ‖ 非色。初共心[1]生殺罪是色。第二殺罪第三第
096a03 ‖ 四非是色。九或作或非作。有色是作。餘者
096a04 ‖ 無[2]作。十或有緣或無緣。色是有緣餘者是無
096a05 ‖ 緣。問曰。是心為有緣為無緣。答曰。非有
096a06 ‖ 緣。問曰。若心非有緣身不動口不言時但
096a07 ‖ 心生念我從今日當作殺眾生者。如是
096a08 ‖ 罪業云何名為非緣。答曰。若殺罪是心則
096a09 ‖ 應有緣。今實殺罪非是心。若心是殺罪即
096a10 ‖ 是身業。而心實非身業。是故殺生罪不名
096a11 ‖ 有緣。但殺生罪共心

简体字

当作杀众生者。如是夺他命罪。是名不共心生。又是不离夺他命者。若睡若觉常积习增长。亦名不共心生。八或色或非色。初共心生杀罪是色。第二杀罪第三第四非是色。九或作或非作。有色是作。余者无作。十或有缘或无缘。色是有缘余者是无缘。问曰。是心为有缘为无缘。答曰。非有缘。问曰。若心非有缘身不动口不言时但心生念我从今日当作杀众生者。如是罪业云何名为非缘。答曰。若杀罪是心则应有缘。今实杀罪非是心。若心是杀罪即是身业。而心实非身业。是故杀生罪不名有缘。但杀生罪共心

Chapter 28 — *Distinctions in the 2nd Ground's Courses of Karmic Action*

shall become someone who kills beings." This instance of the karmic offense of killing is one wherein [the actual act of taking a life] does not take place directly in conjunction with the mind.

Also, in an instance where this [ideational] non-abandonment of taking others' lives always accumulates habitual karmic propensities that continue to increase whether one is asleep or awake, this too qualifies as an instance where [the act of killing] does not arise in conjunction with the mind.

Eighth, it may be [an offense] involving either form or non-form.

That initial case [directly above] in which the act of killing occurred in conjunction with the mind—that is one that involved form. That second [immediately subsequent] example of the karmic offense of killing as well as the third and the fourth—these are all instances not involving form.

Ninth, it may involve performing an action or it may not involve performing an action.

That which involves form is one that does involve performing an action whereas any others do not involve the performing of an action.

Tenth, it may or may not involve the presence of objective conditions.

That involving form does involve objective conditions whereas the rest are circumstances devoid of objective conditions.

Question: Are these states of mind that are possessed of objective conditions or devoid of objective conditions?

Response: They do not necessarily involve objective conditions.

Question: If these states of mind do not necessarily involve objective conditions, and we have a case of the body not moving and the mouth not speaking wherein there is only the production of the thought, "From this day forward, I shall be one who takes the lives of beings," how can it be that karmic offenses such as these do not involve an objective condition?

Response: If it is an instance wherein the karmic offense of killing takes place, then this mind should indeed have associated objective conditions. However, now, in truth, the karmic offense of killing is not [merely] mental. If the mind was what actually commits the karmic offense of killing, then that would itself involve a physical action. But, in truth the mind's actions are not physical actions. Therefore, this [merely mental] karmic offense of killing beings is not defined by the presence of objective conditions. Rather, [an actual] karmic offense of killing occurs in conjunction with the mind and arises within the

正體字

在身中生。以是無作
故言非緣。十一是業。十二非業相應。十三不
隨業行。十四或共業生或不共業生。如共
心生無異。但除心與思共生為異。十五非
先世業報。十六不可修。十七應善知。十八應
以慧證不以身證。十九可斷。二十可知見。
不離劫盜罪。不離邪婬罪。不離妄語罪中。但
[3]一共心生二不共心生。一有色二無色。一作
二[4]無作。一有緣二無緣。餘如殺中說。不離
兩舌不離惡口亦如是。不離散亂語。

简体字

在身中生。以是无作故言非缘。十一是业。十二非业相应。十三不随业行。十四或共业生或不共业生。如共心生无异。但除心与思共生为异。十五非先世业报。十六不可修。十七应善知。十八应以慧证不以身证。十九可断。二十可知见。不离劫盗罪。不离邪淫罪。不离妄语罪中。但一共心生二不共心生。一有色二无色。一作二无作。一有缘二无缘。余如杀中说。不离两舌不离恶口亦如是。不离散乱语。

Chapter 28 — *Distinctions in the 2nd Ground's Courses of Karmic Action*

physical body. It is because this [merely mental] instance does not involve any action that it is referred to as being one not involving objective conditions.

> Eleventh, it may involve performing a karmic action.
> Twelfth, it may not correspond to the commission of a karmic action.
> Thirteenth, it may occur in a manner not in direct linkage with the commission of a karmic action.
> Fourteenth, it may or may not be generated in conjunction with the commission of a given karmic action.

This is analogous to the case involving arising in conjunction with the mind and is no different than that. The only difference here is that it is not arising in conjunction with mind, but is instead arising in conjunction with volition.[136]

> Fifteenth, it may not be a karmic result of actions carried out in previous existences.
> Sixteenth, it is not to be cultivated.
> Seventeenth, it is to be well understood.[137]
> Eighteenth, it should be realized by wisdom and is not realized by the body.
> Nineteenth, it can be severed.[138]
> Twentieth, it can be known and seen.

[Now, as for the application of these factors to] the karmic offense of "not abandoning stealing," the karmic offense of "not abandoning sexual misconduct," and the karmic offense of "not abandoning false speech," these are just the same as when they were applied to the karmic offense of "killing" except that these involve:[139]

> One instance that occurs in conjunction with the mind and two instances that do not occur in conjunction with the mind;
> One instance that involves form and two instances that do not involve form;
> One instance that involves the performance of an action and two instances that do not involve the performance of an action;
> One instance that involves objective conditions and two instances that do not involve objective conditions.

As for "not abandoning divisive speech" and "not abandoning harsh speech," [the relevant distinctions] are just the same [as with the above-discussed actions].

In the case of "not abandoning scattered or inappropriate speech," [the relevant distinctions are as follows]:

正體字	或不善 096a21 ‖ 或無記從不善心生。是不善從無記心生。 096a22 ‖ 是無記或欲界繫。或色界繫。欲界繫者。以 096a23 ‖ 欲界身心。散亂語是欲界繫。色界繫亦如是。 096a24 ‖ 餘如妄語中說。貪取欲界繫。是有漏心數法。 096a25 ‖ 非心相應。非隨心行。心共生。無色無作。有 096a26 ‖ 緣。非業相應。非隨業行。非共業生。非先世業 096a27 ‖ 報。除因報。非可修。應善知。應以慧證。身證。 096a28 ‖ 可斷。可見知。瞋惱。或心相應。或心不相應。纏 096a29 ‖ 所攝名心相應。
简体字	或不善或无记从不善心生。是不善从无记心生。是无记或欲界系。或色界系。欲界系者。以欲界身心。散乱语是欲界系。色界系亦如是。余如妄语中说。贪取欲界系。是有漏心数法。非心相应。非随心行。心共生。无色无作。有缘。非业相应。非随业行。非共业生。非先世业报。除因报。非可修。应善知。应以慧证。身证。可断。可见知。瞋恼。或心相应。或心不相应。缠所摄名心相应。

Chapter 28 — *Distinctions in the 2nd Ground's Courses of Karmic Action*

It may be karmically bad;
It may be karmically neutral;
That which arises from bad intentionality is karmically bad;
That which arises from neutral intentionality is karmically neutral;
It may occur in connection with the desire realm;
It may occur in connection with the form realm.

As for that which occurs in connection with the desire realm, it is scattered or inappropriate speech arising in a desire-realm body and mind that occur in connection with the desire realm;

The basis for being categorized as "connected with the form realm" is similarly determined.

The remaining factors relevant to "scattered or inappropriate speech" are similar to those set forth earlier with regard to "false speech."

As for "covetousness," [the relevant distinctions are as follows]:[140]

It arises in connection with the desire realm;
It is a mental dharma influenced by the contaminants;
It is not associated with the mind;
It does not follow the actions of the mind;
It occurs in conjunction with the mind;
It is formless;
It does not involve an action;
It does involve an objective condition;
It does not correspond to a karmic action;
It does not follow and correspond to karmic action;
It does not arise in conjunction with karmic action;
It is not itself a karmic result from actions committed in a prior existence except when it is a karmic result of a [prior] cause;[141]
It cannot be cultivated;
It should be thoroughly understood;
It should be the object of wisdom-based realization;
It may involve realizations pertaining to the body;
It is subject to severance;
It is subject to being perceived and understood.

As for "ill will," [the relevant distinctions are as follows]:

It may be associated with the mind;
It may not be associated with the mind;
In instances where it is associated with the mind, it is included in the obsessions;

正體字	使所攝名心不相應。隨心行 096b01 ‖ 不隨心行亦如是。共心生不共心生。有覺眾 096b02 ‖ 生與心共生。無覺眾生不與心共生。如心 096b03 ‖ 相應。隨心行共心生業相應。隨業行共業生 096b04 ‖ 亦如是。如心不相應不隨心行不共心生業 096b05 ‖ 不相應不隨業行不與業共生亦如是。餘分 096b06 ‖ 別如貪取中說。如瞋惱邪見亦如是。十善 096b07 ‖ 道中離奪他命是善性。或欲界繫。或不繫三 096b08 ‖ 界。欲界繫[5]者以欲界身離奪他命。是欲界 096b09 ‖ 繫。非三界繫者。學無學人八聖道所攝。離殺 096b10 ‖ 生正業。是或有漏或無漏。
简体字	使所摄名心不相应。随心行不随心行亦如是。共心生不共心生。有觉众生与心共生。无觉众生不与心共生。如心相应。随心行共心生业相应。随业行共业生亦如是。如心不相应不随心行不共心生业不相应不随业行不与业共生亦如是。余分别如贪取中说。如瞋恼邪见亦如是。十善道中离夺他命是善性。或欲界系。或不系三界。欲界系者以欲界身离夺他命。是欲界系。非三界系者。学无学人八圣道所摄。离杀生正业。是或有漏或无漏。

Chapter 28 — *Distinctions in the 2nd Ground's Courses of Karmic Action* 989

In instances where it is not associated with the mind, it is included among the latent afflictions;[142]

The cases are just the same with reference to its following or not following actions of the mind.

As for instances in which it occurs in conjunction with the mind or, alternatively, does not occur in conjunction with the mind, it is when it occurs in beings possessed of ideation that it occurs in conjunction with the mind and it is when it occurs in beings not possessed of ideation that it does not occur in conjunction with the mind.

Just as it is with occurrences associated with the mind, with occurrences following actions of the mind, with occurrences arising in conjunction with the mind, so too it is with occurrences associated with karmic actions, with occurrences following karmic action, and with occurrences in conjunction with the arising of karmic action.

And just as it is with occurrences unassociated with the mind, with occurrences not following actions of the mind, and with occurrences not arising in conjunction with the mind, so too it is with occurrences unassociated with karmic actions, with occurrences not following karmic action, and with occurrences not in conjunction with the arising of karmic action.

The remaining distinctions that could be made here [with regard to "ill will"] may be deduced from the earlier discussion of "covetousness."

[The distinctions that could be made regarding] "wrong views" are just the same as those already described above with regard to "ill will."

As for "abandonment of taking others' lives" among the ten courses of good karmic action, [the relevant distinctions are as follows]:

It is good in nature.

It may occur in connection with the desire-realm planes of existence.

It may be unconnected to the three realms of existence.[143]

In instances connected to the desire realm, one abides in a desire-realm body and abandons taking other beings' lives. This is what is meant by being "connected to the desire realm."

In instances "unconnected to the three realms of existence," this corresponds to actions included in the eightfold path of the Āryas engaged in by those at and beyond the stages of training who practice "right action" by abandoning the killing of beings.

It may involve the contaminants.

It may not involve the contaminants.

| 正體字 | 欲界繫是有漏。非
三界繫是無漏。非心數法。非心相應。非隨心
行。或共心生或不共心生。何等是共心生。如
行人見虫而作是念。我當身業遠離不傷
害。是名離奪命善行共心生。何等是離殺生
善不共心生。有人身不動口不言但心
念從今日不殺生。是名不共心生。又有人
先遠離殺生。若睡若覺心緣餘事。於念念
中不殺生。福常得增長。亦不共心生。或是
色或非色。一是色二非色。一是作二非作。一
有緣二無緣。是業非業相應。不隨業行。或
共業生或不共業生。如共心生不共心生
[6]除心與思為異。 |

| 簡體字 | 欲界系是有漏。非三界系是无漏。非心数法。非心相应。非随心行。或共心生或不共心生。何等是共心生。如行人见虫而作是念。我当身业远离不伤害。是名离夺命善行共心生。何等是离杀生善不共心生。有人身不动口不言但心念从今日不杀生。是名不共心生。又有人先远离杀生。若睡若觉心缘余事。于念念中不杀生。福常得增长。亦不共心生。或是色或非色。一是色二非色。一是作二非作。一有缘二无缘。是业非业相应。不随业行。或共业生或不共业生。如共心生不共心生除心与思为异。 |

Chapter 28 — *Distinctions in the 2nd Ground's Courses of Karmic Action*

When it is "connected to the desire realm," it involves the contaminants. When it is "unconnected to the three realms," it is free of the contaminants.

> It is not a mental dharma.
> It is not a dharma associated with the mind.
> It is not [a dharma that] follows the mind.
> It may arise in conjunction with the mind.
> It may not arise in conjunction with the mind.

What all is implied by arising in conjunction with the mind? This is a circumstance like that of someone who is walking along, sees a bug, and thinks, "Through physical actions that abandon killing, I shall refrain from injuring it." This is what is meant by a good action of abandoning killing arising in conjunction with the mind.

How is it that the good action of abandoning killing other beings does not occur in conjunction with the mind? Take an instance where there is a person whose body does not move, whose mouth does not speak, and who only thinks, "From this very day forward, I shall no longer kill beings." This is a case in which [the action itself] does not occur in concert with the mind.

Then again, we may have a person who, from early on, has abandoned the killing of beings. Whether sleeping or awake, when his mind takes various other circumstances as objective conditions, in thought after thought, as he refrains from killing beings, his merit always increases and at the same time, this does not take place in conjunction with the mind.

This may or may not involve form. One instance involves form and two other instances do not involve form. One instance involves the performance of an action and two other instances do not involve the performance of an action. One instance involves objective conditions and two other instances do not involve objective conditions.

> It may constitute an action.
> It may not occur in conjunction with an action.
> It does not follow an action.

In instances where it may occur in conjunction with an action or may not occur in conjunction with an action, the determining factor is just the same [as in the case explained above] involving the issue of whether the action occurs in conjunction with the mind or does not occur in conjunction with the mind. The only difference is with regard to the presence of mind versus the presence of volition.

正體字	非先業報。除因報。可修 096b23 ‖ [7]可善知[8]可以身證。慧證[9]或可斷或不可斷 096b24 ‖ 有漏則可斷。無漏不可斷。可知見亦如是。 096b25 ‖ 離劫盜。離邪婬。離妄語。離兩舌。離惡口亦如 096b26 ‖ 是。離散亂語。或欲界繫。或色界繫。或不繫 096b27 ‖ 三界。欲界繫者。以欲界身心離散亂語。色 096b28 ‖ 界繫亦如是。不繫三界者。如不殺中說。或 096b29 ‖ 有漏或無漏。有漏者繫。無漏者不繫。餘如離 096c01 ‖ 妄語中說。不貪取者是善性。或欲界繫。或非 096c02 ‖ 繫三界。欲界繫者。欲界凡夫不貪取及
简体字	非先业报。除因报。可修可善知可以身证。慧证或可断或不可断有漏则可断。无漏不可断。可知见亦如是。离劫盗。离邪淫。离妄语。离两舌。离恶口亦如是。离散乱语。或欲界系。或色界系。或不系三界。欲界系者。以欲界身心离散乱语。色界系亦如是。不系三界者。如不杀中说。或有漏或无漏。有漏者系。无漏者不系。余如离妄语中说。不贪取者是善性。或欲界系。或非系三界。欲界系者。欲界凡夫不贪取及

Chapter 28 — *Distinctions in the 2nd Ground's Courses of Karmic Action*   993

It is not itself a karmic result from actions committed in a prior [existence] except when it is a karmic result of a prior cause.

It can be cultivated.

It can be thoroughly understood.

It can be the object of physical realization or wisdom-based realization.

It may be subject to severance or may not be subject to severance.

If it is associated with the contaminants, then it may be subject to severance. If it is unassociated with the contaminants, then it is not subject to severance. So too with respect to its amenability to being known and seen.

[The relevant distinctions applicable to] "abandonment of stealing," "abandonment of sexual misconduct," "abandonment of false speech," "abandonment of divisive speech," and "abandonment of harsh speech" are all similar.

As for [the good karmic action of] "abandonment of scattered or inappropriate speech," [the relevant distinctions are as follows]:

It may be connected to the desire realm.

It may be connected to the form realm.

It may not be connected to any of the three realms.

When connected with the form realm, it is with a desire-realm body and mind that one abandons scattered and inappropriate speech. So too, when connected with the form realm, [it is with a form-realm body and mind that one abandons scattered and inappropriate speech]. When not connected with any of the three realms, [the distinguishing factors] are as explained above in the discussion of the good karmic action of abstaining from killing.

It may be associated with the contaminants.

It may be unassociated with the contaminants.

When associated with the contaminants, it is connected [with the three realms]. When unassociated with the contaminants, it is not connected [with any of the three realms]. The other applicable distinctions are as explained in the above discussion of "abandoning false speech."

As for [the good karmic action of] "abandonment of covetousness," [the relevant distinctions are as follows]:

It is good in nature.

It may be connected with the desire realm.

It may not be connected to any of the three realms.

When connected to the desire realm, this may be a desire-realm common person refraining from covetousness or else this may be someone

正體字	賢聖 096c03 ‖ 不貪取善行。是欲界繫。非三界繫者。諸賢聖 096c04 ‖ 不貪取無漏善行。是或有漏或無漏。欲界繫 096c05 ‖ 是有漏。不繫三界是無漏。是心數法。心相 096c06 ‖ 應。隨心行。共心生。無色無作。有緣。非業。業 096c07 ‖ 相應。隨業行。共業生。非先業報。除因報。可 096c08 ‖ 修。可善知。可以身證。慧證。或可斷。或不可 096c09 ‖ 斷。有漏可斷。無漏不可斷。[10]知見亦如是。 096c10 ‖ 離瞋惱是善性。或欲界繫。或色界繫。
简体字	贤圣不贪取善行。是欲界系。非三界系者。诸贤圣不贪取无漏善行。是或有漏或无漏。欲界系是有漏。不系三界是无漏。是心数法。心相应。随心行。共心生。无色无作。有缘。非业。业相应。随业行。共业生。非先业报。除因报。可修。可善知。可以身证。慧证。或可断。或不可断。有漏可断。无漏不可断。知见亦如是。离瞋恼是善性。或欲界系。或色界系。

Chapter 28 — *Distinctions in the 2nd Ground's Courses of Karmic Action*

who is a worthy or an *ārya* practicing the good karmic action of abstaining from covetousness. This is what is meant by being "connected with the desire realm."

When not connected to any of the three realms, this is an instance of refraining from covetousness that is a good karmic action unassociated with the contaminants done by either a worthy or an *ārya*.

This may be associated with the contaminants.
It may be unassociated with the contaminants.

When it is connected with the desire realm, it is associated with the contaminants. When not connected [to any of the three realms], it is unassociated with the contaminants.

This is a mental dharma.
It is associated with the mind.
It may follow actions of the mind.
It may arise in conjunction with the mind.
It is formless.
It does not involve performance of an action.
It has objective conditions.
It is not a karmic action.
It is associated with karmic actions.
It may follow karmic actions.
It may arise in conjunction with karmic actions.
It is not itself a karmic result from actions committed in a prior [existence] except when it is a karmic result of a prior cause.
It can be cultivated.
It can be thoroughly known.
It is amenable to physical realization.
It is amenable to wisdom-based realization.
It may be subject to severance.
It may not be subject to severance.

When associated with the contaminants, it is subject to severance. When unassociated with the contaminants, it is not subject to severance. So too with the distinctions regarding amenability to being directly known and seen.

As for [the good karmic action of] "abandoning ill will," [the relevant distinctions are as follows]:

It is good in nature.
It may be connected with the desire realm.
It may be connected with the form realm.

正體字

或無色
096c11 ‖ 界繫。或不繫三界。欲界繫者。欲界不瞋惱善
096c12 ‖ 根。餘二界亦如是。不繫者。餘不繫是或有漏
096c13 ‖ 或無漏繫三界者。是有漏。餘是無漏。心數法。
096c14 ‖ 或心相應。或心不相應。與纏相違不瞋善根
096c15 ‖ 與心相應。與使相違不瞋善根與心不相
096c16 ‖ 應。隨心行共心生亦如是。無色無作。或有緣
096c17 ‖ 或無緣。心相應是有緣。心不相應是無緣。非
096c18 ‖ 業或與業相應。或不與業相應。或隨業行
096c19 ‖ 或不隨業行。或共業生。或不共業生。亦如
096c20 ‖ 心說

简体字

或无色界系。或不系三界。欲界系者。欲界不嗔恼善根。余二界亦如是。不系者。余不系是或有漏或无漏系三界者。是有漏。余是无漏。心数法。或心相应。或心不相应。与缠相违不嗔善根与心相应。与使相违不嗔善根与心不相应。随心行共心生亦如是。无色无作。或有缘或无缘。心相应是有缘。心不相应是无缘。非业或与业相应。或不与业相应。或随业行或不随业行。或共业生。或不共业生。亦如心说

Chapter 28 — *Distinctions in the 2nd Ground's Courses of Karmic Action*

> It may be connected to the formless realm.
> It may be that it is not connected with any of the three realms.

When connected with the desire realm, it is in a desire-realm existence with roots of goodness arising [from previous practice] of restraint from ill will. When connected with existence in either of the other two realms, the bases are just the same.

As for when it is "not connected to any of the three realms," all other instances [aside from the above] are "not connected [to any of the three realms]."

> This may be associated with the contaminants or it may be unassociated with the contaminants.

When connected to any of the three realms, it is associated with the contaminants. All other instances are unassociated with the contaminants.

> It is a mental dharma.
> It may be associated with the mind.
> It may be unassociated with the mind.

When opposing obsession, roots of goodness arising from refraining from ill will are associated with the mind. When opposing latent tendencies, roots of goodness arising from refraining from ill will are unassociated with the mind. The distinctions are the same with respect to following actions of the mind and arising in conjunction with the mind.

> It is formless.
> It does not involve performance of an action.
> It may have objective conditions.
> It may not have objective conditions.

When it is associated with the mind it has objective conditions. When it is unassociated with the mind it does not have objective conditions.

> It is not a karmic action.
> It may be associated with a karmic action.
> Or it may not be associated with a karmic action.
> It may follow the enactment of a karmic action.
> Or it may not follow the enactment of a karmic action.
> It may arise in conjunction with a karmic action.
> Or it may not arise in conjunction with a karmic action.

[The distinctions applicable to this arising or not arising in conjunction with a karmic action] are the same as those that applied above when discussing mind.

正體字	非業。報除因報。可以身證慧證。或可斷 096c21 ‖ 或不可斷。有漏可斷。無漏不可斷。可[*]知見 096c22 ‖ 亦如是。正見是善性。或欲界繫。或色界繫。 096c23 ‖ 或無色界繫。或非三界繫。欲界繫者。若凡夫 096c24 ‖ 若賢聖。欲界念相應正見。是色無色界亦如 096c25 ‖ 是。不繫三界者。[11]賢聖無漏正見。或有漏或 096c26 ‖ 無漏。三界繫是有漏。不繫是無漏。心數法。心 096c27 ‖ 相應。隨心行。共心生。無色無作。有緣。非業。 096c28 ‖ 業相應。隨業行。共業生。非先業報。除因報。
简体字	非业。报除因报。可以身证慧证。或可断或不可断。有漏可断。无漏不可断。可知见亦如是。正见是善性。或欲界系。或色界系。或无色界系。或非三界系。欲界系者。若凡夫若贤圣。欲界念相应正见。是色无色界亦如是。不系三界者。贤圣无漏正见。或有漏或无漏。三界系是有漏。不系是无漏。心数法。心相应。随心行。共心生。无色无作。有缘。非业。业相应。随业行。共业生。非先业报。除因报。

It is not a karmic result from actions [committed in a prior existence] except when it is a karmic result of a prior cause.
It can be the object of physical realization or wisdom-based realization.
It may be subject to severance or may not be subject to severance.

When associated with the contaminants it is subject to severance. When unassociated with the contaminants, it is not subject to severance. So too with regard to its amenability to being known and seen.

As for [the good karmic action of] "right view," [the relevant distinctions are as follows]:

It is good in nature.
It may be connected with the desire realm.
It may be connected with the form realm.
It may be connected with the formless realm.
It may not be connected with any of the three realms.

When connected to the desire realm, it involves thoughts corresponding to right views produced in the desire realm by common persons, worthies, or *āryas*. When connected to the form realm and when connected to the formless realm, the circumstances are just the same.

When not connected to any of the three realms, these are right views unassociated with the contaminants as held by worthies or *āryas*.

It may be associated with the contaminants.
It may be unassociated with the contaminants.

When connected to any of the three realms, it is associated with the contaminants. When not connected to any of the three realms, it is unassociated with the contaminants.

It is a mental dharma.
It is a dharma associated with the mind.
It follows actions of the mind.
It arises in conjunction with the mind.
It is formless.
It does not involve the performance of an action.
It may have objective conditions.
It is not a karmic action.
It may be associated with a karmic action.
It may follow the enactment of a karmic action.
It may arise in conjunction with a karmic action.
It is not a karmic result from actions [committed in a prior existence] except when it is a karmic result of a prior cause.

正體字	096c29 ‖ 可以身證。慧證。或可斷。或不可斷。有漏可 097a01 ‖ 斷。無漏不可斷。可見可知亦如是。是名善 097a02 ‖ 等二十種分別。從何起等十二論者。一從何 097a03 ‖ 起。二起誰。三從何因起。四與誰作因。五何 097a04 ‖ 緣。六與誰作緣。七何所緣。八與誰作緣。九 097a05 ‖ 何增上。十與誰作增上。十一何失。十二何果 097a06 ‖ 殺罪。從何起者。從三不善根起。又從邪念 097a07 ‖ 起。又隨以何心奪眾生命。從是心起。起誰 097a08 ‖ 者。從殺罪邊所有諸法。已生今生當生。是 097a09 ‖ 因緣亦如是。何所緣者。緣眾生。又因何心 097a10 ‖ 奪眾生命。亦緣此心。
简体字	可以身证。慧证。或可断。或不可断。有漏可断。无漏不可断。可见可知亦如是。是名善等二十种分别。从何起等十二论者。一从何起。二起谁。三从何因起。四与谁作因。五何缘。六与谁作缘。七何所缘。八与谁作缘。九何增上。十与谁作增上。十一何失。十二何果杀罪。从何起者。从三不善根起。又从邪念起。又随以何心夺众生命。从是心起。起谁者。从杀罪边所有诸法。已生今生当生。是因缘亦如是。何所缘者。缘众生。又因何心夺众生命。亦缘此心。

Chapter 28 — *Distinctions in the 2nd Ground's Courses of Karmic Action*

It can be the object of physical realization or wisdom-based realization.

It may be subject to severance or may not be subject to severance.

When associated with contaminants, it is subject to severance. When unassociated with the contaminants, it is not subject to severance.

The differentiations here are the same with respect to amenability to knowing and seeing.

This [above discussion illustrates] what is meant by the application of twenty distinguishing factors such as "goodness," and so forth [to the understanding of the ten courses of good karmic action and the ten courses of bad karmic action.]

2. THE TWELVEFOLD DISCUSSION OF ORIGINS AND SUCH

As for the twelvefold discussion of "origins" and so forth, it is as follows:[144]

1) From what did it originate?
2) What does it produce?
3) From what cause did it originate?
4) For whom is it a cause?
5) What are the associated conditions?
6) For what is it a condition?
7) What does it take as an objective condition?
8) What is the benefit?[145]
9) What factors are dominant?
10) For whom is this dominant?
11) What losses does this incur?
12) What karmic effects does this entail?

In the case of the karmic offense of "killing," [these discussions are as follows]:

As for "From what did it originate?," it arises from the three types of bad karmic roots and additionally arises from wrong thought. Further, it arises from whichever thought the act of taking a being's life next followed upon. It originated from this thought.

As for "What does it produce?," these are all of the dharmas proximate to the karmic offense of killing whether those dharmas have already arisen, are now arising, or eventually will arise. So too with these causes and conditions.

As for "What does it take as an objective condition?," it takes a living being as its objective condition. Additionally, whichever thought precipitated the taking of that being's life—it also takes this thought as a condition.

正體字

與誰作緣者。因殺罪
097a11 ‖ 邊所有諸法。若已生若今生若當生。是法緣
097a12 ‖ 於殺生罪。何失者。今世惡名人所不信等。
097a13 ‖ 何果者。墮地獄畜生餓鬼阿修羅等及餘惡
097a14 ‖ 處。受苦惱報。增上與誰增上者。如從何處
097a15 ‖ 起中說。劫盜邪婬妄語兩舌惡口散亂語貪
097a16 ‖ 取瞋惱邪見亦如是。但所緣有異。劫盜罪
097a17 ‖ 緣所用物。邪婬緣眾生。妄語兩舌惡口散亂
097a18 ‖ 語緣於名字。貪取緣所用物。瞋惱緣眾生。
097a19 ‖ 邪見緣名字。餘殘亦如上。不殺生從三善
097a20 ‖ 根起。又從正念起。又隨以何心離殺生。
097a21 ‖ 從是心起。起誰者。從是法所有諸法。若已
097a22 ‖ 生若今生若當生。是因緣亦如是。所緣者。緣
097a23 ‖ 於眾生。與誰作緣者。因是不殺生邊所有諸
097a24 ‖ 法。若已生若今生

简体字

与谁作缘者。因杀罪边所有诸法。若已生若今生若当生。是法缘于杀生罪。何失者。今世恶名人所不信等。何果者。堕地狱畜生饿鬼阿修罗等及余恶处。受苦恼报。增上与谁增上者。如从何处起中说。劫盗邪淫妄语两舌恶口散乱语贪取嗔恼邪见亦如是。但所缘有异。劫盗罪缘所用物。邪淫缘众生。妄语两舌恶口散乱语缘于名字。贪取缘所用物。嗔恼缘众生。邪见缘名字。余残亦如上。不杀生从三善根起。又从正念起。又随以何心离杀生。从是心起。起谁者。从是法所有诸法。若已生若今生若当生。是因缘亦如是。所缘者。缘于众生。与谁作缘者。因是不杀生边所有诸法。若已生若今生

Chapter 28 — *Distinctions in the 2nd Ground's Courses of Karmic Action*

As for "For what is it a condition?," all of the peripheral dharmas caused by the karmic offense of killing, whether already arisen, now arising, or eventually arising—these are all conditions associated with the karmic offense of killing.

As for "What losses does this incur?," this includes having a bad reputation in the present lifetime, being the object of others' distrust, and so forth.

As for "What karmic effects does this entail?," these include falling into the hell realm, the animal realm, the hungry-ghost realm, the *asura* realm, and other wretched destinies wherein one undergoes suffering and anguish.

As for "What factors are dominant?" and "For whom is this dominant?," these are the same as with above statement on the bases of origination.

These distinctions are the same in their application to stealing, sexual misconduct, false speech, divisive speech, harsh speech, scattered or inappropriate speech, covetousness, ill will, and wrong views. There are only differences with regard to what in each case serves as an objective condition.

For instance, in the case of stealing, it is the object that one appropriates to one's own use that serves as the objective condition. Sexual misconduct takes a being as the objective condition.

False speech, divisive speech, harsh speech, and scattered or inappropriate speech all take words as their objective condition.

Covetousness takes as its objective condition the particular object that one would appropriate to one's own use.

Ill will takes a being as the objective condition.

Wrong views take words as their objective condition.

All of the remaining distinctions are deducible from the differentiations described above.

"Refraining from killing beings" arises from the three types of good karmic roots as well as from right mindfulness. It also arises from the thought arising just prior to the act of refraining from killing a being.

As for "What does it produce?," these are all of the dharmas arising from this dharma, whether they have already arisen, are now arising, or eventually will arise. So too with the associated causes and conditions.

As for "What does it take as an objective condition?," it takes a living being as its objective condition.

As for "For what is it a condition?," all of the peripheral dharmas caused by the act of not killing whether already arisen, now arising,

正體字

097a25 ‖ 若當生。緣於不殺生。增上
097a25 ‖ 者。諸善根增上。正念亦增上。隨以何心不
097a26 ‖ 殺生。是心亦增上。與誰作增上者。於是不
097a27 ‖ 殺生邊所有諸法。若已生若今生若當生。何
097a28 ‖ 利益者。與殺罪相違是名為利。何果者。與
097a29 ‖ 殺生相違名為果。不劫盜邪婬妄語兩舌惡
097b01 ‖ 口散亂語不貪不恚正見亦如是。但所緣有
097b02 ‖ 異。不劫盜緣所用物。不邪婬緣眾生。不妄
097b03 ‖ 語不兩舌不惡口不散亂語緣名字。不貪取
097b04 ‖ 緣所用物。不瞋惱緣眾生。正見或緣名字
097b05 ‖ 或緣義。有漏緣於名字。無漏緣於義。是菩
097b06 ‖ 薩於善等論及起等十二論。行十善道。應
097b07 ‖ 如是分別知。又知。

简体字

若当生。缘于不杀生。增上者。诸善根增上。正念亦增上。随以何心不杀生。是心亦增上。与谁作增上者。于是不杀生边所有诸法。若已生若今生若当生。何利益者。与杀罪相违是名为利。何果者。与杀生相违名为果。不劫盗邪淫妄语两舌恶口散乱语不贪不恚正见亦如是。但所缘有异。不劫盗缘所用物。不邪淫缘众生。不妄语不两舌不恶口不散乱语缘名字。不贪取缘所用物。不瞋恼缘众生。正见或缘名字或缘义。有漏缘于名字。无漏缘于义。是菩萨于善等论及起等十二论。行十善道。应如是分别知。又知。

Chapter 28 — Distinctions in the 2nd Ground's Courses of Karmic Action

or eventually arising—these are all conditions associated with the act of not killing.

As for "dominant factors," the roots of goodness are dominant and right mindfulness is also dominant. Also whichever thought was followed by the restraint from killing a particular being—that thought was also dominant.

As for "For whom is this dominant?," this is determined by all of the dharmas peripheral to the act of not taking a being's life, whether they have already arisen, are now arising, or will eventually arise.

As for "What is the benefit?," being opposed to the karmic offense of killing—this is the benefit.

As for "What karmic effects does this entail?," these are whichever karmic effects are opposite to those entailed by killing beings.

These distinctions are the same in their application to not stealing, to not committing sexual misconduct, to not committing false speech, to not engaging in divisive speech, to not engaging in harsh speech, to not engaging in scattered or inappropriate speech, to non-covetousness, to refraining from ill will, and to right views. There are only differences with regard to what in each case serves as an objective condition.

For instance, in the case of not stealing, it is the object that one might otherwise appropriate to one's own use that serves as the objective condition.

Refraining from sexual misconduct takes a being [otherwise susceptible to one's sexual misconduct] as the objective condition.

Refraining from false speech, divisive speech, harsh speech, and scattered or inappropriate speech all take words as their objective condition.

Non-covetousness takes as its objective condition the particular object that one might otherwise desire to have available to one's own use.

Refraining from ill will takes a being as the objective condition.

Right views may take words as the objective condition or may take meaning as the objective conditions. Those associated with the contaminants take words as objective conditions. Those unassociated with the contaminants take meanings as the objective condition.

It is in this manner that this bodhisattva should distinguish and know with respect to the practice of the ten courses of good karmic actions the [twenty] analytic discussions of "goodness" and so forth as well as the twelve analytic discussions of "origination" and so forth.

In addition, he should know:

正體字

097b08 ‖　　七種不善處　　以貪瞋癡生
097b09 ‖　　及四[1]門分別　　業眾生各二
097b10 ‖　是菩薩知七不善業道以貪[2]瞋癡生。而分
097b11 ‖　別於世。又知七種不善業中四門分別。是殺
097b12 ‖　罪或從貪生。或從瞋生。或從癡生。從貪生
097b13 ‖　者。若人見眾生。生貪著心。從是因緣。受用
097b14 ‖　好色聲香味觸。或須齒角毛皮筋肉骨髓等。
097b15 ‖　是人生如是貪心故奪他命。是名從[3]貪
097b16 ‖　生殺罪。若人瞋心不喜殺眾生。是名從瞋
097b17 ‖　生。若人邪見不知後世善惡業殺眾生。是
097b18 ‖　名從癡生殺罪。或以為福德故。或使欲度
097b19 ‖　苦故而殺。如西方安息國等。復有取福德
097b20 ‖　因緣故殺。以是殺業因緣故。欲得生天。
097b21 ‖　如東天竺人於天寺中殺生。以此事故
097b22 ‖　[4]欲生天上。是名從癡生。復有人以貪心
097b23 ‖　故取他物。作是念。以我當隨意得好色
097b24 ‖　聲香味觸。是名從貪生。

简体字

　　七种不善处　　以贪嗔痴生
　　及四门分别　　业众生各二
　是菩萨知七不善业道以贪嗔痴生。而分别于世。又知七种不善业中四门分别。是杀罪或从贪生。或从嗔生。或从痴生。从贪生者。若人见众生。生贪着心。从是因缘。受用好色声香味触。或须齿角毛皮筋肉骨髓等。是人生如是贪心故夺他命。是名从贪生杀罪。若人嗔心不喜杀众生。是名从嗔生。若人邪见不知后世善恶业杀众生。是名从痴生杀罪。或以为福德故。或使欲度苦故而杀。如西方安息国等。复有取福德因缘故杀。以是杀业因缘故。欲得生天。如东天竺人于天寺中杀生。以此事故欲生天上。是名从痴生。复有人以贪心故取他物。作是念。以我当随意得好色声香味触。是名从贪生。

3. The Seven Types of Bad Actions, Their Origins, and Four Distinctions

The bases for the seven types of bad karmic actions,
how they may arise from greed, hatred, or delusion,
and also the application of four types of distinctions
of which two each are linked to karmic actions and to beings.

This bodhisattva knows that seven courses of bad karmic action may arise from greed, hatred, or delusion, and thus applies these distinctions to circumstances in the world. He is also aware of four categorical distinctions applicable to these seven types of bad karmic deeds.

This karmic offense of killing may arise from greed, hatred, or from delusion. [Consider the case in which killing] arises from greed. Suppose for example that a person sees some being, produces a thought of greed, and then, due to these causes and conditions, because he wishes to enjoy the use of that being's visual forms, sounds, fragrances, tastes, or touchables, or because he wants its tusks, horns, fur, hide, sinews, flesh, bones, marrow, and such—this person then, due to having this covetous thought, takes this being's life. This is a case of the karmic offense of killing arising from greed.

In a case where someone kills a being due to hating and being displeased [with that being], this is an instance of killing arising from hatred.

In a case where someone beset by wrong views fails to realize the effects of good and bad karmic actions as they unfold in subsequent lives and then, because of that, kills some being, this is an instance of the karmic offense of killing arising from delusion. In some cases, the killer may kill due to regarding the act as productive of merit. Or he may kill out of a desire to liberate [the being he is killing] from suffering. These cases are reflective of customs in the country of Parthia in the west and other such places.

There are yet other instances of killing motivated by the idea that it may serve as a cause and condition for the acquisition of merit. Thus one may wish to achieve rebirth in the heavens through the karma of killing. This latter situation is exemplified by a practice in East India of sacrificing beings in the temple of their deva, wishing through such deeds to be reborn in the heavens. These are all cases of killing occurring because of delusion.

There are yet other individuals who, because of greed, take the possessions of others, thinking: "This is because I deserve to freely acquire whichever fine visual forms, sounds, fragrances, flavors, or touchables appeal to me." This is just a case of stealing arising from greed.

正體字	復有人以瞋心不 097b25 ‖ 喜彼人故劫盜財物。欲令其惱。是名從 097b26 ‖ 瞋生。復有人邪見不知果報。劫盜他物。是 097b27 ‖ 名從癡生。如諸婆羅門說世間財寶皆是 097b28 ‖ 我物。我力弱故諸小人等以非法取用。若我 097b29 ‖ 取者。自取其物無有過罪。以如是心劫 097c01 ‖ [5]盜他物者。是亦從癡生。若人貪著色因緣 097c02 ‖ 故而邪婬。是名從貪生。若人瞋不喜作是 097c03 ‖ 念。是人犯我母婦姊妹女等。我亦還以婬 097c04 ‖ 事污彼母婦姊妹女等。是名從瞋生邪婬。 097c05 ‖ 若人邪見不知果報而故犯者。是名從癡 097c06 ‖ 生。如有人言。人中無有邪婬。何以故。女人 097c07 ‖ 皆為男子故生。如餘所用物。[6]如有所須。 097c08 ‖ 若與從事無邪婬罪。以是心作婬欲者。是 097c09 ‖ 名從癡生。如劫盜罪妄語亦如是。為貪 097c10 ‖ 財故妄語。是名從貪生。為欲誑彼令得 097c11 ‖ 苦惱。是名從瞋生。邪見不知業果報故妄 097c12 ‖ 語。是名從癡生。兩舌惡口散亂語亦如是。
简体字	复有人以嗔心不喜彼人故劫盗财物。欲令其恼。是名从嗔生。复有人邪见不知果报。劫盗他物。是名从痴生。如诸婆罗门说世间财宝皆是我物。我力弱故诸小人等以非法取用。若我取者。自取其物无有过罪。以如是心劫盗他物者。是亦从痴生。若人贪着色因缘故而邪淫。是名从贪生。若人嗔不喜作是念。是人犯我母妇姊妹女等。我亦还以淫事污彼母妇姊妹女等。是名从嗔生邪淫。若人邪见不知果报而故犯者。是名从痴生。如有人言。人中无有邪淫。何以故。女人皆为男子故生。如余所用物。如有所须。若与从事无邪淫罪。以是心作淫欲者。是名从痴生。如劫盗罪妄语亦如是。为贪财故妄语。是名从贪生。为欲诳彼令得苦恼。是名从嗔生。邪见不知业果报故妄语。是名从痴生。两舌恶口散乱语亦如是。

There are yet other people who, due to hatred and dislike of others steal the wealth and possessions of others, wishing thereby to cause them anguish. These are cases of stealing arising from hatred.

Then again, there are people who, holding wrong views and failing to realize the karmic retribution involved, steal the possessions of others. This is stealing arising from delusion. This is exemplified by brahmans who state, "All the wealth and treasures of the world are rightfully mine. It is only because of the relative weakness of my power that all of these inferior classes of people have been able, using methods contrary to our dharma, to take these things for their own use. If I now seize them, this is just a case of someone retrieving his own possessions. Hence there is no karmic transgression in doing this." When someone uses such rationalizations to steal the belongings of others, this too is just a matter of stealing arising from delusion.

When someone commits sexual misconduct because of desire and attachment to sexual gratification, this is an instance of sexual misconduct arising from greed.

If someone motivated by hatred and aversion toward someone else thinks, "Because this fellow violated my mother, wife, sister, or daughter, I shall get back at him by sexually defiling his mother, wife, sisters, and daughters," this is an instance of sexual misconduct arising from hatred.

In someone holding wrong views and not realizing the karmic retributions involved violates [some woman], this is an instance [of sexual misconduct] arising from delusion. This is exemplified by a man who claims, "There is really no such thing as sexual misconduct between humans. Why? All women were born for the enjoyment of men and thus are just like any other thing we exploit for our own use. Thus, if one has a need for it and therefore becomes involved in this kind of affair, then there is no karmic offense of sexual misconduct involved here." When someone relying on this sort of rationalization goes ahead and indulges his sexual desire in this way, that is a case of sexual misconduct arising from delusion.

Just as it is with the karmic offense of stealing, so too it is with false speech. When someone tells lies because of greed for wealth, then this is referred to as false speech arising from greed. When someone deceives someone else in order to cause them anguish, this is referred to as false speech arising from hatred. When someone with wrong views who does not understand the karmic retributions involved tells a lie, this is referred to as false speech arising from delusion.

Divisive speech, harsh speech, and scattered or inappropriate speech are the same [as the above discussion of "false speech"] in that

正體字

097c13 ‖ 三不善道則是根本。從是分別生七種身口
097c14 ‖ 業[7]果。問曰。不離殺生皆是殺生罪不。若
097c15 ‖ 殺生罪皆是不離殺生耶。答曰。有不離
097c16 ‖ 殺生即是殺生罪。有不離殺生非殺生罪。
097c17 ‖ 何等是不離殺生即是殺生罪。若有眾生
097c18 ‖ 知是眾生故殺奪命起身業。是名不離殺
097c19 ‖ 生亦是殺生罪。何等是不離殺生非殺生
097c20 ‖ 罪。此人先雖作殺因緣而眾生不死又身不
097c21 ‖ 動口不說。但心念我從今日當殺眾生。
097c22 ‖ 是名不離殺生非殺生罪。是二[*]門分別。
097c23 ‖ 為四種分別。所謂善不善各二種。
097c24 ‖ 　不但善不善　　身心二種業
097c25 ‖ 　亦復應當知　　更有餘分別
097c26 ‖ 除身殺生劫盜邪婬。餘殘打縛閉繫鞭杖牽
097c27 ‖ 挽等。但不死而已。如是不善身業非奪命
097c28 ‖ 等所攝。

简体字

三不善道则是根本。从是分别生七种身口业果。问曰。不离杀生皆是杀生罪不。若杀生罪皆是不离杀生耶。答曰。有不离杀生即是杀生罪。有不离杀生非杀生罪。何等是不离杀生即是杀生罪。若有众生知是众生故杀夺命起身业。是名不离杀生亦是杀生罪。何等是不离杀生非杀生罪。此人先虽作杀因缘而众生不死又身不动口不说。但心念我从今日当杀众生。是名不离杀生非杀生罪。是二门分别。为四种分别。所谓善不善各二种。

　不但善不善　　身心二种业
　亦复应当知　　更有余分别

　除身杀生劫盗邪淫。余残打缚闭系鞭杖牵挽等。但不死而已。如是不善身业非夺命等所摄。

these three courses of bad karmic action also have these same foundational bases. From this, one can distinguish the arising of the karmic effects resulting from all seven physical and verbal karmic deeds.

Question: Is it or is it not the case that all instances of not abandoning killing beings constitute the karmic offense of killing? Are all instances of the karmic offense of killing necessarily instances of not abandoning killing?

Response: There are instances of not abandoning killing that constitute instances of the karmic transgression of killing beings and there are also instances of not abandoning killing that do not qualify as instances of the karmic transgression of killing beings.

This being the case, which of these instances of not abandoning killing constitute instances of the karmic transgression of killing? Taking for example a case where there is a being, one knows it is a being, one deliberately kills it, and in taking its life, one produces the associated physical karmic action—this is an instance of not abandoning killing also constituting an instance of the karmic offense of killing.

What would be an example of failure to abandon killing not qualifying as an instance of the karmic offense of killing? Take for instance a case where this person did in fact previously engage in the causes and conditions of killing but the being somehow did not die. Further, take the case in which someone makes no bodily movement and utters no words but merely thinks, "From this day on, I shall kill beings." Both of these instances qualify as cases of failure to abandon killing that do not actually entail the karmic offense of killing. This involves two categorical distinctions through which one makes a total of four distinctions, two for each of these two subcategories of the so-called "good" and "bad."

4. More Subsidiary Distinctions Related to the Good and Bad Actions

This is not just a matter of "good" versus "bad,"
but also of two types of karma, "physical" versus "mental."
One should also know
that there are still other distinctions.

There are other subsidiary physical actions aside from the actual killing of beings, stealing, or sexual misconduct, actions that, in the case of killing, include such abuses as beating, tying up, imprisoning, whipping, striking with staves, dragging [through the streets], and so forth. Because they fall short of actually inflicting death, these sorts of bad physical karmic actions are not subsumed under [the karmic offense of] taking life, and so forth [with the subsidiary physical actions associated with stealing and sexual misconduct].

|正體字| 善中迎送合掌禮拜恭敬問訊洗浴
097c29 ‖ 按摩布施等善身業非不殺生等所攝。意業
098a01 ‖ 中除貪取瞋惱邪見餘所有不守攝心諸結
098a02 ‖ 使等不善法。又意業中除不貪取不瞋惱正
098a03 ‖ 見餘善守攝心信戒聞定捨慧等善法。
098a04 ‖ 　　七業亦業道　　三業道非業
098a05 ‖ 殺生劫盜邪婬妄語兩舌惡口散亂語七。是
098a06 ‖ 業即業道。貪取瞋惱邪見。是業道非業。此三
098a07 ‖ 事相應思是業。問曰。前七事何故亦是業亦
098a08 ‖ 是業道。答曰。習行是七事轉增故。至地獄
098a09 ‖ 畜生餓鬼。以是故名為業道。是七能作故名
098a10 ‖ 業。三是業道非業者。是不善業根本。以是
098a11 ‖ 故名三業道非業。

|简体字|

善中迎送合掌礼拜恭敬问讯洗浴按摩布施等善身业非不杀生等所摄。意业中除贪取嗔恼邪见余所有不守摄心诸结使等不善法。又意业中除不贪取不嗔恼正见余善守摄心信戒闻定舍慧等善法。

　　七业亦业道　　三业道非业

　　杀生劫盗邪淫妄语两舌恶口散乱语七。是业即业道。贪取嗔恼邪见。是业道非业。此三事相应思是业。问曰。前七事何故亦是业亦是业道。答曰。习行是七事转增故。至地狱畜生饿鬼。以是故名为业道。是七能作故名业。三是业道非业者。是不善业根本。以是故名三业道非业。

Chapter 28 — *Distinctions in the 2nd Ground's Courses of Karmic Action*

[So too], among the actions that are good, actions such as welcoming eminences on arrival, escorting them off when they leave, pressing the palms together, bowing down in reverence, greeting with half bows, assisting with bathing, massage, and proffering of gifts, none of these good physical karmic actions are subsumed under non-killing, and so forth [with the wholesome subsidiary physical actions associated with stealing and sexual misconduct].

[So too], among the karmic actions of the mind, [the same principle applies] to all of the rest of the unwholesome [mental] dharmas aside from covetousness, ill will, and wrong views, dharmas such as not guarding or focusing the mind, the fetters, and so forth.

[So too], among the karmic actions of the mind, [the same principle applies] to all of the rest of the good [mental] dharmas aside from non-covetousness, refraining from ill will, and right views, dharmas such as guarding and focusing the mind, faith, observance of moral precepts, learning, meditative concentration, equanimity, wisdom, and so forth.

5. DISTINGUISHING "KARMIC DEEDS" VERSUS "COURSES OF KARMIC ACTION"

Seven of the karmic deeds are also courses of karmic action
and three of the courses of karmic action are not karmic deeds.

These seven "karmic deeds" that consist of killing, stealing, sexual misconduct, false speech, divisive speech, harsh speech, and scattered or inappropriate speech are themselves both "karmic deeds" and "courses of karmic action." Covetousness, ill will, and wrong views are "courses of karmic action," but are not "karmic deeds" as such, for these three phenomena correspond to [intentional] thought, this type of [merely mental] activity.

Question: How is it that the previous seven endeavors qualify both as "karmic deeds" and "courses of karmic action"?

Response: It is due to progressively increasing habitual practice of these endeavors that one therefore arrives in the hell realm, the animal realm, and the realm of the hungry ghosts. It is because of this that they are referred to as "courses of karmic action." Because these seven are also endeavors that one can perform, they are also referred to as "karmic deeds."

As for the three which are "courses of karmic action" but not "karmic deeds" as such, this is because they serve as the foundation for those which do constitute bad karmic deeds. Consequently these three are referred to only as "courses of karmic action" but not as "karmic deeds."

正體字

098a12 ‖ 善中亦如是。所謂離殺
098a12 ‖ 生劫盜邪婬妄語兩舌惡口散亂語亦業亦
098a13 ‖ 業道。餘三不貪[1]取不瞋惱正見是業道非
098a14 ‖ 業。此三相應思是業。問曰。前七事何故是
098a15 ‖ 業亦業道。答曰。常修習此事故。能至人天
098a16 ‖ 好處名為道。是七能作故名為業。問曰。餘
098a17 ‖ 三何故但業道非業耶。答曰。三是諸善業根
098a18 ‖ 本。諸善業從中行故。名為業道非業。復次。
098a19 ‖ 　戒法即是業　　業或戒非戒
098a20 ‖ 　業及於業道　　有四種分別
098a21 ‖ 身口業是戒。意業是業非戒。業及於業道
098a22 ‖ 四種分別者。有業非業道。有業道非業。有
098a23 ‖ 業亦是業道。

简体字

善中亦如是。所谓离杀生劫盗邪淫妄语两舌恶口散乱语亦业亦业道。余三不贪取不瞋恼正见是业道非业。此三相应思是业。问曰。前七事何故是业亦业道。答曰。常修习此事故。能至人天好处名为道。是七能作故名为业。问曰。余三何故但业道非业耶。答曰。三是诸善业根本。诸善业从中行故。名为业道非业。复次。

　戒法即是业　　业或戒非戒
　业及于业道　　有四种分别

身口业是戒。意业是业非戒。业及于业道四种分别者。有业非业道。有业道非业。有业亦是业道。

Chapter 28 — *Distinctions in the 2nd Ground's Courses of Karmic Action* 1015

The same principle applies in the sphere of the "good" [courses of karmic action]. Abandonment of killing, of stealing, of sexual misconduct, of false speech, of divisive speech, of harsh speech, and of scattered or inappropriate speech are all both "karmic deeds" and "courses of karmic action." The other three consisting of non-covetousness, refraining from ill will, and right view are all "courses of karmic action," but are not "karmic deeds" as such, for these three phenomena correspond to [volitional] thought, this type of [merely mental] activity.[146]

Question: How is it that, [within the ten courses of good karmic action] the first seven are both "karmic deeds" and "courses of karmic action"?

Response: They are referred to as "courses" [of karmic action] because it is due to always practicing these endeavors that one becomes able to arrive in good circumstances within the realms of humans and devas. It is because these seven are karmic deeds amenable to being performed that they are also referred to as "karmic deeds."

Question: How is it that, [within the ten courses of good karmic action] the remaining three are only "courses of karmic action," but are not "karmic deeds"?

Response: These three serve as the foundation for those that do qualify as good karmic actions. It is because the practice of all good karmic deeds comes forth from within them that they are referred to as "courses of karmic action," while not being referred to as "karmic deeds" as such.

Furthermore:

6. FOUR DISTINCTIONS: "KARMIC DEEDS" AND "COURSES OF KARMIC ACTION"

[Observances of] moral precept dharmas are karmic deeds.
karmic deeds may or may not be [observances of] moral precepts.
Qualification as a "karmic deeds" or as a "course of karmic action"
is a matter involving the application of four types of distinctions.

Physical and verbal karmic deeds may be [observances of] moral precepts. Mental actions may be karma, but they are not themselves [observances of] moral precepts.

As for the four types of categorical distinctions made with respect to qualification as either "karmic actions" or "courses of karmic action," they are as follows:

There are "karmic deeds" that are not "courses of karmic action."
There are "courses of karmic action" that are not "karmic deeds."
There are "karmic deeds" that are also "courses of karmic action."

正體字

有非業非業道。業非業道者。
三種不善身業。業道所不攝。所謂手拳鞭
杖等。及三種善身業。業道所不攝。所謂迎
[2]逆敬禮等。是[3]二善不善業。非業道所攝。或
有人言。亦是業道。何以故。是二業或時至
善惡處故。名為業道。以不定故不說業
道。業道非業者。後三不善及三善是煩惱性
故非業。能起業故名為業道。三善是善根
性故非業。能起善業故名為業道。亦業亦
業道者。所謂殺生不殺生等七事。是非業非
業道者餘法是。復次。

　　菩薩初地邊　　以三種清淨
　　安住十善道　　則生決定心

简体字

有非业非业道。业非业道者。三种不善身业。业道所不摄。所谓手拳鞭杖等。及三种善身业。业道所不摄。所谓迎逆敬礼等。是二善不善业。非业道所摄。或有人言。亦是业道。何以故。是二业或时至善恶处故。名为业道。以不定故不说业道。业道非业者。后三不善及三善是烦恼性故非业。能起业故名为业道。三善是善根性故非业。能起善业故名为业道。亦业亦业道者。所谓杀生不杀生等七事。是非业非业道者余法是。复次。

　　菩萨初地边　　以三种清净
　　安住十善道　　则生决定心

Chapter 28 – *Distinctions in the 2nd Ground's Courses of Karmic Action*

There are [actions] that are neither "karmic deeds" nor "courses of karmic action."

As for those "karmic deeds" that are not "courses of karmic action," these are three types of bad physical deeds not subsumable within the sphere of "courses of karmic action," namely the wielding of fists to strike, whips to lash, cudgels to beat, and so forth. So too in the case of the three corresponding types of good physical deeds not subsumable in one of the categories of "courses of karmic action," namely: welcoming eminences on arrival, bowing down in reverence, and so forth. These two subcategories of good and bad deeds are not subsumable within the "courses of karmic action."

There are those who state that [these two subcategories of good and bad deeds] *are* also "courses of karmic action." Why? [They claim that], because these two types of deeds may have times when they lead one to [rebirth in] good or bad stations of rebirth, they are therefore "courses of karmic action." However, because this is not a fixed matter, we do not claim here that they constitute "courses of karmic action."

As for those that are "courses of karmic action" but which are not "karmic deeds," because the final three bad karmic deeds [of the ten courses of bad karmic action] and the final three good karmic deeds [of the ten courses of good karmic action] are, by nature, associated with the presence [or absence of] afflictions, they are not "karmic deeds" as such. However, because they are able to instigate the production of karmic deeds, they do therefore constitute "courses of karmic action."

[Among these], the three that are good, because they are, by nature, roots of goodness, they are not "karmic deeds" as such. But, because they are able to instigate the production of good karmic deeds, they do therefore constitute "courses of karmic action."

As for those that are both "karmic deeds" and "courses of karmic action," they are the seven deeds consisting of killing or not killing and the others [as well as their opposites].

As for those that are neither "karmic deeds" nor "courses of karmic action," they are all of the dharmas [not otherwise subsumed in the first three of these four categories].

In addition:

7. THREE KINDS OF PURITY USED TO MOVE BEYOND THE FIRST GROUND

If a bodhisattva still at the border with the first ground
uses three kinds of purity
to abide securely in the ten courses of good karmic action,
he will then be able to bring forth decisive resolve.

正體字

098b07 ‖ 是菩薩於第二地中了了分別知如是十
098b08 ‖ 善十不善道。知已以三種清淨住十善道。
098b09 ‖ 所謂自不殺生不教他殺。於殺生罪[4]心
098b10 ‖ 不喜悅。乃至正見亦如是。問曰。菩薩初地
098b11 ‖ 中已住十善道。此中何故重說。答曰。初地
098b12 ‖ 中。非不住十善道。但此中轉勝增長。以三
098b13 ‖ 種清淨故。先初住中雖作閻浮提王不能
098b14 ‖ 行此[5]三種清淨。是故此中說三種清淨。菩
098b15 ‖ 薩住是二地。知如是分別諸業。生決定心。
098b16 ‖ 　世所有惡道　　皆十不善生
098b17 ‖ 　世所有善道　　因於十善生
098b18 ‖ 世間所有惡道者。所謂三種地獄道。熱地獄
098b19 ‖ 冷地獄。黑地獄。三種畜生道。水行畜生。陸行
098b20 ‖ 畜生。空行畜生。種種鬼道。有飢餓鬼者食不
098b21 ‖ 淨鬼者火口者阿修羅夜叉等。皆由行十不
098b22 ‖ 善道。

简体字

　　是菩萨于第二地中了了分别知如是十善十不善道。知已以三种清净住十善道。所谓自不杀生不教他杀。于杀生罪心不喜悦。乃至正见亦如是。问曰。菩萨初地中已住十善道。此中何故重说。答曰。初地中。非不住十善道。但此中转胜增长。以三种清净故。先初住中虽作阎浮提王不能行此三种清净。是故此中说三种清净。菩萨住是二地。知如是分别诸业。生决定心。

　　世所有恶道　　皆十不善生
　　世所有善道　　因于十善生

　　世间所有恶道者。所谓三种地狱道。热地狱冷地狱。黑地狱。三种畜生道。水行畜生。陆行畜生。空行畜生。种种鬼道。有饥饿鬼者食不净鬼者火口者阿修罗夜叉等。皆由行十不善道。

Chapter 28 — *Distinctions in the 2nd Ground's Courses of Karmic Action*

Once this bodhisattva comes to dwell on the second ground, he then distinguishes with utter clarity these ten good and bad courses of karmic action. Having come to know these matters, he applies three kinds of purity to his abiding in the ten courses of good karmic action, namely:

He does not personally kill any being;
He does not instruct others to kill any being;
And he does not delight in the karmic offense of killing.

In this same way, he also [applies these three kinds of purity to the rest of the courses of good karmic action] up to and including "right view."

Question: A bodhisattva dwelling on the first ground already abides in the ten courses of good karmic action. Why is this matter being discussed yet again here [in the context of the second ground]?

Response: It is not that he does not abide in the ten courses of good karmic action when dwelling on the first ground. However, due to the application of these three kinds of purity, such practice becomes ever more superior and ever more greatly increased here [on the second ground]. Previously, when still abiding on the first ground, although he might indeed become a monarch reigning over all of Jambudvīpa, he was still unable at that point to implement these three kinds of purity. It is for this reason that we discuss the three kinds of purity here. The bodhisattva who abides here on the second ground knows these distinctions as they apply to all sorts of karmic actions and thus brings forth decisive resolve.

8. THE 10 COURSES OF GOOD AND BAD KARMA AS ARBITERS OF ONE'S DESTINY

All the world's wretched destinies
are produced from the ten bad deeds.
All the world's good destinies
are produced because of the ten good deeds.

"All the world's wretched destinies" refers to:

The three types of hell-realm destinies, namely the hot hells, cold hells, and hells of blackness;

The three types of animal-realm destinies, namely the animals that live in the water, the animals that live on land, and the animals that fly through the air;

And the different types of ghost-realm destinies, namely the hungry ghosts, the ghosts who eat impure things, and those with flaming mouths, *asuras*, *yakṣas*, and so forth.

All of these arise from engaging in the ten courses of bad karmic action.

| 正體字

098b23 ｜　　　有上中下因緣故。出世間所有善道若
098b23 ‖ 天若人。皆由行十善道生。三界所
098b24 ‖ 攝。天有二十八。人者四天下人是。如是決定知已。
098b25 ‖ 作是念。我欲自生善處。亦令眾生生於善
098b26 ‖ 處。
098b27 ‖ 　　是故我自應　　住於十善道
098b28 ‖ 　　亦令餘眾生　　即住此善道
098b29 ‖ 若生善處若生惡處。皆屬十善[6]十不善道。
098c01 ‖ 我知是世間諸業因緣有無有定主。是故我
098c02 ‖ 應先自行十善道。然後令諸眾生亦住十
098c03 ‖ 善道。問曰。何以故。要先自住十善道後乃
098c04 ‖ 令他住耶。答曰。
098c05 ‖ 　　行於惡業者　　令他善不易
098c06 ‖ 　　自不行善故　　他則不信受
098c07 ‖ 若惡人自不行善。欲令他行善者則為甚
098c08 ‖ 難。何以故。是人自不行善。他人不信受其
098c09 ‖ 語。如偈說。
098c10 ‖ 　　若人自不善　　不能令他善

簡體字

有上中下因缘故。出世间所有善道若天若人。皆由行十善道生。三界所摄。天有二十八。人者四天下人是。如是决定知已。作是念。我欲自生善处。亦令众生生于善处。

　　是故我自应　　住于十善道
　　亦令余众生　　即住此善道

若生善处若生恶处。皆属十善十不善道。我知是世间诸业因缘有无有定主。是故我应先自行十善道。然后令诸众生亦住十善道。问曰。何以故。要先自住十善道后乃令他住耶。答曰。

　　行于恶业者　　令他善不易
　　自不行善故　　他则不信受

若恶人自不行善。欲令他行善者则为甚难。何以故。是人自不行善。他人不信受其语。如偈说。

　　若人自不善　　不能令他善

Chapter 28 — *Distinctions in the 2nd Ground's Courses of Karmic Action*

It is because of the presence of relatively superior, middling, or inferior causes and conditions that all of the world's good destinies are produced. Whether it be the deva realm or the human realm, they all arise from the practice of the ten courses of good karmic action. They are all included within the three realms of existence wherein there are the twenty-eight deva realms and, in the case of the human realm, these are all those peoples that inhabit the four continents.

9. Resolving to Abide in the 10 Good Actions & Teach This to Others

Having come to definitely know such matters, [this bodhisattva] reflects, "I wish that I myself will be born within these good stations of rebirth and wish also that I may be able to influence other beings to be reborn in these good stations of rebirth."

> Therefore I should abide
> within the ten courses of good karmic action
> while also influencing other beings
> to immediately abide within these courses of good karmic action.

Whether one is reborn in the good stations of rebirth or is instead born into bad stations of rebirth, this is all due to the ten courses of good karmic action or ten courses of bad karmic action. [Hence one reflects]:

> I realize that this world exists on the basis of all of the karmic causes and conditions and that there is no fixed subjective agent [involved in its creation].[147] Therefore, I should first ensure that I myself have become established in the practice of the ten courses of good karmic action and then, afterward, I should influence other beings to also abide in the practice of the ten courses of good karmic action.

Question: Why is it that one must first see that he himself abides within the ten courses of good karmic action and only later influences others to abide therein as well?

Response:

> It is not easy for one who engages in bad deeds
> to influence others toward goodness,
> for, if one does not practice goodness oneself,
> others will not believe and accept [one's teaching].

If someone who is a bad person does not practice goodness himself even as he wishes to influence others to practice goodness, this will be a very difficult to accomplish. Why? If this person does not practice goodness himself, other people will not believe in or accept his instruction. This is as described in a verse:

> If one is not good oneself,
> one will be unable to influence others toward goodness.

正體字	098c11 ‖ 　　若自不寂滅　　不能令他寂 098c12 ‖ 　　以是故汝當　　先自行善寂 098c13 ‖ 　　然後教他人　　令行善寂滅 098c14 ‖ 是菩薩當如是行善法。 098c15 ‖ 　　從阿鼻地獄　　乃至於有頂 098c16 ‖ 　　分別十業果　　及其受報處 098c17 ‖ 當如是正知。下從阿鼻地獄。上至非有想 098c18 ‖ 非無想處。皆是善不善種種業受果報處。於 098c19 ‖ 中習[7]行上十不善道故生阿鼻地獄。小減 098c20 ‖ 生大炙地獄。小減生小炙地獄。小減生大 098c21 ‖ 叫喚地獄。小減生小叫喚地獄。小減生僧伽 098c22 ‖ 陀地獄。小減生大陌地獄。小減生黑繩地 098c23 ‖ 獄。小減生活地獄。小減生劍林等小眷屬地 098c24 ‖ 獄中。亦應如是轉小分別。行中十不善道 098c25 ‖ 生畜生中。畜生中亦應轉少分別。行下不善 098c26 ‖ 道生餓鬼中。
简体字	若自不寂灭　　不能令他寂 　　以是故汝当　　先自行善寂 　　然后教他人　　令行善寂灭 是菩萨当如是行善法。 　　从阿鼻地狱　　乃至于有顶 　　分别十业果　　及其受报处 当如是正知。下从阿鼻地狱。上至非有想非无想处。皆是善不善种种业受果报处。于中习行上十不善道故生阿鼻地狱。小减生大炙地狱。小减生小炙地狱。小减生大叫唤地狱。小减生小叫唤地狱。小减生僧伽陀地狱。小减生大陌地狱。小减生黑绳地狱。小减生活地狱。小减生剑林等小眷属地狱中。亦应如是转小分别。行中十不善道生畜生中。畜生中亦应转少分别。行下不善道生饿鬼中。

Chapter 28 — *Distinctions in the 2nd Ground's Courses of Karmic Action*

> If one has not reached quiescence oneself,
> one will be unable to influence others to reach quiescence.
>
> It is for this reason that you should
> first practice goodness and quiescence yourself
> and then afterward instruct other people
> to influence them to practice goodness and reach quiescence.

It is in this way that this bodhisattva should practice good dharmas.

10. One Should Learn the Rebirth Results of the 10 Good & Bad Actions

> From the Avīci Hells
> on up to the summit of existence,
> one distinguishes the effects of ten courses of karmic action
> as well as the places in which one undergoes their retribution.

In just this manner, one should rightly realize that, from down below in the Avīci Hells all the way on up to the station of neither perception nor non-perception, all of these are but places wherein one undergoes the resulting retribution from all of the many different sorts of good and bad karmic deeds. Among these [stations of rebirth]:

> It is by habitually practicing the worst of the ten courses of bad karmic action that one is reborn in the Avīci Hells;
>
> When the extent of evil karma is somewhat less, one is reborn instead in the Great Broiling Hell;
>
> When somewhat less than that, one is reborn in the Lesser Broiling Hell;
>
> When somewhat less again, one is reborn in the Great Screaming Hell;
>
> When even less, one is reborn in the Lesser Screaming Hell;
>
> When yet less than that, one is reborn in the Saṃgata Hell;
>
> When less again, rebirth is in the Great Road Hell;
>
> A yet lesser level brings birth in the Black Line Hell;
>
> When lesser yet, one is reborn in the Living Hell;
>
> Yet another increment less brings rebirth in the Sword Forest Hell or other lesser subsidiary hells for which one should also make ever finer distinctions [in these subcategories of hell-realm retributions].

It is through practicing an intermediate level of the ten courses of bad karmic action that one is reborn into the animal realm. One should also make ever finer distinctions regarding [the levels of karmic retribution as manifested within] the animal realm.

It is through practicing a relatively lesser level of the ten courses of bad karmic action that one is reborn into the realm of the hungry ghosts.

|正體字|

098c27 如是總相說。是中應廣分別
098c27 差別。有諸阿修羅夜叉生鬼道中。有諸龍
098c28 王生畜生中。所受快樂或與諸天同。是諸
098c29 眾生以不善因緣故生。生已受善業果報。
099a01 行最下十善道生閻浮提人中在貧窮下
099a02 賤家。所謂[1]栴陀羅邊地工巧小人等。轉勝生
099a03 居士家。轉勝生婆羅門家。轉勝生剎利家。
099a04 轉勝生大臣家。轉勝生國王家。於十善道
099a05 轉復勝者生瞿陀尼。轉勝生弗婆提。轉勝
099a06 生欝單越。轉勝生四天王處。轉勝生忉利
099a07 天炎摩天兜率陀天化樂天。習行上十善道
099a08 生他化自在天。於是中亦應種種分別小
099a09 大差別。如人中小王大王閻浮提王轉輪聖
099a10 王。四天王處有四天王。忉利天中有釋提桓
099a11 因。炎摩天上有須炎摩天王。兜率陀天上有
099a12 珊兜率陀天王。化樂天上有善化天王。他化
099a13 自在天上有他化自在天王。過是以上。要
099a14 行禪定思得生上界。

|简体字|

如是总相说。是中应广分别差别。有诸阿修罗夜叉生鬼道中。有诸龙王生畜生中。所受快乐或与诸天同。是诸众生以不善因缘故生。生已受善业果报。行最下十善道生阎浮提人中在贫穷下贱家。所谓栴陀罗边地工巧小人等。转胜生居士家。转胜生婆罗门家。转胜生刹利家。转胜生大臣家。转胜生国王家。于十善道转复胜者生瞿陀尼。转胜生弗婆提。转胜生郁单越。转胜生四天王处。转胜生忉利天炎摩天兜率陀天化乐天。习行上十善道生他化自在天。于是中亦应种种分别小大差别。如人中小王大王阎浮提王转轮圣王。四天王处有四天王。忉利天中有释提桓因。炎摩天上有须炎摩天王。兜率陀天上有珊兜率陀天王。化乐天上有善化天王。他化自在天上有他化自在天王。过是以上。要行禅定思得生上界。

Chapter 28 — *Distinctions in the 2nd Ground's Courses of Karmic Action*

This represents only a general discussion of these matters. We should present a more expansive range of differentiating distinctions among these. There are the *asuras* and *yakṣas* born into the ghost realms, *nāga* kings reborn into the animal-realm wherein the bliss they enjoy may be identical to that experienced by the devas. All of these beings take these rebirths because of bad karma and then, having taken such rebirths, they may also enjoy the karmic fruits of their past good karmic actions.

In the case of those who have practiced only the very lowest level of the ten courses of good karmic action, they take rebirth in Jambudvīpa within poverty-stricken low-caste clans, namely among the *caṇḍālas*, or in remote regions, or as artisans, or as people of low social stature.

With a somewhat more superior level [of practice of the ten courses of good karmic action], one may be reborn into merchant-class families. When somewhat more superior, one is reborn into brahman clans. When more superior yet, one is reborn into a *kṣatriyan* clan. When more superior than that, one is reborn into a family of high governmental officials. When more superior yet, rebirth occurs into royal families.

When one's practice of the ten courses of good karmic action has been at a yet more superior level, one is reborn on the continent of Avara-godānīya. When more superior yet, rebirth is on the continent of Pūrva-videha. and when superior to that, rebirth is on the continent of Uttara-kuru.

When more superior yet, rebirth is into the abodes of the Four Heavenly Kings. At increasing levels of superiority to that, rebirth is into the Trāyastriṃśa Heaven, the Yāma Heaven, the Tuṣita Heaven, and the Nirmāṇarati Heaven. At the most superior level of practice of the ten courses of good karmic action, one is reborn in the Paranirmita Vaśavartin Heaven.

Here we should make all kinds of distinctions with regard to the minor and major differences. For instance, among humans, there are minor kings, major kings, the kings ruling over all of Jambudvīpa, and wheel-turning kings. The abode of the Four Heavenly Kings has Four Heavenly Kings. In the Trāyastriṃśa Heaven, there is Śakra, ruler of the devas. In the Yāma Heaven, there is the Suyāma Deva King. In the Tuṣita Heaven, there is the Saṃtuṣita Heaven King. In the Nirmāṇarati Heaven, there is the Skillful Transformations Heaven King. In the Paranirmita Vaśavartin Heaven, there is the Paranirmita Vaśavartin Heaven King. Beyond this, one must utilize volition associated with cultivation of the *dhyāna* absorptions to gain rebirth into the higher [celestial] realms.

正體字	問曰。若以禪定思得 099a15 ‖ 生上界者。何以故。說乃至非有想非無想 099a16 ‖ 處皆以十善道故得生。答曰。雖修禪定 099a17 ‖ 生色界無色界。要當先堅住十善道然後 099a18 ‖ 得修禪定。以是故。彼處以十善業道為大 099a19 ‖ 利益。以是故。說乃至非有想非無想處皆 099a20 ‖ 以[2]十善道因緣故得生。所以者何。先行清 099a21 ‖ 淨十善道離欲。修初禪下思得生梵眾天。 099a22 ‖ 修初禪中思生梵輔天。修初禪上思故得 099a23 ‖ 生大梵天。修二禪下思生少光天。修二禪 099a24 ‖ 中思得生無量光天。修二禪上思得生妙 099a25 ‖ 光天。修三禪下思得生小淨天。修三禪中 099a26 ‖ 思故得生無量淨天。修三禪上思得生遍 099a27 ‖ 淨天。修四禪下思故生阿那婆伽天。修四 099a28 ‖ 禪中思故生福生天。修四禪上思故生廣 099a29 ‖ 果天
简体字	问曰。若以禅定思得生上界者。何以故。说乃至非有想非无想处皆以十善道故得生。答曰。虽修禅定生色界无色界。要当先坚住十善道然后得修禅定。以是故。彼处以十善业道为大利益。以是故。说乃至非有想非无想处皆以十善道因缘故得生。所以者何。先行清净十善道离欲。修初禅下思得生梵众天。修初禅中思生梵辅天。修初禅上思故得生大梵天。修二禅下思生少光天。修二禅中思得生无量光天。修二禅上思得生妙光天。修三禅下思得生小净天。修三禅中思故得生无量净天。修三禅上思得生遍净天。修四禅下思故生阿那婆伽天。修四禅中思故生福生天。修四禅上思故生广果天

Chapter 28 – *Distinctions in the 2nd Ground's Courses of Karmic Action*

Question: If in fact it is essential to utilize volition associated with the *dhyāna* absorptions, why was it just stated that, in every case, it is because of the ten courses of good karmic action that one gains every place of rebirth all the way up to the station of neither perception nor non-perception?

Response: Although one must cultivate the *dhyāna* absorptions to gain rebirth in the stations of either the form or formless realm, one must still first become solidly established in the practice of the ten courses of good karmic action. Only after this can one succeed in the cultivation of the *dhyāna* absorptions. It is for this reason that [acquisition of] those stations relies upon the great benefit provided by the ten courses of good karmic action. It is for this reason as well that it was stated here that, in every case, it is because of the ten courses of good karmic action that one attains every station of rebirth all the way up to the station of neither perception nor non-perception.

How is this so? After having first cultivated purity in the ten courses of good karmic action, by separating from sensual desire and cultivating the first *dhyāna* with relatively inferior volition, one may succeed in taking rebirth in the Brahma-kāyika Heaven. By cultivating the first *dhyāna* with relatively middling volition, one may take rebirth in the Brahma-purohita Heaven. And by cultivating the first *dhyāna* with relatively superior volition, one may succeed in taking rebirth in the Mahābrahma Heaven.

By cultivating the second *dhyāna* with relatively inferior volition, one may take rebirth in the Lesser Light Heaven. By cultivating the second *dhyāna* with relatively middling volition, one may succeed in taking rebirth in the Limitless Light Heaven. And by cultivating the second *dhyāna* with relatively superior volition, one may succeed in taking rebirth in the Sublime Light Heaven.

By cultivating the third *dhyāna* with relatively inferior volition, one may succeed in taking rebirth in the Lesser Purity Heaven. By cultivating the third *dhyāna* with relatively middling volition, one may succeed in taking rebirth in the Limitless Light Heaven. And by cultivating the third *dhyāna* with relatively superior volition, one may succeed in taking rebirth in the Universal Purity Heaven.

By cultivating the fourth *dhyāna* with relatively inferior volition, one may take rebirth in the Anabhraka Heaven. By cultivating the fourth *dhyāna* with relatively middling volition, one may take rebirth in the Puṇya-prasava Heaven. And by cultivating the fourth *dhyāna* with relatively superior volition, one may take rebirth in the Bṛhatphala Heaven.

正體字

099b01 ‖ 修無想定中思得生無想天。以無漏
099b01 ‖ 熏修四禪下思故生不廣天。以無漏熏修四
099b02 ‖ 禪勝思故生不熱天。以無漏熏修四禪勝
099b03 ‖ 思故生喜見天。以無漏熏修四禪勝思故
099b04 ‖ 生妙見天。以無漏熏修四禪最上思故生
099b05 ‖ 阿迦膩吒天。修虛空處定相應思得生空
099b06 ‖ 處天。修識處定相應思得生識處天。修無
099b07 ‖ 所有處定相應思得生無所有處天。修非
099b08 ‖ 有想非無想處定相應思得生非有想非無
099b09 ‖ 想處天。是名生死世間眾生往來之處。[3]

简体字

修无想定中思得生无想天。以无漏熏修四禅下思故生不广天。以无漏熏修四禅胜思故生不热天。以无漏熏修四禅胜思故生喜见天。以无漏熏修四禅胜思故生妙见天。以无漏熏修四禅最上思故生阿迦腻吒天。修虚空处定相应思得生空处天。修识处定相应思得生识处天。修无所有处定相应思得生无所有处天。修非有想非无想处定相应思得生非有想非无想处天。是名生死世间众生往来之处。

Chapter 28 — *Distinctions in the 2nd Ground's Courses of Karmic Action*

By cultivating the non-perception absorption with relatively middling volition, one may succeed in taking rebirth in the Non-perception Heaven.

By repeated cultivation of contaminant-free concentration in the fourth *dhyāna* with relatively inferior volition, one may take rebirth in the "Non-Extensive"[148] or Avṛha Heaven. By repeated cultivation of contaminant-free concentration in the fourth *dhyāna* with [more] superior volition, one may take rebirth in the "Non-Hot" or Atapās Heaven. By repeated cultivation of contaminant-free concentration in the fourth *dhyāna* with [yet more] superior volition, one may take rebirth in the "Delightful Vision" or Sudarśana Heaven. By repeated cultivation of contaminant-free concentration in the fourth *dhyāna* with [even more] superior volition, one may take rebirth in the "Sublime Vision" or Sudṛśa Heaven. By repeated cultivation of contaminant-free concentration in the fourth *dhyāna* with the most superior volition, one may take rebirth in the Akaniṣṭha Heaven.

By cultivating the concentration associated with the station of infinite space with the corresponding volition, one may take rebirth in the Infinite Space Heaven. By cultivating the concentration associated with the station of infinite consciousness with the corresponding volition, one may take rebirth in the Infinite Consciousness Heaven. By cultivating the concentration associated with the station of nothing whatsoever with the corresponding volition, one may take rebirth in the Station of Nothing Whatsoever Heaven. By cultivating the concentration associated with the station of neither perception nor non-perception with the corresponding volition, one may take rebirth in the Neither Perception Nor Non-Perception Heaven.

The above discussion shows the stations to which beings go and from which they come as they undergo birth and death in the world, [as determined by their differing levels of cultivation of either the ten courses of bad karmic action or the ten courses of good karmic action].

The End of Chapter Twenty-Eight

正體字

099b10 ‖　　**[4]分別聲聞辟支佛品第[5]二**
099b11 ‖ 問曰。是十善業道。但是生人天因緣。更有
099b12 ‖ 餘利益耶。答曰有。
099b13 ‖ 　所有聲聞乘　　辟支佛大乘
099b14 ‖ 　皆以十善道　　而為大利益
099b15 ‖ 凡出生死因緣唯有三乘。聲聞辟支佛大乘。
099b16 ‖ 是三乘皆以十善道為大利益。何以故。[6]是
099b17 ‖ 十善道能令行者至聲聞地。亦能令至辟
099b18 ‖ 支佛地。亦能令人至於佛地。問曰。是十善
099b19 ‖ 道。能令何等眾生至聲聞地。答曰。
099b20 ‖ 　隨他無大悲　　畏怖於三界
099b21 ‖ 　樂少功德分　　其志甚劣弱
099b22 ‖ 　心樂於厭離　　常觀世無常
099b23 ‖ 　及知一切法　　皆亦無有我
099b24 ‖ 　乃至一念頃　　不樂於受生
099b25 ‖ 　常不信世間　　而有安隱法

简体字

十住毗婆沙论卷第十三
分别声闻辟支佛品第二十九

　　问曰。是十善业道。但是生人天因缘。更有余利益耶。答曰有。

　　　所有声闻乘　　辟支佛大乘
　　　皆以十善道　　而为大利益

　　凡出生死因缘唯有三乘。声闻辟支佛大乘。是三乘皆以十善道为大利益。何以故。是十善道能令行者至声闻地。亦能令至辟支佛地。亦能令人至于佛地。问曰。是十善道。能令何等众生至声闻地。答曰。

　　　随他无大悲　　畏怖于三界
　　　乐少功德分　　其志甚劣弱
　　　心乐于厌离　　常观世无常
　　　及知一切法　　皆亦无有我
　　　乃至一念顷　　不乐于受生
　　　常不信世间　　而有安隐法

CHAPTER 29
Distinctions Pertaining to Śrāvakas & Pratyekabuddhas

IX. CHAPTER 29: DISTINCTIONS PERTAINING TO THE TWO VEHICLES
   A. THE EFFECTIVENESS OF ALL 3 VEHICLES DEPENDS ON THE 10 GOOD COURSES

Question: Do these ten courses of good karmic action function solely as causes and conditions for rebirths among humans and devas or do they also confer other additional benefits?

Response: They do have [additional benefits, as below]:

All of those cultivating the Śrāvaka Disciple Vehicle,
the Pratyekabuddha Vehicle, or the Great Vehicle,
in every instance rely upon the ten courses of good karmic action
to provide immense benefit for them.

Generally speaking, there are only three vehicles that serve as means for escaping *saṃsāra*'s cycle of births and deaths: the Śrāvaka Disciple Vehicle, the Pratyekabuddha Vehicle, and the Great Vehicle. These three vehicles all rely upon the ten courses of good karmic action to provide immense benefit for them. And how is this the case? These ten courses of good karmic action enable the practitioner to reach the grounds of the *śrāvaka* disciples, also enable him to reach the ground of the *pratyekabuddhas*, and also enable him to reach the ground of the Buddhas.

   1. Q: WHICH BEINGS CAN USE THE 10 COURSES TO FULFILL THE ŚRĀVAKA PATH?

Question: Which kinds of beings do these ten courses of good karmic action enable to reach the grounds of *śrāvaka* disciples?

Response:

Those reliant on others' teachings, who have no great compassion,
who are frightened by existence within the three realms,
who delight in but a minor measure of meritorious qualities,
and whose resolve is too inferior and weak—

Those whose minds delight in renunciation,
who always contemplate the impermanence of the world,
and who also know that all dharmas
have no self—

Those who do not for even a single mind-moment
wish to take on any rebirths,
and who always disbelieve that the world
is possessed of a stable and secure nature—[149]

正體字

099b26 ‖	觀大如毒蛇	陰如拔[7]刃賊
099b27 ‖	六入如空聚	不樂世富樂
099b28 ‖	貴於堅持戒	而為禪定故
099b29 ‖	常樂於安禪	修習諸善法
099c01 ‖	唯觀於涅槃	第一救護者
099c02 ‖	常求盡苦慧	樂集行解脫
099c03 ‖	但貴於自利	[8]一一勝處來
099c04 ‖	善道令是人	能[9]至聲聞地

099c05 ‖ 隨他音聲者。聞他所說隨順而行。不能自
099c06 ‖ 生智慧。問曰。十善道能令一切從他聞者
099c07 ‖ 皆作聲聞耶。答曰。不爾。若無大悲心十善
099c08 ‖ 道能令此人至聲聞地。若有菩薩從諸佛
099c09 ‖ 聞法。以有大悲心故十善道不能令至
099c10 ‖ 聲聞地。問曰。一切無大悲心者。十善道皆
099c11 ‖ 能令至聲聞地耶。答曰。不然。怖畏三界者
099c12 ‖ 十善道能令此人至聲聞道。餘不怖畏者
099c13 ‖ 令生

简体字

观大如毒蛇　　阴如拔刃贼
六入如空聚　　不乐世富乐
贵于坚持戒　　而为禅定故
常乐于安禅　　修习诸善法
唯观于涅槃　　第一救护者
常求尽苦慧　　乐集行解脱
但贵于自利　　一一胜处来
善道令是人　　能至声闻地

随他音声者。闻他所说随顺而行。不能自生智慧。问曰。十善道能令一切从他闻者皆作声闻耶。答曰。不尔。若无大悲心十善道能令此人至声闻地。若有菩萨从诸佛闻法。以有大悲心故十善道不能令至声闻地。问曰。一切无大悲心者。十善道皆能令至声闻地耶。答曰。不然。怖畏三界者十善道能令此人至声闻道。余不怖畏者令生

Chapter 29 — *Distinctions Pertaining to Śrāvakas & Pratyekabuddhas*

Those who contemplate the great elements as like venomous snakes,
the aggregates as like knife-wielding thieves,
and the six sense bases as like a mere empty village,
and who do not delight in worldly wealth or pleasure—

Those who esteem solid observance of the moral precepts
and, for the sake of gaining the *dhyāna* absorptions,
always delight in sitting in *dhyāna* meditation
and in cultivating good dharmas—

Those who look only to nirvāṇa
to serve as the foremost rescuer and protector,
who always seek the wisdom that puts an end to suffering,
and who delight in accumulating the practices leading to liberation—

And those who only esteem the accomplishment of self-benefit
as they come forth through one or another of the supreme bases.
The courses of good karmic action cause these people
to have the ability to reach the grounds of Śrāvaka Disciples.

a. Stanza #1 Commentary

As for these [*śrāvaka* disciples] who accord with what is taught them by others,[150] they listen to what is taught them by others and practice in accordance with that, but are not otherwise able to develop wisdom of their own.

Question: Are the ten courses of good karmic action able in every case to cause all who hear the teachings from others to become *śrāvaka* disciples?

Response: No, that is not the way it is. For those who do not have the great compassion, the ten courses of good karmic action are indeed able to cause them to reach the grounds of the *śrāvaka* disciples. However, in the case of the bodhisattvas who have heard the Dharma from the Buddhas, because they are possessed of the great compassion, the ten courses of good karmic action cannot influence them to enter onto the grounds of the *śrāvaka* disciples.

Question: Is it the case then that whosoever does not possess the great compassion can be caused by the ten courses of good karmic action to reach the grounds of the *śrāvaka* disciples?

Response: No. It is not that way. For those who are frightened at the prospect of continued existence within the three realms, the ten courses of good karmic action are indeed able to cause them to reach the grounds of the *śrāvaka* disciples. For all of those others who are not fearful of existence in the three realms, the ten courses of good karmic action are able to cause them to gain rebirth in good stations

正體字	人天善處。以樂三界故。問曰。一切怖 099c14 ‖ 畏三界者。十善道皆能令至聲聞[10]地。若爾 099c15 ‖ 者菩薩亦怖畏三界為身故。復為眾生勤 099c16 ‖ 行精進求於涅槃。如是十善道。亦應令至 099c17 ‖ 聲聞地。答曰。不必一切怖畏三界者盡墮 099c18 ‖ 聲聞地。何等為墮。樂習行功德少分者。於 099c19 ‖ 佛所教化六波羅蜜中受行少分。如是之 099c20 ‖ 人墮聲聞地。若人能取諸佛功德遍學智 099c21 ‖ 慧十善道必令此人徑至佛道。[11]隨他聞 099c22 ‖ 聲怖畏三界取[12]功德少分。是人有二種十 099c23 ‖ 善道。能令至聲聞地者。至辟支佛地者。問 099c24 ‖ 曰。是人云何[13]俱從他聞怖畏三界取功德 099c25 ‖ 少分十善道能令至聲聞地至辟支佛地。 099c26 ‖ 答曰。志劣弱者作阿羅漢。小堅固者作辟支 099c27 ‖ 佛。
简体字	人天善处。以乐三界故。问曰。一切怖畏三界者。十善道皆能令至声闻地。若尔者菩萨亦怖畏三界为身故。复为众生勤行精进求于涅槃。如是十善道。亦应令至声闻地。答曰。不必一切怖畏三界者尽堕声闻地。何等为堕。乐习行功德少分者。于佛所教化六波罗蜜中受行少分。如是之人堕声闻地。若人能取诸佛功德遍学智慧十善道必令此人径至佛道。随他闻声怖畏三界取功德少分。是人有二种十善道。能令至声闻地者。至辟支佛地者。问曰。是人云何俱从他闻怖畏三界取功德少分十善道能令至声闻地至辟支佛地。答曰。志劣弱者作阿罗汉。小坚固者作辟支佛。

Chapter 29 – Distinctions Pertaining to Śrāvakas & Pratyekabuddhas

of existence among humans and devas. This is because they delight in [continued existences within] the three realms.

Question: The ten courses of good karmic action are able to cause all who are frightened at the prospect of continued existences within the three realms to reach the grounds of the *śrāvaka* disciples. That being the case, bodhisattvas too are fearful of continued existence in the three realms. It is just that, in their diligent and vigorous striving for nirvana, they do so for the sake of both themselves and other beings. Therefore it must be that the ten courses of good karmic action are also able to cause even the bodhisattvas to reach the grounds of the Śrāvaka Disciples.

Response: It is not necessarily the case that everyone who is fearful of continued existence in the three realms is bound to fall down onto the grounds of the Śrāvaka Disciples. Who then is bound to fall? Those who delight in cultivation of but a minor measure of [the requisite] meritorious qualities and who take on but a minor measure of the six *pāramitās* as it was taught them by the Buddhas—it is people of this sort who are bound to fall down onto the grounds of the *śrāvaka* disciples.

In the case of a person who is able to acquire the meritorious qualities of the Buddhas and who is able as well to thoroughly train in their wisdom, the ten courses of good karmic action will definitely propel them directly to the realization of buddhahood.

Among those who rely upon what they have been taught by others, who are fearful of continued existence in the three realms, and who acquire only a minor measure of the meritorious qualities—these people are of two different types. There are those for whom the ten courses of good karmic action are able to cause them to reach the grounds of the *śrāvaka* disciples and there are those who are thereby caused to reach the ground of the *pratyekabuddhas*.

Question: Among these [two types of persons] who rely upon what they have been taught by others, who are fearful of continued existence in the three realms, and who acquire only a minor measure of the meritorious qualities, how is it that the ten courses of good karmic action cause some of them to reach the grounds of the *śrāvaka* disciples whereas others are instead caused to reach the grounds of the *pratyekabuddhas*?

Response: Those of [relatively] inferior and weak resolve end up becoming arhats whereas those whose resolve is somewhat more solid become *pratyekabuddhas*.

正體字

問曰。十善道令一切志劣弱者至聲聞
099c28 ‖ [14]地。答曰。不然。何以故。所謂志弱樂厭離
099c29 ‖ 生死者。非但志劣無厭離者。問曰。觀何
100a01 ‖ 事得知樂厭離心。答曰。觀有為法無常一
100a02 ‖ 切法無我。當知是必樂於厭離。問曰。已知
100a03 ‖ 樂厭離。菩薩亦如是觀有為無常一切法
100a04 ‖ 無我。是十善道何得不令此人墮聲聞地
100a05 ‖ 耶。答曰。是人深厭離離大悲故。乃至一念
100a06 ‖ 中不樂受生。不信世間有安隱相。如經
100a07 ‖ [1]中佛告諸比丘。譬如少糞尚臭穢不淨。何
100a08 ‖ 況多也。如是一念中受生尚苦。何況多也。
100a09 ‖ 諸比丘。當學斷生莫令更受。聲聞人信受
100a10 ‖ 是語故。乃至一念中不樂受生。是人復作
100a11 ‖ 是念。世間無常。於所作事及受命都無安
100a12 ‖ 隱相。死常逐人誰能知死時節。不知死時
100a13 ‖ 為受何業果報。為生何心。如是事中不安
100a14 ‖ 隱故。不可信故。當疾求盡苦。

简体字

问曰。十善道令一切志劣弱者至声闻地。答曰。不然。何以故。所谓志弱乐厌离生死者。非但志劣无厌离者。问曰。观何事得知乐厌离心。答曰。观有为法无常一切法无我。当知是必乐于厌离。问曰。已知乐厌离。菩萨亦如是观有为无常一切法无我。是十善道何得不令此人堕声闻地耶。答曰。是人深厌离离大悲故。乃至一念中不乐受生。不信世间有安隐相。如经中佛告诸比丘。譬如少粪尚臭秽不净。何况多也。如是一念中受生尚苦。何况多也。诸比丘。当学断生莫令更受。声闻人信受是语故。乃至一念中不乐受生。是人复作是念。世间无常。于所作事及受命都无安隐相。死常逐人谁能知死时节。不知死时为受何业果报。为生何心。如是事中不安隐故。不可信故。当疾求尽苦。

Chapter 29 — *Distinctions Pertaining to Śrāvakas & Pratyekabuddhas*

b. Stanza #2 Commentary

Question: Is it the case then that the ten courses of good karmic action cause all such people whose resolve is inferior and weak to reach the grounds of the *śrāvaka* disciples?

Response: No, that is not the way it is. Why? This refers to those whose resolve is relatively weak, but who still do delight in renouncing *saṃsāra*. It is not the case that this refers to those whose resolve is weak but who do not delight in renunciation [of *saṃsāra*], either.

Question: Through contemplation of which matters can one know whether one's mind delights in renunciation?

Response: If one contemplates conditioned dharmas as impermanent and contemplates all dharmas as having no self, one should then realize that he definitely delights in renunciation.

c. Stanza #3 Commentary

Question: Now that we know the bases for delighting in renunciation, since the bodhisattva also contemplates in the same way conditioned dharmas as impermanent and all dharmas as having no self, why do the ten courses of good karmic action not cause this person to fall down onto the grounds of the *śrāvaka* disciples?

Response: Because these people [who are drawn to the Śrāvaka Disciple and Pratyekabuddha Vehicles] have brought forth deep renunciation and have distanced themselves from the great compassion, they do not wish for even a single mind-moment to take on any further rebirths and they do not believe that the world is characterized by stability or security. As the Buddha told the bhikshus in a sutra:

> Just as even a small amount of excrement is smelly, defiled, and unclean, how much the more so a lot of it, so too, even a single mind-moment of rebirth existence is suffering, how much the more so a lot of it. Bhikshus, you should train in the severance of rebirths. Do not allow yourselves to undergo any more of them.[151]

Because *śrāvaka* disciples believe and accept these instructions, they do not wish for even a single mind-moment to undergo any further rebirths. These individuals additionally think thus:

> The world is impermanent. Whether it be the endeavors one pursues or the life span one experiences, these are all characterized by instability and insecurity. Given that death is always pursuing people, who can know the time of their own death? At the time of one's death, one cannot know what kind of karmic retribution one will undergo or what sort of thoughts will arise.[152] Because all such matters are unstable and insecure and because they cannot be trusted, one should urgently strive to put an end to suffering.

正體字

```
          菩薩則不
100a15 || 爾。於恒河沙無量阿僧祇劫受生。為得阿
100a16 || 耨多羅三藐三菩提度諸眾生。是故偈中說。
100a17 || 乃至一念頃不樂[2]於受生。善道[3]令是人能
100a18 || 至聲聞地。問曰。是人樂修[4]集何事故不
100a19 || 樂受生。答曰。是人觀地水火風四大喜生
100a20 || 瞋恨故。不淨臭穢不知恩故。生毒蛇想。
100a21 || 色受想行識五陰。能奪智慧命故。生怨賊
100a22 || 想。眼耳鼻舌身意。入離常離不動不變不壞
100a23 || 無我無我所故。生空聚想。若人於世間一
100a24 || 切受生及資生樂具。以無常虛誑無須臾住
100a25 || 故不生喜悅心。如是之人於一切生處生
100a26 || 無安隱想。但涅槃一法能為救護。如經中
100a27 || 說。諸比丘世間皆是熾然。所謂眼然色然
100a28 || 眼識然眼觸然。及眼觸因緣生受皆亦是然。
100a29 || 以何事故然。所謂貪欲火瞋恚火愚癡火。生
100b01 || 老病死憂悲[5]苦惱火之所熾然。耳鼻舌身意
100b02 || 亦如是。
```

简体字

菩萨则不尔。于恒河沙无量阿僧祇劫受生。为得阿耨多罗三藐三菩提度诸众生。是故偈中说。乃至一念顷不乐于受生。善道令是人能至声闻地。问曰。是人乐修集何事故不乐受生。答曰。是人观地水火风四大喜生瞋恨故。不净臭秽不知恩故。生毒蛇想。色受想行识五阴。能夺智慧命故。生怨贼想。眼耳鼻舌身意。入离常离不动不变不坏无我无我所故。生空聚想。若人于世间一切受生及资生乐具。以无常虚诳无须臾住故不生喜悦心。如是之人于一切生处生无安隐想。但涅槃一法能为救护。如经中说。诸比丘世间皆是炽然。所谓眼然色然眼识然眼触然。及眼触因缘生受皆亦是然。以何事故然。所谓贪欲火瞋恚火愚痴火。生老病死忧悲苦恼火之所炽然。耳鼻舌身意亦如是。

Chapter 29 — Distinctions Pertaining to Śrāvakas & Pratyekabuddhas

The bodhisattva, on the other hand, does not act in this manner, but rather commits himself to undergoing rebirths as numerous as the sands of the Ganges across the course of countless *asaṃkhyeya* kalpas for the sake of attaining *anuttarasamyaksaṃbodhi* and liberating beings.

Thus the verse says [of *śrāvaka* disciples] that they "do not for even a single mind-moment delight in taking on any rebirths." The [ten] courses of good karmic action enable these individuals to reach the grounds of the *śrāvaka* disciples.

d. Stanza #4 Commentary

Question: What sorts of endeavors do these people delight in cultivating and accumulating that they therefore so dislike undergoing further rebirth?

Response: Because, in contemplating the four great elements of earth, water, fire, and air, these people are fond of regarding them with animosity, and because they regard them as forming what is unlovely, foul-smelling, defiled, and ungrateful for kindnesses,[153] they therefore see them as analogous to poisonous snakes.

Because the five aggregates of form, feeling, perception, formative factors, and consciousness are able to rob one of one's wisdom life, they contemplate them as analogous to hostile bandits.

Because the sense bases of eye, ear, nose, tongue, body, and mind are destitute of permanence, unshakability, immutability, and indestructibility, and because they are devoid of self and are devoid of anything belonging to a self, they perceive them as like an empty village.

[They realize that], even if one were to have the advantage of every sort of natural endowment and life-enhancing provision for enjoyment, because those things are impermanent, false, deceptive, and do not abide for even a moment, they are not moved to delight in this. Hence people of this sort think of all stations of rebirth as devoid of any stability or security and they look only to the single dharma of nirvāṇa as their rescuer and protector. This is as described in a sutra:

> Bhikshus, the world is entirely ablaze, that is to say: The eye is ablaze, visual forms are ablaze, eye consciousness is ablaze, eye contact is ablaze, and whatever feeling is produced with eye contact as the causal condition—that too is ablaze.
>
> And with what is it ablaze? It is ablaze with the fire of desire, the fire of hatred, the fire of delusion, the fire of birth, aging, sickness, death, grief, lamentation, anguish, and torment. So too is this the case with the ear, nose, tongue, body, and mind faculty.[154]

正體字

觀一切有為法皆是熾然。[6]唯涅槃
100b03 ‖ 寂滅[7]法能為救護。貴涅槃一法故捨一切
100b04 ‖ 事勤習坐禪。問曰。若觀一切有為法皆是
100b05 ‖ 熾然。唯涅槃寂滅能為救護者。十善道皆令
100b06 ‖ 至聲聞地耶。答曰。不然。佛所結戒。為禪
100b07 ‖ 定故貴重此戒。有決定心而不毀犯。捨一
100b08 ‖ 切事但樂坐禪。求盡苦智常勤修習解脫
100b09 ‖ 因緣。於先世中或從一勝處來二勝處來
100b10 ‖ 者。十善道能令此人至聲聞地。何以故。持
100b11 ‖ 戒清淨則心不悔。心不悔故得歡喜。得歡
100b12 ‖ 喜故身輕軟。身輕軟故心快樂。心快樂故攝
100b13 ‖ 心得定。攝心得定故。生如實智慧。生如
100b14 ‖ 實智慧故即生厭。從厭生離從離得解脫。
100b15 ‖ 若一若二勝處來者。如尊者羅睺羅從諦勝
100b16 ‖ 處來。如尊者施曰羅從捨勝處來。如尊者
100b17 ‖ 離跋多從寂滅勝處來。如尊者舍利弗從
100b18 ‖ 慧勝處來。

简体字

观一切有为法皆是炽然。唯涅槃寂灭法能为救护。贵涅槃一法故舍一切事勤习坐禅。问曰。若观一切有为法皆是炽然。唯涅槃寂灭能为救护者。十善道皆令至声闻地耶。答曰。不然。佛所结戒。为禅定故贵重此戒。有决定心而不毁犯。舍一切事但乐坐禅。求尽苦智常勤修习解脱因缘。于先世中或从一胜处来二胜处来者。十善道能令此人至声闻地。何以故。持戒清净则心不悔。心不悔故得欢喜。得欢喜故身轻软。身轻软故心快乐。心快乐故摄心得定。摄心得定故。生如实智慧。生如实智慧故即生厌。从厌生离从离得解脱。若一若二胜处来者。如尊者罗睺罗从谛胜处来。如尊者施曰罗从舍胜处来。如尊者离跋多从寂灭胜处来。如尊者舍利弗从慧胜处来。

Chapter 29 — Distinctions Pertaining to Śrāvakas & Pratyekabuddhas

e. STANZA #5–6 COMMENTARY

They contemplate all conditioned dharmas as ablaze and regard only nirvāṇa's dharma of quiescent cessation as able to provide a source of rescue. Because they so esteem this single dharma of nirvāṇa, they abandon all other endeavors in favor of diligent practice of sitting in *dhyāna* meditation.

Question: If one contemplates all conditioned dharmas as ablaze and the quiescent cessation of nirvāṇa as the only source of rescue and protection, is it the case then that the ten courses of good karmic action are able in every case to cause these people to reach the grounds of the *śrāvaka* disciples?

Response: No, that is not so. Consider the moral precepts formulated by the Buddha. It is for the sake of attaining the *dhyāna* absorptions that these moral precepts are esteemed as so important. [Hence we refer here instead to] those with resolute aspiration who refrain from transgressing against the precepts, who abandon all other endeavors, who delight solely in sitting in *dhyāna* meditation, who seek the wisdom that extinguishes suffering, and who always diligently cultivate the causes and conditions for liberation. It is people of this sort who have come forth from cultivating one or two of the supreme bases [of meritorious qualities] in previous lives that the ten courses of good karmic action thus enable to reach the grounds of the *śrāvaka* disciples.

And how does this come about? If one upholds the moral precepts purely, one's mind becomes free of any regrets. Because one's mind is free of regrets, one becomes suffused with joyfulness. Having gained this state of joyfulness, one's body experiences a state of pliancy. Because one's body experiences this state of pliancy, one's mind becomes blissful. Because one's mind becomes blissful, one focuses the mind and gains meditative absorption. Because one focuses the mind and gains meditative absorption, one develops wisdom that accords with reality. Because one develops wisdom that accords with reality, one immediately develops disenchantment. From disenchantment, one develops detachment, and from detachment, one attains liberation.[155]

f. STANZA #7 COMMENTARY

As for "coming forth from one or perhaps two of the supreme bases [of meritorious qualities]," this is exemplified by the Venerable Rāhula who came forth from the supreme basis of truthfulness, by the Venerable Sivali[156] who came forth from the supreme basis of relinquishment, by the Venerable Revata who came forth from the supreme basis of quiescence, and as exemplified by the Venerable Śāriputra who came forth from the supreme basis of wisdom.

100b19	或從諦捨二勝處來。或從諦寂
100b20	滅二勝處來。或從諦慧二勝處來。或從捨
100b21	寂滅二勝處來。或從捨慧二勝處來。或從
100b22	寂滅慧二勝處來。如是十善道。能令至聲 聞地。[8]
100b23	十住毘婆沙論卷第十四　100c02 ‖十住毘婆沙論卷第十五
100c03 ‖ 100c04 ‖聖者龍樹造 100c05 ‖後秦龜茲國三藏鳩摩羅什譯
100c06	分別聲聞辟支佛品之餘
100c07	[9]問曰。十善道令何等人至辟支佛地。答曰。
100c08	於聲聞所行　　十善道轉勝
100c09	深禪不隨他　　常憙於遠離
100c10	恒樂善修習　　甚深因緣法
100c11	遠離方便力　　及以大悲心
100c12	少欲及少事　　惡賤憒閙語
100c13	常樂遠離處　　威德深重人
100c14	喜為福田地　　常觀於出性
100c15	成辦有理事　　恭敬於諸主
100c16	已成就繫心　　知心在所緣
100c17	常樂於禪定　　中人之勢力
100c18	樂於出家法　　善心不縮沒
100c19	得慧光明者　　或從二勝處

或从谛舍二胜处来。或从谛寂灭二胜处来。或从谛慧二胜处来。或从舍寂灭二胜处来。或从舍慧二胜处来。或从寂灭慧二胜处来。如是十善道。能令至声闻地。

问曰。十善道令何等人至辟支佛地。答曰。
　于声闻所行　　十善道转胜
　深禅不随他　　常喜于远离
　恒乐善修习　　甚深因缘法
　远离方便力　　及以大悲心
　少欲及少事　　恶贱愦闹语
　常乐远离处　　威德深重人
　喜为福田地　　常观于出性
　成办有理事　　恭敬于诸主
　已成就系心　　知心在所缘
　常乐于禅定　　中人之势力
　乐于出家法　　善心不缩没
　得慧光明者　　或从二胜处

Chapter 29 – Distinctions Pertaining to Śrāvakas & Pratyekabuddhas

Then again, it may perhaps be that one comes forth from the two supreme bases consisting of truthfulness and relinquishment, that one comes forth from the two supreme bases consisting of truthfulness and quiescence, that one comes forth from the two supreme bases consisting of truthfulness and wisdom, that one comes forth from the two supreme bases consisting of relinquishment and quiescence, that one comes forth from the two supreme bases consisting of relinquishment and wisdom, or that one comes forth from the two supreme bases consisting of quiescence and wisdom.

It is in this way that the ten courses of good karmic action may enable one to reach the grounds of the *śrāvaka* disciples.

2. Q: WHO CAN USE THE TEN COURSES TO BECOME A PRATYEKABUDDHA?

Question: What sorts of people do the ten courses of good karmic action cause to enter the grounds of the *pratyekabuddhas*?

Response:

In the ten courses of good karmic action
practiced by *śrāvaka* disciples, they are even more superior.
They cultivate deep *dhyāna*, don't rely on others' teaching,
and are always fond of abiding in seclusion, far from others.

They always delight in the thorough cultivation
of the extremely deep dharma of causes and conditions.
They remain detached from the power of skillful means
as well as from the mind of great compassion.

They pursue lesser aspirations and lesser endeavors.
They abhor and disdain boisterous chatter,
always enjoy abiding in secluded places,
and are possessed of awe-inspiring virtue and deep solemnity.

They delight in serving as fields of merit
and always contemplate what by nature promotes transcendence.
They accomplish those endeavors that are principled
and accord reverence to the Lords [of the Dharma].

Having already perfected anchoring of the mind,
the knowing mind focuses on whatever is taken as the object.
They always delight in *dhyāna* concentration
and in this possess the power of men of intermediate capacities.

They delight in the dharmas of the monastic
and in them the mind of goodness does not shrink or sink away.
Those who gain the light of wisdom
may come forth from two of the supreme bases.

| 100c20 ‖ 　　或三勝處來　　十善之業道
| 100c21 ‖ 　　能令如是人　　至於緣覺地
| 100c22 ‖ 於聲聞所行十善道轉勝者。過聲聞人所
| 100c23 ‖ 行十善道。而不及菩薩所行。作是念。聲聞
| 100c24 ‖ 人應隨他聞而行道然後得自證智慧。我
| 100c25 ‖ 則不然。不樂隨他人。以是故。我應令十
| 100c26 ‖ 善道轉勝。以是因緣故。我樂不隨他十善
| 100c27 ‖ 道。令我至辟支佛地。如是思惟已常樂於
| 100c28 ‖ 遠離。作是念。若我常樂憒閙則為集諸惡
| 100c29 ‖ 不善法。以近可染可瞋可癡事故。於是遠
| 101a01 ‖ 離中應修習甚深因緣法。復作是念。若我
| 101a02 ‖ 不修習甚深因緣法者則不得不隨他智。
| 101a03 ‖ 我今何故不常修習甚深因緣。然後可得
| 101a04 ‖ 不隨他智。甚深者。難得其底不可通達。
| 101a05 ‖ 一切凡夫從無始生死中所有經書及其[1]技
| 101a06 ‖ 藝皆可得其邊底。唯甚深因緣不可得底。

　　或三胜处来　　十善之业道
　　能令如是人　　至于缘觉地
于声闻所行十善道转胜者。过声闻人所行十善道。而不及菩萨所行。作是念。声闻人应随他闻而行道然后得自证智慧。我则不然。不乐随他人。以是故。我应令十善道转胜。以是因缘故。我乐不随他十善道。令我至辟支佛地。如是思惟已常乐于远离。作是念。若我常乐愦闹则为集诸恶不善法。以近可染可嗔可痴事故。于是远离中应修习甚深因缘法。复作是念。若我不修习甚深因缘法者则不得不随他智。我今何故不常修习甚深因缘。然后可得不随他智。甚深者。难得其底不可通达。一切凡夫从无始生死中所有经书及其技艺皆可得其边底。唯甚深因缘不可得底。

Chapter 29 — Distinctions Pertaining to Śrāvakas & Pratyekabuddhas

Or perhaps they come forth from three of the supreme bases.
The ten courses of good karmic action
enable persons of this sort
to reach the ground of the Pratyekabuddhas.

a. STANZA#1 COMMENTARY

As for "In the ten courses of good karmic action practiced by *śrāvaka* disciples, they are even more superior," they surpass that level of accomplishment in the ten courses of good karmic action reached by the *śrāvaka* disciples, but still do not approach the level of accomplishment in such dharmas as practiced by the bodhisattvas.

They reflect in this manner:

> The *śrāvaka* disciple practitioners respond to and accord with what they are taught by others in their practice of the path, after which they attain personal realizations of wisdom. As for myself, I am not thus inclined, for I do not delight in following others. Therefore I should cause the practice of the ten courses of good karmic action to become even more superior. For this reason I shall delight in the ten courses of good karmic action without relying on others and this shall enable me to reach the ground of the *pratyekabuddhas*.

Having reflected in this manner, they always delight in seclusion, thinking thus:

> If I forever delight in the boisterousness [of the common crowd], then that is bound to lead to the accumulation of all manner of evil and unwholesome dharmas due to close proximity to circumstances that can cause defilement, can cause hatred, and can cause delusion. In this seclusion, I should cultivate the extremely deep dharma of causes and conditions.

b. STANZA#2 COMMENTARY

They additionally reflect in this way:

> If I do not cultivate the extremely deep dharma of causes and conditions, then I will be unable to gain that wisdom that is not reliant on the teachings of others. Why should I not now always cultivate the extremely deep dharma of causes and conditions so that I can later gain the wisdom that is not reliant on the teachings of others?

"Extremely deep" refers in this context to that which is difficult to fathom and that with regard to which one cannot reach an utterly penetrating comprehension. One can completely fathom all of the scriptures, texts, skills, and arts possessed by all common people across the beginningless course of *saṃsāra*. It is only the extremely deep dharma of causes and conditions that one cannot completely fathom. [The

正體字

101a07 ‖ 如兔等小虫不能得大海邊底。若人有方
101a08 ‖ 便大悲心及修[2]集甚深因緣即得阿耨多
101a09 ‖ 羅三藐三菩提。若離此二事修[*]集甚深因
101a10 ‖ 緣智則成辟支佛。方便名於成就教化眾
101a11 ‖ 生中種種思惟而不錯謬。亦於甚深法不
101a12 ‖ 取相大悲名深。憐愍眾生。勝聲聞辟支佛。
101a13 ‖ 何況凡夫。少欲少事惡賤憒鬧語。如是則
101a14 ‖ 得辟支佛地。若大欲大事好聚眾人。為方
101a15 ‖ 便大悲所護者。阿耨多羅三藐三菩提則為
101a16 ‖ 易得。何以故。求辟支[3]佛人少欲者作是
101a17 ‖ 念但自度身。少事者但自成就善根不及
101a18 ‖ 餘人。是人捨離教化眾生事故不親近眾
101a19 ‖ 鬧。菩薩大欲大事作是念。我應度一切眾生。
101a20 ‖ 以此大欲因緣故則為大事教化眾生。教
101a21 ‖ 化眾生此非小事。若憎惡憒鬧語則不成
101a22 ‖ 此事。是故菩薩入憒鬧中亦用憒鬧之語
101a23 ‖ 但無所著。復次覆真實功德故是為

简体字

如兔等小虫不能得大海边底。若人有方便大悲心及修集甚深因缘即得阿耨多罗三藐三菩提。若离此二事修集甚深因缘智则成辟支佛。方便名于成就教化众生中种种思惟而不错谬。亦于甚深法不取相大悲名深。怜愍众生。胜声闻辟支佛。何况凡夫。少欲少事恶贱愦闹语。如是则得辟支佛地。若大欲大事好聚众人。为方便大悲所护者。阿耨多罗三藐三菩提则为易得。何以故。求辟支佛人少欲者作是念但自度身。少事者但自成就善根不及余人。是人舍离教化众生事故不亲近众闹。菩萨大欲大事作是念。我应度一切众生。以此大欲因缘故则为大事教化众生。教化众生此非小事。若憎恶愦闹语则不成此事。是故菩萨入愦闹中亦用愦闹之语但无所著。复次覆真实功德故是为少欲。

Chapter 29 — *Distinctions Pertaining to Śrāvakas & Pratyekabuddhas* 1047

difficulty of fathoming it] is comparable to a rabbit's or other small creature's inability to fathom the very bottom of a great ocean.

If one possesses skillful means and the mind of great compassion while also increasingly cultivating the extremely deep dharma of causes and conditions, then he can proceed directly toward the attainment of *anuttarasamyaksaṃbodhi*. However, if one abandons these two requisites while increasingly cultivating the extremely deep knowledge of causes and conditions, then he will instead become a *pratyekabuddha*.

"Skillful means" refers here to perfecting in a manner free of error all the different sorts of thought used in teaching beings while also not seizing on merely superficial aspects of extremely profound dharmas.

"Great compassion" refers here to abiding in a deep and kindly sympathy for beings, one that is superior even to that of *śrāvaka* disciples and *pratyekabuddhas*, how much the more so common people.

c. STANZA #3 COMMENTARY

As for "pursuing lesser aspirations and lesser endeavors," and "abhorring and disdaining boisterous chatter," those possessed of these qualities can reach the ground of the *pratyekabuddhas*.

If one is inclined toward great aspirations and great endeavors, if one enjoys gatherings of many people, and if one is protected by skillful means and great compassion, then it will become easy to reach *anuttarasamyaksaṃbodhi*.

Why is this so? One who pursues *pratyekabuddhahood*, possessed as he is of lesser aspirations, thinks: "One need only see to one's own liberation."

As for his "pursuing lesser endeavors," this practitioner devotes himself solely to the perfection of his own roots of goodness and does not extend his concern to other people. Because this person abandons the endeavor of teaching beings, he does not draw near to any of the many sorts of commotion.

The bodhisattva, being inclined toward great aspirations and great endeavors, thinks: "I should liberate all beings." It is because of this great aspiration that he then takes on the great endeavor of teaching beings. This teaching of beings is no minor endeavor. If one abhors boisterousness and talkativeness, then he will not succeed in this work. Therefore the bodhisattva enters into the midst of such commotion and resorts to discourse appropriate to such commotion, but he still has nothing to which he is attached.

Moreover, it is because [the *pratyekabuddha* practitioners] reject the cultivation of genuine meritorious qualities that they are said to have

正體字

少欲。
101a24 ‖ 少事務故名為少事。惡賤憒鬧名少欲。
101a25 ‖ 樂獨處故名為少事。如是之人少欲少事。
101a26 ‖ 不樂眾鬧語。樂於親近遠離可畏深邃之
101a27 ‖ 處其心深大。是人作是念。若我住遠離可
101a28 ‖ 畏深邃之處人則不來。以遠離處住故。心
101a29 ‖ 亦深遠。若人自不深遠喜戲調者。外人往
101b01 ‖ 來則不為難。如是人不與眾生和合。雖
101b02 ‖ 捨眾生亦欲令眾生種諸善根為大利益
101b03 ‖ 作是念。我云何不與眾生和合亦能利益
101b04 ‖ 眾生。如是思惟知已。我當為眾生作福田
101b05 ‖ 之利受其供養。如是雖不與眾生和合。
101b06 ‖ 而能作大利益。是人復思惟。我云何當得
101b07 ‖ 福田地。即自見知。若我深樂為福田地。常
101b08 ‖ 觀出性。然後福田地法自然而來。[4]乃至出
101b09 ‖ 性之法亦自然而來。所謂持戒禪定智慧等。
101b10 ‖ 復作是念。我當云何疾至福田地及

简体字

少事务故名为少事。恶贱愦闹名少欲。乐独处故名为少事。如是之人少欲少事。不乐众闹语。乐于亲近远离可畏深邃之处其心深大。是人作是念。若我住远离可畏深邃之处人则不来。以远离处住故。心亦深远。若人自不深远喜戏调者。外人往来则不为难。如是人不与众生和合。虽舍众生亦欲令众生种诸善根为大利益作是念。我云何不与众生和合亦能利益众生。如是思惟知已。我当为众生作福田之利受其供养。如是虽不与众生和合。而能作大利益。是人复思惟。我云何当得福田地。即自见知。若我深乐为福田地。常观出性。然后福田地法自然而来。乃至出性之法亦自然而来。所谓持戒禅定智慧等。复作是念。我当云何疾至福田地及

"lesser aspirations." It is because they take on but few responsibilities that these are referred to as "lesser endeavors." It is because of their abhorrence and disdain for commotion that they are said to have "lesser aspirations." And it is because they delight in residing in solitude that they are said to engage in "lesser endeavors."

As for persons such as these who have lesser aspirations, engage in lesser endeavors, do not delight in the commotion and chatter of the multitudes, and who delight in proximity to far away, fearsome, and very remote places, their determination is extremely great. These individuals reflect thus:

> If I dwell in a faraway, fearsome, and very remote place, then nobody will come there, and thus, by virtue of that abiding at a great distance, the mind itself will also be able to abide at an especially great distance. If one does not dwell extremely far from those who delight in frivolousness, then outsiders will not find it difficult to come and go there.

d. STANZA #4 COMMENTARY

People of this sort do not live together with other beings. Although they have abandoned beings, they still wish to influence beings to plant roots of goodness and do wish to be of great benefit to them. Hence they reflect in this manner: "How might I not live together with other beings and yet still benefit beings?" Having pondered in this manner, they realize: "I should benefit beings by serving as a field of merit for them, doing so by accepting offerings from them. Thus, even though I do not live together with other beings, I shall still be able to be of great benefit to them."

Continuing in this vein, this person reflects: "How then might I become a field of karmic merit for others?" He then immediately sees and realizes the following, thinking:

> If I deeply delight in serving as a field of merit and in always contemplating whatever naturally leads to transcendence, then, later on, the means for serving as a field of merit will spontaneously come forth and whatever dharmas naturally lead to transcendence will spontaneously come forth as well.

These [dharmas that naturally lead to transcendence] are what we refer to as the observance of moral precepts, cultivation of *dhyāna* absorptions, development of wisdom, and so forth.

He also has this thought:

> How might I be able to swiftly reach that ground in which I may become a field of merit and acquire the dharmas leading to

出性
101b11 ‖ 法。我當為正觀者於諸現有理趣事中皆
101b12 ‖ 悉成辦供養恭敬諸主。如是福田地及出性
101b13 ‖ 法不久疾得。何以故。我當成辦有理之事
101b14 ‖ 正觀諸法能得不隨他智。又供養恭敬諸
101b15 ‖ 主故令善根增厚。善根增厚故智慧深厚。
101b16 ‖ 智慧深厚故能通達實事。能通達實事故能
101b17 ‖ 生厭。從厭則生離。從離得解脫。得解脫
101b18 ‖ 故前後所集善根得為福田。然後得證出
101b19 ‖ 性之法。諸主者諸佛世尊。是種諸善根時
101b20 ‖ 是最大因緣。是人復思惟。我云何能疾成有
101b21 ‖ 理趣事。是人即自知見。若我集繫心一處
101b22 ‖ 知其所緣。常樂禪定。是人能繫心一處則
101b23 ‖ 能得三昧。得三昧故有理事皆能成辦。如
101b24 ‖ 經中說。

出性法。我当为正观者于诸现有理趣事中皆悉成办供养恭敬诸主。如是福田地及出性法不久疾得。何以故。我当成办有理之事正观诸法能得不随他智。又供养恭敬诸主故令善根增厚。善根增厚故智慧深厚。智慧深厚故能通达实事。能通达实事故能生厌。从厌则生离。从离得解脱。得解脱故前后所集善根得为福田。然后得证出性之法。诸主者诸佛世尊。是种诸善根时是最大因缘。是人复思惟。我云何能疾成有理趣事。是人即自知见。若我集系心一处知其所缘。常乐禅定。是人能系心一处则能得三昧。得三昧故有理事皆能成办。如经中说。

Chapter 29 — Distinctions Pertaining to Śrāvakas & Pratyekabuddhas

transcendence? I should become one who is grounded in right contemplation, should accomplish all endeavors that are manifestly principled and of meaningful significance, and should make offerings to and demonstrate reverence for the Lords [of the Dharma]. If I proceed in this manner, then before too long I shall swiftly acquire that ground on which I can serve as a field of merit and shall also acquire the dharmas that naturally lead to transcendence.

Why should I proceed in this manner? I should accomplish those endeavors that are principled and should rightly contemplate dharmas for this shall enable me to realize the wisdom that is not reliant on the teachings of others.

Furthermore, it is because of making offerings to and revering the Lords [of the Dharma] that one's roots of goodness are able to increase and grow ever more fully developed. Due to such growth in one's roots of goodness, wisdom too shall then become extremely deep and full in its development.

It is because of wisdom's becoming extremely deep and full in its development that one is then able to gain an utterly penetrating comprehension of the true character of all phenomena. When one is able to gain an utterly penetrating comprehension of the true character of all phenomena, one can then generate disenchantment. It is from this disenchantment that one is then able to generate detachment. It is through this detachment that one gains liberation. And it is because of gaining liberation that the roots of goodness one has accumulated in the past and later on finally enable one to serve as a field of merit. Afterward, one then attains the realization of the dharmas naturally leading to transcendence.

As for "the Lords," this is a specific reference to the Buddhas, the Bhagavats. During the time that one is planting roots of goodness, this matter [of reverence for the Buddhas] is the very greatest of all causes and conditions in that endeavor.

e. Stanza #5 Commentary

This practitioner continues pondering these matters, thinking, "Now, how exactly will I be able to swiftly succeed in those endeavors that are principled and of meaningful significance?"

This person then immediately understands and sees: "If I anchor the mind in a single place, directly know what it takes as its object, and always delight in the cultivation of the *dhyāna* absorptions, [my aims may be accomplished in this way]."

If this practitioner is able to anchor his mind in a single place, he is then able to gain samādhi. Due to acquiring samādhi, all principled endeavors can then be accomplished. This is as described in the sutras:

正體字

```
         得禪定能如實知如實見。若人已
101b25 || 行繫心則疾入三昧。疾入三昧故名禪定
101b26 || 者常定者。若能如是修[*]集諸法則為供養
101b27 || 恭敬諸佛。若人以香華四事供養佛不名
101b28 || 供養佛。若能一心不放逸親近修[*]集聖
101b29 || 道是名供養恭敬諸佛。如經說。般涅槃時
101c01 || 佛告阿難。天雨[5]文陀羅華及栴檀末香作
101c02 || 天伎樂。不名供養恭敬如來也。阿難。若
101c03 || 比丘比丘尼優婆塞優婆夷一心不放逸親近
101c04 || 修[*]集聖法。是名真供養佛。是故阿難。汝
101c05 || 當修學真供養佛。如是眾功德。皆是中勢
101c06 || 力人樂出家善心不縮沒者。最上勢力能
101c07 || 得成佛。下勢力者作聲聞。以是故中勢力
101c08 || 人作辟支佛。樂出家故能成眾功德。何以
101c09 || 故。若在居家則不能少欲少事。不能身心
101c10 || 遠離。亦不能禪定。若心縮沒不清淨者。
```

简体字

得禅定能如实知如实见。若人已行系心则疾入三昧。疾入三昧故名禅定者常定者。若能如是修集诸法则为供养恭敬诸佛。若人以香华四事供养佛不名供养佛。若能一心不放逸亲近修集圣道是名供养恭敬诸佛。如经说。般涅槃时佛告阿难。天雨文陀罗华及栴檀末香作天伎乐。不名供养恭敬如来也。阿难。若比丘比丘尼优婆塞优婆夷一心不放逸亲近修集圣法。是名真供养佛。是故阿难。汝当修学真供养佛。如是众功德。皆是中势力人乐出家善心不缩没者。最上势力能得成佛。下势力者作声闻。以是故中势力人作辟支佛。乐出家故能成众功德。何以故。若在居家则不能少欲少事。不能身心远离。亦不能禅定。若心缩没不清净者。

"By gaining *dhyāna* concentration, one becomes able to know in accordance with reality and see in accordance with reality."

If one has already practiced anchoring of the mind, then he will swiftly enter samādhi. It is through this ability to swiftly enter samādhi that one becomes an adept in the *dhyāna* absorptions, one who always abides in meditative absorption.

If one becomes able in this manner to cultivate these dharmas, then this itself constitutes offerings and reverence to the Buddhas. If someone were to make offerings of incense, flowers, and the four requisites to the Buddhas, this would not truly qualify as making offerings to the Buddhas. Rather, if one can single-mindedly draw close to and cultivate the path of the Āryas, doing so without falling into neglectfulness, this would truly constitute offerings and reverence to the Buddhas. As stated in the sutras, at the time of his *parinirvāṇa*, the Buddha told Ānanda:

> The raining down of *mandārava* flowers and powdered *candana* incense accompanied by the music of the devas—this does not truly qualify as offerings and reverence to the Tathāgata Ānanda, if a bhikshu, bhikshuni, *upāsaka*, or *upāsikā* were to single-mindedly and without neglectfulness draw close to and cultivate the dharmas of the Āryas, it is this that would truly constitute the making of offerings to the Buddha. Therefore, Ānanda, you should cultivate and train in this true offering to the Buddha.

Many meritorious qualities such as these characterize the practitioner of intermediate strength who delights in leaving the household life and who does not allow his devotion to goodness to retreat or fall away.

Those of the most superior strength are able to succeed in attaining buddhahood whereas those possessed of a lesser degree of strength become *śrāvaka* disciples. Hence it is those of intermediate strength who become *pratyekabuddhas*.

f. Stanza #6–7 Commentary

Because they delight in leaving behind the household life they are able to perfect a multitude of meritorious qualities. And why is this so? If one continues to abide within the household, one is unable to have but few desires and take on but few endeavors. One is unable to remain physically and mentally detached nor can one acquire the *dhyāna* absorptions.

If one's resolve retreats and sinks into impurity, one will be unable to successfully accomplish many endeavors, one will be unable to understand the extremely deep dharma of causes and conditions, one

正體字

不
能成辦眾事。不能知甚深因緣法。不能
證出性。不能如法真供養恭敬諸佛。如
是眾[6]生是中勢力。作是念。我中勢力人。常
樂出家心不縮沒。諸所願功德事皆自然
來。復作是思惟。是中勢力樂為得何果。即
知當得智慧果。何以故。智慧能為照明。如
經中說。諸比丘一切光明中智慧光為勝。復
作是念。我所樂慧光云何當得。即知若從
二勝處來。若三勝處來。二勝處者先已說。三
勝處者。所謂諦捨寂滅。或諦捨慧。或諦寂滅
慧。以是故我當修[*]集如是諸勝處。我修
[*]集是已得智慧光明。所願智慧自然而至。
如是相如是修[*]集助道法者。十善道能令
至辟支佛[7]地。

简体字

不能成办众事。不能知甚深因缘法。不能证出性。不能如法真供养恭敬诸佛。如是众生是中势力。作是念。我中势力人。常乐出家心不缩没。诸所愿功德事皆自然来。复作是思惟。是中势力乐为得何果。即知当得智慧果。何以故。智慧能为照明。如经中说。诸比丘一切光明中智慧光为胜。复作是念。我所乐慧光云何当得。即知若从二胜处来。若三胜处来。二胜处者先已说。三胜处者。所谓谛舍寂灭。或谛舍慧。或谛寂灭慧。以是故我当修集如是诸胜处。我修集是已得智慧光明。所愿智慧自然而至。如是相如是修集助道法者。十善道能令至辟支佛地。

will be unable to achieve the realization of the nature of transcendence, and one will be unable to truly make offerings to and revere the Buddhas in a manner that accords with the Dharma.

Beings such as these possess an intermediate level of strength. They think, "I am a person of intermediate strength. If I always delight in leaving the household life and maintain a resolve that does not retreat or fall away, all the meritorious circumstances that I wish for will naturally come forth for me."

He also reflects, "Being one of middling capacities, which of the fruits of the path should I delight in acquiring?" He immediately realizes that he should acquire the fruit of wisdom. And why? Because wisdom can bring about brilliant illumination. This is as stated in the sutras where it says: "Bhikshus, of all the different sorts of illumination, the light of wisdom is supreme."[157]

He then also thinks: "How should I go about acquiring this light of wisdom in which I delight?" He then realizes that it will come forth through perfection of either two or three of the supreme bases [of meritorious qualities]. As for the twofold acquisitions of the supreme bases, those combinations were already discussed above.

As for threefold acquisitions of the supreme bases, those may consist of truth, relinquishment, and quiescence, may consist of truth, relinquishment, and wisdom, or may consist of truth, quiescence, and wisdom. [He thinks,] "Therefore I should cultivate and accumulate these supreme bases. Once I have cultivated and accumulated these [supreme bases], I shall gain the light of wisdom and thus that wisdom that I have vowed to gain will naturally arrive here for me."

When someone possessed of such characteristics as these cultivates and accumulates these path-assisting dharmas in this way, the ten courses of good karmic action will enable him to reach the ground of the *pratyekabuddha*.

The End of Chapter Twenty-Nine

正體字

101c25 ‖	大乘品第[8]三
101c26 ‖	問曰。如仁已說。十善道能令人至聲聞辟
101c27 ‖	支佛地。十善業道。復令何等眾生至[9]於佛
101c28 ‖	地。答曰。
101c29 ‖	所行十善道　　勝於二種人
102a01 ‖	無量希有修　　勝一切世間
102a02 ‖	發堅善二願　　成大悲無礙
102a03 ‖	善受行方便　　忍[1]辱諸苦惱
102a04 ‖	不捨諸眾生　　深愛諸佛慧
102a05 ‖	於佛力自在　　樂盡遍行者
102a06 ‖	能破邪見意　　受護佛正法
102a07 ‖	健堪受精進　　堅心化眾生
102a08 ‖	不貪著自樂　　及無量身命
102a09 ‖	一切事中上　　所作無過咎
102a10 ‖	一切種清淨　　一切勝處來
102a11 ‖	善道令此人　　至十力世尊

简体字

大乘品第三十

问曰。如仁已说。十善道能令人至声闻辟支佛地。十善业道。复令何等众生至于佛地。答曰。

　　所行十善道　　胜于二种人
　　无量希有修　　胜一切世间
　　发坚善二愿　　成大悲无碍
　　善受行方便　　忍辱诸苦恼
　　不舍诸众生　　深爱诸佛慧
　　于佛力自在　　乐尽遍行者
　　能破邪见意　　受护佛正法
　　健堪受精进　　坚心化众生
　　不贪着自乐　　及无量身命
　　一切事中上　　所作无过咎
　　一切种清净　　一切胜处来
　　善道令此人　　至十力世尊

CHAPTER 30
[Distinctions Pertaining to] the Great Vehicle

X. CHAPTER 30: [DISTINCTIONS PERTAINING TO] THE GREAT VEHICLE
   A. Q: WHICH BEINGS CAN USE THE TEN COURSES TO BECOME BUDDHAS?

Question: As you have already explained, the ten courses of good karmic action enable one to reach the grounds of the *śrāvaka* disciples and *pratyekabuddha*s. Which sorts of beings can the ten courses of good karmic action also cause to reach the ground of buddhahood?

   B. A: THE TEN COURSES ENABLE BUDDHAHOOD FOR BEINGS OF THIS SORT (VERSE)

Response:

> The way they practice the ten courses of good karmic action
> is superior to that of the two other classes of practitioners,
> for they engage in measureless extraordinary cultivation
> superior to that of anyone else in the world.
>
> They bring forth vows that are both solid and good,[158]
> perfect the great compassion that cannot be impeded,
> thoroughly take on the practice of skillful means,
> and patiently endure every sort of pain and anguish.
>
> They do not abandon any being,
> deeply cherish the wisdom of the Buddhas,
> and delight in those who completely and thoroughly practice
> the Buddhas' powers and sovereign masteries.
>
> They are able to refute all ideas involving wrong views
> and accept and protect the Buddhas' right Dharma.
> They are valiant, able to endure, and vigorous,
> and are possessed of solid resolve in teaching beings.
>
> They do not covet or become attached to their own happiness
> or to living a measurelessly long life.
> They are supreme in all their endeavors
> and free of fault in all the works they do.
>
> They possess every kind of purity
> and come forth through the practice of all the supreme bases.
> The courses of good karmic action enable these persons
> to reach the ground of the Bhagavats who possess the ten powers.

正體字

102a12 ‖ 所修十善道勝二種人者。菩薩修十善道。
102a13 ‖ 於求聲聞辟支佛者為轉勝。轉勝者。一心
102a14 ‖ 修行常修行。為自利故修行。為他利故修
102a15 ‖ 行。清淨修行。一心行者用意修行。常修行者
102a16 ‖ 不中休息。為自利故修行者。生天人因緣
102a17 ‖ 泥洹因緣。為他利修行者。菩薩修行十善
102a18 ‖ 道。迴向利安[2]一切眾生故。以是因緣故。
102a19 ‖ 能度過算數眾生。清淨修行者。不壞行無
102a20 ‖ 雜行。不濁行自在行。具足行不貪著行。智者
102a21 ‖ 所讚行。壞者有行有不行。與此相違名不
102a22 ‖ 壞行。雜者自不作令他作。與此相違名不
102a23 ‖ 雜行。濁者與煩惱罪業合行。與此相違名
102a24 ‖ 為不濁行。自在者。破戒人為田業妻子財
102a25 ‖ 物所繫不得自在。持戒者無如是事。隨
102a26 ‖ 意自在

简体字

　　所修十善道胜二种人者。菩萨修十善道。于求声闻辟支佛者为转胜。转胜者。一心修行常修行。为自利故修行。为他利故修行。清净修行。一心行者用意修行。常修行者不中休息。为自利故修行者。生天人因缘泥洹因缘。为他利修行者。菩萨修行十善道。回向利安一切众生故。以是因缘故。能度过算数众生。清净修行者。不坏行无杂行。不浊行自在行。具足行不贪着行。智者所赞行。坏者有行有不行。与此相违名不坏行。杂者自不作令他作。与此相违名不杂行。浊者与烦恼罪业合行。与此相违名为不浊行。自在者。破戒人为田业妻子财物所系不得自在。持戒者无如是事。随意自在

Chapter 30 — [Distinctions Pertaining to] the Great Vehicle

C. AN EXTENSIVE LINE-BY-LINE EXPLANATION OF THE VERSE'S DEEP MEANING

1. "SUPERIORITY OF THE BODHISATTVA'S CULTIVATION OF THE TEN COURSES"

As for "the way they practice the ten courses of good karmic action is superior to that of the two other classes of practitioners,"[159] this refers to the fact that the bodhisattvas have become superior to the *śrāvaka* disciple and *pratyekabuddha* aspirants in the quality of their cultivation of the ten courses of good karmic action. "Becoming superior," [in their cultivation of the ten courses of good karmic action] means that the bodhisattvas cultivate them with single-minded focus, that they always cultivate them, that they cultivate them to benefit themselves, that they cultivate them to benefit others, and that they cultivate them purely.

"Cultivating them with single-minded focus" means that they employ full mental intention in their cultivation.

"Always cultivate them" means that they never rest in their cultivation of them.

"Cultivating them to benefit themselves" means that they do this to establish the causes and conditions for birth among humans and devas and to establish the causes and conditions for the attainment of nirvāṇa.

"Cultivating them to benefit others" means that, as the bodhisattvas cultivate the ten courses of good karmic action, they dedicate the merit to the benefit and peace of all beings. It is for this reason that they can liberate an incalculable number of beings.

"Cultivating them purely" means theirs is undamaged practice, unmixed practice, unsullied practice, practice in which one has sovereign mastery, perfectly complete practice, practice free of covetousness and attachment, and practice that is praised by the wise.

"Damaged" practice refers here to that in which some aspects of the practice are cultivated whereas others are left aside and not practiced. Practice that is opposite to this is "undamaged" practice.

"Mixed" practice refers here to that wherein one encourages others to practice what one does not practice oneself. Practice that is opposite to this is "unmixed" practice.

"Sullied" practice is practice that occurs in conjunction with afflictions and karmic offenses. Practice that is opposite to this is "unsullied" practice.

As for "sovereign mastery," because they are tied down by agricultural work, wives, children, or material possessions, those who are prone to breaking the precepts are unable to achieve a state of sovereign mastery [in their practice]. Having no such [encumbering] circumstances, those who uphold the precepts may freely achieve a state

正體字

```
         無所繫屬。具足者。盡行一切大小
102a27 ‖ 戒。遮止諸煩惱。常[3]憶念守護。為禪定作
102a28 ‖ [4]因緣。迴向佛道能令同真際法性。是名
102a29 ‖ 具足。不貪著者。不向世間不取戒相自
102b01 ‖ 高卑他。智者所讚者。聲聞法中不隨生死。
102b02 ‖ 但為涅槃故名智者所讚。此大乘法中。尚
102b03 ‖ 不迴向聲聞辟支佛乘。何況生死。但向阿
102b04 ‖ 耨多羅三藐三菩提。是名智者所讚十善道。
102b05 ‖ 問曰。修有何相名為善修。答[5]曰。以無量
102b06 ‖ 希有修十善道。勝一切世間。是名善修。問
102b07 ‖ 曰。云何菩薩。以此修勝一切世間。答曰。諸
102b08 ‖ 菩薩以五事修故。勝一切世間。一願二堅
102b09 ‖ 心三深心四善清淨五方便。
```

简体字

无所系属。具足者。尽行一切大小戒。遮止诸烦恼。常忆念守护。为禅定作因缘。回向佛道能令同真际法性。是名具足。不贪著者。不向世间不取戒相自高卑他。智者所赞者。声闻法中不随生死。但为涅槃故名智者所赞。此大乘法中。尚不回向声闻辟支佛乘。何况生死。但向阿耨多罗三藐三菩提。是名智者所赞十善道。问曰。修有何相名为善修。答曰。以无量希有修十善道。胜一切世间。是名善修。问曰。云何菩萨。以此修胜一切世间。答曰。诸菩萨以五事修故。胜一切世间。一愿二坚心三深心四善清净五方便。

Chapter 30 — [Distinctions Pertaining to] the Great Vehicle

of sovereign mastery in which they are not tied down by anything at all.

"Perfectly complete" practice refers to exhaustively complete observance of all the major and minor moral precepts that blocks off the afflictions, that involves constant mindfulness of the need to preserve them and guard against transgression, that serves as a cause and condition for the *dhyāna* absorptions, that is dedicated to realization of buddhahood, and that enables one to unite with ultimate reality and the nature of dharmas. This is what is meant by "perfectly complete" in this context.

Practice "free of covetousness and attachment" does not direct its focus toward worldly priorities, does not seize on merely superficial aspects of the moral precepts, and remains free of any tendency to elevate oneself and disparage others.

As for practice "praised by the wise," in the Dharma of *śrāvaka* disciples, it is because it does not follow the cycle of births and deaths and is implemented solely for the sake of nirvāṇa that it is referred to as "praised by the wise."

In this Dharma of the Great Vehicle, its practitioners do not even dedicate their practice to success in the Śrāvaka Disciple Vehicle or the Pratyekabuddha Vehicle, how much the less could their practice be dedicated to *saṃsāra*? Rather, it is dedicated solely to the realization of *anuttarasamyaksaṃbodhi*. This is what is meant by practice of the ten courses of good karmic action that is "praised by the wise."

Question: What are the marks of cultivation that qualify it as "good" cultivation?

Response: It is that which incorporates countless extraordinary qualities into cultivation of the ten courses of good karmic action in a manner superior to the cultivation practiced by anyone else in the world. This is what is meant by "good" cultivation.

a. Five Ways in Which the Bodhisattva's Practice is Superior

Question: How do the bodhisattvas, employing this sort of cultivation, cultivate in a manner "superior to anyone else in the entire world"?

Response: It is on the basis of five aspects of their cultivation that the bodhisattvas' cultivation is "superior to that of anyone else in the world":[160]

First, their vows;
Second, their solid resolve;
Third, their resolute intentions;
Fourth, their thoroughgoing purity;[161]
And fifth, their use of skillful means.

正體字

　　　　願者菩薩所行
願。一切凡夫人及聲聞辟支佛人所無。以
是故。菩薩所行願勝一切世間。如大智經
毘摩羅達多女問中。佛因目揵連說。菩薩
從初發願乃至道場。能為一切世間天及
人作福田。又勝一切聲聞辟支佛。又如淨
毘尼中。摩訶迦葉於佛前說。世尊善說希
有。所謂菩薩初一發願勝一切聲聞辟支佛。
又如偈中說。

　　菩薩初發心　　與大慈悲合
　　為於無上道　　即是心為勝
　　是故以此願　　住於世間上

堅心者。菩薩於諸苦惱所謂活地獄。黑繩地
獄。合會地獄。小叫喚地獄。大叫喚地獄。小炙
地獄。大炙地獄。阿鼻地獄。[6]沸[7]屎。劍林。灰
河。阿浮陀。尼羅浮陀。阿波[8]簸。阿羅邏。休休。
欝鉢羅。拘勿陀。須曼[9]那。分陀利。鉢頭摩。
寒熱地獄中種種拷掠。如是苦惱。畜生餓鬼
阿修羅人天。共相食噉互相恐怖。飢餓穀貴。
從天退失。慳妬

简体字

愿者菩萨所行愿。一切凡夫人及声闻辟支佛人所无。以是故。菩萨所行愿胜一切世间。如大智经毗摩罗达多女问中。佛因目揵连说。菩萨从初发愿乃至道场。能为一切世间天及人作福田。又胜一切声闻辟支佛。又如净毗尼中。摩诃迦葉于佛前说。世尊善说希有。所谓菩萨初一发愿胜一切声闻辟支佛。又如偈中说。

　　菩萨初发心　　与大慈悲合
　　为于无上道　　即是心为胜
　　是故以此愿　　住于世间上

坚心者。菩萨于诸苦恼所谓活地狱。黑绳地狱。合会地狱。小叫唤地狱。大叫唤地狱。小炙地狱。大炙地狱。阿鼻地狱。沸屎。剑林。灰河。阿浮陀。尼罗浮陀。阿波簸。阿罗逻。休休。郁钵罗。拘勿陀。须曼那。分陀利。钵头摩。寒热地狱中种种拷掠。如是苦恼。畜生饿鬼阿修罗人天。共相食啖互相恐怖。饥饿谷贵。从天退失。悭妒

Chapter 30 — [Distinctions Pertaining to] the Great Vehicle

1) Superiority of Vows

As for "their vows," the vows implemented by the bodhisattvas do not even exist among all common people, *śrāvaka* disciple practitioners, or *pratyekabuddha* practitioners. It is for this reason that the vows implemented by the bodhisattvas are superior to those of anyone else in the world. This is as described in the questions of the woman Vimaladattā in the *Mahāprajñāpāramitā Sūtra* in which the Buddha, because of Maudgalyāyana, said, "From the point of his initial generation of the vow all the way on forward to his arrival at the *bodhimaṇḍa*, the bodhisattva is able to serve the entire world's devas and humans as a field of merit, doing so in a manner that is superior to all *śrāvaka* disciples or *pratyekabuddhas*."

This is also as set forth in the *Pure Vinaya Sutra* in which Mahākāśyapa said in the Buddha's presence, "The Bhagavat has here so well described this rarity, that is to say, the bodhisattva's initial generation of the vow which is superior to that of all *śrāvaka* disciples and *pratyekabuddhas*."

This also accords with a verse in which it is proclaimed that:

As for the bodhisattva's initial generation of his resolve
conjoined to the great kindness and great compassion
for the sake of the unsurpassable path,
it is just this very resolve that is supreme.
It is therefore the case that, because of this vow,
he abides in a position superior to those in the world.

2) Superiority of Solid Resolve

As for his "solid resolve," the bodhisattva maintains it even in the midst of every sort of pain and torment, that is to say he maintains it even in the Living Hells, Black-line Hells, Unification Hells, Lesser Screaming Hells, Great Screaming Hells, Lesser Roasting Hells, Great Roasting Hells, Avīci Hells, Boiling Excrement Hells, Sword Forest Hells, River of Coals Hells, Abhuta Hells, Nirarbuda Hells, Aṭaṭa Hells, Apalāla Hells, Huhuva Hells, Utpala Hells, Kumuda Hells, Sumanā Hells, Puṇḍarīka Hells, and the Padma Hells. He maintains it even when tortured and whipped in these various cold and hot hells.

He maintains it even in the midst of the anguish and torment in the animal realms, the hungry ghost realms, the asura realms, and the realms of humans and devas in which beings devour each other, exist in a state of mutual fearfulness, and go hungry when food has become too expensive.

And he maintains it when he falls back from and loses celestial realm rebirth and when he then encounters jealousy, the torment of

正體字

瞋惱。恩愛別離。怨憎合會。
102b29 ‖ 生老病死憂悲惱等。此六道中。所有諸苦若
102c01 ‖ 見若聞若受。修十善道。為阿耨多羅三藐三
102c02 ‖ 菩提時心終不壞。以是故此菩薩以堅心
102c03 ‖ 修十善道。勝一切世間。如說。
102c04 ‖ 　地獄及畜生　　餓鬼阿修羅
102c05 ‖ 　天人六趣苦　　不能動其心
102c06 ‖ 　是故諸菩薩　　以此堅固心
102c07 ‖ 　所修十善道　　勝一切世間
102c08 ‖ 深心者。大心用心愛心念心。諸菩薩以如是
102c09 ‖ 等心修十善道。勝一切世間。除諸佛世尊
102c10 ‖ 及久行菩薩。如說。
102c11 ‖ 　深心及用心　　利益世間心
102c12 ‖ 　菩薩以是心　　勝一切世間
102c13 ‖ 善清淨者。菩薩修十善業道三種清淨。餘人
102c14 ‖ 所無。以是故。勝一切世間。如說。
102c15 ‖ 　菩薩人中寶　　具深心淨心
102c16 ‖ 　以是善法力　　世間所不及

简体字

瞋恼。恩爱别离。怨憎合会。生老病死忧悲恼等。此六道中。所有诸苦若见若闻若受。修十善道。为阿耨多罗三藐三菩提时心终不坏。以是故此菩萨以坚心修十善道。胜一切世间。如说。

　地狱及畜生　　饿鬼阿修罗
　天人六趣苦　　不能动其心
　是故诸菩萨　　以此坚固心
　所修十善道　　胜一切世间

深心者。大心用心爱心念心。诸菩萨以如是等心修十善道。胜一切世间。除诸佛世尊及久行菩萨。如说。

　深心及用心　　利益世间心
　菩萨以是心　　胜一切世间

善清净者。菩萨修十善业道三种清净。余人所无。以是故。胜一切世间。如说。

　菩萨人中宝　　具深心净心
　以是善法力　　世间所不及

Chapter 30 — [Distinctions Pertaining to] the Great Vehicle

hatred, separation from those one loves, association with those one detests, birth, aging, sickness, death, sorrow, lamentation, misery, and the like.

Thus he maintains his resolve even in the midst of all these sufferings in the six destinies of rebirth. Whether observing them, whether hearing them occur, or whether actually undergoing them himself, the bodhisattva still continues to cultivate the ten courses of good karmic action for the sake of realizing *anuttarasamyaksaṃbodhi*. During that entire time, his resolve continues on and never deteriorates.

It is on these bases that this bodhisattva, by cultivating the ten courses of good karmic action with solid resolve, thereby surpasses everyone else in the entire world. This is as described here:

> Even when in the hells, among the animals,
> the hungry ghosts, the asuras,
> the devas, or the humans, the sufferings of these six destinies,
> are still incapable of shaking their resolve.
>
> Therefore the bodhisattvas,
> through such solid resolve as this,
> are superior to the entire world
> in their cultivation of the ten courses of good karmic action.

3) Superiority of Resolute Intentions

Regarding their "resolute intentions," they also possess great intentions, useful intentions, affectionate intentions, and mindful intentions. The bodhisattvas rely on such types of intentions as these in their cultivation of the ten courses of good karmic action and, in this, they are superior to everyone in the entire world with the exception of the Buddhas, the Bhagavats, and those bodhisattvas of long-enduring practice. This is as described here:

> They possess resolute intentions, useful intentions,
> and intentions that strive to benefit the world,
> it is through their use of these types of intentions
> that the bodhisattvas surpass the entire world.

4) Superiority of Thoroughgoing Purity

As for "their thoroughgoing purity,"[162] in cultivating the courses of good karmic action, the bodhisattvas maintain the three types of karmic purity to a degree not found in such cultivation as carried on by anyone else.[163] Consequently, they are superior in this to everyone else in the entire world. This is as described here:

> The bodhisattvas are treasures of the human realm
> completely possessed of resolute intentions and pure intentions.
> It is because of the power of these good dharmas
> that they are unequaled by anyone in the world.

正體字

102c17 ‖ 方便者。菩薩以方便力修於善法。餘人所
102c18 ‖ 無。是故勝一切世間。無量修者。菩薩以五
102c19 ‖ 因緣故名無量修。一時無量。二善根無量。
102c20 ‖ 三緣無量。四究竟無量。五迴向無量。時無量
102c21 ‖ 者。[10]謂菩薩修行善業道過於時量。時量過
102c22 ‖ 故。所修善業道亦無量。是故勝一切世間。如
102c23 ‖ 說。
102c24 ‖ 　諸菩薩師子　　所修善業道
102c25 ‖ 　過諸算數時　　故修善最勝
102c26 ‖ 善根無量者。諸菩薩[11]修無量無邊善根。從
102c27 ‖ 是善根所修善業道亦無量。是故勝一切世
102c28 ‖ 間。如大乘法中淨毘尼經。佛告迦葉。譬如
102c29 ‖ 生[12]酥滿四大海。菩薩有為善根資糧亦如
103a01 ‖ 是。是福德迴向無為智則大利益一切眾
103a02 ‖ 生。是故菩薩雖處有為能勝一切世間。如
103a03 ‖ 說。

简体字

　　方便者。菩萨以方便力修于善法。余人所无。是故胜一切世间。无量修者。菩萨以五因缘故名无量修。一时无量。二善根无量。三缘无量。四究竟无量。五回向无量。时无量者。谓菩萨修行善业道过于时量。时量过故。所修善业道亦无量。是故胜一切世间。如说。
　　　诸菩萨师子　　所修善业道
　　　过诸算数时　　故修善最胜
　　善根无量者。诸菩萨修无量无边善根。从是善根所修善业道亦无量。是故胜一切世间。如大乘法中净毗尼经。佛告迦叶。譬如生酥满四大海。菩萨有为善根资粮亦如是。是福德回向无为智则大利益一切众生。是故菩萨虽处有为能胜一切世间。如说。

Chapter 30 — [Distinctions Pertaining to] the Great Vehicle

5) Superiority in the Use of Skillful Means

As for "their use of skillful means," the bodhisattvas use the power of skillful means to cultivate good dharmas that others do not possess. Consequently, they are superior in this to everyone else in the entire world.

2. The Bodhisattva's "Measureless Cultivation"

Regarding their "measureless" cultivation,[164] it is on the basis of five types of causes and conditions that the cultivation of the bodhisattva qualifies as "measureless," namely:

First, immeasurability of time;
Second, immeasurability of roots of goodness;
Third, immeasurability of objective conditions;
Fourth, immeasurability of ultimate ends;
And fifth, immeasurability of dedication of merit.

a. Immeasurability of Time

As for "immeasurability of time," the cultivation of the courses of good karmic action as practiced by the bodhisattvas exceeds the very bounds of time. Because it exceeds the bounds of time, their cultivation of the courses of good karmic action is itself measureless. Therefore, in this, they are superior to everyone else in the entire world. This is as described here:

As for the cultivation of the courses of good karmic action
as practiced by the bodhisattvas, those lions among men,
because its duration surpasses the bounds of calculable time,
their cultivation of goodness is the most superior of all.

b. Immeasurability of Roots of Goodness

As for "immeasurability of roots of goodness," bodhisattvas cultivate measureless and boundless roots of goodness. Because the courses of good karmic action they cultivate in reliance upon these roots of goodness are also immeasurable, the bodhisattvas are in this respect superior to everyone else in the world.

As stated in the Great Vehicle Dharma's *Pure Vinaya Sutra*: "The Buddha told Kāśyapa, 'It is as if the four great seas were filled to the brim with buttermilk. Just so extensive are the bodhisattva's conditioned roots of goodness and provisions for the path.'" Because this merit is dedicated to the knowledge that cognizes the unconditioned, it is able to provide immense benefit to all beings. Therefore, even though the bodhisattva abides in the midst of conditioned existence, he is able to surpass everyone else in the world in this respect. This is as described here:

正體字	103a04 ‖	為一切眾生　　及求佛道故
	103a05 ‖	善根則無量　　以是勝世間
	103a06 ‖	緣無量者。菩薩不緣有量眾生故修[*]集善
	103a07 ‖	根。而所修善根不言為利益若干[1]眾生。
	103a08 ‖	菩薩但緣一切眾生故修[*]集善根。是故菩
	103a09 ‖	薩緣無量眾生所修善業道亦無量。勝一切
	103a10 ‖	世間。如淨毘尼經中。佛告諸天子。如大菩
	103a11 ‖	薩薄有慈悲心求利益他。是心能令無量
	103a12 ‖	眾生得利樂。深發心菩薩。勤行精進亦如
	103a13 ‖	是。能教化無量阿僧祇眾生令得涅槃樂。
	103a14 ‖	如說。
	103a15 ‖	菩薩無量善　　功德自莊嚴
	103a16 ‖	皆為度眾生　　無量之大苦
	103a17 ‖	究竟無量者。初地中為發願故。已說十究
	103a18 ‖	竟。是究竟無量故。菩薩所修善業道亦無量。
	103a19 ‖	是故勝一切世間。如說。
	103a20 ‖	[2]菩薩修善道　　從十究竟生
	103a21 ‖	是故勝一切　　無有能壞者

简体字

　　为一切众生　　及求佛道故
　　善根则无量　　以是胜世间

　缘无量者。菩萨不缘有量众生故修集善根。而所修善根不言为利益若干众生。菩萨但缘一切众生故修集善根。是故菩萨缘无量众生所修善业道亦无量。胜一切世间。如净毗尼经中。佛告诸天子。如大菩萨薄有慈悲心求利益他。是心能令无量众生得利乐。深发心菩萨。勤行精进亦如是。能教化无量阿僧祇众生令得涅槃乐。如说。

　　菩萨无量善　　功德自庄严
　　皆为度众生　　无量之大苦

　究竟无量者。初地中为发愿故。已说十究竟。是究竟无量故。菩萨所修善业道亦无量。是故胜一切世间。如说。
　　　　　　解大乘品第三十一
　　菩萨修善道　　从十究竟生
　　是故胜一切　　无有能坏者

Chapter 30 — [Distinctions Pertaining to] the Great Vehicle

[Accumulated] for the sake of all beings
as well as for the sake of buddhahood,
their roots of goodness are immeasurable.
Because of this, they are superior to all others in the world.

c. Immeasurability of Objective Conditions

As for the "immeasurability of objective conditions," in his accumulation of roots of goodness, the bodhisattva does not take as his objective condition a merely measurable number of beings. He does not say that the roots of goodness he has cultivated are for benefiting some particular number of beings. Rather, the bodhisattva simply takes all beings as the objective condition for his accumulation of roots of goodness. Therefore, since the bodhisattva takes a measureless number of beings as the objective condition on which he focuses, the courses of good karmic action that he cultivates are also measureless. Consequently, he is superior in this respect to everyone else in the world. As stated in the *Pure Vinaya Sutra*:

> The Buddha told the *devaputras*, "This is just as in the case of the great bodhisattva possessed of the mind of kindness and compassion who strives to benefit others. This resolve of his is able to cause countless beings to receive benefit and happiness. So too it is with the bodhisattva who is deeply earnest in bringing forth his resolve. Being like this in his diligent application of vigor, he can thereby teach measurelessly many *asaṃkhyeyas* of beings, enabling them to gain the bliss of nirvāṇa."

This is as described here:

> The bodhisattva adorns himself
> with measurelessly many fine meritorious qualities,
> all for the purpose of liberating beings
> from their measureless great suffering.

d. Immeasurability of Ultimate Ends

As for "immeasurability of ultimate ends," "the ten ultimate ends" were already discussed during the explanation of the first ground when discussing the making of [the ten bodhisattva] vows.[165] It is because of this immeasurability of ultimate ends that the courses of good karmic action as cultivated by the bodhisattva are measureless. He is therefore superior in this respect to anyone in the world. This is as described here:

> The bodhisattva's cultivation of the courses of good karmic action
> comes forth from the ten ultimate ends.
> Therefore it is superior to that of everyone else
> and such that no one is able to ruin it.

正體字

103a22 ‖ 迴向無量者。如初地中說。菩薩迴向果報無
103a23 ‖ 量。以是迴向果報無量。所修善業亦無量。
103a24 ‖ 是故勝一切世間。如說。
103a25 ‖ 　以無量因緣　　修於善業道
103a26 ‖ 　迴向佛乘故　　是以為最上
103a27 ‖ 希有者。諸菩薩修善道。以五因緣故名希
103a28 ‖ 有。一堪受故。二精進故。三心堅故。四慧故。
103a29 ‖ 五果故。堪受者。我當作天人中尊一切智慧
103b01 ‖ 者。能如是堪受。是為希有。若人以指舉三
103b02 ‖ 千大千世界。於虛空中令住百千萬劫。是
103b03 ‖ 事可成。不足為難。若發願言我當作佛。
103b04 ‖ 是為希有甚難。如說。
103b05 ‖ 　為無量佛法　　立誓當作佛
103b06 ‖ 　是人無有比　　何況有勝者
103b07 ‖ 精進者。多有人堪受發阿耨多羅三藐三菩
103b08 ‖ 提心。不能精進行六波羅蜜。若人以堪受
103b09 ‖ 發阿耨多羅三藐三菩提心。

简体字

　　回向无量者。如初地中说。菩萨回向果报无量。以是回向果报无量。所修善业亦无量。是故胜一切世间。如说。
　　以无量因缘　　修于善业道
　　回向佛乘故　　是以为最上
　　希有者。诸菩萨修善道。以五因缘故名希有。一堪受故。二精进故。三心坚故。四慧故。五果故。堪受者。我当作天人中尊一切智慧者。能如是堪受。是为希有。若人以指举三千大千世界。于虚空中令住百千万劫。是事可成。不足为难。若发愿言我当作佛。是为希有甚难。如说。
　　为无量佛法　　立誓当作佛
　　是人无有比　　何况有胜者
　　精进者。多有人堪受发阿耨多罗三藐三菩提心。不能精进行六波罗蜜。若人以堪受发阿耨多罗三藐三菩提心。

Chapter 30 — [Distinctions Pertaining to] the Great Vehicle

e. Immeasurability of Dedication of Merit

"Immeasurability of dedication of merit" is as described earlier in the explanation of the first ground. The karmic fruits of the bodhisattva's dedication of merit are measureless. Because the karmic fruits of dedication of merit are measureless, the courses of good karmic action he cultivates are also measureless. He is therefore superior in this respect to anyone in the world. This is as described here:

> On the basis of measureless causes and conditions,
> they cultivate the courses of good karmic action.
> Because they dedicate this to [the realization of] the Buddha Vehicle,
> they are therefore the most superior of all.

3. The Bodhisattva's "Extraordinary Cultivation"

As for the "extraordinary" nature of their cultivation,[166] it is because of five causes and conditions that the bodhisattvas' cultivation of the courses of good karmic action is said to be "extraordinary":

> First, because of their capacity to endure;
> Second, because of their vigor;
> Third, because of the solidity of their resolve;
> Fourth, because of their wisdom;
> Fifth, because of the karmic fruits.

a. His Extraordinary Capacity to Endure

As for [the extraordinary nature of] their capacity to endure, [they reflect], "I ought to become one who is the most revered among all devas and humans, one who is possessed of all-knowledge." If one is able to have a capacity such as this, this is extraordinary. Were someone to use his finger to lift a great trichiliocosm's worlds and hold them aloft in space for a hundred thousand myriads of kalpas, even this might be considered possible to do and not worthy of being deemed truly difficult. Yet if one makes the vow: "I shall become a buddha," it is this that is extraordinary and extremely difficult. This is as described here:

> As for he who, for the sake of a buddha's measureless dharmas,
> would make the vow: "I shall become a buddha,"
> this person is one who is beyond compare,
> how much the less could there be anyone who might surpass him?

b. His Extraordinary Vigor

Regarding [the extraordinary nature of] their vigor, there are many people who can bring forth the resolve to attain *anuttarasamyaksaṃbodhi* but who are then unable to vigorously practice the six *pāramitās*. If someone can bring forth the resolve to attain *anuttarasamyaksaṃbodhi*

正體字

能精進行六波
103b10 ‖ 羅蜜。是名實堪受無量功德。精進希有故。
103b11 ‖ 所修善業道亦希有。如說。
103b12 ‖ 　希有大精進　　凡人念已怖
103b13 ‖ 　菩薩實行之　　何得不希有
103b14 ‖ 心堅者。有人發精進心修[*]集佛道。若有
103b15 ‖ 障礙心不堅固則不能成。是[3]故發精進
103b16 ‖ 安住希有。堅心中則成其事。壞諸障礙。是
103b17 ‖ 為菩薩修善業道第一希有。如說。
103b18 ‖ 　若人無堅心　　尚不成小事
103b19 ‖ 　何況成佛道　　世間無上者
103b20 ‖ 慧者。是堪受精進堅心皆以慧為根本。是故
103b21 ‖ 菩薩慧為第一希有。能生如是堪受精進堅
103b22 ‖ 心故。以慧為希有[4]以慧為希有故。所修
103b23 ‖ 善業亦希有。如說。
103b24 ‖ 　如有人堪受　　欲得於佛法
103b25 ‖ 　精進得堅心　　皆以慧為本
103b26 ‖ 果者。修善業故得無量無邊諸佛之法。是
103b27 ‖ 故

简体字

能精进行六波罗蜜。是名实堪受无量功德。精进希有故。所修善业道亦希有。如说。

　希有大精进　　凡人念已怖
　菩萨实行之　　何得不希有

心坚者。有人发精进心修集佛道。若有障碍心不坚固则不能成。是故发精进安住希有。坚心中则成其事。坏诸障碍。是为菩萨修善业道第一希有。如说。

　若人无坚心　　尚不成小事
　何况成佛道　　世间无上者

慧者。是堪受精进坚心皆以慧为根本。是故菩萨慧为第一希有。能生如是堪受精进坚心故。以慧希有以慧为希有故。所修善业亦希有。如说。

　如有人堪受　　欲得于佛法
　精进得坚心　　皆以慧为本

果者。修善业故得无量无边诸佛之法。是故

Chapter 30 — [Distinctions Pertaining to] the Great Vehicle

and then also be able to vigorously practice the six *pāramitās*, this is what is meant by truly having the capacity to take on the attainment of the measureless meritorious qualities. It is because of the extraordinary nature of their vigor that the courses of good karmic action they cultivate are also extraordinary in nature. This is as described here:

> Their practice of great vigor is so extraordinary that,
> having merely contemplated it, the common man is frightened.
> The bodhisattva actually practices it.
> How could this not be regarded as extraordinary?

c. His Solidity of Resolve

As for [the extraordinary nature of] their solidity of resolve, there are those who bring forth vigorous resolve to cultivate the path to buddhahood. However, if upon encountering obstacles, their resolve is not solid, they will be unable to succeed. Therefore, if they bring forth vigor and become securely established in extraordinarily solid resolve, they will succeed in their endeavors and demolish all obstacles. It is this that is the most extraordinary accomplishment in bodhisattvas' cultivation of the courses of good karmic action. This is as described here:

> If one has no solidity of resolve,
> he will be unable to succeed in even minor endeavors.
> How much the less could one attain buddhahood
> and become the one unsurpassed by anyone in the world?

d. His Extraordinary Wisdom

As for [the extraordinary nature of] their wisdom, this capacity to endure, this vigor, and this solidity of resolve all take wisdom as their foundation. Therefore it is the wisdom of the bodhisattva that is the most extraordinary. Because it is able to produce this capacity to endure, this vigor, and this solidity of resolve, wisdom is itself deemed to be extraordinary. It is because this wisdom is extraordinary that the courses of good karmic action that are cultivated are also extraordinary. This is as described here:

> If someone has the capacity to endure
> in pursuing his aspiration to realize the Buddha's Dharma,
> and if he possesses vigor and has achieved solidity of resolve,
> all of these capacities take wisdom as their foundation.

e. His Extraordinary Karmic Fruits

As for [the extraordinary nature of] the karmic fruits they achieve, due to their cultivation of the courses of good karmic actions, they gain all the measureless and boundless dharmas of the Buddhas. Therefore

正體字
希有。如說。 103b28 ‖ 　行此善得道　　無量功德力 103b29 ‖ 　為諸眾生師　　誰聞而不行 103c01 ‖ 堅願者。菩薩以五因緣故名為堅願。一於 103c02 ‖ 聲聞乘心不轉。二於辟支佛乘不轉。三於 103c03 ‖ 外道事不轉。四於一切魔事不轉。五無因 103c04 ‖ 緣不轉。如說。 103c05 ‖ 　聞二乘解脫　　何不為此道 103c06 ‖ 　若未入於位　　則失菩薩道 103c07 ‖ 　又貪外道事　　或為魔所壞 103c08 ‖ 　或復無因緣　　自捨菩薩道 103c09 ‖ 善願者。菩薩以五因緣故名善願。一先籌 103c10 ‖ 量得失者。二知道者。三知道果者。四不 103c11 ‖ 貪惜自樂者。五欲滅眾生大苦者。

简体字
希有。如说。 　行此善得道　　无量功德力 　为诸众生师　　谁闻而不行 　坚愿者。菩萨以五因缘故名为坚愿。一于声闻乘心不转。二于辟支佛乘不转。三于外道事不转。四于一切魔事不转。五无因缘不转。如说。 　闻二乘解脱　　何不为此道 　若未入于位　　则失菩萨道 　又贪外道事　　或为魔所坏 　或复无因缘　　自舍菩萨道 　善愿者。菩萨以五因缘故名善愿。一先筹量得失者。二知道者。三知道果者。四不贪惜自乐者。五欲灭众生大苦者。

Chapter 30 — [Distinctions Pertaining to] the Great Vehicle

[the karmic fruits] are extraordinary in nature. This is as described here:

> By practicing this goodness, one realizes buddhahood,
> acquires the power of its measureless meritorious qualities,
> and then serves as the teacher of all beings.
> Who, on hearing this, could fail to practice them?

4. The Bodhisattva's Vows

a. The "Solidity" of His Vows

Regarding their "solid" vows,[167] it is for five reasons that the bodhisattva is deemed to have made solid vows, namely:

First, his resolve does not turn back toward the Śrāvaka Disciple Vehicle;

Second, his resolve does not turn back toward the Pratyekabuddha Vehicle;

Third, his resolve does not turn back in favor of the endeavors of the followers of non-Buddhist paths;

Fourth, his resolve does not turn back due to any of the works of Māra;

And fifth, his resolve does not turn back due to an absence of [conducive] causes and conditions.

This is as described here:

> One might hear of the liberations won through the Two Vehicles
> and think, "Why not take up these paths instead?"
> If one has not yet entered the station [of irreversibility],[168]
> then one might fall away from the bodhisattva path.

> Or one might covet the endeavors of followers of non-Buddhist paths,
> or one might be destroyed by the works of Māra,
> or else, due to an absence of conducive causes and conditions,
> one might voluntarily abandon the bodhisattva path.

b. The "Goodness" of His Vows

As for the "goodness" of their vows,[169] it is for five reasons that the bodhisattva's vows are said to be "good" vows, namely:

First, they reflect a prior assessment of gains or losses;

Second, they are based on a knowledge of the path;

Third, they reflect a knowledge of the fruits of the path;

Fourth, they reflect an absence of any selfish attachment to one's own pleasure;

Fifth, they reflect the wish to extinguish the immense sufferings endured by all beings.

如是
作願名為善願。如說。
先見世過患　　佛道大利益
知行無上道　　及其無量果
捨自寂滅樂　　欲除眾生苦
發是無比願　　為諸佛所讚
大悲無礙者。以五因緣故。知菩薩有大悲。
一利安無量眾生故。於資生之物不生貪
惜。二不惜身。三不惜命。四不觀時久遠。
五欲怨親中等心利益。如說。
內外所愛物　　於中不貪著
為利眾生故　　及捨於身命
生死無量[5]劫　　猶如一眴頃
怨親中平等　　名菩薩大悲
無礙者。菩薩以五因緣故。悲心有礙。一以
地獄苦故。二以畜生苦故。三以餓鬼苦故。

如是作愿名为善愿。如说。
先见世过患　　佛道大利益
知行无上道　　及其无量果
舍自寂灭乐　　欲除众生苦
发是无比愿　　为诸佛所赞

大悲无碍者。以五因缘故。知菩萨有大悲。一利安无量众生故。于资生之物不生贪惜。二不惜身。三不惜命。四不观时久远。五欲怨亲中等心利益。如说。
内外所爱物　　于中不贪着
为利众生故　　及舍于身命
生死无量劫　　犹如一眴顷
怨亲中平等　　名菩萨大悲

无碍者。菩萨以五因缘故。悲心有碍。一以地狱苦故。二以畜生苦故。三以饿鬼苦故。

Chapter 30 — [Distinctions Pertaining to] the Great Vehicle

Vows made in this manner are deemed to be good vows. This is as described here:

> One first observes the faults and misery of the world
> and the immense benefit bestowed by the path to buddhahood.
> One knows and practices the unsurpassable path
> as well as its measureless fruits.
>
> One relinquishes the bliss of entering one's own quiescent cessation,
> and wishes to rid beings of their sufferings.
> One who brings forth such peerless vows as these
> is someone who is praised by all buddhas.

5. The Bodhisattva's "Great Compassion"

Regarding "the great compassion" that cannot be impeded,[170] there are five grounds for knowing a bodhisattva is possessed of the great compassion, namely:

> First, because he is devoted to benefiting and conferring happiness on countless beings, he does not covet or selfishly cherish any of the life-sustaining requisites;
> Second, he does not selfishly cherish his own physical well-being;
> Third, he does not selfishly cherish his own life-span;
> Fourth, he is not concerned with the extensively long period of time involved;
> Fifth, he maintains a mind of equal regard and motivation to benefit both adversaries and friends.

This is as described here:

> He has no covetous attachment for any of those things
> that people cherish, whether personal or external.
> In order to be of benefit to beings,
> he would even sacrifice his body and life.
>
> The countless kalpas spent amidst *saṃsāra*
> are for him like the mere blinking of an eye.
> He acts with uniformly equal regard for both enemy and friend.
> These are the factors defining a bodhisattva's great compassion.

6. The "Unimpeded" Nature of the Bodhisattva's Compassion

As for [their compassion's] being "unimpeded,"[171] there are five reasons why a bodhisattva's compassion might [otherwise] become impeded, namely:

> First, by the sufferings of the hell realms;
> Second, by the sufferings of the animal realms;
> Third, by the sufferings of the hungry ghost realms;

正體字

103c27 ‖	四以惡人無返復故。五以生死過惡故。若
103c28 ‖	此五事不障其心是名無礙大悲。如說。
103c29 ‖	第一地獄苦　　畜生餓鬼苦
104a01 ‖	惡人及生死　　不障名大悲
104a02 ‖	菩薩能如是　　佛說無礙悲
104a03 ‖	善受行方便者。菩薩以五因緣故。名善受
104a04 ‖	行方便。一知方時。二知他心所樂。三知轉
104a05 ‖	入道。四知事次第。五知引導眾生。
104a06 ‖	知方時者知是方處。應以如是說法。知
104a07 ‖	是[1]時中。應以如是說[2]法知是方處。應
104a08 ‖	以如是因緣度眾生。知是時中應以如
104a09 ‖	是因緣度眾生菩薩先知是事已隨順而
104a10 ‖	行。如說。
104a11 ‖	若以世尊意　　為他人解說
104a12 ‖	先應知二事　　後隨時方說
104a13 ‖	若不知時方　　而欲說佛[3]意
104a14 ‖	不得所為利　　而更有過咎

简体字

四以恶人无返复故。五以生死过恶故。若此五事不障其心是名无碍大悲。如说。

　　第一地狱苦　　畜生饿鬼苦
　　恶人及生死　　不障名大悲
　　菩萨能如是　　佛说无碍悲

善受行方便者。菩萨以五因缘故。名善受行方便。一知方时。二知他心所乐。三知转入道。四知事次第。五知引导众生。

知方时者知是方处。应以如是说法。知是时中。应以如是说法知是方处。应以如是因缘度众生。知是时中应以如是因缘度众生菩萨先知是事已随顺而行。如说。

　　若以世尊意　　为他人解说
　　先应知二事　　后随时方说
　　若不知时方　　而欲说佛意
　　不得所为利　　而更有过咎

Fourth, by evil people's ingratitude [for kindnesses bestowed on them];

Fifth, by the faults and evils encountered amidst *saṃsāra*.

If even these five circumstances fail to impede his resolve, then he qualifies as possessing the unimpeded great compassion. This is as described here:

> If even the foremost sufferings encountered in the hell realms,
> the sufferings met in the animal realms or hungry ghost realms,
> [the ingratitude of] evil people, and *saṃsāra*
> still fail to impede him, he is one possessed of the great compassion.
> The bodhisattva who is able to be one who is like this
> has been declared by the Buddha to possess unimpeded compassion.

7. The Bodhisattva's "Thorough Practice of Skillful Means"

Regarding "thoroughly taking on the practice of skillful means,"[172] there are five bases for a bodhisattva's qualification as "thoroughly taking on the practice of skillful means," namely:

First, he knows the correct place and time;
Second, he knows what delights the minds of others;
Third, he knows what will cause others to turn and enter the path;
Fourth, he knows what constitutes the correct sequence of events;
Fifth, he knows how to lead and guide beings.

a. His Knowledge of "the Correct Place and Time"

As for "knowing the correct place and time," he knows that, in this particular place, one should explain Dharma in this particular way and knows that, at this particular time, one should explain the Dharma in this other way. He knows that, in this particular place, one should employ these specific causes and conditions to bring about the liberation of these particular beings. And he knows that, at this particular time, one should employ just these particular causes and conditions to bring about the liberation of these other beings. Having assessed these specific factors in advance, the bodhisattva then proceeds to act accordingly. This is as described here:

> If one takes up the intent of the Bhagavat
> wishing then to explain it for others,
> one should first know these two factors,
> and then speak in accordance with the correct time and place.

> Should one fail to know the correct time and place
> and yet wish to proclaim the intent of the Buddhas,
> he will [not only] fail to accomplish the intended benefit,
> but moreover may thus commit a blameworthy error.

正體字

104a15 ‖ 知他心所樂者。知他深心為在何事為何
104a16 ‖ 所樂。菩薩先知已。入眾生所知所樂。隨順起
104a17 ‖ 發度脫方便。如是則不虛也。如說。
104a18 ‖ 　菩薩知眾生　　深心難測意
104a19 ‖ 　先知其意已　　漸令住佛[*]意
104a20 ‖ 　遍知世間事　　自利亦利他
104a21 ‖ 　若能如是者　　說名善方便
104a22 ‖ 知轉入道者。能轉外道凡夫意令入佛道。
104a23 ‖ 亦轉眾生惡事令住善事中。亦知轉聲聞
104a24 ‖ 辟支佛道令入大乘中。已在佛法者不令
104a25 ‖ 入外道。先知是事已隨順而修行。如說。
104a26 ‖ 　若人令眾生　　遠離外道法
104a27 ‖ 　及諸不善者　　入佛上寂滅
104a28 ‖ 　[4]若知諸眾生　　上中下之心
104a29 ‖ 　知已能引導　　是名善方便
104b01 ‖ 知事次第者。如聲聞乘中。

简体字

　　知他心所乐者。知他深心为在何事为何所乐。菩萨先知已。入众生所知所乐。随顺起发度脱方便。如是则不虚也。如说。
　　　菩萨知众生　　深心难测意
　　　先知其意已　　渐令住佛意
　　　遍知世间事　　自利亦利他
　　　若能如是者　　说名善方便
　　知转入道者。能转外道凡夫意令入佛道。亦转众生恶事令住善事中。亦知转声闻辟支佛道令入大乘中。已在佛法者不令入外道。先知是事已随顺而修行。如说。
　　　若人令众生　　远离外道法
　　　及诸不善者　　入佛上寂灭
　　　若知诸众生　　上中下之心
　　　知已能引导　　是名善方便
　　知事次第者。如声闻乘中。

Chapter 30 — [Distinctions Pertaining to] the Great Vehicle

b. His Knowledge of "What Delights the Minds of Others"

As for "knowing what delights the minds of others," this involves knowing, due to their mental dispositions, which endeavors and which experiences will cause them to be pleased. Having known this in advance, the bodhisattva acquires a penetrating understanding of what beings know and delight in and then brings forth the appropriate skillful means to facilitate their liberation. If one acts in this way, then his efforts will not be in vain. This is as described here:

> The bodhisattva knows with respect to beings
> the difficult-to-assess intentions present in their mental dispositions,
> and, having already first known the character of their intentions,
> he gradually influences them to dwell in the Buddha's intent.
>
> Through thoroughly knowing the affairs of the world,
> he benefits himself while also benefiting others.
> One who is able to proceed in this manner
> is said to be adept in the practice of skillful means.

c. His Knowledge of "What Causes Others to Turn & Enter the Path"

As for their "knowing what will cause others to turn and enter the path," this refers to knowing whatever may induce the minds of common persons following non-Buddhist paths to turn away from them and instead enter the path of the Buddha. It also refers to knowing whatever will induce beings to turn away from evil deeds and instead engage in good deeds. And it also refers to knowing whatever will induce followers of the *śrāvaka* disciple and *pratyekabuddha* paths to turn away from them and instead enter into the Great Vehicle.

This refers as well to knowing with respect to those already abiding within the Buddha's Dharma, just what will prevent them from entering into non-Buddhist paths. Having first come to know these matters, one then implements the practice accordingly. This is as described here:

> If one is able to induce beings
> to abandon non-Buddhist paths
> while also inducing those devoted to what is bad
> to enter the Buddha's way to the supreme quiescent cessation,
>
> and if one knows with respect to beings
> the superior, middling, or inferior character of their minds,
> and, having known this, one is then able to lead and guide them,
> this is what is meant by being adept in the practice of skillful means.

d. His Knowledge of "What Constitutes the Correct Sequence"

As for "knowing what constitutes the correct sequence," take for instance the priorities in the Śrāvaka Disciple Vehicle wherein they

正體字	初說布施。次持戒。次生天。次五欲過患。次在家苦惱。次出家利樂。次說苦諦。次集諦。次滅諦。次道諦。次須陀洹果。次斯陀含果。次阿那含果。次阿羅漢果。次不壞解脫。次說諸無礙。辟支佛乘中亦說。我我所物多有過患。捨此過患之物得大利益。在家為過惡。出家為利益。次眾鬧亂語為過惡。獨行為善利。聚落為過惡。阿練若處為善利。厭離多欲多事。樂[5]於少欲少事。守護諸根。飲食知節。初夜後夜隨時覺悟。觀緣取相樂住空舍。貴於持戒禪定智慧不現奇異。令他歡喜但自利益。樂於深法不隨他智。[6]如大乘中次第者。初說檀波羅蜜。次尸羅波羅蜜。羼提波羅蜜。毘梨耶波羅蜜。禪波羅蜜。般若波羅蜜。初說諦勝處。次說捨勝處滅勝處慧勝處。
简体字	初说布施。次持戒。次生天。次五欲过患。次在家苦恼。次出家利乐。次说苦谛。次集谛。次灭谛。次道谛。次须陀洹果。次斯陀含果。次阿那含果。次阿罗汉果。次不坏解脱。次说诸无碍。辟支佛乘中亦说。我我所物多有过患。舍此过患之物得大利益。在家为过恶。出家为利益。次众闹乱语为过恶。独行为善利。聚落为过恶。阿练若处为善利。厌离多欲多事。乐于少欲少事。守护诸根。饮食知节。初夜后夜随时觉悟。观缘取相乐住空舍。贵于持戒禅定智慧不现奇异。令他欢喜但自利益。乐于深法不随他智。如大乘中次第者。初说檀波罗蜜。次尸罗波罗蜜。羼提波罗蜜。毗梨耶波罗蜜。禅波罗蜜。般若波罗蜜。初说谛胜处。次说舍胜处灭胜处慧胜处。

Chapter 30 – [Distinctions Pertaining to] the Great Vehicle

first speak of giving, then of upholding the moral precepts, then of being reborn in the heavens, then of the faults and misery in pursuing the five kinds of sensual pleasures, then of the suffering and distress of the household life, and then of the benefits and bliss of abandoning the home life [in favor of the monastic path]. Following this, they explain the truth of suffering, then the truth of its origination, then the truth of its cessation, and then the truth of the path. After this, they speak of the stream enterer's fruit of the path, the fruit of the *sakṛdāgāmin*, the fruit of the *ānagamin*, and the fruit of arhatship. They next speak of the indestructible liberation and then speak of those that are unimpeded.

Beyond that, within the Pratyekabuddha Vehicle, they also speak of the faults and misery inherent in the self and everything deemed to be possessed by the self and speak as well of the immense benefit in the abandonment of such faults and misery. They then speak of the life of the householder as possessed of serious faults and of leaving behind the household life as beneficial.

They next explain that the many sorts of disputation and conceptual elaboration involve serious faults, that solitary practice bestows wholesome benefits, that village life involves serious faults, that abiding in a forest hermitage brings wholesome benefits, that one should renounce the many desires and the many sorts of [worldly] endeavors and instead delight in having but few wants and but few endeavors. [They teach that] one is to carefully guard the sense faculties, know moderation in drink and food, maintain vigilance at all times throughout the first watch and the last watch of the night,[173] contemplate an object, focus on its characteristics, and take delight in dwelling in an empty hut.

They esteem the upholding of the moral precepts, the cultivation of *dhyāna* absorptions, and the development of wisdom. They refrain from displaying idiosyncratic or strange personal appearances. Although they do inspire happiness in others [who observe them on the daily alms round], they are only concerned with benefiting themselves. They delight in profound dharmas and acquire wisdom that does not rely on [teachings provided by] others.

According to the Great Vehicle's priorities regarding the correct sequencing of events, one first speaks of the perfection of giving, then the perfection of moral virtue, then the perfection of patience, then the perfection of vigor, then the perfection of meditative concentration, and then the perfection of wisdom.[174]

[The Great Vehicle also] first speaks of the truthfulness supreme basis [for the generation of meritorious qualities], then the relinquishment basis, then the quiescence basis, and then the wisdom basis.

正體字	復次初 104b17 ‖ 讚歎發菩提心。次十種願。次十究竟。次讚 104b18 ‖ 歎遠離退失菩提心法。次修集不退失菩 104b19 ‖ 提心法。次堅心精進。次堅固堪受。次堅誓。 104b20 ‖ 復次初說能得諸地法。次說能住諸地法。 104b21 ‖ 次說能得諸地底法。次說遠離諸地垢法。 104b22 ‖ 次[7]說能作[8]淨地法。次說諸地久住法。次 104b23 ‖ [*]說能到諸地邊法。次說能作不退失諸 104b24 ‖ 地法。次說諸地果。次說諸地果勢力。復次 104b25 ‖ 或初說歡喜地。次說離垢地。次說明地。次 104b26 ‖ 說炎地。次說難勝地。次說現前地。次說深 104b27 ‖ 遠地。次說不動地。次說善慧地。次說法雲 104b28 ‖ 地。如說。 104b29 ‖ 　　初施次持戒　　果報得生天
简体字	复次初赞叹发菩提心。次十种愿。次十究竟。次赞叹远离退失菩提心法。次修集不退失菩提心法。次坚心精进。次坚固堪受。次坚誓。复次初说能得诸地法。次说能住诸地法。次说能得诸地底法。次说远离诸地垢法。次说能作净地法。次说诸地久住法。次说能到诸地边法。次说能作不退失诸地法。次说诸地果。次说诸地果势力。复次或初说欢喜地。次说离垢地。次说明地。次说炎地。次说难胜地。次说现前地。次说深远地。次说不动地。次说善慧地。次说法云地。如说。 　　初施次持戒　　果报得生天

Chapter 30 — [Distinctions Pertaining to] the Great Vehicle

Then again, they also first praise the generation of the resolve to attain bodhi, then the ten vows, and then the ten ultimate ends. They then praise the renunciation of whatsoever dharma might conduce to retreat from the resolve to attain bodhi, then they praise cultivation of those dharmas that prevent retreat from the resolve to attain bodhi, followed by promoting vigor buttressed by solid resolve, solidly established capacity for endurance, and then solidity in sustaining one's vows.

Yet again, [the Great Vehicle]:

First speaks of the dharmas that enable acquisition of all the [bodhisattva] grounds;
Next speaks of the dharmas that enable dwelling on the grounds;
Next speaks of the dharmas that enable acquisition of the deepest aspects of the grounds;
Next speaks of the dharmas by which one abandons defilements on the grounds;
Next speaks of the dharmas enabling purification of the grounds;
Next speaks of the dharmas conducive to abiding for a long time on the grounds;
Next speaks of the dharmas enabling one to reach the most extreme limits of each of the grounds;
Next speaks of the dharmas enabling nonregression from the grounds;
Next speaks of the fruits associated with each of the grounds;
And then speaks of the powers associated with the fruits of each of the grounds.

Then again, it may be that [the Great Vehicle]:

First speaks of the Ground of Joyfulness;
Next speaks of the Ground of Stainlessness;
Next speaks of the Ground of Shining Light;
Next speaks of the Ground of Blazing Brilliance;
Next speaks of the Difficult-to-Conquer Ground;
Next speaks of the Ground of Direct Presence;
Next speaks of the Far-Reaching Ground;
Next speaks of the Ground of Immovability;
Next speaks of the Ground of Excellent Intelligence;
And then speaks of the Ground of the Dharma Cloud.

These [various Three-Vehicle sequences] are as described below:

[Śrāvakas] first speak of giving, next of upholding moral precepts, and then their karmic fruition in gaining rebirth in the heavens.

	正體字
104c01 ‖	無常在家過　　出家為大利
104c02 ‖	次無上四諦　　斷結證四果
104c03 ‖	是方便次第　　令人住初[9]乘
104c04 ‖	初說生死過　　次說涅槃利
104c05 ‖	守護於諸根　　持戒及禪定
104c06 ‖	不隨他智慧　　功德樂獨處
104c07 ‖	自依不依他　　樂求自利樂
104c08 ‖	亦不捨他人　　深行頭陀法
104c09 ‖	其求中乘者　　教法相如是
104c10 ‖	以四十不共　　說佛無量德
104c11 ‖	亦說菩薩時　　一切所行法
104c12 ‖	為利眾生故　　次第說是法
104c13 ‖	自利及利他　　說種種功德
104c14 ‖	亦說諸佛子　　所樂十種地
104c15 ‖	求法大乘者　　如是次第度
104c16 ‖	引導者。隨眾生所樂門。知是門已。以是門
104c17 ‖	引導眾生。隨其所樂任其勢力而令得度。
104c18 ‖	如說。
104c19 ‖	或有諸眾生　　可以深經書
104c20 ‖	難事及工巧　　呪術以愛語

简体字

无常在家过　　出家为大利
次无上四谛　　断结证四果
是方便次第　　令人住初乘
初说生死过　　次说涅槃利
守护于诸根　　持戒及禅定
不随他智慧　　功德乐独处
自依不依他　　乐求自利乐
亦不舍他人　　深行头陀法
其求中乘者　　教法相如是
以四十不共　　说佛无量德
亦说菩萨时　　一切所行法
为利众生故　　次第说是法
自利及利他　　说种种功德
亦说诸佛子　　所乐十种地
求法大乘者　　如是次第度
引导者。随众生所乐门。知是门已。以是门引导众生。随其所乐任其势力而令得度。如说。
或有诸众生　　可以深经书
难事及工巧　　咒术以爱语

Chapter 30 — [Distinctions Pertaining to] the Great Vehicle

Next, impermanence, the faults of the household life,
and then the immense benefits achieved by leaving the home life.

Next, they speak of the unsurpassed dharma of the four truths,
the severance of the fetters, and attaining the four fruits [of the path].
This sequence of skillful means
induces people to abide in the first of the [Three] Vehicles.

[*Pratyekabuddhas*] first speak of the faults in *saṃsāra*
and then speak of the benefits associated with nirvāṇa,
guarding and restraining the sense faculties,
maintaining the moral precepts, the *dhyāna* absorptions,

the wisdom not reliant on [the teachings] of others,
the excellent qualities associated with delighting in dwelling alone,
relying upon oneself, not relying on others,
delighting in striving for one's own benefit and happiness

while still not abandoning others,
and deeply cultivating the dharmas of the *dhūta* austerities.
In the case of those who cultivate this mid-level vehicle,
such are the features of the dharmas they teach.

[The Great Vehicle] refers to the forty exclusive dharmas
in describing the measureless qualities of the Buddha,
speaks as well of all of the dharmas that he practiced
when he was a bodhisattva

in order to be of benefit to beings,
speaking of these dharmas according to their correct sequence,
describing self-benefit as well as the benefiting of others,
explaining all of his different sorts of meritorious qualities,

explaining also with regard to all the Buddha's sons
the ten grounds in which they delight.
Those who seek Dharma as set forth in the Great Vehicle
achieve liberation in accordance with just such a sequence as this.

e. His Knowledge of "How to Lead and Guide Beings"

"Leading and guiding beings" involves adapting to whatever subjects beings delight in, and then, having understood precisely what those subjects are, using those very subjects as the means by which one leads and guides them. By adapting to whatever they delight in, allowing for their individual strengths, one influences them toward the achievement of liberation. This is as described here:

There may be cases where there are beings
amenable [to being led and guided] through profound classics,
through recondite subjects, through trades or artisanal skills,
through techniques involving mantras, through pleasing words,

正體字

104c21 ‖	善說及資財　　布施戒定慧
104c22 ‖	如是籌量已　　引來入大乘
104c23 ‖	或現於女身　　引導諸男子
104c24 ‖	復現男子身　　引導於女人
104c25 ‖	示[10]眾五欲樂　　然後說欲過
104c26 ‖	而令一切人　　得離於五欲
104c27 ‖	善行是五事。是名菩薩善受行方便。能忍
104c28 ‖	苦惱者。若有人過算數劫於生死中能忍
104c29 ‖	諸苦惱。十善業道能令此人住於阿耨多羅
105a01 ‖	三藐三菩提。問曰。一切人皆樂樂惡苦。是
105a02 ‖	人云何能忍苦惱。答曰。以五因緣故。一樂
105a03 ‖	無我。二信樂空。三籌量世法。四[1]觀業果
105a04 ‖	報。五念過算數劫唐受苦惱。如說。
105a05 ‖	樂無我空法　　又知業果報
105a06 ‖	利衰等八法　　處世必應受
105a07 ‖	亦念過去世　　空受無量苦
105a08 ‖	何況為佛道　　而當不受耶

简体字

　　善说及资财　　布施戒定慧
　　如是筹量已　　引来入大乘
　　或现于女身　　引导诸男子
　　复现男子身　　引导于女人
　　示众五欲乐　　然后说欲过
　　而令一切人　　得离于五欲

善行是五事。是名菩萨善受行方便。能忍苦恼者。若有人过算数劫于生死中能忍诸苦恼。十善业道能令此人住于阿耨多罗三藐三菩提。问曰。一切人皆乐乐恶苦。是人云何能忍苦恼。答曰。以五因缘故。一乐无我。二信乐空。三筹量世法。四观业果报。五念过算数劫唐受苦恼。如说。

　　乐无我空法　　又知业果报
　　利衰等八法　　处世必应受
　　亦念过去世　　空受无量苦
　　何况为佛道　　而当不受耶

Chapter 30 — *[Distinctions Pertaining to] the Great Vehicle*

through skillful discourse, through resources or wealth,
or through giving, moral virtue, meditation, or wisdom.
After [the bodhisattva] has assessed such factors,
he leads them to enter into the Great Vehicle.

He might manifest in a woman's body
to lead and guide men,
or he might manifest in the body of a man
to lead and guide women,

first showing the many pleasures of the five types of sensual desire,
and, afterward, speaking of the faults inherent in those desires,
thereby leading every sort of person
to then abandon the five types of sensual desire.

It is just such a skillful implementation of [his awareness of] these five matters that constitutes the bodhisattva's "adeptly taking on the practice of skillful means."

8. The Bodhisattva's "Patient Endurance of Pain and Anguish"

Regarding "patiently enduring every sort of pain and anguish,"[175] this refers to the case of a person who, through an incalculable number of kalpas in the cycle of births and deaths, can endure all sorts of pain and anguish as he cultivates the ten courses of good karmic action that enable this person to eventually abide in *anuttarasamyaksaṃbodhi*.

Question: Every person delights in happiness and detests suffering. How then could such a person be able to endure [such an immense amount of] pain and anguish?

Response: There are five reasons for his ability to accomplish this:
First, delight in nonself;
Second, resolute belief in emptiness;
Third, assessment of the nature of worldly dharmas;
Fourth, contemplation of retributions resulting from karmic actions;
Fifth, mindfulness of an incalculable number of kalpas already spent
   fruitlessly undergoing pain and anguish.

These are as described here:

He delights in the dharmas of nonself and emptiness,
and also understands the retributions resulting from karmic actions
as well as gain, loss, and the rest of the eight worldly dharmas
that one must certainly endure while dwelling in the world.

He is also mindful of his past lives
in which he endured in vain a measureless amount of suffering,
[thinking], "How much the more so should I be willing to undergo it
when this would be for the sake of realizing buddhahood?"

正體字

105a09 ‖ 不捨於一切者。或有眾生第一弊惡無有
105a10 ‖ 功德不可利益。菩薩於此終不生捨心。問
105a11 ‖ 曰。若是惡人不可度者。云何不捨。答曰。以
105a12 ‖ 五因緣故。一賤小人法故。二貴大人法故。
105a13 ‖ 三畏誑諸佛故。四知恩故。五為是[2]世間
105a14 ‖ 事故出世間。如說。
105a15 ‖ 　欲度眾生故　　生心持重擔
105a16 ‖ 　於惡怨賊中　　心常不應捨
105a17 ‖ 　[3]賤小貴大人　　是小大差別
105a18 ‖ 　不應眾生中　　愍憐心還息
105a19 ‖ 　於諸急難中　　無事而利益
105a20 ‖ 　擔於重擔時　　而不中懈廢
105a21 ‖ 　若發無上心　　或有捨眾生
105a22 ‖ 　若自心疲苦　　及惡人所[4]害
105a23 ‖ 　即為欺誑於　　十方三世佛
105a24 ‖ 　諸佛世中尊　　為利益眾生
105a25 ‖ 　行種種苦行　　修[*]集於佛道
105a26 ‖ 　佛於恒沙劫　　捨樂作福業

简体字

不舍于一切者。或有众生第一弊恶无有功德不可利益。菩萨于此终不生舍心。问曰。若是恶人不可度者。云何不舍。答曰。以五因缘故。一贱小人法故。二贵大人法故。三畏诳诸佛故。四知恩故。五为是世间事故出世间。如说。

　欲度众生故　　生心持重担
　于恶怨贼中　　心常不应舍
　贱小贵大人　　是小大差别
　不应众生中　　愍怜心还息
　于诸急难中　　无事而利益
　担于重担时　　而不中懈废
　若发无上心　　或有舍众生
　若自心疲苦　　及恶人所害
　即为欺诳于　　十方三世佛
　诸佛世中尊　　为利益众生
　行种种苦行　　修集于佛道
　佛于恒沙劫　　舍乐作福业

Chapter 30 — [Distinctions Pertaining to] the Great Vehicle

9. The Bodhisattva's "Never Abandoning Any Being"

As for "They do not abandon any being,"[176] sometimes there are beings who engage in the most extreme sorts of pernicious evil, who are utterly devoid of meritorious qualities, and whom it is impossible to benefit. Nonetheless, the bodhisattva still never thinks to abandon such beings.

Question: If these sorts of evil people cannot be brought to liberation, why should one not simply abandon them?

Response: There are five reasons, namely:

First, because of disdain for the dharmas of petty people;
Second, because of esteem for the dharmas of the great men;
Third, because of fear of cheating the Buddhas;
Fourth, because of gratitude for the kindnesses one has received;
Fifth, it is because of these works within the world that one transcends the world.

These are as described here:

Because of one's aspiration to liberate beings,
one brings forth the resolve to carry a heavy burden.
Thus, even in the midst of evil adversaries,
one's mind should never be inclined to abandon them.

To disdain petty people and esteem those who are great[177]
is [to conceive of] some difference between the petty and the great.
When in the midst of beings, one should not allow
one's mind of kindly sympathy to withdraw or cease.

In the midst of [others'] urgent difficulties
wherein one has no personal interests, one still provides help.
When it is the time to bear a heavy burden,
one does not shrink from or diminish one's efforts in that work.

In a case where one has brought forth the unsurpassable resolve,
but may still have instances in which one abandons beings,
either due to mental weariness or anguish
or because of being harmed by evil men,
those are instances of cheating and deceiving
all buddhas of the ten directions and three periods of time.

The Buddhas, the honored ones within the world,
for the sake of bestowing benefit on beings,
engaged in all manner of austerities
in their cultivation of the path to buddhahood.
For kalpas in number as the sands of the Ganges, the Buddhas
sacrificed happiness as they performed meritorious karmic deeds.

正體字	105a27 ‖　　若捨一惡人　　　則為背佛恩
105a28 ‖　　是故惡眾生　　　不應於中捨
105a29 ‖　　若人於無量　　　阿僧祇劫中
105b01 ‖　　所修[*]集佛道　　大悲為根本
105b02 ‖　　若以貪欲心　　　瞋恚怖畏心
105b03 ‖　　捨一可度者　　　是斷佛道根
105b04 ‖ [5]是故善業道能令不捨者至阿耨多羅三
105b05 ‖ 藐三菩提。深樂佛慧者。若人深樂佛慧。便疾
105b06 ‖ 得阿耨多羅三藐三菩提。以五因緣故。深
105b07 ‖ 樂佛慧。一佛慧無與等。二佛智能令人為
105b08 ‖ 世中尊。三佛以佛智自度其身。四佛智亦
105b09 ‖ 度他人。五佛智是一切功德住處。如說。
105b10 ‖　　諸佛之智慧　　　天上及世間
105b11 ‖　　一切無與等　　　何況而得勝
105b12 ‖　　諸佛以此智　　　為天阿修羅
105b13 ‖　　一切世間人　　　恭敬而作禮
105b14 ‖　　佛以智自度　　　亦度於他人		
简体字	若舍一恶人　　　则为背佛恩
是故恶众生　　　不应于中舍
若人于无量　　　阿僧祇劫中
所修集佛道　　　大悲为根本
若以贪欲心　　　瞋恚怖畏心
舍一可度者　　　是断佛道根
是故善业道能令不舍者至阿耨多罗三藐三菩提。深乐佛慧者。若人深乐佛慧。便疾得阿耨多罗三藐三菩提。以五因缘故。深乐佛慧。一佛慧无与等。二佛智能令人为世中尊。三佛以佛智自度其身。四佛智亦度他人。五佛智是一切功德住处。如说。
诸佛之智慧　　　天上及世间
一切无与等　　　何况而得胜
诸佛以此智　　　为天阿修罗
一切世间人　　　恭敬而作礼
佛以智自度　　　亦度于他人		

Were one to abandon even a single evil person,
that would be to turn one's back on the kindness of the Buddhas.
Therefore one must not abandon in mid-course
even those beings who are evil.

In an instance where someone,
throughout countless *asaṃkhyeyas* of kalpas,
cultivates the path to buddhahood,
the great compassion is the very root of that endeavor.

If due to thoughts rooted in desire
or thoughts founded on hatred or fear,
one were to abandon even one being who could attain liberation,
this would be to sever the root of the Buddha path.

Therefore [one should realize that] the courses of good karmic action can enable one who does not abandon [any beings] to eventually reach *anuttarasamyaksaṃbodhi*.

10. The Bodhisattva's "Deep Delight in the Buddhas' Wisdom"

As for "deeply delighting in the wisdom of the Buddhas,"[178] if one deeply delights in the wisdom of the Buddhas, then he will thereby swiftly attain *anuttarasamyaksaṃbodhi*. There are five reasons why [the bodhisattva] feels deep delight in the wisdom of the Buddhas, namely:

First, the wisdom of the Buddhas is unequaled by any other;

Second, the wisdom of the Buddhas is able to cause someone to become one who is honored throughout the world;

Third, the Buddhas use the wisdom of the Buddhas to bring about their own liberation;

Fourth, the wisdom of the Buddhas also enables the liberation of others;

Fifth, the wisdom of the Buddhas is the abode of all meritorious qualities.

These are as described below:

As for this wisdom of all the Buddhas,
no matter whether it be up in the heavens or in the world,
there is no wisdom anywhere that can even equal it,
how much the less might there be any superior to it.

It is because of this very wisdom that all buddhas
receive deep respect and reverential obeisance
from the devas, from the *asuras*,
and from all the world's humans.

The Buddhas use this wisdom to liberate themselves
and also use it to liberate other people.

正體字

105b15 ‖　　若得是佛智　　是功德藏者
105b16 ‖ 於諸佛力及自在法中樂盡遍行者。遍行
105b17 ‖ 名久習。一切行力名十種智力。自在名隨
105b18 ‖ 意所作。若人深樂佛十力及自在法中盡遍
105b19 ‖ 行。如是人阿耨多羅三藐三菩提不久疾得。
105b20 ‖ 以五因緣故樂盡遍行。一尊重諸佛教勅。
105b21 ‖ 二諸佛有大弟子故。三身證一切法故。四
105b22 ‖ 攝取墮落者。五已墮落者能拔濟之。如說。
105b23 ‖　　尊佛教無比　　佛子有四八
105b24 ‖　　及以六三種　　堪為諸天師
105b25 ‖　　以佛智慧眼　　見諸法現前
105b26 ‖　　逆惡斷善根　　及諸破戒等
105b27 ‖　　如是墜落人　　攝取而濟度
105b28 ‖　　若人於佛力　　自在中遍行
105b29 ‖　　涅槃及天福　　常在此人手
105c01 ‖ 於是中諸佛以佛力能為五種事。一令眾
105c02 ‖ 生學聲聞乘。[6]二令眾生學辟支佛乘。

简体字

　　若得是佛智　　是功德藏者

于诸佛力及自在法中乐尽遍行者。遍行名久习。一切行力名十种智力。自在名随意所作。若人深乐佛十力及自在法中尽遍行。如是人阿耨多罗三藐三菩提不久疾得。以五因缘故乐尽遍行。一尊重诸佛教敕。二诸佛有大弟子故。三身证一切法故。四摄取堕落者。五已堕落者能拔济之。如说。

　　尊佛教无比　　佛子有四八
　　及以六三种　　堪为诸天师
　　以佛智慧眼　　见诸法现前
　　逆恶断善根　　及诸破戒等
　　如是坠落人　　摄取而济度
　　若人于佛力　　自在中遍行
　　涅槃及天福　　常在此人手

于是中诸佛以佛力能为五种事。一令众生学声闻乘。二令众生学辟支佛乘。

Chapter 30 — [Distinctions Pertaining to] the Great Vehicle

If one acquires this wisdom of the Buddhas,
this is someone who is a treasury of meritorious qualities.

11. "Delight in Those Who Practice the Buddhas' Powers & Masteries"

Regarding "delight in those who completely and thoroughly practice the Buddhas' powers and the sovereign masteries,"[179] "thorough practice" refers to long-enduring practice of all the practices. "The powers" refers to the ten wisdom powers. "Sovereign masteries" refers to the ability to do precisely as one wishes in whatever one does. If one feels profound delight in the complete and thorough practice of the dharmas of the Buddhas' ten powers and sovereign masteries, such a person will be able before long to swiftly attain *anuttarasamyaksaṃbodhi*.

There are five reasons for delighting in the complete and thorough practice [of the powers and sovereign masteries], namely:

First, due to reverential esteem for the teachings and directives of all buddhas;
Second, due to the fact that all buddhas have such great disciples;
Third, due to their personal realization of all dharmas;
Fourth, due to their ability to draw in those who have fallen away;
Fifth, due to their ability to then rescue those who have fallen away.

These are as described below:

[They delight] due to revering the Buddhas' incomparable teachings,
due to the existence of the fourfold and eightfold classes
of the Buddha's sons of six and threefold types,
due to their capacity to become the teachers even of the devas,
due to the Buddhas' wisdom eye
with which they see all dharmas manifest directly before them,

and due to their ability to draw in and rescue, bringing to liberation
even those people who have fallen away such as
those who, by heinous evil deeds, have severed roots of goodness,
those who have broken the moral precepts, and other such beings.

If there be a person who [delights] in those who thoroughly practice
the Buddhas' powers and sovereign masteries,
then nirvāṇa as well as the merit of the heavens
will always be as if resting in the palm of his hand.

12. The Buddhas' "Practice of the Powers"

[Regarding the "Buddhas' powers"],[180] in circumstances such as these, the Buddhas are able to use a buddha's powers to accomplish five types of endeavors, namely:

First, they may induce beings to train in the Śrāvaka Disciple Vehicle;

正體字

```
              三令
105c03 ‖ 眾生學大乘法。四力具足者令得解脫。五
105c04 ‖ 力劣者令住世樂。如說。
105c05 ‖   諸佛以[7]神力    令厭離眾生
105c06 ‖   或令學小乘      中乘及大乘
105c07 ‖   有力具足者      令其得解脫
105c08 ‖   力不具足者      生天[8]令世樂
105c09 ‖ 自在者。諸佛於五事中自在。一諸神通自
105c10 ‖ 在。二自心中得自在。三滅盡中得自在。四
105c11 ‖ 聖如意中得自在。五壽命中得自在。如說。
105c12 ‖   飛行等自在      自心得自在
105c13 ‖   於滅禪定中      如入出自舍
105c14 ‖   一切淨不淨      隨心而能轉
105c15 ‖   命不為他害      自緣亦無盡
105c16 ‖   如是等自在      一切法亦爾
105c17 ‖   是故人師子      名為自在者
```

简體字

三令众生学大乘法。四力具足者令得解脱。五力劣者令住世乐。如说。

　　诸佛以神力　　令厌离众生
　　或令学小乘　　中乘及大乘
　　有力具足者　　令其得解脱
　　力不具足者　　生天令世乐

自在者。诸佛于五事中自在。一诸神通自在。二自心中得自在。三灭尽中得自在。四圣如意中得自在。五寿命中得自在。如说。

　　飞行等自在　　自心得自在
　　于灭禅定中　　如入出自舍
　　一切净不净　　随心而能转
　　命不为他害　　自缘亦无尽
　　如是等自在　　一切法亦尔
　　是故人师子　　名为自在者

Chapter 30 — [Distinctions Pertaining to] the Great Vehicle

Second, they may induce beings to train in the Pratyekabuddha Vehicle;

Third, they may induce beings to train in the Dharma of the Great Vehicle;

Fourth, in the case of those whose powers have become perfectly complete, they may enable their attainment of liberation;

Fifth, in the case of those whose powers are as yet inferior, they may enable them to abide in worldly happiness.

These are as described below:

> The Buddhas use their spiritual powers
> to influence beings who have developed renunciation,
> perhaps influencing them to train either in the Small Vehicle,
> or in the Intermediate Vehicle, or in the Great Vehicle.
>
> In the case of those whose powers are completely fulfilled,
> they enable them to attain liberation.
> For those whose powers are still incomplete,
> they assist their celestial rebirth or their happiness within the world.

13. The Buddhas' "Practice of the Sovereign Masteries"

As for "their sovereign masteries,"[181] there are five matters in which the Buddhas possess sovereign mastery, namely:

First, sovereign mastery in the spiritual superknowledges;

Second, the attainment of sovereign mastery over their own minds;

Third, the attainment of sovereign mastery in complete cessation;

Fourth, the attainment of sovereign mastery in the psychic powers of the Āryas;[182]

Fifth, sovereign mastery in determining their own life spans.

These are as described below:

> They have sovereign mastery in flying and other [superknowledges]
> and they have sovereign mastery over their own minds
> as well as in the *dhyāna* absorption of complete cessation
> that for them is [as easy] as entering and exiting their own abodes.
>
> They can transform all things, whether pure or impure,
> in accordance with their own minds.[183]
> Their life spans cannot be diminished by others,
> for, so long as they sustain the conditions, their lives will be endless.
>
> Just as it is for such sovereign masteries as these,
> so too it is with respect to all dharmas.
> It is for these reasons that [the Buddhas], the lions among men,
> are known as those who possess the sovereign masteries.

正體字

| 105c18 ‖ 能破惡意者。所謂遠離正道。凡夫九十六
| 105c19 ‖ 種外道等。略說惡意者。說五陰為我。或言
| 105c20 ‖ 我有五陰。或言五陰中有我。或言我中有
| 105c21 ‖ 五陰。或言離五陰有我。如說。
| 105c22 ‖ 　若五陰是我　　即為墮斷滅
| 105c23 ‖ 　則失業因緣　　無功而解脫
| 105c24 ‖ 　餘殘有四種　　異陰無有相
| 105c25 ‖ 　無相無有法　　皆應如是破
| 105c26 ‖ 復次五邪見名為惡意。所謂邪見身見邊見
| 105c27 ‖ 見取戒取。如說。
| 105c28 ‖ 　破因果邪見　　二十種身見
| 105c29 ‖ 　有見及無見　　下事以為最
| 106a01 ‖ 　但以戒力故　　而得於解脫
| 106a02 ‖ 　如先一異破　　此見如是破
| 106a03 ‖ 　正意八道破　　說名得解脫
| 106a04 ‖ 守護諸佛正法者。若人能守護諸佛所教法
| 106a05 ‖ 所謂十二部經。以其心能信能受。十善業道
| 106a06 ‖ 能令此人至阿耨多羅三藐三菩提。

简体字

能破恶意者。所谓远离正道。凡夫九十六种外道等。略说恶意者。说五阴为我。或言我有五阴。或言五阴中有我。或言我中有五阴。或言离五阴有我。如说。

　若五阴是我　　即为堕断灭
　则失业因缘　　无功而解脱
　余残有四种　　异阴无有相
　无相无有法　　皆应如是破

复次五邪见名为恶意。所谓邪见身见边见见取戒取。如说。

　破因果邪见　　二十种身见
　有见及无见　　下事以为最
　但以戒力故　　而得于解脱
　如先一异破　　此见如是破
　正意八道破　　说名得解脱

守护诸佛正法者。若人能守护诸佛所教法所谓十二部经。以其心能信能受。十善业道能令此人至阿耨多罗三藐三菩提。

Chapter 30 — [Distinctions Pertaining to] the Great Vehicle

14. The Bodhisattva's "Ability to Refute All Wrong Views"

Regarding being "able to refute all ideas involving wrong views,"[184] this is a reference to whatever strays far from the right path such as the ninety-six kinds of non-Buddhist paths favored by common people, and other such wrong views. A general characterization of such wrong ideas would include the claim that the five aggregates constitute a self, that there is a self that possesses the five aggregates, that there is a self contained within the five aggregates, that the five aggregates are contained within a self, or that there exists a self apart from the five aggregates. These ideas are as described below:

> If [one posits that] the five aggregates constitute a self,
> thereby falling into the annihilationist [fallacy],
> one thus dispenses with the efficacy of karmic causes and conditions
> and posits liberation in the absence of the requisite efforts.

> As for the rest [of the wrong views], they are of four types.
> As for those positing a signless self distinct from the aggregates,
> whatsoever is signless is necessarily a nonexistent dharma.
> All [of the other fallacies] should be refuted in this same way.

Then again, it is the five erroneous views that constitute wrong ideas, namely: wrong views, the view of [the five-aggregate] "person" as constituting a self, extreme views, seizing upon views, and views that seize on precept observance [alone as constituting the path]. These are as described below:

> One demolishes the wrong views about cause and effect,
> the twenty kinds of views referencing a "person,"
> views positing the ultimacy of existence or nonexistence,
> [views esteeming] inferior endeavors as supreme,
> and [the view that] it is solely by the power of precept observance
> that one succeeds in achieving liberation.

> As with the earlier refutation [of a self] identical to or distinct
> [from the five aggregates], these views are refuted in just such a way.
> Using right thought and the eightfold path to refute them,
> one explains that these are the bases for attaining liberation.

15. The Bodhisattva's "Preservation and Protection of Right Dharma"

Regarding "preserving and protecting the Buddhas' right Dharma,"[185] this refers to someone who is able to preserve and protect the Dharma as taught by all buddhas, namely the twelve categories of scriptural text. Because his mind is able to believe and accept them, the ten courses of good karmic action can cause this person to succeed in reaching *anuttarasamyaksaṃbodhi*.

正體字	
	以五因
106a07 ‖	緣故應[1]受護正法。一知報諸佛恩故。二
106a08 ‖	令法久住故。三以最上供養供養諸佛故。
106a09 ‖	四利益無量眾生故。五正法第一難得故。
106a10 ‖	如說。
106a11 ‖	若人欲施作　　諸佛所[*]受事
106a12 ‖	亦令法久住　　以上供養佛
106a13 ‖	為欲療治於　　眾生之重病
106a14 ‖	亦知諸世尊　　從苦得是法
106a15 ‖	以是因緣故　　知法為難得
106a16 ‖	是故有智者　　應當愛護法
106a17 ‖	於是中。以五因緣故。名為愛護正法。一如
106a18 ‖	所說行。二令他人如法行。三除破佛法刺
106a19 ‖	蕀故。四離四黑印。五行四大印。如說。
106a20 ‖	自於佛法中　　如佛所教住
106a21 ‖	悲心不悋法　　亦令他得住
106a22 ‖	又破於魔眾　　及外道論師
106a23 ‖	若憎佛法者　　以無瞋心破

简体字

以五因缘故应受护正法。一知报诸佛恩故。二令法久住故。三以最上供养供养诸佛故。四利益无量众生故。五正法第一难得故。如说。

　　若人欲施作　　诸佛所受事
　　亦令法久住　　以上供养佛
　　为欲疗治于　　众生之重病
　　亦知诸世尊　　从苦得是法
　　以是因缘故　　知法为难得
　　是故有智者　　应当爱护法

于是中。以五因缘故。名为爱护正法。一如所说行。二令他人如法行。三除破佛法刺蕀故。四离四黑印。五行四大印。如说。

　　自于佛法中　　如佛所教住
　　悲心不吝法　　亦令他得住
　　又破于魔众　　及外道论师
　　若憎佛法者　　以无瞋心破

Chapter 30 — [Distinctions Pertaining to] the Great Vehicle

There are five reasons why one should accept and protect right Dharma, namely:

First, because one realizes the obligation to repay the kindness of all buddhas;

Second, in order to cause the Dharma to abide for a long time;

Third, in order to perform the most supreme form of offering, thus making an offering to the Buddhas themselves;

Fourth, in order to be of benefit to an incalculable number of beings;

Fifth, because right Dharma is the rarest of all things.

These are as described below:

If a person wishes to devote himself
to those endeavors bequeathed by all buddhas
and also wishes to cause the Dharma to remain for a long time
by presenting the most supreme offering to the Buddhas,

then, because he wishes to heal
the serious diseases that afflict beings,
because he has realized that all the Bhagavats
obtained this Dharma through having to undergo suffering,

and because, understanding these conditions of its origination,
he realizes that the Dharma is a rarity difficult to come by—
[for all these reasons], he who is wise
should therefore cherish and protect the Dharma.

In this connection, there are five bases by which one's actions might qualify as "cherishing and protecting right Dharma," namely:

First, one cultivates [the path] according to the way it was taught;

Second, one influences others to practice in accordance with the Dharma;

Third, one extricates any thorns that might destroy the Buddha's Dharma;

Fourth, one abandons the four seals of darkness;

Fifth, one practices [in accordance with] the four seals of greatness.[186]

These are as described below:

In one's own relationship with the Dharma of the Buddhas,
one abides in accordance with how the Buddha taught it.
One retains a mind of compassion, is not miserly with Dharma,
and also influences others to abide within it.

Moreover, one crushes the armies of Māra
and also refutes the claims of the non-Buddhist treatise masters.
On encountering those who detest the Dharma of the Buddhas,
with a mind free of hatred, one refutes their claims.

正體字

106a24 ‖	遠離四黑印　　受行四大印
106a25 ‖	如是則名為　　愛護於正法
106a26 ‖	勇健者。菩薩以五因緣故名為勇健。一破
106a27 ‖	魔賊[2]故。二破外道賊故。三破煩惱賊故。
106a28 ‖	四破諸根賊故。五破五陰賊故。如說。
106a29 ‖	惡魔起兵眾　　道樹欲害佛
106b01 ‖	常求於佛便　　[3]嬈亂聽者心
106b02 ‖	佛日出世[4]間　　魔請令涅槃
106b03 ‖	常亂受學者　　破於解脫道
106b04 ‖	乃至於今日　　其心猶不息
106b05 ‖	是憎涅槃者　　善人之大賊
106b06 ‖	應以戒定慧　　摧破魔力怨
106b07 ‖	自謂有智慧　　常輕慢於佛
106b08 ‖	以種種因緣　　滅佛法故出
106b09 ‖	常憎佛弟子　　自失教他失
106b10 ‖	是諸外道輩　　世間之大賊
106b11 ‖	當以無瞋心　　應以多聞慧
106b12 ‖	及以大心力　　摧破外道怨

简体字

远离四黑印　　受行四大印
如是则名为　　爱护于正法
勇健者。菩萨以五因缘故名为勇健。一破魔贼故。二破外道贼故。三破烦恼贼故。四破诸根贼故。五破五阴贼故。如说。
　　恶魔起兵众　　道树欲害佛
　　常求于佛便　　娆乱听者心
　　佛日出世间　　魔请令涅槃
　　常乱受学者　　破于解脱道
　　乃至于今日　　其心犹不息
　　是憎涅槃者　　善人之大贼
　　应以戒定慧　　摧破魔力怨
　　自谓有智慧　　常轻慢于佛
　　以种种因缘　　灭佛法故出
　　常憎佛弟子　　自失教他失
　　是诸外道辈　　世间之大贼
　　当以无瞋心　　应以多闻慧
　　及以大心力　　摧破外道怨

Chapter 30 — *[Distinctions Pertaining to] the Great Vehicle*

One departs from the four seals of blackness
while taking on the practice of the four seals of greatness.
One who is able to act in such a way is deemed to be
someone who cherishes and protects right Dharma.

16. The Bodhisattva's "Valor"

As for their being "valiant,"[187] there are five bases because of which the bodhisattva is deemed to be valiant, namely:

First, because he crushes Māra's thieves;
Second, because he crushes the non-Buddhist partisan thieves;
Third, because he crushes the thieves of the afflictions;
Fourth, because he crushes the thieves of the sense faculties;
Fifth, because he crushes the thieves of the five aggregates.

These are as described below:

Māra the Evil One marshaled his armies
and, at the bodhi tree, sought to harm the Buddha.
Always seeking opportunities to take advantage of the Buddha
and disturb the minds of his audience.
Once the Buddha sun had arisen and shone upon the world,
Māra made the request intended to cause him to enter nirvāṇa.

He is forever confusing those who take on the training,
attempting to destroy their paths to liberation,
even to the point that, to this very day,
his determination to accomplish this still never ceases.

These who detest nirvāṇa
are the great thieves of good people.
One must use moral virtue, *dhyāna* concentration, and wisdom
to crush adversaries possessed of Māra's powers.

There are those who, of the opinion that they are wise,
always slight the Buddhas out of arrogance
and use all different sorts of tactics
to destroy the Buddha's Dharma, manifesting for that very reason.

They always detest the Buddha's disciples
and, having become failures themselves, they teach others to fail.
These various classes of non-Buddhists
are the great thieves in the world.

One ought to use a mind free of hatred
and one should use the wisdom based on extensive learning.
Then, availing oneself of the power of the great resolve,
one should utterly demolish these non-Buddhist adversaries.

正體字	106b13 ‖ 煩惱力起業	輪轉墮惡道
	106b14 ‖ 煩惱力障故	不能行大道
	106b15 ‖ 以煩惱力故	墮種種邪見
	106b16 ‖ 以煩惱力故	不行甘露道
	106b17 ‖ 以是因緣故	煩惱最大賊
	106b18 ‖ 以正念定慧	破此煩惱賊
	106b19 ‖ 若為根賊牽	令人墮惡道
	106b20 ‖ 又墮天人中	不得至涅槃
	106b21 ‖ 今此諸根賊	何不以慚愧
	106b22 ‖ 正念及智慧	摧破諸根賊
	106b23 ‖ 譬如世間人	以軟語欺誑
	106b24 ‖ 財物及刀矟	以此四除賊
	106b25 ‖ 以此五陰故	受生老病死
	106b26 ‖ 亦墮大怖畏	得諸急苦惱
	106b27 ‖ 五陰因緣故	憂悲及啼哭
	106b28 ‖ 五陰因緣故	受種種諸苦
	106b29 ‖ 是故汝當知	應以知見法
	106c01 ‖ 摧破此五陰	猶如破怨賊
	106c02 ‖ 堪受者。心志力強有大人相。	

简体字	烦恼力起业	轮转堕恶道
	烦恼力障故	不能行大道
	以烦恼力故	堕种种邪见
	以烦恼力故	不行甘露道
	以是因缘故	烦恼最大贼
	以正念定慧	破此烦恼贼
	若为根贼牵	令人堕恶道
	又堕天人中	不得至涅槃
	今此诸根贼	何不以惭愧
	正念及智慧	摧破诸根贼
	譬如世间人	以软语欺诳
	财物及刀矟	以此四除贼
	以此五阴故	受生老病死
	亦堕大怖畏	得诸急苦恼
	五阴因缘故	忧悲及啼哭
	五阴因缘故	受种种诸苦
	是故汝当知	应以知见法
	摧破此五阴	犹如破怨贼
	堪受者。心志力强有大人相。	

Chapter 30 — [Distinctions Pertaining to] the Great Vehicle

The power of the afflictions brings forth karmic actions,
cyclic existence, and descent into the wretched destinies.
It is because of obstacles caused by the power of the afflictions
that one remains unable to practice the great path.

It is because of the power of the afflictions
that one falls into all sorts of wrong views.
It is because of the power of the afflictions
that one does not practice the path to the elixir of immortality.

It is because of all these reasons
that the afflictions are the worst of all the great thieves.
Through right mindfulness, concentration, and wisdom,
one becomes able to crush the thieves of the afflictions.

If one is dragged along by the thieves of the sense faculties,
they cause a person to descend into the wretched destinies
and also cause one to fall into celestial and human realms
wherein one does not succeed in reaching nirvāṇa.

Now, given [the plight caused by] these sense-faculty thieves,
how could one fail to use a sense of shame, dread of blame,
and right mindfulness as well as wisdom
to utterly crush the thieves of the sense faculties.

These are analogous to [the stratagems of] people of the world
who may resort to gently persuasive words, or to deception,
or to wealth and valuables, or even to swords and lances,
using these four means to drive away the thieves.

It is because of these five aggregates
that one undergoes birth, aging, sickness, and death,
also falls into the realms of immense terror,
and becomes subject to undergoing intense suffering and anguish.

It because of the five aggregates
that one is plunged into grief and then sobs and weeps.
It is also because of the five aggregates
that one undergoes all the different sorts of sufferings.

Therefore you should realize
the need to use the dharmas of knowledge and vision
to utterly crush [the ruinous power of] the five aggregates
just as one would defeat adversaries or thieves.

17. The Bodhisattva's "Ability to Endure"

As for [the bodhisattva's] being "able to endure,"[188] he is one whose resolve is strong, who is possessed of the marks of a great man, and

見事深遠。以
五因緣故。名為堪受者。一所願事成其心不
高。二所願不成心亦不下。三苦惱切己其
心不動。四樂事加身心亦不異。五其心深
遠。若瞋若喜難可得知。如說。

身心[5]新苦至　　其意亦不動
隨意樂事至　　大智心不異
若瞋喜怖畏　　他人不能測
如是深心相　　是說堪受者

勤精進者。於五事中勤行精進。一未生惡法
為不生故勤行精進。二已生惡法為斷滅
故勤行精進。三未生善法為令生故勤行
精進。四已生善法為增長故勤行精進。五
於世間事中有所作無能障礙故勤行精
進。如說。

斷已生惡法　　猶如除毒蛇
斷未生惡法　　如預斷流水

见事深远。以五因缘故。名为堪受者。一所愿事成其心不高。二所愿不成心亦不下。三苦恼切己其心不动。四乐事加身心亦不异。五其心深远。若嗔若喜难可得知。如说。

身心新苦至　　其意亦不动
随意乐事至　　大智心不异
若嗔喜怖畏　　他人不能测
如是深心相　　是说堪受者

勤精进者。于五事中勤行精进。一未生恶法为不生故勤行精进。二已生恶法为断灭故勤行精进。三未生善法为令生故勤行精进。四已生善法为增长故勤行精进。五于世间事中有所作无能障碍故勤行精进。如说。

断已生恶法　　犹如除毒蛇
断未生恶法　　如预断流水

Chapter 30 — *[Distinctions Pertaining to] the Great Vehicle*

who is possessed of a profound and distant vision. There are five grounds for his being deemed "able to endure," namely:

First, when he succeeds in the endeavors he has vowed to achieve, his mind does not become elated;

Second, when he does not succeed in the endeavors he has vowed to achieve, his mind does not become dejected;

Third, when pain and anguish cut close, his mind remains unmoved;

Fourth, when his body is beset by pleasurable experiences, his mind still remains unchanged;

Fifth, his state of mind runs deep and sees far. Thus whether he has been given cause for anger or cause for joy, his mind remains inscrutable.

These are as described below:

When his body or mind experience some new suffering,
his mind still remains unmoved.
No matter what sort of pleasurable experience comes,
his greatly wise mind does not change.

Even where he is given cause for anger, joy, or fear,
no one else can fathom [his state of mind].
Wherever one possesses marks of resolute intentions such as these,
this person is said to be one who is "able to endure."

18. The Bodhisattva's "Vigor"

Regarding [the bodhisattva's] diligent "vigor,"[189] there are five circumstances in which he is diligent in his practice of vigor, namely:

First, he is diligently vigorous in preventing the arising of bad dharmas that have not yet arisen;

Second, he is diligently vigorous in cutting off and destroying bad dharmas that may already have arisen;

Third, he is diligently vigorous in causing the arising of good dharmas that have not yet arisen;

Fourth, he is diligently vigorous in increasing any good dharmas that have already arisen;

Fifth, he is diligently vigorous in ensuring that nothing can obstruct whatever endeavors he has taken up in the world.

These are as described below:

He cuts off evil dharmas that have already arisen
just as one might get rid of a venomous snake.
He cuts off any evil dharmas that have not yet arisen
just as one might block off the waters of a flood.

正體字	106c19 ‖ 　　增長於善法　　如溉甘果栽 106c20 ‖ 　　未生善為生　　如[6]攢木出火 106c21 ‖ 　　世間善事中　　精進無障礙 106c22 ‖ 　　諸佛說是人　　名為勤精進 106c23 ‖ 堅心化眾生者。若菩薩於五乘中教[7]化眾 106c24 ‖ 生時。供養輕慢憎愛怖畏苦樂疲極等事中 106c25 ‖ 其心不轉。是名堅心化眾生。五乘者。一者 106c26 ‖ 佛乘。二者辟支佛乘。三者聲聞乘。四者天乘。 106c27 ‖ 五者人乘。如說。 106c28 ‖ 　[8]如應以一心　　一切諸力勢 106c29 ‖ 　　依種種方便　　離於憎愛心 107a01 ‖ 　　教化諸眾生　　離垢心清淨 107a02 ‖ 　　令得無量世　　難得無上乘 107a03 ‖ 　　若入無勢力　　不堪住大乘 107a04 ‖ 　　次教辟支佛　　聲聞天人乘 107a05 ‖ 不貪自樂者。所謂不著一切諸樂。菩薩以 107a06 ‖ 五因緣故不貪自樂。	
简体字	增长于善法　　如溉甘果栽 　　未生善为生　　如攒木出火 　　世间善事中　　精进无障碍 　　诸佛说是人　　名为勤精进 坚心化众生者。若菩萨于五乘中教化众生时。供养轻慢憎爱怖畏苦乐疲极等事中其心不转。是名坚心化众生。五乘者。一者佛乘。二者辟支佛乘。三者声闻乘。四者天乘。五者人乘。如说。 　　如应以一心　　一切诸力势 　　依种种方便　　离于憎爱心 　　教化诸众生　　离垢心清净 　　令得无量世　　难得无上乘 　　若入无势力　　不堪住大乘 　　次教辟支佛　　声闻天人乘 不贪自乐者。所谓不着一切诸乐。菩萨以五因缘故不贪自乐。	

Chapter 30 — [Distinctions Pertaining to] the Great Vehicle

He brings about the growth of [already arisen] good dharmas
just as one might water a sweet fruit's seedling.
He strives to bring forth goodness that has not yet arisen
just as one might use a wooden friction drill to light a fire.

In pursuing his good endeavors in the world,
he acts with such diligent vigor as permits no obstruction.
All buddhas say of a person such as this
that he is to be known as one who is diligently vigorous.

19. The Bodhisattva's "Solid Resolve in Teaching Beings"

As for "solid resolve in the teaching of beings,"[190] if, during all that time in which he teaches beings in the five vehicles, the bodhisattva's mind remains unturned even as he experiences at the hands of others the giving of offerings, slighting, arrogance, detestation, love, terror, suffering, bliss, extreme exhaustion, and other such situations, he thereby qualifies as one who "proceeds with solid resolve in the teaching of beings."

As for the five vehicles, they are:

First, the Buddha Vehicle;
Second, the Pratyekabuddha Vehicle;
Third, the Śrāvaka Disciple Vehicle;
Fourth, the Deva Vehicle;
Fifth, the Human Vehicle.

These are as described below:

You should use single-minded focus[191]
and all your powers,
while relying on many different sorts of skillful means
and abandoning any thoughts of hate or love

as you proceed to teach every sort of being,
doing so with a pure mind that has abandoned defilement,
thereby influencing them to gain what in countless lifetimes
is a rarity: the unsurpassable [Buddha] Vehicle.

If one enters among those who have no such strength
and thus have no capacity to abide in the Great Vehicle,
one may in sequence teach either the Pratyekabuddha Vehicle,
the Śrāvaka Disciple Vehicle, or the vehicles of devas or humans.

20. The Bodhisattva's "Not Coveting His Own Happiness"

As for "not coveting their own happiness,"[192] this refers to not being attached to any sort of bliss. There are five reasons why the bodhisattva does covet his own happiness, namely:

正體字	一[1]樂無常如水泡。二 107a07 ‖ 世樂變苦。三從眾緣生故。四從渴愛起故。 107a08 ‖ 五少樂如蜜[2]渧故。如說。 107a09 ‖ 　　樂少住如泡　　變苦如毒食 107a10 ‖ 　　三合從觸有　　貪欲[3][病-丙+(瓜-、)]故生 107a11 ‖ 　　若離於貪愛　　更無有別樂 107a12 ‖ 　　如枯井蜜[*]渧　　樂少而苦多 107a13 ‖ 　　利益眾生者　　不應有貪著 107a14 ‖ 及無量身命者。菩薩以五因緣故不貪惜 107a15 ‖ 身。一身不從先世來。二不去至後世。三 107a16 ‖ 不堅牢。四是身無我。[4]五無我所。如說。 107a17 ‖ 　　汝身眾穢聚　　不淨遍充滿 107a18 ‖ 　　不從先世來　　不持至後世 107a19 ‖ 　　雖久好供[5]事　　而破大恩分 107a20 ‖ 　　是身不堅固　　如沫不久壞 107a21 ‖ 　　緣生無定性　　無性不自在 107a22 ‖ 　　是故應當知　　非我非我所 107a23 ‖ 　　是身無量過　　不應有貪惜
簡体字	一乐无常如水泡。二世乐变苦。三从众缘生故。四从渴爱起故。 五少乐如蜜渧故。如说。 　　乐少住如泡　　变苦如毒食 　　三合从触有　　贪欲[病-丙+(瓜-、)]故生 　　若离于贪爱　　更无有别乐 　　如枯井蜜渧　　乐少而苦多 　　利益众生者　　不应有贪着 及无量身命者。菩萨以五因缘故不贪惜身。一身不从先世 来。二不去至后世。三不坚牢。四是身无我。五无我所。如说。 　　汝身众秽聚　　不净遍充满 　　不从先世来　　不持至后世 　　虽久好供事　　而破大恩分 　　是身不坚固　　如沫不久坏 　　缘生无定性　　无性不自在 　　是故应当知　　非我非我所 　　是身无量过　　不应有贪惜

Chapter 30 — [Distinctions Pertaining to] the Great Vehicle

First, all pleasures are just as ephemeral as a bubble on the water;
Second, worldly pleasures transform into suffering;
Third, they are a product of the conjunction of many conditions;
Fourth, they are a product of cravings;
Fifth, they are but a minor bliss like that of a mere drop of honey.

These are as described below:

Pleasures abide for but a short time, like a bubble
and they transform into suffering like food laced with poison.
Relying on a three-part conjunction, they exist through contact
and arise because of the ulcerous boil of desire.

If one abandons desire and craving,
then there is no pleasure that exists apart from them.
[Pleasures] are like a dry well or a drop of honey,
for there is but little bliss and an abundance of suffering.

Whosoever aims to be of benefit to beings
should not have any sort of covetous attachment.

21. THE BODHISATTVA'S "NOT COVETING A MEASURELESSLY LONG LIFE"

Regarding [their refraining from covetous attachment] "to living a measurelessly long life,"[193] there are five reasons why the bodhisattva does not covet or selfishly cherish his own body, namely:

First, the body did not come forth from previous lives;
Second, it shall not go on to future lives;
Third, it is not a durable entity;
Fourth, it is devoid of any self;
Fifth, there is nothing in it qualifying as the property of a self.

These are as described below:

Your body is but a collection of many sorts of filth
entirely filled up with impurities.
It did not come forth to the present from previous lives,
and it will not be taken forth to one's future lives.

Even though one might provide for and serve it well for a long time,
it will still break its obligation to repay great kindness.
This body is not a durable entity,
for, like a foam bubble, it will be destroyed before long.

Whatsoever is the product of conditions has no fixed nature.
Having no fixed nature, it is therefore not a self-existent entity.
Therefore, one should realize that [the body]
is not a self and is not the possession of a self.

This body is possessed of countless faults.
Thus one should not selfishly cherish it.

正體字

107a24 ‖ 菩薩以五因緣故不貪惜壽命。一樂慧命
107a25 ‖ 故。二怖畏罪故。三念無始生死中無量死
107a26 ‖ 故。四與一切眾生共受故。五不可免故。如
107a27 ‖ 說。
107a28 ‖ 　從多聞正論　　生貪慧命故
107a29 ‖ 　怖畏失命時　　而起於罪惡
107b01 ‖ 　又見一切人　　無脫死[6]王者
107b02 ‖ 　不可以財智　　方便力所免
107b03 ‖ 　修[*]集善法者　何得惜是命
107b04 ‖ 一切事中上者。若人有所作事必能究竟。是
107b05 ‖ 名為上人。菩薩[7]以五事發必得究竟。一者
107b06 ‖ 財物。二者布施。三持戒。四修定。五道德。如
107b07 ‖ 說。
107b08 ‖ 　勤求聚財利　　慇懃行布施
107b09 ‖ 　次第淨持戒　　精[8]進求禪定
107b10 ‖ 　行種種方便　　生八道解脫
107b11 ‖ 　是名諸事中　　名之為上人

简体字

菩萨以五因缘故不贪惜寿命。一乐慧命故。二怖畏罪故。三念无始生死中无量死故。四与一切众生共受故。五不可免故。如说。

　从多闻正论　　生贪慧命故
　怖畏失命时　　而起于罪恶
　又见一切人　　无脱死王者
　不可以财智　　方便力所免
　修集善法者　　何得惜是命

一切事中上者。若人有所作事必能究竟。是名为上人。菩萨以五事发必得究竟。一者财物。二者布施。三持戒。四修定。五道德。如说。

　勤求聚财利　　殷勤行布施
　次第净持戒　　精进求禅定
　行种种方便　　生八道解脱
　是名诸事中　　名之为上人

Chapter 30 — [Distinctions Pertaining to] the Great Vehicle

There are five reasons why the bodhisattva does not selfishly cherish a long life span, namely:

First, because he delights in the life of wisdom;
Second, because he is frightened at the prospect of committing any karmic transgression [in order to preserve it];
Third, because he is mindful of the countless deaths one has undergone throughout the course of beginningless *saṃsāra*;
Fourth, because [death] is an experience jointly shared by all beings;
Fifth, because [death] is unavoidable.

These are as described below:

Because, through abundant learning and right discourse about it,
one comes to prize one's life of wisdom,
because one fears that, when [trying to avoid] losing one's life,
one might produce the evil of karmic transgressions,

and also, because one observes that no one
can escape [the clutches of] the king of death
and hence it cannot be avoided through the power
of expedients dependent on wealth or knowledge—

How then could anyone devoted to cultivating good dharmas
still continue to cherish this life?

22. The Bodhisattva's "Supremacy in All Endeavors"

As for "They are supreme in all their endeavors,"[194] if one absolutely must be able to complete whatever endeavor he begins, this is the mark of a superior person. There are five endeavors that, once the bodhisattva has begun them, he absolutely must bring to completion, namely:

First, [the accumulation of] wealth;
Second, giving;
Third, the observance of the moral precepts;
Fourth, the cultivation of meditative concentration;
Fifth, [the cultivation of] the virtues associated with the path.

These are as described below:

One strives diligently to accumulate wealth
and, with utmost sincerity, [uses it] to engage in giving.
In their sequence, he purifies his observance of the moral precepts
and then vigorously strives to acquire the *dhyāna* absorptions.

He implements many different skillful means
for bringing forth liberation through the eightfold path.
This is how, in all the endeavors that one takes up,
one comes to be known as a superior person.

<table>
<tr><td rowspan="2">正體字</td><td>

107b12 ‖ 所作無過咎者。是菩薩所作智者不呵。以
107b13 ‖ 五因緣故。所作無過智者不呵。一作可作
107b14 ‖ 事。二[9]大果利。三不壞法。四次後無過。五
107b15 ‖ 大名聲。如說。
107b16 ‖ 　　先種種籌量　　自作易作事
107b17 ‖ 　　從是事所得　　無量大果利
107b18 ‖ 　　不妨於善法　　作已無惡隨
107b19 ‖ 　　善人所讚歎　　名聞廣流布
107b20 ‖ 　　智者所起業　　名為無過咎
107b21 ‖ 　　[10]可作及易作　自屬於己身
107b22 ‖ 　　無量大功德　　疾得果利益
107b23 ‖ 　　智者如是知　　後無有過咎
107b24 ‖ 　　應加勤精進　　而作如是事
107b25 ‖ 一切種清淨一切勝處來者。以五因緣故
107b26 ‖ 諸勝處一切種清淨。一深心清淨。二迴向清
107b27 ‖ 淨。三自如說行勝處。四令他人行。

</td></tr>
</table>

<table>
<tr><td rowspan="2">简体字</td><td>

所作无过咎者。是菩萨所作智者不呵。以五因缘故。所作无过智者不呵。一作可作事。二大果利。三不坏法。四次后无过。五大名声。如说。
　　先种种筹量　　自作易作事
　　从是事所得　　无量大果利
　　不妨于善法　　作已无恶随
　　善人所赞叹　　名闻广流布
　　智者所起业　　名为无过咎
　　可作及易作　　自属于己身
　　无量大功德　　疾得果利益
　　智者如是知　　后无有过咎
　　应加勤精进　　而作如是事
一切种清净一切胜处来者。以五因缘故诸胜处一切种清净。一深心清净。二回向清净。三自如说行胜处。四令他人行。

</td></tr>
</table>

Chapter 30 — [Distinctions Pertaining to] the Great Vehicle

23. THE BODHISATTVA'S "FREEDOM FROM FAULT IN ALL THE WORKS THEY DO"

Regarding being "free of fault in all the works they do,"[195] whatever endeavors this bodhisattva engages in is of the sort that is not criticized by the wise. There are five reasons that whatever he does is free of fault and is not criticized by the wise, namely:

> First, he engages in works that he is capable of accomplishing;
> Second, they produce a greatly beneficial result;
> Third, they do no damage to the Dharma;
> Fourth, they are free of any subsequently resulting faults;
> Fifth, they result in an immensely fine reputation.

These are as described below:

> He first makes all different sorts of assessments
> regarding matters of his own ability and the ease of accomplishment,
> ensuring that what is gained by this endeavor
> will constitute an immeasurably great resulting benefit,

> that it will not interfere with the good Dharma,
> that, once it has been accomplished, nothing bad will follow from it,
> that it will be of a sort that is praised by good people,
> and that it will cause a fine reputation to spread widely.

> Whichever works are initiated by the wise
> are of a sort that they are free of any fault.
> Issues of feasibility and ease of accomplishment
> are matters for which one is individually responsible.
> Those possessed of measureless great qualities,
> will swiftly bring about a resulting benefit.

> It is in this manner that the wise come to know
> that there will be no subsequent fault arising from this,
> and that they should devote diligent vigor to this task,
> whereupon they then engage in endeavors such as these.

24. THE BODHISATTVA'S "COMPLETE PURITY" & "SUCCESS IN SUPREME BASES"

Regarding "They abide in purity of every kind and come forth through the practice of all the supreme bases [of meritorious qualities],"[196] there are five causal bases for [the bodhisattva's coming forth through] all the supreme bases and for his possessing every kind of purity, namely:

> First, he has resolute intentions that are pure;
> Second, his dedications of merit are pure;
> Third, his own practice of the supreme bases [of meritorious qualities] accords with the way he explains them to others;
> Fourth, he influences others to practice them;

|正體字|

```
         五離諸
107b28 ‖ 勝處相違法所謂妄語慳貪戲調愚癡。如說。
107b29 ‖   菩薩深淨心    遠離於諂曲
107c01 ‖   皆以四勝處    迴向於佛道
107c02 ‖   先自修善法    後令他人行
107c03 ‖   菩薩如是者    四勝處清淨
107c04 ‖ 十善道能令至十力世尊者。如是修習十
107c05 ‖ 善業道。能令人至十力。十力者名為正遍
107c06 ‖ 知。正遍知者則是佛。以[11]五因緣故名世尊。
107c07 ‖ 一斷過去世疑。二斷未來世疑。三斷現[12]在
107c08 ‖ 世疑。四斷過三世法疑。五斷不可說法疑。
107c09 ‖ 如說。
107c10 ‖   無始過去世    通達無有疑
107c11 ‖   無邊未來世    知通達無疑
107c12 ‖   十方無有邊    現在一切世
107c13 ‖   出過於三世    無為微妙法
107c14 ‖   十四不可說    亦通無有疑
107c15 ‖   是故功德藏    諸佛名世尊
```

|简体字|

五离诸胜处相违法所谓妄语悭贪戏调愚痴。如说。

　　菩萨深净心　　远离于谄曲
　　皆以四胜处　　回向于佛道
　　先自修善法　　后令他人行
　　菩萨如是者　　四胜处清净

十善道能令至十力世尊者。如是修习十善业道。能令人至十力。十力者名为正遍知。正遍知者则是佛。以五因缘故名世尊。一断过去世疑。二断未来世疑。三断现在世疑。四断过三世法疑。五断不可说法疑。如说。

　　无始过去世　　通达无有疑
　　无边未来世　　知通达无疑
　　十方无有边　　现在一切世
　　出过于三世　　无为微妙法
　　十四不可说　　亦通无有疑
　　是故功德藏　　诸佛名世尊

Chapter 30 — [Distinctions Pertaining to] the Great Vehicle

Fifth, he abandons all dharmas contrary to the supreme bases [of meritorious qualities], namely false speech, miserliness, covetousness, frivolous restlessness, and delusion.

These are as described below:

> The bodhisattva possesses profound and pure intentions,
> abandons flattery and deviousness,
> always relies upon the four supreme bases,
> and dedicates his merit to the realization of buddhahood.
>
> He first cultivates good dharmas himself
> and thereafter influences others to practice them.
> The bodhisattva who proceeds in this manner
> is one for whom the four supreme bases are pure.

25. How the Ten Courses Enable the Attainment of Buddhahood

As for "The ten courses of good karmic action enable these persons to reach the station of the Bhagavats who possess the ten powers,"[197] if one cultivates the ten courses of good karmic action in this manner, they enable a person to reach that state wherein he is possessed of the ten powers. "The ten powers" refers to the possession of right and universal knowledge. One who acquires right and universal knowledge is then himself a buddha. There are five causal bases for one's being referred to as a "*bhagavat*,"[198] namely:

First, [through his right and universal knowledge], he has severed all doubts with respect to the past;

Second, he has severed all doubts with respect to the future;

Third, he has severed all doubts with respect to the present;

Fourth, he has severed all doubts with respect to dharmas that transcend the three periods of time;

Fifth, he has severed all doubts regarding the ineffable dharmas.

These are as described below:

> With regard to the beginningless past,
> they have an utterly penetrating comprehension free of doubts.
> With regard to the boundless future,
> they know it with a penetrating comprehension free of doubts.
>
> All of the boundless worlds
> throughout the ten directions of the present
> as well as what transcends the three periods of time,
> including the sublime dharmas of the unconditioned
>
> and also the fourteen ineffable dharmas—[199]
> they know those too with a comprehension free of doubts.
> They are therefore treasuries of meritorious qualities,
> the Buddhas, those renowned as the World Honored Ones.

正體字

107c16 ‖ 如是功德成就者十善業道能令菩薩至阿
107c17 ‖ 耨多羅三藐三菩提。是故求佛道者。應
107c18 ‖ 如是修十善[13]業。
107c19 ‖ 十住毘婆沙論卷第十[14]五

简体字

　　如是功德成就者十善业道能令菩萨至阿耨多罗三藐三菩提。是故求佛道者。应如是修十善业。

The ten courses of good karmic action are able to cause bodhisattvas who perfect such meritorious qualities as these to reach *anuttarasamyaksaṃbodhi*. Therefore whoever seeks to attain buddhahood should cultivate the ten courses of good karmic action in this manner.

The End of Chapter Thirty

正體字

| 107c21 ‖ 十住毘婆沙論卷第十[15]六 107c22 ‖
| 107c23 ‖   [*]聖者龍樹造
| 107c24 ‖   [*]後秦龜茲國三藏鳩摩羅什譯
| 107c25 ‖   護戒品第[16]四
| 107c26 ‖ 是菩薩如是行諸善道。
| 107c27 ‖   於善不善道   總相及別相
| 107c28 ‖   各各分別知   有二種果報
| 107c29 ‖ 十善業道總相果報者。若生天上若生人
| 108a01 ‖ 中。別相果報者。離殺生善行。有二種果報。
| 108a02 ‖ 一者長壽。二者少病。離劫盜善行。有二種
| 108a03 ‖ 果報。一者大富。二者獨有財物。離邪婬善
| 108a04 ‖ 行。有二種果報。一者妻婦貞良。二者不為
| 108a05 ‖ 外人所壞。離妄語善行。有二種果報。一者
| 108a06 ‖ 不為人所謗毀。二者不為人所欺誑。離
| 108a07 ‖ 兩舌善行。有二種果報。一者得好眷屬。二
| 108a08 ‖ 者不為人所壞。離惡口善行。有二種果
| 108a09 ‖ 報。一者得聞隨意所樂音聲。二者無有鬪
| 108a10 ‖ 諍。

简体字

十住毗婆沙论卷第十四
护戒品第三十二

是菩萨如是行诸善道。
　于善不善道　　总相及别相
　各各分别知　　有二种果报

十善业道总相果报者。若生天上若生人中。别相果报者。离杀生善行。有二种果报。一者长寿。二者少病。离劫盗善行。有二种果报。一者大富。二者独有财物。离邪淫善行。有二种果报。一者妻妇贞良。二者不为外人所坏。离妄语善行。有二种果报。一者不为人所谤毁。二者不为人所欺诳。离两舌善行。有二种果报。一者得好眷属。二者不为人所坏。离恶口善行。有二种果报。一者得闻随意所乐音声。二者无有斗诤。

Chapter 31
Guarding the Moral Precepts

XI. Chapter 31: Guarding the Moral Precepts

It is in this way that this bodhisattva practices the courses of good karmic action.

A. General and Specific Results of the Ten Courses of Karmic Action

In both good and bad courses of karmic action,
there are general characteristics as well as specific characteristics.
Each of these are to be clearly distinguished and known
as possessing two corresponding types of karmic results.

1. The Ten Courses of Good Karmic Action
    a. General Karmic Results of the Ten Courses of Good Karmic Action

As for the general characteristics of the resulting retributions of the ten courses of good karmic action, these may consist of either rebirth in the heavens or rebirth among humans.

   b. Specific Karmic Results of the Ten Courses of Good Karmic Action

As for the specific characteristics of the resulting retributions, they are as follows:

In the case of the good karmic action of abandoning the killing of beings, there are two resultant karmic retributions: First, long life span. Second, having but little illness.

From the good karmic action of abandoning stealing, there are two resultant karmic retributions: First, one obtains great wealth. Second, one becomes independently wealthy.

From the good karmic action of abandoning sexual misconduct, there are two resultant karmic retributions: First, one's wife will be chaste and good. Second, she cannot be "ruined" by others.[200]

From the good karmic action of abandoning false speech, there are two resultant karmic retributions: First, one will not be slandered by anyone. Second, one will not be cheated or deceived by others.

From the good karmic action of abandoning divisive speech, there are two resultant karmic retributions: First, one will gain a fine following. Second, one's [reputation] will not be ruined by others.

From the good karmic action of abandoning harsh speech, there are two resultant karmic retributions: First, one will hear whichever sounds one delights in hearing. Second, one will not become embroiled in disputes.

正體字

```
108a11 ||   離散亂語善行。有二種果報。一者人信
108a11 ||   受其語。二者所言決定。離貪取善行。有二
108a12 ||   種果報。一者知足。二者少欲。離瞋惱善行。
108a13 ||   有二種果報。一者在所生處常求他好事。
108a14 ||   二者不喜惱害眾生。正見善行。有二種果
108a15 ||   報。一者離諂曲。二者所見清淨。十不善道亦
108a16 ||   如是。總相果報者。上行墮地獄。中行墮畜
108a17 ||   生。不行墮餓鬼。別相果報者。殺生不善行。
108a18 ||   有二種果報。一者短命。二者多病。劫盜不善
108a19 ||   行。有二種果報。一者貧窮。二者[1]失財。邪婬
108a20 ||   不善行。有二種果報。一者得醜惡妻婦。又
108a21 ||   不貞良。二者為他所壞。妄語不善行。有二
108a22 ||   種果報。一者人所謗毀。二者為人欺誑。兩
108a23 ||   舌不善行。有二種果報。一者得惡眷屬。二
108a24 ||   者眷屬可壞。
```

简体字

离散乱语善行。有二种果报。一者人信受其语。二者所言决定。离贪取善行。有二种果报。一者知足。二者少欲。离瞋恼善行。有二种果报。一者在所生处常求他好事。二者不喜恼害众生。正见善行。有二种果报。一者离谄曲。二者所见清净。十不善道亦如是。总相果报者。上行堕地狱。中行堕畜生。不行堕饿鬼。别相果报者。杀生不善行。有二种果报。一者短命。二者多病。劫盗不善行。有二种果报。一者贫穷。二者失财。邪淫不善行。有二种果报。一者得丑恶妻妇。又不贞良。二者为他所坏。妄语不善行。有二种果报。一者人所谤毁。二者为人欺诳。两舌不善行。有二种果报。一者得恶眷属。二者眷属可坏。

Chapter 31 — *Guarding the Moral Precepts*

From the good karmic action of abandoning scattered or inappropriate speech, there are two resultant karmic retributions: First, people will trust and accept whatever one says. Second, whatever one says will be definitely decisive.

From the good karmic action of abandoning covetousness, there are two resultant karmic retributions: First, one will be easily contented. Second, one will have but few wants.

From the good karmic action of abandoning ill will, there are two resultant karmic retributions: First, wherever one is reborn, one will always seek to bring about fine circumstances for others. Second, one will not delight in tormenting or harming other beings.

From the good karmic action of maintaining right views, there are two resultant karmic retributions: First, one will abandon flattery and deviousness. Second, whatever one sees will be pure in character.

2. The Ten Courses of Bad Karmic Action
    a. General Karmic Results of the Ten Courses of Bad Karmic Action

The same principles apply in the matter of the ten courses of bad karmic action. As for the general characteristics of their resulting karmic retributions, if one has engaged in them to a high degree, one falls into the hell realms. If one has engaged in them to a middling degree, one will fall into the animal realms. If one has engaged in them to a lesser[201] degree, then one will to fall into the realms of the hungry ghosts.

b. Specific Karmic Results of the Ten Courses of Bad Karmic Action

As for the specific karmic retributions [associated with the ten courses of bad karmic action], they are as follows:

From the bad karmic action of killing beings, there are two resultant retributions: First, a short life span. Second, much illness.

From the bad karmic action of stealing, there are two resultant karmic retributions: First, poverty. Second, loss of wealth.

From the bad karmic action of sexual misconduct, there are two resultant karmic retributions: First, one will have an ugly and evil wife who is also unchaste. Second, one will be ruined by her.

From the bad karmic action of false speech, there are two resultant karmic retributions: First, one will be slandered by others. Second, one will be cheated and deceived by others.

From the bad karmic action of divisive speech, there are two resultant karmic retributions: First, one will gain a bad following. Second, one will have a following vulnerable to destruction.

正體字

惡口不善行。有二種果報。一
者耳聞惡聲。二者常有鬪諍。散亂語不善
行。有二種果報。一者語不信受。二者言無
本末。貪取不善行。有二種果報。一者心不
知足。二者多欲無厭。瞋惱不善行。有二種
果報。一者惡性。二者喜惱眾生。邪見不善
行。有二種果報。一者其心諂曲。二者墮在
邪見。

　　知已愛樂法　　於法心不動
　　於諸眾生中　　慈悲心轉勝

愛法者。但愛於法更無勝事。此中法者。先
說十善業道。樂法者。但樂於法更無餘事。
於法心不動者。乃至失命終不捨法。菩薩
行如是法。於眾生中慈悲轉勝。初地中雖
有慈悲不及此地。以通達罪福業因緣
故。眾生可愍皆屬於業不得自在。則無瞋
恨憎恚之心。

简体字

恶口不善行。有二种果报。一者耳闻恶声。二者常有斗诤。散乱语不善行。有二种果报。一者语不信受。二者言无本末。贪取不善行。有二种果报。一者心不知足。二者多欲无厌。瞋恼不善行。有二种果报。一者恶性。二者喜恼众生。邪见不善行。有二种果报。一者其心谄曲。二者堕在邪见。

　　知已爱乐法　　于法心不动
　　于诸众生中　　慈悲心转胜

爱法者。但爱于法更无胜事。此中法者。先说十善业道。乐法者。但乐于法更无余事。于法心不动者。乃至失命终不舍法。菩萨行如是法。于众生中慈悲转胜。初地中虽有慈悲不及此地。以通达罪福业因缘故。众生可愍皆属于业不得自在。则无瞋恨憎恚之心。

From the bad karmic action of harsh speech, there are two resultant karmic retributions: First, one will have to listen to sounds that one loathes. Second, one will be forever embroiled in disputes.

From the bad karmic action of scattered or inappropriate speech, there are two resultant karmic retributions: First, one's words will not be trusted and accepted. Second, one's speech will have neither beginning nor end.

From the bad karmic action of covetousness, there are two resultant karmic retributions: First, one's mind will never know contentment. Second, one will have an abundance of insatiable desires.

From the bad karmic action of ill will, there are two resultant karmic retributions: First, one will be bad-natured. Second, one will delight in tormenting other beings.

From the bad karmic action of maintaining wrong views, there are two resultant karmic retributions: First, one's mind will tend toward flattery and deviousness. Second, one will tend to fall into wrong views.

B. The Bodhisattva's Implementation of Moral Virtue on the Path
1. Cherishing the Dharma and Increasing Kindness and Compassion

Having known the Dharma, one cherishes and delights in it
and one's mind becomes unshakable in the Dharma.
When in the midst of beings,
one's mind of kindness and compassion becomes ever greater.

As for "cherishing the Dharma," one cherishes only the Dharma and sees nothing superior to the Dharma. In this context, "Dharma" refers to the ten courses of good karmic action discussed earlier.

As for "delighting in the Dharma," one delights only in the Dharma and in nothing else.

As for "one's mind remains unshakable in the Dharma," the bodhisattva never abandons the Dharma even when threatened with the loss of his life.

As the bodhisattva practices dharmas such as these, when he is in the midst of other beings, his kindness and compassion toward them become ever greater. Although kindness and compassion do exist on the first ground, their quality therein cannot match their quality as they exist on this ground. This is because he now has a penetrating comprehension of the causes and conditions for karmic offenses and karmic merit.

Beings are pitiable, for they are all under the influence of their own karma and are unable to gain independence from it. This being the case, one's mind then remains free of any thoughts affected by hatred

正體字

　　　　如是行者慈悲轉勝。作是念。
108b12 ‖ 　咄哉諸眾生　　深墮於邪見
108b13 ‖ 　我應說正見　　令得入正道
108b14 ‖ 菩薩通達罪福業因緣。於諸眾生深行慈
108b15 ‖ 悲。作是念。眾生可愍不知諸法實相故。多
108b16 ‖ 行妄想生諸邪見。因邪見故起諸煩惱。
108b17 ‖ 因煩惱故而起諸業。起業因緣故輪轉生
108b18 ‖ 死。我先發心求阿耨多羅三藐三菩提。為
108b19 ‖ 度眾生故當說正見。是諸眾生是我應度。
108b20 ‖ 今當為說正見令入真道使得度脫。如
108b21 ‖ 是念已。知諸眾生有種種煩惱。所謂。
108b22 ‖ 　觀所起煩惱　　及諸煩惱垢
108b23 ‖ 　種種黑惡業　　受種種苦惱
108b24 ‖ 　愍念諸眾生　　多有所闕少
108b25 ‖ 　種種觀察已　　是皆如我有
108b26 ‖ 　即時以悲心　　方便發大願
108b27 ‖ 　云何令眾生　　得滅是諸苦
108b28 ‖ 煩惱煩惱垢者。使所攝名為煩惱

简体字

　　　　如是行者慈悲转胜。作是念。
　　咄哉诸众生　　深堕于邪见
　　我应说正见　　令得入正道
　　菩萨通达罪福业因缘。于诸众生深行慈悲。作是念。众生可愍不知诸法实相故。多行妄想生诸邪见。因邪见故起诸烦恼。因烦恼故而起诸业。起业因缘故轮转生死。我先发心求阿耨多罗三藐三菩提。为度众生故当说正见。是诸众生是我应度。今当为说正见令入真道使得度脱。如是念已。知诸众生有种种烦恼。所谓。
　　观所起烦恼　　及诸烦恼垢
　　种种黑恶业　　受种种苦恼
　　愍念诸众生　　多有所阙少
　　种种观察已　　是皆如我有
　　即时以悲心　　方便发大愿
　　云何令众生　　得灭是诸苦
　　烦恼烦恼垢者。使所摄名为烦恼

or anger. For one who practices in this way, kindness and compassion do indeed become ever greater. He reflects in this manner:

2. THE MOTIVATION TO TEACH BEINGS AND CAUSE THEM TO ENTER THE PATH

> Alas! These beings!
> They have fallen so very deeply into wrong views.
> I must explain right views for them
> and thus cause them to gain entry into the path of what is right.

Having gained this penetrating comprehension of the causes and conditions for karmic offenses and karmic merit, the bodhisattva engages in the deep practice of kindness and compassion for all beings, thinking thus:

> Beings are so pitiable. Because they do not know the true character of dharmas, for the most part they engage in false thinking and thus develop all manner of wrong views. It is because of their wrong views that they produce all manner of afflictions, and it is because of their afflictions that then create all sorts of karma. And it is because they produce these karmic causes and conditions that they then turn about in *saṃsāra*'s cycle of births and deaths.
>
> I previously brought forth the resolve to seek *anuttara-samyak-saṃbodhi*. In order to bring about the liberation of beings, I should explain right views for them. I should liberate all of these beings and influence them to enter the true path so that are then caused to attain liberation.

Having reflected thus, one comes to realize that all beings are beset by all manner of afflictions, as described below:

3. THE GENESIS OF A BODHISATTVA'S WISH TO RESCUE BEINGS FROM SUFFERING

> One contemplates the afflictions they have brought forth
> as well as the defilement associated with those afflictions,
> all of the different sorts of black and evil karmic actions they do,
> and all the diverse sorts of suffering and anguish they undergo.

> One bears in mind all of these beings, feeling pity for their plight
> and for the many ways in which they have become so deficient.
> Having taken up all of these different contemplations,
> one realizes, "They are all just as I myself have been."

> One then immediately brings forth the mind of compassion
> and uses the skillful means of bringing forth a great aspiration:
> "Oh, how might I be able to influence these beings
> to succeed in extinguishing all their many sufferings?"

Regarding "afflictions" and "defilement associated with those afflictions," "afflictions" refers to any of the dharmas subsumed by the

正體字

纏所攝名
為垢。使所攝煩惱者。貪瞋[2]慢無明身見邊
見見取戒取邪見疑。是十根本隨三界見諦
思惟所斷分別故名九十八使。非使所攝
者。不信無慚無愧諂曲戲[3]侮堅執懈怠退沒
睡眠[4]佷戾慳嫉憍不忍食不知[5]足。亦以三
界見諦思惟所斷分別故有一百九十六纏
垢。有言人。煩惱在深心垢在淺心。有人言。
諸障蓋名為纏垢。餘皆名煩惱。黑惡業者。
即是[6]七不善業道。及貪取瞋惱邪見相應思。
能生苦報。種種苦惱者。身中種種惡事名為
苦。心中種種惡事名為惱。又今世苦名為
苦。後墮惡道名為惱。

简体字

缠所摄名为垢。使所摄烦恼者。贪瞋慢无明身见边见见取戒取邪见疑。是十根本随三界见谛思惟所断分别故名九十八使。非使所摄者。不信无惭无愧谄曲戏侮坚执懈怠退没睡眠佷戾慳嫉憍不忍食不知足。亦以三界见谛思惟所断分别故有一百九十六缠垢。有言人。烦恼在深心垢在浅心。有人言。诸障盖名为缠垢。余皆名烦恼。黑恶业者。即是七不善业道。及贪取瞋恼邪见相应思。能生苦报。种种苦恼者。身中种种恶事名为苦。心中种种恶事名为恼。

fetters whereas "defilement" refers to [whatever arises from] being "obsessed"[202] [by the afflictions].

[More specifically], those afflictions subsumed by the fetters include greed, hatred, conceit, ignorance, the view of a real self in association with the body [or any of the other four aggregates],[203] extreme views, seizing on views, seizing on unprincipled precepts, wrong views, and doubt. These ten [consisting of three] root and [seven] subsidiary afflictions are distinguished according to their relationship to the three realms of existence and according to whether they are to be severed by directly seeing the [four] truths or whether they are to be severed by meditative cultivation.[204] As a consequence [of these distinctions], there are ninety-eight latent tendencies.[205]

Those not subsumed by the fetters include non-faith, absence of a sense of shame, absence of a dread of blame, flattery, deviousness, restlessness, regretfulness,[206] rigid attachment, indolence, neglectfulness, drowsiness, malice, miserliness, jealousy, arrogance, impatience, and gluttony. These too are distinguished according to their relationship to the three realms of existence and according to whether they are to be severed by directly seeing the [four] truths or whether they are to be severed by meditative cultivation. As a consequence [of these distinctions], there are one hundred and ninety-six obsessive defilements.

There are others who explain "afflictions" as phenomena residing in deep mental dispositions and explain "defilements" as phenomena abiding at a more superficial level of mind.

There are yet others who explain that it is all of the hindrances that constitute "obsessive defilements" whereas all else falls within the sphere of "afflictions."

Regarding "black and evil karmic actions," this refers to those seven courses of karmic action [among the ten courses of bad karmic action] that actually do constitute [physical or verbal] karmic actions together with thought that has come under the influence of covetousness, ill will, or wrong views. These are able to engender painful karmic retributions.

As for "all the different sorts of suffering and anguish," whatsoever bad experiences are undergone by the body correlate with "suffering" whereas whatsoever bad experiences are undergone by the mind correlate with "anguish." Alternatively, one may explain that present-life sufferings are what correlate with "suffering" whereas "anguish" corresponds to later experiences occurring through descent into the wretched destinies.

正體字

```
              多有所少者。或諸
108c12 ||  根支體。或資生所須。或信戒等諸功德不具
108c13 ||  故名為少。餘句易解如偈中所說。不復須
108c14 ||  釋。如是思惟已。[7]眾生甚可愍。墮在於二
108c15 ||  乘。我當為發願令住於大乘。是事如[8]此
108c16 ||  十地經中金剛藏菩薩自說。是菩薩離十不
108c17 ||  善業道。亦令眾生住十善業道。為眾生深
108c18 ||  求勝心好心樂心憐愍心慈悲心利益心守
108c19 ||  護心我所有心大師心攝取心受取心。作是
108c20 ||  念。此諸眾生甚可憐愍。墮種種邪意邪見
108c21 ||  行邪險道。我今應令住在真實正見道中。
108c22 ||  是諸眾生種類不同互相諍競。常懷忿恚瞋
108c23 ||  惱熾盛。然我當令住無上大慈。是[9]諸眾生
108c24 ||  無有厭足。貪求他利邪命自活。我當令
108c25 ||  住清淨身口意業。是諸眾生在貪欲瞋恚愚
108c26 ||  癡因緣中常起種種煩惱結使而不方便求
108c27 ||  欲自出。我當滅其諸苦惱事令住無苦惱
108c28 ||  處。
```

简体字

又今世苦名为苦。后堕恶道名为恼。多有所少者。或诸根支体。或资生所须。或信戒等诸功德不具故名为少。余句易解如偈中所说。不复须释。如是思惟已。众生甚可愍。堕在于二乘。我当为发愿令住于大乘。是事如此十地经中金刚藏菩萨自说。是菩萨离十不善业道。亦令众生住十善业道。为众生深求胜心好心乐心怜愍心慈悲心利益心守护心我所有心大师心摄取心受取心。作是念。此诸众生甚可怜愍。堕种种邪意邪见行邪险道。我今应令住在真实正见道中。是诸众生种类不同互相诤竞。常怀忿恚嗔恼炽盛。然我当令住无上大慈。是诸众生无有厌足。贪求他利邪命自活。我当令住清净身口意业。是诸众生在贪欲嗔恚愚痴因缘中常起种种烦恼结使而不方便求欲自出。我当灭其诸苦恼事令住无苦恼处。

Regarding "the many ways in which they have become so deficient," "deficiencies" refers here to inadequacies in sense faculties, limbs, or physical bodies, in what is essential to sustain life, or in faith, observance of the moral precepts, or other such meritorious qualities.

Because the remaining lines are easy to interpret in accordance with the verse statements, no further explanation is necessary.

Once one has contemplated in this manner, one realizes:

4. The Vow to Cause 2 Vehicles Practitioners to Enter the Mahāyāna

Beings are ever so pitiable.
For those who have fallen into the Two Vehicles,
I shall make a vow for their sakes
to cause them to dwell in the Great Vehicle.[207]

This circumstance accords with this *Ten Grounds Sutra* wherein Vajragarbha Bodhisattva himself said:[208]

> This bodhisattva abandons the ten courses of bad karmic action while also influencing beings to abide in the ten courses of good karmic action. For the sake of these beings, he strives profoundly to gain the supreme mind, the fine mind, the delighting mind, the pitying mind, the kind and compassionate mind, the beneficial mind, the protective mind, the mind that sees other beings as one's own, the mind that acts as a great teacher, the mind that draws in others, and the mind that accepts others. He thinks:
>
> All of these beings are so very pitiable. They have fallen into all different sorts of wrong thought and wrong views, and thus travel along in wrong and hazardous paths. I should now influence them to abide in the true path of right views.
>
> All these different groups of beings engage in mutual disputation and fighting. They always feel anger toward one another as mutual hatred and torment blaze up between them. This being the case, I should influence them to instead abide in the unsurpassably great kindness.
>
> These beings are insatiable, so much so that they covet any advantages enjoyed by others and pursue wrong livelihoods as their means of survival. I should influence them to instead abide in the pure actions of body, speech, and mind.
>
> Abiding among causes and conditions associated with greed, hatred, and delusion, these beings are forever generating all the different sorts of afflictions and fetters while never availing themselves of the means whereby they might seek to escape their plight. I should extinguish their sufferings and anguish and influence them to instead abide in the state that is free of sufferings and anguish.

正體字	108c29 ‖ 是諸眾生為無明所翳入黑闇稠林。不能自出離。智慧明入在諸見險惡道中。我 109a01 ‖ 應救之使得無礙智慧之眼。以是慧眼不 109a02 ‖ 隨他人。於一切法知如實相。是諸眾生墮 109a03 ‖ 在生死長流。欲墮地獄畜生餓鬼阿修羅坑 109a04 ‖ 入邪曲網中。種種煩惱惡草所覆無有導 109a05 ‖ 師不生[1]出心。道言非道非道言道。魔民 109a06 ‖ 怨賊常共隨逐無有善師。隨順魔意遠離 109a07 ‖ 佛法。如是眾生我應令度此諸生死險惡道 109a08 ‖ 得住無畏無衰一切智慧城。是諸眾生為欲 109a09 ‖ 流有流見流無明流所漂種種罪業濤波所 109a10 ‖ 覆沒在愛河。隨生死波浪。為[2]洄澓所轉 109a11 ‖ 不能自出。為欲覺瞋覺惱覺醎水淹爛為 109a12 ‖ 身見羅剎之所執持。入五欲深林為喜染 109a13 ‖ 所著吹。在我慢陸地。甚可憐愍。無洲無 109a14 ‖ 救。於六入空聚落不能動發。無善度者。
简体字	是诸众生为无明所翳入黑闇稠林。不能自出离。智慧明入在诸见险恶道中。我应救之使得无碍智慧之眼。以是慧眼不随他人。于一切法知如实相。是诸众生堕在生死长流。欲堕地狱畜生饿鬼阿修罗坑入邪曲网中。种种烦恼恶草所覆无有导师不生出心。道言非道非道言道。魔民怨贼常共随逐无有善师。随顺魔意远离佛法。如是众生我应令度此诸生死险恶道得住无畏无衰一切智慧城。是诸众生为欲流有流见流无明流所漂种种罪业涛波所覆没在爱河。随生死波浪。为洄澓所转不能自出。为欲觉嗔觉恼觉碱水淹烂为身见罗刹之所执持。入五欲深林为喜染所著吹。在我慢陆地。甚可怜愍。无洲无救。于六入空聚落不能动发。无善度者。

These beings have had their vision obscured by ignorance and thus have wandered into a dense forest of darkness so deeply that they are unable to escape from it by themselves. Having abandoned the light of wisdom, they have strayed into the hazardous and evil path of the various [wrong] views. I should rescue them and cause them then to acquire the eye of unimpeded wisdom. Using this wisdom eye, they will not follow other people, but rather will know all dharmas in accordance with their true character.

These beings have fallen into the long river of births and deaths and are about to descend into the pit of the hell realms, animal realms, hungry ghost realms, and *asura* realms. They are on the verge of falling into the net trap of perversity and deviousness hidden from their view by the weeds of the many different afflictions.

Having no guide, they are not even motivated to escape from their predicament. They claim that the path is not the path and that what is not the path is indeed the path. The minions of Māra, their adversaries, always pursue them. Having no good guide, they obey the ideas of Māra and stray far from the Dharma of the Buddha.

I should cause beings such as these to pass beyond these hazardous and evil roads in the cycle of births and deaths so that they may be able to dwell in the city of all-knowledge that is free of fear and free of decay.

All these beings have become caught and carried along, drifting, in the current of the flood of desire, the flood of existence, the flood of [wrong] views, and the flood of ignorance in which they are pulled under by the great waves of the many different karmic offenses and are submerged in the river of craving. They are swept along by the waves of the cycle of births and deaths, caught in a swirling whirlpool that pulls them around and around in a current from which they cannot escape.

They are drowned and rotted by the salty waves of desirous ideation, hate-filled ideation, and tormenting ideation.[209] They are seized and held by that *rākṣasa* of the view of a real self in association with the body. They enter into the deep woods of the five desires, are seized by the defilements of sensual enjoyments, and are blown about on the high plateau of conceit.

[Beings] are so extremely pitiable. There is no island [of respite] for them, nor do they have any means of rescue. They are stuck in the empty village of the six sense bases from which they are unable to move. There is no one with the skill to take

正體字

109a15 ‖ 如是眾生我今應以大悲牢堅智慧之船
109a16 ‖ 載至諸安隱無怖畏一切智洲。是諸眾生多
109a17 ‖ 苦可愍。閉在生死憂悲苦惱牢獄。多懷貪
109a18 ‖ 恚愛憎墮四顛倒為四大毒蛇所害。為五
109a19 ‖ 陰怨家所殘。喜染詐賊所陷。在六入空聚
109a20 ‖ 受無量苦惱。我應破其生死牢獄令得自
109a21 ‖ 在無礙涅槃安隱快樂。是諸眾生甚可憐愍。
109a22 ‖ 狹劣小心樂於少利。縮沒無有一切智心。
109a23 ‖ 設求出者則樂聲聞辟支佛乘。我應令得
109a24 ‖ 大心使樂佛廣大之法。
109a25 ‖ 　菩薩如是行　　則得持戒力
109a26 ‖ 　善知起善業　　使令得增長
109a27 ‖ 　是則為佛子　　深入離垢地
109a28 ‖ 持戒力者。一心清淨具足十善道。戒則得
109a29 ‖ 修集福德力。能起善業者。善知自生增
109b01 ‖ 長善道。亦令他眾生

简体字

如是众生我今应以大悲牢坚智慧之船载至诸安隐无怖畏一切智洲。是诸众生多苦可愍。闭在生死忧悲苦恼牢狱。多怀贪恚爱憎堕四颠倒为四大毒蛇所害。为五阴怨家所残。喜染诈贼所陷。在六入空聚受无量苦恼。我应破其生死牢狱令得自在无碍涅槃安隐快乐。是诸众生甚可怜愍。狭劣小心乐于少利。缩没无有一切智心。设求出者则乐声闻辟支佛乘。我应令得大心使乐佛广大之法。

　菩萨如是行　　则得持戒力
　善知起善业　　使令得增长
　是则为佛子　　深入离垢地

　持戒力者。一心清净具足十善道。戒则得修集福德力。能起善业者。善知自生增长善道。亦令他众生

them on beyond. I should now transport all such beings in the sturdy and durable ship of the great compassion and wisdom, taking them to the continent of all-knowledge where they shall become safe, secure, and free of fear.

These beings produce such an abundance of suffering that they are indeed pitiable. They are confined within the prison of birth, death, sorrow, lamentation, suffering, and anguish wherein they are much inclined toward greed, anger, craving, and hatred. They fall into the four inverted views, are harmed by the venomous snakes of the four great elements, are tortured by their five-aggregate enemies, are ensnared by the deceptive thief of sensual enjoyments' defilements, and undergo measureless suffering and anguish in the empty village of the six sense bases.

I should demolish their prison of *saṃsāra* and cause them to attain unimpeded sovereign mastery in the security and bliss of nirvāṇa.

These beings are so extremely pitiable. With such narrow, inferior, and petty minds, they have come to delight in paltry sorts of benefit. They have shrunken back from, fallen away from, and become bereft of the resolve to attain all-knowledge. Even when they do seek a means of escape, they then only delight in the vehicles of *śrāvaka* disciples or *pratyekabuddhas*. I should cause them to gain the truly great resolve by influencing them to delight in the vast and magnificent dharmas of a buddha.

[Next, we have]:

5. THE POWER OF THE PRECEPTS AND DEEP ENTRY INTO THE SECOND GROUND

If the bodhisattva carries forth his practice in this manner,
he will gain the power arising from upholding the moral precepts.
Having thoroughly known how to bring forth good karmic actions,
he strives to cause them to increase.
If one proceeds thus, he will thereby become a son of the Buddha
and will deeply enter the Ground of Stainlessness.

Regarding "the power arising from upholding the moral precepts," if one is single-minded in purely fulfilling the moral precepts associated with the ten courses of good karmic action, then he will acquire the power derived from cultivating and accumulating merit.

As for the ability "to bring forth good karmic actions," one knows well how to personally bring forth and increase the courses of good karmic action and also knows how to cause other beings to do so as well.

正體字

```
         深入者。所行轉遠盡
109b02 ‖ 其邊底。佛子者。能隨法行名為佛子。於初
109b03 ‖ 地始生。至二地增長。是菩薩應如是勤行
109b04 ‖ 精進。
109b05 ‖   菩薩若得至    離垢地邊際
109b06 ‖   爾時則得見    百種千種佛
109b07 ‖ 初地中已說。般舟三昧。見現在佛助三昧法。
109b08 ‖ 所謂以三十二相八十種好四十不共法念
109b09 ‖ 佛。於一切法無所貪著。亦說利益三昧。
109b10 ‖ 能成就果報勢力。問曰。若菩薩於初地中
109b11 ‖ 已到其邊能見諸佛。初入第二地。即應見
109b12 ‖ 諸佛。云何言乃至第二地邊乃見諸佛。若爾
109b13 ‖ 者。入第二地初中應失此三昧。至後乃得。
109b14 ‖ 答曰。初入第二地中亦見諸佛亦不退失
109b15 ‖ 是三昧。汝不能善解偈義故作此難。第二
109b16 ‖ 地初中。但見百種佛。乃至其邊得見百種
109b17 ‖ 千種佛。見諸佛已心大歡喜。欲得佛法故。
109b18 ‖ 勤行精進。
```

简体字

深入者。所行转远尽其边底。佛子者。能随法行名为佛子。于初地始生。至二地增长。是菩萨应如是勤行精进。

　　菩萨若得至　　离垢地边际
　　尔时则得见　　百种千种佛

初地中已说。般舟三昧。见现在佛助三昧法。所谓以三十二相八十种好四十不共法念佛。于一切法无所贪着。亦说利益三昧。能成就果报势力。问曰。若菩萨于初地中已到其边能见诸佛。初入第二地。即应见诸佛。云何言乃至第二地边乃见诸佛。若尔者。入第二地初中应失此三昧。至后乃得。答曰。初入第二地中亦见诸佛亦不退失是三昧。汝不能善解偈义故作此难。第二地初中。但见百种佛。乃至其边得见百种千种佛。见诸佛已心大欢喜。欲得佛法故。勤行精进。

Chapter 31 — *Guarding the Moral Precepts*

As for his "deeply entering" [the Ground of Stainlessness], his practices become ever more far-reaching to the point that they exhaust its very limits and depths.

As for the term "son of the Buddha," whosoever is able to carry on his practice in accordance with the Dharma is one who is known as "a son of the Buddha."

From the point of its initial arising on the first ground on through to the second ground in which it increases, this bodhisattva should diligently practice vigor in this manner.

6. REACHING THE 2ND GROUND, THE BODHISATTVA MAY SEE A 1000 BUDDHAS

When the bodhisattva succeeds in reaching
the boundaries of the Ground of Stainlessness,
he will then be able to see
a hundred or a thousand buddhas.

In discussing the first ground, we already explained the *pratyutpanna* samādhi and the dharmas assisting acquisition of the samādhi in which one sees the buddhas of the present era. Specifically, these included using the thirty-two major marks, eighty secondary characteristics, and forty dharmas exclusive to the Buddhas in practicing mindfulness of the Buddha without having any attachment to any dharma. We also discussed the means to enhance the samādhi and enable the complete development of the powers arising from its fruition.

Question: If, by virtue of having already reached the limits of the first ground, a bodhisattva is able to see the Buddhas, then, on entering the second ground, he should then be able to see the Buddhas. Why then do you now state that, only upon reaching the limits of the second ground, does one, then and only then, see the Buddhas? If that is truly the case, then it must be that one loses this samādhi on first entering the second ground and only then regains it later on.

Response: When first entering the second ground, one still sees the Buddhas and still does not fall back from this samādhi. It is only because you have not well understood the intended meaning of the verse that you have posed this challenge.

In the beginning and middle phases of the second ground, one still only sees a hundred buddhas. It is only when one reaches its very limits that one is then able to see from a hundred up to a thousand buddhas. Once one has seen the Buddhas, one's mind is filled with immense joy. It is because of one's zeal to achieve success in the Buddha's Dharma that one then becomes diligent in practicing vigor.

正體字

```
109b19 ||     即能以四事      供養於諸佛
109b20 ||     能於諸佛所      復受十[3]業道
109b21 || 四事者。衣服飲食臥具醫藥。餘義則可知。
109b22 ||     作如是行已      從佛受善道
109b23 ||     至百千萬劫      不毀亦不失
109b24 || 不毀者。不令戒羸弱。或以清淨事名不
109b25 || 毀。都不復行名為[4]失。是菩薩如是。過初
109b26 || 地[5]入第二地已。如說。
109b27 ||     [6]善離慳貪垢      樂行清淨捨
109b28 ||     [*]善離慳貪垢      深愛清淨戒
109b29 || 清淨名但以善心行捨。不雜諸煩惱。深愛
109c01 || 名堅住其中。究竟不捨。此地中慳貪垢。破
109c02 || 戒垢無有遺餘。是故此地名為離垢。菩薩
109c03 || 如是無慳貪破戒心。於四攝法中愛語偏
109c04 || 利。六波羅蜜中戒度偏利。
```

简体字

即能以四事　　供养于诸佛
能于诸佛所　　复受十业道

四事者。衣服饮食卧具医药。余义则可知。

作如是行已　　从佛受善道
至百千万劫　　不毁亦不失

不毁者。不令戒羸弱。或以清净事名不毁。都不复行名为失。是菩萨如是。过初地入第二地已。如说。

善离悭贪垢　　乐行清净舍
善离悭贪垢　　深爱清净戒

清净名但以善心行舍。不杂诸烦恼。深爱名坚住其中。究竟不舍。此地中悭贪垢。破戒垢无有遗余。是故此地名为离垢。菩萨如是无悭贪破戒心。于四摄法中爱语偏利。六波罗蜜中戒度偏利。

7. ONE MAKES OFFERINGS TO THE BUDDHAS & RECEIVES THE 10 COURSES AGAIN

One immediately becomes able to use the four requisites
to make offerings to the Buddhas.
He is then able to receive again the ten courses of karmic action
in the abodes of the Buddhas.

"The four requisites" refers to robes, food and drink, bedding, and medicines. One may deduce for himself the meaning of the rest of the verse.

8. HAVING RECEIVED THEM AGAIN, ONE FOREVER UPHOLDS THE PRECEPTS

Having performed acts such as these,
one receives the courses of good karmic action from the Buddhas
and, even throughout a hundred thousand myriads of kalpas,
one never allows his practice to become damaged or lost.

"Never allowing this practice to become damaged" means that one does not allow one's practice of the moral precepts to become scant or weak. One may also say that it is purity in one's endeavors that defines non-damage. "Loss" refers to complete discontinuance of one's practice.

It is in this manner that this bodhisattva has passed through the first ground and entered the second ground. This matter is as described below:

9. ONE ABANDONS MISERLINESS, PRACTICES GIVING, & DELIGHTS IN PRECEPTS

One thoroughly abandons the defilement of miserliness
and delights in the practice of pure giving.
By thoroughly abandoning the defilement of miserliness,
one gains a deep love of purity in upholding the moral precepts.

"Purity" refers to practicing giving with a mind devoted exclusively to goodness, one that is not mixed with any of the afflictions. "Deep love" [of purity in the moral precepts] refers to abiding so solidly in it that one never relinquishes that practice.

On this ground, there are no further residual traces of the defilement associated with miserliness or the defilement associated with breaking precepts. It is because of this that this ground is referred to as "stainless."

The bodhisattva who in this manner remains free of thoughts inclined toward miserliness or the breaking of moral precepts is especially proficient in the practice within the four means of attraction known as "pleasing words" and is also especially proficient in the practice within the six *pāramitās* referred to as "the perfection of moral virtue."

正體字

利名多行勢力轉
109c05 ‖ 深。問曰。若第二地中。尸羅波羅蜜已得勢
109c06 ‖ 力。今此地中。應解說尸羅波羅蜜分生力淨
109c07 ‖ 差別。答曰。
109c08 ‖ 　略說尸羅度　　有六十五分
109c09 ‖ 　生力淨差別　　處處論中說
109c10 ‖ 尸羅波羅蜜無量無邊。但略說有六十五分。
109c11 ‖ 餘戒生戒力戒淨戒差別。論中先後處處說
109c12 ‖ 相。如寶頂經中和合佛法品中。無盡意菩薩
109c13 ‖ 於佛前說六十五種尸羅波羅蜜分。尸羅名
109c14 ‖ 不惱。一切眾生於他物中無劫盜想不著
109c15 ‖ 外色不誑眾生。眷屬具足故不兩舌。多忍
109c16 ‖ 惡言故無有惡口。常思惟籌量利益語
109c17 ‖ 故無散亂語。喜人樂故心無貪取。忍諸
109c18 ‖ 苦故無有瞋惱。

简体字

利名多行势力转深。问曰。若第二地中。尸罗波罗蜜已得势力。今此地中。应解说尸罗波罗蜜分生力净差别。答曰。
　略说尸罗度　　有六十五分
　生力净差别　　处处论中说
　尸罗波罗蜜无量无边。但略说有六十五分。余戒生戒力戒净戒差别。论中先后处处说相。如宝顶经中和合佛法品中。无尽意菩萨于佛前说六十五种尸罗波罗蜜分。尸罗名不恼。一切众生于他物中无劫盗想不着外色不诳众生。眷属具足故不两舌。多忍恶言故无有恶口。常思惟筹量利益语故无散乱语。喜人乐故心无贪取。忍诸苦故无有嗔恼。

Chapter 31 — *Guarding the Moral Precepts*

"Proficient" refers here to having engaged in extensive practice whereby one's power in that practice has becomes ever more deeply developed.

C. Śīla Pāramitā's Aspects, Arising, Powers, Purification & Distinctions

Question: If on the second ground one has already acquired strength in one's practice of *śīla pāramitā*, the perfection of moral virtue, now, as one discusses this ground, one should explain the aspects, the arising, the powers, the purification, and the distinctions associated with *śīla pāramitā*.

Response:
> In a general discussion of the perfection of *śīla*,
> there are sixty-five aspects.
> As for its arising, powers, purification, and distinctions,
> these are discussed in place after place elsewhere in this treatise.

1. The Sixty-Five Aspects of the Perfection of Moral Virtue

Śīla pāramitā, as a topic of discussion, is measureless and boundless. To speak of it only in general terms, there are sixty-five aspects. As for the other subtopics, in particular the arising of moral virtue, the powers of moral virtue, the purification of moral virtue, and distinctions to be made with regard to moral virtue, these factors are discussed in detail both earlier and later on in this treatise.

[This interpretive approach] is in accordance with the "The Harmonious Dharma of the Buddha" chapter of *The Jeweled Summit Sutra* wherein, in the presence of the Buddha, Akṣayamati Bodhisattva spoke of the sixty-five aspects of *śīla pāramitā*, stating that *śīla* refers to the following:[210]

> It is not [physically] tormenting any being;[211]
> It is not having any thought of stealing the possessions of others;
> It is not being attached to any outward visual forms;
> It is not deceiving beings;
> Through ensuring the complete unity of retinues, it is not engaging in divisive speech;
> Through being well able to patiently endure harsh words [from others], it is being free of harsh speech;
> Through always contemplating and evaluating whether one's speech is beneficial, it is being free of scattered or inappropriate speech;
> Through delighting in the continued happiness of others, it is being free of covetousness;
> Through patiently enduring every sort of suffering, it is being free of ill will;

正體字	109c19 ‖ 　　　　不稱譽[7]餘師故名為正 109c19 ‖ 見。信淨心故信佛。知法真實故信法。樂 109c20 ‖ 尊重恭敬賢聖眾故信僧。念佛以五體投 109c21 ‖ 地供養禮敬。乃至小戒深心怖畏故。戒不羸 109c22 ‖ 弱。不依餘乘故不毀戒。離邪行故戒不 109c23 ‖ 缺損。不起惡煩惱故名不雜戒。畢竟常 109c24 ‖ 樂增長善法故名不濁戒。隨意行故名自 109c25 ‖ 在戒。不為智者所呵故名為聖所讚戒。常 109c26 ‖ 在念安慧故名為易行戒。一切無過故名 109c27 ‖ 不可呵戒。守護諸根故名為善護戒。諸佛 109c28 ‖ 所念故名為名聞戒。如法物中知量取故 109c29 ‖ 名為少欲戒。斷慳貪故名知足戒。身心遠 110a01 ‖ 離故名遠離戒。離眾鬧語故名阿蘭若戒。
简体字	不称誉余师故名为正见。信净心故信佛。知法真实故信法。乐尊重恭敬贤圣众故信僧。念佛以五体投地供养礼敬。乃至小戒深心怖畏故。戒不羸弱。不依余乘故不毁戒。离邪行故戒不缺损。不起恶烦恼故名不杂戒。毕竟常乐增长善法故名不浊戒。随意行故名自在戒。不为智者所呵故名为圣所赞戒。常在念安慧故名为易行戒。一切无过故名不可呵戒。守护诸根故名为善护戒。诸佛所念故名为名闻戒。如法物中知量取故名为少欲戒。断悭贪故名知足戒。身心远离故名远离戒。离众闹语故名阿兰若戒。

Through not praising teachers of other paths, it is right view;
Through faith in purification of the mind, it is faith in the Buddha;[212]
Through knowing that the Dharma is genuine, it is faith in the Dharma;
Through delighting in venerating and revering the assemblies of worthies and *āryas*, it is faith in the Sangha;
Through full prostrations, the making of offerings, and other expressions of reverential respect, it is mindfulness of the Buddha;
Through having mental dispositions by which one is fearful of transgressing against even the most minor moral precept, it is moral virtue that does not become diminished or weak;
Through not relying on any of the other vehicles, it is moral virtue that is undamaged;
Through abandoning erroneous practice, it is moral virtue that does not become deficient;
Through the non-arising of evil afflictions, it is moral virtue that does not become admixed [with impure aspects];
Through the most ultimate and constant delight in increasing and strengthening good dharmas, it is moral virtue that remains unsullied;
Through practicing in accordance with one's wishes, it is moral virtue characterized by sovereign mastery;
Through not doing anything criticized by the wise, it is moral virtue that is praised by the Āryas;
Through always abiding in mindfulness guided by stable wisdom, it is easily practiced moral virtue;
Through the complete absence of karmic transgressions in all that one does, it is irreproachable moral virtue;
Through guarding the sense faculties, it is skillfully guarded moral virtue;
Through being one of whom all buddhas are mindful, it is illustrious moral virtue;
Through receiving in proper measure things obtained in accordance with the Dharma,[213] it is moral virtue characterized by but few wants;
Through the severance of covetousness, it is moral virtue that knows contentment;
Through renunciation in both body and mind, it is moral virtue characterized by renunciation;
Through abandoning the many sorts of boisterous speech, it is moral virtue appropriate to a forest hermitage;

正體字

110a02 ‖ 不視他面望有所得故名為具足聖種戒。
110a03 ‖ 屬善根故名細行頭陀戒。生人天中故
110a04 ‖ 名隨說行戒。救一切眾生故名為慈戒。忍
110a05 ‖ 一切苦故名為悲戒。心不退沒故名為喜
110a06 ‖ 戒。離憎愛故名為捨戒。降伏心故名為
110a07 ‖ 自見過戒。護彼心故名為不錯戒。善護戒
110a08 ‖ 故名為善攝戒。成熟眾生故名為布施戒。
110a09 ‖ 無所願故名忍辱戒。不懈退故名精進
110a10 ‖ 戒。集助禪法故名為禪戒。多聞善根無厭
110a11 ‖ 足故名為智慧戒。從多聞得智慧故名
110a12 ‖ 為求多聞戒。集助七覺法故名親近善知
110a13 ‖ 識戒。捨邪道故名離惡知識戒。觀無常
110a14 ‖ 故名不貪身戒。勤集善根故名不信命戒。

简体字

不视他面望有所得故名为具足圣种戒。属善根故名细行头陀戒。生人天中故名随说行戒。救一切众生故名为慈戒。忍一切苦故名为悲戒。心不退没故名为喜戒。离憎爱故名为舍戒。降伏心故名为自见过戒。护彼心故名为不错戒。善护戒故名为善摄戒。成熟众生故名为布施戒。无所愿故名忍辱戒。不懈退故名精进戒。集助禅法故名为禅戒。多闻善根无厌足故名为智慧戒。从多闻得智慧故名为求多闻戒。集助七觉法故名亲近善知识戒。舍邪道故名离恶知识戒。观无常故名不贪身戒。勤集善根故名不信命戒。

Through having no need to look to anyone else in the hope of obtaining anything, it is moral virtue perfectly complete in the lineage bases of the Āryas;

Through being one who possesses roots of goodness, it is moral virtue characterized by refined practice of the *dhūta* austerities;

Through [its efficacy in bringing about] rebirth among humans and devas, it is moral virtue characterized by practice consistent with the manner in which it has been taught;

Through devotion to rescuing all beings, it is moral virtue characterized by kindness;[214]

Through enduring every sort of suffering, it is moral virtue characterized by compassion;

Through resolve that does not retreat and sink away, it is moral virtue characterized by joy;

Through abandoning both hatred and affection, it is moral virtue characterized by equanimity;

Through subduing the mind, it is moral virtue marked by seeing one's own faults;

Through protecting the minds of others, it is unerring moral virtue;

Through skillfully guarding the precepts, it is moral virtue that is well restrained.[215]

Through devotion to the ripening of beings, it is moral virtue characterized by giving;

Through having nothing for which one wishes, it is moral virtue characterized by patience;

Through not desisting and withdrawing from endeavors, it is moral virtue characterized by vigor;

Through accumulating the dharmas assisting *dhyāna*, it is moral virtue characterized by *dhyāna*;

Through insatiable pursuit of abundant learning and roots of goodness, it is moral virtue characterized by wisdom;

Through gaining wisdom from abundant learning, it is moral virtue that seeks abundant learning;

Through accumulating the dharmas that assist the seven limbs of enlightenment, it is moral virtue that draws close to good spiritual guides;

Through relinquishing erroneous paths, it is moral virtue characterized by the abandonment of bad spiritual guides;

Through contemplating impermanence, it is moral virtue characterized by non-attachment to the body;

Through diligently accumulating roots of goodness, it is moral virtue characterized by not trusting [in the durability of] one's life;

正體字

110a15 ‖ 深心清淨故名不悔戒。行清淨故名不假
110a16 ‖ 偽戒。深心無垢故名無熱戒。善起業故名
110a17 ‖ 無憂戒。不自高故。名無慢戒。離染欲故
110a18 ‖ 名不戲調戒。心質直故名不[1]自高戒。心調
110a19 ‖ 和故名有羞戒。惡心不發故名調善戒。滅
110a20 ‖ 諸煩惱故名為寂滅戒。如說行故名為隨
110a21 ‖ 所教戒。行四攝法故名教化眾生戒。不失
110a22 ‖ 自法故名為護法戒。本來清淨故名一切
110a23 ‖ 願滿戒。迴向無上道故名至佛法戒。等心
110a24 ‖ 一切眾生故名得佛三昧戒。大德舍利弗是
110a25 ‖ 六十五分。諸菩薩清淨戒。則為無盡。生戒者
110a26 ‖ 處處說。略說有八種生戒。四從身生。

简体字

深心清净故名不悔戒。行清净故名不假伪戒。深心无垢故名无热戒。善起业故名无忧戒。不自高故。名无慢戒。离染欲故名不戏调戒。心质直故名不自高戒。心调和故名有羞戒。恶心不发故名调善戒。灭诸烦恼故名为寂灭戒。如说行故名为随所教戒。行四摄法故名教化众生戒。不失自法故名为护法戒。本来清净故名一切愿满戒。回向无上道故名至佛法戒。等心一切众生故名得佛三昧戒。大德舍利弗是六十五分。诸菩萨清净戒。则为无尽。生戒者处处说。略说有八种生戒。四从身生。

Chapter 31 — *Guarding the Moral Precepts*

Through purity in one's resolute intentions, it is moral virtue characterized by freedom from regrets;

Through purity in one's actions, it is moral virtue that is not false;

Through resolute intentions that are free of defilement, it is moral virtue that is free of heat;

Through skillfulness in initiating karmic actions, it is moral virtue that is free of sorrow;

Through not elevating oneself [above others], it is moral virtue that is free of conceit;

Through abandoning defiled desires, it is moral virtue that does not indulge frivolous restlessness;

Through maintaining a straightforward mind, it is moral virtue that does not elevate oneself [above others];

Through maintaining a well-regulated mind, it is moral virtue possessed of a sense of shame;

Through not bringing forth evil thoughts, it is moral virtue trained in goodness;

Through extinguishing all afflictions, it is moral virtue characterized by quiescence;

Through practicing in accordance with [the original] explanations, it is moral virtue that follows what has been taught;

Through practicing the dharmas constituting the four means of attraction, it is moral virtue characterized by the transformative teaching of beings;

Through not erring in [the practice of] one's own dharma, it is moral virtue that protects the Dharma;

Through [maintaining one's] fundamental purity, it is moral virtue in which all vows are fulfilled;

Through dedicating [one's merit] to realization of the unsurpassed path, it is moral virtue that leads to acquiring the dharmas of the Buddha;

Through maintaining a mind of uniformly equal regard for all beings, it is moral virtue that leads to acquiring the Buddha's samādhis.

Venerable Śāriputra, as for these sixty-five aspects [of the perfection of *śīla*], [were one to exhaustively list them], the aspects of all bodhisattva's pure moral virtue would be endlessly numerous.

2. The Arising of the Moral Precepts

Now, as for the arising of the moral precepts, this is a matter discussed in place after place [elsewhere in this treatise].

Briefly stated, there are eight categories involved in the arising of the moral precepts, four arising from association with the body and

正體字

　　　　四從
110a27 ‖ 口生。從身生者。離奪命離[2]惱苦眾生離
110a28 ‖ 劫盜離邪婬。從口生者。離妄語兩舌惡口
110a29 ‖ 散亂語。是名八。是八種戒從受生。是受法。
110b01 ‖ 若以身若以口若以心受和合為二十四
110b02 ‖ 教。他受亦二十四。隨喜受亦二十四。修習行
110b03 ‖ 時亦二十四。合九十六。皆是欲界繫。從是晝
110b04 ‖ 夜生。何以故。初受心已滅。是第二心晝夜常
110b05 ‖ 生。用福德亦如是。所以者何。初布施心滅
110b06 ‖ 已。從第二心後。用時[3]當生。是名善身業。
110b07 ‖ 有十善業道所攝。有不攝。欲界所繫如是。
110b08 ‖ 色界繫有二種。一從身生[4]二從口生。從身
110b09 ‖ 生者。離十不善道。所不攝罪。

简体字

四从口生。从身生者。离夺命离恼苦众生离劫盗离邪淫。从口生者。离妄语两舌恶口散乱语。是名八。是八种戒从受生。是受法。若以身若以口若以心受和合为二十四教。他受亦二十四。随喜受亦二十四。修习行时亦二十四。合九十六。皆是欲界系。从是昼夜生。何以故。初受心已灭。是第二心昼夜常生。用福德亦如是。所以者何。初布施心灭已。从第二心后。用时当生。是名善身业。有十善业道所摄。有不摄。欲界所系如是。色界系有二种。一从身生二从口生。从身生者。离十不善道。所不摄罪。

Chapter 31 — *Guarding the Moral Precepts*

four arising from association with speech. Those arising from association with the body are the abandonment of taking life, the abandonment of inflicting torment and suffering on beings, the abandonment of stealing, and the abandonment of sexual misconduct. Those associated with the mouth are the abandonment of lying, divisive speech, harsh speech, and scattered or inappropriate speech. These are the eight.

These eight categories of moral precepts arise by taking them on [as ongoing obligations]. These dharmas associated with taking them on, when separately distinguished in terms of taking them on physically, taking them on verbally, and taking them on mentally result in a combined total of twenty-four subcategories. When further considered in terms of the twenty-four associated with [the injunction against] instructing others [to commit any of these transgressions], the twenty-four associated with [the injunction against] rejoicing in [transgressions directly committed by others], and the twenty-four associated with [the injunction against] carrying them out oneself, this results in a total of ninety-six, all of which occur in connection with the desire realm.

These [moral precepts] arise commencing with this very day and night. How is this the case? After the initial mental moment of taking on [the obligation imposed by the moral precept] has expired, throughout the entire day and night, during the second [and all subsequent] mental moments thereafter [the force of that moral precept] constantly arises.

One's use of the associated merit is also just the same. How is this the case? After the initial mind-moment associated with an act of giving expires, beginning with the second mind-moment, as one uses [this merit], it is constantly produced.[216] This is the nature of the process as it occurs in association with good physical karmic actions.

There are those [instances of the arising of the moral precepts] that are subsumed within the ten courses of good karmic action and those that are not subsumed therein. This is the situation as it occurs in connection with the desire realm.

As for those [instances of the arising of moral precepts] that occur in connection with the form realm, there are two kinds: first, those [moral precepts] arising from association with the body, and second, those [moral precepts] arising from association with speech. As for those arising from association with the body, this refers to the abandonment of karmic offenses not subsumed among the ten courses of bad karmic action.[217]

正體字

從口生者。
110b10 ‖ 離散亂語。是戒以身受口受心受。二三為
110b11 ‖ 六。教他亦六。隨喜亦六。習行時亦六。四六
110b12 ‖ 二十四。先說九十六合為百二十。如是從
110b13 ‖ 行生戒。復有證道時生戒。退道時生戒。初
110b14 ‖ 生時生戒。以事廣故今但略說。戒力者。
110b15 ‖ 隨波羅蜜增長。戒轉得力。隨所得地戒亦
110b16 ‖ 堅固得力。戒淨者。不毀壞缺減等如先說。
110b17 ‖ 復次戒淨不淨相。[5]七梵行法中說。如經說。
110b18 ‖ 以七種婬欲名戒不淨。一者雖斷婬欲而
110b19 ‖ [6]以染心受女人洗浴按摩。

简体字

从口生者。离散乱语。是戒以身受口受心受。二三为六。教他亦六。随喜亦六。习行时亦六。四六二十四。先说九十六合为百二十。如是从行生戒。复有证道时生戒。退道时生戒。初生时生戒。以事广故今但略说。戒力者。随波罗蜜增长。戒转得力。随所得地戒亦坚固得力。戒净者。不毁坏缺减等如先说。复次戒净不净相。七梵行法中说。如经说。以七种淫欲名戒不净。一者虽断淫欲而以染心受女人洗浴按摩。

In the case of those [moral precepts] arising from association with speech, this refers to the abandonment of scattered or inappropriate speech.[218] Taking on this moral precept involves taking it on physically, taking it on verbally, and taking it on mentally. Taking all of these categories into account, this amounts to two times three, a subtotal of six.

Similarly, there are thus also another six associated with the injunction against instructing others [to carry out any given karmic transgression], another six associated with [the injunction against] rejoicing [in transgressions committed by others], and another six associated with [the injunction against] carrying out [any given transgression] oneself. This yields in total four times six, for a net total of twenty-four. When these are added to the previously cited ninety-six, this brings the grand total to one hundred and twenty.

In much the same fashion, moral precepts also arise in association with the character of one's actions. Thus there is also an arising of moral precepts at the time one attains the realization of the path and there is also an arising of moral precepts at the time one retreats from the path. So too, there may also be an arising of moral precepts in association with one's first taking on birth.

Because this subject [of the arising of moral precepts] is so very expansive in its scope, we now only present this condensed explanation.

3. The Powers of the Moral Precepts

As for the powers associated with the moral precepts, as growth occurs in the corresponding *pāramitā*, one's practice of moral virtue becomes ever stronger. Also, in direct correlation with whichever of the grounds one has entered, there will also be a corresponding enhancement in the solidity of one's practice of moral virtue and hence also in the powers associated with it.

4. The Purification of the Moral Precepts

As for the purification of the moral precepts, not damaging or destroying moral precepts, not allowing deficiencies or diminishment in their practice, and so forth—these are all just as previously explained.

Additionally, the characteristic features of purity or impurity in one's practice of moral virtue correspond to their treatment in the dharma of the seven types of brahmacarya.[219] As related in the sutras, it is by virtue of seven manifestations of sexual desire[220] that the moral virtue [of one who practices *brahmacarya*] is impure, namely:

> First, although one may indeed have cut off sexual relations, with a defiled mind, one might nonetheless still accept either bathing or massage performed by a woman;

正體字

```
           二以染心聞
110b20 ‖ 女人香共語戲笑。三以染心目共相視。四
110b21 ‖ 雖有障礙。以染心聞女人音聲。五先共女
110b22 ‖ 人語笑。後雖相離憶念不捨。六自限爾所
110b23 ‖ 時斷婬欲然後當作。七期生天上受天
110b24 ‖ 女樂及後身富樂。是故斷婬欲是名不淨。
110b25 ‖ 離此七事名戒清淨。戒差別者。有二種。一
110b26 ‖ 有漏。二無漏。三種欲界繫色界繫不繫。四種
110b27 ‖ 正命所攝二種正語正業。正命所不攝亦二
110b28 ‖ 種正語正業。五種凡夫戒菩薩戒聲聞戒辟
110b29 ‖ 支佛戒無上佛戒。六種欲界正命所攝身口。
110c01 ‖ 一。正命所不攝二。
```

简体字

二以染心闻女人香共语戏笑。三以染心目共相视。四虽有障碍。以染心闻女人音声。五先共女人语笑。后虽相离忆念不舍。六自限尔所时断淫欲然后当作。七期生天上受天女乐及后身富乐。是故断淫欲是名不净。离此七事名戒清净。戒差别者。有二种。一有漏。二无漏。三种欲界系色界系不系。四种正命所摄二种正语正业。正命所不摄亦二种正语正业。五种凡夫戒菩萨戒声闻戒辟支佛戒无上佛戒。六种欲界正命所摄身口。一。正命所不摄二。

Second, with a defiled mind, one might smell the perfume of a woman, engage in conversation with her, or participate in mutual joking with her;

Third, with a defiled mind, one might engage in mutual gazing with her;

Fourth, even though there might be a physical barrier separating one from a woman, with a defiled mind, he might still listen to her voice;

Fifth, one might have earlier talked and joked with a woman and later, even though separate from her, he might still recall that experience, being unable to let it go;

Sixth, one has restricted oneself from sexual relations [only] for a particular period of time, after which one will indulge in it again later on;[221]

Seventh, someone might temporarily cut off all sexual relations, doing so hoping that he will thereby be reborn in the heavens and enjoy sexual pleasures there together with celestial maidens while also gaining wealth and pleasure in future lives.

Therefore, [in cases such as these, even though] one has cut off sexual relations, these are still instances of impurity [in moral virtue]. Apart from these seven types of situations, [the practice of *brahmacarya*] does constitute purity in the practice of moral virtue.

5. DISTINCTIONS IN THE MORAL PRECEPTS

Regarding distinctions in moral virtue, a twofold distinction consists of, first, that characterized by the presence of the contaminants, and second, that characterized by the absence of the contaminants.

A threefold distinction consists of that connected with the desire realm, that connected with the form realm, and that with no connections [anywhere in the three realms].

A fourfold distinction consists of two types of right speech and right karmic action subsumed within right livelihood together with a different two types of right speech and right karmic action not subsumed within right livelihood.

A fivefold distinction consists of the common person's moral virtue, a bodhisattva's moral virtue, a *śrāvaka* disciple's moral virtue, a *pratyekabuddha's* moral virtue, and the unsurpassable moral virtue of a buddha.

A sixfold distinction consists of:

First, desire realm [moral virtue] of body and speech subsumed within right livelihood;

Second, [desire realm moral virtue of body and speech] not subsumable within right livelihood;

正體字

　　　色界繫正命所攝身口
業三。正命所不攝四。無漏正命所攝身口
五。正命所不攝六。七種七善業道。八種如
先說。身四種口四種。九種七欲界繫七善業
道二種如先說。十種道戒三種。對治戒三
種。但戒三種。是九種。無漏戒有漏戒為十。
如是等種種分別差別。問曰。聲聞乘中。說
身業口業名為尸羅。此二善業名好。二不
善業名惡。是善身口業名尸羅。此論中即以
此為尸羅。為更有尸羅。答曰。
　　不但身口業　　名之為尸羅
　　修親近樂行　　亦名為尸羅
此三事一義。所謂修習親近樂行。

简体字

色界系正命所摄身口业三。正命所不摄四。无漏正命所摄身口五。正命所不摄六。七种七善业道。八种如先说。身四种口四种。九种七欲界系七善业道二种如先说。十种道戒三种。对治戒三种。但戒三种。是九种。无漏戒有漏戒为十。如是等种种分别差别。问曰。声闻乘中。说身业口业名为尸罗。此二善业名好。二不善业名恶。是善身口业名尸罗。此论中即以此为尸罗。为更有尸罗。答曰。
　　不但身口业　　名之为尸罗
　　修亲近乐行　　亦名为尸罗
此三事一义。所谓修习亲近乐行。

Third, form realm [moral virtue] of body and speech subsumed within right livelihood;
Fourth, [form realm moral virtue of body and speech] not subsumable within right livelihood;
Fifth, [moral virtue] of body and speech that is free of the contaminants and which is subsumed within right livelihood;
Sixth, [moral virtue of body and speech that is free of the contaminants] but not subsumed within right livelihood.

A seven-fold distinction consists of the seven [physical and verbal] courses of good karmic action.

An eightfold distinction consists of the previously-mentioned eight [types of arising of moral virtue] consisting of those four associated with the body and those four associated with speech.

A ninefold distinction consists of the seven [physical and verbal] courses of good karmic action in addition to the twofold distinction [according to presence or absence of the contaminants] cited earlier.

A tenfold distinction consists of three types of moral virtue associated with the path, three types of antidotal moral virtue, and three types of simple moral virtue. These nine types are all free of the contaminants. With the addition of moral virtue involving the contaminants, the total number of types comes to ten.

So it is that we have all these many different categories of moral virtue.

D. The Essential Constituents of Śīla (Moral Virtue)
1. Q: Does Moral Virtue Consist Only of Good Actions of Body & Speech?

Question: The Śrāvaka Disciple Vehicle claims that karmic actions of body and speech are the bases of *śīla*, moral virtue. Where these two consist of good karmic actions, they are deemed to be good. Where these two consist of bad karmic actions, they are deemed to be bad. Thus they hold that good karmic actions of body and speech constitute [the practice of] *śīla*. Does this treatise take these to constitute *śīla* or does it instead take *śīla* to involve some other additional factor?

2. A: No, There Are Other Factors Integral to Moral Virtue

Response:
It is not merely karmic actions of body and speech
that constitute *śīla*.
Cultivation, close personal engagement, and delight in practice
also constitute what is meant by *śīla*.

These three factors each contribute to the meaning of this single concept: cultivation, close personal engagement, and delight in practice.

正體字

問曰。若以
修習親近樂行。名為尸羅者。一切法皆應
名尸羅。何以故。常修習親近樂行故汝今
應說最勝修習尸羅答曰。
　　若無我我所　　遠離諸戲論
　　一切無所得　　是名上尸羅
若不知內外法實相。即因尸羅生憍慢貪
著[7]故。開諸罪門。是故若於內法不見有
我。於外法中不得我所。知內外法畢竟空
無所得。亦於畢竟空不取相戲論是名最
勝尸羅。何以故。如是尸羅中尚無心錯。何
況身口。是故諸佛菩薩。第一能行尸羅者。
於一切法無所得。名為上尸羅。如迦葉經
中[8]說。佛告迦葉。尸羅名無我無非我無作
無所作。無作者。無行無不行。無名無色無
相無無相。非善非非善。非寂滅非非寂
滅。

简体字

问曰。若以修习亲近乐行。名为尸罗者。一切法皆应名尸罗。何以故。常修习亲近乐行故汝今应说最胜修习尸罗答曰。
　　若无我我所　　远离诸戏论
　　一切无所得　　是名上尸罗
若不知内外法实相。即因尸罗生憍慢贪着故。开诸罪门。是故若于内法不见有我。于外法中不得我所。知内外法毕竟空无所得。亦于毕竟空不取相戏论是名最胜尸罗。何以故。如是尸罗中尚无心错。何况身口。是故诸佛菩萨。第一能行尸罗者。于一切法无所得。名为上尸罗。如迦葉经中说。佛告迦葉。尸罗名无我无非我无作无所作。无作者。无行无不行。无名无色无相无无相。非善非非善。非寂灭非非寂灭。

Chapter 31 — *Guarding the Moral Precepts*

3. THE SUPREME CULTIVATION OF MORAL VIRTUE
   a. Q: PLEASE EXPLAIN THE BASES OF SUPREME CULTIVATION OF MORAL VIRTUE

Question: If one takes cultivation, close personal engagement, and delight in practice as [also] determining what is meant by *śīla*, then all dharmas could be considered as associated with *śīla*. How so? Because they may all be associated with constant cultivation, close personal engagement, and delight in practice. Therefore, you should explain what constitutes the supreme cultivation of *śīla*.

   b. A: NO "I," NO "MINE," NO ELABORATION, AND INAPPREHENSIBILITY

Response:
If it is based on the nonexistence of "I" and "mine,"
the renunciation of conceptual elaboration,
and realizes nothing at all is apprehensible as [inherently existent],
then this is what is meant by *śīla*.

If one does not know the true character of all inward and outward dharmas, then, because one may generate arrogance and clinging attachment due to one's attachment to *śīla*, one may thereby open the door to all sorts of karmic offenses.

Therefore, if one does not perceive any self among the inward dharmas, does not perceive anything belonging to a self among the outward dharmas, if one realizes that all these inward and outward dharmas are ultimately empty and devoid of anything that is apprehensible, and if one also refrains from conceptual elaboration seizing on any characteristics in what is ultimately empty, then this is what constitutes the supreme [practice of] *śīla*.

And why is this so? In *śīla* such as this, there is not even the slightest mental error, how much the less could there be any [error in the actions] of either body or speech? Therefore, the Buddhas and the Bodhisattvas are those who are foremost in their ability to practice *śīla*, for they do not apprehend any [inherent existence] in any dharma. This is what constitutes the supreme practice of *śīla*. As related in the *Kāśyapa Sutra*, the Buddha told Kāśyapa:[222]

   c. SCRIPTURAL DESCRIPTIONS OF SUPREME CULTIVATION OF MORAL VIRTUE

Śīla refers to the nonexistence of self, to the nonexistence of nonself, to the nonexistence of doing, to the nonexistence of anything that is done, to the nonexistence of a doer, to the nonexistence of practice, to the nonexistence of non-practice, to the nonexistence of name, to the nonexistence of form, to the nonexistence of characteristics, and to the nonexistence of the absence of characteristics. There is neither goodness nor non-goodness. There is neither quiescent cessation nor nonexistence of quiescent cessation. There is no grasping and

正體字	111a01 ‖ 非取非捨。無眾生無眾生因緣。無身 111a01 ‖ 無口無心。無世間無世間法不依世間。 111a02 ‖ 不以尸羅自高。不以尸羅下人不以尸 111a03 ‖ 羅起增上慢。不以尸羅分別此彼。迦葉。 111a04 ‖ 是名諸賢聖尸羅。離於三界無漏無繫。如 111a05 ‖ 無盡意菩薩尸羅品中。語舍利弗。尸羅名不 111a06 ‖ 分別是眾生不說是我。不說是壽者命者。 111a07 ‖ 不說是人。不說是養育者。不說是色陰受 111a08 ‖ 想行識陰。不說是地種水火風種。尸羅名 111a09 ‖ 不分別是眼相不分別是色相不分別是 111a10 ‖ 耳相聲相鼻相香相舌相味相身相觸相意相 111a11 ‖ 法相。尸羅名不分別是身是口是心。尸羅 111a12 ‖ 名攝心故是一心相。選擇諸法故是慧相。 111a13 ‖ 尸羅名到空至無相際不雜三界。無作無 111a14 ‖ 起無生忍。尸羅名不從先際來不至後際 111a15 ‖ 亦不住中際。尸羅名不住。心意識不與念 111a16 ‖ 和合。
简体字	非取非舍。无众生无众生因缘。无身无口无心。无世间无世间法不依世间。不以尸罗自高。不以尸罗下人不以尸罗起增上慢。不以尸罗分别此彼。迦叶。是名诸贤圣尸罗。离于三界无漏无系。如无尽意菩萨尸罗品中。语舍利弗。尸罗名不分别是众生不说是我。不说是寿者命者。不说是人。不说是养育者。不说是色阴受想行识阴。不说是地种水火风种。尸罗名不分别是眼相不分别是色相不分别是耳相声相鼻相香相舌相味相身相触相意相法相。尸罗名不分别是身是口是心。尸罗名摄心故是一心相。选择诸法故是慧相。尸罗名到空至无相际不杂三界。无作无起无生忍。尸罗名不从先际来不至后际亦不住中际。尸罗名不住。心意识不与念和合。

no relinquishing. There are no beings and no causes and conditions for the existence of any being. There is no body, no speech, and no mind, no world, no worldly dharmas, no reliance on the world. There is no elevation of oneself by virtue of one's *śīla*, no belittling of others because of [their absence of] *śīla*, no development of overweening pride because of one's *śīla*, and no distinguishing between this one and that one because of *śīla*.

Kāśyapa, this is what constitutes the *śīla* of all worthies and *āryas*, the *śīla* that has gone beyond the three realms, that is free of all contaminants, and that retains no connections [anywhere within the three realms].

This also accords with Akṣayamati Bodhisattva's statement to Śāriputra in the chapter on *śīla*:[223]

Śīla refers to not making any discriminating assertion claiming the existence of any being. One does not claim that any self exists, does not claim that anyone possessed of a soul or anyone possessed of a life exists. One does not claim that there is any person, does not claim that there is anyone who has been raised up, does not claim that there is any form aggregate or any feeling, perception, formative-factor, or consciousness aggregate. One does not claim that there exists any earth element or any water, fire, or wind element;

Śīla refers to not discriminating the existence of any eye characteristic, to not discriminating the existence of any visual form characteristic, to not discriminating the existence of any ear characteristic, any sound characteristic, any nose characteristic, any smell characteristic, any tongue characteristic, any flavor characteristic, any body characteristic, any characteristic of tangible objects, any mind characteristic, or any characteristic of dharmas as objects of mind;

Śīla refers to not discriminating the existence of body, speech, or mind;

Because *śīla* involves maintaining a focused mind, it is therefore characterized by single-mindedness;

Because it involves skillful selection among dharmas, it is therefore characterized by wisdom;

Śīla refers to arriving at emptiness, to reaching the ultimate limit of signlessness that does not involve any admixture with the three realms of existence, and to wishlessness, non-arising, and the unproduced dharmas patience;

Śīla refers to not coming forth from the past, not going forth to the future, and not abiding between them, either;

Śīla refers to not dwelling in the conjunction of mind faculty, mind consciousness, and thoughts [as objects of mind];

正體字	尸羅名不依欲界不依色界不依無 111a17 ‖ 色界。尸羅名離貪塵除瞋垢滅無明闇。非 111a18 ‖ 常非斷不違眾緣生相。尸羅名離我心捨 111a19 ‖ 我所心不住身見。尸羅名不貪著名相不 111a20 ‖ 與名色和合。尸羅名不為結使所使。不 111a21 ‖ 為諸纏所覆。不住障礙疑悔中。尸羅名 111a22 ‖ 貪不善根所不住過瞋不善根斷[1]癡不善 111a23 ‖ 根。尸羅名無急無熱[2]猗心快樂。尸羅名不 111a24 ‖ 斷諸佛種故不破法身。不分別法性故不 111a25 ‖ 斷法種。無為相故不斷僧種。舍利弗。是 111a26 ‖ 名諸菩薩最勝無上尸羅。如是尸羅則不可 111a27 ‖ 盡唯除諸佛尸羅皆有盡也所謂。 111a28 ‖ 　從凡夫尸羅　　後至辟支佛 111a29 ‖ 　是皆有盡相　　菩薩則無盡 111b01 ‖ 從凡夫來所有尸羅雖久受果報終歸於 111b02 ‖ 盡。諸阿羅漢辟支佛所有尸羅皆亦有盡。菩 111b03 ‖ 薩尸羅無我無我所
简体字	尸罗名不依欲界不依色界不依无色界。尸罗名离贪尘除瞋垢灭无明闇。非常非断不违众缘生相。尸罗名离我心舍我所心不住身见。尸罗名不贪著名相不与名色和合。尸罗名不为结使所使。不为诸缠所覆。不住障碍疑悔中。尸罗名贪不善根所不住过瞋不善根断痴不善根。尸罗名无急无热猗心快乐。尸罗名不断诸佛种故不破法身。不分别法性故不断法种。无为相故不断僧种。舍利弗。是名诸菩萨最胜无上尸罗。如是尸罗则不可尽唯除诸佛尸罗皆有尽也所谓。 　从凡夫尸罗　　后至辟支佛 　是皆有尽相　　菩萨则无尽 　从凡夫来所有尸罗虽久受果报终归于尽。诸阿罗汉辟支佛所有尸罗皆亦有尽。菩萨尸罗无我无我所

Chapter 31 — Guarding the Moral Precepts

Śīla refers to not relying on the desire realm, to not relying on the form realm, and to not relying on the formless realm;

Śīla refers to abandoning the dust of greed, to ridding oneself of the defilement of hatred, to extinguishing the darkness of ignorance, to not falling into either eternalism or annihilationism, and to not contradicting production as characterized by [the conjunction of] multiple conditions;

Śīla refers to abandoning the conception of a self, to relinquishing the conception of anything belonging to a self, and to not dwelling in the view of a real self in association with the body;

Śīla refers to not being attached to designations and characteristics being incompatible with name-and-form;[224]

Śīla refers to not being under the direction of any of the fetters;

[*Śīla* refers to] not being overpowered by any of the obsessions;

[*Śīla* refers to] not abiding in any of the hindering doubts or regrets;

Śīla refers to not abiding in roots of bad action associated with greed, to transcending roots of bad action associated with hatred, and to severing roots of bad action associated with delusion;

Śīla refers to the happiness of the delighted mind free of anxiety and free of mental fever;

Śīla refers to not destroying the Dharma body, this through not severing the lineage of the Buddhas, to not severing the lineage of the Dharma, this through not making discriminations regarding the nature of dharmas, and to not severing the lineage of the Sangha, this through being characterized by [cultivation of] the unconditioned.[225]

Śāriputra, this is what is meant by the supreme and unsurpassed *śīla* of bodhisattvas. *Śīla* of this sort is inexhaustible. With the sole additional exception of the Buddhas, *śīla* [as practiced by all others] is in every case exhaustible.

This is as stated herein:

d. THE INEXHAUSTIBILITY OF THE BODHISATTVAS' MORAL VIRTUE

Beginning with the *śīla* of the common person
and ending with that practiced by a *pratyekabuddha*,
all of these are characterized by exhaustibility.
It is only that of bodhisattvas that is inexhaustible.

Even though all of the *śīla* practice coming forth from the common person results in their long-enduring enjoyment of its karmic fruits, it is all finally completely exhausted. Even all *śīla* ever practiced by all arhats and *pratyekabuddhas* is finally exhausted as well.

However, because the bodhisattva's practice of *śīla* is based on the realization of the nonexistence of a self or anything belonging to a

離一切所得滅諸戲
論。是故無盡。如無盡意菩薩尸羅品中說。
諸凡夫尸羅隨生處盡故。尸羅則盡。外道五
通退轉時盡故。尸羅則盡。人以十善業道盡
故。尸羅則盡。欲界諸天福德盡故。尸羅則盡。
色界諸天四禪四無量盡故。尸羅則盡。無色
界諸天隨定生處盡故。尸羅則盡。諸學無學
人入涅槃盡故。尸羅則盡。諸辟支佛無大
悲故。尸羅則盡。大德舍利弗。但諸菩薩尸羅
無有盡。何以故。從菩薩尸羅出諸尸羅差
別因無盡故果亦無盡。菩薩尸羅無盡故。如
來尸羅亦無盡。是故諸大人尸羅名為無盡。
問曰。汝解麁尸羅時。說六十五種尸羅。聲
聞中有八種尸羅。四種從身生。四種從口
生。如是事者何得不相違。答曰。不相違
也。何以故。

雖非尸羅體　　益故名為分

离一切所得灭诸戏论。是故无尽。如无尽意菩萨尸罗品中说。诸凡夫尸罗随生处尽故。尸罗则尽。外道五通退转时尽故。尸罗则尽。人以十善业道尽故。尸罗则尽。欲界诸天福德尽故。尸罗则尽。色界诸天四禅四无量尽故。尸罗则尽。无色界诸天随定生处尽故。尸罗则尽。诸学无学人入涅槃尽故。尸罗则尽。诸辟支佛无大悲故。尸罗则尽。大德舍利弗。但诸菩萨尸罗无有尽。何以故。从菩萨尸罗出诸尸罗差别因无尽故果亦无尽。菩萨尸罗无尽故。如来尸罗亦无尽。是故诸大人尸罗名为无尽。问曰。汝解粗尸罗时。说六十五种尸罗。声闻中有八种尸罗。四种从身生。四种从口生。如是事者何得不相违。答曰。不相违也。何以故。

虽非尸罗体　　益故名为分

self, on the abandonment of the idea that any dharma can be apprehended at all, and on the extinguishing of all conceptual elaboration, it is therefore utterly inexhaustible. This is as described by Akṣayamati Bodhisattva in the chapter on *śīla*:[226]

> Because [the karmic fruits of] the *śīla* practiced by common people come to an end in accordance with the stations of rebirth into which they are reborn, [the karmic fruits of] their *śīla* become exhausted. Because the five spiritual powers acquired by non-Buddhist practitioners come to an end when they regress, [the karmic fruits of] their *śīla* become exhausted. Because [the karmic fruits of] the ten courses of good karmic action as practiced by humans are exhaustible, [the karmic fruits of] their *śīla* become exhausted
>
> Because the merit of the devas in the desire realm is exhaustible, [the karmic fruits of] their *śīla* become exhausted. Because the four *dhyānas* and the four immeasurable minds as practiced by devas in the form realm are exhaustible, [the karmic fruits of] their *śīla* become exhausted. Because the stations into which the devas of the formless realm may be reborn in accordance with their meditative absorptions are exhaustible, [the karmic fruits of] their *śīla* become exhausted.
>
> Because learners and those beyond learning [in the Śrāvaka Disciple Vehicle] come to an end with their entry into nirvāṇa, [the karmic fruits of] their *śīla* are exhaustible. Because the *pratyekabuddhas* do not possess the great compassion, [the karmic fruits of] their *śīla* are exhaustible.
>
> Venerable Śāriputra, only the *śīla* of bodhisattvas is inexhaustible. Why? It is from the bodhisattva's practice of *śīla* that there emerge all the different manifestations of *śīla*. Because those karmic causes are inexhaustible, the associated karmic fruits are also inexhaustible. Because the *śīla* of bodhisattvas is inexhaustible, the *śīla* of the Tathāgatas is also inexhaustible. As a consequence, the *śīla* as practiced by all these great men is inexhaustible.

4. A CLARIFICATION REGARDING ASPECTS VERSUS ESSENCE OF MORAL VIRTUE

Question: When you explained the more general aspects of *śīla*, you spoke of sixty-five different aspects of *śīla* [*pāramitā*] and stated that, among *śrāvaka* disciples, there are eight kinds of *śīla*, four arising in association with the body and four arising in association with speech. How is there no contradiction between these [two different ways of enumerating the types of *śīla*]?

Response: They are not mutually contradictory. How is this so?

Although [those aspects] are not the very essence of *śīla*,
because they are beneficial, they are referred to as its aspects.

正體字

111b20 ||　　八種身口業　　　即是尸羅體
111b21 || 雖六十五種分非尸羅體而利益身口八種
111b22 || 麁尸羅故名尸羅分。凡能有所利益皆名
111b23 || 為分。如象馬扇蓋名為王分。是故禪定智
111b24 || 慧等雖非尸羅體以利益尸羅故。亦名尸
111b25 || 羅分。

简体字

　　八种身口业　　　即是尸罗体
　　虽六十五种分非尸罗体而利益身口八种粗尸罗故名尸罗分。凡能有所利益皆名为分。如象马扇盖名为王分。是故禅定智慧等虽非尸罗体以利益尸罗故。亦名尸罗分。

As for those eight kinds of physical and verbal karmic actions, those do constitute the essence of *śīla*.

Although those sixty-five aspects do not constitute the very essence of *śīla*, because they are nonetheless beneficial to those eight relatively coarse categories of physical and verbal *śīla*, they are therefore referred to as aspects of *śīla*. In general, whatever is able to be of benefit [to this practice] is regarded as an aspect [of *śīla*]. This is analogous to the custom of referring to all the [monarch's] elephants, horses, feather fans, and canopies as aspects of kingship. Consequently, although the *dhyāna* absorptions, wisdom, and so forth are not themselves the very essence of *śīla*, because they are beneficial to the practice of *śīla*, they too are regarded as aspects of *śīla*.

The End of Chapter Thirty-One

正體字

111b26 ‖　　　解頭陀品第[3]五
111b27 ‖ 菩薩如是行尸羅法。
111b28 ‖　　見十利應著　　二六種衣法
111b29 ‖　　又以見十利　　盡形應乞食
111c01 ‖ 比丘欲具足行持戒品。應著二六種衣。以
111c02 ‖ 見十利故。何等十。一以慚愧故。二障寒
111c03 ‖ 熱蚊虻毒虫故。三以表示沙門儀法故。四
111c04 ‖ 一切天人見法衣恭敬尊貴如塔寺故。五
111c05 ‖ 以厭離心著染衣非為貪好故。六以隨
111c06 ‖ 順寂滅非為熾然煩惱故。七著法衣有惡
111c07 ‖ 易見故。八著法衣更不須餘物莊嚴故。九
111c08 ‖ 著法衣隨順修八聖道故。十我當精進行
111c09 ‖ 道不以染污心於須臾間著壞色衣。以
111c10 ‖ 見是十利故。應著二種衣。一者居士衣。二
111c11 ‖ 者糞掃衣。

简体字

解头陀品第三十三之一

菩萨如是行尸罗法。
　　见十利应着　　二六种衣法
　　又以见十利　　尽形应乞食

比丘欲具足行持戒品。应着二六种衣。以见十利故。何等十。一以惭愧故。二障寒热蚊虻毒虫故。三以表示沙门仪法故。四一切天人见法衣恭敬尊贵如塔寺故。五以厌离心着染衣非为贪好故。六以随顺寂灭非为炽然烦恼故。七着法衣有恶易见故。八着法衣更不须余物庄严故。九着法衣随顺修八圣道故。十我当精进行道不以染污心于须臾间着坏色衣。以见是十利故。应着二种衣。一者居士衣。二者粪扫衣。

Chapter 32
An Explanation of the Dhūta Austerities

XII. Chapter 32: An Explanation of the Dhūta Austerities
  A. Having Seen 10 Benefits, Wear Correct Robes and Go on Alms Round

The bodhisattva practices the dharma of *śīla* in this way:[227]

> Having observed its ten benefits, one should wear
> the two and six types of robes in accordance with that dharma.
> Additionally, due to having observed its ten benefits,
> one should obtain food on the alms round for one's entire life.

Wishing to completely fulfill the practice of upholding the various categories of moral precepts and having observed that there are ten associated benefits from doing so, one should take up the practice of wearing the two types and the six types of robes. What are those ten benefits? They are:

  1. The Ten Benefits of the Appropriate Robes

First, because this assists a sense of shame and a dread of blame;
Second, because this allows one to protect oneself from cold, heat, mosquitoes, horseflies, and poisonous insects;
Third, because this displays the proper deportment of a *śramaṇa*;
Fourth, because, whenever devas or humans lay eyes on the Dharma robes, they are moved to respect and veneration comparable to what they would feel when coming upon a stupa or temple;
Fifth, because one wears the dyed robes with the mind of renunciation and not out of some desire to wear what is considered fine;
Sixth, because one wears the robes to accord with the ideal of quiescence and not to be ablaze with the fire of afflictions.
Seventh, because when one wears the Dharma robes, if there is something bad in one's character, this is easy for others to observe.
Eighth, because when one wears the Dharma robes, one requires no additional adornments;
Ninth, because in wearing the Dharma robes, one acts in accordance with the eightfold path of the Āryas;
Tenth, because I should be vigorous in practice of the path, I should not wear the *kāṣāya* robes for even a moment during which I am beset with defiled thoughts.

Having observed these ten benefits, one should wear the two types of robes: First, robes contributed by a householder. Second, cast-off robes.

正體字

```
          六種者。一劫[4]貝。二芻摩。三憍[5]絺
111c12 ║  耶。四氀衣。五赤麻衣。六白麻衣。見有十利
111c13 ║  盡形乞食者。一所用活命自屬不[6]屬他。
111c14 ║  二眾生施我食者令住三寶然後當食。三
111c15 ║  若有施我食者當生悲心我當勤行精進
111c16 ║  令善住布施作已乃食。四隨順佛教行故。
111c17 ║  五易滿易養。六行破憍慢法。七無見頂善
111c18 ║  根。八見我乞食餘有修善法者亦當效
111c19 ║  我。九不與男[7]女大小有諸因緣事。十次
111c20 ║  第乞食故。於眾生中生平等心。即種助一
111c21 ║  切種智。
111c22 ║     佛雖聽請食     欲以自利己
111c23 ║     亦利他人故     則不受請食
111c24 ║  自利者。能具諸波羅蜜。利他者教化眾生
111c25 ║  令住
```

简体字

六种者。一劫贝。二刍摩。三憍絺耶。四氀衣。五赤麻衣。六白麻衣。见有十利尽形乞食者。一所用活命自属不属他。二众生施我食者令住三宝然后当食。三若有施我食者当生悲心我当勤行精进令善住布施作已乃食。四随顺佛教行故。五易满易养。六行破憍慢法。七无见顶善根。八见我乞食余有修善法者亦当效我。九不与男女大小有诸因缘事。十次第乞食故。于众生中生平等心。即种助一切种智。

　　佛虽听请食　　欲以自利己
　　亦利他人故　　则不受请食

　　自利者。能具诸波罗蜜。利他者教化众生令住

As for the six types of robes, they are: First, *kārpāsa* (cotton) cloth robes. Second, *kṣaumā* (linen) cloth robes. Third, *kauśeya* (silk) cloth robes. Fourth, animal hair robes. Fifth, red hemp robes. Sixth, white hemp robes.

2. The Ten Benefits of Obtaining One's Food from the Alms Round

As for, "having observed its ten benefits, one should obtain food on the alms round for one's entire life," [those ten benefits are]:

First, that what I obtain [on the alms round] is able to sustain my life is my own responsibility and no one else's;[228]

Second, [having reflected], "May those beings who provide me with food be caused to find refuge in the Three Jewels," one may then go ahead and eat;

Third, [one reflects], "Whenever someone provides me with food, I should bring forth a thought of compassion for them and resolve to be diligent in practicing vigor so they may abide well in their practice of giving." Having reflected thus, one may then eat;

Fourth, this is a practice that accords with the instructions of the Buddha;

Fifth, one is easily satisfied and easily nourished through this practice.

Sixth, one practices a dharma that crushes potential arrogance;

Seventh, this practice plants roots of goodness for gaining the invisible summit mark [of a buddha's body];

Eighth, by observing the practice of obtaining food on the alms round, others engaged in the cultivation of good dharmas will emulate my practice;

Ninth, through this practice one refrains from forming close ties with particular men or women, whether old or young;

Tenth, by practicing the strictly sequential method of obtaining food on the alms round, one develops a mind of uniformly equal regard for all beings that assists the acquisition of the knowledge of all modes.

B. Dwelling in a Forest Hermitage

1. To Derive the Benefits of Dhūta Practice, Do Not Accept Invitations

Although the Buddha did permit accepting invitations for meals,
if one wishes to provide for one's own benefit
while also benefiting other people,
one should not accept invitations for meals.

"One's own benefit" refers here to the ability to perfect [the cultivation of] all the *pāramitās*. "Benefiting others" refers here to teaching beings in such a way that one induces them to abide in [accordance with] the

正體字	三寶。行者如是自利利他。 111c26 ‖　　見有十利故　　常不捨空閑 111c27 ‖　　問疾及聽法　　教化乃至寺 111c28 ‖　受阿練若處比丘。雖增長種種功德。略說 111c29 ‖　見十利故。盡形不應捨。何等為十。一自 112a01 ‖　在來去。二無我無我所。三隨意所住無有 112a02 ‖　障礙。四心轉樂習阿練若住處。五住處少欲 112a03 ‖　少事。六不惜身命。為具足功德故。七遠 112a04 ‖　離眾鬧語故。八雖行功德不求恩報。九 112a05 ‖　隨順禪定易得一心。十於空處住易生 112a06 ‖　無障礙想。問訊病等來至寺者。 112a07 ‖　　若有因緣事　　來在塔寺住 112a08 ‖　　於一切事中　　不捨空閑想 112a09 ‖　比丘雖受盡形阿練若法。有因緣事至則 112a10 ‖　入塔寺。
简体字	三宝。行者如是自利利他。 　　见有十利故　　常不舍空闲 　　问疾及听法　　教化乃至寺 　受阿练若处比丘。虽增长种种功德。略说见十利故。尽形不应舍。何等为十。一自在来去。二无我无我所。三随意所住无有障碍。四心转乐习阿练若住处。五住处少欲少事。六不惜身命。为具足功德故。七远离众闹语故。八虽行功德不求恩报。九随顺禅定易得一心。十于空处住易生无障碍想。问讯病等来至寺者。 　　若有因缘事　　来在塔寺住 　　于一切事中　　不舍空闲想 　比丘虽受尽形阿练若法。有因缘事至则入塔寺。

Chapter 32 — *An Explanation of the Dhūta Austerities*

Three Jewels. A practitioner who acts accordingly will benefit himself while also benefiting others.

2. Having Observed Ten Benefits, Remain in Solitude with 3 Exceptions

Because one has observed its ten benefits,
one never abandons residing in a solitary wilderness dwelling.
In order to visit and console the sick, to listen to Dharma,
or to provide teachings, one may then go to a temple.

For the bhikshu who has taken up the practice of dwelling in a forest hermitage, although it may increase many different sorts of meritorious qualities, generally speaking, it is due to seeing ten benefits from this that, for the rest of his life, he should never abandon this practice. What are the ten benefits? They are as follows:

3. The Ten Benefits of Dwelling in Solitude in Forest Hermitage

First, one retains complete freedom to come and go at will;
Second, one thus easily does away with conceptions of "I" and "mine";
Third, there is nothing to impede one's dwelling wherever one wishes;
Fourth, one's mind increasingly delights in forest hermitage practice;
Fifth, one's dwelling place conduces to but few wants and few responsibilities;
Sixth, for the sake of perfecting the meritorious qualities, one should give up any selfish cherishing for his own body or life;[229]
Seventh, one departs far from the boisterous chatter of the crowds;
Eighth, even though one's practice is [devoted to perfecting] the meritorious qualities, one seeks no kindness in return;
Ninth, it becomes easy to achieve single-mindedness in accordance with one's cultivation of *dhyāna* concentration;
Tenth, through abiding in a solitary wilderness location, one easily develops unimpeded reflections.[230]

4. When Leaving, One Should Maintain the Perception of Emptiness

As for coming to the temple to visit and console the sick or for the other above-mentioned reasons:

If there are situations where, for particular reasons,
one comes and abides at the stupa or temple,
Still, in every such situation,
one never abandons one's perception of emptiness and serenity.

Although a bhikshu may have taken on the dharma of lifetime forest hermitage dwelling, if situations emerge involving particular causes and conditions, he may then go and enter the stupa or temple, for the

正體字	佛法有通有塞。非如外道阿練 112a11 ‖ 若。名常樂空閑靜處。於一切法不捨空 112a12 ‖ 想。以一切法體究竟皆空故。問曰。有何因 112a13 ‖ 緣故來至塔寺。答曰。一供給病人。二為[1]病 112a14 ‖ 求醫藥具。三為病者求看病人。四為病 112a15 ‖ 者說法。五為餘比丘說法。六聽法教化。 112a16 ‖ 七為供養恭敬大德者。八為供給聖眾。九 112a17 ‖ 為讀誦深經。十教他令[2]讀深經。有如是 112a18 ‖ 等諸因來至塔寺。 112a19 ‖ 　精進行諸覺　　隨阿練若法 112a20 ‖ 　比丘已住於　　阿練若處者 112a21 ‖ 　常應精勤生　　種種諸善法 112a22 ‖ 　大膽心無我　　滅除諸怖畏 112a23 ‖ 阿練若精進者。若比丘斷貪。不惜身命利 112a24 ‖ 養故。晝夜常勤精進如救頭然。
简体字	佛法有通有塞。非如外道阿练若。名常乐空闲静处。于一切法不舍空想。以一切法体究竟皆空故。问曰。有何因缘故来至塔寺。答曰。一供给病人。二为病求医药具。三为病者求看病人。四为病者说法。五为余比丘说法。六听法教化。七为供养恭敬大德者。八为供给圣众。九为读诵深经。十教他令读深经。有如是等诸因来至塔寺。 　　精进行诸觉　　随阿练若法 　　比丘已住于　　阿练若处者 　　常应精勤生　　种种诸善法 　　大胆心无我　　灭除诸怖畏 　阿练若精进者。若比丘断贪。不惜身命利养故。昼夜常勤精进如救头然。

Chapter 32 — An Explanation of the Dhūta Austerities

Dharma of the Buddha has both exceptions and restrictions in such cases. In this respect, it is not like the non-Buddhist approaches to forest hermitage dwelling. [This practice] is defined by always delighting in abiding in an empty and serenely quiet place. Hence one never relinquishes the perception of all dharmas as empty. This is because the very essence of all dharmas is that they are all ultimately empty [of any inherent existence of their own].

5. Ten Reasons a Forest Dweller Might Come to a Temple or Stupa

Question: What are the reasons for which one might come to the stupa or temple?
Response:

First, to provide for the care of the sick;
Second, to seek medical supplies to treat one's own sickness;
Third, for one who is sick to search for a physician to treat his illness;
Fourth, to teach the Dharma to the sick;
Fifth, to teach the Dharma to the other bhikshus;
Sixth, to listen to teachings on Dharma;
Seventh, in order to pay respects and make offerings to greatly virtuous monastics;
Eighth, in order to provide for the needs of the Ārya Sangha;
Ninth, to study and recite profound scriptures;
Tenth, to instruct others in the study of profound scriptures.

There are reasons such as these that justify coming to the stupa or temple.

6. The Forest Dweller's Vigorous Cultivation of Right Dharma

One is vigorous in cultivating the various types of thought
as one accords with the dharma of the forest hermitage.
The bhikshu who has been residing
in a forest hermitage abode

should always be vigorous and diligent in bringing forth
the many different good dharmas,
in great courageousness in one's resolve to realize nonself,
and in extinguishing every sort of fear.

Regarding the application of vigor in a forest hermitage, this is exemplified by the bhikshu who, because he has cut off covetousness and does not cherish his body, life, or offerings, always strives with diligence and vigor both day and night as, for his entire life,[231] he accords with forest hermitage practice, doing so with the same urgency one would feel in putting out a fire in one's own turban.

正體字

[3] 身依隨

112a25 ‖ 阿練若。覺者所謂出覺不瞋覺不惱覺等諸
112a26 ‖ 善覺。復次念佛是正遍知者。眾生中尊。佛法
112a27 ‖ 是善說。弟子眾隨順正行。復次隨順空隨
112a28 ‖ 順無相隨順無願諸覺名隨阿練若覺。復
112a29 ‖ 次隨順四勝處。隨順六波羅蜜諸覺。是名
112b01 ‖ 隨順阿練若覺。復次如佛為郁伽長者說
112b02 ‖ 在家出家菩薩行。若出家菩薩受阿練若法。
112b03 ‖ 應如是思惟。我何故住阿練若處。我非但
112b04 ‖ 住阿練若處故名為沙門。而阿練若處。多
112b05 ‖ 有眾生。多惡不善。不護諸根不精進不
112b06 ‖ 修習善法者。如麞鹿猿猴眾鳥惡[4]賊旃陀
112b07 ‖ 羅等不名為比丘。我今為何事故住阿練
112b08 ‖ 若處。應成辦其事。長者何等為事。一謂念
112b09 ‖ 不散亂。二得諸陀羅尼。三行慈心。四行悲
112b10 ‖ 心。五自在住五神通。

简体字

身依随阿练若。觉者所谓出觉不嗔觉不恼觉等诸善觉。复次念佛是正遍知者。众生中尊。佛法是善说。弟子众随顺正行。复次随顺空随顺无相随顺无愿诸觉名随阿练若觉。复次随顺四胜处。随顺六波罗蜜诸觉。是名随顺阿练若觉。复次如佛为郁伽长者说在家出家菩萨行。若出家菩萨受阿练若法。应如是思惟。我何故住阿练若处。我非但住阿练若处故名为沙门。而阿练若处。多有众生。多恶不善。不护诸根不精进不修习善法者。如獐鹿猿猴众鸟恶贼旃陀罗等不名为比丘。我今为何事故住阿练若处。应成办其事。长者何等为事。一谓念不散乱。二得诸陀罗尼。三行慈心。四行悲心。五自在住五神通。

Chapter 32 — An Explanation of the Dhūta Austerities   1175

As for "[cultivating the various types of] thought," this refers to the thought of renunciation, the thought of non-ill will, and the thought of nonharming as well as to the other types of wholesome thought.[232]

Then again, this also refers to:

Cultivating mindfulness of the Buddha as the possessor of right and universal knowledge and as the most revered among all beings;
Cultivating mindfulness of the Buddha's Dharma as well spoken;
Cultivating mindfulness of his Sangha of disciples as according with right practice [of the path].

Furthermore, cultivating thought appropriate to dwelling in a forest hermitage refers as well to cultivating all of the various contemplative ideation that accords with emptiness, that accords with signlessness, and that accords with wishlessness.

Additionally, this refers to contemplative thought accordant with the four supreme bases [for the development of meritorious qualities] and concordant with the six *pāramitās*.

These are the various sorts of thought that are accordant with the dharma for abiding in a forest hermitage.

Then again, this is similar to what the Buddha told Ugra, the Elder, when explaining the bodhisattva path practices of both laity and monastics:[233]

7. SCRIPTURAL CITATION ON THE CORRECT PURPOSES OF A FOREST DWELLER

If a monastic bodhisattva takes on the dharma of forest hermitage practice, he should reflect in this manner:

"Why am I choosing to abide in a forest hermitage setting? It is not solely because I abide in a forest hermitage setting that I qualify as a *śramaṇa*, for there are many sorts of beings who abide in a forest hermitage setting. Mostly inclined toward evil and not toward goodness, they do not guard the sense faculties, do not cultivate with vigor, and do not cultivate the good dharmas. Take for example the musk deer, monkeys, the many sorts of birds, evil bandits, *caṇḍālas*, and other such people, none of whom are bhikshus. So, for what purpose am I choosing to abide in a forest hermitage setting?"

One must indeed accomplish one's purpose. Elder, what sorts of things constitute one's purpose? [They include the following]:

1) So that one's thoughts will not be scattered;
2) To acquire [consummate practice of] the *dhāraṇīs*;
3) To cultivate the mind of kindness;
4) To cultivate the mind of compassion;
5) To abide with sovereign mastery in the five types of spiritual superknowledges;

正體字	六具足六波羅蜜。七 112b11 ∥ 不捨一切智心。八修習方便智。九攝取眾 112b12 ∥ 生。十成就眾生。十一不捨四攝法。十二常 112b13 ∥ 念六思念。十三為多聞故不捨精進。十四 112b14 ∥ 正觀擇諸法。十五應正解脫。十六知得果。 112b15 ∥ 十七住於正位。十八守護佛法。十九信業 112b16 ∥ 果報故名正見。二十離一切憶想分別思 112b17 ∥ 惟故名正思惟。二十一隨眾生所信樂為 112b18 ∥ 說法故名為正語。二十二滅諸業故起業 112b19 ∥ 名為正業。二十三破煩惱氣故名為正命。 112b20 ∥ 二十四得無上道故名正精進。二十五觀 112b21 ∥ 不虛妄法故名正念二十六得一切智慧 112b22 ∥ 故名正定。二十七於空不怖。二十八於無 112b23 ∥ 相不畏。二十九於無願不沒。三十故以智 112b24 ∥ 受身。三十一依義不依語。三十二依智不 112b25 ∥ 依識。三十三依了義經不依不了義經。三 112b26 ∥ 十四依法不依人。長者如是等名為出家 112b27 ∥ 菩薩比丘。利益事應生。
简体字	六具足六波罗蜜。七不舍一切智心。八修习方便智。九摄取众生。十成就众生。十一不舍四摄法。十二常念六思念。十三为多闻故不舍精进。十四正观择诸法。十五应正解脱。十六知得果。十七住于正位。十八守护佛法。十九信业果报故名正见。二十离一切忆想分别思惟故名正思惟。二十一随众生所信乐为说法故名为正语。二十二灭诸业故起业名为正业。二十三破烦恼气故名为正命。二十四得无上道故名正精进。二十五观不虚妄法故名正念二十六得一切智慧故名正定。二十七于空不怖。二十八于无相不畏。二十九于无愿不没。三十故以智受身。三十一依义不依语。三十二依智不依识。三十三依了义经不依不了义经。三十四依法不依人。长者如是等名为出家菩萨比丘。利益事应生。

Chapter 32 — An Explanation of the Dhūta Austerities

6) To completely fulfill the practice of the six *pāramitās*;
7) To avoid abandoning the resolve to realize all-knowledge;
8) To cultivate the knowledge of skillful means;
9) To attract beings [into the Dharma];
10) To facilitate beings' success [in cultivating the path];
11) To avoid abandoning the four means of attraction;
12) To become ever mindful of the six objects of mindfulness;[234]
13) To avoid abandoning vigor in the acquisition of extensive learning;
14) To engage in correct contemplative analysis of dharmas;
15) To practice in accordance with right liberation;
16) To achieve the realization of the fruits [of the path];
17) To abide in the right and definite position (*samyaktva-niyāma*);
18) To preserve and protect the Buddha's Dharma;
19) To abide in right views through faith in karmic retributions;
20) To abide in right intentional thought through abandoning all recollective and discriminating thought;
21) To abide in right speech through teaching Dharma for beings in accordance with their own resolute beliefs;
22) To abide in right action through acting in ways that extinguish [bad] karma;
23) To abide in right livelihood through extinguishing affliction driven habitual karmic propensities;
24) To abide in right effort through striving for the attainment of the unsurpassed path;
25) To abide in right mindfulness through contemplation of dharmas that are not false;
26) To abide in right meditative concentration through the attainment of comprehensive wisdom;
27) To not be frightened by emptiness;
28) To not be made fearful by signlessness;
29) To not be overwhelmed by wishlessness;
30) To be guided by wisdom in taking on one's bodies;
31) To rely on the meaning, not merely on the words;
32) To rely on wisdom, not merely on consciousness;
33) To rely on sutras of ultimate meaning, not on sutras whose meaning is non-ultimate;
34) To rely on Dharma, not on persons.

Elder, it is [purposes] such as these that constitute the beneficial endeavors that the renunciant bodhisattva bhikshu should bring forth.

正體字

隨順阿練若法者。
112b28 ‖ 所謂四禪四無量心。天耳天眼他心智宿命
112b29 ‖ 智神通等。滅諸怖畏者。是人以三因緣能
112c01 ‖ 滅怖畏。一見無我我所法相故能除怖畏。
112c02 ‖ 二以方便力故。三以心膽力故能除怖畏。
112c03 ‖ 見無我我所者。如初地中所說。除五種怖
112c04 ‖ 畏方便力者。此論中念正思惟業果報故。
112c05 ‖ 名方便力。應作是念。諸大國王在深宮殿。
112c06 ‖ 象馬車步四兵[5]侍衛業因緣盡。亦受種種諸
112c07 ‖ 衰惱事。又業因緣守護者。雖行險道中入
112c08 ‖ 大海水在大戰陣亦安隱無患。我先世業
112c09 ‖ 因緣。若在聚落。若在阿練若處。業因緣必
112c10 ‖ 受其報。如是思惟已除滅怖畏。復作是念。
112c11 ‖ 若我為守護身故。入城邑聚落。捨阿練若
112c12 ‖ 處者。無有

简体字

随顺阿练若法者。所谓四禅四无量心。天耳天眼他心智宿命智神通等。灭诸怖畏者。是人以三因缘能灭怖畏。一见无我我所法相故能除怖畏。二以方便力故。三以心胆力故能除怖畏。见无我我所者。如初地中所说。除五种怖畏方便力者。此论中念正思惟业果报故。名方便力。应作是念。诸大国王在深宫殿。象马车步四兵侍卫业因缘尽。亦受种种诸衰恼事。又业因缘守护者。虽行险道中入大海水在大战阵亦安隐无患。我先世业因缘。若在聚落。若在阿练若处。业因缘必受其报。如是思惟已除灭怖畏。复作是念。若我为守护身故。入城邑聚落。舍阿练若处者。无有

Chapter 32 — An Explanation of the Dhūta Austerities

8. THE APPROPRIATE DHARMAS OF A FOREST DWELLER

As for "according with the dharma of the forest hermitage," this refers to cultivation of the four *dhyānas*, the four immeasurable minds, the heavenly ear, the heavenly eye, cognition of others' thoughts, cognition of past lives, the spiritual superknowledges, and so forth.

9. THE MEANS FOR EXTINGUISHING FEAR

As for "extinguishing every sort of fear," there are three reasons for this practitioner's ability to extinguish fear:

> First, because he sees that dharmas are characterized by nonexistence of self and the nonexistence of anything belonging to a self, he is therefore able to dispel fear;
> Second, because he has the power of skillful means;
> Third, because he has the power of mental courage, he is able to dispel fear.

Regarding this matter of "seeing the nonexistence of self and the nonexistence of anything belonging to a self," this is just as presented earlier, in the [third chapter's] treatment of the first ground, where ridding oneself of five kinds of fear was discussed.[235]

As for "the power of skillful means," in this treatise, it is mindfulness that rightly reflects upon karma and its retributions that constitutes the power of skillful means. One should reflect in this way:

> All of the great kings may be deep in their palaces where their security is ensured by the fourfold elephant, cavalry, chariot, and infantry battalions that surround and serve them. Even so, once the karmic causes and conditions sustaining their rule finally come to an end, even they are compelled to undergo all of the different events that eventually bring about their ruin and anguish.
>
> Also, in the case of those who are protected by the causes and conditions of their karmic actions, even though they might travel a hazardous road, sail far out onto the waters of the great sea, or walk amidst the ranks of battling armies, they will still remain entirely safe and free of any personal calamities.
>
> Given the karmic causes and conditions established in my previous lives, no matter whether I reside in the village or in a forest hermitage, I will still definitely be compelled to undergo its karmic retribution.

Having contemplated matters in this way, one thereby succeeds in extinguishing fear. Furthermore, one thinks:

> If, to protect myself, I choose to go forth into the city or village, thus abandoning this living in a forest hermitage, there will be nothing

正體字

能勝善身業善口業善意業守
112c13 ‖ 護者。如佛告波斯匿王。若人行身善業行
112c14 ‖ 口善業行意善業。是名為人善自守護。是
112c15 ‖ 人若言我善自守護者是為實說。大王是
112c16 ‖ 人雖無四兵衛護亦可名為善好守護。何
112c17 ‖ 以故。如是守護名內守護。非外守護。是故
112c18 ‖ 我以身業善行口業善行意業善行故名為
112c19 ‖ 善自守護。復作是念。是諸鳥獸腹行虫等
112c20 ‖ 在阿練若處。身不行善口不行善意不行
112c21 ‖ 善。以遠聚落住故而無所畏。我之心智
112c22 ‖ 豈不如此鳥獸等耶。如是思惟除諸怖畏。
112c23 ‖ 又以念佛故。在阿練若處。能破一切諸怖
112c24 ‖ 畏事。如經說。汝諸比丘阿練若處。若在樹
112c25 ‖ 下若在空舍。或生怖畏。心沒毛豎者。汝當
112c26 ‖ 念我是如來應正遍知明行足善逝世間解
112c27 ‖ 無上士調御丈夫

简体字

能胜善身业善口业善意业守护者。如佛告波斯匿王。若人行身善业行口善业行意善业。是名为人善自守护。是人若言我善自守护者是为实说。大王是人虽无四兵卫护亦可名为善好守护。何以故。如是守护名内守护。非外守护。是故我以身业善行口业善行意业善行故名为善自守护。复作是念。是诸鸟兽腹行虫等在阿练若处。身不行善口不行善意不行善。以远聚落住故而无所畏。我之心智岂不如此鸟兽等耶。如是思惟除诸怖畏。又以念佛故。在阿练若处。能破一切诸怖畏事。如经说。汝诸比丘阿练若处。若在树下若在空舍。或生怖畏。心没毛竖者。汝当念我是如来应正遍知明行足善逝世间解无上士调御丈夫

there that is able to exceed the protection afforded me by good physical karmic actions, good verbal karmic actions, and good mental karmic actions.

This is just as told to King Prasenajit by the Buddha himself when he said:[236]

> If a person practices good physical karmic actions, practices good verbal karmic actions, and practices good mental karmic actions, this is what affords a person the best personal protection. Were this person to claim of himself, "I am hereby well protected," this would indeed be a proclamation of the truth.
>
> Great King, even though this man would not be surrounded and guarded by the fourfold battalions of the army, he can still be regarded as being well protected. And why is this so? It is because this form of protection is inward protection, not mere outward protection.

[Thus one may be moved to reflect]:

> Therefore I do in fact qualify as personally well protected by virtue of my practice of good physical karmic actions, good verbal karmic actions, and good mental karmic actions.

One may additionally reflect thus:

> All of these birds, beasts, snakes, and such that abide in the vicinity of this forest hermitage—even without practicing good physical karmic actions, good verbal karmic actions, or good mental karmic actions, they are free of fear due to dwelling far from the village. How could one as knowledgeable as I fail to even match [the fearlessness of] these birds, beasts, and other creatures?

Through reflecting in these various ways, one does away with all of one's fears.

Additionally, by resorting to mindfulness of the Buddha, one can dispel all fear-inducing circumstances that may arise in a forest hermitage. As is stated in a sutra:[237]

> When any of you bhikshus are dwelling in a forest hermitage setting, whether beneath a tree, or in some empty building, it could happen that you might be overcome with fear, even to the point that your heart sinks and your hair stands on end. At just that very point, you should become mindful of me [by my ten names]: the Thus Come One (*tathāgata*), Worthy of Offerings (*arhat*), of Right and Universal Enlightenment (*samyak-saṃbuddha*), Perfect in the Clear Knowledges and Conduct (*vidyā-caraṇa-saṃpanna*), the Well Gone One (*sugata*), the Knower of the Worlds (*lokavid*), the Unsurpassed Tamer of Those to

正體字

天人師佛世尊。如是念時
112c28 ‖ 怖畏即滅。大膽名心不怯弱決定求道。如
112c29 ‖ 說。
113a01 ‖ 　比丘住空閑　　當以心膽力
113a02 ‖ 　除滅諸怖畏　　念佛無畏者
113a03 ‖ 　若人自起業　　怖畏不得脫
113a04 ‖ 　不怖亦不脫　　怖則失正利
113a05 ‖ 　如是知不免　　而破餘利者
113a06 ‖ 　則行小人事　　比丘所不應
113a07 ‖ 　若有怖畏者　　應畏於生死
113a08 ‖ 　一切諸怖畏　　生死皆為因
113a09 ‖ 　是故行道者　　欲脫於生死
113a10 ‖ 　亦救於他人　　不應生怖畏
113a11 ‖ 如佛離怖畏經中說怖畏法。有沙門婆羅
113a12 ‖ 門。住阿練若處。應如是念。以不淨身業
113a13 ‖ 故。不淨口業故。不淨意業故。[1]念不清
113a14 ‖ 淨故。自高卑人故。懈怠心故。妄憶念故。心
113a15 ‖ 不定故。愚癡故怖畏。與此相違。身業清淨
113a16 ‖ 等則無怖畏。又佛為郁伽長者說。出家菩
113a17 ‖ 薩在阿練若處。應作是念。我何故在此。

简体字

天人师佛世尊。如是念时怖畏即灭。大胆名心不怯弱决定求道。如说。

　比丘住空闲　　当以心胆力
　除灭诸怖畏　　念佛无畏者
　若人自起业　　怖畏不得脱
　不怖亦不脱　　怖则失正利
　如是知不免　　而破余利者
　则行小人事　　比丘所不应
　若有怖畏者　　应畏于生死
　一切诸怖畏　　生死皆为因
　是故行道者　　欲脱于生死
　亦救于他人　　不应生怖畏

如佛离怖畏经中说怖畏法。有沙门婆罗门。住阿练若处。应如是念。以不净身业故。不净口业故。不净意业故。念不清净故。自高卑人故。懈怠心故。妄忆念故。心不定故。愚痴故怖畏。与此相违。身业清净等则无怖畏。又佛为郁伽长者说。出家菩萨在阿练若处。应作是念。我何故在此。

be Tamed (*anuttara-puruṣa-damya-sārathi*), the Teacher of Devas and Humans (*śāstā-deva-manuṣyāṇām*), the Enlightened One (*buddha*), the World Honored One (*bhagavat*). When you become mindful in this way, your fear will immediately disappear.

As for "great courageousness," this refers to possessing resolve that is not timid or weak and which is decisive in seeking the path. This is as described here:

> The bhikshu who abides in the wilderness
> should draw upon the power of courageous resolve
> to extinguish all fears,
> being mindful of the Buddha as the one who is fearless.

> In a case where someone has created karma
> and fears that he will be unable to escape [its retribution],
> even if he is not fearful, he will still not escape it.
> Hence, if one is fearful, then one loses his rightful benefit.

> Thus, if one realizes that he cannot avoid it,
> and yet allows this to destroy other benefits one might achieve,
> then one thereby involves himself in the affairs of petty men
> and engages in behavior a bhikshu should never adopt.

> If one is to have something that one fears,
> then one should instead fear *saṃsāra*.
> All the various forms of fear
> have this cycle of births and deaths as their cause.

> Therefore, one who practices the path
> wishing to gain liberation from *saṃsāra*
> while also rescuing others
> should not give rise to fear.

As stated by the Buddha in *The Sutra on Abandoning Fear* when discussing the dharma of fearfulness:[238]

> In an instance where a *śramaṇa* or brahman is abiding in a forest hermitage, he should reflect as follows: "It is because of impure physical karma, because of impure verbal karma, because of impure mental karma, because of thoughts devoted to what is impure, because of elevating self and diminishing others, because of an indolent mind, because of false recollective thinking, because of an unconcentrated mind, and because of one's delusions that one is overcome by fear. And it is because of the very opposite qualities consisting of purity of physical karma and so forth that one then becomes free of fear."

Additionally, for the sake of Ugra, the Elder, the Buddha said:[239]

> The monastic bodhisattva who resides in a forest hermitage should reflect thus: "For what purpose am I here?"

正體字

即 113a18 ‖ 時自知。欲離怖畏故。來至於此。怖畏於
113a19 ‖ 誰。畏眾憒閙。畏眾語言。畏貪欲瞋恚愚癡。
113a20 ‖ 畏憍慢恚恨嫉他利養。畏色聲香味觸。畏
113a21 ‖ 五陰魔。畏諸愚癡障礙處。畏非時語。畏不
113a22 ‖ 見言見。畏不聞言聞。畏不覺而覺。畏不
113a23 ‖ 知而知。畏諸沙門垢。畏共相憎惡。畏欲界
113a24 ‖ 色界無色界一切生處。畏墮地獄畜生餓鬼
113a25 ‖ 及諸難處。略說畏一切惡不善法故。來在
113a26 ‖ 此住。若人在家樂在眾閙不修習道。住
113a27 ‖ 在邪念不能得離如是怖畏所。有過去
113a28 ‖ 諸菩薩。皆在阿練若處。離諸怖畏得無畏
113a29 ‖ 處。得一切智慧。所有當來諸菩薩亦在阿練
113b01 ‖ 若處離諸怖畏得一切智慧。今現在諸菩
113b02 ‖ 薩。住阿練若處離諸怖畏。得無畏處成一
113b03 ‖ 切智慧。以是故。我怖畏一切諸惡度諸怖
113b04 ‖ 畏故。應住阿練若處。復次一切怖畏皆從
113b05 ‖ 著我生。貪著我故。愛受我故。生我想故。
113b06 ‖ 見我故。貴我故。分別我故。守護我故。若
113b07 ‖ 我住阿練若處不捨貪著我者。則為空在
113b08 ‖ 阿練若處。復次長者見有所得者。則不住阿
113b09 ‖ 練若處。住我我所心者。則不住阿練若處。
113b10 ‖ 住顛倒者。則不住阿練若處。

简体字

即时自知。欲离怖畏故。来至于此。怖畏于谁。畏众愦闹。畏众语言。畏贪欲嗔恚愚痴。畏憍慢恚恨嫉他利养。畏色声香味触。畏五阴魔。畏诸愚痴障碍处。畏非时语。畏不见言见。畏不闻言闻。畏不觉而觉。畏不知而知。畏诸沙门垢。畏共相憎恶。畏欲界色界无色界一切生处。畏堕地狱畜生饿鬼及诸难处。略说畏一切恶不善法故。来在此住。若人在家乐在众闹不修习道。住在邪念不能得离如是怖畏所。有过去诸菩萨。皆在阿练若处。离诸怖畏得无畏处。得一切智慧。所有当来诸菩萨亦在阿练若处离诸怖畏得一切智慧。今现在诸菩萨。住阿练若处离诸怖畏。得无畏处成一切智慧。以是故。我怖畏一切诸恶度诸怖畏故。应住阿练若处。复次一切怖畏皆从着我生。贪着我故。爱受我故。生我想故。见我故。贵我故。分别我故。守护我故。若我住阿练若处不舍贪着我者。则为空在阿练若处。复次长者见有所得者。则不住阿练若处。住我我所心者。则不住阿练若处。住颠倒者。则不住阿练若处。

Chapter 32 — An Explanation of the Dhūta Austerities

He should then immediately realize, "It is because of a desire to abandon fear that I have come here. Fear of what? It is fear of the many sorts of befuddling disturbances, fear of the chattering of crowds, fear of greed, hatred, and delusion, fear of arrogance, fear of anger and hostility, fear of jealousy over offerings received by others, fear of visual forms, sounds, smells, tastes, touchables, fear of the *māra* of the five aggregates, fear of all circumstances involving delusion-induced obstacles, fear of untimely speech, fear of claiming to have seen what one has not seen, fear of claiming to have heard what one has not heard, fear of claiming to have awakened when one has not yet awakened, fear of claiming to know what one does not know, fear of the *śramaṇa*'s defilements, fear of mutual detestation, fear of all the places of rebirth throughout the desire realm, the form realm, and the formless realm, and fear of falling into the hell realms, the animal realms, the hungry ghost realms, or any of the other difficulties.[240] To state it briefly, it is because of fear of all evil and unwholesome dharmas that I have come to abide here.

"If one lives as a householder, delights in its many sorts of commotion, does not cultivate the path, and abides in wrong thought, he will not be able to achieve emancipation from such points of fear as these.

"There were the bodhisattvas of the past, all of whom resided in a forest hermitage, abandoned all fears, reached the state of fearlessness, and gained all-knowledge. So too, all bodhisattvas of the future shall also dwell in a forest hermitage, abandon all fears, and gain all-knowledge. All of the bodhisattvas of the present also undertake the practice of residing in a forest hermitage and thereby abandon all fears, reach the station of fearlessness, and gain all-knowledge.

"Therefore, given that I fear all of these sorts of bad circumstances, in order to transcend all fears, I too should take up the practice of abiding in a forest hermitage dwelling.

"Furthermore, all fears arise due to attachment to a self, due to affection for and acceptance of a self, due to the conception of a self, due to the perception of a self, due to esteeming a self, due to discriminations conceiving of a self, and due to protection of a self.

"Were I to take up the practice of abiding in a forest hermitage dwelling but still fail to abandon this attachment to a self, then this would amount to abiding in a forest hermitage in vain."

Furthermore, Elder, whosoever perceives that there is anything at all that is apprehensible [as inherently existent] does not truly reside in a forest hermitage. Whosoever abides in the conception of a self or anything belonging to a self does not truly reside in a forest hermitage. Whosoever abides in thoughts affected by the inverted views does not truly abide in a forest hermitage.

正體字

```
         長者乃至生
113b11 ‖ 涅槃想者。尚不住阿練若處。何況起煩惱
113b12 ‖ 想者。長者譬如草木在阿練若處。無有驚
113b13 ‖ 畏。菩薩如是。在阿練若處。應生草木想
113b14 ‖ [2]石瓦想水中影想鏡中像想。於語言生響
113b15 ‖ 想。於心生幻想。此中誰驚誰畏。菩薩爾時
113b16 ‖ 則正觀身。無我無我所。無眾生無壽者命
113b17 ‖ 者。無養育者。無男無女。無知者見者。怖
113b18 ‖ 畏名為虛妄分別。我則不應隨虛妄分別。
113b19 ‖ 菩薩如是應如草木住阿練若處。又知一
113b20 ‖ 切法皆亦如是。斷鬪諍名阿練若處。無我
113b21 ‖ 無我所無所屬名阿練若處。不應樂在
113b22 ‖ 家出家眾鬧處住。諸佛不聽阿練若處比丘
113b23 ‖ 與在家出家者和合。
113b24 ‖ 問曰。佛不聽與一切眾人和合耶。答曰。不
113b25 ‖ 然。
113b26 ‖   佛聽四和合     餘者則不聽
113b27 ‖   是故應親近     餘者則遠離
```

简体字

长者乃至生涅槃想者。尚不住阿练若处。何况起烦恼想者。长者譬如草木在阿练若处。无有惊畏。菩萨如是。在阿练若处。应生草木想石瓦想水中影想镜中像想。于语言生响想。于心生幻想。此中谁惊谁畏。菩萨尔时则正观身。无我无我所。无众生无寿者命者。无养育者。无男无女。无知者见者。怖畏名为虚妄分别。我则不应随虚妄分别。菩萨如是应如草木住阿练若处。又知一切法皆亦如是。断斗诤名阿练若处。无我无我所无所属名阿练若处。不应乐在家出家众闹处住。诸佛不听阿练若处比丘与在家出家者和合。

问曰。佛不听与一切众人和合耶。答曰。不然。
　　佛听四和合　　余者则不听
　　是故应亲近　　余者则远离

Elder, so it goes even up to the point that, not even one who conceives of nirvāṇa [as inherently existent] truly abides in a forest hermitage, how much the less could it be that someone who conceives of afflictions [as inherently existent] truly abides in a forest hermitage.

Elder, just as the grass and trees in the vicinity of a forest hermitage are entirely free of fear, so too is the bodhisattva. When abiding in a forest hermitage, one should envision oneself as like the grass and trees, envision oneself as like stones or tiles, envision oneself as like a reflection in a pool of water, and envision oneself as like an image in a mirror. One should imagine speech to be echoes and should imagine one's thoughts to be like magical illusions. In any of this, who is it that could possibly be frightened? And who is it that could be struck with fear?

The bodhisattva then undertakes right contemplation of the body, observing the nonexistence of self and the nonexistence of anything belonging to a self. He observes that there is no being, no one possessed of a soul, no one possessed of a life, no one who has been raised up, no one identifiable as male, no one identifiable as female, no knower, and no perceiver.

Fear itself is but a product of false discriminations. Thus one reflects: "Then I should not simply follow along with false discriminations."

In just this way, the bodhisattva should be just like the grass or trees as he abides in a forest hermitage. He should also be aware that all dharmas are also just like this.

It is the cutting off of all forms of struggle and disputation that truly qualifies as abiding within a forest hermitage. It is the nonexistence of self, the nonexistence of anything belonging to a self, and the not belonging to anything at all that truly qualify as the bases of abiding in a forest hermitage.

One should not delight in the many sorts of noisy dwelling places of either householders or monastics. The Buddhas do not permit a bhikshu dwelling in a forest hermitage to abide together with either a householder or a monastic.

10. Four Cases in Which a Forest Dweller May Gather with Others

Question: Did the Buddha forbid one to gather together with anyone else in the community?

Response: No. He did not.

The Buddha permitted meeting with others in four circumstances but did not permit it otherwise.
Therefore one should draw close [to others] in those situations, while still abiding well apart in other circumstances.

正體字

113b28 ‖ 菩薩在阿練若處。聽與四眾和合。所謂入
113b29 ‖ 聽法眾。教化眾生供養於佛。不離一切智
113c01 ‖ 心和合。是故唯聽此四事和合。餘者不應
113c02 ‖ 親近。復次菩薩應作是念。云何諸佛所聽。
113c03 ‖ 阿練若住處。我當親近。我或非阿練若住
113c04 ‖ 處。謂是住阿練若處。或有錯謬。問曰。何等
113c05 ‖ 是阿練若住處。菩薩應當[3]和合。答曰。佛自
113c06 ‖ 經中說阿練若住處。名不住一切法。不
113c07 ‖ [4]歸諸塵。不取一切法相。不貪色聲香味
113c08 ‖ 觸。一切法平等故。無所依止住名阿練若
113c09 ‖ 處住。[5]自心善故。不相違住處。名阿練若
113c10 ‖ 住。捨一切擔[*]猗樂住故。名阿練若住。脫
113c11 ‖ 一切煩惱。無怖畏住故。名阿練若住。度
113c12 ‖ 諸流住故。名阿練若住。住聖種故名阿
113c13 ‖ 練若住。知足趣得故。名阿練若住。易滿
113c14 ‖ 易養少欲住故。名阿練若住。

简体字

菩萨在阿练若处。听与四众和合。所谓入听法众。教化众生供养于佛。不离一切智心和合。是故唯听此四事和合。余者不应亲近。复次菩萨应作是念。云何诸佛所听。阿练若住处。我当亲近。我或非阿练若住处。谓是住阿练若处。或有错谬。问曰。何等是阿练若住处。菩萨应当和合。答曰。佛自经中说阿练若住处。名不住一切法。不归诸尘。不取一切法相。不贪色声香味触。一切法平等故。无所依止住名阿练若处住。自心善故。不相违住处。名阿练若住。舍一切担猗乐住故。名阿练若住。脱一切烦恼。无怖畏住故。名阿练若住。度诸流住故。名阿练若住。住圣种故名阿练若住。知足趣得故。名阿练若住。易满易养少欲住故。名阿练若住。

Chapter 32 — An Explanation of the Dhūta Austerities 1189

Thus the bodhisattva who abides in a forest hermitage is permitted to join in four types of assemblies. Specifically, he may enter assemblies gathered to hear the teaching of Dharma, may enter assemblies to teach beings, may enter assemblies to make offerings to the buddha, and may enter assemblies gathered to prevent abandoning the resolve to gain all-knowledge.

Therefore one is only permitted to gather together with others in these four circumstances. [The bhikshu dwelling in a forest hermitage] should not draw close to others in other circumstances.

11. THE ASPECTS DEFINING HERMITAGE DWELLING APPROVED BY THE BUDDHAS

Additionally, the bodhisattva should reflect in this manner: "How should I establishing a forest hermitage dwelling that is closely adherent to those permitted by all buddhas? Could it perhaps be that this is not actually a forest hermitage dwelling and that I merely suppose it to be a forest hermitage dwelling? Could I perhaps be mistaken about the meaning of this?"

Question: What then are the aspects of a forest hermitage dwelling that a bodhisattva should know?[241]

Response: In the sutras, the Buddha himself declared:

Abiding in a forest hermitage refers to not abiding in any dharma, to not taking refuge in any of the sense objects, to not seizing on any mark of any dharma, and to not coveting any visual forms, sounds, smells, tastes, or tangible objects;

Abiding in a forest hermitage refers to dwelling in a manner wherein one has nothing upon which one relies, this because [one realizes that] all dharmas are uniformly equal;

Dwelling in a forest hermitage refers to abiding in a manner free of contradictions because of the goodness of one's own mind;

Dwelling in a forest hermitage refers to dwelling in a manner whereby one relinquishes all the burdens and abides in delighted happiness;

Dwelling in a forest hermitage refers to abiding in a manner whereby one becomes liberated from all afflictions and one becomes free of all fears;

Dwelling in a forest hermitage refers to dwelling in a manner whereby one crosses beyond the floods;[242]

Dwelling in a forest hermitage refers to abiding in the lineage bases of the Āryas;[243]

Dwelling in a forest hermitage refers to being satisfied with what one obtains in the course of things;

Dwelling in a forest hermitage refers to dwelling in way that one is easily satisfied, easily supported, and inclined to but few wants;

正體字	智慧足住故。 113c15 ‖ 名阿練若住。正行多聞住故。名阿練若住。 113c16 ‖ 空無相無願解脫門現前故。名阿練若住。 113c17 ‖ 斷諸縛得解脫住故。名阿練若住。順十二 113c18 ‖ 因緣隨順住故。名阿練若住。畢竟寂滅所 113c19 ‖ 作已作[6]住故。名阿練若住。阿練若住處者。 113c20 ‖ 隨順戒品[7]佐助定品。利益慧品易得解 113c21 ‖ 脫品。易得解脫知見品。易行諸助菩提法。 113c22 ‖ 能攝諸頭陀功德。阿練若住處通達諸諦。 113c23 ‖ 阿練若處見知諸陰。阿練若處。諸性同為法 113c24 ‖ 性。阿練若處出離十二入。阿練若處不忘 113c25 ‖ 失菩提心。阿練若處觀空不畏。阿練若處能 113c26 ‖ 護佛法。阿練若處。求解脫者不失功德。
简体字	智慧足住故。名阿练若住。正行多闻住故。名阿练若住。空无相无愿解脱门现前故。名阿练若住。断诸缚得解脱住故。名阿练若住。顺十二因缘随顺住故。名阿练若住。毕竟寂灭所作已作住故。名阿练若住。阿练若住处者。随顺戒品佐助定品。利益慧品易得解脱品。易得解脱知见品。易行诸助菩提法。能摄诸头陀功德。阿练若住处通达诸谛。阿练若处见知诸阴。阿练若处。诸性同为法性。阿练若处出离十二入。阿练若处不忘失菩提心。阿练若处观空不畏。阿练若处能护佛法。阿练若处。求解脱者不失功德。

Chapter 32 — An Explanation of the Dhūta Austerities

Dwelling in a forest hermitage refers to abiding in a manner whereby one achieves the fulfillment of wisdom;

Dwelling in a forest hermitage refers to abiding in a manner whereby one rightly practices [what one has acquired through] extensive learning;

Dwelling in a forest hermitage refers to directly manifest realization of the emptiness, signlessness, and wishlessness gates to liberation;

Dwelling in a forest hermitage refers to abiding in a manner wherein one severs all the bonds and gains liberation;

Dwelling in a forest hermitage refers to abiding in a manner that accords with the twelvefold chain of causation;

Dwelling in a forest hermitage refers to abiding in a manner whereby one reaches the state of ultimate quiescence in which one has already done what is to be done;

Dwelling in a forest hermitage refers to abiding in a manner compliant with all classes of moral precepts, compliant with all types of practice assisting acquisition of the meditative absorptions, compliant with all types of practice beneficial to wisdom, compliant with all types of practice that facilitate easy achievement of liberation, compliant with all classes of practice facilitating easy acquisition of the knowledge and vision of liberation, compliant with whatever practices facilitate easy practice of the dharmas conducive to realization of bodhi, and compliant with whatever is able to conduce to accumulating all meritorious qualities associated with the *dhūta* austerities;

Dwelling in a forest hermitage refers to achieving a penetrating comprehension of the truths;

Dwelling in a forest hermitage refers to seeing and knowing the aggregates;

Dwelling in a forest hermitage refers to [realizing that] the nature of all things is identical to the nature of dharmas;[244]

Dwelling in a forest hermitage refers to abandoning the twelve sense bases;

Dwelling in a forest hermitage refers to never forgetting one's resolve to attain bodhi;

Dwelling in a forest hermitage refers to contemplating emptiness without being frightened by it;

Dwelling in a forest hermitage refers to being able to protect and preserve the Buddha's Dharma;

Dwelling in a forest hermitage refers to [practicing in a manner whereby] one who seeks liberation does not err with regard to the the meritorious qualities;

正體字

```
              阿
113c27 ‖ 練若處。能得一切智者則能增益阿練若
113c28 ‖ 處。[8]菩薩如是行。疾得具六度。
113c29 ‖ 何以故。若菩薩在阿練若處住。不貪惜身
114a01 ‖ 命是名檀波羅蜜行。三種善業清淨[1]入細
114a02 ‖ 頭陀行法。是名尸波羅蜜。不瞋恨心於諸
114a03 ‖ 眾生慈心普遍。但忍樂薩婆若乘不在餘
114a04 ‖ 乘。是名羼提波羅蜜。自立誓願於阿練若
114a05 ‖ 處不得正法忍終不捨此處是名毘梨耶
114a06 ‖ 波羅蜜。得禪定故不觀生處修習善根是
114a07 ‖ 名禪波羅蜜。如身阿練若亦如是。如身
114a08 ‖ 菩提亦如是。如實中無差別。是名般若波
114a09 ‖ 羅蜜。
114a10 ‖    佛聽有四法    住阿練若處
114a11 ‖ 何等四。如佛告長者。一者多聞。二善知決
114a12 ‖ 定義。三樂修正憶念。四隨順如所說行。
```

简体字

阿练若处。能得一切智者则能增益阿练若处。菩萨如是行。疾得具六度。

何以故。若菩萨在阿练若处住。不贪惜身命是名檀波罗蜜行。三种善业清净入细头陀行法。是名尸波罗蜜。不瞋恨心于诸众生慈心普遍。但忍乐萨婆若乘不在余乘。是名羼提波罗蜜。自立誓愿于阿练若处不得正法忍终不舍此处是名毗梨耶波罗蜜。得禅定故不观生处修习善根是名禅波罗蜜。如身阿练若亦如是。如身菩提亦如是。如实中无差别。是名般若波罗蜜。

　　佛听有四法　　住阿练若处

何等四。如佛告长者。一者多闻。二善知决定义。三乐修正忆念。四随顺如所说行。

Chapter 32 — An Explanation of the Dhūta Austerities

Dwelling in a forest hermitage refers to [practicing in a manner whereby], if one is a person capable of gaining all-knowledge, he will thus achieve increased benefit.

12. Hermitage Dwelling as a Means to Fulfill the Six Perfections

If a bodhisattva dwelling in a forest hermitage is able to practice in this way, he will swiftly achieve complete fulfillment of the six perfections. How might this be so?

> If a bodhisattva abiding in a forest hermitage does not have a selfish cherishing even for his own body or life, this is the practice of *dāna pāramitā*, the perfection of patience;
>
> If he maintains purity in the three kinds of good karmic actions and enters the refined practice of the *dhūta* austerities, this is the practice of *śīla pāramitā*, the perfection of moral virtue;
>
> If he does not generate any hatred toward any other beings but rather extends a mind of universally inclusive kindness to all of them, and if he only accepts and delights in the vehicle of all-knowledge and no other vehicle, this is the practice of *kṣānti pāramitā*, the perfection of patience;
>
> If he makes the solemn personal vow to abide in a forest hermitage and never leave this place so long as he has not yet rightly realized the [unproduced] dharmas patience, this is the practice of *vīrya pāramitā*, the perfection of vigor;
>
> If, having gained the *dhyāna* absorptions, his cultivation of roots of goodness is not done with an eye toward taking rebirth in the stations of rebirth to which they correspond,[245] this is the practice of *dhyāna pāramitā*, the perfection of *dhyāna* meditation;
>
> If one's person and the forest hermitage have become of the same suchness, if one's person and bodhi have become of the same suchness, and if these are all indistinguishable from ultimate reality, this is the practice of *prajñā-pāramitā*, the perfection of wisdom.

13. The Buddha's Four Prerequisite Dharmas for Hermitage Dwelling

> The Buddha permitted those possessed of four dharmas
> to abide in a forest hermitage.

What then are those four dharmas? As the Buddha told [Ugra], the Elder, they are:

> First, extensive learning;
> Second, thorough knowledge of the definitive meaning;
> Third, delight in the cultivation of right mindfulness;
> Fourth, practice accordant with the manner in which [the Dharma] was taught.

正體字

	如
114a13 ‖	是人應住阿練若處。復有菩薩煩惱深厚。
114a14 ‖	是人若在眾鬧則發煩惱。應在阿練若處
114a15 ‖	住降伏煩惱。
114a16 ‖	復次菩薩得五神通。是人欲教化成就天
114a17 ‖	龍夜叉乾闥婆故。應住阿練若處。復有菩
114a18 ‖	薩作是念。諸佛所讚聽處。是阿練若處。復
114a19 ‖	次住阿練若處。助滿一切善法增長善根。
114a20 ‖	然後入聚落。為眾生說法。成就如是功
114a21 ‖	德。乃可住阿練若處。復次。
114a22 ‖	決定王經中　　佛為阿難說
114a23 ‖	阿練若比丘　　應住四四法
114a24 ‖	菩薩住阿練若處者。一遠離在家出家。二
114a25 ‖	欲讀誦深經。三引導眾生使得阿練若處
114a26 ‖	功德。四晝夜不離念佛。復有四法。一乃至
114a27 ‖	彈指頃於眾生中不生瞋恨心。二不應一
114a28 ‖	時頃使眠睡覆心。

简体字

如是人应住阿练若处。复有菩萨烦恼深厚。是人若在众闹则发烦恼。应在阿练若处住降伏烦恼。

复次菩萨得五神通。是人欲教化成就天龙夜叉乾闼婆故。应住阿练若处。复有菩萨作是念。诸佛所赞听处。是阿练若处。复次住阿练若处。助满一切善法增长善根。然后入聚落。为众生说法。成就如是功德。乃可住阿练若处。复次。

　　决定王经中　　佛为阿难说
　　阿练若比丘　　应住四四法

菩萨住阿练若处者。一远离在家出家。二欲读诵深经。三引导众生使得阿练若处功德。四昼夜不离念佛。复有四法。一乃至弹指顷于众生中不生瞋恨心。二不应一时顷使眠睡覆心。

People of this sort should take up the practice of dwelling in a forest hermitage.

14. Other Bodhisattvas for Whom Hermitage Dwelling Is Beneficial

Additionally, there are bodhisattvas whose afflictions are deep and dense. If such a person abides in the midst of noisy crowds, he will bring forth yet more afflictions. Therefore he should dwell in a forest hermitage in order to subdue afflictions.

Then again, there are bodhisattvas who have acquired the five spiritual superknowledges. Because these practitioners may wish to teach devas, dragons, *yakṣas*, or *gandharvas* and assist their success [on the path], they should dwell in a forest hermitage.

Yet again, there are bodhisattvas who think thus: "Dwelling in a forest hermitage is the circumstance praised and permitted by all buddhas."

Moreover, dwelling in a forest hermitage assists the fulfillment of all good dharmas and increases roots of goodness. Afterward, one may then enter the village and teach Dharma for the welfare of beings. If one's intention is to develop such meritorious qualities, one may then dwell in a forest hermitage.

Also:

15. Four Fourfold Dharmas for the Forest Dweller

In the Sutra of the Resolute King,
The Buddha told Ānanda:
"The bhikshu who dwells in a forest hermitage
should dwell in four fourfold dharmas."

A bodhisattva who wishes to abide in a forest hermitage [may do so for these purposes]:

First, to depart far from both laypeople and monastics;
Second, out of a wish to study and recite profound scriptures;
Third, as a means of leading forth other beings, thereby influencing them to develop the meritorious qualities arising from dwelling in a forest hermitage;
Fourth, to engage in uninterrupted day and night practice of mindfulness of the Buddha.

There are another four dharmas:

First, one does not generate a thought of hatred toward other beings even for the duration of a finger snap;
Second, one should not allow drowsiness to blanket one's mind even for the briefest moment;

正體字

	三於一念頃不應生眾
114a29 ‖	生想。四於一念頃不應忘捨菩提心。復有
114b01 ‖	四法。一常應閑坐不應聚眾。二常樂經行。
114b02 ‖	三常觀諸法無新故想。四不應離深空無
114b03 ‖	相無願法。復有四法。一行四禪不行世間
114b04 ‖	禪。行四無量緣眾生生悲心而不取眾
114b05 ‖	生相。二雖行慈心而不緣眾生。雖行喜
114b06 ‖	心而不貪樂。雖行捨心而不捨眾生。三
114b07 ‖	自見身有四聖種行而不自高卑下他人。
114b08 ‖	四自行多聞如所聞行。是為四。復次。
114b09 ‖	無智無精進　　而住空閑處
114b10 ‖	即得於四法　　復得餘四法
114b11 ‖	又復得三事　　如是佛所說

简体字

三于一念顷不应生众生想。四于一念顷不应忘舍菩提心。复有四法。一常应闲坐不应聚众。二常乐经行。三常观诸法无新故想。四不应离深空无相无愿法。复有四法。一行四禅不行世间禅。行四无量缘众生生悲心而不取众生相。二虽行慈心而不缘众生。虽行喜心而不贪乐。虽行舍心而不舍众生。三自见身有四圣种行而不自高卑下他人。四自行多闻如所闻行。是为四。复次。

　　无智无精进　　而住空闲处
　　即得于四法　　复得余四法
　　又复得三事　　如是佛所说

Chapter 32 — An Explanation of the Dhūta Austerities

Third, one should not conceive of [an inherently existent] being even for the briefest moment;

Fourth, one should not forget one's resolve to attain bodhi even for the briefest moment.

There are yet four more dharmas:

First, one should always engage in quiet sitting [meditation] and refrain from joining together with groups;

Second, one should always delight in meditative walking;

Third, one always contemplates all dharmas without any conception of their being either new or old;

Fourth, one should never depart from the profound dharmas of emptiness, signlessness, and wishlessness.

Again, there are four additional dharmas:

First, one cultivates the four *dhyānas* but does not cultivate worldly *dhyāna* meditation. Thus, in one's cultivation of the four immeasurable minds, one brings forth thoughts of compassion focusing on beings as the objective condition, but without seizing on any mark [of the existence] of any being;

Second, although one cultivates the [immeasurable] mind of kindness, one does not perceive any [inherently existent] being as the object. Although one cultivates the [immeasurable] mind of sympathetic joy, one does not crave happiness [for oneself]. And, although one cultivates the [immeasurable] mind of equanimity, one never forsakes any being;

Third, although one may perceive oneself as compliant with the four lineage bases of the Āryas, one does not take that as a basis for elevating oneself and looking down on others;

Fourth, one personally engages in the accumulation of extensive learning while also practicing in accordance with what one has learned.

These are the [four sets of] four dharmas [as presented in that scripture]. There is an additional related topic, as below:

16. THE BAD RESULTS OF FOREST DWELLING WITHOUT WISDOM AND VIGOR

One who has no wisdom and has no vigor
and yet dwells alone in an isolated place
then acquires four dharmas
and also acquires yet another four dharmas.
He also encounters three additional situations.
Circumstances such as these are as described by the Buddha.

正體字

114b12 ‖ 阿練若比丘於諸功德中應勤修習。何以
114b13 ‖ 故。阿練若功德中。此二事能生諸功德故。
114b14 ‖ 若比丘愚癡懈怠在阿練若處住者則得四
114b15 ‖ 非法。一多眠睡。二多貪利養。三以[2]因緣現
114b16 ‖ 矯異相。四現不樂阿練若處復有四法。一
114b17 ‖ 增上慢未得謂得。二於深經心懷憎惡。三
114b18 ‖ 壞空無相無願法。四於持深經者心生瞋
114b19 ‖ 恨。復有三事。一若在阿練若處。不精進無
114b20 ‖ 智慧。或值女人墮在非法。若得僧殘。若得
114b21 ‖ 重罪。若反戒還俗。是為三。[3]
114b22 ‖ [4]復次。[5]
114b23 ‖   [6]廣說空閑法　　及與乞食法
114b24 ‖   餘十頭陀德　　皆亦應廣說
114b25 ‖ 十二頭陀法。上來[*]以廣解二事。餘十頭陀
114b26 ‖ 功德亦應如是知。何以故。是二則為開十
114b27 ‖ 頭陀門。餘則易解。十頭陀者。

简体字

　　阿练若比丘于诸功德中应勤修习。何以故。阿练若功德中。此二事能生诸功德故。若比丘愚痴懈怠在阿练若处住者则得四非法。一多眠睡。二多贪利养。三以因缘现矫异相。四现不乐阿练若处复有四法。一增上慢未得谓得。二于深经心怀憎恶。三坏空无相无愿法。四于持深经者心生嗔恨。复有三事。一若在阿练若处。不精进无智慧。或值女人堕在非法。若得僧残。若得重罪。若反戒还俗。是为三。

十住毗婆沙论卷第十五
解头陀品三十三之二

　　复次。
　　广说空闲法　　及与乞食法
　　余十头陀德　　皆亦应广说
　　十二头陀法。上来以广解二事。余十头陀功德亦应如是知。何以故。是二则为开十头陀门。余则易解。十头陀者。

Chapter 32 — An Explanation of the Dhūta Austerities

Of all the meritorious qualities, the bhikshu who dwells in a forest hermitage should diligently cultivate these, [namely wisdom and vigor]. Why? Because, of all the meritorious qualities associated with a forest hermitage, it is these two factors that are able to generate all of the [other] meritorious qualities.

If a bhikshu were instead to give into delusion and indolence while abiding in a forest hermitage, he will acquire four wrong dharmas:

First, he will spend much of his time sleeping;
Second, he will become much inclined to want offerings;
Third, he will take advantage of these [special] circumstances[246] to pretend to be extraordinary;
Fourth, he will become unhappy with dwelling in a forest hermitage.

He will also acquire four additional dharmas:

First, he will develop overweening pride due to which he will think he has already attained what he has not yet attained;
Second, he will come to abhor profound scriptures;
Third, he will ruin [his ability to realize] the dharmas of emptiness, signlessness, and wishlessness;
Fourth, his mind will generate hatred for those who uphold the profound scriptures.

There are three additional circumstances that might occur. If he abides in a forest hermitage while failing in vigor and having no wisdom, he may meet some woman and fall into behavior contrary to the Dharma due to which he either becomes a ruined member of the Sangha, commits a grave offense, or transgresses against the moral precepts and returns to lay life.[247] These are the three.

C. Additional Discussions of the Dhūta Austerities

There are additional related topics, as below:

Extensive discussion of dharmas practiced in solitary wilderness life
as well as the dharmas associated with the alms round
and the virtues of practicing the other ten *dhūta* austerities—
all of these should also be extensively explained.

In the course of the preceding discussion, we have presented an extensive explanation of two of the twelve *dhūta* austerities.[248] The meritorious qualities of the other ten *dhūta* austerities should be similarly understood. How so? This is because these two practices have served to open the door into the other ten *dhūta* austerities. Thus the others may now be easily understood. As for those other ten *dhūta* austerities, they are:

正體字

```
            一著糞掃衣。
114b28 ‖ 二一坐。三常坐。四食後不受非時飲食。五
114b29 ‖ 但有三衣。六毳衣。七隨敷坐。八樹下住。九
114c01 ‖ 空地住。十死人間住。糞掃衣者。人所棄捨
114c02 ‖ 受而後著。受者。若心生若口言。一坐者。先
114c03 ‖ 受食處更不復食。常坐者。夜常不臥。食後
114c04 ‖ 不飲漿者。食後不受非時飲。石蜜等可食
114c05 ‖ 之物。但有三衣者。唯受三衣更不畜餘
114c06 ‖ 衣。毳衣者。從毳所成麁毛毳衣[7]褐氈欽婆
114c07 ‖ 羅等。隨敷坐者。隨所得坐處不令他起。
114c08 ‖ 樹下住者。樂住樹下不入覆處。空地坐者。
114c09 ‖ 露地止住。住死人間者。隨順厭離心故。常
114c10 ‖ 止宿死人間法。是名十二頭陀。令戒清淨。
```

简体字

一着粪扫衣。二一坐。三常坐。四食后不受非时饮食。五但有三衣。六毳衣。七随敷坐。八树下住。九空地住。十死人间住。粪扫衣者。人所弃舍受而后着。受者。若心生若口言。一坐者。先受食处更不复食。常坐者。夜常不卧。食后不饮浆者。食后不受非时饮。石蜜等可食之物。但有三衣者。唯受三衣更不畜余衣。毳衣者。从毳所成粗毛毳衣褐毡钦婆罗等。随敷坐者。随所得坐处不令他起。树下住者。乐住树下不入覆处。空地坐者。露地止住。住死人间者。随顺厌离心故。常止宿死人间法。是名十二头陀。令戒清净。

Chapter 32 — *An Explanation of the Dhūta Austerities*

1. A Listing and Brief Discussion of The Other Ten Dhūta Austerities

First, wearing robes made [only] of cast-off rags;
Second, [taking one's daily meal in but] a single sitting;
Third, always sitting, [even when sleeping];
Fourth, having taken the meal, not accepting food or drink at the wrong times;
Fifth, possessing only a single three-part set of robes;
Sixth, wearing an animal-hair robe;
Seventh, laying out one's sitting mat wherever one happens to be.
Eighth, dwelling at the foot of a tree;
Ninth, dwelling out in the open;
Tenth, dwelling in a charnel field.

"Cast-off rag robes" refers to those that have been thrown away by others. After having accepted them, one then wears them. "Accepting" refers here to either mental or verbal assent.

"In but a single sitting" refers to taking one's meal at the first place one accepted it and then refraining from taking any further food [for that entire day].

"Always sitting" means one never lies down, even at night.

"After the meal, refraining from any beverages" refers to not accepting any beverage at the wrong time,[249] not even those made merely with crystalized sugar or other nutritional substances.

"Possessing only the single set of three robes" means one only accepts that single set of three robes and does not collect any other clothing whatsoever.

"Wearing an animal-hair robe" refers to wearing an animal-hair robe made of cloth woven from coarse animal hairs such as felt cloth or *kambala* (wool) cloth.

"Laying out one's sitting mat wherever one happens to be" refers to simply going along with whatever sitting spot is available that does not involve causing someone else to get up and move.

"Dwelling at the foot of a tree" refers to delighting in dwelling out beneath the trees, never going into a sheltered location.

"Dwelling out in the open" simply refers to living out on the open ground.

"Dwelling in a charnel field" refers to always spending the night in the area where the dead bodies are cast off in order to accord with the mind of renunciation.

This is what is meant by the twelve *dhūta* austerities that facilitate purity in the observance of the moral precepts.

正體字

114c11 ‖ 糞掃衣有十利。一不以衣故與在家者和
114c12 ‖ 合。二不以衣故現乞衣相。三亦不方便說
114c13 ‖ 得衣相。四不以衣故四方求索。五若不得
114c14 ‖ 衣亦不憂。六得亦不喜。七賤物易得無有
114c15 ‖ 過患。八[8]是順行初受四依法。九入在麁衣
114c16 ‖ 數中。十不為人所貪著。一坐食亦有十利。
114c17 ‖ 一無有求第二食疲苦。二於所受輕少。三
114c18 ‖ 無有所用疲苦。四食前無疲苦。五入在
114c19 ‖ 細行食法。六食消後食。七少妨患。八少疾
114c20 ‖ 病。九身體輕便。十身快樂。

简体字

粪扫衣有十利。一不以衣故与在家者和合。二不以衣故现乞衣相。三亦不方便说得衣相。四不以衣故四方求索。五若不得衣亦不忧。六得亦不喜。七贱物易得无有过患。八是顺行初受四依法。九入在粗衣数中。十不为人所贪着。一坐食亦有十利。一无有求第二食疲苦。二于所受轻少。三无有所用疲苦。四食前无疲苦。五入在细行食法。六食消后食。七少妨患。八少疾病。九身体轻便。十身快乐。

2. The Benefits of the Other Ten Dhūta Austerities
a. The Ten Benefits of Wearing Cast-Off Robes

There are ten benefits from wearing cast-off rag robes, namely:

First, one does not have to mix with the laity simply to acquire robes;
Second, one need not appear to solicit robes simply to acquire clothing;
Third, nor is one compelled to present the appearance of finding some expedient to discuss obtaining robes;
Fourth, one is not compelled to go off and search in the four directions in order to obtain robes;
Fifth, even if one does not obtain a robe, one is still free of distress;
Sixth, even if one does obtain a robe, one is not elated;
Seventh, worthless material is easily come by in a way that does not risk committing transgressions;
Eighth, this practice accords with the initially received explanation of the methods for obtaining the four requisites;[250]
Ninth, one thereby becomes just another one of those who wear coarse [and common] clothing;
Tenth, one thereby avoids becoming the object of others' covetousness.

b. The Ten Benefits of Taking One's Single Meal in a Single Sitting

[Taking one's meal in but] a single sitting also has ten benefits, as follows:

First, one does not experience the weariness and inconvenience of going off in search of a second meal;
Second, as a consequence, one accepts but little [food];
Third, there is none of the weariness and inconvenience entailed by what one would consume [by compelling others to provide additional meals];
Fourth, one is spared the weariness and inconvenience of readying oneself [for an additional meal];
Fifth, one adopts an approach to eating that is consistent with more refined practice;
Sixth, one eats only after one's previous meal has been entirely digested;
Seventh, one devotes less effort to fending off difficulties [associated with obtaining food];
Eighth, one has fewer illnesses;
Ninth, one's body feels lighter and more at ease;
Tenth, one's experience of the body is pleasant.

正體字	常坐亦有十利。 114c21 ‖ 一不貪身樂。二不貪睡眠樂。三不貪臥具 114c22 ‖ 樂。四無臥時脇著席苦。五不隨身欲。六易 114c23 ‖ 得坐禪。七易讀誦經。八少睡眠。九身輕易 114c24 ‖ 起。十求坐臥具衣服心薄。食後不受非時 114c25 ‖ 飲食亦有十利。一不多食。二不滿食。三 114c26 ‖ 不貪美味。四少所求欲。五少妨患。六少疾 114c27 ‖ 病。七易滿。八易養。九知足。十坐禪讀經 114c28 ‖ 身不疲極。但三衣亦有十利。一於三衣外 114c29 ‖ 無求受疲苦。二無有守護疲苦。三所畜物 115a01 ‖ 少。四唯身所著為足。五細戒行。
简体字	常坐亦有十利。一不贪身乐。二不贪睡眠乐。三不贪卧具乐。四无卧时胁着席苦。五不随身欲。六易得坐禅。七易读诵经。八少睡眠。九身轻易起。十求坐卧具衣服心薄。食后不受非时饮食亦有十利。一不多食。二不满食。三不贪美味。四少所求欲。五少妨患。六少疾病。七易满。八易养。九知足。十坐禅读经身不疲极。但三衣亦有十利。一于三衣外无求受疲苦。二无有守护疲苦。三所畜物少。四唯身所著为足。五细戒行。

Chapter 32 — An Explanation of the Dhūta Austerities

c. The Ten Benefits of Always Sitting and Never Lying Down

Always sitting [and never lying down to sleep] also has ten benefits, as follows:[251]

First, one does not seek physical pleasure;
Second, one does not seek pleasure from sleeping;
Third, one does seek pleasure from [good] bedding;
Fourth, one is spared the aches associated with lying down on a sleeping mat;
Fifth, one does not pursue physical desires;
Sixth, it becomes easy to achieve success in sitting in *dhyāna* meditation;
Seventh, it becomes easy to study and recite scriptures;
Eighth, one spends less time sleeping;
Ninth, one's body feels light and rises easily;
Tenth, one devotes but little mental effort to seeking sitting cushions, bedding, and clothing;

d. The Ten Benefits of Not Accepting Food at the Wrong Time

There are also ten benefits of refraining from accepting food or drink at the wrong time,[252] after one has already eaten, as follows:

First, one thereby avoids excessive eating;
Second, one does not become full when eating;
Third, one avoids desire for fine flavors;
Fourth, one has fewer things one otherwise desires;
Fifth, one has fewer interfering difficulties;
Sixth, one has fewer illnesses;
Seventh, one easily feels full;
Eighth, one is easily supported;
Ninth, one is easily satisfied;
Tenth, one's body remains free of weariness when sitting in *dhyāna* meditation or studying scriptures.

e. The Ten Benefits of Possessing Only One Three-Part Set of Robes

Possessing only the single three-part set of robes also has ten benefits, as follows:

First, one is spared the weariness and inconvenience associated with seeking robes beyond the single three-part set of robes;
Second, one is spared the weariness and inconvenience of storing and protecting [additional clothing];
Third, one collects fewer things;
Fourth, one is satisfied with whatever one is wearing;
Fifth, this refines one's practice of the moral precepts;

正體字

```
            六行來無
115a02 ‖ 累。七身體輕便。八隨順阿練若處住。九處
115a03 ‖ 處所住無所顧惜。十隨順道行。受毳衣亦
115a04 ‖ 有十利。一在麁衣數。二少所求索。三隨意
115a05 ‖ 可坐。四隨意可臥。五浣濯則易。六染時亦
115a06 ‖ 易。七少有虫壞。八難壞。九更不受餘衣。
115a07 ‖ 十不[1]廢求道。隨敷坐亦有十利。一無求
115a08 ‖ 好精舍住疲苦。二無求好坐臥具疲苦。三
115a09 ‖ 不惱上座。四不令下坐愁惱。五少欲。六少
115a10 ‖ 事。七趣得而用。八少用則少務。九不起諍
115a11 ‖ 訟因緣。十不奪他所用。樹下坐亦有十利。
115a12 ‖ 一無有求房舍疲苦。
```

简体字

六行来无累。七身体轻便。八随顺阿练若处住。九处处所住无所顾惜。十随顺道行。受毳衣亦有十利。一在粗衣数。二少所求索。三随意可坐。四随意可卧。五浣濯则易。六染时亦易。七少有虫坏。八难坏。九更不受余衣。十不废求道。随敷坐亦有十利。一无求好精舍住疲苦。二无求好坐卧具疲苦。三不恼上座。四不令下坐愁恼。五少欲。六少事。七趣得而用。八少用则少务。九不起诤讼因缘。十不夺他所用。树下坐亦有十利。一无有求房舍疲苦。

Chapter 32 — An Explanation of the Dhūta Austerities

Sixth, one remains free of encumbrances when traveling;
Seventh, one's body feels lighter and more at ease;
Eighth, this practice accords with standards of practice for dwelling in a forest hermitage;
Ninth, no matter where one goes, one has nothing that one treasures;
Tenth, one's practice accords with the path.

f. THE TEN BENEFITS OF ACCEPTING ROBES WOVEN FROM ANIMAL HAIR

Accepting robes made of animal hair also has ten benefits, as follows:

First, one is a wearer of coarse clothes;
Second, one seeks but little;
Third, one can sit down anywhere;
Fourth, one can lie down anywhere;
Fifth, it is easy to wash;
Sixth, it is easy to dye;
Seventh, it is seldom ruined by insects;
Eighth, it is difficult to ruin;
Ninth, one has no need of any additional clothing;
Tenth, one does not neglect one's pursuit of the path.

g. THE TEN BENEFITS OF LAYING OUT ONE'S SITTING MAT WHEREVER ONE IS

Laying out one's sitting mat wherever one happens to be also has ten benefits, as follows:

First, one is spared the weariness and difficulty of seeking out a good monastic dwelling in which to live;
Second, one is spared the weariness and difficulty of seeking out a good seat and bed;
Third, one avoids aggravating those of senior monastic rank;
Fourth, one gives no cause for distress to those of junior monastic rank;
Fifth, one has few wants;
Sixth, one has few tasks;
Seventh, one uses whatever is available in the course of things;
Eighth, since one uses but little, one has but few responsibilities;
Ninth, one avoids the creation of causes or conditions for disputes;
Tenth, one avoids appropriating a spot used by someone else.

h. THE TEN BENEFITS OF DWELLING BENEATH A TREE

Dwelling beneath a tree also has ten benefits, as follows:

First, one is spared the weariness and inconvenience of seeking out a sheltered dwelling;

正體字

　　二無有求坐臥具
115a13 ‖ 疲苦。三無有所[2]愛疲苦。四無有受用疲
115a14 ‖ 苦。五無處名字。六無鬪諍事。七隨順四依
115a15 ‖ 法。八少而易得無過。九隨順修道。十無眾
115a16 ‖ 鬧行。死人間住亦有十利。一常得無常想。
115a17 ‖ 二常得死想。三常得不淨想。四常得一切
115a18 ‖ 世間不可樂想。五常得遠離一切所愛人。六
115a19 ‖ 常得悲心。七遠離戲調。八心常厭離。九勤
115a20 ‖ 行精進。十能除怖畏。空地坐者亦有十利。
115a21 ‖ 一不求樹下。二遠離我所有。三無有諍訟。
115a22 ‖ 四若餘去無所顧惜。五少戲調。六能忍風
115a23 ‖ 雨寒熱蚊虻毒虫等。七不為音聲刺蕀所
115a24 ‖ 刺。八不令眾生瞋恨。

简体字

二无有求坐卧具疲苦。三无有所爱疲苦。四无有受用疲苦。五无处名字。六无斗诤事。七随顺四依法。八少而易得无过。九随顺修道。十无众闹行。死人间住亦有十利。一常得无常想。二常得死想。三常得不净想。四常得一切世间不可乐想。五常得远离一切所爱人。六常得悲心。七远离戏调。八心常厌离。九勤行精进。十能除怖畏。空地坐者亦有十利。一不求树下。二远离我所有。三无有诤讼。四若余去无所顾惜。五少戏调。六能忍风雨寒热蚊虻毒虫等。七不为音声刺蕀所刺。八不令众生瞋恨。

Chapter 32 — An Explanation of the Dhūta Austerities

Second, one is spared the weariness and inconvenience of seeking lodging;[253]

Third, one is spared the weariness and inconvenience of indulging one's own preferences;

Fourth, one is spared the weariness and inconvenience of appropriating things for one's own use;

Fifth, one does not even have an address;

Sixth, one has no disputes;

Seventh, one complies with the dharma regulating the four necessities;

Eighth, one uses but little, uses only what is easily obtained, and avoids transgressions;

Ninth, one accords with correct cultivation of the path;

Tenth, one need not practice amidst the noisiness of groups.

i. THE TEN BENEFITS OF DWELLING IN A CHARNEL FIELD

Dwelling in a charnel field also has ten benefits, as follows:

First, one is always acquiring the perception of impermanence;

Second, one is always acquiring the perception of death;

Third, one is always acquiring the perception of the unloveliness [of the body];

Fourth, one is always acquiring the perception of the unenjoyability of all worldly existence;

Fifth, one is always developing renunciation of all who are dear to oneself;

Sixth, one is always attaining the mind of compassion;

Seventh, one abandons all frivolous restlessness;

Eighth, one's mind always abides in renunciation;

Ninth, one remains diligent in the cultivation of vigor;

Tenth, one is able to dispel all fears.

j. THE TEN BENEFITS OF DWELLING OUT IN THE OPEN

Dwelling out in the open also has ten benefits, as follows:

First, one does not have to find a tree to dwell beneath;

Second, one abandons everything one owns;

Third, one remains free of disputes;

Fourth, when going elsewhere, one has nothing one treasures;

Fifth, one seldom indulges frivolous restlessness;

Sixth, one is able to endure wind, rain, cold, heat, mosquitoes, horseflies, poisonous insects, and such;

Seventh, one remains unpierced by the thorn of noise;[254]

Eighth, one avoids arousing the hatred of other beings;

九自亦無有愁恨。十 ‖無眾閙行處。[3]

‖ 十住毘婆沙論卷第十六
‖ 十住毘婆沙論卷第十七 ‖
‖ 　　聖者龍樹造
‖ 　　後秦龜茲國三藏鳩摩羅什譯
‖ 　　解頭陀品之餘
‖ [4]如五空閑說　　餘功德亦爾
‖ 　自讀誦教他　　得捨空閑處
‖ 阿練若比丘有五種分別。一以惡意欲求
‖ 利養。二愚癡鈍根故行阿練若。三狂癡失意
‖ 作阿練若。四為行頭陀行故作阿練若。五
‖ 以諸佛菩薩賢聖所稱讚故作阿練若。於
‖ 此五阿練若中為行頭陀行故作阿練若。
‖ 以諸佛菩薩賢聖所稱讚故作阿練若。是
‖ 二為善。餘三可呵。如五種分別阿練若法
‖ 餘十一頭陀行亦應如是分別[5]知。問曰。佛
‖ 說[6]若已受阿練若法終不應捨。若有因
‖ 緣得捨去不。答曰。
‖ 　讀誦經因緣　　可捨阿練若
‖ 若比丘欲從他受[7]讀誦經法。若欲教他讀
‖ 誦。應從阿練若處

九自亦无有愁恨。十无众闹行处。

　　如五空闲说　　余功德亦尔
　　自读诵教他　　得舍空闲处

　　阿练若比丘有五种分别。一以恶意欲求利养。二愚痴钝根故行阿练若。三狂痴失意作阿练若。四为行头陀行故作阿练若。五以诸佛菩萨贤圣所称赞故作阿练若。于此五阿练若中为行头陀行故作阿练若。以诸佛菩萨贤圣所称赞故作阿练若。是二为善。余三可呵。如五种分别阿练若法余十一头陀行亦应如是分别知。问曰。佛说若已受阿练若法终不应舍。若有因缘得舍去不。答曰。

　　读诵经因缘　　可舍阿练若

　　若比丘欲从他受读诵经法。若欲教他读诵。应从阿练若处

Chapter 32 — An Explanation of the Dhūta Austerities

Ninth, one is himself also able to enjoy freedom from sorrow and hostility;

Tenth, one is able to avoid places frequented by noisy crowds;

3. Additional Discussion of Matters Related to Hermitage Dwelling

As explained for the five types of solitary wilderness dweller, just so understand correctness in the other meritorious qualities. In instances where one is to study, recite, or teach others, one may leave one's solitary wilderness dwelling.

a. Five Types of Monks Who Dwell in a Forest Hermitage

There are five distinct categories of bhikshus who dwell in a forest hermitage, namely:

First, there are those who, with evil intentions, seek gain and offerings;

Second, there are those who practice in a forest hermitage because of their own stupidity and dull faculties;

Third, there are those who establish a forest hermitage because they are insane, deluded, or deranged;

Fourth, there are those who establish a forest hermitage in order to practice the *dhūta* austerities;

Fifth, there are those who establish a forest hermitage because it is a practice praised by all buddhas, bodhisattvas, worthies, and *āryas*.

Of these five categories of forest hermitage dwellers, those taking up the practice in order to cultivate the *dhūta* austerities and those taking up the practice because it has been praised by all buddhas, bodhisattvas, worthies, and *āryas* are both good, whereas the other three may be reprimanded.

Just as with this fivefold distinction among those dwelling in a forest hermitage, so too should one distinguish and know [the differences among] the practitioners of the other eleven *dhūta* austerities.

b. Additional Discussion of When One May Leave a Hermitage

Question: The Buddha said that whosoever has taken up the practice of dwelling in a forest hermitage should never abandon it. If there are extenuating circumstances, is it or is it not permissible to abandon it?

Response:

One may leave one's forest hermitage
in order to study or recite scriptures.

If a bhikshu wishes to receive others' teachings on the study or recitation of the Dharma of the scriptures, or, alternatively, if he wishes to instruct others in such study or recitation, he may leave his forest

	來入塔寺。以是因緣可
115b22 ‖	得捨離。
115b23 ‖	教他讀誦時　　不應望供給
115b24 ‖	即時應念佛　　佛[8]常有所作
115b25 ‖	阿練若從空閑處來。教他讀誦。不應求敬
115b26 ‖	心供給。應當念[9]佛。尚自有所作。何況於
115b27 ‖	我。念佛者。佛是多陀阿伽[10]陀三藐三佛陀。
115b28 ‖	諸天龍神乾闥婆阿修羅迦樓羅緊那羅摩睺
115b29 ‖	羅伽釋提桓因四天王人非人所供養。一切
115c01 ‖	眾生無上福田。尚不求他供給身自執事。
115c02 ‖	我今未有所知。始欲求學。云何受他供給。
115c03 ‖	復應作是念。
115c04 ‖	我應善供給　　一切諸眾生
115c05 ‖	不望彼供給　　自利利他故
115c06 ‖	云何為自利。若貴供給則失法施功德。
115c07 ‖	若不貴供給者則得法施功德。云何為利
115c08 ‖	他。若貴彼供給而教令讀誦者。彼則生念
115c09 ‖	師直以世利故而教誨我

来入塔寺。以是因缘可得舍离。

　教他读诵时　　不应望供给
　即时应念佛　　佛常有所作

阿练若从空闲处来。教他读诵。不应求敬心供给。应当念佛。尚自有所作。何况于我。念佛者。佛是多陀阿伽陀三藐三佛陀。诸天龙神乾闼婆阿修罗迦楼罗紧那罗摩睺罗伽释提桓因四天王人非人所供养。一切众生无上福田。尚不求他供给身自执事。我今未有所知。始欲求学。云何受他供给。复应作是念。

　我应善供给　　一切诸众生
　不望彼供给　　自利利他故

云何为自利。若贵供给则失法施功德。若不贵供给者则得法施功德。云何为利他。若贵彼供给而教令读诵者。彼则生念师直以世利故而教诲我

Chapter 32 — An Explanation of the Dhūta Austerities

hermitage and come into the stupa or temple. It is permissible to leave for these purposes.

1) Proper Motivation When Leaving the Forest Hermitage

When teaching others in study and recitation,
one should not do so wishing to attract offerings or support.
Rather, one should immediately bring to mind the Buddha, [thinking],
"Even[255] the Buddha had endeavors he was intent on accomplishing."

When one emerges from his isolated forest hermitage to teach others in study and recitation, one should not do so seeking to attract respect or offerings of support. Rather, one should bring to mind the Buddha, thinking, "If even the Buddha[256] had endeavors he was intent on accomplishing, how much the more should this be so for someone like me?"

"Bringing to mind the Buddha" in this context refers to recalling that the Buddha is the Tathāgata, the One of Right and Universal Enlightenment, one to whom even the devas, dragons, spirits, *gandharvas*, *asuras*, *garudas*, *kinnaras*, *mahoragas*, Śakra, ruler of the devas, the Four Heavenly Kings, humans, and nonhumans all make offerings, one who serves as the unsurpassable field of merit for all beings. [One recalls that] not even he seeks offerings or support from anyone. He just continues on in devotion to the endeavors he has taken up. [Thus one reflects]: "Now I am one who still does not know anything, one who is just a beginner in the training. How then could I be worthy to receive anyone's offerings?"

Additionally, one should reflect as follows:

2) Generating the Motivation to Benefit Both Self and Others

I am the one who should be devoted
to making offerings to all beings,
for, rather than expecting them to make offerings,
I should be benefiting myself while also benefiting others.

What then is meant by "benefiting oneself"? If one esteems the receiving of offerings [from others], then he loses the merit that would otherwise arise through giving the gift of Dharma. If, on the other hand, one refrains from esteeming the receiving of offerings, then one may acquire the meritorious qualities arising from giving the Dharma to others.

What then is meant by "benefiting others"? If one esteems others' offerings and then teaches them to study and recite scriptures, they will then think, "The teacher instructs us only in order to gain worldly

正體字

115c10 ‖ 不以法故。是人
115c10 ‖ 若以是心供給師者則不得大利。若但
115c11 ‖ 恭敬法故尊重師者則得大利是名利
115c12 ‖ 他。
115c13 ‖ 　從他求智慧　　應不惜身命
115c14 ‖ 若行者欲從他[11]求智慧應捨身命。捨者
115c15 ‖ 為智慧故。勤心精進恭敬於師不惜身命。
115c16 ‖ 問曰。何以故。為智慧恭敬師而不惜身
115c17 ‖ 命。答曰。
115c18 ‖ 　若一字一心　　以此為劫數
115c19 ‖ 　恭敬於師所　　能說[12]此論者
115c20 ‖ 　離諸諂曲心　　深愛而[13]恭敬
115c21 ‖ 　晝夜不休息　　盡於爾所劫
115c22 ‖ 隨師所教論[14]義字數及爾所心念。若受法
115c23 ‖ 者心無諂曲不惜身命。晝夜恭敬始終無
115c24 ‖ 異。雖能如是猶不報師所益論議智慧之
115c25 ‖ 恩。

简体字

不以法故。是人若以是心供给师者则不得大利。若但恭敬法故尊重师者则得大利是名利他。

　　从他求智慧　　应不惜身命

若行者欲从他求智慧应舍身命。舍者为智慧故。勤心精进恭敬于师不惜身命。问曰。何以故。为智慧恭敬师而不惜身命。答曰。

　　若一字一心　　以此为劫数
　　恭敬于师所　　能说此论者
　　离诸谄曲心　　深爱而恭敬
　　昼夜不休息　　尽于尔所劫

随师所教论义字数及尔所心念。若受法者心无谄曲不惜身命。昼夜恭敬始终无异。虽能如是犹不报师所益论议智慧之恩。

Chapter 32 – An Explanation of the Dhūta Austerities

benefit for himself and not for the sake of the Dharma." If someone makes offerings to his spiritual teacher when under the influence of these sorts of thoughts, he will not reap a great amount of merit. If, on the other hand, he were to feel profound esteem for the teacher solely out of reverence for the Dharma, he would acquire an immense amount of merit. This is what constitutes "benefiting others."

In one's striving to acquire wisdom from others,
one should not cherish even one's own body or life.

If the practitioner wishes to seek wisdom from others, he should then be willing even to sacrifice his own body and life in this quest. "Sacrifice" means that, for the sake of acquiring wisdom, one is so diligent, vigorous, and reverently respectful of his spiritual teacher that he does not even cherish his own body and life.

c. On the Importance of Revering One's Spiritual Teacher

Question: Why should one, in striving for wisdom, revere the spiritual teacher even to the point that one does not even cherish one's own body and life?

1) On the Difficulty of Repaying the Kindness of One's Teacher

Response:
If every one of his words and every one of his thoughts
were to be accorded that very number of kalpas
during which one might bow in reverence to the spiritual teacher
able to teach this treatise,

as one also took care to avoid any flattering or devious thought,
and, suffused with deep affection, [bowed in] reverence to him
day and night without cease, [one should indeed wish to do so],
continuing on even to the end of just such a number of kalpas.

[If one allotted a number of kalpas of devotion] corresponding to however many words are in the treatises taught by one's spiritual teacher in addition to however many thoughts he used in providing that instruction, and if the mind of the beneficiary of the teachings remained entirely free of any flattery and deviousness in his demonstrations of reverence performed without cherishing his own body and life, and if he carried on with that reverence day and night with earnestness that remained undiminished from beginning to end—although one might indeed carry through with just such devotion, one still would be unable to adequately repay the kindness of the spiritual teacher's benefiting one with the wisdom of this treatise.

正體字

	是故弟子應離諂曲心捨貪惜身命破
115c26 ‖	於憍慢。若師輕蔑及以[15]敬愛心無有異。
115c27 ‖	當生深愛心[16]第一恭敬心。應生父母心。應
115c28 ‖	生大師心。應生善知識想。應生能為難事
115c29 ‖	想。應生難報心。若師聽則受[17]所常行事。
116a01 ‖	不須師勅餘事則相望師意隨事而行。師
116a02 ‖	所愛重隨而愛重。不應因師求於世利。莫
116a03 ‖	求師讚歎。莫求名聞。但求智慧法寶。師
116a04 ‖	有謬失常應隱藏。若師過釁若彰露者。當
116a05 ‖	方便覆之。師有功德稱揚流布。深心愛樂
116a06 ‖	聽受持解。[1]思惟義趣如所說行。求自利
116a07 ‖	利他者。莫為[2]秕弟子。莫為[3]大弟子。莫
116a08 ‖	為垢弟子。莫為衰弟子。莫為

简体字

是故弟子应离谄曲心舍贪惜身命破于憍慢。若师轻蔑及以敬爱心无有异。当生深爱心第一恭敬心。应生父母心。应生大师心。应生善知识想。应生能为难事想。应生难报心。若师听则受所常行事。不须师敕余事则相望师意随事而行。师所爱重随而爱重。不应因师求于世利。莫求师赞叹。莫求名闻。但求智慧法宝。师有谬失常应隐藏。若师过衅若彰露者。当方便覆之。师有功德称扬流布。深心爱乐听受持解。思惟义趣如所说行。求自利利他者。莫为秕弟子。莫为大弟子。莫为垢弟子。莫为衰弟子。莫为

Chapter 32 — An Explanation of the Dhūta Austerities

2) On Maintaining the Proper Attitude toward One's Teacher

The disciple should therefore abandon any thoughts of flattery or deviousness, should not selfishly cherish his own body and life, and should crush any arrogance. Even were the teacher to slight him, his thoughts of reverence and affectionate regard should remain undiminished. Rather, he should bring forth thoughts of deep affection for him, should bring forth the most profoundly sincere reverence for him, should think of the spiritual teacher as he would his own parents, should think of him as a great teaching master, should think of him as his good spiritual guide, should think of him as someone able to do what is most difficult, and should realize that [the teacher's kindness] is something difficult to ever adequately repay.

3) On Taking Direction from One's Teacher

If one's spiritual teacher has already permitted them, then one should take up the tasks one usually does, for one does not need the teacher's [additional] permission to do so. If there are other tasks that arise, then one is to consult the teacher for his opinion, whereupon one performs the tasks accordingly. Thus one should also cherish and esteem whatever one's teacher cherishes and esteems.

4) On Not Seeking Praise or Benefit in Relating to a Teacher

One must not seek to reap any worldly advantage from one's relationship with one's spiritual teacher. One must not seek the teacher's praise and must also not seek name and fame [on account of that relationship]. Rather, one should seek only to obtain the Dharma jewel of wisdom.

5) On Making the Teacher's Good Qualities Well Known

In the event the teacher makes some mistake, one should allow it to always remain a private matter. If the teacher has committed some infraction and it has come to light, one should use some expedient to conceal it.

One should proclaim and make widely known the meritorious qualities possessed by one's teacher while also sincerely delighting in listening to, accepting, upholding, comprehending, contemplating, and practicing in accord with the import of his teachings.

6) On the Need to Become a Good Lineage-Preserving Disciple

As for striving to "benefit oneself and also benefit others," one must not become a mere straw disciple, must not become a disastrous disciple,[257] must not become a defiled disciple, must not become a disciple who allows [the lineage to go to] ruin, and must not become a

正體字

無益弟子。
116a09 ‖ 無如是等過。但住善弟子法中。供給於師。
116a10 ‖ 如般舟經說。佛告[4]颰陀婆羅。若菩薩欲得
116a11 ‖ 是三昧者。應勤精進於諸師所生尊重心
116a12 ‖ 難遭心。若從口聞。若得經卷處。於是師所
116a13 ‖ 應深心恭敬生父母心善知識心大師心。以
116a14 ‖ 能說如是法助菩提故。颰陀婆羅。若求菩
116a15 ‖ 薩道者。若求聲聞者。所從師讀誦是法
116a16 ‖ 處。不生深恭敬心父母心善知識心大師心。
116a17 ‖ 能得[5]誦利是法。令不忘失久住不滅者。
116a18 ‖ 無有是處。何以故。颰陀婆羅以不恭敬因
116a19 ‖ 緣故。佛法則滅。[6]是故颰陀婆羅。若求菩薩
116a20 ‖ 道者。若求聲聞者。於所從聞。讀誦書寫
116a21 ‖ 是法處。生恭敬心父母心善知識心大師心
116a22 ‖ 者。於所讀誦書寫未得者令得已得久住
116a23 ‖ 則有是處。何以故。以恭敬心故佛法不滅。

简体字

无益弟子。无如是等过。但住善弟子法中。供给于师。如般舟经说。佛告颰陀婆罗。若菩萨欲得是三昧者。应勤精进于诸师所生尊重心难遭心。若从口闻。若得经卷处。于是师所应深心恭敬生父母心善知识心大师心。以能说如是法助菩提故。颰陀婆罗。若求菩萨道者。若求声闻者。所从师读诵是法处。不生深恭敬心父母心善知识心大师心。能得诵利是法。令不忘失久住不灭者。无有是处。何以故。颰陀婆罗以不恭敬因缘故。佛法则灭。是故颰陀婆罗。若求菩萨道者。若求声闻者。于所从闻。读诵书写是法处。生恭敬心父母心善知识心大师心者。于所读诵书写未得者令得已得久住则有是处。何以故。以恭敬心故佛法不灭。

Chapter 32 — An Explanation of the Dhūta Austerities

useless disciple. One must not allow oneself to fall into any such transgressions as these.

i) Scriptural Instructions on Right Behavior toward Teachers

One must abide solely within the dharma appropriate to a good disciple. One should make offerings to one's spiritual teacher. This is as described in *The Pratyutpanna [Samādhi] Sūtra* in which the Buddha told Bhadrapāla:

> If a bodhisattva wishes to acquire this samādhi, he should be diligent and vigorous in bringing forth thoughts of reverential esteem toward all his teachers, thoughts recognizing the rare good fortune to encounter them. In the case of those from whom one has received teachings personally spoken by them or those from whom one has obtained volumes of scriptural texts, one should express deeply sincere reverence for these teachers, regarding them as one would one's own parents, regarding them as one's good spiritual guides, and regarding them as great teaching masters. This is because they are able to teach Dharma such as this which is able to assist one's realization of bodhi.
>
> Bhadrapāla, whether one strives to follow in the bodhisattva path or one seeks the way of a *śrāvaka* disciple, if one were to fail to bring forth thoughts of deep reverence for the teacher as the source of one's becoming able to study and recite this Dharma, if one were to fail to think of one's teacher as one would one's own parents, regarding him as one's good spiritual guide, and regarding him as a great teaching master, it would then be impossible for one to correctly understand[258] this Dharma in such a way that it would not perish but rather would abide for a long time without disappearing.
>
> Why is this? Bhadrapāla, it is because of just such failure to accord reverence that the Buddha's Dharma disappears.
>
> Therefore, Bhadrapāla, whether one strives to follow in the bodhisattva path or one seeks the way of a *śrāvaka* disciple, were one to bring forth thoughts of reverential respect for whoever one heard this Dharma from and whoever was the source of one's being able to study, recite, or write out this Dharma, bringing forth thoughts regarding him as one would one's own parents, regarding him as one's good spiritual guide, and regarding him as a great master of the teachings—if one were able to do that, then it is indeed possible that whatsoever one has studied, recited, and written out, and whatsoever one had not obtained but has now obtained might now be able to remain [in this world] for a long time.
>
> And why is this? Because it is due to having a mind of reverential respect that the Buddha's Dharma does not disappear. Therefore,

正體字

116a24 ‖ 是故颰陀婆羅。我今告汝。於是師所應生
116a25 ‖ 深恭敬心父母心善知識心大師心。是則隨
116a26 ‖ 我所教。

简体字

是故颰陀婆罗。我今告汝。于是师所应生深恭敬心父母心善知识心大师心。是则随我所教。

Bhadrapāla, I am now telling you: One must bring forth thoughts of profound reverential respect toward teachers such as this, bringing forth thoughts regarding them as one would one's own parents, regarding them as good spiritual guides, and regarding them as great masters of the teachings. This being so, one is to comply with what I have herein instructed.

The End of Chapter Thirty-Two

正體字

116a27 ‖　　　助尸羅果品第[7]六
116a28 ‖ 如是菩薩。為求多聞知多聞義已隨說行
116a29 ‖ 故。能令尸羅清淨。清淨尸羅法應當修行。
116b01 ‖ 問曰。何等法能令尸羅清淨。答曰。
116b02 ‖ 　護身口意業　　亦不得護法
116b03 ‖ 　終不令我見　　及以餘見雜
116b04 ‖ 　迴向薩婆若　　此四淨尸羅
116b05 ‖ 行者修此四法。尸羅自然清淨。護身口意
116b06 ‖ 業者。常應正念身口意業乃至小罪不令
116b07 ‖ 錯謬。譬如龜鼈常護頭足。此人深樂空故。
116b08 ‖ 於第一義中而亦不得護三業法。有人
116b09 ‖ 雖見法空謂知空者在。是故說不[8]雜
116b10 ‖ 我見眾生見人見壽[9]者見知者見。迴向薩婆
116b11 ‖ 若者。持戒果報不求餘福。

简体字

助尸罗果品第三十四

如是菩萨。为求多闻知多闻义已随说行故。能令尸罗清净。清净尸罗法应当修行。问曰。何等法能令尸罗清净。答曰。

　护身口意业　　亦不得护法
　终不令我见　　及以余见杂
　回向萨婆若　　此四净尸罗

行者修此四法。尸罗自然清净。护身口意业者。常应正念身口意业乃至小罪不令错谬。譬如龟鳖常护头足。此人深乐空故。于第一义中而亦不得护三业法。有人虽见法空谓知空者在。是故说不杂我见众生见人见寿者见知者见。回向萨婆若者。持戒果报不求余福。

Chapter 33
Aids to Gaining the Fruits of Śīla

XIII. Chapter 33: Aids to Gaining the Fruits of Śīla
   A. On the Purification of Śīla, Moral Virtue

In order to pursue extensive learning and then practice in accord with the way it was taught after understanding the meaning of that extensive learning, a bodhisattva such as this becomes able to purify his practice of *śīla*. Thus one should cultivate the dharmas used to purify one's practice of *śīla* (moral virtue).

    1. Four Dharmas Enabling Purification of Moral Virtue

Question: Which dharmas are able to purify one's practice of *śīla*?
Response:
> Guard the actions of body, speech, and mind
> while also not apprehending any dharma by which one guards it.
> Never permit any admixture of the view of a self
> or any of the other views.
> Dedicate the merit from this to the attainment of all-knowledge.
> These four methods purify one's practice of *śīla*.

If the practitioner cultivates these four dharmas, his observance of *śīla* will naturally become pure. "Guarding the actions of body, speech, and mind" refers to always using right mindfulness in one's physical, verbal, and mental actions even to the point that one does not allow oneself to err through committing even the most minor transgressions, acting in this like the tortoise who always takes such care in guarding his head and feet.

Because this practitioner deeply delights in emptiness, in his comprehension of the supreme meaning, he does not even apprehend [the existence of] any dharma by which one guards the three types of actions. There are others who, although they do indeed perceive the emptiness of dharmas, they are still of the opinion that the knower of emptiness remains [as an existent entity]. It is for this reason that [the verse] says, "Never permit any admixture of the view imputing a self," the view of a being, the view of a person, the view of a soul, the view of a life,[259] or the view of a knower.

"Dedicating [merit to the realization of] all-knowledge" means one does not dedicate the merit arising from upholding the moral precepts to any other sort of fortunate result, but rather only dedicates it to the

正體字

```
            但為度一切眾
116b12 ‖ 生。以求佛道。是為四。復有四法。能令尸羅
116b13 ‖ 清淨。所謂。
116b14 ‖   無我我所心    亦無斷常見
116b15 ‖   入於眾緣法    則能淨尸羅
116b16 ‖ 無我我所心者。不貪著我我所心。但知此
116b17 ‖ 心虛妄顛倒而無我法。無斷常見者。以斷
116b18 ‖ 常見多過故。入眾緣法者。知諸法從眾緣
116b19 ‖ 生無有定性。行於中道。如是四法能淨尸
116b20 ‖ 羅。復有四法能淨尸羅。所謂。
116b21 ‖   行四聖種[10]行    及十二頭陀
116b22 ‖   亦不樂眾鬧    念何故出家
116b23 ‖ 四聖種者。所謂趣得衣服而足。趣得飲食
116b24 ‖ 而足。趣得坐臥具而足。樂斷樂修行。十二
116b25 ‖ 頭陀者。所謂受阿練若法。受乞食法。糞掃
116b26 ‖ 衣。一坐。
```

简体字

但为度一切众生。以求佛道。是为四。复有四法。能令尸罗清净。所谓。

　　无我我所心　　亦无断常见
　　入于众缘法　　则能净尸罗

无我我所心者。不贪着我我所心。但知此心虚妄颠倒而无我法。无断常见者。以断常见多过故。入众缘法者。知诸法从众缘生无有定性。行于中道。如是四法能净尸罗。复有四法能净尸罗。所谓。

　　行四圣种行　　及十二头陀
　　亦不乐众闹　　念何故出家

四圣种者。所谓趣得衣服而足。趣得饮食而足。趣得坐卧具而足。乐断乐修行。十二头陀者。所谓受阿练若法。受乞食法。粪扫衣。一坐。

Chapter 33 — Aids to Gaining the Fruits of Śīla

liberation of all beings through one's quest to attain buddhahood. These are the four [dharmas that enable the purification of moral virtue].

2. Four More Dharmas Enabling Purification of Moral Virtue

There are yet another four dharmas by which one is able to bring about the purification of one's practice of śīla, namely:

If one has no conceptions of a self or anything belonging to a self,
if one also has no annihilationist or eternalist views,
and if one penetrates the dharma explaining multiple conditions,
one will then be able to purify one's practice of śīla.

"Freedom from conceptions of a self or anything belonging to a self" refers to not being attached to thoughts imputing the existence of a self or anything belonging to a self. One need only realize that these ideas are empty, false, and inverted and hence there is no dharma of [the existence of] a self.

One "has no annihilationist or eternalist views" because annihilationist and eternalist views are possessed of numerous faults.

As for "penetrating the dharma that explains multiple conditions," by knowing that all dharmas are products of many conditions and hence are devoid of any fixed nature of their own, one practices the Middle Way.

[By availing oneself of] four such dharmas such as these, one is able to purify one's practice of śīla.

3. Four More Dharmas Enabling Purification of Moral Virtue

There are four additional dharmas through which one is able to purify one's practice of śīla, namely:

One practices the four lineage bases of the Āryas,
adopts the twelve *dhūta* austerities,
also does not delight in the noise of crowds,
and bears in mind why one left home [to become a monastic].

"The four lineage bases of the Āryas" refers to being satisfied with whatever robes one has already obtained, to being satisfied with whatever food and drink one has already obtained, to being satisfied with whatever dwelling place[260] one has already obtained, and to delighting in severance and delighting in cultivation.

"The twelve *dhūta* austerities" are:

Adopting the dharma of dwelling in a forest hermitage;
Obtaining one's food through the alms round;
Wearing robes made of cast-off rags;
[Taking one's daily meal in but] a single sitting;

正體字

常坐。食後不受非時飲食。但有三
衣。毛氀衣。隨敷坐。樹下住。空地住。死人間
住。亦不樂眾鬧者。不與在家出家者和
合。有人雖行阿練若法。多知多識故。多人
往來。是故說不樂眾鬧。若至餘處。若心不
與和合。何故出家者。行尸羅者作是念。我
何故而出家。念已。隨出家事欲成就故。如
所說行。是為四。復有四法能淨尸羅。所
謂。

　　五陰無生滅　　六性如法性
　　見六情亦空　　不著世俗語
　　如是之四法　　亦能淨尸羅

五陰無生滅者。思惟五陰本末故。見五陰
無生滅[11]者。見地等六性如法性。如法性不
可得六性亦不可得。知六情雖是苦樂等。心
心數法因緣。

简体字

常坐。食后不受非时饮食。但有三衣。毛氀衣。随敷坐。树下住。空地住。死人间住。亦不乐众闹者。不与在家出家者和合。有人虽行阿练若法。多知多识故。多人往来。是故说不乐众闹。若至余处。若心不与和合。何故出家者。行尸罗者作是念。我何故而出家。念已。随出家事欲成就故。如所说行。是为四。复有四法能净尸罗。所谓。

　　五阴无生灭　　六性如法性
　　见六情亦空　　不着世俗语
　　如是之四法　　亦能净尸罗

五阴无生灭者。思惟五阴本末故。见五阴无生灭者。见地等六性如法性。如法性不可得六性亦不可得。知六情虽是苦乐等。心心数法因缘。

Chapter 33 — Aids to Gaining the Fruits of Śīla

Always sitting [to sleep, never lying down];
Having taken the meal, not accepting food or drink at the wrong times;
Possessing only a single three-part set of robes;
Wearing only an animal-hair robe;
Laying out one's sitting mat wherever one happens to be;
Dwelling at the foot of a tree;
Dwelling out in the open (lit. "on empty ground");
Dwelling in a charnel field.

"Not delighting in the noise of crowds" refers to avoiding meeting together with either laypeople or monastics. There are those who, although they have taken up the dharma of dwelling in a forest hermitage, because they have many acquaintances and friends, often have many people coming and going. Therefore, it refers here to "not delighting in the noise of crowds," whether through not going off to other places or through being disinclined to gather together with others.

As for "bearing in mind why one left home [to become a monastic]," one who is focused on *śīla* practice reflects thus: "Why did I leave the home life to become a monastic?" Having pondered this, because one accords with the endeavors appropriate to the monastic's life and wishes to succeed in these, he practices in a manner that accords with the way [monastic cultivation] was taught. These are the four.

4. Four More Dharmas Enabling Purification of Moral Virtue

There are another four dharmas by which one can purify one's practice of *śīla*, namely:

[One sees that] the five aggregates have no arising or destruction,
[sees] the six elements[261] as like the nature of dharmas,
sees that the six sense faculties are empty [of inherent existence],
and does not become attached to worldly expressions.
[Practice] that accords with these four dharmas
also enables one to purify one's practice of *śīla*.

As for "[seeing that] the five aggregates have no arising or destruction," this means that, by contemplating the five aggregates from root to branch, one perceives their absence of arising and destruction.

As for "[seeing that] the six elements" consisting of earth and so forth "are like the nature of dharmas,"[262] this means that, just as the nature of dharmas cannot be apprehended, so too, the six elements cannot be apprehended, either.

One realizes that, although the six sense faculties involve pain, pleasure, and such, they do so through causes and conditions linked

正體字

	以正智推求。亦知是空。了達
116c13 ‖	三種皆知是空。有行者貪著於空則還妨
116c14 ‖	道。是故說莫貪著空。隨於世俗說空名
116c15 ‖	字。如是法者能淨尸羅。問曰。若爾者云何
116c16 ‖	言五陰諸法。答曰。以空故。五陰諸法空。最
116c17 ‖	後言莫著於空者。空亦應捨。如是無有
116c18 ‖	邪疑法妨礙尸羅。問曰。五陰諸法。以有相
116c19 ‖	可相故。決定有。如說色是苦惱相覺苦樂
116c20 ‖	是受相。現有如是等諸相。云何言非空非
116c21 ‖	不空。答曰。
116c22 ‖	惱壞是色相　　何等為是色
116c23 ‖	若惱是色相　　離相無可相
116c24 ‖	此相在何處　　無相無可相
116c25 ‖	世界終無有　　無相有可相
116c26 ‖	相與及可相　　非合非不合
116c27 ‖	其來無所從　　去亦無所至
116c28 ‖	若有合非合　　成於相可相

简体字

以正智推求。亦知是空。了达三种皆知是空。有行者贪着于空则还妨道。是故说莫贪着空。随于世俗说空名字。如是法者能净尸罗。问曰。若尔者云何言五阴诸法。答曰。以空故。五阴诸法空。最后言莫着于空者。空亦应舍。如是无有邪疑法妨碍尸罗。问曰。五阴诸法。以有相可相故。决定有。如说色是苦恼相觉苦乐是受相。现有如是等诸相。云何言非空非不空。答曰。

　恼坏是色相　　何等为是色
　若恼是色相　　离相无可相
　此相在何处　　无相无可相
　世界终无有　　无相有可相
　相与及可相　　非合非不合
　其来无所从　　去亦无所至
　若有合非合　　成于相可相

Chapter 33 — Aids to Gaining the Fruits of Śīla

to the mind and mental dharmas. Thus, by resorting to investigative applications of right wisdom, one realizes that they are empty [of any inherent existence].

One then utterly comprehends the nature of all three of these associated categories, realizing that in every case they are entirely empty [of inherent existence].

There are practitioners who develop an attachment to emptiness that then also hinders cultivation of the path. Hence it states here that one must not develop an attachment to emptiness that simply conforms to worldly uses of the word "emptiness."

Dharmas such as these enable one to purify one's practice of *śīla*.

Question: If this is truly so, why do you speak here of the dharmas of the five aggregates?

Response: It is because they are empty. All dharmas of the five aggregates are empty. As for the very last part where it states that one must not become attached to emptiness, this means that even "emptiness" should be relinquished. If one accords with this, then there will be no dharma of erroneous doubtfulness impeding one's practice of *śīla*.

Question: Because the dharmas of the five aggregates are possessed of characteristic marks and that which can be marked, they do therefore definitely exist. Take for instance the [canonical] declarations that "the form aggregate is characterized by being assailed by what is painful"[263] and "awareness of pain and pleasure is the characteristic of the feeling aggregate." Given that they obviously possess such characteristics, how can one claim that [the aggregates] are neither empty nor non-empty?

Response:

Affliction and destruction are marks of the form aggregate.
What all goes into making this form?
If affliction is indeed a characteristic mark of form,
apart from its marks, there is nothing amenable to being marked.

And where then do these characteristic marks abide?
There is no mark nor anything that can be marked.
The entire world is finally nonexistent.
There is neither any mark nor anything that can be marked.

Characteristic marks and that which can be marked
are neither conjoined nor not conjoined.
In their coming forth, they have no place from which they come.
In going away, they also have no place to which they go.

If one posits either a conjoining or a nonconjoining
through which one establishes either marks or what is markable,

正體字	116c29 ‖	如是則為失　　相及可相相
	117a01 ‖	以相成可相　　相亦不自成
	117a02 ‖	相自不能成　　云何成可相
	117a03 ‖	世界甚可愍　　分別相可相
	117a04 ‖	迷惑諸[1]邪徑　　邪師所欺誑
	117a05 ‖	相可相則是　　無相無可相
	117a06 ‖	如是眼見事　　如何不能知
	117a07 ‖	隨計相可相　　有如是戲論
	117a08 ‖	隨起戲論時　　則[2]隨煩惱處
	117a09 ‖	復次行者以不來不去門觀諸陰性入空。
	117a10 ‖	如說。
	117a11 ‖	生老病死法　　生時無從來
	117a12 ‖	生老病死法　　滅時無所去
	117a13 ‖	諸陰界入性　　生時無從來
	117a14 ‖	滅時無所去　　佛法義如是
	117a15 ‖	如火非人功　　亦不在鑽木
	117a16 ‖	和合中亦無　　而因和合有
	117a17 ‖	薪盡則火滅　　滅[3]時無所去
	117a18 ‖	諸緣合故有　　緣散則皆無
	117a19 ‖	眼識亦如是　　不在於眼中
简体字		如是则为失　　相及可相相
		以相成可相　　相亦不自成
		相自不能成　　云何成可相
		世界甚可愍　　分别相可相
		迷惑诸邪径　　邪师所欺诳
		相可相则是　　无相无可相
		如是眼见事　　如何不能知
		随计相可相　　有如是戏论
		随起戏论时　　则随烦恼处
		复次行者以不来不去门观诸阴性入空。如说。
		生老病死法　　生时无从来
		生老病死法　　灭时无所去
		诸阴界入性　　生时无从来
		灭时无所去　　佛法义如是
		如火非人功　　亦不在钻木
		和合中亦无　　而因和合有
		薪尽则火灭　　灭时无所去
		诸缘合故有　　缘散则皆无
		眼识亦如是　　不在于眼中

Chapter 33 — Aids to Gaining the Fruits of Śīla

then to proceed in this way is mistaken
with regard to both marks and what is markable.

This would be to use marks to establish what is markable.
[However], marks themselves are not self established.
Since even marks themselves cannot be established,
how then could they [be used to] establish what is markable?

The beings of the world are so extremely pitiable,
for they distinguish marks and what is markable,
become deluded in pursuing all manner of deviant paths,
and are cheated and deceived by deviant teachers.

Marks and what is markable then are just
devoid of marks and devoid of anything that can be marked.
Given such a visibly apparent situation as this,
how could one fail to realize [what is so obvious]?

Pursuant to imputations of the existence of marks and the markable,
there exist such [merely] conceptual elaborations as these.
And whenever such conceptual elaborations as these arise,
one then falls into a position associated with afflictions.[264]

Moreover, the practitioner employs the gateway of [understanding that all phenomena] neither come into existence nor pass away to facilitate the contemplation of the aggregates, sense realms, and sense bases as empty [of inherent existence]. This is as described here:

The dharmas of birth, aging, sickness, and death,
when arising, have no place from which they come.
The dharmas of birth, aging, sickness, and death,
when extinguished, have no place to which they go.

It is the nature of the aggregates, sense realms, and sense bases that,
when arising, they have no place from which they come,
and, when extinguished, they have no place to which they go.
Just so is the meaning of the Buddha's Dharma.

So too with fire, which is not in the human effort used to make it,
is also not present in the friction drill or wood,
and is not in their coming together, either,
even as it still does exist due to their all having come together.

If the fuel is entirely consumed, the fire will then die out.
Yet, when it does die out, there is no place to which it goes.
It exists due to the coming together of conditions,
yet, if those conditions scatter, it becomes entirely nonexistent.

So too is this the case with the eye consciousness
that does not abide in the eye,

117a20 ‖	不在於色中	亦不在中間
117a21 ‖	不在和合中	亦不離和合
117a22 ‖	亦不從餘來	而因和合有
117a23 ‖	和合散則無	諸法亦如是
117a24 ‖	生時無從來	滅時無所至
117a25 ‖	如彼龍心力	而有陰雲現
117a26 ‖	不從龍身出	亦不餘處來
117a27 ‖	而[4]此大陰雲	雨流滿世界
117a28 ‖	然後乃消滅	亦無有去處
117a29 ‖	如雲無來去	諸法亦如是
117b01 ‖	生時無從來	滅時無所去
117b02 ‖	如壁上畫人	不在一一[5]彩
117b03 ‖	亦不在和合	壁中亦復無
117b04 ‖	畫師所亦無	畫筆中亦無
117b05 ‖	不從餘處來	而因和合有
117b06 ‖	和合散則無	諸法亦如是
117b07 ‖	有時無從來	無時無所去
117b08 ‖	燈炎不在油	亦不從炷出
117b09 ‖	亦不餘處來	而因油炷有
117b10 ‖	因緣盡則滅	滅時無去處

正體字

不在于色中　亦不在中間
不在和合中　亦不离和合
亦不从余来　而因和合有
和合散则无　诸法亦如是
生时无从来　灭时无所至
如彼龙心力　而有阴云现
不从龙身出　亦不余处来
而此大阴云　雨流满世界
然后乃消灭　亦无有去处
如云无来去　诸法亦如是
生时无从来　灭时无所去
如壁上画人　不在一一彩
亦不在和合　壁中亦复无
画师所亦无　画笔中亦无
不从余处来　而因和合有
和合散则无　诸法亦如是
有时无从来　无时无所去
灯炎不在油　亦不从炷出
亦不余处来　而因油炷有
因缘尽则灭　灭时无去处

简体字

also does not abide in visual forms,
also does not abide between them,

also does not abide in their combination,
also is not found apart from them,
also does not come thither from elsewhere,
yet does exist due to such a combination,

and which, when the combining scatters, then becomes nonexistent.
So too it also is with all dharmas.
When arising, there is no place from which they come,
and when extinguished, there is no place to which they go.

This is analogous to a dragon's mental powers
through which the dark clouds appear.
They do not emerge from the body of the dragon,
nor do they arrive from some other place,

and yet the rain from these great dark clouds
pours down throughout the entire world,
after which it then evaporates,
yet has no place to which it goes.

Just as such clouds neither come nor go,
so too it is with all dharmas.
When they arise, there is no place from which they come,
and, when destroyed, there is no place to which they go.

They are also like a man who has been painted on a wall
that does not reside in any or all of the colors,
also does not reside in their combination,
and also does not abide in the wall.

It does not abide in the painter,
nor does it abide in the paintbrush.
It does not come forth from elsewhere,
yet it exists because of all of these coming together.

When that combination scatters, it then no longer exists.
So too it is with all dharmas.
When they exist, there is no place from which they come.
When they cease to exist, there is no place to which they go.

The lamp flame does not abide in its oil,
also does not emerge from its wick,
and also does not arrive from some other place,
and yet, because of the oil and the wick, it exists.

If its causes and conditions end, it is extinguished.
When it is extinguished, there is no place to which it goes.

正體字

117b11 ‖　　諸法來去相　　皆亦復如是
117b12 ‖ 復有四法。能淨尸羅。所謂。
117b13 ‖　　能自思量身　　不自高下他
117b14 ‖　　此二無所得　　心[6]猗無有慢
117b15 ‖　　觀諸法平等　　是四淨尸羅
117b16 ‖ 能自思量者。行者作是念。我身不淨無常死
117b17 ‖ 相為何所直。如是念已。即不自高下於他
117b18 ‖ 人。信解身及他無我我所故無所得。猗者。
117b19 ‖ 得如是法故。心輕柔軟堪任受法。以此猗
117b20 ‖ 樂心不自高。觀諸法平等者。以空觀有為
117b21 ‖ 無為法一切悉等無上中下差別。如說。
117b22 ‖　　若當因於下　　而有中上者
117b23 ‖　　下不作中上　　云何因下有
117b24 ‖　　下自作下者　　中上先定有
117b25 ‖　　若當因於中　　而有下上者
117b26 ‖　　中不作下上　　云何因中有
117b27 ‖　　中自作中者　　下上先定有

简体字

　　诸法来去相　　皆亦复如是
复有四法。能净尸罗。所谓。
　　能自思量身　　不自高下他
　　此二无所得　　心猗无有慢
　　观诸法平等　　是四净尸罗
能自思量者。行者作是念。我身不净无常死相为何所直。如是念已。即不自高下于他人。信解身及他无我我所故无所得。猗者。得如是法故。心轻柔软堪任受法。以此猗乐心不自高。观诸法平等者。以空观有为无为法一切悉等无上中下差别。如说。
　　若当因于下　　而有中上者
　　下不作中上　　云何因下有
　　下自作下者　　中上先定有
　　若当因于中　　而有下上者
　　中不作下上　　云何因中有
　　中自作中者　　下上先定有

All dharmas' characteristics of coming forth and departing
are in every case also just like this.

5. FOUR MORE DHARMAS ENABLING PURIFICATION OF MORAL VIRTUE

There are another four dharmas by which one can purify one's practice of *śīla*, namely:

One is able to contemplate the nature of one's own body
and refrains from elevating oneself or diminishing others.
Since these two cannot be apprehended,
one abides in mental pliancy, free of any conceit.
One contemplates all dharmas as uniformly equal.
These four serve to purify one's *śīla*.

As for being "able to contemplate the nature of one's own body," the practitioner has this thought: "This body of mine is characterized by impurity, impermanence, and mortality. What true worth[265] does it possess?"

Having reflected in this manner, one does not elevate oneself and look down on others.

Because one has a resolute belief that both self and others are devoid of "I" and "mine," one realizes that they cannot be apprehended at all.

As for "mental pliancy," having acquired these dharmas, one's mind then abides in lightness, suppleness, and the capacity to endure and acquiesce in dharmas. It is due to this mental pliancy and delight that one does not elevate himself above others.

As for "contemplating all dharmas as uniformly equal," this means that, because [one realizes] they are empty, one contemplates all conditioned and unconditioned dharmas as equal and devoid of any distinctions as to those which are superior, those which are middling, and those which are inferior. This is as described here:

If one would posit that, because of the inferior,
there thereby exist the middling and the superior,
since the inferior does not itself create the middling or the superior,
how then could they exist because of the inferior?
And for the inferior itself to have become "inferior,"
middling and superior would definitely have existed beforehand.

If one would posit that, because of the middling,
there thereby exist the inferior and the superior,
since the middling does not itself create the inferior or the superior,
how could they exist because of the middling?
And for the middling itself to have become "middling,"
inferior and the superior would definitely have existed beforehand.

正體字	117b28 ‖ 若當因於上　而有中下者 117b29 ‖ 上不作中下　云何因上有 117c01 ‖ 上自作上者　中下先定有 117c02 ‖ 因下不得作　不因亦不得 117c03 ‖ 若先定有者　不應因於下 117c04 ‖ 若先定無者　云何成中上 117c05 ‖ 因中不得作　不因亦不得 117c06 ‖ 若先定有者　不應因於中 117c07 ‖ 若先定無者　云何成下上 117c08 ‖ 因上不得作　不因亦不得 117c09 ‖ 若先定有者　不應因於上 117c10 ‖ 若先定無者　云何成中下 117c11 ‖ 復次以空一相故。觀諸法皆平等眾生亦 117c12 ‖ 如是。如說。 117c13 ‖ 智者於空中　不說分別相 117c14 ‖ 空一而無異　能如是見空 117c15 ‖ 是則為見佛　佛不異空故 117c16 ‖ 說言諸佛一　一切眾生一 117c17 ‖ 一切法一法　無上中下別 117c18 ‖ 一切佛世尊　離自性他性 117c19 ‖ 一切諸眾生　亦離自他性
简体字	若当因于上　而有中下者 上不作中下　云何因上有 上自作上者　中下先定有 因下不得作　不因亦不得 若先定有者　不应因于下 若先定无者　云何成中上 因中不得作　不因亦不得 若先定有者　不应因于中 若先定无者　云何成下上 因上不得作　不因亦不得 若先定有者　不应因于上 若先定无者　云何成中下 复次以空一相故。观诸法皆平等众生亦如是。如说。 智者于空中　不说分别相 空一而无异　能如是见空 是则为见佛　佛不异空故 说言诸佛一　一切众生一 一切法一法　无上中下别 一切佛世尊　离自性他性 一切诸众生　亦离自他性

Chapter 33 – *Aids to Gaining the Fruits of Śīla*

If one would posit that, because of the superior,
there thereby exist the middling and the inferior,
since the superior does not itself create the middling or the inferior,
how could they exist because of the superior?
And for the superior itself to have become "superior,"
middling and inferior would definitely have existed beforehand.

It cannot be that, due to the inferior, [middling and superior exist].
Nor can it be that it is *not* because of it [that they exist].
If [the middling and superior] already existed previously,
they could not exist because of the inferior.
And if [the middling and superior] were previously nonexistent,
how could they succeed in becoming the middling and superior?

It cannot be that, due to the middling, [inferior and superior exist].
Nor can it be that it is *not* because of it [that they exist].
If [the inferior and the superior] already existed previously,
they could not exist because of the middling.
And if [the inferior and the superior] were previously nonexistent,
how could they succeed in becoming the inferior and the superior?

It cannot be that, due to the superior, [inferior and middling exist].
Nor can it be that it is *not* because of it [that they exist].
If [the middling and the inferior] definitely already existed,
they could not exist because of the superior.
And if [middling and inferior] were certainly previously nonexistent,
how could they succeed in becoming middling and inferior?

Additionally, because their emptiness is of a singular character, one contemplates all dharmas as uniformly equal. So too it is with beings. This is as described here:

In the midst of what is empty, the wise
do not speak of any distinguishable characteristic signs.
In the singularity of emptiness, there are no differentiations.
If one is able to perceive emptiness in this manner
this then is to see the Buddha,
for the Buddha is no different from emptiness.

It is said that all buddhas are one,
all beings are one,
all dharmas are but a single dharma,
and no distinctions exist between superior, middling, or inferior.

All of the Buddhas, the Bhagavats,
transcend both inherently existent and externally created nature.
So too do all beings
transcend both inherently existent and externally created nature.

正體字	117c20 ‖	一切法亦爾	離自性他性
	117c21 ‖	以是因緣故	是故名一相
	117c22 ‖	有諸佛則非	無諸佛亦非
	117c23 ‖	有諸眾生非	無諸眾生非
	117c24 ‖	有諸法[7]則非	無諸法亦非
	117c25 ‖	離於有無故	名之為平等
	117c26 ‖	一切佛世尊	眾生及諸法
	117c27 ‖	一切不可取	名諸法平等
	117c28 ‖	一切佛眾生	及法無差別
	117c29 ‖	不可分別故	名之為平等
	118a01 ‖	諸佛與眾生	并及一切法
	118a02 ‖	入生住滅中	寂滅無所有
	118a03 ‖	亦無所從來	亦復無所去
	118a04 ‖	以無來去故	名之為平等
	118a05 ‖	諸佛與眾生	并及一切法
	118a06 ‖	悉皆無所有	過一切有道
	118a07 ‖	此三非是等	亦復非非等
	118a08 ‖	非等非非等	非非等不等
	118a09 ‖	如是說諸法	皆等無差別
简体字		一切法亦尔	离自性他性
		以是因缘故	是故名一相
		有诸佛则非	无诸佛亦非
		有诸众生非	无诸众生非
		有诸法则非	无诸法亦非
		离于有无故	名之为平等
		一切佛世尊	众生及诸法
		一切不可取	名诸法平等
		一切佛众生	及法无差别
		不可分别故	名之为平等
		诸佛与众生	并及一切法
		入生住灭中	寂灭无所有
		亦无所从来	亦复无所去
		以无来去故	名之为平等
		诸佛与众生	并及一切法
		悉皆无所有	过一切有道
		此三非是等	亦复非非等
		非等非非等	非非等不等
		如是说诸法	皆等无差别

All dharmas are also just so
in transcending inherently existent and externally created natures.
It is because of just such causes and conditions
that they are said to be of a singular character.

If one claims that buddhas exist, this is wrong.
If one claims no buddhas exist, this is also wrong.
If one claims that beings exist, this is wrong.
If one claims that no beings exist, this is also wrong.

If one claims dharmas exist, that is wrong.
If one claims that no dharmas exist, that is also wrong.
It is because they transcend both "existence" and "nonexistence"
that they are said to be uniformly equal.

All the Buddhas, the Bhagavats,
all beings, and also all dharmas
are in every case ungraspable.
This is what is meant by the uniform equality of all dharmas.

All buddhas, beings,
and dharmas have no differences.
Because one cannot make any distinctions among them,
they are said to be of a single uniform equality.

All buddhas, all beings,
and all dharmas,
even as they enter into arising, enduring, and destruction,
abide in quiescent cessation and do not exist at all.

Nor do they have any place from which they have come,
nor do they have any place to which they go.
It is because of their neither coming nor going
that they are said to be of a single uniform equality.

All buddhas, all beings,
and all dharmas
are, in every case, entirely nonexistent
and utterly beyond all of the paths of existence.

These three are not equal,
are not unequal,
are not both equal and unequal,
and are neither equal nor unequal.
It is in this way that one explains all dharmas
as being in every case equal and devoid of distinctions.

正體字

118a10 ‖	復有四法。能淨尸羅。如說。
118a11 ‖	善能信解空　　不驚無相法
118a12 ‖	眾生中大悲　　能忍於無我
118a13 ‖	[1]如是之四法　　亦能淨尸羅
118a14 ‖	行者了達諸法無自性無他性故。名為信
118a15 ‖	解空。如說。
118a16 ‖	一切所有法　　終不自性生
118a17 ‖	若從眾緣生　　則應從他有
118a18 ‖	不從自性生　　云何從他生
118a19 ‖	自性已不成　　他性亦復無
118a20 ‖	若離自性[2]生　　則無有自性
118a21 ‖	若離於自性　　則無有自相
118a22 ‖	自性自性相　　不以合故有
118a23 ‖	不以散故[3]無　　二定有則無
118a24 ‖	他不能生法　　自亦不能生
118a25 ‖	自他亦不能　　離二亦不生
118a26 ‖	若無有自者　　云何從他生
118a27 ‖	離於世俗法　　則無有自他
118a28 ‖	若他從他生　　他即無[4]自體
118a29 ‖	無體則非有　　以何物生他

简体字

复有四法。能净尸罗。如说。
善能信解空　　不惊无相法
众生中大悲　　能忍于无我
如是之四法　　亦能净尸罗
行者了达诸法无自性无他性故。名为信解空。如说。
一切所有法　　终不自性生
若从众缘生　　则应从他有
不从自性生　　云何从他生
自性已不成　　他性亦复无
若离自性生　　则无有自性
若离于自性　　则无有自相
自性自性相　　不以合故有
不以散故无　　二定有则无
他不能生法　　自亦不能生
自他亦不能　　离二亦不生
若无有自者　　云何从他生
离于世俗法　　则无有自他
若他从他生　　他即无自体
无体则非有　　以何物生他

Chapter 33 — Aids to Gaining the Fruits of Śīla

6. Four More Dharmas Enabling Purification of Moral Virtue

There are another four dharmas by which one can purify one's practice of *śīla*. They are as described below:

> Being well able to maintain a resolute belief in emptiness,
> not being frightened by the dharma of signlessness,
> maintaining the great compassion toward beings,
> and being able to acquiesce in the nonexistence of self—
> It is through four dharmas such as these
> that one is also able to purify one's practice of *śīla*.

It is because of a practitioner's complete comprehension of all dharmas as devoid of any self-existent nature or any externally created nature that he is referred to as having "a resolute belief in emptiness." This is as described here:

> All dharmas whatsoever
> never arise on the basis of any inherently existent nature.
> If they arise from multiple conditions,
> they should then exist through that which is other.

> Given they do not arise through any inherently existent nature,
> how then could they arise through that which is other?
> If an inherently existent nature is not established,
> then any nature existing through some "other" is also nonexistent.

> If they transcend any arising from an inherently existent nature,
> then they are devoid of any inherently existent nature.
> If they have transcended any inherently existent nature,
> then they are [also] devoid of any mark of inherent existence.

> An inherently existent nature and marks of inherent existence
> do not exist on the basis of conjoining
> and do not become nonexistent through separation.
> Hence they are both devoid of any fixed existence.

> Dharmas cannot be produced from that which is other,
> nor can they be produced from themselves,
> nor can they be produced by both self and other,
> and yet, apart from those two, they cannot be produced, either.

> If no inherent existence can be established for itself,
> how then could it possibly be produced from what is other?
> If one departs from dharmas that are mere worldly conventions,
> then "self" and "other" are entirely nonexistent.

> If that which is other were produced from that which is other,
> then that "other" would have no substance of its own.
> If it had no substance, then it could not even exist.
> From what thing then can there be the arising of what is other?

<table>
<tr><td rowspan="20">正體字</td><td>118b01 ‖</td><td>以無自體故　　他生亦復無</td></tr>
<tr><td>118b02 ‖</td><td>四種皆空故　　無法定生滅</td></tr>
<tr><td>118b03 ‖</td><td>不驚無相者。信樂遠離諸相故不驚。</td></tr>
<tr><td>118b04 ‖</td><td>[5]如說。</td></tr>
<tr><td>118b05 ‖</td><td>　一切若無相　　一切即有相</td></tr>
<tr><td>118b06 ‖</td><td>　寂滅是無相　　即為是有法</td></tr>
<tr><td>118b07 ‖</td><td>　若觀無相法　　無相即為相</td></tr>
<tr><td>118b08 ‖</td><td>　若言修無相　　即非修無相</td></tr>
<tr><td>118b09 ‖</td><td>　若捨諸計著　　名之為無相</td></tr>
<tr><td>118b10 ‖</td><td>　取是捨著相　　則為無解脫</td></tr>
<tr><td>118b11 ‖</td><td>　凡以有取故　　因取而有捨</td></tr>
<tr><td>118b12 ‖</td><td>　離取取何事　　名之以為捨</td></tr>
<tr><td>118b13 ‖</td><td>　取者所用取　　及以可取法</td></tr>
<tr><td>118b14 ‖</td><td>　共離俱無有　　是皆名寂滅</td></tr>
<tr><td>118b15 ‖</td><td>　若法相因成　　此即為無性</td></tr>
<tr><td>118b16 ‖</td><td>　若無有性者　　此即無有相</td></tr>
<tr><td>118b17 ‖</td><td>　若法無有性　　此即無相者</td></tr>
<tr><td>118b18 ‖</td><td>　云何言無性　　即名為無相</td></tr>
<tr><td>118b19 ‖</td><td>　若用有與無　　亦遮亦應聽</td></tr>
<tr><td>118b20 ‖</td><td>　雖言心不著　　是則無有過</td></tr>
</table>

<table>
<tr><td rowspan="23">简体字</td><td>以无自体故　　他生亦复无</td></tr>
<tr><td>四种皆空故　　无法定生灭</td></tr>
<tr><td>不惊无相者。信乐远离诸相故不惊。如说。</td></tr>
<tr><td>　一切若无相　　一切即有相</td></tr>
<tr><td>　寂灭是无相　　即为是有法</td></tr>
<tr><td>　若观无相法　　无相即为相</td></tr>
<tr><td>　若言修无相　　即非修无相</td></tr>
<tr><td>　若舍诸计着　　名之为无相</td></tr>
<tr><td>　取是舍着相　　则为无解脱</td></tr>
<tr><td>　凡以有取故　　因取而有舍</td></tr>
<tr><td>　离取取何事　　名之以为舍</td></tr>
<tr><td>　取者所用取　　及以可取法</td></tr>
<tr><td>　共离俱无有　　是皆名寂灭</td></tr>
<tr><td>　若法相因成　　此即为无性</td></tr>
<tr><td>　若无有性者　　此即无有相</td></tr>
<tr><td>　若法无有性　　此即无相者</td></tr>
<tr><td>　云何言无性　　即名为无相</td></tr>
<tr><td>　若用有与无　　亦遮亦应听</td></tr>
<tr><td>　虽言心不着　　是则无有过</td></tr>
</table>

Chapter 33 — *Aids to Gaining the Fruits of Śīla*

Because it has no substance of its own,
production from some other is also a nonexistent [possibility].
Since all four [tetralemma ideas] are empty [of inherent existence],
no dharma whatsoever has any fixed arising or destruction.

As for "not being frightened by signlessness," it is because of one's resolute belief [in signlessness] and one's utter transcendence of all signs that one is not frightened. This is as described here:[266]

If everything is signless,
then everything is identical with whatever possesses signs.
Quiescent cessation is signless
and is identical with whatever is an existent dharma.[267]

If one contemplates the dharma of signlessness,
whatever is signless is [seen as] the same as what possesses signs.
If one says that one is cultivating signlessness,
that is just a non-cultivation of signlessness.

Were one to relinquish all strategizing and attachments[268]
and designate that as constituting signlessness,
such seizing on this sign of having relinquished attachments
then becomes the very absence of liberation.

In general, it is because of the existence of grasping,
that then, because of that grasping, there then is relinquishing.
It is the abandonment of grasping and whatever thing is grasped[269]—
It is on this basis that one then refers to "relinquishing."

As for the one who grasps, the grasping to which he resorts,
as well as that dharma that is subject to being grasped,
whether as conjoined or separate, they are all entirely nonexistent,[270]
for these are all synonymous with quiescent cessation.

If any dharma's signs are established on the basis of causes,
this is just something devoid of any [inherently existent] nature.
Whatever is devoid of any [inherently existent] nature—
this is just something that is devoid of any [inherently existent] signs.

If a dharma has no [inherently existent] nature—
this is just something that is signless.
How can one assert that it has no [inherently existent] nature?
It is precisely because it is synonymous with signlessness.[271]

If one uses [such terms as] "existence" and "nonexistence,"
"both" and "neither" should be permissible as well,[272] for,
although one may speak thus, so long as one's mind is not attached,
one thereby remains free of any fault in doing so.

正體字	118b21 ‖	何處先有法	而後不滅者
	118b22 ‖	何處先有然	而後有滅者
	118b23 ‖	此有相寂滅	同無相寂滅
	118b24 ‖	是故寂滅語	及寂滅語者
	118b25 ‖	先來非寂滅	亦非不寂滅
	118b26 ‖	亦非寂不寂	非非寂不寂

118b27 ‖ 眾生中大悲者。眾生無量無邊故。悲心亦廣
118b28 ‖ 大。復次諸佛法無量無邊無盡如虛空。悲心
118b29 ‖ 是諸佛法根本。能得大法故名為大悲。一
118c01 ‖ 切眾生中最大者名為佛。佛所行故名為大
118c02 ‖ 悲。忍無我法者。信樂實法故。諸佛皆一涅
118c03 ‖ 槃道故。名為無我法。若入此法中心則不
118c04 ‖ 忍。如小草入火則燒盡。若真金入火能堪
118c05 ‖ 忍無失如是。若凡夫人不修習善根入無
118c06 ‖ 我中不能堪忍即生邪疑。是菩薩無量世
118c07 ‖ 來修習善根智慧猛利諸佛護念。雖未斷
118c08 ‖ 結使入無我法中心能忍受。無我法者陰界
118c09 ‖ 入十二因緣等諸法是。破我因緣如先說。

简体字

何处先有法　　而后不灭者
何处先有然　　而后有灭者
此有相寂灭　　同无相寂灭
是故寂灭语　　及寂灭语者
先来非寂灭　　亦非不寂灭
亦非寂不寂　　非非寂不寂

众生中大悲者。众生无量无边故。悲心亦广大。复次诸佛法无量无边无尽如虚空。悲心是诸佛法根本。能得大法故名为大悲。一切众生中最大者名为佛。佛所行故名为大悲。忍无我法者。信乐实法故。诸佛皆一涅槃道故。名为无我法。若入此法中心则不忍。如小草入火则烧尽。若真金入火能堪忍无失如是。若凡夫人不修习善根入无我中不能堪忍即生邪疑。是菩萨无量世来修习善根智慧猛利诸佛护念。虽未断结使入无我法中心能忍受。无我法者阴界入十二因缘等诸法是。破我因缘如先说。

Where has there ever first existed some dharma
that, afterward, was not destroyed?
Wherever there was first some fire
that, afterward, was then extinguished,
the quiescent cessation of these existent signs
is identical to the quiescent cessation of whatsoever is signless.

Therefore, as for these words about quiescent cessation
as well as the one who speaks about quiescent cessation,
from the beginning onward, they have not been quiescent[273]
nor have they been nonquiescent,
nor have they been both quiescent and nonquiescent,
nor have they been neither quiescent nor nonquiescent.

Regarding "maintaining compassion toward beings," because beings are countless and boundless, one's mind of compassion is also expansive in that very same way. Also, the Dharma of all buddhas is measureless, boundless, and endless, like empty space. The mind of compassion is the very foundation of the Dharma of all buddhas. It is because it is able to bring about the realization of the great Dharma that it is referred to as the "great" compassion. Among all beings, the one who is the greatest is the Buddha. It is because it is practiced by the Buddha that it is referred to as the "great" compassion.

As for "acquiescence in the dharma of nonself," one accomplishes this because one has a resolute faith in the true Dharma. It is because it is the one path to nirvāṇa taken by all buddhas that it is known as "the Dharma of nonself."

If one enters into this dharma and one's mind is unable to endure it, this is like putting a small plant into a fire, whereupon it is entirely burned up. However, if one puts real gold into a fire, it is able to endure it and it remains entirely undiminished.

In the same way, if a common person, one who has not cultivated roots of goodness, attempts to enter [the dharma of] nonself, he will be unable to bear it and will immediately bring forth erroneous doubts about it. This bodhisattva, however, has cultivated roots of goodness for countless lifetimes. His wisdom has become fiercely sharp and he is sustained by the protective mindfulness of all buddhas. Although he may not yet have cut off the fetters, when he enters into the dharma of nonself, his mind is able to endure and accept it.

"The dharma of nonself" is a reference to all such dharmas as the aggregates, the sense realms, the sense bases, and the twelvefold chain of causation. The causes and conditions through which one demolishes [the view of] self are as discussed earlier.

正體字

118c10 ‖	是故欲淨尸羅。當行此四法。復次。
118c11 ‖	有四破尸羅　　而似持尸羅
118c12 ‖	行[6]者當精進　　自制慎莫為
118c13 ‖	寶頂經迦葉品中。佛告迦葉。四種破戒比丘
118c14 ‖	似如持戒比丘。何等四。迦葉。有比丘。於經
118c15 ‖	戒中盡能具行而說有我。迦葉是名破戒
118c16 ‖	似如持戒。復次迦葉。有比丘。誦持律經守
118c17 ‖	護戒行。於身見中不動不離。是名破戒似
118c18 ‖	如持戒。復次迦葉。有比丘。具行十二頭陀。
118c19 ‖	而見諸法定有。是名破戒似如持戒。復次
118c20 ‖	迦葉。有比丘。緣眾生行慈心。聞諸行無
118c21 ‖	生相心則驚畏。是名破戒似如持戒。迦葉。
118c22 ‖	此四破戒人似如持戒。復次。
118c23 ‖	世尊之所說　　沙門有四品

简体字

是故欲净尸罗。当行此四法。复次。

　　有四破尸罗　　而似持尸罗
　　行者当精进　　自制慎莫为

　　宝顶经迦葉品中。佛告迦葉。四种破戒比丘似如持戒比丘。何等四。迦葉。有比丘。于经戒中尽能具行而说有我。迦葉是名破戒似如持戒。复次迦葉。有比丘。诵持律经守护戒行。于身见中不动不离。是名破戒似如持戒。复次迦葉。有比丘。具行十二头陀。而见诸法定有。是名破戒似如持戒。复次迦葉。有比丘。缘众生行慈心。闻诸行无生相心则惊畏。是名破戒似如持戒。迦葉。此四破戒人似如持戒。复次。

　　世尊之所说　　沙门有四品

Therefore, if one wishes to purify one's practice of *śīla*, one should practice these four dharmas.
Furthermore:

7. Four Kinds of Monks Who Break the Moral Precepts

There are four individuals who destroy *śīla*
even when seeming to uphold *śīla*.
The practitioner should be vigorous
in exerting self-control and taking care not to act [as they do].

In the "Kāśyapa" chapter of *The Jeweled Summit Sutra*, the Buddha told Kāśyapa:[274]

> There are four kinds of bhikshus who break the moral precepts while seeming as if they are bhikshus who uphold the moral precepts. What are those four? Kāśyapa, there are bhikshus who are completely able to perfectly practice the moral precepts of the scriptures and yet claim that a self exists. Kāśyapa, this is what is meant by breaking the moral precepts while seeming as if one is upholding the moral precepts.
>
> Then again, Kāśyapa, there are bhikshus who recite and retain the moral precept scriptures and guard their practice of the moral precepts, but who do not move from and never abandon their view of a real self in association with the body. This is what is meant by breaking the moral precepts while seeming as if one is upholding the moral precepts.
>
> Yet again, Kāśyapa, there are bhikshus who are perfect in their practice of the twelve *dhūta* austerities while nonetheless maintaining the view that dharmas have a fixed existence. This is what is meant by breaking the moral precepts while seeming as if one is upholding the moral precepts.
>
> Then again, Kāśyapa, there are bhikshus who focus on beings as the objective condition in their cultivation of the mind of kindness but who, on hearing that all conditioned things[275] are characterized by nonproduction, their minds are filled with terror. This is what is meant by breaking the moral precepts while seeming as if one is upholding the moral precepts.
>
> Kāśyapa, these are the four kinds of persons who break the moral precepts even while seeming as if they are upholding the moral precepts.

Furthermore:

8. Four Kinds of Monks of Which One Should Become the Fourth

According to what the Bhagavat has taught,
there are four types of *śramaṇas*

正體字

118c24 ‖　　應為第四者　　遠離前三種
118c25 ‖ 迦葉品中說四種比丘[7]者。應學第四沙門。
118c26 ‖ 不應為三。何等為四。佛告迦葉。有四種
118c27 ‖ 沙門。一者形色相沙門。二者威儀矯異沙門。
118c28 ‖ 三者貪求名利沙門。四者真實行沙門。云何
118c29 ‖ 名為形色相沙門。有沙門形沙門色相。所謂
119a01 ‖ 著僧伽梨剃除鬚髮。執持黑鉢。而行不淨
119a02 ‖ 身業不淨口業不淨意業。不[1]求寂滅。不[2]求
119a03 ‖ 善。慳貪懈怠行惡法。破[3]戒不樂修道。是
119a04 ‖ 名形色相沙門。云何威儀矯異沙門。[4]具四
119a05 ‖ 種威儀。審諦安詳趣得衣食。行聖種行。不
119a06 ‖ 與在家出家和合。少於語言。以是所行。欲
119a07 ‖ 取人意心不清淨。如此威儀不為善。不
119a08 ‖ 為寂滅。而見諸法定有。於空無所有法畏
119a09 ‖ 如墮坑。見說空者生怨家想。是名威儀矯
119a10 ‖ 異沙門。

简体字

　　应为第四者　　远离前三种

迦叶品中说四种比丘者。应学第四沙门。不应为三。何等为四。佛告迦叶。有四种沙门。一者形色相沙门。二者威仪矫异沙门。三者贪求名利沙门。四者真实行沙门。云何名为形色相沙门。有沙门形沙门色相。所谓着僧伽梨剃除须发。执持黑钵。而行不净身业不净口业不净意业。不求寂灭。不求善。悭贪懈怠行恶法。破戒不乐修道。是名形色相沙门。云何威仪矫异沙门。具四种威仪。审谛安详趣得衣食。行圣种行。不与在家出家和合。少于语言。以是所行。欲取人意心不清净。如此威仪不为善。不为寂灭。而见诸法定有。于空无所有法畏如堕坑。见说空者生怨家想。是名威仪矫异沙门。

Chapter 33 — Aids to Gaining the Fruits of Śīla

of which one should become the fourth
while distancing oneself from the first three kinds.[276]

As for these four kinds of bhikshus referred to here that are found in the "Kāśyapa" chapter, one should learn to become the fourth kind of śramaṇa while avoiding becoming any of the other three kinds. What then are those four? The Buddha told Kāśyapa:

There are four kinds of śramaṇas, namely:

First, those who, merely in form and appearance, seem to be śramaṇas;

Second, those śramaṇas who merely feign extraordinary deportment;

Third, those who are śramaṇas simply because they covet fame and self-benefit;

Fourth, śramaṇas who genuinely carry on right practice.

a. He Who Is a Monk Only in Form and Appearance

What is meant by one who is a śramaṇa merely in form and appearance? He adopts the form of the śramaṇa and adopts the appearance of a śramaṇa, doing so specifically through wearing a saṃghāṭī robe, shaving off his hair and beard, and carrying a blackened bowl, while nonetheless still engaging in impure physical actions, impure verbal actions, and impure mental actions. He does not seek to reach nirvāṇa and does not seek to become good. He is miserly and indolent and practices evil dharmas. He breaks the moral precepts and does not delight in cultivation of the path. This is what is meant by one who is a śramaṇa merely in form and appearance.

b. He Who Merely Feigns Extraordinary Deportment

What is meant by the śramaṇa who merely feigns extraordinary deportment? He is perfect in the four kinds of deportment. He investigates the truths, is comfortable and serene in getting by on whatever robes and food he has already acquired, is devoted to the practice of the [four] lineage bases of the Āryas, avoids gathering together with either laypeople or monastics, and speaks but little, but he does all these things in order to seize the attentions of others with a mind that is not pure.

Deportment of this sort is not done for the sake of goodness, is not done for the sake of reaching nirvāṇa, and is done with an implicit view that seizes on all dharmas as having a fixed and definite existence. [Such a practitioner] fears the dharmas of emptiness and nonexistence in just the same way as one might fear falling into a pit. Whenever he sees anyone who speaks of emptiness, he thinks of him as an enemy. This is what is meant by the śramaṇa who merely feigns extraordinary deportment.

	云何為貪求名利沙門。有沙門雖
119a11 ‖	強能持戒。作是念。云何令人知我持戒。強
119a12 ‖	求多聞。云何令人知我多聞。強作阿練若
119a13 ‖	法。云何令人知我是阿練若。強行少欲知足
119a14 ‖	遠離。云何令人知我少欲知足行遠離法。
119a15 ‖	非為厭離心故。非為滅煩惱故。非以求
119a16 ‖	[5]八直聖道故。非為涅槃故。非度一切眾
119a17 ‖	生故。是名求名利沙門。云何真實行沙門。
119a18 ‖	有沙門尚不貪惜身。何況惜名利聞諸法
119a19 ‖	空無所有。心大歡喜隨說而行。尚不貪惜
119a20 ‖	涅槃而行梵行。何況貪惜三界。尚不著空
119a21 ‖	見。何況著我人眾生壽者命者知者見者見。
119a22 ‖	[6]於諸煩惱中而求解脫。不於外求。觀一
119a23 ‖	切法本來清淨無垢。此人但依於身不依
119a24 ‖	於餘。以諸法實相尚不貪法身。何況色身。
119a25 ‖	見法離相

云何为贪求名利沙门。有沙门虽强能持戒。作是念。云何令人知我持戒。强求多闻。云何令人知我多闻。强作阿练若法。云何令人知我是阿练若。强行少欲知足远离。云何令人知我少欲知足行远离法。非为厌离心故。非为灭烦恼故。非以求八直圣道故。非为涅槃故。非度一切众生故。是名求名利沙门。云何真实行沙门。有沙门尚不贪惜身。何况惜名利闻诸法空无所有。心大欢喜随说而行。尚不贪惜涅槃而行梵行。何况贪惜三界。尚不着空见。何况着我人众生寿者命者知者见者见。于诸烦恼中而求解脱。不于外求。观一切法本来清净无垢。此人但依于身不依于余。以诸法实相尚不贪法身。何况色身。见法离相

c. He Who Is a Monk Only for Fame and Self-Benefit

What is meant by one who is a *śramaṇa* simply because he covets fame and self-benefit? There are those *śramaṇas* who, although they are able to force themselves to uphold the moral precepts, [as they do so, they think], "How can I cause other people to know me as one who upholds the moral precepts?"

Although they are able to force themselves to strive after extensive learning, [as they do so, they think], "How can I cause other people to know me as someone possessed of extensive learning?"

Although they are able to force themselves to take up the dharma of abiding in a forest hermitage, [as they do so, they think], "How can I cause other people to know that I am a forest hermitage dweller?"

Although they are able to force themselves to have but few wants, to be easily satisfied, and to practice the dharmas of one who dwells in solitude, as they do so, they think, "How can I cause other people to know that I have but few wants, am easily satisfied, and practice the dharmas of one who dwells in solitude?"

They do not do these things in order to develop a mind of renunciation, do not do them in order to destroy the afflictions, do not do them in order to strive in the eightfold right path of the Āryas, do not do them in order to reach nirvāṇa, and do not do them in order to bring about the liberation of all beings. This is what is meant by the *śramaṇa* who covets fame and self-benefit.

d. The Monk Who Genuinely Carries on Right Practice

What is meant by the *śramaṇa* who genuinely carries on right practice? There is a type of *śramaṇa* who does not retain any selfish cherishing even of his own body, how much the less might he cherish fame or self-benefit? On being taught that all dharmas are empty and that nothing whatsoever exists, his mind is filled with great joy and he proceeds to practice in accordance with that teaching.

He does not have any selfish cherishing even of nirvāṇa as he carries on his practice of *brahmacarya*, how much the less might he have any selfish cherishing of [any station of rebirth within] the three realms?

He is not even attached to the view that sees the emptiness [of all dharmas], how much the less might he become attached to the existence of a self, a person, a being, a soul, a life, a knower, or a seer?

He seeks liberation even in the midst of the afflictions and does not seek it anywhere outside. He contemplates all dharmas as fundamentally pure and undefiled. This person relies only on himself and does not rely on anyone else. Through [his direct knowing of] the true character of all dharmas, he does not even covet the Dharma body, how much the less the form body. He sees dharmas as transcending

正體字

|| 不以言說。尚不分別無為聖眾。
119a26 || 何況眾[7]人。不為斷不為修習故。不惡生
119a27 || 死不樂涅槃無縛無解。知諸佛法無有
119a28 || 定相。知己不往來生死亦復不滅。迦葉。是
119a29 || [8]名隨真實行沙門。迦葉。汝等應勤行真實
119b01 || 行。沙門莫為名字所害。復次。
119b02 ||　　不為王等法　　而持於尸羅
119b03 ||　　亦不依生等　　而持於尸羅
119b04 || 行者欲淨尸羅。不應為王等法。王等法者。
119b05 || 佛為淨德力士說。善男子。菩薩尸羅者。乃至
119b06 || 失命因緣猶不破戒。不期為國王故持戒。
119b07 || 不期生天故持戒。不期為釋提桓因不
119b08 || 為梵天王不為富樂自在力故持戒不為
119b09 || 名聞稱讚故。不為利養故持戒。不為壽
119b10 || 命故。不為飲食衣服臥具醫藥資生物故
119b11 || 持戒。不依生等法者。不為生天人持戒。
119b12 || 不自依持戒。

简体字

不以言说。尚不分别无为圣众。何况众人。不为断不为修习故。不恶生死不乐涅槃无缚无解。知诸佛法无有定相。知己不往来生死亦复不灭。迦葉。是名随真实行沙门。迦葉。汝等应勤行真实行。沙门莫为名字所害。复次。
　　不为王等法　　而持于尸罗
　　亦不依生等　　而持于尸罗

行者欲净尸罗。不应为王等法。王等法者。佛为净德力士说。善男子。菩萨尸罗者。乃至失命因缘犹不破戒。不期为国王故持戒。不期生天故持戒。不期为释提桓因不为梵天王不为富乐自在力故持戒不为名闻称赞故。不为利养故持戒。不为寿命故。不为饮食衣服卧具医药资生物故持戒。不依生等法者。不为生天人持戒。不自依持戒。

marks and as inexpressible in words. He does not even make any discriminating distinctions among those in the community of Āryas who course in the unconditioned, how much the less might he do so among those in the common multitude of people? He does not for the sake of severance or for the sake of cultivation abhor *saṃsāra* on the one hand and delight in nirvāṇa on the other. For him, there is neither bondage nor liberation. He realizes that the Dharma of the Buddhas has no fixed aspects and, having realized this, he neither comes and goes in *saṃsāra*, nor opts to enter nirvāṇa, either.

Kāśyapa, this is what is meant by the *śramaṇa* who accords with genuine practice. Kāśyapa, you should all be diligent in the practice of the genuine-practice *śramaṇa*. Do not allow yourselves to be harmed for the sake of a reputation.

9. WRONG MOTIVATIONS FOR UPHOLDING THE PRACTICE OF MORAL VIRTUE

Moreover:

> Do not uphold the practice of *śīla*
> merely for the sake of kingship or other such things.
> Also, do not uphold the practice of *śīla*
> to obtain a particular rebirth or other such aims.

The practitioner who wishes to purify his practice of *śīla* should not practice it for the sake of such things as kingship. With regard to such things as becoming a king, when speaking for the benefit of the stalwart, Pure Virtue, the Buddha said, "Son of Good Family, as for the bodhisattva who practices *śīla*:

> He will never break a moral precept even at the cost of his own life;
> He does not uphold the moral precepts hoping to become a king;
> He does not uphold the moral precepts hoping to achieve celestial rebirth;
> He does not uphold the moral precepts hoping to become Śakra, ruler of the devas, hoping to become the Brahma Heaven King, or hoping to gain wealth, happiness, or unconstrained and independent power;
> He does not uphold the moral precepts for the sake of fame or praise, for the sake of offerings, for the sake of a long life span, or for the sake of drink, food, robes, bedding, medicines, or other life-sustaining things;
> He does not uphold the moral precepts in reliance on dharmas concerned with rebirths and such. Hence he does not do so for the sake of being reborn among devas or humans;
> He does not uphold the moral precepts because of concerns having to do with himself;

|正體字|

119b13 ‖ 不依他持戒。不依今世持
119b13 ‖ 戒。不依後世持戒。不依色不依受想行
119b14 ‖ 識不依眼不依入不依耳鼻舌身意故
119b15 ‖ 持戒。不依欲界色界無色界故持戒。不為
119b16 ‖ 得脫地獄畜生餓鬼阿修羅惡道故持戒。不
119b17 ‖ 為畏天中貧故持戒。不為畏人中貧故
119b18 ‖ 持戒。不為畏夜叉貧故持戒。問曰。若不
119b19 ‖ 為如此等法者。為何法故持戒。答曰。
119b20 ‖ 　為欲令三寶　　久住故持戒
119b21 ‖ 　為欲得種種　　利益故持戒
119b22 ‖ 三寶久住者。為不斷佛種故持戒。為轉法
119b23 ‖ 輪故持戒。為攝聖眾故持戒。為脫生老病
119b24 ‖ 死憂悲苦惱故持戒。

|简体字|

不依他持戒。不依今世持戒。不依后世持戒。不依色不依受想行识不依眼不依入不依耳鼻舌身意故持戒。不依欲界色界无色界故持戒。不为得脱地狱畜生饿鬼阿修罗恶道故持戒。不为畏天中贫故持戒。不为畏人中贫故持戒。不为畏夜叉贫故持戒。问曰。若不为如此等法者。为何法故持戒。答曰。

　为欲令三宝　　久住故持戒
　为欲得种种　　利益故持戒

　三宝久住者。为不断佛种故持戒。为转法轮故持戒。为摄圣众故持戒。为脱生老病死忧悲苦恼故持戒。

He does not uphold the moral precepts because of concerns having to do with others;

He does not uphold the moral precepts because of present-life concerns;

He does not uphold the moral precepts because of future-life concerns;

He does not uphold the moral precepts out of concerns associated with his physical form, out of concerns associated with feelings, perceptions, formative factors, or consciousnesses, out of concerns associated with the eyes, out of concerns associated with the sense bases, or out of concerns associated with the ears, nose, tongue, body, or mind faculty;

He does not uphold the moral precepts out of concerns associated with the desire realm, form realm, or formless realm;

He does not uphold the moral precepts to be liberated from the wretched destinies of the hell realm, the animal realm, the hungry ghost realm, or the *asura* realm;

He does not uphold the moral precepts out of fear of being poverty-stricken when reborn among the devas;

He does not uphold the moral precepts out of fear of being poverty-stricken when reborn among humans;

He does not uphold the moral precepts out of fear of being poverty-stricken when reborn among the *yakṣas*."

10. Right Motivations for Upholding the Practice of Moral Virtue

Question: If [this bodhisattva] does not [uphold the moral precepts] out of concern for these sorts of things, then for the sake of which sorts of things does he uphold the moral precepts?

Response:

It is because he wishes to cause the Three Jewels
to abide for a long time that he upholds the moral precepts.
It is because he wishes to obtain the many different sorts
of benefits that he upholds the moral precepts.

As for "causing the Three Jewels to abide for a long time":

It is in order to prevent the cutting off of the lineage of the Buddhas that he upholds the moral precepts;

It is in order to turn the wheel of Dharma that he upholds the moral precepts;

It is in order to attract a community of *āryas* that he upholds the moral precepts;

It is in order to gain liberation from birth, aging, sickness, death, lamentation, grief, pain, and melancholy that he upholds the moral precepts;

|正體字|

為度一切眾生故持
戒。為令一切眾生得安樂故持戒。為令眾
生到安[9]樂處故持戒。為修禪定故持戒。
為智慧解脫解脫知見故持戒。是事如淨德
經中廣說。

菩薩能如是　　成就於尸羅
不失於十利　　及餘種種利
亦復不墮於　　四難處邪道
不得四失法　　不值四壞法
又得不欺誑　　諸佛等四法
能過墮地獄　　十事諸怖畏

不失於十利者。不失常為轉輪聖王。常
於彼中不失不放逸心。不失常作釋提桓
因。常於彼中不失不放逸心。常不失求
諸佛道。常不失諸菩薩所教化事。常不失
樂說辯才。常不失種諸善根福德滿足所
願。常不失為諸佛菩薩賢聖所讚。常不
失疾能具足一切智慧。是為十。

|简体字|

为度一切众生故持戒。为令一切众生得安乐故持戒。为令众生到安乐处故持戒。为修禅定故持戒。为智慧解脱解脱知见故持戒。是事如净德经中广说。

　　菩萨能如是　　成就于尸罗
　　不失于十利　　及余种种利
　　亦复不堕于　　四难处邪道
　　不得四失法　　不值四坏法
　　又得不欺诳　　诸佛等四法
　　能过堕地狱　　十事诸怖畏

不失于十利者。不失常为转轮圣王。常于彼中不失不放逸心。不失常作释提桓因。常于彼中不失不放逸心。常不失求诸佛道。常不失诸菩萨所教化事。常不失乐说辩才。常不失种诸善根福德满足所愿。常不失为诸佛菩萨贤圣所赞。常不失疾能具足一切智慧。是为十。

It is in order to facilitate the liberation of all beings that he upholds the moral precepts;

It is in order to cause all beings to gain peace and happiness that he upholds the moral precepts;

It is in order to cause beings to reach a peaceful and secure[277] place that he upholds the moral precepts;

It is in order to cultivate the *dhyāna* absorptions that he upholds the moral precepts;

It is in order to gain wisdom, liberation, and the knowledge and vision of liberation that he upholds the moral precepts.

These matters are just as extensively discussed in *The Pure Virtue Sutra*.

11. The Benefits of Perfecting the Practice of Moral Virtue

The bodhisattva who is able in this fashion
to perfect the practice of *śīla*
will not lose the ten benefits
or the many other different types of benefits.

Additionally, he will not fall down into
erroneous paths associated with the four difficulties.
He will not encounter the four dharmas associated with loss and
he will not encounter the four dharmas associated with destruction,

He will also gain the four dharmas
by which one does not deceive the Buddhas or others.
He is able to pass beyond susceptibility to falling into the hells
and the rest of the ten terror-inducing circumstances.

"Will not lose the ten benefits" refers to:

Not losing the ability to always become a wheel-turning king;
Not losing the non-neglectful mind when acting in that capacity;
Not losing the ability to always become Śakra, ruler of the devas;
Not losing the non-neglectful mind when acting in that capacity;
Never losing one's quest to seek the path of all buddhas;
Never losing those things that all bodhisattvas are taught;
Never losing the unimpeded knowledge of eloquence;
Never losing [the pursuit of] the planting of roots of goodness and merit and the fulfillment of whatsoever one has vowed to accomplish;
Never losing that due to which one is praised by all buddhas, bodhisattvas, worthies and *āryas*;
Never losing the ability to swiftly perfect the attainment of all-knowledge.

These are the ten [benefits of perfecting the practice of *śīla*.

正體字	種種利 119c13 ‖ 者。於種種功德不退失。如經中說。菩薩善 119c14 ‖ 守持戒。常為諸天所讚。諸龍王善護諸人 119c15 ‖ 供養。常為諸佛所念。常為世[10]間大師。愍 119c16 ‖ 念眾生。不墮四難處等邪道者。菩薩能如 119c17 ‖ 是成就尸羅者。不墮四難處。一不生無 119c18 ‖ 佛處。二不生邪見家。三不生長壽天。四不 119c19 ‖ 墮一切惡道。得四不失法者。一不失菩提 119c20 ‖ 心。二不失念佛。三不失常求多聞。四不 119c21 ‖ 失念無量世事。不值四壞法者。一不值 119c22 ‖ 法壞。二不值刀兵。三不值惡毒。四不值 119c23 ‖ 飢餓。得四不誑法者。一不欺誑十方諸佛。 119c24 ‖ 二不欺誑諸天神等。三不欺誑眾生。四不 119c25 ‖ 自欺誑身。
简体字	种种利者。于种种功德不退失。如经中说。菩萨善守持戒。常为诸天所赞。诸龙王善护诸人供养。常为诸佛所念。常为世间大师。愍念众生。不堕四难处等邪道者。菩萨能如是成就尸罗者。不堕四难处。一不生无佛处。二不生邪见家。三不生长寿天。四不堕一切恶道。得四不失法者。一不失菩提心。二不失念佛。三不失常求多闻。四不失念无量世事。不值四坏法者。一不值法坏。二不值刀兵。三不值恶毒。四不值饥饿。得四不诳法者。一不欺诳十方诸佛。二不欺诳诸天神等。三不欺诳众生。四不自欺诳身。

Chapter 33 — Aids to Gaining the Fruits of Śīla

"The many other different types of benefits" refers to never retreating from or losing one's many different sorts of meritorious qualities. This is as described in the sutras:

The bodhisattva who skillfully guards his ability to uphold the moral precepts:

Is always praised by the devas;
Is well protected by the dragon kings;
Is the beneficiary of people's offerings;
Is always borne in mind by all buddhas;
Always serves as a great teacher of those in the world;
And is sympathetically mindful of beings.

As for "not falling down into erroneous paths associated with the four difficulties," the bodhisattva who is able to perfect the practice of śīla in this manner will not fall into places [of rebirth] beset with the four difficulties, namely:

First, he will not be born into a place in which the Buddha is not present;
Second, he will not be born into a household in which wrong views hold sway;
Third, he will not take rebirth among the long-lived devas;
Fourth, he will not be reborn into any of the wretched destinies.
"The four dharmas associated with loss" are:
First, he never loses the resolve to attain bodhi;
Second, he never loses his mindfulness of the Buddha;
Third, he never loses his constant quest for extensive learning;
Fourth, he never loses his ability to call to mind the events experienced across the course of countless lifetimes.

Regarding "not encountering the four dharmas associated with destruction" this refers to:

First, never encountering the destruction of the Dharma;
Second, never encountering weapons or war;
Third, never encountering noxious poisons;
Fourth, never encountering hunger.

As for "gaining the four dharmas of non-deception," they are:

First, one does not deceive the Buddhas of the ten directions;
Second, one does not deceive devas, spirits, or other such beings;
Third, one does not deceive beings;
Fourth, one does not deceive oneself.

正體字	119c26 ‖ 又過十怖畏者。菩薩如是清淨 119c26 ‖ 持戒。能過墮地獄等十怖畏。何等十。一能 119c27 ‖ 過地獄怖畏。二能過畜生怖畏。三能過餓 119c28 ‖ 鬼怖畏。四能過貧窮怖畏。五能過誹謗呵罵 119c29 ‖ 惡名怖畏。六能過諸煩惱所覆怖畏。七能過 120a01 ‖ 聲聞辟支佛正位怖畏。八能過天人龍神夜 120a02 ‖ 叉乾闥婆阿修羅迦樓羅緊那羅摩睺羅伽等 120a03 ‖ 怖畏。九能過刀兵惡毒水火師子虎狼他人 120a04 ‖ 所害怖畏。十能過邪見怖畏。菩薩如是淨 120a05 ‖ 持於戒。則能住諸佛法。所謂四十不共法。 120a06 ‖ 堪[1]任為法器。
简体字	又过十怖畏者。菩萨如是清净持戒。能过堕地狱等十怖畏。何等十。一能过地狱怖畏。二能过畜生怖畏。三能过饿鬼怖畏。四能过贫穷怖畏。五能过诽谤呵骂恶名怖畏。六能过诸烦恼所覆怖畏。七能过声闻辟支佛正位怖畏。八能过天人龙神夜叉乾闼婆阿修罗迦楼罗紧那罗摩睺罗伽等怖畏。九能过刀兵恶毒水火师子虎狼他人所害怖畏。十能过邪见怖畏。菩萨如是净持于戒。则能住诸佛法。所谓四十不共法。堪任为法器。

Chapter 33 — Aids to Gaining the Fruits of Śīla

Also, regarding "passing beyond the ten terror-inducing circumstances," the bodhisattva who purifies the moral precepts in this way thereby becomes able to pass beyond any vulnerability to falling down into the hells or into any of the other situations contained in the ten terror-inducing circumstances. What then are those ten? They are:

First, one is able to pass beyond the fear of falling into the hell realms;

Second, one is able to pass beyond the fear of falling into the animal realms;

Third, one is able to pass beyond the fear of falling into the hungry ghost realms;

Fourth, one is able to pass beyond the fear of becoming poverty-stricken;

Fifth, one is able to pass beyond the fear of slander, rebuke, and bad reputation;

Sixth, one is able to pass beyond the fear of being overcome by the various sorts of afflictions;

Seventh, one is able to pass beyond the fear of reaching the [irreversible] "right and definite position" (*samyaktva niyāma*) [in the paths] of the *śrāvaka* disciples and the *pratyekabuddhas*;

Eighth, one is able to pass beyond the fear of [falling into the destinies of] devas, men, dragons, spirits, *yakṣas*, *gandharvas*, *asuras*, *garuḍas*, *kinnaras*, *mahoragas*, and others;

Ninth, one is able to pass beyond the fear of weapons or war, noxious poisons, water, fire, lions, tigers, wolves, and injury by other men;

Tenth, one is able to pass beyond the fear of adopting wrong views.

If the bodhisattva is able in this manner to purify his observance of the moral precepts, then he will be able to abide within the Dharma of all Buddhas, namely the forty exclusive dharmas, and he will also be able to become a Dharma vessel.

The End of Chapter Thirty-Three

讚戒品第[2]七

菩薩如是淨持尸羅。能攝種種功德諸利。如無盡意菩薩說。復次略讚尸羅少分。尸羅者。是出家人第一所喜樂處。如年少富貴最可喜樂。能增長善法。如慈母養子。能防護衰患如父護子。尸羅能成就諸出家者一切大利。如白衣多財尸羅能救一切苦惱。如正行順理。尸羅善人所敬。如報恩法。尸羅人所愛重。猶如壽命。尸羅智者所貴。如智慧。求解脫者善護尸羅。如王密事大臣守護。樂道利者。愛重尸羅。如樂涅槃。愛重佛法。智慧之人善守尸羅。如惜壽者護安身法救死時急。尸羅為最如遇急難得善知識。尸羅清淨莊嚴賢人。如貴家女慚愧無穢。

赞戒品第三十五

　　菩萨如是净持尸罗。能摄种种功德诸利。如无尽意菩萨说。复次略赞尸罗少分。尸罗者。是出家人第一所喜乐处。如年少富贵最可喜乐。能增长善法。如慈母养子。能防护衰患如父护子。尸罗能成就诸出家者一切大利。如白衣多财尸罗能救一切苦恼。如正行顺理。尸罗善人所敬。如报恩法。尸罗人所爱重。犹如寿命。尸罗智者所贵。如智慧。求解脱者善护尸罗。如王密事大臣守护。乐道利者。爱重尸罗。如乐涅槃爱重佛法。智慧之人善守尸罗。如惜寿者护安身法救死时急。尸罗为最如遇急难得善知识。尸罗清净庄严贤人。如贵家女惭愧无秽。

Chapter 34
In Praise of the Moral Precepts

XIV. CHAPTER 34: IN PRAISE OF THE MORAL PRECEPTS

The bodhisattva who purifies his observance of the moral precepts in this manner is able to gather together all sorts of meritorious qualities and derive all manner of benefits. This is as stated by Akṣayamati Bodhisattva when he said:

> Then again, to offer but a brief praise of a few aspects of *śīla*:
>
> *Śīla* is the basis for the monastic's experiencing the foremost joyous delight that is comparable to the most supreme delight enjoyed by a youth who has both wealth and noble birth;
>
> [*Śīla*] brings about the proliferation and growth of good dharmas just as when a kind mother raises her child;
>
> [*Śīla*] is able to protect one from ruinous calamity just as when a father protects his child;
>
> *Śīla* is able to bring about for monastics complete accomplishment in all forms of great benefit just as great wealth is able to bring about great benefit for a householder;
>
> *Śīla* is as able to rescue one from all forms of suffering torment just as when right action accords with what is principled;
>
> *Śīla* is as revered by good people as the dharma of repaying others' kindnesses;
>
> *Śīla* is just as cherished and esteemed by people as a long life span;
>
> *Śīla* is as esteemed by the wise as wisdom itself;
>
> Those who strive to gain liberation thoroughly guard their practice of *śīla* just as carefully as high officials guard the secrets of the king;
>
> Those who delight in the benefits of the path cherish and value *śīla* just as deeply as those who delight in nirvāṇa cherish and value the Dharma of the Buddha;
>
> The wise thoroughly guard their practice of *śīla* with the same urgency as those who cherish their own lives guard their physical safety and urgently seek rescue when death threatens;
>
> The supreme [good fortune] of encountering *śīla* is comparable to that of meeting a good guide in the midst of grave danger;
>
> *Śīla* adorns the worthy ones with purity and, in this, it is analogous to the daughter of nobility who, possessed of a sense of shame and dread of blame, remains undefiled;

正體字	尸羅即是功德[3]之初門。如不諂曲 120a22 ‖ 開諸善利。尸羅最是梵行之本。如直心則是 120a23 ‖ 正見之本。諸大人法以尸羅為本。如求重 120a24 ‖ 位以直心為本。尸羅即是功德寶[卄/積]。如不 120a25 ‖ 放逸。亦如正念能生諸利。亦如賢友初中 120a26 ‖ 後善。學正法者不得過越。如海常限。尸羅 120a27 ‖ 即是功德住處。亦如大地萬物依止。尸羅潤 120a28 ‖ 益諸善功德。亦如天雨潤益種子能成五 120a29 ‖ 根。如火熟物能生諸利。如風成身。尸羅能 120b01 ‖ 受一切道果。亦如虛空含受萬物亦如吉 120b02 ‖ 瓶隨願皆得。亦如美饍利益諸根。尸羅善 120b03 ‖ 能通利諸道。能令諸根清淨無礙。智慧壽命 120b04 ‖ 以尸羅為本。猶如身命以氣息為本。尸 120b05 ‖ 羅即是最上依處如民依王。尸羅即是諸功 120b06 ‖ 德主。如軍大將。尸羅得眾快樂。如隨意婦 120b07 ‖ 能稱夫心。若求涅槃及生天上。尸羅即是 120b08 ‖ 學道資用。
简体字	尸罗即是功德之初门。如不谄曲开诸善利。尸罗最是梵行之本。如直心则是正见之本。诸大人法以尸罗为本。如求重位以直心为本。尸罗即是功德宝[卄/積]。如不放逸。亦如正念能生诸利。亦如贤友初中后善。学正法者不得过越。如海常限。尸罗即是功德住处。亦如大地万物依止。尸罗润益诸善功德。亦如天雨润益种子能成五根。如火熟物能生诸利。如风成身。尸罗能受一切道果。亦如虚空含受万物亦如吉瓶随愿皆得。亦如美膳利益诸根。尸罗善能通利诸道。能令诸根清净无碍。智慧寿命以尸罗为本。犹如身命以气息为本。尸罗即是最上依处如民依王。尸罗即是诸功德主。如军大将。尸罗得众快乐。如随意妇能称夫心。若求涅槃及生天上。尸罗即是学道资用。

Śīla is the initial entryway into meritorious qualities just as not engaging in flattery and deviousness opens the way to acquiring fine benefits;

Śīla is the most important foundation of *brahmacarya* just as the straight mind is the foundation of right views;

Śīla is the origin of all dharmas of great people just as the straight mind is the origin of success in seeking an important position;

Śīla is a treasure trove of meritorious qualities comparable to non-negligence and right mindfulness in their ability to bring forth every sort of benefit;

[Śīla] is also comparable to a worthy friend who is good in the beginning, good in the middle, and good to the end;

[Śīla] is something beyond which one who trains in right Dharma must never go and, in this, he is like the ocean which always remains within its boundaries;[278]

Śīla is the dwelling place of meritorious qualities and, in this, it is also like the great earth upon which the myriad things depend;

Śīla serves to moisten all of the meritorious qualities of goodness and, in this, it is analogous to the rain falling down from the sky that moistens and benefits the seeds and enables the growth of the five kinds of roots;

[Śīla] is like fire in its ability to cook things and provide all sorts of benefits and, in this, it is like the [energetic] winds that sustain the body;

Śīla is able to accommodate all fruits of the path and, in this, it is also like empty space that contains and takes in the myriad things.

[Śīla] is also like the magically-auspicious vase that is able to bring forth anything that one might wish for, and it is also like fine cuisine in its ability to benefit all of one's faculties;

Śīla is well able to open all paths and it is able to cause all one's faculties to become purified and unimpeded;

One's wisdom life relies upon *śīla* as its foundation just as the life of the body depends upon the breath as its very foundation;

Śīla is the most superior of all points of reliance just as it is the king upon whom all his subjects rely;

Śīla serves as the lord of all the meritorious qualities just as the chief general commands the entire army;

Śīla is the source of the many varieties of happiness and, in this, it is like the compliant wife who is well able to satisfy all the wishes of her husband;

Whether it be in striving to reach nirvāṇa or in gaining rebirth in the heavens, *śīla* constitutes the provisions sustaining those training

正體字		如彼遠行必持衣糧。尸羅將人令
	120b09	至善處。如經險路得善導師。尸羅度人
	120b10	從生死過。猶如牢船[4]得渡大海。尸羅能
	120b11	滅諸煩惱患。猶如良藥能消眾病。尸羅器仗
	120b12	能[5]御魔賊。如善兵器能對敵陣。如所愛親
	120b13	經難不捨。尸羅將人諸衰惱中隨護不捨。
	120b14	尸羅能照後世癡冥。如大燈明能除黑闇。
	120b15	尸羅度人出諸惡道。如[6]度深水得好橋
	120b16	梁。尸羅能除煩惱熱急。如清涼室能除毒
	120b17	熱。欲墮惡趣尸羅能救。如勇士持[7]刃救
	120b18	人怖畏。諸[8]凡夫人應深愛尸羅如諸菩薩
	120b19	學諦勝處。行者善行尸羅如諸菩薩行捨
	120b20	勝處得果之人善修尸羅亦[9]如菩薩修滅
	120b21	勝處護持尸羅令[10]人得果。亦如菩薩修
	120b22	慧勝處。不壞法者能淨尸羅如諸菩薩清淨
	120b23	無垢。諸惡人等捨離尸羅如彼諂曲捨離直
	120b24	心。
简体字	如彼远行必持衣粮。尸罗将人令至善处。如经险路得善导师。尸罗度人从生死过。犹如牢船得渡大海。尸罗能灭诸烦恼患。犹如良药能消众病。尸罗器仗能御魔贼。如善兵器能对敌阵。如所爱亲经难不舍。尸罗将人诸衰恼中随护不舍。尸罗能照后世痴冥。如大灯明能除黑闇。尸罗度人出诸恶道。如度深水得好桥梁。尸罗能除烦恼热急。如清凉室能除毒热。欲堕恶趣尸罗能救。如勇士持刃救人怖畏。诸凡夫人应深爱尸罗如诸菩萨学谛胜处。行者善行尸罗如诸菩萨行舍胜处得果之人善修尸罗亦如菩萨修灭胜处护持尸罗令人得果。亦如菩萨修慧胜处。不坏法者能净尸罗如诸菩萨清净无垢。诸恶人等舍离尸罗如彼谄曲舍离直心。	

on the path and, in this, it is like the essential clothing and provisions that one traveling afar must take along on his travels;

Śīla leads people along in such a way that they are caused to reach a good place and, in this, it is like finding a good guide who escorts one along a hazardous road;

Śīla delivers people from the faults of *saṃsāra* and, in this, it is like a sturdy ship by which one is able to cross a great ocean;

Śīla is well able to put an end to all calamities wrought by the afflictions and, in this, it is like a good medicine that is able to eliminate the many sorts of diseases;

Śīla's weapons are able to defend one against Māra's thieves and, in this, they are like the weapons of a good army that are able to counter an enemy's troops;

Just as a beloved relative leads one through hardships and does not desert one, so too, *śīla* leads people through all manner of ruinous torment, continues to protect them, and never abandons them;

Śīla is able to illuminate even the darkness of delusion in one's future lives and, in this, it is like the light of a great lamp that is able to dispel the darkness;

Śīla is able even to deliver one out of the wretched destinies and, in this, it is like finding a good bridge when crossing deep waters;

Śīla is able to dispel the extreme fever of the afflictions and, in this, it is like a cool room that is able to get rid of scorching heat;

Even when on the verge of falling into the wretched destinies, *śīla* is able to come to the rescue and, in this, it is like a fierce sword-brandishing warrior rescuing someone in terror;

Every common person should feel a deeply cherishing fondness for *śīla* like that of the bodhisattvas training in the supreme basis of truthfulness;[279]

The practitioner's skillful practice of *śīla* is just like all bodhisattvas' practice of the supreme basis of relinquishment;

The skillful cultivation of *śīla* on the part of the practitioner who has gained the fruits [of the path] is just like all bodhisattvas' cultivation of the supreme basis of quiescence;

Guarding and upholding the practice of *śīla* causes one to attain the fruits [of the path] just like a bodhisattva who cultivates the wisdom supreme basis;

One who refrains from damaging the Dharma is able to purify his practice of *śīla* in a manner comparable to the purity and stainlessness of the bodhisattvas;

Bad people abandon *śīla* just as flattering and devious people abandon the straight mind;

正體字

```
         放逸之人不行尸羅如慳貪者不行惠
120b25 ‖ 施。放逸之人捨離尸羅如戲論者離寂滅
120b26 ‖ 法。愚癡之人無有尸羅猶如盲者不見五
120b27 ‖ 色。無思惟者去尸羅遠。如離八道去[11]涅
120b28 ‖ 槃遠。善愛身者深樂尸羅如阿羅漢深愛
120b29 ‖ 樂法。尸羅能使無[12]惱善法相續不斷。如佛
120c01 ‖ 出世善事不絕。尸羅能令諸道果住。如
120c02 ‖ 佛神力令法久住。尸羅如佛自利利人。尸
120c03 ‖ 羅善護諸善功德。如王知時能護國界。尸
120c04 ‖ 羅安行者心。如須陀洹果。如時發事後
120c05 ‖ 則無悔。尸羅究竟必得涅槃。如菩薩願究
120c06 ‖ 竟得佛。尸羅亦如良田好澤投之以種疾
120c07 ‖ 得增長。尸羅是正行之因。如知時方等是
120c08 ‖ 成諸事因。如人端嚴福德智慧人所尊貴。
120c09 ‖ 尸羅如是自他所敬。如福德熟時心則安
120c10 ‖ 隱。尸羅能使心得安隱受諸利報。尸羅能
120c11 ‖ 令行者歡喜。猶如好兒令父心悅。
```

简体字

放逸之人不行尸罗如悭贪者不行惠施。放逸之人舍离尸罗如戏论者离寂灭法。愚痴之人无有尸罗犹如盲者不见五色。无思惟者去尸罗远。如离八道去涅槃远。善爱身者深乐尸罗如阿罗汉深爱乐法。尸罗能使无恼善法相续不断。如佛出世善事不绝。尸罗能令诸道果住。如佛神力令法久住。尸罗如佛自利利人。尸罗善护诸善功德。如王知时能护国界。尸罗安行者心。如须陀洹果。如时发事后则无悔。尸罗究竟必得涅槃。如菩萨愿究竟得佛。尸罗亦如良田好泽投之以种疾得增长。尸罗是正行之因。如知时方等是成诸事因。如人端严福德智慧人所尊贵。尸罗如是自他所敬。如福德熟时心则安隐。尸罗能使心得安隐受诸利报。尸罗能令行者欢喜。犹如好儿令父心悦。

Neglectful people do not practice *śīla* and, in this, they are like miserly people who do not practice kindly giving;

Neglectful people abandon *śīla* and, in this, they are like those prone to inappropriate and frivolous speech who abandon the dharma of quiescence;

Stupid people are bereft of *śīla* just as a blind man does not see the five colors;

An unreflective person is as far from *śīla* as one who has abandoned the eightfold right path is far from nirvāṇa;

Those who truly love themselves deeply delight in *śīla* just as an arhat deeply loves the Dharma;

Śīla is able to ensure that the good dharmas by which one remains free of afflictions continue on uninterruptedly just as the Buddha's emergence in the world ensures that goodness will continue without cease;

Śīla is able to cause the fruits of the path to abide [in the world] just as the Buddha's spiritual power causes the Dharma to remain for a long time;

Śīla is just like the Buddha in that it benefits both oneself and others;

Śīla thoroughly protects all good meritorious qualities just as a king who understands right timing, is able to defend the country's borders;

Śīla quiets the mind of the practitioner just as when a stream-enterer,[280] by revealing in timely fashion [moral code infractions] remains free of subsequent regrets;

Śīla ensures that one shall ultimately and definitely reach nirvāṇa just as the bodhisattva vow ensures that one will ultimately become a buddha;

Śīla is also like a good plot of farmland that is well irrigated which, when sown with seeds, produces a rapidly-growing crop;

Śīla is the cause of right conduct just as knowing the right time, knowing the right place, and so forth are the causes of success in all endeavors;

Just as a handsome man possessed of merit and wisdom is revered and esteemed by others, so too is *śīla* respected by both self and others;

Just as when one's merit has become ripe, one's mind is peaceful and secure, so too is *śīla* able to cause one's mind to become peaceful and secure and to enjoy all its beneficial rewards;

Śīla is able to cause the practitioner to be delighted just as a fine son is able to inspire delight in his father's mind;

正體字	尸羅則 120c12 ‖ 是無有過失無畏之法。如人無過心則無 120c13 ‖ 畏。尸羅令人今世後世無有怖畏無諸罪 120c14 ‖ 惡。供養稱讚持尸羅者餘者亦喜自知有 120c15 ‖ 分。尸羅親愛眾生。如修慈定。尸羅滅苦如 120c16 ‖ 修悲定。尸羅與喜如修喜定。尸羅無憎無 120c17 ‖ 愛。如修捨定。尸羅為人所信。如四種善語 120c18 ‖ 能令人信。尸羅樂行。如世法中常歡喜心。 120c19 ‖ 如多聞是樂說因。尸羅則是言行相應因。尸 120c20 ‖ 羅是無畏因。如辯才無畏。尸羅是名聞因。 120c21 ‖ 如通諸經有好名稱。尸羅是能救法。如易 120c22 ‖ 與語者為人所救。尸羅能成明解脫法。如 120c23 ‖ 隨所說行。尸羅是諸佛相。如阿耨多羅三 120c24 ‖ 藐三菩提。尸羅助修道法。如定助慧。尸羅 120c25 ‖ 令人無所畏難。如大心膽無所畏懼。尸羅 120c26 ‖ 是諸功德聚處。猶如雪山寶物積聚信等功 120c27 ‖ 德。諸希有事[13]所可依止。
简体字	尸罗则是无有过失无畏之法。如人无过心则无畏。尸罗令人今世后世无有怖畏无诸罪恶。供养称赞持尸罗者余者亦喜自知有分。尸罗亲爱众生。如修慈定。尸罗灭苦如修悲定。尸罗与喜如修喜定。尸罗无憎无爱。如修舍定。尸罗为人所信。如四种善语能令人信。尸罗乐行。如世法中常欢喜心。如多闻是乐说因。尸罗则是言行相应因。尸罗是无畏因。如辩才无畏。尸罗是名闻因。如通诸经有好名称。尸罗是能救法。如易与语者为人所救。尸罗能成明解脱法。如随所说行。尸罗是诸佛相。如阿耨多罗三藐三菩提。尸罗助修道法。如定助慧。尸罗令人无所畏难。如大心胆无所畏惧。尸罗是诸功德聚处。犹如雪山宝物积聚信等功德。诸希有事所可依止。

Chapter 34 — *In Praise of the Moral Precepts*

- Śīla is a dharma that causes fearlessness in one who is free of faults just as when a person becomes free of faults, his mind then becomes free of fear;
- Śīla causes one to become free of all fear and free of the evil of moral transgressions in both the present life and future lives;
- Others are inspired to make offerings and give praise to whoever upholds the practice of śīla, for others are moved by him to feel joy and realize that they too have some part in it;
- Śīla causes one to feel affection for other beings, just as when one cultivates the meditation on [measureless] kindness;
- Śīla motivates one to do away with the sufferings of others, just as when one cultivates the meditation on [measureless] compassion;
- Śīla bestows joyfulness, just as when one cultivates the meditation on [measureless] sympathetic joy;
- Śīla causes one to become free of both hatred and desire, just as when one cultivates the meditation on [measureless] equanimity;
- Śīla inspires faith on the part of others, just as the four kinds of good speech are able to win the trust of others;
- Śīla brings delight in its practice just as dharmas of the world always bring delight to the mind [of a worldly person];
- Just as extensive learning is the cause of delight in speech, śīla is the cause of consistency between one's words and one's actions;
- Śīla is the cause of fearlessness just as eloquence also brings about fearlessness;
- Śīla is the cause of renown just as complete comprehension of all scriptures brings a fine reputation;
- Śīla is a dharma capable of bringing about one's rescue just as being one who is easy to converse with ensures one will be rescued by them;
- Śīla is a dharma that is able to bring about successful attainment of the clear knowledges and liberation and, in this, it is comparable to practicing in accordance with the teachings;
- Śīla is the characteristic feature of all buddhas and, in this, it is comparable to *anuttarasamyaksaṃbodhi*;
- Śīla is a dharma that aids cultivation of the path and, in this, it is like samādhi's role in assisting the attainment of wisdom;
- Śīla causes a person to have no difficulties that he fears just as someone possessed of great courage has nothing that he fears;
- Śīla is the gathering place of every form of meritorious quality, for just as the Himalayas are the repository of precious things, faith, the other meritorious qualities, and all marvelous phenomena[281] rely on śīla for their very existence;

正體字	尸羅猶如大海有 120c28 ‖ 諸奇異。亦如美果依止於樹。尸羅與人隨 120c29 ‖ 所樂果。如隨正智慧者如行即得。尸羅名 121a01 ‖ 為無水而淨。尸羅則是最上妙香。不從根 121a02 ‖ 莖枝葉華果中出。尸羅莊嚴過諸寶飾。常住 121a03 ‖ 其身無能却者。尸羅大樂不從五欲生。後 121a04 ‖ 世亦有諸妙樂報。尸羅是一切世間天人魔 121a05 ‖ 梵沙門婆羅門所讚歎者。尸羅快樂自在 121a06 ‖ 身中不從他得生天涅槃之善方便。尸羅即 121a07 ‖ 是信河正濟。無有泥陷瓦石刺蕀。隨意可 121a08 ‖ 入善渡無礙。尸羅是寶財無諸衰惱。尸羅是 121a09 ‖ 淨道無能壞者猶如平路行[1]旅無難。尸羅 121a10 ‖ 是好田不種不穫自然獲實。尸羅是甘露 121a11 ‖ 果。不從樹草生。香美無比。尸羅是[2]沙華 121a12 ‖ 不從水陸生常不萎壞。尸羅除煩惱熱。 121a13 ‖ 如冷水洗浴。尸羅善守護勝諸刀[3]杖行尸 121a14 ‖ 羅者不以人畏故而得恭敬。尸羅是自在 121a15 ‖ 處無有諍競。尸羅是好寶不從山生。不從 121a16 ‖ 大海出。而寶價無量。
简体字	尸罗犹如大海有诸奇异。亦如美果依止于树。尸罗与人随所乐果。如随正智慧者如行即得。尸罗名为无水而净。尸罗则是最上妙香。不从根茎枝叶华果中出。尸罗庄严过诸宝饰。常住其身无能却者。尸罗大乐不从五欲生。后世亦有诸妙乐报。尸罗是一切世间天人魔梵沙门婆罗门所赞叹者。尸罗快乐自在身中不从他得生天涅槃之善方便。尸罗即是信河正济。无有泥陷瓦石刺蕀。随意可入善渡无碍。尸罗是宝财无诸衰恼。尸罗是净道无能坏者犹如平路行旅无难。尸罗是好田不种不获自然获实。尸罗是甘露果。不从树草生。香美无比。尸罗是沙华不从水陆生常不萎坏。尸罗除烦恼热。如冷水洗浴。尸罗善守护胜诸刀杖行尸罗者不以人畏故而得恭敬。尸罗是自在处无有诤竞。尸罗是好宝不从山生。不从大海出。而宝价无量。

Chapter 34 — *In Praise of the Moral Precepts* 1273

Śīla is like the great sea in that it contains the many sorts of extraordinary things;

Also, just as, to obtain fine fruit, one relies on a tree, so too *śīla* is what provides people with whichever fruit they find pleasing. This is just as when one who pursues right wisdom then acquires [its fruits] in accordance with his practice;

Śīla is that by which one is cleansed even without the aid of water;

Śīla is the most superior of sublime incenses, one that does not come forth from some root, trunk, branch, leaf, blossom, or fruit;

Śīla is an adornment that surpasses that of any jewelry, for it always remains with one's person and cannot be stolen by anyone;

Śīla provides a great bliss not born of any of the five desires and it bestows the reward of sublime bliss in future lives as well;

Śīla is that which is praised by all worlds' devas, humans, *māras*, Brahmās, *śramaṇas*, and brahmans;

The happiness produced by *śīla* abides independently in one's own person for it is not obtained from anyone else and it is also the excellent means for gaining celestial rebirth or nirvāṇa;

Śīla is the right ford for crossing the river of faith, one that is free of quicksand, tiles, stones, thorns, or brambles, and one that may be entered at will so as to skillfully cross without being impeded by anything;

Śīla is a form of precious wealth free of ruin or anguish;

Śīla is the indestructible path of purity that is comparable to a level road that can be traveled without difficulty;

Śīla is a fine farm field that, even without having to plant it or harvest it, one naturally obtains its fruits;

Śīla is the fruit tasting of the elixir of immortality that, even though not obtained from a tree or produced from a plant, is incomparably delicious;

Śīla is a *mañjūṣaka* flower that does not grow forth from either water or land and never wilts;

Śīla dispels the fever of the afflictions and, in this, it is like bathing in cool waters;

Śīla provides complete protection superior to that of even swords or staves, hence the practitioner of *śīla* is respected, but not because others fear him;

Śīla is a station of sovereign mastery that is free of any disputation or struggle;

Śīla is a fine jewel not extracted from the mountains or drawn forth from the great sea, one whose value is incalculable;

121a17 ‖ 尸羅能過不活畏入眾
畏考掠畏墮惡道畏。尸羅常隨逐人。今世後
121a18 ‖ 世如影隨形。

尸罗能过不活畏入众畏考掠畏堕恶道畏。尸罗常随逐人。今世后世如影随形。

Śīla is able to take one beyond the fear of not surviving, beyond the fear of entering the assembly, beyond the fear of interrogation and beating, and beyond the fear of falling into the hells.[282]

Śīla always follows along with a person in present and future lives just as a shadow follows its form.

The End of Chapter Thirty-Four

正體字

121a19 ‖	戒報品第[4]八
121a20 ‖	[5]菩薩離垢地。清淨具說已。菩薩住此地。常
121a21 ‖	作轉輪王。第二地於十地中名為離垢。慳
121a22 ‖	貪十惡根本永盡故名為離垢。菩薩於是地
121a23 ‖	中深行尸羅波羅蜜。是菩薩若未離欲。此
121a24 ‖	地果報因緣故。作四天下轉輪聖王。得千輻
121a25 ‖	金輪種種珍寶莊嚴。其[6]輞真琉璃為轂。周
121a26 ‖	圓十五里。百種夜[7]叉神所共守護。能飛行
121a27 ‖	虛空導四種兵。輕[8]健迅疾如金翅鳥王。如
121a28 ‖	風如念。所詣之處滅諸衰患降伏怨賊。一
121a29 ‖	切小王皆來歸伏。親族人民莫不愛敬。普能
121b01 ‖	照明。聖王姓族種種華鬘[9]瓔珞間錯莊校。五
121b02 ‖	種伎樂常隨逐之。以奇妙寶蓋羅覆其上。
121b03 ‖	行時有種種華香碎末旃檀常雨供養。燒真
121b04 ‖	黑沈水牛頭旃檀黃旃檀以塗其身。其輪兩
121b05 ‖	邊天女執持白拂侍立。

简体字

戒报品第三十六

　　菩萨离垢地。清净具说已。菩萨住此地。常作转轮王。第二地于十地中名为离垢。悭贪十恶根本永尽故名为离垢。菩萨于是地中深行尸罗波罗蜜。是菩萨若未离欲。此地果报因缘故。作四天下转轮圣王。得千辐金轮种种珍宝庄严。其辋真琉璃为毂。周圆十五里。百种夜叉神所共守护。能飞行虚空导四种兵。轻健迅疾如金翅鸟王。如风如念。所诣之处灭诸衰患降伏怨贼。一切小王皆来归伏。亲族人民莫不爱敬。普能照明。圣王姓族种种华鬘瓔珞间错庄校。五种伎乐常随逐之。以奇妙宝盖罗覆其上。行时有种种华香碎末旃檀常雨供养。烧真黑沉水牛头旃檀黄旃檀以涂其身。其轮两边天女执持白拂侍立。

Chapter 35
The Karmic Rewards of the Moral Precepts

XV. Chapter 35: The Karmic Rewards of the Moral Precepts
   A. The Second Ground Bodhisattva as a Wheel-Turning King

The comprehensive explanation of purification related to the bodhisattva's Ground of Stainlessness is hereby concluded. The bodhisattva dwelling on this ground always becomes a wheel-turning king. This second of the ten grounds is referred to as the Ground of Stainlessness. It is because covetousness and the rest of the ten bad karmic actions are all cut off at the very root that it is referred to as "stainless." A bodhisattva on this ground engages in the deep practice of *śīla pāramitā*. In the event that this bodhisattva has not yet abandoned the desires, the causes and conditions associated with this ground's karmic rewards result in his becoming a wheel-turning king ruling over the four continents who obtains a thousand-spoked gold wheel.

   B. The Wheel-Turning King's Treasures
   1. His Gold Wheel Treasure

Its rim is adorned with many different sorts of precious jewels and its hub is made of real beryl. It has a circumference of fifteen *li*.[283] It is protected by a hundred kinds of *yakṣas*. It is able to fly through the air leading a fourfold army with agility, strength, and speed like that of the king of the golden-winged [*garuḍa*] birds, like that of the wind, or like that of a single thought, so that it is then able, wherever it goes, to put an end to all calamities and conquer any enemies.

All of the lesser kings come and declare their allegiance and submission. Of all of his relatives, clans, and subject peoples, there are none who do not both love and revere him. He is able to emanate radiance that illuminates everywhere. The sage king's clan members wear many different kinds of floral chaplets with interspersed adornments of pearls. The five kinds of music follow him wherever he goes. An extraordinarily marvelous jeweled canopy hangs down over and around him. As he walks along, many different sorts of flower blossoms, incenses, and powdered sandalwood rain down as offerings as there also burn genuine black aloewood incense and ox-head sandalwood incense. His body is scented with yellow sandalwood fragrance. On both sides of that wheel, heavenly maidens stand in attendance, holding white whisks. The canopy above him is composed of all sorts

正體字	121b06 ‖ 121b07 ‖ 121b08 ‖ 121b09 ‖ 121b10 ‖ 121b11 ‖ 121b12 ‖ 121b13 ‖ 121b14 ‖ 121b15 ‖ 121b16 ‖ 121b17 ‖ 121b18 ‖ 121b19 ‖	種種珍寶以為其 蓋。其輪有種種希有之事而用莊嚴。是名 金輪寶具足。一切[10]象相。身大而白如真銀 山[11]王出神嶽。大象[12]眾中能飛行虛空。伊羅 婆那安闍那王摩那等諸大象王皆能摧却。 是名白象寶具足。馬相色如孔雀頸。其體 輕疾如金翅鳥王飛行無礙。是名馬寶。貴家 中生身無疾病。有大勢力形體淨潔憶念 深遠直心柔軟。持戒堅固深敬愛王。能通達 種種經書[13]技術。是名主兵臣寶。如財主 天王富相具足千萬億種諸寶伏藏常隨逐行。 千萬億種諸夜叉神眷屬隨從。皆是先世行 業之報。善知分別。金銀帝青大青金剛摩羅竭 [14]車璖馬瑙珊瑚[15]頗梨摩尼真珠琉瑠等種種 寶物。悉能善知出入多少。隨宜能用。
简体字		种种珍宝以为其盖。其轮有种种希有之事而用庄严。是名金轮宝具足。一切象相。身大而白如真银山王出神岳。大象众中能飞行虚空。伊罗婆那安阁那王摩那等诸大象王皆能摧却。是名白象宝具足。马相色如孔雀颈。其体轻疾如金翅鸟王飞行无碍。是名马宝。贵家中生身无疾病。有大势力形体净洁忆念深远直心柔软。持戒坚固深敬爱王。能通达种种经书技术。是名主兵臣宝。如财主天王富相具足千万亿种诸宝伏藏常随逐行。千万亿种诸夜叉神眷属随从。皆是先世行业之报。善知分别。金银帝青大青金刚摩罗竭车磲马瑙珊瑚颇梨摩尼真珠琉琉等种种宝物。悉能善知出入多少。随宜能用。

of precious jewels. The wheel itself has all sorts of different rare things adorning it. This is what is meant by his "gold wheel treasure."

2. HIS ELEPHANT TREASURE

[As for his elephant treasure] it possesses all the characteristics of an elephant and its body is huge and white like a king of mountains made of real silver. It comes from a herd of great elephants in the magic mountains. It is able to fly through the air, decisively defeat, and drive away in retreat all of the other great elephant kings, including Airāvaṇa, Añjana, Vāmana, and the rest. This is what is meant by his "white elephant treasure."

3. HIS HORSE TREASURE

[As for his horse treasure], it possesses all the characteristics of horses and is the color of a peacock's neck. Its body has agility and speed like that of the king of the golden-winged [*garuḍa*] birds and it can fly unimpeded through the air. This is what is meant by his "horse treasure."

4. HIS PRIME MINISTER OF MILITARY AFFAIRS TREASURE

[As for his prime minister of military affairs treasure], he is one who has been born into a noble clan with a body that is free of illness, possessed of great strength, and a physical form of pristine appearance. His memory and thought are deep and far-reaching and he is possessed of a straight and resilient mind. He is solid in his observance of the precepts and he has deep reverence and affection for the king. He is able to penetrate the meaning of the many different classic scriptures as well as the technical skills and arts. This is what is meant by his "prime minister of military affairs treasure."

5. HIS TREASURY MINISTER TREASURE

As for his treasury minister treasure, like the heavenly king of great wealth, he is characterized by such repletion in wealth that a thousand myriads of *koṭis* of kinds of precious jewels form a treasury that always follows along with him wherever he goes, attended by retinue of a thousand myriads of *koṭis* of *yakṣas*. All of this is the karmic reward for his karmic actions in previous lives. [All of the precious jewels in the treasury] are well known and distinguished, including the gold, silver, *indranīla* sapphires, *mahānīla* sapphires, diamonds, malachite, *musāragalva*, carnelian, coral, *sphaṭika*, *maṇi* jewels, real pearls, beryl, and all of the other different kinds of precious things. Precisely how much goes out and how much comes in is also well known. In accordance with whatever is fitting, he is able to use these so that he is able

正體字		能滿
	121b20 ‖	王願。是名居士寶。光明如日月照十六由
	121b21 ‖	旬。形如大鼓能滅種種毒虫惡氣疾病苦
	121b22 ‖	痛。人天見者莫不珍愛。好華[*]瓔珞以為莊
	121b23 ‖	嚴。處在高幢威光奇特。能令眾生發希有
	121b24 ‖	心生大歡喜。是名珠寶。其手爪甲紅赤而
	121b25 ‖	薄。其形脩直高隆。潤澤不肥不瘦。身肉次第
	121b26 ‖	肌膚厚實細密薄皮不堪苦事。身安堅牢如
	121b27 ‖	多羅樹。身上處處吉字明了。吉樹文畫[16]嚴
	121b28 ‖	莊其身。象王牛王馬王畫文幡蓋文魚文園
	121b29 ‖	林等文現其身上。踝平不現。足如龜背。足
	121c01 ‖	邊俱赤。足跟圓廣。[蹲-酋+(十/田/厶)]傭柔軟。膝圓不現。髀
	121c02 ‖	如金柱如芭蕉樹。如象王鼻軟澤光潤。傭
	121c03 ‖	圓而直。橫文有三。腹傭不現。臍圓而深。脊背
	121c04 ‖	平直。乳如頻[17]婆果。如雙鴛鴦圓起不垂柔
	121c05 ‖	軟鮮淨。又其臂纖傭圓[18]且長節隱不現。其
	121c06 ‖	鼻端直不偏現出不大不小孔[19]覆不現。
简体字	能满王愿。是名居士宝。光明如日月照十六由旬。形如大鼓能灭种种毒虫恶气疾病苦痛。人天见者莫不珍爱。好华瓔珞以为庄严。处在高幢威光奇特。能令众生发希有心生大欢喜。是名珠宝。其手爪甲红赤而薄。其形修直高隆。润泽不肥不瘦。身肉次第肌肤厚实细密薄皮不堪苦事。身安坚牢如多罗树。身上处处吉字明了。吉树文画严庄其身。象王牛王马王画文幡盖文鱼文园林等文现其身上。踝平不现。足如龟背。足边俱赤。足跟圆广。[跳-兆+專]佣柔软。膝圆不现。髀如金柱如芭蕉树。如象王鼻软泽光润。佣圆而直。横文有三。腹佣不现。脐圆而深。脊背平直。乳如频婆果。如双鸳鸯圆起不垂柔软鲜净。又其臂纤佣圆且长节隐不现。其鼻端直不偏现出不大不小孔覆不现。	

to fulfill the wishes of the king. This is what is meant by his "treasury minister treasure."[284]

6. His Jewel Treasure

[As for his jewel treasure, it emanates] light like the sun or moon that produces illumination that extends for sixteen *yojanas*. It is shaped like a huge drum and it is able to extinguish many different kinds of insect venom, noxious energies, pestilences, and pain. Of all the humans and devas who see it, none fail to cherish it. It is adorned with fine flowers and necklaces, and, wherever it is placed, a banner is flown on high. It radiates an awe-inspiring and extraordinary radiance that is able to cause beings to bring forth thoughts of wonder and immense joy. This is what is meant by his "jewel treasure."

7. His Jade Maiden Treasure

[Regarding a wheel-turning king's "jade maiden" treasure], her fingernails are vermillion-colored and thin. Her physical form is straight, tall, and imposing. Her complexion is smooth, soft, and neither plump nor thin. Variations in the contours of her flesh are gradual in the transitions of her muscles and skin from dense and full to fine and delicate. Her tender skin would be ill-suited for coarse tasks. Her body is as stable and firm in its stance as the trunk of a *tāla* tree. In place after place on her body, auspicious characters are clearly visible. The silhouette outline of the auspicious tree adorns her body as well. The insignias of the king of elephants, king of bulls, and king of horses, as well as other such emblems as the imperial canopy emblem, the fish emblem, and the parks and forests emblems grace her body as adornments.

Her ankle bones appear flat and not prominent. Her feet have a profile like the shell of a tortoise. The sides of her feet are entirely red. Her heels are round and broad. Her calves are soft and smooth. Her knees are rounded and not prominent. Her thighs are shaped like golden pillars, like a plantain tree's trunk, or like an elephant's trunk while also being soft, smooth, radiantly lustrous, even, round, straight, and graced by three horizontal creases. Her belly is even and not prominent. Her umbilicus is round and deep. Her back is flat and straight. Her breasts are like *bimba* fruit or like [the breasts of] a pair of mandarin ducks. They are rounded and prominent, but not sagging, while also being soft, smooth, and fresh and pristine in appearance.

Also, her arms are slender, even, round, and long, with joints that are hidden and hence not apparent. The profile of her nose is straight and not jutting prominently outward. It is neither large nor small, and its nostrils are hidden and hence not visible.

正體字	兩
121c07 ‖ 頰不深平滿不高兩邊俱滿。額平而長有吉
121c08 ‖ 畫文。耳軟而垂著無價環。齒如真珠貫如
121c09 ‖ 月初生。如雪如[20]珂。脣如丹霞。如頻婆果
121c10 ‖ 上下相當不麁不細。如赤真珠貫。眼白黑
121c11 ‖ [21]睛二色分明。莊嚴長廣光明清淨。其睫青緻
121c12 ‖ 長而不亂。眉毛不厚不薄不高不下如月
121c13 ‖ 初生。高曲而長兩邊相似。髮軟而細潤澤不
121c14 ‖ 亂。其身芬馨常有香氣。如開種種上好香
121c15 ‖ 奩。身諸毛孔常出真妙栴檀名香能悅人
121c16 ‖ 心。口中常有青蓮華香。身體柔軟如伽陵伽。
121c17 ‖ 天衣細滑之事一切具足。心無諂曲直信慚
121c18 ‖ 愧深愛敬王。知時知方善有方便攝取王
121c19 ‖ 心坐起言語能得王意隨王意行常出愛
121c20 ‖ 語。如人間德女眾好具足。色如提盧多摩天
121c21 ‖ 女清淨分明。如月十五日畫文炳現。如帝
121c22 ‖ 釋夫人舍脂。著天衣天鬘天香。多以天光明
121c23 ‖ 金摩尼珠莊校其身。善知歌舞伎樂娛樂戲
121c24 ‖ 笑之事。善有方便隨意能令王發歡喜。
简体字	两颊不深平满不高两边俱满。额平而长有吉画文。耳软而垂着无价环。齿如真珠贯如月初生。如雪如珂。唇如丹霞。如频婆果上下相当不粗不细。如赤真珠贯。眼白黑睛二色分明。庄严长广光明清净。其睫青致长而不乱。眉毛不厚不薄不高不下如月初生。高曲而长两边相似。发软而细润泽不乱。其身芬馨常有香气。如开种种上好香奁。身诸毛孔常出真妙栴檀名香能悦人心。口中常有青莲华香。身体柔软如伽陵伽。天衣细滑之事一切具足。心无谄曲直信惭愧深爱敬王。知时知方善有方便摄取王心坐起言语能得王意随王意行常出爱语。如人间德女众好具足。色如提卢多摩天女清净分明。如月十五日画文炳现。如帝释夫人舍脂。着天衣天鬘天香。多以天光明金摩尼珠庄校其身。善知歌舞伎乐娱乐戏笑之事。善有方便随意能令王发欢喜。

Her two cheeks are not sunken, but rather are even and full. They are not high, but rather are full on both sides.

Her forehead is flat, broad, and graced with an auspicious emblem. Her ears are soft, hang downward, and wear priceless earrings.

Her teeth appear like a strand of real pearls or like a new crescent moon and are the color of snow or alabaster. Her lips, a rosy cinnabar-red, appear like *bimba* fruits, are well matched above and below, and are neither coarse nor fine. They resemble strands of red pearls.

Her eyes are white with dark blue[285] [irises] and the margin between the two colorations is clearly defined. [Her eyes] are graceful, long and wide. They glisten with brightness and clarity. The lashes are bluish, with close-grown hairs that are long, but not disarrayed.

Her eyebrows are neither too thick nor too thin, neither too high nor too low, and they form the shape of new crescent moons. They are prominent and long with their two sides symmetrical.

Her hair is soft while also being fine, smooth, glossy, and not disarrayed.

Her body always emanates an incense-like scent similar to the fragrance rising forth from newly opened containers of various fine perfumes. All of the pores of her body always emit a truly sublime *candana* sandalwood's famous scent that is well able to please anyone's mind.

Her mouth always has the fragrance of a blue lotus.

Her body is as soft as a *kalaviṅka* bird and she is perfectly adorned with the sublimely smooth raiment of the devas.

Her mind is free of any tendency toward flattery or deviousness. She is straightforward, trustworthy, and endowed with a sense of shame and dread of blame. She deeply loves and reveres the king. She knows the right time, knows the right place, and is well equipped with means for drawing the king's attentions. Whether sitting or standing, her words are well able to match the king's intentions and accord with the course of the king's thoughts. She always speaks pleasing words and, like a virtuous maiden among humans, she is replete in the many sorts of fine qualities. Her appearance is comparable to that of the heavenly maiden, *Tiluduoma*,[286] for it has a purity and clarity that shines like the moon on the fifteenth night of the month. Her appearance is also comparable to that of Indra's consort, Śacī. She wears heavenly raiment, a floral chaplet of the devas, celestial scents, and has many [strands of] radiant heavenly gold, *maṇi* jewels, and pearls adorning her body. She is well versed in singing, dancing, music, and all of the other arts of pleasurable entertainment and humor while also being well possessed of all the ways to be freely able to cause the king to be

正體字

```
121c25 ||    切女中是女為最。是名玉女寶。又轉輪聖
121c26 || 王有四如意德。一者色貌端嚴。於四天下
121c27 || 第一無比。二無病痛。三人民深愛。四壽命
121c28 || 長遠。教誨眾生以十善業。能令諸天宮殿
121c29 || 充滿。能減阿修羅眾。能薄諸惡趣增益善
122a01 || 處。能為眾生多求利事有所施作。不用
122a02 || 兵仗以法治化天子安樂。外無敵國畏內
122a03 || 無陰謀畏。又其國內無疫病飢餓及諸災
122a04 || [1]蝗衰惱之事。一切邊[2]王皆所歸伏。多有眷
122a05 || 屬能疾攝人。更無有能侵害國界。其四種
122a06 || 兵勢力具足。諸婆羅門居士庶人皆共愛敬。
122a07 || 甘香美食自然而有。國界日增無有損減善
122a08 || 能通達經書[3]技藝算數呪術皆悉受持。巧
122a09 || 能論說分別義趣。群臣具足悉有威德。常
122a10 || 行財施無能及者。
```

简体字

一切女中是女为最。是名玉女宝。又转轮圣王有四如意德。一者色貌端严。于四天下第一无比。二无病痛。三人民深爱。四寿命长远。教诲众生以十善业。能令诸天宫殿充满。能减阿修罗众。能薄诸恶趣增益善处。能为众生多求利事有所施作。不用兵仗以法治化天子安乐。外无敌国畏内无阴谋畏。又其国内无疫病饥饿及诸灾蝗衰恼之事。一切边王皆所归伏。多有眷属能疾摄人。更无有能侵害国界。其四种兵势力具足。诸婆罗门居士庶人皆共爱敬。甘香美食自然而有。国界日增无有损减善能通达经书技艺算数咒术皆悉受持。巧能论说分别义趣。群臣具足悉有威德。常行财施无能及者。

Chapter 35 — The Karmic Rewards of the Moral Precepts

delighted. Among all women, this woman is the very best. Such is the description of the king's "jade-maiden treasure."

C. Four Qualities of the Wheel Turning King

The wheel-turning king also has four spontaneously manifesting qualities:

First, his physical appearance is handsome and dignified and, in this, he is foremost, unmatched by anyone living on any of the four continents;

Second, he remains free of sickness and pain;

Third, he is deeply loved by his people;

Fourth, he has a very long life span.

D. A Description of a Wheel-Turning King's Domain, Rule & Qualities

He teaches beings that, through abiding by the ten courses of good karmic action, they are able to keep the heavenly palaces full, are able to diminish the *asura* hordes, are able to diminish the number of beings in the wretched destinies, and are able to increase their numbers in the good stations of rebirth.

In whatever endeavors he undertakes, he primarily seeks what is most beneficial to beings. Thus, without using armies and weapons, he institutes order in accordance with the Dharma and ensures peace and happiness among all the feudal princes.

Outwardly, he has no fear of hostile countries on his borders. Inwardly, he has no fear of secret plots against his reign. Additionally, his country remains free of plague, famine, or any of the disasters, locusts, or other ruinous and anguishing circumstances.

All the kings in the border regions pledge their allegiance and submit to him. He is attended by a large retinue and is able to swiftly gather people [to become loyal followers]. Thus there are none able to attack and damage his domain. His fourfold army is possessed of abundant might. He is loved and respected by all brahmans, merchants, and common people.

Sweet, fragrant, and delectable food comes to him spontaneously. The boundaries of his domain increase by the day and never shrink. He is well able to reach a penetrating comprehension of all the classic scriptures, arts, mathematics, and spiritual incantations, all of which he can retain and invoke. He is skilled in his ability to debate, discuss, and clearly distinguish their meaning and import. Those in his assembly of officials are all well possessed of awe-inspiring virtue. He is always devoted to philanthropic giving that no one can match.

正體字	千子端嚴如諸天子威 122a11 ‖ 德勇健能破強敵。所住宮殿堂閣樓觀如四 122a12 ‖ 天王帝釋勝殿。王所教誨無有能壞於四 122a13 ‖ 天下。唯有此王威相具足故無能及者。音 122a14 ‖ 聲深遠易聽易解不散不亂。如迦羅頻伽 122a15 ‖ 鳥美軟和雅聞者悅耳。眷屬同心不可沮 122a16 ‖ 壞。所住之處地水虛空無有障礙。威力猛 122a17 ‖ [4]盛能堪大事。念問[5]耆老不欺誑人。心無 122a18 ‖ 妬嫉不忍非法無有瞋恨。威儀安詳而不 122a19 ‖ 輕躁。所言誠實未曾兩舌。行施持戒常修 122a20 ‖ 善心。進止知時不失方便。神色和悅言常 122a21 ‖ 含笑。未曾皺眉惡眼視人。退失利者為 122a22 ‖ 之作利。已有利者令深知報懷慚愧心。 122a23 ‖ 有大智慧威德尊嚴而能忍辱。大丈夫相其 122a24 ‖ 性猛厲。諸所為事疾能成辦。先正思量然後 122a25 ‖ 乃行。王有法眼所為殊勝。
简体字	千子端严如诸天子威德勇健能破强敌。所住宫殿堂阁楼观如四天王帝释胜殿。王所教诲无有能坏于四天下。唯有此王威相具足故无能及者。音声深远易听易解不散不乱。如迦罗频伽鸟美软和雅闻者悦耳。眷属同心不可沮坏。所住之处地水虚空无有障碍。威力猛盛能堪大事。念问耆老不欺诳人。心无妒嫉不忍非法无有嗔恨。威仪安详而不轻躁。所言诚实未曾两舌。行施持戒常修善心。进止知时不失方便。神色和悦言常含笑。未曾皱眉恶眼视人。退失利者为之作利。已有利者令深知报怀惭愧心。有大智慧威德尊严而能忍辱。大丈夫相其性猛厉。诸所为事疾能成办。先正思量然后乃行。王有法眼所为殊胜。

Chapter 35 — The Karmic Rewards of the Moral Precepts

His thousand sons are all as handsome as the sons of the devas and they are possessed of awe-inspiring virtue, courage, strength, and the ability to crush even the strongest of enemies.

The palace in which he dwells is replete with halls, towers, and pavilions like those supreme palaces enjoyed by the Four Heavenly Kings and Indra.

Whatsoever the king instructs is unable to be subverted by anyone anywhere on the four continents. It is only this one king whose marks of awe-inspiring power are so complete that none are able to match him.

His voice is deep, carries far, is easily heard, easily understood, and is never scattered or disordered. And, like the sound of the *kalaviṅka* bird, it is beautiful, soft, harmonious, refined, and pleasing to the ear of the hearer.

His retinue is of like mind and incapable of obstructiveness. Wherever he abides, whether on the land, the water, or moving through the air, there is no one able to impede his travel. He has awesome power that is courageous and abundant with which he can undertake and succeed in great endeavors.

He thinks of and asks after the welfare of the aged. He never deceives anyone. His mind has no jealousy. He does not tolerate anything contrary to Dharma and he has no hatred.

His personal deportment is serene and dignified and it is neither restless nor impetuous. Whatever he says is sincere and true and he never utters divisive speech. In whatever he does, he upholds the moral precepts and cultivates a mind imbued with goodness. In initiating or halting endeavors, he knows the right time and never fails to employ appropriate methods.

His facial expression is amiable and, in speaking, he is always inclined to a subtle smile. He never scowls or glowers at anyone. For those who have encountered misfortune, he does whatever is beneficial for them. Those who have already been benefited thereby come to feel deep gratitude and to feel disposed toward a sense of shame and dread of blame.

He is possessed of great wisdom, awe-inspiring virtue, and a dignified manner while also being able to abide in patience. He has the marks of the great man and his nature is such that he may manifest fierce severity. He is able to swiftly complete every endeavor he takes up. He first assesses circumstances correctly and then acts accordingly. Because the King has the Dharma eye, whatever he does is exceptional.

正體字	
	善思量者乃與從
122a26 ‖	事。若不任者更求賢明。善集福德財物。清
122a27 ‖	淨能自防護不破禁戒。多饒財寶如毘沙
122a28 ‖	門王。有大勢力如天帝釋。端嚴可愛猶如
122a29 ‖	滿月。能照如日。能忍如地。心深如海不為
122b01 ‖	苦樂之所傾動。如須彌山王風不能搖。諸
122b02 ‖	寶妙事之所住處。諸善福德之所依止。是諸
122b03 ‖	一切世間親族。諸苦惱者之所歸趣。無歸作
122b04 ‖	歸無舍作舍。有怖畏者[6]能除怖畏。轉輪
122b05 ‖	聖王有如是等相。
122b06 ‖	能轉破戒者　　令住於善法
122b07 ‖	其餘所行事　　如初地中說
122b08 ‖	轉破戒者。能令眾生捨惡行善得安樂事。
122b09 ‖	令住善法者。能轉眾生惡身口意業令行
122b10 ‖	善身口意業。此事如初地中說。所謂見諸
122b11 ‖	佛得諸三昧。但彼數百此地數千以為差
122b12 ‖	別。
122b13 ‖	十住毘婆沙論卷第十[7]七

简体字

善思量者乃与从事。若不任者更求贤明。善集福德财物。清净能自防护不破禁戒。多饶财宝如毗沙门王。有大势力如天帝释。端严可爱犹如满月。能照如日。能忍如地。心深如海不为苦乐之所倾动。如须弥山王风不能摇。诸宝妙事之所住处。诸善福德之所依止。是诸一切世间亲族。诸苦恼者之所归趣。无归作归无舍作舍。有怖畏者能除怖畏。转轮圣王有如是等相。

　　能转破戒者　　令住于善法
　　其余所行事　　如初地中说

转破戒者。能令众生舍恶行善得安乐事。令住善法者。能转众生恶身口意业令行善身口意业。此事如初地中说。所谓见诸佛得诸三昧。但彼数百此地数千以为差别。

Chapter 35 — The Karmic Rewards of the Moral Precepts

Where he has those who are possessed of good judgment, he delegates tasks to them. If they are incapable of fulfilling their duties, he then seeks further for other surrogates who are worthy and wise.

He is skillful in accumulating karmic merit and wealth. By virtue of his own purity, he is able to guard his own actions and defend against breaking any of the moral precepts.

He bestows much wealth and treasure and, in this, he is comparable to King Vaiśravaṇa. He possesses great strength like Śakra, ruler of the devas.

He is as majestic and entrancing as the full moon and as radiant as the sun. He has the capacity to endure of the earth and his mind is as deep as the ocean. He is not shaken in the least by either pain or pleasure, and, like Sumeru, king of the mountains, none of the winds can make him quaver and he is the repository of all jewels and marvelous things.

He is one in whom all the excellent meritorious qualities reside. He acts as the close friend and relative of everyone in the entire world and he is a place of refuge for all who are beset by suffering or affliction. He is a refuge for those who have no refuge and a shelter for those who have no shelter. He can dispel the fear of those beset by fear.

Such are the characteristics of the wheel-turning sage king.

He is able to reverse the path of those who break moral precepts
and then influence them to abide in good dharmas.
All the other endeavors to which he is devoted
are as previously explained in the discussion of the first ground.

As for "reversing the path of those who break moral precepts," he is able to influence beings to relinquish evil actions and take up those endeavors that are conducive to peace and happiness.

As for "influencing them to abide in good dharmas," he is able to turn beings away from evil actions of body, speech, and mind and influence them to take up the good karmic actions of body, speech, and mind.

As for these endeavors being "as previously explained in the discussion of the first ground," this refers to being able to see the buddhas and acquire the samādhis. The only difference is that, on that ground, hundreds of buddhas are seen, whereas on this ground, thousands of buddhas are seen.

The End of Chapter Thirty-Five

The End of theTreatise on the Ten Grounds

Volume Two Endnotes

1. Because the received text's listing of these 40 exclusive dharmas presents them in a somewhat different order than occurs as they are actually presented and discussed in the text, I reorder and renumber them here to follow the actual order of their presentation. I do so based on the usually factual assumption that the section titles and preliminary lists in translations of Sanskrit texts are for the most part *not* part of the original text, but rather are added by the Sanskrit-to-Chinese translator to assist the reader, or, in this case, perhaps by the editors and scribes in Kumārajīva's translation bureau. For those interested in the erroneously ordered and numbered list found here in the received text, it is as follows:

    1) Sovereign mastery of the ability to fly;
    2) [The ability to manifest] countless transformations;
    3) Boundless psychic powers of the sort possessed by *āryas*;
    4) Sovereign mastery of the ability to hear sounds;
    5) Immeasurable power of knowledge to know others' thoughts;
    6) Sovereign mastery in [training and subduing] the mind;
    7) Constant abiding in stable wisdom;
    8) Never forgetting;
    9) Possession of the powers of the *vajra* samādhi;
    10) Thorough knowing of matters that are unfixed;
    11) Thorough knowing of matters pertaining to the formless realm's meditative absorptions;
    12) The completely penetrating knowledge of all matters associated with eternal cessation;
    13) Thorough knowing of the non-form dharmas unassociated with the mind;
    14) The great powers *pāramitā*;
    15) The [four] unimpeded [knowledges] *pāramitā*;
    16) The *pāramitā* of perfectly complete replies and predictions in response to questions;
    17) Perfectly complete implementation of the three turnings in speaking Dharma;
    18) Their words are never spoken without a purpose;
    19) Their speech is free of error;
    20) Invulnerability to harm by anyone;
    21) They are the great generals among all *āryas*;
    22–25) They are able to remain unguarded in four ways;
    26–29) They possess the four fearlessnesses;
    30–39) They possess the ten powers;
    40) They possess the unimpeded liberations.

2. VB notes: "This is a category in Sarvāstivāda Abhidharma (not in the Theravāda Abhidharma), which indicates the author is familiar with the Sarvāstivāda system."
3. "Without a purpose" here is literally "empty" (in the sense of "in vain" or "fruitlessly").
4. VB notes: "See Anguttara Nikaya 7:58. The four are: conduct of body, speech, and mind, and livelihood."
5. To correct an apparent graphic-similarity scribal error, I emend the reading of the *Taisho* text here by preferring the SYMG editions' *neng* (能), "able to," to the *Taisho* edition's *suo* (所), "that which."
6. VB notes: "See *Anguttara Nikaya*, Sevens, no. 40 (see, too, Sixes, no. 24):
    'Bhikkhus, possessing seven qualities, a bhikkhu exercises mastery over his mind and is not a servant of his mind. What seven? Here, (1) a bhikkhu is skilled in concentration; (2) skilled in the attainment of concentration; (3) skilled in the duration of concentration; (4) skilled in emergence from concentration; (5) skilled in fitness for concentration; (6) skilled in the range of concentration; and (7) skilled in resolution regarding concentration. Possessing these seven qualities, a bhikkhu exercises mastery over his mind, and is not a servant of his mind.'"
7. This appears to be yet another instance of KJ's use of *xing* (性), usually translated as "nature," as a translation for *dhātu* which is more ordinarily translated into Sino-Buddhist Classical Chinese as *jie* (界), "realm."
8. VB notes: "In the above [passage: '諸相諸觸諸覺諸念亦知起知住知生知滅'], 相 is clearly another instance of the confusion between 相 and 想 so common in Chinese texts. The Pali part parallel has *saññā*. See the end of Majjhima Nikāya 123, where the Buddha says he knows the arising, persistence, and passing away of *vedanā*, *saññā*, and *vitakka*."
9. In response to my earlier draft translation of *emo* (惡魔) here as "an evil demon," VB notes: Here there is no doubt that 惡魔 is none other than the infamous Māra, a particular individual, not just any "evil demon." See *Samyutta Nikāya* 4:24 "Seven Years of Pursuit":
    "On one occasion the Blessed One was dwelling at Uruvelā on the bank of the river Nerañjarā at the foot of the Goatherd's Banyan Tree. Now on that occasion Māra the Evil One had been following the Blessed One for seven years, seeking to gain access to him but without success....
    "Then Māra the Evil One, in the presence of the Blessed One, recited these verses of disappointment:
    "There was a crow that walked around
    A stone that looked like a lump of fat.

> 'Let's find something tender here,' [he thought,]
> 'Perhaps there's something nice and tasty.'
>
> But because he found nothing tasty there,
> The crow departed from that spot.
> Just like the crow that attacked the stone,
> We leave Gotama disappointed."

10. These five are: past dharmas, present dharmas, future dharmas, unconditioned dharmas (referred to below as "those that transcend the three periods of time"), and ineffable dharmas.

11. I emend the text here to correct an apparent graphic-similarity scribal error, preferring SYMG's *san* (三), "three," to the *Taisho* text's *er* (二), "two." The rationale for the emendation is evident in the paragraph's discussion of "three" dharmas that are "strung together," not merely "two."

12. I have made the same emendation here as in the immediately previous note.

13. VB notes that this incident involving the elephant named Nālagiri is described in the Vinaya, Cūlavagga, II 194 foll. of PTS Pali edition.

14. As described later in the text, "The twelve *dhūta* austerities" are:
    Adopting the dharma of dwelling in a forest hermitage;
    Obtaining one's food through the alms round;
    Wearing robes made of cast-off rags;
    [Taking one's daily meal in but] a single sitting;
    Always sitting to sleep, [never lying down];
    Having taken the meal, not accepting food or drink at the wrong times;
    Possessing only a single set of three robes;
    Wearing only an animal-hair robe;
    Laying out one's sitting mat wherever one happens to be;
    Dwelling at the foot of a tree;
    Dwelling out in the open (lit. "on empty ground");
    Dwelling in a charnel field.

15. VB notes: "In the Pali these are laid out as parallel descriptive terms. The Pali actually has nine synonymous terms. See AN 1:174."

16. Based on VB's very sensible suggestion that "quiescent cessation" (寂滅) is probably here as elsewhere simply a somewhat opaque sounding sino-Buddhist translation of "*nirvāṇa*," I have gone ahead and rendered it as such throughout this entire passage as well as in other places throughout the text where the context demands it.

17. I have been unable to find a Sanskrit antecedent for this Chinese transliteration of a type of rishi, a *"pisuo"* (脾娑) rishi. VB suggests that this may be a transliteration of *viśvarśi (viś ṛṣi)*.
18. VB notes that one can find approximate Pali Canon parallels at MN 110.4, MLDB p. 892, and AN 3:3.
19. VB notes: "The story of Ciñcā the brahman girl occurs in the Dhammapada Commentary, commenting on verse 176. See Burlingame, *Buddhist Legends* III 19 foll."
20. VB notes: "In the Pali Canon, this incident is referred to in Udāna Section 38."
21. VB notes: "The incident is at SN 4:18 (PTS ed. I 113–14)."
22. VB notes: "The story is in the Pāli Vinaya in Cullavagga, chapter 7; PTS ed II 194–96."
23. VB notes: "This [story] is at the beginning of the Pārājika chapter of the Vinaya."
24. VB notes: "His departure from the Sangha and denunciation of the Buddha are mentioned at the beginning of MN 12. MN 105 is spoken to him, and his arguments with the Buddha about arahants are at DN 23."
25. VB notes: "See AN 7:58: Four things that the Tathāgata does not have to guard: conduct of body, speech, and mind, and livelihood."
26. "The *upoṣadha* dharma" is a reference to spiritual purification, in particular the two days of the month when monastics recite the precepts and the days of the month in which pious lay people voluntarily take on a semi-monastic level of moral precept observance.
27. This is verse 183 of the *Dhammapada*.
28. The first four lines here correspond to *Dhammapada* 361.
29. This corresponds to verse 362 of the *Dhammapada*.
30. VB notes: "See AN 5:181 foll.: 'Bhikkhus, there are these five kinds of forest dwellers. What five? (1) One who becomes a forest dweller because of his dullness and stupidity; (2) one who becomes a forest dweller because he has evil desires, because he is driven by desire; (3) one who becomes a forest dweller because he is mad and mentally deranged; (4) one who becomes a forest dweller, [thinking]: "It is praised by the Buddhas and the Buddhas' disciples"; (5) and one who becomes a forest dweller for the sake of fewness of desires, for the sake of contentment, for the sake of eliminating [defilements], for the sake of solitude, for the sake of simplicity. The fifth is pronounced the best.'"

31. VB notes: "I think the author here is referring to the Buddha's hesitation, immediately after his enlightenment, about going out and teaching the Dharma. See MN 26.19, SN 6:1, etc."
32. VB notes: "This is at MN 26.22–23. Interestingly the author here takes a similar perspective on *sarvajñatā* as the Theravāda commentaries, that knowledge arises when the Buddha directs his attention to some issue (*āvajjanapaṭibaddhaṃ buddhassa bhagavato ñāṇaṃ*), in contrast to the later Mahāyāna view that the Buddha perpetually knows everything simultaneously."
33. The second part of the Chinese text's title, "Forty Dharmas Exclusive to Buddhas: The Exclusive Dharma of Thoroughly Knowing What is Unfixed," is misleading because "the exclusive dharma of thoroughly knowing what is unfixed" only describes the first few pages of this long chapter that in fact discusses all of the remaining exclusive dharmas (nos. 10–40). I have therefore dropped this misleading phrase from the chapter title. One should be aware that these chapter titles almost certainly do not originate with Nāgārjuna but rather with Kumārajīva's translation team.
34. VB notes: "The above corresponds to Majjhima Nikaya no. 136."
35. Commenting on the corresponding passages as preserved in the Pali canon, VB notes: "The Pāli sutta with the simile of the raft mentions all four fruits (MN 22; see the end). But the proposition about one of two fruits occurs in a number of other suttas, such as the Satipaṭṭhāna Sutta (see end of MN 10)."
36. Regarding this "*Ekottara Āgama's Shejiali Sutra*" (舍迦梨經), I have so far been unable to locate the Sanskrit for its title.
37. VB comments: "The above corresponds to Anguttara Nikāya 10:217 (also 10:218). Note that there are three modes in which the karmic results may be received, both in Pāli and Chinese versions: in the present life (現受報), upon rebirth (that is, the next life; 生受), or in a subsequent life (after the next one; 後受). Here is the Pāli followed by my rendering:

> 217. "*Nāhaṃ, bhikkhave, sañcetanikānaṃ kammānaṃ katānaṃ upacitānaṃ appaṭisaṃviditvā byantībhāvaṃ vadāmi. Tañca kho diṭṭheva dhamme upapajje vā apare vā pariyāye. Na tvevāhaṃ, bhikkhave, sañcetanikānaṃ kammānaṃ katānaṃ upacitānaṃ appaṭisaṃveditvā dukkhass'antakiriyaṃ vadāmi.*"
>
> "Bhikkhus, I do not say that there is a termination of volitional kamma that has been done and accumulated so long as one has not experienced [its results], and that may be in this very life, or in the [next] rebirth, or on some subsequent occasion. But I do not say that there is making an end of suffering so long as one has not

experienced [the results of] volitional kamma that has been done and accumulated."

38. Again, I have so far been unable to find the Sanskrit name for this transliterated title.
39. VB notes: "The Pāli parallel is *Majjhima* 58: *Abhayarājakumāra Sutta*."
40. These "three groups" refers to the *tri-skandha* (三聚) as that term is used to categorize the karmic destinies of beings. Those who are "definitely deviant" or "erroneous" are definitely bound to be unsuccessful in reaching enlightenment whereas those who are "definitely righteous" or "correct" are definitely bound to succeed in becoming enlightened. In his Mppu, in commenting on a passage in the Great Perfection of Wisdom Sutra that brings up the topic of these three groups, N points out that it is the ability or inability to destroy the inverted views that is pivotal in determining one's position in this threefold categorization. It is those who may or may not encounter the karmic conditions enabling the destruction of these inverted views who are categorized as "indefinite." (See T25.n1509.647c27–648a01.)
41. These four "repositories of Dharma" (*dharma-piṭaka*) are identified by Nāgārjuna in his Mppu as: 1) the Sutra Piṭaka; 2) the Vinaya Piṭaka; 3) the Abhidharma Piṭaka; and 4) the Kṣudraka-piṭaka (T12; No. 1509; 143c23–25).
42. These are "delectable absorptions" (*āsvādana-samādhi*) which are characterized by the arising of extremely pleasurable meditation states to which the unskilled or unwise meditator is vulnerable to becoming attached.
43. VB notes: "The Pāli parallel is the opening passage of Dīgha Nikāya no. 14, almost verbatim the same."
44. I emend the reading of the *Taisho* text here by preferring on sensibility grounds the SYMG editions' *ci jing* (此經), "this sutra," to the *Taisho* edition's *jing ci* (經此), "sutra this."

    The sutra to which this text refers is obviously the Ten Grounds Sutra upon which Nāgārjuna's SZPPS comments. This topic of the expansiveness of the Buddha's knowledge and vision is treated at great length in the sutra itself.
45. VB notes: "The names of *pratyekabuddhas* are mentioned in MN 116. I would posit the following equivalents [for a few of the *pratyekabuddhas* mentioned here]:

    無垢 = Ariṭṭha
    華相 = Tagarasikhī
    喜見 = Piyadassī

46. VB notes: "Parallel to the above is AN 6:62 Section 6: (6) 'Then, Ānanda, having encompassed his mind with my own mind, I understand some person thus: "Wholesome qualities and unwholesome qualities are found in this person." On a later occasion, having encompassed his mind with my own mind, I understand him thus: "This person does not have even a mere fraction of a hair's tip of an unwholesome quality. This person possesses exclusively bright, blameless qualities. He will attain *nibbāna* in this very life."'"
47. VB notes: "[This passage is found] in MN 12."
48. VB notes: "The following passage comes toward the end of MN 12."
49. This long paragraph (beginning with "Supposing…") has the appearance of language quoted from a sutra. However, having failed to locate it, I frame it here as simply Nāgārjuna's amplification of the meaning of the immediately preceding passage that VB recognized as having a Pali analogue in MN 12.
50. This is the name as recorded in the Pali canon. I'm not sure about the Sanskrit for this name.
51. Ibid.
52. VB notes that the following passage is found in the beginning of MN 136.
53. Rāhula was the Buddha's son whereas Devadatta was someone intent on killing the Buddha.
54. VB suggest that this passage may be alluding to AN 4:111, "Kesi the Horse Trainer."
55. This refers to *satkāyadṛṣṭi*.
56. Again, although in these last two cases, the Chinese is literally "gain the path" (得道), per Hirakawa (p. 451, column 2) this corresponds to: "*bodhi, abhisaṃbuddha, saṃbodhi-prāpta.*" Edgerton in turn suggests "becoming perfectly enlightened" for *abhisambuddhana* (Page 58, column 2).
57. Although "*brahmacarya*" (梵行) generally refers to celibate spiritual practice, it may just as well be thought of as "the holy life" or "the spiritual life. VB notes that this scriptural quote "is found in many places in the Nikāyas: e.g., beginning of MN 148: "*Bhagavā etadavoca – 'dhammaṃ vo, bhikkhave, desessāmi ādikalyāṇaṃ majjhe kalyāṇaṃ pariyosānakalyāṇaṃ sātthaṃ sabyañjanaṃ. kevalaparipuṇṇaṃ parisuddhaṃ brahmacariyaṃ pakāsessāmi.'"*
58. VB notes: "In the Pali suttas, the second wonder is being able to declare another person's thoughts. For the three wonders, see AN 3:60: "There are, brahman, these three kinds of wonders. What three?

The wonder of psychic potency, the wonder of mind-reading, and the wonder of instruction (*iddhipāṭihāriyaṃ ādesanāpāṭihāriyaṃ anusāsanī-pāṭihāriyaṃ*; also at DN 11.3–8, I 212–14). The second is explained thus: There is one who ... declares: 'Your thought is thus, such is what you are thinking, your mind is in such and such a state.' And even if he makes many declarations, they are exactly so and not otherwise."

59. I have been unable to locate either the Sanskrit or Pali antecedents for the titles of these scriptures. VB also notes: "I'm not sure of the references here. Perhaps the former is the Potaliya Sutta, MN 54, but I'm not sure."

60. VB notes: "[The Pali canon analogue for] the following is at MN 12 and AN 4:8."

61. I emend the reading of the *Taisho* text here by preferring on sensibility grounds the SYMG editions' *wei wei* (微畏, "slightest fear," to the *Taisho* edition's *shi* (是), "this."

62. VB notes that the analogue passage in the Pali canon is found at DN no. 20.

63. VB notes: "See MN 115 and AN 1:277."

64. VB notes: "The above, too, is in MN 115 and AN 1:284 foll."

65. VB notes: "On this, see MN 45, 46."

66. VB notes: "This may be an allusion to AN 5:28."

67. VB notes: "This may be an allusion to AN 5:27."

68. This is a concept with numerous similar alternative explanations, most of which refer to the immense amount of merit and time required to acquire the thirty-two marks and eighty minor characteristics of a buddha's body and finally achieve buddhahood. This is discussed in greater detail in Nāgārjuna's commentary on the Great Perfection of Wisdom Sutra. See T25.1509.57b05–27.

69. Nārāyaṇa is a powerful celestial eminence regarded as a Dharma protector in Buddhism.

70. As is quite common with the syntax of multi-line Classical Chinese verses, this quatrain has require the rearrangement of its lines to produce a sensible and naturally flowing statement in English.

71. "Eight classes in four pairs" (四雙八輩) refers to the four preliminary phases and four fruition stages on the individual-liberation path of the *śrāvaka* disciples.

72. VB notes: "見聞覺知 = Pāli *diṭṭhaṃ, sutaṃ, mutaṃ, viññātaṃ*, where *mutaṃ* is explained as things sensed through the other three sense faculties: smell, taste, and touch."

Hence, in "seen, heard, sensed, and known," (per Hirakawa's BCSD: *dṛṣṭa-śruta-mata-jñāta* or *dṛṣṭa-śruta-mata-vijñāta*) "sensed" (*mata*) refers to the sensory function of the olfactory, gustatory, and tactile sense faculties. Therefore this series is intended to refer to the functions of all six sense faculties and their corresponding consciousnesses.

73. To correct an apparent scribal error very likely originating in homophony, I emend the reading of the text here, preferring on sensibility grounds the homophonous *de* (得), "achieved" of the SYMG editions to the *Taisho* text's *de* (德), "qualities."

74. "Five characteristics" here is slightly ambiguous. It could refer particularly to the five types of desire which together constitute the first of the five hindrances (visible forms, sounds, smells, tastes, and touchables, or wealth, sex, fame, food, and leisure). Alternatively, it may be intended to refer to all five of the "five hindrances" that must be eliminated to access deep states of meditation (desire, ill will, lethargy-and-sleepiness, excitedness-and-regretfulness, and afflicted doubtfulness).

75. To correct an apparent graphic-similarity scribal error, I emend the reading of the *Taisho* text here by preferring the SYMG editions' *li* (力), "power," to the *Taisho* edition's *fen* (分), "portion."

76. I am not sure precisely what Nāgārjuna intended by "the six categories of meanings associated with the forty exclusive Dharmas," set forth in his preceding praise verses.

77. The Sanskrit antecedent of *shixiang* (實相) in KJ translations is usually *dharmatā*, i.e. the true nature of all dharmas, i.e. *śūnyatā*, i.e. the utter absence of inherent existence in any and all phenomena.

78. To correct an apparent graphic-similarity scribal error, I emend the reading of the *Taisho* text here by preferring the SYMG editions' *shen* (深), "deep" or "profound," to the *Taisho* edition's *ran* (染), "defiled." Nāgārjuna's discussion of this line corroborates the correctness of the emendation.

79. When translated into Chinese, "Tathāgata" means "Thus Come One."

80. Again, this most likely refers to "The Pratyutpanna Samādhi Sūtra" preserved in the *Taisho* Canon as the *Banzhou Sanmei Jing* (般舟三昧經 / T13.no. 0418.902c23–919c05).

81. "Overweening pride," *zeng shang man* (增上慢), corresponds to the Sanskrit *adhimāna*.

82. To correct an obvious graphic-similarity scribal error, I emend the reading of the *Taisho* text here by preferring the SYMG editions' *zeng* (增), "increase," to the *Taisho* edition's *zeng* (憎), "detest."
83. "Characteristic sign" refers here to any of the signs associated with three sequential levels of practice described at the very beginning of this chapter:
    1) The thirty-two marks and eighty secondary characteristics of a buddha's form body;
    2) The Dharma body of the Buddhas;
    3) The true character [of all dharmas], i.e. "emptiness of inherent existence" (*śūnyatā*). This "emptiness of inherent existence" is evidenced by: a) their being merely composite constructs of subsidiary conditions; b) their being merely evanescently transient states in a chain of serial causality; and c) their being mere names attached to a) and b) to which one falsely imputes individual reality.
84. To correct an obvious graphic-similarity scribal error, I emend the reading of the *Taisho* text here by preferring the SYMG editions' *zhai* (齋), "ritual purification," to the *Taisho* edition's *qi* (齊), "uniform."

    Also, "Precepts of abstinence" refers here to the *aṣṭāṅgasamanvāgataṃ upavāsaṃ*, the laity's formal acceptance and observance of the practice of upholding the eight precepts that include celibacy and not eating after midday. One observes this enhanced level of lay precept practice either continuously or on the eighth, fourteenth, fifteenth, twenty-third, twenty-ninth, and thirtieth days of each lunar month.
85. This reference to laypeople staying in a monastery probably refers most usually to the not uncommon practice of allowing laypeople to live in separate quarters on monastery grounds when they are continuously training in these eight lay precepts for a predetermined period of time.
86. I translate here as "monastic preceptor" and "monastic Dharma teacher" what the KJ text retains in transliteration as *"upādhyāya"* and *"ācārya"* respectively.
87. KJ retained the Sanskrit term for "benefactor" (*dānapati*) which I have opted to translate here.
88. VB notes: "This is the practice of seeking alms at every door, without skipping over houses where the people do not give or give poor quality food." The rationale for observing this "proper sequence" is that, since providing alms to monks and nuns produces karmic merit, one would not want to deny that opportunity to anyone.

89. Lest "unwholesome remorsefulness" seem somewhat opaque, this would refer first and foremost to regretting having done something good or regretting not having done something bad.
90. "Demolishing through separation" most likely refers to the "deconstructive analysis" involved in such contemplations as the contemplation of the thirty-two (or 36) parts of the body, the nine stages of the decomposition of a rotting corpse, the white-boned skeleton contemplation, etc. All of these contemplations serve as powerful antidotes to sensual desire.
91. This attainment of the sign of unloveliness refers to directly perceiving the unloveliness of sensually attractive physical forms so completely that the image of their unloveliness is retained even in the absence of the initially contemplated meditation object. This is often accomplished by deeply practicing the contemplations of the parts of the body, the stages of decomposition of a rotting corpse, or the white-boned skeleton.
92. Hirakawa gives the Sanskrit as: *"saṃrañjanīyaṃ dharmam."* These six dharmas refer to mutual harmoniousness, respect, equality, and fairness in matters pertaining to: body, speech, mind, precepts, views, and benefits received (food, robes, shelter, etc.).
93. These five bases of liberation (Skt. *vimukty-āyatanāni*) are five different circumstances under which, with or without the advantage of correct teaching from a qualified Dharma teacher or fellow practitioner, a practitioner may come to engage with and find success in cultivation, establish his mind in concentration, and then finally achieve liberation. VB refers us to AN 5:26 for the precise canonical explanation.
94. VB refers us to AN 9:29.
95. VB refers us to AN 8:80.
96. VB refers us to AN 8:80, noting that this is found in the second part of that sutta.
97. These are the *navasaṃjñā* for which VB refers us to AN 9:16.
98. VB refers us to AN 8:30.
99. "No apprehensible reality" (無所得) refers to emptiness of inherent existence, i.e. there is nothing in or about these *dhyāna* absorptions that can be gotten at as ultimately real.
100. VB notes: "Items 43-45 are at SN 35:238, 'The Simile of the Vipers.'"
101. VB notes: "This may also be in SN 35:238: 'The further shore, which is safe and free from danger': this is a designation for Nibbāna."

102. This appears to be a quotation from the "Pratyutpanna Samādhi Sūtra."
103. "Compulsory karmic retributions" most likely refers here to heinous karmic offenses that entail immediate retribution during or at the end of this very life such as: patricide, matricide, killing an arhat, drawing the blood of a buddha, or causing a schism in the monastic sangha.
104. This statement seems contradictory. As such, I am not particularly confident that this sentence is not corrupted or that I have interpreted its intent correctly.
105. The immediately preceding abhidharmic analytic categories are in some cases phrased so tersely in the Chinese as to be mildly obscure. Hence I may not have rendered all of them with definitively precise accuracy.
106. These eight verse lines are a verbatim quote from the very beginning of Chapter Three on the characteristic features of the first bodhisattva ground (26a19–22).
107. Again, the first two of these five verses roughly correspond to the KB translation of the *Ten Grounds Sutra* (500b08-11).
108. As noted in chapter two, again, *biding* (必定),"stage of certainty," is a translation of the Sanskrit *avaivartika*, the stage of irreversibility from which one can never again fall back in one's progress on the path.
109. These twenty verse lines are a verbatim quote from the very beginning of Chapter Two on entry into the first of the ten bodhisattva grounds (23a23-b03).
110. KJ retained the Sanskrit *sarvajña* which I have chosen here to translate as "all-knowledge."
111. With the exception of a minor phrase variation in the second of these twenty-eight lines, this is a verbatim quote from the opening lines of Chapter Four, "On the Purification of the Ground" (28c24–29a08).
112. Each of these seven are clearly explained at the very beginning of Chapter Three.
113. Again, these were: "disbelief, breaking of precepts, having but little learning, covetousness, indolence, chaotic thoughts, and absence of wisdom."
114. The Chinese text here simply transliterates a Sanskrit term for "passport" as *weipotuo* (韋婆陀), which I prefer to translate.
115. At this point in N's text, there is an interpolated note, most likely inserted by the KJ translation team: "The Chinese translation of the Sanskrit *"weituo"* (韋陀) is "unopposed" and it means 'passport.'"

116. Again, "the five hindrances" is a reference to desire, ill will, lethargy-and-sleepiness, excitedness-and-regretfulness, and afflicted doubtfulness, hindrances that must be overcome in order to successfully enter deep states of meditation.
117. "…the other [forms of wisdom]" most likely refers to "wisdom that arises from contemplation" and "great wisdom," both of which were mentioned just above in discussing the metaphoric significance of "firewood" in this extended analogy that forms the basis of two thirds of this chapter.
118. *Zhengwei* (正位), "right and fixed position," seems to usually correspond to the Sanskrit *samyaktva-niyāma* for which Conze's MDPL gives "certainty to have got safely out of this world," or, in the case of "*samyaktva-niyata*," "destined for salvation."
119. "Faculties" here is a reference to "the five root faculties" that, once developed, become "the five powers": faith, vigor, mindfulness, concentration, and wisdom.
120. I emend the reading per the SYMG editions to correct the *Taisho* edition's mistaken inclusion here of *bu* (不), "not." Absent this correction, the statement would result in the exact opposite of the obviously intended meaning.
121. This line could also be plausibly rendered as: "the hazardous and bad road of *saṃsāra*."
122. In other words: "This is tantamount to committing suicide [on the path to spiritual liberation]."
123. In this particular passage, especially following on the heels of his warning about "neglectfulness," N. is presenting a very close paraphrase of five verses from his own Bodhisaṃbhāra Śāstra, verses 24–28. I quote them here from my own complete translation of that treatise along with its early Indian commentary:

> Until one develops the great compassion and the patiences,
> Even though he may have gained irreversibility,
> The bodhisattva is still subject to a form of "dying"
> Occurring through the arising of negligence.

> The grounds of the Śrāvakas or the Pratyekabuddhas,
> If entered, constitute "death" for him
> Because he would thereby sever the roots
> Of the bodhisattva's understanding and awareness.

> At the prospect of falling into the hell-realms,
> The bodhisattva would not be struck with fright.
> The grounds of the Śrāvakas and the Pratyekabuddhas
> Do provoke great terror in him.

> It is not the case that falling into the hell realms
> Would create an ultimate obstacle to bodhi.
> If one fell onto the grounds of the Śrāvakas or Pratyekabuddhas,
> That would create an ultimate obstacle.
>
> Just as is said of one who loves long life
> That he is frightened at the prospect of being beheaded,
> So too the grounds of the Śrāvakas and Pratyekabuddhas
> Should provoke in one this very sort of fear.

124. The Chinese translation preserved a short-hand rendering of the third hindrance (as "drowsiness") and fourth hindrance (as "excitedness") for which I have supplied the standard complete rendering of these classic Indian Buddhist technical terms, the third and fourth of which are dual-component hindrances.
125. This is most likely referring to the fact that his adherence to moral virtue is not pursued in order to achieve rebirth in the heavens.
126. This most likely refers to preventing oneself from taking rebirth in the form realm heavens because they constitute an obstacle to cultivation of the bodhisattva path.
127. "Four means of attraction" refers to giving, pleasing words, beneficial actions, and joint endeavors.
128. The four immeasurable minds are kindness, compassion, sympathetic joy, and equanimity.
129. As revealed by the DSBC Sanskrit of the Ten Grounds Sutra's discussion of the second bodhisattva ground, *shi zhong xin* (十種心) "ten types of *resolute intentions*" here and in the ensuing SZPPS discussion correspond to the Sanskrit *cittāśaya*.
130. The DSBC Sanskrit of the Ten Grounds Sutra accords fairly closely with the SZPPS order of this list of ten "resolute intentions" (*cittāśaya*) as it is presented in the following explanation. It records the Sanskrit antecedents as: *ṛjvāśaya* (= *ārjava*?), *mṛdvāśaya, karmaṇyāśaya, damāśaya, śamāśaya, kalyāṇāśaya, asaṃsṛṣṭāśaya, anapekṣāśaya, udārāśaya, māhātmyāśaya*.
131. These six verses correspond to verses 12 through 17 of N's *Bodhisaṃbhāra Śāstra*. I quote them here from my own complete translation of that treatise along with its early Indian commentary:

> From the very beginning, the bodhisattva
> Should accord with the power of his abilities
> And use skillful means to instruct beings,
> Causing them to enter the Great Vehicle.
>
> Even if one taught beings as numerous as the Ganges' sands
> So that they were caused to gain the fruit of arhatship,

> Still, by instructing but a single person to enter the Great Vehicle,
> One would generate merit superior to that.
>
> Instructing through resort to the Śrāvaka Vehicle
> Or through resort to the Pratyekabuddha Vehicle
> Is undertaken where, on account of lesser abilities,
> Beings are unable to accept instruction in the Great Vehicle.
>
> Where even when relying on Śrāvaka or Pratyekabuddha Vehicles
> In addition to the Great Vehicle teachings,
> There are those who still cannot accept any such instruction,
> One should strive to establish them in merit-creating situations.
>
> If there be persons unable to accept
> Instruction conducing either to the heavens or to liberation,
> Favor them through bestowing present-life benefits.
> Then, as befits one's powers, one should draw them in.
>
> Where, with regard to particular beings, a bodhisattva
> Has no conditions through which to instruct them,
> He should draw forth the great kindness and compassion
> And should refrain from abandoning them.

132. To correct an apparent graphic-similarity scribal error, I emend the reading of the *Taisho* text here by preferring the SYMG editions' *guo* (果), "resultant," to the *Taisho* edition's *yi* (異), "different." (The immediately following question in the ensuing text echoes this word choice and corroborates the validity of the emendation.)

133. Although this teaching seems to be addressed exclusively to men regarding their behaviors vis-à-vis women, that is only because most women were illiterate at the time and never would have encountered this treatise outside of a lecture format where its universal applicability would have been made clear.

134. In Buddhist texts, "restricted orifice" refers to oral sex, anal sex, etc.

135. This "scattered or inappropriate speech" usually translates *saṃbhinnapralāpa* which, in addition to the definitions mentioned here, is usually also interpreted to include "lewd, dirty, or off-color speech." This traditional subdefinition is implicitly and euphemistically referenced here a few lines below as one of the traditional meanings of "speech contrary to Dharma."

136. "Volition" (思) could be referring here to premeditation, i.e. deliberate intentionality.

137. VB notes: "Items sixteen and seventeen here correspond to functions relating to the four noble truths: the truth of the path is *bhāvetabba*, 'to be cultivated.' The truth of suffering is *pariññeyya*, 'to be well understood.'"

138. VB notes: "[This refers to] *pahātabba*: the function pertaining to the second noble truth."
139. I am not entirely sure about the accuracy of my translation of the following fourfold list. I may have misunderstood it or it may be slightly corrupted.
140. Because some of these listed distinctions seem contradictory, I am not confident that I have correctly rendered the intended meaning of the abhidharmic technical terms here. It may also be the case that the text has become somewhat corrupted.
141. Because this would seem to be a contradiction, I am not sure I have translated this correctly. There are five instances of this same statement (with minor variations) in this chapter.
142. VB notes: "The above [two cases] refer to two stages or degrees of an affliction: the stage of *anuśaya*, where it remains as a latent tendency; and the stage of obsession, where it arises and dominates the mind."
143. VB notes: "This latter alternative presumably refers to abandoning the taking of life in world-transcendent (*lokottara*) states of mind."
144. This twelvefold list has become slightly corrupted at some point, but not irretrievably so. (As noted below, I correct the corruption by emendation.) As received, it duplicates the sixth member of the list ("For what is it a condition?" ["與誰作緣?"]) and leaves out another member of the list which we encounter in the ensuing discussion ("What is the benefit?" ["何利益?"]).
145. The received editions of this text mistakenly duplicate list item number six here as "8) For what is it a condition?". I have emended the text to correct this obvious scribal error by inserting the missing list item ("What is the benefit?" ["何利益?"]) which is found in the ensuing discussion at 97a27–8.)
146. VB notes: "This may be alluding to a passage in the early sutras, see AN 6.63: 'It is volition, O monks, that I call karma. For having willed, one acts by body, speech, or mind.' Thus covetousness, etc., are here considered not to be karma (in the sense of actual action) because they are mental states associated with or corresponding to volition rather than actions in their own right. The Theravada Abhidhamma differs, considering covetousness, etc., both karma and paths of karma. They are mental karma (*manokamma*)."
147. The phrase "there is no fixed subjective agent [involved in its creation]" (無有定主) can refer to one or both of two ideas: a) The absence of any sort of creator god involved in the creation of the world; or b) The absence of any inherently existent "self" in oneself or in any of the other beings who collectively create all the causes and conditions

for the creation, abiding, and destruction of the world, this through the causal power of their good and bad karmic deeds.

148. In referring to it as the "Non-extensive Heaven (不廣天), N uses an extremely rare name for this Avṛha Heaven. (There is only one other use of this name in the entire *Taisho* canon.) The more common Chinese name is the "No Affliction Heaven" (無煩天).

149. In commenting on this line that I might otherwise translate as "and who always disbelieve that the world / is possessed of *the dharma of stability and security—*," VB notes: "In Sanskrit and Pali, *-dharma / -dhamma* is often used as a suffix to indicate 'having the nature of' or 'subject to.' Thus (P) *sabbe sattā maraṇadhammā*, 'all beings are subject to death / have the nature of dying.' I suspect that the Sanskrit original of this line used *'dharma'* [法] in that function, thus [the sense of this may be] 'The world does not have a stable and secure nature.'"

150. "*Śrāvaka*" means, in essence, "auditor," i.e. "those who learn by listening."

151. VB notes: The Pali version, AN 1:328 NDB p.121: "Bhikkhus, just as even a trifling amount of feces is foul smelling, so too I do not praise even a trifling amount of existence, even for a mere finger snap."

152. N seems to be referring here to the pivotal importance of one's last thoughts at the moment of death that may so strongly influence whether or not one then enters good or bad rebirth circumstances.

153. Lest it not be so obvious, "what is unlovely, stinking, defiled, and ungrateful for kindnesses" is intended to refer to the human body.

154. VB notes: "See SN 35:28, Connected Discourses p. 1143."

155. VB notes: "This sequence is found in several places in the *Nikāyas*, especially in the *Anguttara*. See AN 10:1–4 and 11:1–4. Here, 厭 = *nibbidā*, which I render 'disenchantment,' while 離 is *virāga*, 'dispassion' or 'detachment.'"

156. VB notes: "尊者施曰羅. This is probably Ven. Sivali. Since 捨 can mean either 'generosity' or 'relinquishment,' the two connect Sivali's past-life merits with his special facility as a monk.

From Dictionary of Pali Proper Names: 'In Padumuttara Buddha's time he made the resolve to be pre-eminent among recipients of gifts, like Sudassana, disciple of Padumuttara. To this end he gave alms for seven days to the Buddha and his monks. In the time of Vipassī Buddha he was a householder near Bandhumatī. The people gave alms to the Buddha and the Order in competition with the king, and when they were in need of honey, curds and sugar, Sīvalī gave enough of these for sixty-eight thousand monks.... Sīvalī was declared by the Buddha (A.i.24) pre-eminent among recipients of gifts.... Sīvalī went to the Himālaya with five hundred others, to test his good luck. The gods provided them with everything. On Gandhamādana a deva, named Nāgadatta, entertained them for seven days on milk rice."

For more, see:

http://www.palikanon.com/english/pali_names/s/siivalii.htm."

157. VB notes: *"Anguttara* 4: 143 : 'Bhikkhus, there are these four lights. What four? The light of the moon, the light of the sun, the light of fire, and the light of wisdom. These are the four lights. Of these four lights, the light of wisdom is foremost.'"

158. Although slightly ambiguous, their "twofold vows" most likely refers to their vows to accomplish both self-benefit and other-benefit, i.e. to become buddhas themselves while also facilitating the awakening of all other beings.

159. See the chapter-commencing verse, line 1–2.

160. See the chapter-commencing verse, line 4.

161. As noted by VB, here this *shan* (善) does not have its somewhat more usual meaning of "goodness" (*kuśala*). Rather, as in many places in KJ translations, it serves here as an intensifying modifier. When modifying "purity," as in the "*su*" of *suviśuddha*, it would instead mean "thorough," "thoroughgoing," or "complete" purity.

162. See the preceding note for an explanation of this somewhat less usual use of the *shan* (善) in *shan qingjing* (善清淨).

163. Although not explicitly stated here, the "three types of purity" may refer to either (or both) of two explanations offered earlier in the sutra. Here are the two previous explanations:

1) In Chapter Five, we had: "As for 'purity,' this means that one has completely developed the three types of purity, namely purity in physical actions, purity in verbal actions, and purity in mental actions."

2) In Chapter Twenty-eight, specifically referring to the bodhisattva's practice of these ten courses of good karmic action on this second bodhisattva ground, we had a verse and the prose explanation immediately following it, as follows:

"If a bodhisattva still at the border with the first ground
employs three kinds of purity
to abide securely in the ten courses of good karmic action,
he will then be able to bring forth decisive resolve.

Once this bodhisattva comes to dwell on the second ground, he then distinguishes with utter clarity these ten good and bad courses of karmic action. Having come to know these matters, he applies three kinds of purity to his abiding in the ten courses of good karmic action, namely:

He does not personally kill any being;
He does not instruct others to kill any being;
And he does not delight in the karmic offense of killing."

164. See the chapter-commencing verse, line 3.
165. See Chapter Five, "The Explanation of the Vows," in which these ten "ultimate ends" that define the infinity of the bodhisattva vows are listed as follows:

"[Hence these vows are made]:

First, until the end of the realms of beings;
Second, until the end of the realms of worlds;
Third, until the end of the realms of empty space;
Fourth, until the end of the Dharma realm;
Fifth, until the end of the realm of nirvāṇa;
Sixth, until the end of the realms in which buddhas are born;
Seventh, until the end of the realms of all buddhas' knowledge;
Eighth, until the end of everything that can be taken as an object of mind;
Ninth, until the end of the knowledge associated with the range of all buddhas' actions;
And tenth, until the end of the permutations of the knowledge of worldly dharmas.

These are the ten [ways in which vows are] ultimately enduring."

166. See chapter-commencing verse, line 3.
167. See chapter-commencing verse, line 5.
168. This is clearly a reference to "the right and fixed position" (*samyaktva-niyāma*) wherein the bodhisattva becomes immune to the temptations of opting for the nirvāṇa prized by adherents of the Śrāvaka Disciple Vehicle and Pratyekabuddha Vehicles.
169. See chapter-commencing verse, line 5.
170. See chapter-commencing verse, line 6.
171. See chapter-commencing verse, line 6.
172. See chapter-commencing verse, line 7.
173. VB points out that this "... *maintaining vigilance* at all times throughout the first watch and the last watch of the night" is stock material in the early suttas that should not be misunderstood as referencing "achieving awakening" (覺悟) as such. See NDB pp. 212, 427, etc.
174. I prefer here to translate what the KJ text preserves as the transliterations of the Sanskrit for the perfections: "One first speaks of *dāna*

pāramitā, then *śīla pāramitā*, then *kṣānti pāramitā*, then *vīrya pāramitā*, then *dhyāna pāramitā*, and then *prajñā pāramitā*."

175. See chapter-commencing verse, line 8.
176. See chapter-commencing verse, line 9.
177. Having already made it clear in the above fivefold list that it is a good thing to disdain the *dharmas* of petty people and esteem the *dharmas* of great men, here one is reminded to still retain completely equal compassionate regard for the people themselves.
178. See chapter-commencing verse, line 10. ("[They] deeply cherish the wisdom of the Buddhas ....")
179. See chapter-commencing verse, line 11–12.
180. See chapter-commencing verse, line 12.
181. See chapter-commencing verse, line 12.
182. VB notes: "For these, see AN 5:144 (NDB pp. 761–62 along with note 1144. Paṭisambhidāmagga calls them "powers of the noble ones" (*ariy'iddhi*)."
183. This is a reference to number four, "the psychic powers of the Āryas."
184. See chapter-commencing verse, line 13.
185. See chapter-commencing verse, line 14.
186. A search of the *Taisho* Canon indicates that, in both cases (whether "dark" or "great"), these "four seals" refer to four levels of trustworthiness in determining whether or not any given teaching that one has received is to be trusted as truly originating with the Buddha.
187. See chapter-commencing verse, line 15.
188. See chapter-commencing verse, line 15.
189. See chapter-commencing verse, line 15.
190. See chapter-commencing verse, line 16.
191. I emend the text here to accord with four other editions by substituting 汝 for 如 to correct an apparent homophonic scribal error, this because the resulting reading is much more plausible than the extremely forced reading that retaining 如 would yield.
192. See chapter-commencing verse, line 17.
193. See chapter-commencing verse, line 18.
194. See chapter-commencing verse, line 19.
195. See chapter-commencing verse, line 20.
196. See chapter-commencing verse, lines 21–22.
197. See chapter-commencing verse, lines 23–24.

198. Although, per MW, the meaning of the Sanskrit word *bhagavat* is "possessing fortune, fortunate, prosperous, happy" or "glorious, illustrious, divine, adorable, venerable," in Buddhism, it is one of the ten primary names of any and all buddhas that is intended to call to mind all of the Buddha's qualities including his perfect wisdom and virtue. The Chinese translation is "World Honored One" (世尊). Other common English translations (per PDB) are "Blessed One," "Exalted One," or "Lord." It is because of the wide range of connotations of the name that, rather than translate the Chinese honorific, I usually prefer to simply use the now fairly common Sanskrit name "Bhagavat." (I *do* translate it in the following verse, however.) "Bhagavan" is essentially the same word that one encounters in other translations and other traditions as (again per PDB) *bhagavān, bhagavad, bhagawan,* and *bhagwan.*
199. "The fourteen ineffable dharmas" is a reference to the fourteen "unanswered" or "undeclared" (*avyākṛta*) dharmas.
200. Although the language itself is not specific, the implicit reference is to extramarital relationships, perhaps voluntary, perhaps not.
201. I emend the text here (at 108a17, second character) by replacing the clearly erroneous *bu* (不), "not," with the doubtlessly intended *xia* (下), "lesser," to correct an obvious graphic-similarity scribal error not noticed in either *Taisho* or in any of its recorded alternate editions).
202. "Obsessed" (纏) corresponds to the Sanskrit *paryavasthāna* and refers to the active phase of entanglement by the afflictions.
203. "...the view of a real self in association with the body [or any of the other four aggregates]" (身見) corresponds to the Sanskrit *satkāya-dṛṣṭi*.
204. VB notes that, on the Śrāvaka Vehicle path, this severance via seeing the four truths occurs upon realizing stream-entry, whereas severance through meditative cultivation occurs on the three higher stages of the path to arhatship.
205. What is referred to here as "the ninety-eight fetters" (九十八使) is elsewhere rendered somewhat more precisely as "the ninety-eight latent tendencies" (九十八隨眠 [*anuśaya*]), hence I translate accordingly.
206. I emend the reading here to correct a fairly obvious graphic-similarity scribal error by preferring on doctrinal sensibility grounds SYMG's *hui* (悔), "regret," to the *Taisho* edition's *wu* (侮), "to insult."
207. I have followed four other editions (SYMG) in placing these four lines into verse format. The correctness of this couldn't be clearer, especially given the combination of even line length, context, and

unavoidably obvious Chinese rhyming of the quatrain's third line with the first line and fourth line with the second line.

208. This very long quotation (2.5 pages, ending at the next set of stanza lines) corresponds fairly closely to a second-ground passage in the KB Ten Grounds Sutra translation (T10n0286_0505b05–c20) and also to the corresponding second-ground passage in the Śikṣānanda translation of the Avataṃsaka Sutra's "Ten Grounds" chapter (T10n0279_0186a10–b22).

209. VB notes: "This is a reference to the three wrong thoughts (*vitarka*): sensual thought, thought of ill will, and thought of harming."

210. The following passage corresponds quite closely with a long passage in the "Akṣayamati" Chapter of the *Mahāsaṃnipāta Sūtra* (in the *Taisho* canon's Chinese translation by Dharmakṣema in 413 CE: 大方等大集經卷第二十七 –無盡意菩薩品第十二之一 T13n0397_p0189c27–190b10). However, that translation lists "sixty-seven" rather than the "sixty-five" to which Nāgārjuna refers in this treatise probably authored two centuries before Dharmakṣema's translation.

211. This aspect of moral virtue together with the next nine correspond to the ten courses of good karmic action.

212. This aspect of moral virtue together with the next two correspond to the Three Refuges.

213. VB points out that "things that accord with Dharma" (如法物) is probably best construed as "things *obtained* in accordance with the Dharma," this because it directly corresponds to "*yathādhammaṃ lābha*" in the Pali scriptures.

214. This aspect of moral virtue and the next three correspond to the four immeasurable minds.

215. This aspect of moral virtue together with the next five correspond to the six perfections. Here the first two perfections are listed in reverse order.

216. I emend the reading here to correct a fairly obvious graphic-similarity scribal error by preferring (due to issues of doctrinal sensibility and explicitly stated parallelism) the SYMG editions' *chang* (常), "constantly," to the *Taisho* edition's *dang* (當), "should."

217. VB notes: "This is referring to the abandoning of physical bad karma not included in the ten karmic paths, for, in the form realm, there is no killing, stealing, and sexual misconduct—indeed, there is no sexuality there, no private property, and the beings have fixed life spans. Since the three transgressions are impossible there, there is no abandoning them; but minor types of unwholesome physical conduct might exist there, and one must abstain from these."

218. VB offers a clarifying note here with respect to bad karmic actions associated with speech in the form realm: "This [mention of scattered or inappropriate speech] is not just an example; apparently there is no lying, divisive speech, or harsh speech in the form realm, but there is scattered speech."
219. "*Brahmacarya*," literally "brahman conduct" refers to the celibate spiritual life.
220. VB notes: "See *Anguttara Nikāya* 7:50, NDB pp. 1038–39. The sixth is different from the Pali version."
221. As mentioned in the above note, the Pali version of number six is different, as follows: "(6) '...he does not recollect laughing, talking, and playing with women in the past...but he looks at a householder or a householder's son enjoying himself furnished and endowed with the five objects of sensual pleasure....'"
222. VB located what appears to be very nearly this same passage in the Mahāratnakuta collection (大寶積經) at T11n0310_p0636c28.
223. VB located this passage in the *Mahāvaipulya-mahāsaṃnipāta Sūtra* (大方等大集經) at T13n0397_p0190b11.
224. "Name and form" (名色 = *nāmarūpa*) is a reference to the five aggregates.
225. The *Mahāvaipulya-mahāsaṃnipāta Sūtra* translation's version of this passage clarifies this Sangha-related clause with "by *cultivation* of the unconditioned" (T13n0397_p0190b28: 不斷僧種, [17]修無為故。[Note 17 in that edition tells us that the SYMG reading has 以修 instead of just 修]).
226. The *Mahāvaipulya-mahāsaṃnipāta Sūtra* translation's version of this passage is found at T13n0397_p0190c01.
227. VB offers the following supplementary note on the austerities:

"Ten ascetic practices are mentioned in the *Anguttara Nikāya* at 5:181–90, each distinguished as fivefold in accordance with the reasons they are undertaken. In the Theravada tradition, the standard list of ascetic practices is expanded to thirteen, described and analyzed in *Visuddhimagga*, Chapter 2. Ten agree with those in this chapter. They differ in that the *Daśabhūmika-vibhāṣā-śāstra* includes two not in the *Visuddhimagga* system: wearing robes made of animal hairs, and not accepting drinks other than water after midday. The *Visuddhimagga* list includes three not in this *Daśabhūmika-vibhāṣā-śāstra*: walking on alms round by going to every house, without skipping any (a narrowing of the ascetic practice of eating only food collected on alms round); eating only from the alms bowl (refusing the use of other plates and saucers); and refusing food brought after one has started one's meal (but still within the time limits). The latter seems to be a different interpretation of the ascetic practice the *Daśabhūmika-vibhāṣā-śāstra* system interprets as refusing drinks after mid-day."

228. The Chinese text for this first reflection is ambiguous. It seems to allude to the idea that whatever one receives [or doesn't receive] on the alms round is a direct reflection of whether or not one has created enough merit, hence being able to continue in this is one's own responsibility and no one else's.

229. The implication here is that one should be willing to abandon any concerns for personal comfort as one vigorously pursues very rigorous bodhisattva path practices.

230. "Unimpeded reflections" here likely refers to such reflections as those devoted to deep understanding and realization of the three gates to liberation, the four immeasurables, the four bases of meritorious qualities, and the six perfections (as implied just below at 112a27–29).

231. Due to the requirements of sensibility, I emend the reading of the text here in accordance with the SYMG editions by adding a missing *ji* (及) before *Taisho's shen* (身) to produce *jishen* (及身) which I take here to mean "for one's entire life."

232. VB notes: "What is mentioned here are the three kinds of wholesome thought, namely, thought of renunciation, thought of non-ill will, and thought of nonharming. Note that *chujue* (出覺) is *nekkhammavitakka*, 'thought of renunciation.' See for example MN 19, on the three kinds of wholesome thought: '*Tassa mayhaṃ, bhikkhave, evaṃ appamattassa ātāpino pahitattassa viharato uppajjati nekkhammavitakko … abyāpādavitakko … pe … avihiṃsāvitakko.*'"

233. VB notes that this is Ugra, the subject of the *Ugraparipṛcchā Sūtra* and that this passage can be found in the *Mahāratnakūṭa Sūtra* (大寶積經 卷第八十二, 郁伽長者會第十九), beginning at T11n0310_p0477c24.

234. This likely refers to the "six recollections" (*anusmṛti*) of the Buddha, the Dharma, the Sangha, moral virtue, generosity, and the devas.

235. The relevant verse from chapter three (T26, no. 1521, 27a15–18) is:
>   He is free of the fear of not surviving,
>   the fear of death, the fear of the wretched destinies,
>   the fear of the Great Assembly's awesome virtue,
>   the fear of ill repute, and the fear of being disparaged.
>
>   As for fear of imprisonment, shackles, and manacles,
>   and the fear of beatings or capital punishment,
>   given that he is free of a self or any possessions of self,
>   how then could he have any such fears as these?

Endnotes

236. VB notes that the Pali parallel is *Samyutta Nikāya* 3:5.
237. VB notes: "The Pali parallel is *Saṃyutta Nikāya* 11: 3. The author of this work is evidently very familiar with the *Nikāyas/Āgama* collections."
238. VB notes: "The Pali parallel for this passage is the first part of *Majjhima Nikāya Sutta* 4; see MLDB pp.102–3."
239. As noted earlier by VB, again, this is Ugra, the subject of the *Ugraparipṛcchā Sūtra*. This particular passage can be found in the *Mahāratnakūṭa Sūtra* (大寶積經卷第八十二, 郁伽長者會第十九), beginning at T11n0310_p0478a20.
240. "Difficulties" here is probably a reference to the eight difficulties of which the hells, animals, and hungry ghosts are the first three list members.
241. I emend the reading of the *Taisho* text here by preferring on sensibility grounds the SYMG editions' *zhi* (知), "to know," to the *Taisho* edition's *hehe* (和合), "to harmonize."
242. This is probably meant to refer to the four floods (Skt. *catvāra oghāḥ, catur-ogha*): sensual desire (*kāmarāga*), [craving for] continuing existence (*bhāva*), ignorance (*avidyā*), and views (*dṛṣṭi*). (These are identical to the "contaminants" [*āsrava*]).
243. Again, the four lineage bases of the Āryas (*catur-āryavaṃśa*) are: delighting in mere sufficiency in clothing, delighting in mere sufficiency of food and drink, delighting in mere sufficiency of bedding, and delighting in the severance [of evil] and the cultivation [of goodness].
244. "Nature of dharmas" usually corresponds to the Sanskrit *dharmatā*. Still, although somewhat less likely, given that KJ very regularly uses *xing* (性) to translate *dhātu*, this might also be construed to mean: "Dwelling in a forest hermitage refers to [realizing that] all realms together constitute the Dharma realm."
245. "The stations of rebirth to which they correspond" refers to rebirth in the heavens of the form realm.
246. I emend the reading of the *Taisho* text here by preferring on sensibility grounds the SYMG editions' *ci yinyuan* (此因緣), "these [special] circumstances," to the *Taisho* edition's *yinyuan* (因緣), "[special] circumstances."
247. A saṃghāvaśeṣa offense is a serious offense (such as touching a woman motivated by a thought of desire) that requires a meeting of the bhikshu sangha to determine the disciplinary penalty. "Grave offense" here is a euphemism for sexual intercourse, a pārājika offense entailing expulsion from the monastic community. The third case, "transgressing against the precept and returning to lay

life," refers to committing either of the above sorts of offenses and then voluntarily setting aside the robes (rather than waiting for the bhikshu sangha's formal judgment on the matter).

248. These first two *dhūta* austerities just discussed at length were always gaining one's sustenance from the alms round and dwelling in a forest hermitage.

249. "Not accepting any beverage at the wrong time" means that that one does not accept any beverage but water outside of that very mealtime. "Wrong time" has the additional meaning of "not after midday."

250. VB notes: "When one first receives full ordination, the teacher explains the ideal form of the four requisites: using cast off robes, food obtained on alms round, dwelling at the foot of a tree, and using cow's urine for medicine. Then he explains the more lenient alternatives. Thus *chushou* (初受), ["the initially received explanation"], refers to what was first explained at one's ordination."

251. Lest it not be obvious, this in no way restricts standing or walking. It is entirely a matter of never lying down, not even when one sleeps.

252. Again, although it is not mentioned here, in addition to its otherwise referenced meanings, "at the wrong time" also means "not after midday."

253. VB notes that this *zuo wo ju* (坐臥具), *senāsana*, literally "seats and beds" is a term of convenience for "a dwelling place."

254. VB notes: "This is an allusion to a sutra in which the Buddha says that "noise is a thorn for one attaining the first dhyāna." See *Anguttara Nikaya* 10:72 "Thorns": ... (5) Noise is a thorn to the first *jhāna*. (6) Thought and examination are a thorn to the second *jhāna*. (7) Rapture is a thorn to the third *jhāna*. (8) In-and-out breathing is a thorn to the fourth *jhāna*."

255. To correct an apparent graphic-similarity and/or homophonic scribal error, I emend the reading of the *Taisho* text here by preferring the SYMG editions' *shang* (尚), "even," to the *Taisho* edition's *chang* (常), "always." The correctness of the emendation is corroborated by the commentary in the next paragraph.

256. To correct an apparent omission, I emend the reading of the *Taisho* text here by preferring on sensibility grounds the SYMG editions' insertion of an additional *fo* (佛), "Buddha," to begin this sentence. The emended reading then exactly echoes the text of the verse upon which this sentence comments.

257. I emend the reading of the *Taisho* text here by preferring on sensibility grounds the SYMG editions' *yang* (映), "disastrous," to the *Taisho* edition's *da* (大), "great."
258. I emend the reading of the text here in accordance with the SYM (but not G) editions by preferring on sensibility grounds *tong* (通) "understand" to the *Taisho* edition's *song* (誦) "recite."
259. I emend the reading of the text here in accordance with the SYMG editions by preferring on sensibility grounds the inclusion of an apparently lost member of the often-encountered rather standard list that is found later on in this same chapter that includes *mingzhe jian* (命者見), "the view of a life."
260. Again, even though this *zuo wo ju* (坐臥具) would seem to refer to "seats and beds," it is a hyperliteral translation of the Sanskrit *senāsana* which is just a term of convenience for "a lodging" or "a dwelling place."
261. Yet again, both here and directly below, KJ is translating *xing* (性) (more usually "nature") as *dhātu* (usually "realms" or "elements." We know this both from context and from comparisons of his Ten Grounds Sutra translation with a much later Sanskrit edition of that sutra. This rendering of *xing* is somewhat inconsistently applied by the KJ translation team, hence we must rely on context sensibility to determine which Sanskrit antecedent is being referenced in any given passage. This line presents a perfect example of that inconsistency of usage, for it is used in *both* senses here, first as "elements," then as "nature."
262. "The six elements" (*ṣaḍ-dhātu*) are: earth, water, fire, wind / air, space, and consciousness.
263. Regarding this statement that "the form aggregate is characterized by being assailed by what is painful," VB notes:

> "'如說色是苦惱相': There is a word play in the Pali (and, presumably its Sanskrit counterpart) that [although successfully captured in this passage translated by KJ], wasn't reflected in the Chinese translation [of the *Saṃyukta Āgama*]. A Pali sutta (SN 22:79) playfully tried to derive *rūpa* = material form from the verb *ruppati*, meaning something like "to be molested, to be assailed."—"assailed by cold, by heat, by hunger and thirst, etc." There is no real etymological connection between *rūpa* and *ruppati*, but the pun works. Here is the Pali: "*Kiñca, bhikkhave, rūpaṃ vadetha? Ruppatī ti kho, bhikkhave, tasmā 'rūpna' ti vuccati. Kena ruppati? Sītenapi ruppati, uṇhenapi ruppati, jighacchāyapi ruppati, pipāsāyapi ruppati, ḍaṃsamakasavātātapasiriṃsapasamphassenapi ruppati.*"

The Chinese parallel is *Saṃyukta Āgama* 46 (雜阿含經-T02n0099_ p0011b26–29): "若可閡可分, 是名色受陰。指所閡, 若手、若石、若杖、若刀、若冷、若暖、若渴、若飢、若蚊、虻、諸毒虫、風、雨觸, 是名觸閡, 是故閡是色受陰。"

264. To correct an apparent graphic-similarity scribal error, I emend the reading of the *Taisho* text here by preferring the SYMG editions' *duo* (墮), "to fall," to the *Taisho* edition's *sui* (隨), "to follow."
265. In Classical Chinese literature, *zhi* (直), "straight, direct, etc.," is interchangeable with *zhi* (值), "worth, value, etc.," and I have translated it accordingly here as this is clearly the meaning intended by the KJ translation team.
266. This very long verse is a nearly verbatim repetition of the verse found earlier in the treatise in Chapter Eight, at 39c21–40a13. There are eight variant characters as endnoted directly below.
267. The Chapter Eight version of this verse has "and is identical with whatever is possessed of signs" instead of "and is identical with whatever is an existent dharma" (即為是有相 instead of 即為是有法).
268. The Chapter Eight version of this verse has "Were one to relinquish all covetousness" instead of "Were one to relinquish all strategizing and attachments" (若捨諸貪著 instead of 若捨諸計著).
269. The Chapter Eight version of this verse has "There is someone who grasps and something that is grasped" instead of "It is the abandonment of grasping and whatever thing is grasped" (誰取取何事 instead of 離取取何事).
270. The Chapter Eight version of this verse has "whether as conjoined or separate, they are all entirely nonexistent" instead of "whether as conjoined or separate, they are all devoid of existence" (共離俱不有 instead of 共離俱無有).
271. The Chapter Eight version of this verse has "It is precisely because it is signless" instead of "It is precisely because it is synonymous with signlessness" (即為是無相 instead of 即名為無相).
272. These first two verse lines are referring to the four alternative propositions of the tetralemma, as in: 1) It exists; 2) It does not exist; 3) It both exists and does not exist; and 4) It neither exists nor does not exist.
273. The Chapter Eight version of this verse has a fairly nonconsequential variant for one of the characters in this line (先亦非寂滅 instead of 先來非寂滅).
274. The following passage corresponds to a section of the *Great Jeweled Summit Sutra* (大寶積經: T11n0310_p0636c17–29).

275. *Xing* (行), more usually "action(s)," refers here instead to *saṃskāras*, hence here the translation as "all conditioned things."
276. This verse and the very long passage that follow are also found in the *Great Jeweled Summit Sutra* (大寶積經: T11n0310_p0636a29–b29).
277. I emend the reading of the text here in accordance with the SYMG editions by preferring on sensibility grounds *anwen* (安隱), "peaceful and secure" to the *Taisho* edition's *anle* (安樂), "peaceful and happy" which appears to be a result of scribal absent-mindedness reflexively repeating the immediately preceding concept which would produce an unlikely redundancy.
278. VB notes: "See AN 8:19, [where this is listed as] one of the qualities of the ocean."
279. Here and in the following three paragraphs, the text is referring to the four supreme bases for the generation of meritorious qualities, namely truth, relinquishment, quiescence, and wisdom.
280. "Stream enterer" here is literally "one who has acquired the fruit of the path of a *srota-āpanna*."
281. "Marvelous phenomena" (希有事) is generally intended to refer to miraculous occurrences brought about by spiritual powers. (希有= *adbhuta*, "supernatural.")
282. VB notes: "AN 9:5 mentions these four fears. See NDB p. 1255." This topic of the fears to which a bodhisattva is invulnerable is also extensively treated in Chapter Three of this treatise in the discussion of the characteristics of the bodhisattva who has reached the second bodhisattva ground.
283. As of the Tang Dynasty, a couple hundred years after Kumārajīva made this translation, a Chinese mile (*li* = 里) was roughly 1060 feet, i.e. a fifth of a U.S. mile or a third of kilometer. As of the end of the Han Dynasty, a couple hundred years before this translation was made, it was roughly 1365 feet, i.e. a quarter of a U.S. mile or four tenths of a kilometer. Using these measures as a basis, the circumference of this wheel would be between 3.0 and 3.9 U.S. miles, or between 5 and 6 kilometers.
284. Although this is literally the "householder treasure," (居士寶 / *gṛhapati ratna*), the literature makes it clear that this is a minister of the treasury.
285. To correct an apparent graphic-similarity scribal error, I emend the reading of the *Taisho* text here by preferring the SYMG editions' *qing* (青), "blue," to the *Taisho* edition's *jing* (睛), "eye."
286. A search of Cbeta suggests that this is the only place in the entire Chinese Buddhist canon that this transliteration appears, hence any

Sanskrit reconstructions I might suggest for this celestial maiden's name would be mere conjecture.

Variant Readings from Other Chinese Editions

Fascicle One Variant Readings

[0020004] 聖者龍樹＝龍樹菩薩【宋】【元】【明】【宮】＊
[0020005] 後秦龜茲國三藏＝姚秦三藏法師【宋】【元】【明】【宮】＊
[0020006] 〔序品第一〕－【宮】
[0020007] 洄澓＝迴復【宮】
[0020008] 明註曰汙南藏作汁
[0020009] 地＝住【宋】【元】【明】【宮】
[0020010] 若有＝有若【宋】【元】【明】【宮】
[0020011] 至＝五【宋】【元】【明】【宮】
[0020012] 億＝世【宋】【元】【明】，〔億〕－【宮】
[0020013] 有＋(差)【明】
[0020014] 悲＝愍【宋】【元】【明】【宮】
[0020015] 三＝二【宋】【元】【明】【宮】
[0020016] 他＝彼【宋】【元】【明】【宮】
[0020017] 死畏＝畏死【宮】
[0020018] 極＝拯【宋】【元】【明】【宮】
[0020019] 纏＝縛【宋】【元】【明】【宮】
[0021001] 礙＝閡【明】
[0021002] 柱＝橛【宋】【元】【明】【宮】
[0021003] 矛＝鉾【元】【宮】，＝稍【明】
[0021004] ((鏘[金*疾]…曰))八字＝((槍蒺[廾/梨]刀劍鑺網))七　字【宋】【元】【明】，((槍蒺[廾/梨]刀僉鐵曰))七字【宮】
[0021005] 考＝栲【宋】【元】【明】【宮】
[0021006] [口*(隹/乃)]＝[此/束]【宋】【元】【明】【宮】
[0021007] 鏒＝釘【宋】【元】【明】【宮】
[0021008] 勃＝[火*字]【宋】【元】【明】【宮】
[0021009] 弗＝鏺【宋】【元】【明】【宮】
[0021010] 身＝體【宋】【元】【明】【宮】
[0021011] 鏘＝槍【宋】【元】【明】【宮】
[0021012] 鹹＝酸【宋】【元】【明】【宮】
[0021013] 搥＝埠【宋】【元】【宮】
[0021014] 埠＝搥【明】
[0021015] 麁＝[盧-(田/皿)+且]【宮】 [0021016] 剝創夷＝剄瘡痍【宋】【元】，＝剝瘡痍【明】，　明註曰剝南藏作剄，＝剝瘡痍【宮】
[0021017] 裂＝冽【明】
[0021018] 蝎＝蠍【宋】【元】【明】【宮】
[0021019] 烏＝鳥【明】
[0021020] 鴿＝鵒【宋】【元】【明】【宮】
[0021021] 弶＝㢭【宋】【元】【明】【宮】

[0021022] 乘＝重【宋】【元】【明】【宮】
[0021023] 火＝大【宋】【元】【明】【宮】
[0021024] （屎）＋屎【宋】【元】【明】，屎＝屎屎【宮】
[0021025] 涕＝洟【宋】【元】【明】【宮】
[0021026] （無）＋護【宮】
[0021027] 十＋（住）【宋】【元】【明】【宮】
[0022001] 餘＝饒【宋】【元】【明】
[0022002] 嚴＝校【宋】【元】【宮】，＝較【明】
[0022003] 偈＝得【宋】【元】【明】【宮】
[0022004] 波蔗＋（道遮反）【宋】【元】【宮】，（道遮切）【明】
[0022005] 諳＝闇【宋】【元】
[0022006] 照＝昭【元】【宮】
[0022007] 義說十地＝說十地義【宋】【元】【明】【宮】
[0022008] 有＝又【宋】【元】【明】【宮】
[0023001] 〔故〕－【宋】【元】【明】【宮】
[0023002] 障探玄記作除清涼疏作降
[0023003] 大＝天【宋】【元】【宮】
[0023004] 久＝亦【宋】【元】【明】【宮】
[0023005] 〔名〕－【宋】【元】【明】【宮】
[0023006] 七＝十【元】
[0023007] （善）＋行【宋】【元】【明】
[0023008] （善根）＋亦【宋】【元】【明】
[0023009] 佷＝狠【明】
[0023010] 味＝未【宋】【元】【明】【宮】
[0023011] 供養＝親近【宋】【元】【明】【宮】
[0023012] （上）＋頂【宮】
[0023013] 通達＝通違【宮】
[0023014] 受＝定【宋】【元】，明註曰受南藏作定
[0024001] 閡＝礙【宋】【元】【明】【宮】下同
[0024002] （於）＋曲【宋】【元】【明】
[0024003] 於＝質【宋】【元】【明】
[0024004] 真＝直【宮】
[0024005] 〔故〕－【宋】【元】【明】【宮】
[0024006] 諸＋（佛）【宋】【元】【明】【宮】
[0024007] 淤＝於【宋】【元】【明】【宮】
[0024008] ［漂＊寸］＝漂【宋】【元】【明】【宮】
[0024009] 〔如〕－【宋】【元】【明】【宮】
[0024010] 常＝為【宋】【元】【明】【宮】
[0024011] 盡＝量【宋】【元】【明】【宮】
[0024012] 垢＝咎【宮】

Variant Readings in Other Editions

[0024013] 〔向〕－【宮】
[0025001] （智）＋慧【宋】【元】【明】
[0025002] 〔為〕－【宋】【元】【明】【宮】
[0025003] 〔來〕－【宋】【元】【明】【宮】
[0025004] 是如＝以是【宋】【元】【明】
[0025005] （出）＋世間【宋】【元】【明】【宮】
[0025006] 〔如〕－【宮】
[0025007] 〔道〕－【宋】【元】【明】【宮】
[0025008] 惰＝墮【宋】【元】，〔惰〕－【宮】
[0025009] 渧＝滴【宋】【元】【明】【宮】下同

Fascicle Two Variant Readings

[0026001] 〔是〕－【宋】【元】【明】【宮】＊ ［＊ 1］
[0026002] 名為＝多【宋】【元】【明】【宮】
[0026003] 〔名〕－【宋】【元】【明】【宮】
[0026004] 七＝十【宋】【元】
[0026005] 此＝此七【明】，＝七【宮】
[0026006] 聞＝闟【宮】
[0026007] 是＋（名）【宋】【元】【明】【宮】
[0026008] 以＝已【宋】【元】【明】【宮】
[0027001] 〔就〕－【宮】
[0027002] （諸）＋佛【宋】【元】【明】【宮】
[0027003] 故＝畏【宋】【元】【明】【宮】
[0027004] （佛）＋智慧【宋】【元】【明】【宮】
[0027005] 若＝者【宋】【元】【明】【宮】
[0027006] 若＝如【宮】
[0028001] 菩薩＝世尊【宋】【元】【明】【宮】
[0028002] 〔多〕－【宋】【元】【明】【宮】
[0028003] 〔於〕－【宋】【元】【明】【宮】
[0028004] 〔河〕－【宋】【元】【明】【宮】，明註曰南藏無河字
[0028005] 考＝拷【宋】【元】【明】【宮】
[0028006] 我見＝自我【宮】
[0028007] 根本＋（相）【宋】【元】【明】【宮】
[0028008] （是）＋故【宋】【元】【明】【宮】
[0028009] （十住毘婆沙）＋淨地品【宋】【元】【明】【宮】
[0029001] （轉）＋增上【宋】【元】【明】【宮】
[0029002] 想＝心【宋】
[0029003] 〔名〕－【宋】【元】【明】【宮】
[0029004] 檀＝壇【宋】【元】【明】【宮】＊ ［＊ 1］
[0029005] 〔我〕－【宋】【元】【明】【宮】

[0029006] （若）＋僧【宋】【元】【明】【宮】
[0029007] 遠＝進【宋】【元】
[0029008] 說＝謗【宋】【元】【明】【宮】
[0030001] 大＝太【明】
[0030002] （法）＋者【宋】【元】【明】【宮】
[0030003] 〔間〕－【宋】【元】【明】【宮】
[0030004] 善根＝根善【宋】【元】【明】，〔善〕－【宮】
[0030005] 〔得〕－【宋】【元】【明】【宮】
[0030006] 〔道〕－【宋】【元】【明】【宮】
[0030007] （稱）＋名【宋】【元】【明】【宮】
[0030008] 親侍＝觀佛【宮】
[0030009] 術＝率【宋】【元】【明】【宮】
[0030010] 及＝又【宋】【元】【明】【宮】
[0030011] 術＝率【明】【宮】
[0030012] 胎＋（中）【宋】【元】【明】【宮】
[0030013] 及＝乃至【宋】【元】【明】【宮】
[0030014] 樂＝藥【明】
[0030015] 教＋（化）【宋】【元】【明】【宮】
[0031001] 不＝非【宋】【元】【明】【宮】＊ ［＊ 1］
[0031002] 〔復次〕－【宋】【元】【明】【宮】

Fascicle Three Variant Readings

[0031003] 釋願品之餘＝復次【宮】
[0031004] 品＋（第五）【明】
[0031005] 餘＋（復次）【宋】【元】【明】
[0031006] 疑＋（悔）【宋】【元】【明】【宮】
[0031007] 外＋（多）【宋】【元】【明】【宮】
[0031008] 憂＝優【宋】【元】【明】【宮】＊ ［＊ 1］
[0031009] 莾莎＝瓶沙【宋】【元】【明】【宮】
[0031010] 緣＝經【宋】【元】【宮】
[0031011] 尼子＝尼揵子【宋】【元】【宮】，＝尼犍子【明】
[0031012] 明註曰火南藏作失
[0031013] 喜＝苦【宋】【元】【明】【宮】
[0032001] 埠＝搥【明】
[0032002] 閡＝礙【宋】【元】【明】【宮】
[0032003] 〔少〕－【宋】【元】【明】【宮】
[0032004] 晛＝是【宮】
[0032005] 少＋（飲食）【宋】【元】【明】【宮】
[0032006] 〔菩薩〕－【宋】【元】【明】【宮】
[0032007] 諸＝於【宋】【元】【明】【宮】

[0032008] 華+(等)【宋】【元】【明】【宮】
[0032009] 橫＝蝗【宋】【元】【明】【宮】
[0032010] 見+(佛)【宋】【元】【明】【宮】
[0033001] 佛+(經)【宋】【元】【明】【宮】
[0033002] 可+(以)【宋】【元】【明】【宮】
[0033003] 疑＝礙【宮】
[0033004] 之＝趣【宋】【元】【明】【宮】
[0033005] 過+(是)【宋】【元】【明】【宮】
[0033006] 益＝利益者【宋】【元】【明】【宮】
[0033007] 閡＝礙【宋】【元】【明】【宮】下同
[0033008] 喜＝悅【宋】【元】【明】【宮】
[0033009] 寐寤＝寤寐【宋】【元】【明】【宮】
[0033010] 〔那摩樹〕－【宋】【元】【明】【宮】
[0033011] 利＝梨【宋】【元】【明】【宮】
[0033012] 盤＝槃【宋】【元】【宮】
[0033013] 虫蝎＝不為虫蝎之所【宋】【元】【明】【宮】
[0033014] 蔚＝欝【宋】【元】【明】【宮】
[0033015] 蟻＝蛾【宋】【元】【明】【宮】
[0033016] 瓔＝纓【宋】【元】【明】【宮】
[0033017] 巍＝諸【明】
[0033018] 車璖馬＝硨磲瑪【宋】【元】【明】【宮】
[0034001] 頗梨＝玻[王*梨]【宋】【元】【明】【宮】
[0034002] 眾+(俱)【宋】【元】【明】【宮】
[0034003] 我+(當)【宋】【元】【明】【宮】
[0034004] 壽+(命)【宋】【元】【明】【宮】
[0034005] 來＝集【宋】【元】【明】【宮】
[0034006] 獨＝濁【宮】
[0034007] 已＝以【宋】【元】【明】【宮】
[0034008] 〔性〕－【宋】【元】【明】【宮】
[0034009] 諸+(佛)【宋】【元】【明】【宮】
[0035001] 生＝出【宋】【元】【宮】
[0035002] 轉+(無量)【宋】【元】【明】【宮】
[0035003] 當＝常【宋】【元】【明】【宮】
[0035004] 福＝功【宋】【元】【明】【宮】
[0035005] 法忍＝忍法【宋】【元】【明】【宮】
[0036001] 不分卷【宋】【元】【明】【宮】

Fascicle Four Variant Readings

[0036002] 不分卷【宋】【元】【明】【宮】
[0036003] 〔發〕－【宋】【元】【明】【宮】

[0036004] 向＝尚【元】，明註曰向南藏作尚
[0036005] 重＋（重）【宋】【元】【明】【宮】
[0036006] 菩提＝菩薩【明】
[0037001] 為＝若【宋】【元】【明】【宮】
[0037002] 智＝知【宋】【元】【明】【宮】
[0037003] 若於乃至等二十字宋元明宮四本俱作五言四句偈
[0037004] 帥＝師【宋】【元】【明】【宮】
[0037005] 主＝王【元】
[0037006] 又＝或【宋】【元】【明】【宮】
[0037007] 閡＝礙【宋】【元】【明】【宮】
[0037008] 誰＝雖【宋】【元】【明】【宮】
[0037009] 深＝餘【宮】
[0037010] 論＝謗【宋】【元】【明】【宮】
[0037011] 上＝尚【明】
[0037012] 修善＝善修【宋】【元】【明】【宮】
[0038001] 又＝久【宮】
[0038002] 復＝後【宋】【元】【明】【宮】
[0038003] 住＝作【宋】【元】【明】【宮】
[0038004] 卷第三終【宋】【元】【明】【宮】
[0038005] 卷第四首【宋】【元】【明】【宮】
[0038006] 村＝封【宋】【元】【明】【宮】
[0038007] 者＝失【宋】【元】【明】【宮】
[0038008] 名＝者【宋】【元】【明】【宮】
[0038009] 著＝者【元】
[0038010] 威＝是【宮】
[0038011] 此＝是【宋】【元】【明】【宮】
[0038012] 為＝有【宋】【元】【明】【宮】
[0038013] 俱＝但【明】
[0039001] 我＝於【宮】
[0039002] 人＝者【宋】【元】【明】【宮】
[0039003] 非＝不【宋】【元】【明】【宮】
[0039004] 一＝二【宋】【元】【明】【宮】
[0039005] 明註曰合南藏作念
[0040001] 庠＝詳【明】
[0040002] 聞＋（有）【宋】【元】【明】【宮】
[0040003] 〔能〕－【明】
[0040004] 波＝婆【宋】【元】【明】【宮】
[0040005] 可＋（能）【明】
[0040006] 是＝退【宮】
[0040007] 礙＝癡【宋】【元】【明】【宮】

[0040008] 不卑＝卑下【宋】【元】【明】【宮】
[0040009] 疆＝彊【宋】【元】【明】【宮】
[0040010] 明註曰往南藏作住
[0040011] 不分卷【宋】【元】【明】【宮】

Fascicle Five Variant Readings

[0040012] 不分卷【宋】【元】【明】【宮】
[0041001] 行佛＝乘行【明】，＝乘行佛【宮】
[0041002] 〔就〕－【宋】【元】【明】【宮】
[0041003] 其＝道【宋】【元】【明】【宮】
[0041004] 坘＝埠【宋】【元】【宮】，＝塠【明】
[0041005] 〔供〕－【宋】【元】【明】【宮】
[0041006] 廣＝演【宋】【元】【明】【宮】
[0041007] 惑＝或【宋】【元】【明】【宮】
[0041008] 善＋（解）【宋】【元】【明】
[0042001] 〔今現在說法其佛〕－【宮】
[0042002] 弟子福＝福弟子【宋】【元】
[0042003] 〔今〕－【宋】【元】【明】，今＋（現在說法）【宮】
[0042004] （此）＋偈【宋】【元】【明】【宮】
[0042005] 人天＝天人【宋】【元】【明】【宮】
[0042006] 煩＝憂【宋】【元】【明】【宮】
[0042007] 明註曰三乘行南藏作三行佛
[0042008] 阿彌乃至薩十字宋元明三本俱作長行
[0042009] 意＝音【宮】
[0042010] 珠＝殊【宋】【元】【明】【宮】
[0042011] 鬘＝鬚【宮】
[0042012] 生＝王【宋】【元】【明】【宮】
[0043001] 映＝歎【宋】【元】【明】【宮】
[0043002] 齒＝園【宋】【元】【明】【宮】
[0043003] 增＝示【宋】【元】【明】【宮】
[0043004] 威＝功【宋】【元】【明】【宮】
[0043005] 王＝主【宋】【元】【明】【宮】
[0043006] 甚＝具【宋】【元】【明】【宮】
[0043007] 諸＝之【宮】
[0043008] 足＝尼【宋】【元】【明】【宮】
[0043009] 〔伏〕－【宋】【元】【明】【宮】
[0043010] 他＝陀【宋】【元】【明】，＝地【宮】
[0044001] 比＝上【宋】【元】【明】【宮】
[0044002] 弱＝尼【宋】【元】【明】【宮】
[0044003] 廣＝曠【宋】【元】【明】【宮】

[0044004] 閡＝礙【宋】【元】【明】【宮】下同
[0044005] 今＝金【宋】【元】【明】【宮】
[0044006] 目＝自【宋】【元】【明】【宮】
[0044007] 念＝令【明】
[0044008] 薩＝和【宋】【元】【明】【宮】
[0044009] 成＝法【宋】【元】【明】【宮】
[0044010] 莊嚴王＝堅莊【宋】【元】【明】【宮】
[0044011] 意＝益【宋】【元】【明】【宮】
[0045001] 幢＝博【宋】【元】【宮】
[0045002] 地＝也【宋】【元】【明】，地＋(也)【宮】
[0045003] 卷第四終【宋】【元】【明】【宮】
[0045004] 卷第五首【宋】【元】【明】【宮】， 譯號同異如首卷【宋】【元】【明】【宮】
[0045005] 〔食〕－【宋】【元】【明】【宮】
[0045006] 〔行〕－【宋】【元】【明】【宮】
[0045007] 蠡＝螺【宋】【元】【明】【宮】＊ [＊ 1]
[0045008] 罪＝惡【宋】【元】【明】【宮】
[0045009] 破＝故【宋】【元】【明】【宮】
[0045010] 秤＝稱【宋】【元】【明】【宮】
[0045011] 尚＝上【宋】【宮】
[0045012] 佛＝尊【宋】【元】【明】【宮】
[0046001] 人言＝入【宋】【元】【明】【宮】
[0046002] 說＝脫【宋】【元】【明】【宮】
[0046003] 樂＝隱【宋】【元】【明】【宮】
[0046004] 〔是諸佛〕－【宋】【元】【明】【宮】
[0046005] 〔皆〕－【宋】【元】【明】【宮】
[0046006] 量＝重【宋】【元】
[0046007] 〔迴向〕－【宋】【元】【明】
[0046008] 〔迴向〕－【宮】
[0046009] 一一＝十方【宮】
[0046010] 受＝授【宋】【元】【明】【宮】
[0046011] 〔佛〕－【宋】【元】【明】【宮】
[0046012] (解脫品)＋解脫【宋】【元】【明】【宮】
[0046013] 睞＝睢【宋】【元】
[0046014] 說＝知【宋】【元】【明】【宮】
[0046015] 〔亦應如是〕－【宋】【元】【明】【宮】＊
[0047001] 不分卷【宋】【元】【明】【宮】

Fascicle Six Variant Readings

[0047002] 不分卷【宋】【元】【明】【宮】
[0047003] 〔於〕－【宋】【元】【明】【宮】

Variant Readings in Other Editions

[0047004] 〔者〕－【宋】【元】【明】【宮】
[0047005] 支＝友【宮】
[0047006] 〔佛〕－【宋】【元】【明】【宮】
[0047007] 作＝為【宋】【元】【明】【宮】
[0048001] 〔夫〕－【宋】【元】【明】【宮】
[0048002] 分萬分＝萬分萬【宋】【元】【明】【宮】
[0048003] 名＝石【宋】【元】【明】【宮】
[0048004] 〔業〕－【宮】
[0048005] 報果＝果報【宋】【元】【明】【宮】
[0048006] 閡＝礙【宋】【元】【明】【宮】下同
[0049001] 池＝海【宋】【元】【明】
[0049002] 況＝海【宋】【元】，＝至【宮】
[0049003] 火＝大【宋】【元】【明】【宮】
[0049004] 有大＝大慧【宋】【元】【明】【宮】
[0049005] 起＝造【宋】【元】【明】【宮】
[0049006] （若）＋菩薩【宋】【元】【明】【宮】
[0049007] 埿＝泥【宮】
[0049008] 三＝二【宋】【元】【明】【宮】
[0049009] 有外＝求【宋】【元】【明】【宮】
[0049010] 族＝姓【宋】【元】【明】【宮】
[0049011] 兔＝免【明】
[0050001] 〔能〕－【宋】【元】【明】【宮】
[0050002] 膽＝瞻【宋】【元】【明】【宮】
[0050003] 〔老病〕－【宮】
[0050004] 車璖馬腦＝硨磲瑪瑙【宋】【元】【明】【宮】
[0050005] 具則＝其身【宋】【元】【明】【宮】
[0050006] 愛＝受【宋】【元】【明】【宮】
[0050007] 床以＝以床【宋】【元】【明】【宮】
[0050008] 堅＋（慧堅）【元】【明】
[0050009] 久＝文【宋】【元】【宮】
[0050010] 知是＝如此【宋】【元】【明】【宮】
[0050011] 〔脫〕－【宋】【元】【明】【宮】
[0050012] 俾＝[卑*頁]【宋】【元】【明】【宮】
[0050013] 〔請〕－【宋】【元】【明】【宮】
[0050014] 量＝置【宋】【元】【明】【宮】
[0051001] 祝＝呪【宋】【元】【明】【宮】
[0051002] 〔施〕－【宋】【元】【明】【宮】
[0051003] 杖＝仗【宋】【元】【明】【宮】
[0051004] 雜＝離【宋】【元】【明】
[0051005] 者＋（施者）【宋】【元】【明】【宮】

[0051006] （有罪）＋受【宋】【元】【明】【宮】
[0051007] 〔先已說〕－【宮】
[0051008] 〔應〕－【宋】【元】【明】【宮】
[0051009] （應）＋行【宋】【元】【明】【宮】
[0051010] 淨＝事【宮】
[0051011] 〔施者〕－【宋】【元】【明】【宮】
[0051012] 淨＋（淨）【宋】【元】【明】【宮】
[0051013] 二＋（種）【宋】【元】【明】【宮】
[0051014] 肢＝支【宋】【元】【明】，＝枝【宮】
[0051015] 髆＝髀【宋】【元】【明】【宮】
[0051016] 卷第五終【宋】【元】【明】【宮】
[0051017] 卷第六首【宋】【元】【明】【宮】，譯號同異如首卷【宋】　【元】【明】【宮】，（分別布施品之餘）＋總相【宋】【元】，　（分別布施品第十二之餘）＋總相【明】
[0051018] 〔淨〕－【宋】【元】【明】【宮】
[0052001] 四＋（事）【宋】【元】【明】【宮】
[0052002] （一）＋三【宋】【元】【明】
[0052003] 〔一〕－【宮】
[0052004] 入＝得【宋】【元】【明】【宮】
[0052005] 菩薩＝菩提【宋】【元】【明】【宮】
[0052006] 〔為得…施〕二十字－【宋】【元】【明】【宮】
[0052007] （貴）＋人【宋】【元】【明】【宮】
[0052008] 輙＝轉【宋】【元】【明】
[0052009] 吉＝告【宋】【元】【明】【宮】
[0052010] 雖＝離【宋】【元】【明】【宮】
[0052011] 讀＝讚【宋】【元】【明】【宮】
[0052012] 毘＝田【宋】【元】【明】【宮】
[0052013] 殖＝植【宋】【元】【明】【宮】
[0052014] 估＝賈【宋】【元】【明】【宮】
[0052015] 〔背〕－【宋】【元】【明】【宮】
[0053001] 〔大〕－【宋】【元】【明】【宮】
[0053002] 〔足〕－【宋】【元】【明】【宮】
[0053003] 不分卷【宋】【元】【明】【宮】

Fascicle Seven Variant Readings

[0053004] 不分卷【宋】【元】【明】【宮】
[0053005] 異＝黑【宋】【元】【明】【宮】＊［＊ 1 2 3 4］
[0053006] 處＋（中）【宋】【元】【明】【宮】
[0053007] 善＝義【宋】【元】【明】【宮】
[0053008] 財法＝法施財【宋】【元】【明】【宮】
[0053009] （智）＋慧【宋】【元】【明】【宮】

Variant Readings in Other Editions

[0054001] 為＝惑【宋】【元】【宮】
[0054002] 鉢油＝油鉢【宋】【元】【明】【宮】
[0054003] 達＝利【宋】【元】【明】【宮】
[0054004] 人＝者【宋】【元】【明】【宮】
[0054005] 惟心＝唯以【宋】【元】【明】，＝雖異【宮】
[0054006] 三＝二【宮】
[0054007] 所＝依【明】
[0054008] 捨＝離【宋】【元】【明】【宮】
[0054009] 謂＝諸【宋】【元】【明】【宮】
[0054010] 受＝愛【宋】【元】【明】【宮】
[0055001] 四＝依【宋】【元】【明】【宮】
[0055002] 是＝一【宮】
[0055003] 〔者〕－【宋】【元】【明】【宮】
[0055004] （僧）＋者【宋】【元】【明】【宮】
[0055005] 解＋（脫）【宋】【元】【明】【宮】
[0055006] 故＝名【宋】【元】【明】【宮】
[0055007] 性＝姓【宋】【元】【明】【宮】
[0055008] 〔佛〕－【宋】【元】【明】【宮】
[0055009] 無＝不【宋】【元】【明】【宮】
[0056001] （無）＋緣【宋】【元】【明】【宮】
[0056002] 行＝作【宋】【元】【明】【宮】
[0056003] （以）＋成【宋】【元】【明】【宮】
[0056004] 令＝今【明】
[0056005] 想＝相【宋】【元】【明】【宮】
[0056006] 堅牢＝牢堅【宮】
[0056007] 門＝本【宋】【元】【明】【宮】
[0056008] 〔身〕－【宋】【元】【明】【宮】
[0057001] 〔乏〕－【宮】
[0057002] 〔少〕－【宋】【元】【明】
[0057003] 勉＝免【宋】【元】【宮】
[0057004] 罪＝非【宋】【元】
[0057005] 憐＝慈【宋】【元】【明】【宮】
[0057006] 作＝於【宋】【元】【明】【宮】
[0057007] 〔者〕－【宋】【元】【明】【宮】
[0057008] 故＋（是以）【宋】【元】【明】【宮】
[0057009] 卷第六終【宋】【元】【明】【宮】
[0057010] 卷第七首【宋】【元】【明】【宮】，譯號同異如首卷 【宋】【元】【明】【宮】
[0057011] 患＝愚【元】
[0057012] 杖＝仗【宋】【元】【明】【宮】

[0057013] 考＝栲【明】
[0057014] 息＝想【宋】【元】，明註曰息南藏作想
[0057015] 〔多〕－【宮】
[0057016] 技＝伎【宋】【元】，＝假【宮】
[0057017] 明註曰叢南藏作業
[0057018] 鍼[口*(佳/乃)]＝鍼[此/束]【宋】【元】，＝鐵[此/束]【明】【宮】
[0057019] 惡＝怨【宋】【明】【宮】
[0057020] 心歡樂＝止歡喜【宋】【元】【明】【宮】
[0058001] 裨＝埤【宋】【元】【明】【宮】
[0058002] 所施物＝物施所【宋】【元】【明】，＝物施【宮】
[0058003] 後＝復【宋】【元】
[0058004] 苦＝若【宋】【元】【明】【宮】
[0058005] 施＝捨【宋】【元】【明】【宮】
[0058006] 歎＝歡【明】
[0058007] 目＝自【元】【明】【宮】
[0058008] 里＝理【宋】【元】【宮】
[0058009] 客＝僕【明】
[0058010] （諸）＋三【宋】【元】【明】【宮】
[0058011] 定＝乏【宮】
[0058012] 相＝想【宋】【元】【明】【宮】＊［＊ 1 2 3 4 5 6 7 8 9 10 11 12 13 14 15 16 17 18 19 20 21 22 23 24 25 26 27 28 29 30 31 32 33 34 35 36 37 38 39 40 41 42 43 44 45 46 47 48 49 50 51 52 53 54 55 56 57 58 59 60 61 62 63 64 65 66 67 68 69 70 71 72 73 74 75 76 77 78 79 80 81 82 83 84 85 86 87 88 89 90]
[0058013] 耳＝身【宋】【元】【明】【宮】
[0058014] （相）＋畏【宋】【元】【明】【宮】
[0058015] 舍＝捨【宋】【元】【明】【宮】
[0058016] [漂*寸]＝漂【宋】【元】【明】【宮】
[0058017] [米*离]粘＝黐黏【宮】
[0059001] 陵＝凌【宋】【元】【明】【宮】
[0059002] 打＝持【元】【明】
[0059003] 〔以〕－【宋】【元】【明】【宮】
[0059004] 妻＝此【宋】【元】【宮】
[0059005] 不分卷【宋】【元】【明】【宮】

Fascicle Eight Variant Readings

[0059006] 不分卷【宋】【元】【明】【宮】
[0059007] 生＝以【明】
[0060001] 杖＝仗【宋】【元】【明】【宮】
[0060002] 杖＝仗【明】

Variant Readings in Other Editions

[0060003] 泆＝佚【宋】【元】【明】【宮】＊［＊ 1］
[0060004] 淫＝婬【宋】【元】【明】【宮】
[0060005] 鼇＝龜【宋】【元】【明】【宮】
[0060006] 陵＝凌【宋】【元】【明】【宮】
[0060007] 〔生〕－【宋】【元】【明】【宮】
[0060008] 〔受〕－【宋】【元】【明】【宮】
[0061001] 已＝以【宋】【元】【明】【宮】＊［＊ 1］
[0061002] 矛＝牟【宋】【元】【明】【宮】
[0061003] 劬＝拘【宋】【元】【明】【宮】
[0061004] 豫＝預【宋】【元】【明】【宮】
[0061005] 威儀＝威德【宋】【元】【明】，＝德慧【宮】
[0061006] 密＝蜜【宮】
[0061007] 披＝被【宋】【元】【明】【宮】
[0061008] 想＝相【宋】【元】【明】【宮】
[0061009] 飲＝飯【宋】【元】【明】【宮】
[0061010] 祠＝祀【宋】【元】【明】【宮】
[0061011] 我＝民【宋】
[0061012] 潰＝憒【宋】【元】【明】【宮】
[0062001] 果＝卑【宋】
[0062002] ［漂＊寸］＝漂【宋】【元】【明】
[0062003] 樑＝梁【宋】【元】【明】
[0062004] 憧＝幢【宋】【元】【明】【宮】
[0062005] （則）＋有【宋】【元】【明】【宮】
[0062006] 山＝止【宋】【元】【明】【宮】
[0062007] 羅＋（緊那羅）【明】
[0063001] 乏＝之【宮】
[0063002] 波＝婆【宋】【元】【明】【宮】
[0063003] 行＝已習學【宋】【元】【明】【宮】
[0063004] 波羅＋（蜜）【宋】【元】【明】【宮】
[0063005] 修＝其【宋】【元】【明】【宮】
[0063006] 詳＝庠【宮】
[0063007] 匱＝遺【宋】【元】【明】【宮】
[0063008] 六十二＝九十六【宋】【元】【明】【宮】
[0063009] 卷第七終【宋】【元】【明】【宮】
[0063010] 卷第八首【宋】【元】【明】【宮】，譯號同異如首卷 【宋】【元】【明】【宮】
[0064001] 考＝拷【宋】【元】【明】【宮】
[0064002] 〔法〕－【宋】【元】【明】【宮】
[0064003] 〔設〕－【宋】【元】【明】【宮】
[0064004] 住＝信【宋】【元】【宮】

[0064005] 撿＝斂【宋】【元】【明】【宮】
[0064006] 以正願淨土∞乘施獲神足【明】
[0064007] 以正願淨土∞乘施獲神足【明】
[0064008] （法）＋會【宋】【元】【明】【宮】
[0064009] 車璖＝硨磲【宋】【元】【明】【宮】
[0064010] 〔舌〕－【宋】【元】【明】【宮】
[0064011] 法＝相【宋】【元】【明】【宮】
[0064012] 一＋（一）【宮】
[0065001] 網縵＝縵網【宋】【元】【明】【宮】
[0065002] 身餘＝餘身【宋】【元】【明】【宮】
[0065003] 項＝頭【宋】【元】【明】【宮】
[0065004] 駒＝俱【宋】【元】【明】【宮】
[0065005] 坻＝垣【宮】
[0065006] 尼＝泥【宋】【元】【明】【宮】
[0065007] 速疾＝疾得【宋】【元】【明】【宮】
[0065008] 傭＝偏【宋】【元】【宮】
[0065009] 人＝力【宋】【元】【明】【宮】
[0065010] 尚＝上【宋】【元】【明】【宮】
[0065011] 毛＝毫【宋】【元】【明】【宮】
[0065012] 有是相＝是有相【宋】【元】，＝是相有【宮】
[0065013] 不分卷【宋】【元】【明】【宮】

Fascicle Nine Variant Readings

[0065014] 不分卷【宋】【元】【明】【宮】
[0066001] 〔是〕－【宋】【元】【明】【宮】
[0066002] 考＝拷【宋】【元】【明】【宮】
[0066003] 和尚＝和上【宋】【元】【宮】
[0066004] 於＋（諸）【宋】【元】【明】【宮】
[0067001] （廣）＋大【宋】【元】【明】【宮】
[0067002] 閡＝礙【宋】【元】【明】【宮】下同
[0067003] 〔法〕－【宋】【元】【明】【宮】
[0067004] 廣＋（說）【宋】【元】【明】
[0067005] （虛）＋空【宋】【元】【明】【宮】
[0067006] 〔名〕－【宋】【元】【明】【宮】
[0067007] 憎＝增【宋】【元】【明】【宮】
[0067008] 又＝及【宋】【元】【明】【宮】
[0067009] 免＝勉【宋】【元】【明】【宮】
[0067010] 故＋（無有法）【宋】【元】【明】【宮】
[0067011] 惡＝心【元】
[0067012] 於捨＝捨於【宋】【元】【明】【宮】

Variant Readings in Other Editions　　　　　　　　　　　　　　　　1335

[0067013] （說）＋諸【宋】【元】【明】【宮】
[0068001] 有＝所【宮】
[0068002] 尚＝常【宋】【元】【明】【宮】
[0068003] 厭＝倦【宋】【元】【明】【宮】
[0068004] 能淨乃至道十字宋元明宮四本俱作長行
[0068005] 故＝教【宋】【元】【明】【宮】
[0068006] 田＝佃【宋】【元】【明】【宮】
[0068007] 〔間〕－【宋】【元】【明】【宮】
[0068008] 〔歡〕－【宋】【元】【明】【宮】
[0068009] 竟＝盡【宋】【元】【明】【宮】
[0068010] 降＝調【宋】【元】【明】【宮】
[0068011] 〔三昧〕－【宋】【元】【明】【宮】
[0069001] 高＝毫【明】
[0069002] 泥＝尼【宋】【元】【明】【宮】
[0069003] 關＝鋌【宋】【元】【明】【宮】
[0069004] 畏＝界【宋】【元】【明】【宮】
[0069005] 禪＝緻【宋】【元】【明】，＝穊【宮】
[0069006] 緻＝穊【宮】＊［＊１］
[0069007] 主＝生【宋】【元】【明】【宮】
[0069008] （能）＋破【宋】【元】【明】【宮】
[0069009] 〔師〕－【宋】【元】【明】【宮】
[0069010] 〔可〕－【宮】
[0069011] 大＋（法）【宋】【元】【明】【宮】
[0069012] 〔所謂〕－【宋】【元】【明】【宮】
[0069013] 岐＝祇【宋】【元】【明】
[0069014] 授＝受【宋】【元】【宮】
[0069015] 憂＝優【宋】【元】【明】【宮】
[0069016] （毘佛略未曾有論議）＋如是【明】，　明註曰如是上有如是諸經佛羅未曾有論議十一字
[0069017] 〔斐肥儸未曾有經〕－【明】
[0069018] 儸＝似【宮】
[0069019] 主＝王【宋】【元】【宮】
[0069020] 纖＝［月＊鐵］【宋】【元】【宮】＊，　明註曰纖南藏作[月＊鐵]＊［＊１］
[0069021] 念＝命【宋】【元】【明】【宮】
[0069022] 踝＝［蹲-酋+(十/田)]【宋】【元】【明】【宮】
[0069023] 墮＝脫【宋】【元】【明】【宮】
[0069024] 身＋（行）【宋】【元】【明】【宮】
[0069025] 邊＝過【宮】
[0069026] 山＝心【宋】【元】【明】【宮】

[0069027] 順＝煩【宮】
[0069028] 鮮＝淨【宮】
[0069029] 文＝又【元】
[0070001] 度脫＝廣度【宋】【元】【宮】，＝廣受【明】
[0070002] 深紅＝染染【宋】【元】【明】【宮】
[0070003] 鮮淨＝淨鮮【宋】【元】【明】【宮】
[0070004] 已＝以【宋】【元】【明】【宮】
[0070005] 軟＝懦【宋】【元】【明】【宮】
[0070006] （智）＋者【宋】【元】【明】【宮】
[0070007] 講＝稱【宮】
[0070008] 枕＝机【宋】【元】【宮】，＝几【明】＊
[0070009] 幛＝帷【宋】【元】【明】【宮】
[0070010] 以＝有【宋】【元】【明】【宮】
[0070011] 虎＝琥【宋】【元】【明】【宮】
[0070012] 車璩＝硨磲【宋】【元】【明】【宮】
[0070013] 八＋（部）【宋】【元】【明】【宮】
[0070014] 恨＝恚【宋】【元】【明】【宮】
[0070015] 斷＝齭【宋】【元】【明】【宮】
[0070016] 震＝振【宋】【元】【宮】
[0070017] 不故＝事不【宋】【元】【明】【宮】
[0070018] 智＝知【宋】【元】【明】【宮】＊［＊ 1］
[0070019] 〔如〕－【宋】【元】【明】【宮】
[0070020] 恚＝意【宮】
[0070021] 傭＝備【宮】
[0071001] 泥＝尼【明】
[0071002] 滿＝端【宋】【元】【明】【宮】
[0071003] 人＝仁【宋】【元】【明】【宮】
[0071004] 病＝患【宋】【元】【明】【宮】
[0071005] 緻＝穉【宮】下同
[0071006] 脈平＝膝平【宋】【元】【明】，＝膝手【宮】
[0071007] 極柔軟＝柔懦軟【宋】【元】【明】【宮】
[0071008] 緻＝穉【宋】【元】【宮】＊，明註曰緻南藏作穉＊［＊ 1］
[0071009] 正＝整【宋】【元】【明】【宮】
[0071010] 九＝八【宋】【元】【明】【宮】

Fascicle Ten Variant Readings

[0071011] 十＝九【宋】【元】【明】【宮】
[0071012] 聞聲＝聲聞【明】
[0071013] （受）＋記【宋】【元】【明】【宮】
[0071014] 轉＝輪【宋】【元】【明】【宮】

Variant Readings in Other Editions

[0072001] 〔無量〕－【宋】【元】【明】【宮】
[0072002] 〔而〕－【宋】【元】【明】【宮】
[0072003] 〔百千〕－【宋】【元】【明】【宮】
[0072004] 王天＝天王【宋】【元】【明】【宮】
[0072005] 劫＝河【宋】【元】【明】【宮】
[0072006] 〔王〕－【宋】【元】【明】【宮】
[0072007] 相＝想【宋】【元】【明】【宮】
[0072008] 羅＋（迦樓羅）【明】
[0072009] 猶如＝光猶【宋】【元】【明】【宮】
[0072010] 不＝復【宋】【元】【明】
[0072011] 末＝抹【明】
[0072012] 車璩馬瑙＝硨磲瑪瑙【宋】【元】【明】【宮】
[0072013] 〔化〕－【宋】【元】【明】【宮】
[0072014] 技＝伎【宋】【元】【明】【宮】
[0073001] 所＝能【宋】【元】【明】【宮】
[0073002] 聞＝音【宋】【元】【明】【宮】
[0073003] 力＋（勢）【宋】【元】【明】【宮】
[0073004] 犍＝捷【宋】【元】【宮】＊ ［＊ 1 2 3］
[0073005] 量＝上【宋】【元】【明】【宮】
[0073006] 諸＝心【宋】【元】【明】【宮】
[0073007] 行＋（生）【宋】【元】【明】【宮】
[0073008] 〔有〕－【宋】【元】【明】【宮】
[0073009] 閡＝礙【宋】【元】【明】【宮】下同
[0073010] 出＝去【宋】【元】【明】【宮】
[0073011] 二＝三【宋】【元】【明】【宮】＊ ［＊ 1］
[0074001] 〔如〕－【宋】【元】【明】【宮】＊ ［＊ 1］
[0074002] 分＋（分）【宋】【元】【明】【宮】
[0074003] 大＝但【宋】【元】【明】【宮】
[0074004] 智＝知【宋】【元】【明】【宮】＊ ［＊ 1 2 3］
[0074005] 智＋（知不）【宋】【元】【明】【宮】
[0074006] 〔故〕－【宋】【元】【明】【宮】
[0074007] 〔人〕－【宋】【元】【明】【宮】
[0074008] 〔者〕－【宋】【元】【明】【宮】
[0074009] 豫＝預【宋】【元】【明】【宮】＊ ［＊ 1 2 3 4］
[0074010] （是）＋故【明】
[0074011] 〔城〕－【宋】【元】【明】【宮】
[0074012] 故＋（佛）【宋】【元】【明】【宮】
[0074013] 知＋（婆羅門忘請佛及僧者）【宋】【元】【明】【宮】
[0074014] 歲數＝數歲【宋】【元】【明】【宮】
[0074015] 韋＝毘【宋】【元】【明】【宮】

[0074016] 估＝賈【宋】【元】【明】【宮】
[0075001] 〔者〕－【宋】【元】【明】【宮】
[0075002] 具＋（足）【宋】【元】【明】【宮】
[0075003] 智＝根【宋】【元】【明】【宮】
[0075004] 已＝以【宋】【元】【明】【宮】下同
[0075005] 訪＝方【宋】【元】【明】【宮】
[0075006] 邅＝羅【宋】【元】【明】【宮】
[0075007] 蓮＝連【宋】【元】【明】【宮】
[0075008] 訾＝呰【宋】【元】【明】【宮】＊［＊ 1］
[0075009] 法＝汝【宋】【元】【明】【宮】
[0075010] 〔智〕－【宋】【元】【明】【宮】
[0075011] 知他＝他知【宋】【元】【明】【宮】
[0075012] 〔切〕－【宋】【元】【明】【宮】
[0075013] 任＝住【宋】【元】【明】
[0075014] 韋陀＝韋大【宋】【元】【明】【宮】下同
[0075015] 〔曰〕－【宋】【元】【明】【宮】
[0075016] 導＝道【宋】【元】【明】【宮】
[0075017] 〔故〕－【宮】
[0075018] 〔經〕－【宋】【元】【明】【宮】
[0076001] 無＝不【宋】【元】【明】【宮】
[0076002] 無明＋（邪見自古亦然有無明）【宋】【元】【明】【宮】
[0076003] 病＝疾【宋】【元】【明】【宮】
[0076004] 錠＝定【宋】【元】【明】【宮】
[0076005] 〔老〕－【宋】【元】【明】【宮】
[0076006] 真＝直【宋】【元】【明】【宮】
[0076007] 〔故〕－【宋】【元】【明】【宮】
[0076008] 〔道〕－【宋】【元】【明】【宮】
[0076009] 〔瞋恚〕－【宋】【元】【明】【宮】
[0076010] （所）＋說【宋】【元】【明】【宮】
[0076011] 〔處〕－【宋】【元】【明】【宮】
[0076012] 智＝能【宋】【元】【明】【宮】
[0076013] 語＝謂【宋】【元】【明】【宮】
[0076014] 〔者〕－【宮】
[0077001] 雪＝宣【明】
[0077002] 飲＝飯【宋】【元】【明】【宮】
[0077003] 〔佛故〕－【宋】【元】【明】【宮】
[0077004] 洹＝涅【宮】
[0077005] 已＝以【宮】下同
[0077006] 惡＝苦【宮】
[0077007] 〔已〕－【宋】【元】【明】【宮】

[0077008] 不分卷及品【宋】【元】【明】【宮】

Fascicle Eleven Variant Readings

[0077009] 不分卷及品【宋】【元】【明】【宮】
[0077010] 〔又〕－【宋】【元】【明】【宮】
[0077011] 人＋（人）【宋】【元】【明】【宮】
[0078001] 利＝行【宋】【元】【宮】
[0078002] 〔得〕－【宋】【元】【明】【宮】
[0078003] （聞）＋斷【宋】【元】【明】【宮】＊ ［＊ 1］
[0078004] 興＝多【宋】【元】【明】【宮】
[0078005] 任＝住【元】
[0078006] 儻＝倘【明】
[0078007] 命＝令【宋】【元】【明】【宮】
[0078008] 名＋（為）【宋】【元】【明】【宮】
[0079001] 皆＝智【宋】【元】【明】【宮】
[0079002] 卷第九終【宋】【元】【明】【宮】
[0079003] 卷第十首【宋】【元】【明】【宮】，譯號同異如首卷【宋】【元】【明】【宮】 [0079004] 首＝百【元】【明】
[0079005] 水或火＝火或水【宋】【元】【明】【宮】
[0079006] 名為＝為名【宋】【元】【明】【宮】
[0079007] 又若＝若人【宋】【元】【明】【宮】
[0079008] 答＋（曰）【宋】【元】【明】【宮】
[0079009] 〔作〕－【宋】【元】【明】【宮】
[0079010] 畜生餓鬼＝餓鬼畜生【宋】【元】【明】【宮】
[0080001] 應＋（心）【宋】【元】【明】【宮】
[0080002] 經此＝此經【宋】【元】【明】【宮】
[0080003] 色＋（故）【宋】【元】【明】【宮】
[0080004] 十＝七【宮】
[0080005] 第＝弟【宋】＊【元】＊【明】＊【宮】＊【CB】＊ ［＊ 1］
[0080006] 餘＋（諸）【宋】【元】【明】【宮】
[0080007] 愛＋（心）【宋】【元】【明】【宮】
[0080008] 何＝可【元】【明】
[0080009] 而不變＝不變異【宋】【元】【明】【宮】
[0080010] 變＋（異）【宋】【元】【明】【宮】
[0080011] 娑＝婆【元】
[0080012] 報＋（若作）【宋】【元】【明】【宮】
[0080013] 〔佛言〕－【宋】【元】【明】【宮】
[0081001] 色＋（離）【宋】【元】【明】【宮】
[0081002] （世間）＋亦【宋】【元】【明】【宮】
[0081003] （如來）＋身【宋】【元】【明】【宮】

[0081004] 神＝身【明】
[0081005] （諸）＋天【宋】【元】【明】【宮】
[0081006] 空＝害【宮】
[0081007] 應＋（以）【宋】【元】【明】【宮】
[0081008] 須＝復【宋】【元】【明】【宮】
[0081009] 著＝習【宋】【元】【明】【宮】
[0081010] 異＝果【宮】
[0081011] 〔有〕－【宋】【元】【明】【宮】
[0081012] 能＋（全）【宋】【元】【明】【宮】
[0081013] （之）＋分【宋】【元】【明】【宮】
[0082001] （守）＋護【宋】【元】【明】【宮】＊［＊ 1 2］
[0082002] 呵＝阿【元】【明】
[0082003] （是）＋故【宋】【元】【明】【宮】
[0082004] 言＋（如來）【宋】【元】【明】【宮】
[0082005] 微＝疑【宋】【元】【明】【宮】
[0082006] 盡＋（我於此中）【宋】【元】【明】【宮】
[0082007] 是＝微畏【宋】【元】【明】【宮】
[0082008] 〔如〕－【宋】【元】【明】【宮】
[0082009] 〔但〕－【宋】【元】【明】【宮】
[0082010] 但＝俱【宋】
[0082011] 法受＝受法【宋】【元】【明】【宮】
[0082012] 即＋（時）【宋】【元】【明】【宮】
[0082013] 受＝愛【宋】▷＊］【元】▷＊］【明】▷＊］［＊ 1］
[0082014] （禪）＋定【宋】【元】【明】【宮】
[0082015] 如＝知【宋】【元】【明】【宮】
[0083001] 知＝智【宋】【元】【明】【宮】
[0083002] 小＋（力）【明】【宮】
[0083003] 解＋（脫）【宮】
[0083004] 悲＝慧【宋】【元】【明】【宮】
[0083005] 智＝知【宋】【元】【明】【宮】
[0083006] 德＝田【宋】【元】【明】【宮】
[0083007] 摩＝魔【明】
[0083008] 似＝以【宋】【元】【明】【宮】
[0083009] 不分卷【宋】【元】【明】【宮】

Fascicle Twelve Variant Readings

[0083010] 不分卷【宋】【元】【明】【宮】
[0084001] 唯＝惟【宋】【元】【明】【宮】
[0084002] 設＝妄【宋】【元】【明】【宮】
[0084003] 善＝此【宋】【元】【宮】

[0084004] 天中＝中天【宋】【元】【明】【宮】
[0084005] 可＝能【宋】【元】【明】【宮】
[0084006] 蔭＝音【宋】【元】【明】
[0084007] 嫌譏而拒＝譏刺而巨【宋】【元】【明】【宮】
[0084008] 德＝得【宋】【元】【明】【宮】
[0085001] 所＝并【宋】【元】【明】【宮】
[0085002] 骨＝血【宋】【元】【明】【宮】
[0085003] 明註曰南藏無無求惱者施
[0085004] 求惱＝惱求【明】【宮】
[0085005] 垢＝妬【宋】【元】【明】【宮】
[0085006] 住＝性【宋】【元】【明】，＝往【宮】
[0085007] 定＝禪【宋】【元】【明】【宮】
[0085008] 分＝力【宋】【元】【明】【宮】
[0085009] 勢＝施【宋】【元】【明】【宮】
[0085010] 一切眾生＝諸眾生中【宋】【元】【明】【宮】
[0086001] 卷第十終【宋】【元】【明】【宮】
[0086002] 卷第十一首【宋】【元】【明】【宮】，譯號同異如首卷【宋】【元】【明】【宮】
[0086003] 染＝深【宋】【元】【明】【宮】
[0086004] 〔供〕－【宋】【元】【明】【宮】
[0086005] 〔即〕－【宋】【元】【明】【宮】
[0086006] 于＝於【宋】【元】【明】【宮】
[0086007] （大）＋定【宋】【元】【明】【宮】，定＝寶【宮】
[0086008] 恪＝敬【明】
[0086009] 甞＝常【宋】【元】【明】【宮】
[0086010] 已＝以【宋】【元】【明】【宮】
[0086011] 憎＝增【宋】【元】【明】【宮】
[0086012] 復＋（次）【宮】
[0086013] 忍法＝法忍【宋】【元】【明】【宮】
[0086014] 出＝說【宮】
[0086015] 眠睡＝睡眠【明】
[0087001] 啛＝嚌【宋】【元】【明】【宮】
[0087002] 齊＝齋【宋】【元】【明】【宮】
[0087003] 毀＝瑕【宋】【元】【明】【宮】
[0087004] 〔者〕－【宋】【元】【明】【宮】
[0087005] 上＝尚【宋】【元】【明】【宮】
[0087006] 〔生〕－【宋】【元】【明】【宮】
[0087007] 念＝令【宮】
[0087008] 受＝愛【宮】
[0087009] 相＝想【宋】【元】【明】【宮】＊ ［＊ 1 2］

[0087010] 颰＝跋【宋】【元】【明】【宮】下同
[0087011] 碎＝破【宋】【元】【明】【宮】
[0087012] 諷誦＝誦諷【宋】【元】【明】【宮】
[0088001] 搆＝[彀-心+牛]【明】
[0088002] 茶＝荼【明】
[0088003] 聞＝問【明】
[0088004] （也）－【宋】【元】【明】【宮】
[0088005] 薩＝提【宋】【元】【明】【宮】
[0088006] 隨喜＝菩薩【宮】
[0088007] 義＝議【宋】【元】【明】【宮】
[0088008] 口＝曰【宋】【元】【明】【宮】
[0088009] 煉＝練【宋】【元】【明】【宮】＊［＊ 1］
[0088010] 聞＝問【宮】＊［＊ 1］
[0088011] 為＝有【宋】【元】【宮】
[0088012] 聞＝門【宋】【元】，＝問【宮】
[0089001] 生＝用【宮】
[0089002] 具＝且【元】【明】
[0089003] 心＝力【宋】【元】【明】【宮】
[0089004] 明註曰大南藏作太
[0089005] 聞＝問【宋】【元】【宮】
[0089006] 地＝法【宋】【元】【明】【宮】
[0089007] 人＝智【宋】【元】【明】
[0089008] 貪＝食【宮】
[0089009] 生＝心【宮】
[0089010] 行＝得【宋】【元】【明】
[0089011] 一地＝初【宋】【元】【明】【宮】
[0089012] （者）－【宋】【元】【明】【宮】
[0090001] 七＝十【宋】【元】【明】【宮】
[0090002] 不分卷及品【宋】【元】【明】【宮】

Fascicle Thirteen Variant Readings

[0090003] 不分卷及品【宋】【元】【明】【宮】
[0090004] （佛）－【宮】
[0090005] 好＝知【宋】【元】【明】
[0090006] 狼虎＝虎狼【宋】【元】【明】【宮】
[0090007] 岐＝路【宋】【元】【宮】
[0090008] 搏＝揣【宋】【元】【明】【宮】
[0090009] （大）－【宋】【元】【明】【宮】
[0090010] 欲樂＝樂欲【宋】【元】【明】【宮】
[0090011] （知）－【宋】【元】【明】【宮】

Variant Readings in Other Editions 1343

[0090012] 令＝生【宮】
[0090013] 盛＝威【宮】
[0090014] 等＋(是能生智慧等)【宋】【元】【明】【宮】
[0090015] 芽＝牙【宮】
[0090016] 〔枝〕－【宋】【元】【明】【宮】
[0090017] (韋陀秦言無對義)本文＝(韋陀秦言無對義)　夾註【宋】【元】【明】【宮】
[0090018] 〔在〕－【宋】【元】【明】【宮】
[0090019] 〔界〕－【宋】【元】【明】【宮】
[0091001] 灰＝炙【宋】【元】【明】【宮】
[0091002] 冰＝水【宋】【元】【明】【宮】
[0091003] 濕＝潔【宮】
[0091004] 裳＝常【宋】【元】【明】【宮】
[0091005] 〔等〕－【宋】【元】【明】【宮】
[0091006] 〔為〕－【宋】【元】【明】【宮】
[0091007] (於)＋涅槃【宋】【元】【明】【宮】
[0091008] 難＝艱【宋】【元】【明】【宮】
[0091009] 〔如〕－【宋】【元】【明】【宮】
[0091010] 礙＝置【宋】【元】【明】【宮】
[0091011] 若＝苦【宮】
[0091012] (若)＋俱【宋】【元】【明】【宮】
[0091013] 如＋(彼好)【宋】【元】【明】【宮】
[0091014] 〔是〕－【宋】【元】【明】【宮】
[0091015] 可＋(住)【宋】【元】【明】【宮】
[0091016] 轉＝便轉還【宋】【元】【明】【宮】
[0091017] (諸)＋魔【宋】【元】【明】【宮】
[0091018] (普令)＋安隱【宋】【元】【明】【宮】
[0091019] (正)＋法【宋】【元】【明】【宮】
[0091020] 涅槃＋(道)【宋】【元】【明】【宮】
[0091021] 卷第十一終【宋】【元】【明】【宮】
[0091022] 卷第十二首【宋】【元】【明】【宮】，譯號同異如首卷　【宋】【元】【明】【宮】
[0092001] 擇＝釋【宋】【元】【明】【宮】
[0092002] 依＝諸【宋】【元】【明】【宮】
[0092003] 先已＝已先【明】
[0092004] 品＋(中)【宋】【元】【明】【宮】
[0092005] 念＝善處【宋】【宮】
[0092006] 得無上道＝能亦度人【宋】【元】【明】【宮】
[0092007] 善＝惡【宋】【元】【明】【宮】
[0092008] 〔不〕－【宋】【元】【明】【宮】

[0093001] 根＝福【宋】【元】【明】【宮】
[0093002] 不遠離諸蓋＝遠離諸善法不捨是諸惡是名惡菩薩 【宋】【元】【明】【宮】
[0093003] 人愚癡＝愚癡人【宋】【元】【明】【宮】
[0093004] 深＝染【宋】【元】【明】【宮】
[0093005] 渡＝度【宋】【元】【明】【宮】
[0093006] 〔三〕－【明】
[0093007] 〔又〕－【宋】【元】【明】【宮】
[0093008] 又無＝無有【宋】【元】【明】【宮】
[0094001] 二＝一【元】
[0094002] 七＝十【明】
[0094003] 言＝事【明】
[0094004] 〔法〕－【宋】【元】【明】【宮】
[0094005] 一＝二十八【宋】【元】【明】【宮】
[0094006] 習＝集【宋】【元】【明】【宮】
[0094007] 上＝尚【宋】【元】【明】【宮】
[0094008] 令＝念【宮】
[0095001] 異＝果【宋】【元】【明】【宮】
[0095002] 不分卷及品【宋】【元】【明】【宮】

Fascicle Fourteen Variant Readings

[0095003] 不分卷及品【宋】【元】【明】【宮】
[0095004] 〔不〕－【宋】【元】【明】【宮】
[0095005] 身意乃至別二十字宋元明宮四本俱作長行
[0095006] 二＝各【明】
[0095007] 〔眾〕－【宋】【元】【明】【宮】
[0095008] 此＝本【宋】【元】【明】【宮】
[0095009] 〔人〕－【宋】【元】【明】【宮】
[0095010] 他＋（人）【宋】【元】【明】【宮】
[0095011] 〔無〕－【宋】【元】【明】【宮】
[0095012] 後＝彼【宋】【元】【明】【宮】
[0095013] 〔者〕－【宋】【元】【明】【宮】
[0096001] 生＝主【宮】
[0096002] 作＝有【元】【明】
[0096003] 一共＝共一【宋】【元】【明】【宮】
[0096004] 無＝不【宋】【元】【明】【宮】
[0096005] 〔者以欲界身〕－【宋】【元】【明】【宮】
[0096006] 除＋（生）【宋】【元】【明】【宮】
[0096007] 可＝應【宋】【元】【明】【宮】
[0096008] 〔可〕－【宋】【元】【明】【宮】
[0096009] 〔或可斷或不可斷〕－【宋】【元】【明】【宮】

Variant Readings in Other Editions　　　　　　　　　　1345

[0096010] 知見＝見知【宋】【元】【明】【宮】＊［＊1］
[0096011] 賢聖＝聖賢【宋】【元】【明】【宮】
[0097001] 門＝問【宋】【元】【明】【宮】＊［＊1］
[0097002] 瞋＝恚【宋】【元】【明】【宮】
[0097003] 貪＋（心）【宋】【元】【明】【宮】
[0097004] 〔欲〕－【宋】【元】【明】【宮】
[0097005] 盜＝奪【宋】【元】【明】【宮】
[0097006] 如＝各【宋】【元】【明】【宮】
[0097007] 果＋（報）【宋】【元】【明】【宮】
[0098001] （不）＋取【宋】【元】【明】【宮】
[0098002] 逆＝送【宋】【元】【明】【宮】
[0098003] 二＝三【宋】【元】【明】
[0098004] 心＝必【明】
[0098005] 三＝二【宋】【元】【宮】
[0098006] 〔十〕－【宋】【元】【明】【宮】
[0098007] 行＝修【宋】【元】【明】【宮】
[0099001] 枏＝旃【宋】【元】【明】【宮】
[0099002] 十＝中【宮】
[0099003] 卷第十二終【宋】【元】【明】【宮】
[0099004] 卷第十三首【宋】【元】【明】【宮】，譯號同異如首卷　【宋】【元】【明】【宮】
[0099005] 二十（十九）【宋】【元】【明】【宮】
[0099006] （即）＋是【宋】【元】【明】【宮】
[0099007] 刃＝刀【宋】【元】【明】【宮】
[0099008] 一一勝處來＝二勝處來者【宋】【元】【明】【宮】
[0099009] 至＝到【宋】【元】【明】【宮】
[0099010] 地＋（耶）【宋】【元】【明】【宮】
[0099011] 隨他聞聲＝隨從他聞【宮】
[0099012] （佛）＋功德【宋】【元】【明】【宮】
[0099013] 俱＝但【宋】【元】【明】【宮】
[0099014] 地＝耶【宋】【元】【明】【宮】
[0100001] 中＋（說）【宋】【元】【明】【宮】
[0100002] 於受生＝受生十【宋】【元】【明】【宮】
[0100003] 令是人能＝能令是人【宋】【元】【明】【宮】
[0100004] 集＝習【明】
[0100005] 〔苦〕－【宋】【元】【明】【宮】
[0100006] 〔唯〕－【宋】【元】【明】【宮】
[0100007] 〔法〕－【宋】【元】【明】【宋】
[0100008] 不分卷及品【宋】【元】【明】【宮】

Fascicle Fifteen Variant Readings

[0100009] 不分卷及品【宋】【元】【明】【宮】
[0101001] 技＝伎【宋】【元】【宮】
[0101002] 集＝習【明】＊ ［＊ 1 2 3 4 5 6 7 8 9 10 11 12 13］
[0101003] 〔佛〕－【宋】【元】【明】【宮】
[0101004] 乃＝及【宋】【元】【明】【宮】
[0101005] 文＝曼【明】
[0101006] 生＋（生）【宮】
[0101007] 地＝法【宋】【元】【宮】
[0101008] 三＋（十）【宋】【元】【明】【宮】
[0101009] 〔於〕－【宋】【元】【明】【宮】
[0102001] 辱＝受【宋】【元】【明】【宮】
[0102002] （無量）＋一切【宋】【元】【明】【宮】
[0102003] 憶＝屎【宋】
[0102004] 因＝同【宋】【宮】
[0102005] 曰＋（若菩薩）【宋】【元】【明】【宮】
[0102006] 沸＝佛【宮】
[0102007] 屎＝憶【宋】
[0102008] 〔簸阿〕－【宮】
[0102009] 那＝陀【宋】【元】【明】【宮】
[0102010] 謂＝諸【宋】【元】【明】【宮】
[0102011] 修＝有【宋】【元】【明】【宮】
[0102012] 酥＝蘇【宮】
[0103001] 眾生＋（不利益若干眾生）【宋】【元】【明】【宮】
[0103002] （解大乘品之二）＋菩薩【元】【宮】，（解大乘品第三十一）＋菩薩【明】
[0103003] 故＋（說）【宋】【元】【明】【宮】
[0103004] 〔以慧為希有〕－【明】
[0103005] 劫＝時【宋】【元】【明】【宮】
[0104001] 時＝等【宋】【元】【宮】
[0104002] 法＋（知是等中應以如是說法）【明】
[0104003] 意＝慧【宋】【元】【明】【宮】＊ ［＊ 1］
[0104004] 若＝善【宋】【元】【明】【宮】
[0104005] 〔於〕－【宋】【元】【明】【宮】
[0104006] 如＝知【宋】【元】【明】【宮】
[0104007] 〔說〕－【宋】【元】【明】【宮】＊ ［＊ 1］
[0104008] 淨地＝地淨【宋】【元】【明】【宮】
[0104009] 乘＝果【宮】
[0104010] 眾＝現【宋】【元】【明】【宮】
[0105001] 觀＝樂【明】
[0105002] 〔世間〕－【宋】【元】【明】【宮】

Variant Readings in Other Editions

[0105003] 賤＝惡【宋】【元】【明】【宮】
[0105004] 害＝著【宋】【元】【宮】
[0105005] 是故乃至菩提二十字宋元明宮四本俱作五言四句偈
[0105006] 二十（者）【宋】【元】【明】【宮】
[0105007] 神＝佛【宋】【元】【明】【宮】
[0105008] 令＝今【宋】【元】【明】【宮】
[0106001] 受＝愛【宋】【元】【明】【宮】＊［＊ 1］
[0106002] 〔故〕－【宮】
[0106003] 嬈＝惱【宋】【元】【明】【宮】
[0106004] 間＝時【宋】【元】【明】【宮】
[0106005] 新＝辛【宋】【元】【明】【宮】
[0106006] 攢＝鑽【宋】【元】【明】【宮】
[0106007] 〔化〕－【宋】【元】【明】【宮】
[0106008] 如＝汝【宋】【元】【明】【宮】
[0107001] 樂＋（視）【宋】【元】【明】【宮】
[0107002] 浠＝滴【宋】【元】【明】【宮】
[0107003] ［病-丙+(瓜-丶)］＝癩【宋】【元】【明】【宮】
[0107004] 〔五〕－【宋】
[0107005] 事＝養【宋】【元】【明】【宮】
[0107006] 王＝生【元】【明】
[0107007] （應）＋以【宋】【元】【明】【宮】
[0107008] 進＝勤【宋】【元】【明】【宮】
[0107009] （得）＋大果【宋】【元】【明】【宮】
[0107010] 可＝所【明】
[0107011] 五＋（道）【宋】【元】【明】【宮】
[0107012] 〔在〕－【宋】【元】【明】【宮】
[0107013] 業＋（道）【宋】【元】【明】【宮】
[0107014] 五＝三【宋】【元】【明】【宮】

Fascicle Sixteen Variant Readings

[0107015] 六＝四【宋】【元】【明】【宮】
[0107016] 四＝三十一【宋】【元】【宮】，＝三十二【明】
[0108001] 失＝共【宋】【元】【明】【宮】
[0108002] 慢＝漫【明】
[0108003] 侮＝悔【宋】【元】【明】【宮】
[0108004] 很戾＝恨【宋】【元】【明】【宮】
[0108005] 足＝法【宋】【元】【宮】
[0108006] 七＝十【宋】【元】【明】【宮】
[0108007] 眾生乃至大乘二十字宋元明宮四本俱作五言四句偈
[0108008] 〔此〕－【宋】【元】【明】【宮】

[0108009] 〔諸〕－【宋】【元】【明】【宮】
[0109001] 出＝善【宮】
[0109002] 洄＝迴【宋】【元】【宮】
[0109003] 業＝善【宋】【元】【明】【宮】
[0109004] （不）＋失【宋】【元】【明】【宮】
[0109005] 入＝住【宋】【元】【明】【宮】
[0109006] 善＝若【宋】【元】【宮】＊［＊ 1］
[0109007] 〔餘〕－【宋】【元】【明】【宮】
[0110001] 〔自〕－【宋】【元】【明】【宮】
[0110002] 惱苦＝苦惱【宋】【元】【明】【宮】
[0110003] 當＝常【宋】【元】【明】【宮】
[0110004] 二＝一【宋】【元】【明】【宮】
[0110005] 七＝一【宋】【元】【宮】
[0110006] 以＝已【宋】【元】【明】【宮】＊［＊ 1］
[0110007] （心生憍慢貪著）＋故【宋】【元】【明】【宮】
[0110008] 〔說〕－【宋】【元】【明】【宮】
[0111001] 癡＝疑【宋】【元】【明】【宮】
[0111002] 猗＝倚【宋】【元】【明】【宮】＊［＊ 1］
[0111003] 五＝三十二【宋】【元】【宮】，＝三十三之一【明】
[0111004] 貝＝具【明】【宮】
[0111005] 締＝奢【宋】【元】【明】【宮】
[0111006] 屬＝見【宮】
[0111007] 女＝子【宋】【元】【宮】
[0112001] 病＋（者）【宋】【元】【明】【宮】
[0112002] （誦）＋讀【宋】【元】【明】【宮】
[0112003] （及）＋身【宋】【元】【明】【宮】
[0112004] 賊＝賤【宮】
[0112005] 侍＝防【宋】【元】【明】【宮】
[0113001] 念＝命【宮】
[0113002] 石瓦＝瓦石【宋】【元】【明】【宮】
[0113003] 和合＝知【宋】【元】【明】【宮】
[0113004] 歸＝緣【宋】【元】【明】【宮】
[0113005] 自＝息【宋】【元】【明】【宮】
[0113006] 住＝佐【宋】【元】【宮】
[0113007] 佐＝住【宋】【元】【明】
[0113008] 菩薩乃至六度十字宋元明宮四本俱作五言二句偈
[0114001] 入＝人【明】
[0114002] （此）＋因緣【宋】【元】【明】【宮】
[0114003] 卷第十四終【明】

Variant Readings in Other Editions 1349

[0114004] 卷第十五首【明】,譯號同異如首卷【明】, 復前行明本有品題解頭陀品第三十三之二十字
[0114005] 卷第十四終【宋】【元】【宮】
[0114006] 卷第十五首【宋】【元】【宮】,譯號同異如首卷【宋】【元】 【宮】,廣前行宋元宮本俱有品題解頭陀品下之餘七字
[0114007] 褐氈=氀㲪【宋】【元】【明】【宮】
[0114008] 是=不違【宋】【元】【明】【宮】
[0115001] 廢=失【宋】【元】【明】【宮】
[0115002] 愛=受【宋】【元】【明】【宮】
[0115003] 不分卷及品【宋】【元】【明】【宮】

Fascicle Seventeen Variant Readings

[0115004] 不分卷及品【宋】【元】【明】【宮】
[0115005] 知+(見)【宋】【元】【明】【宮】
[0115006] 〔若〕-【宋】【元】【明】【宮】
[0115007] 〔讀〕-【宋】【元】【明】【宮】
[0115008] 常=尚【宋】【元】【明】【宮】
[0115009] 佛+(佛)【宋】【元】【明】【宮】
[0115010] 陀=度【宋】【元】【明】【宮】
[0115011] 求=伏【元】【明】
[0115012] 此=是【宋】【元】【明】【宮】
[0115013] 恭敬=供給【宋】【明】【宮】,=供結【元】
[0115014] 義=議【宋】【元】【明】【宮】
[0115015] 敬愛=愛敬【明】
[0115016] 第=弟【宋】【元】【宮】
[0115017] 所常=常所【宋】【元】【明】【宮】
[0116001] 思=怠【宋】
[0116002] 秇=咎【宋】【元】【明】【宮】
[0116003] 大=殃【宋】【元】【明】【宮】
[0116004] 颺=跂【宋】【元】【明】【宮】下同
[0116005] 誦=通【宋】【元】【明】
[0116006] 〔是故〕-【宋】【元】【明】【宮】
[0116007] 六=三十三【宋】【元】【宮】,=三十四【明】
[0116008] 雜=離【宋】【元】【明】【宮】
[0116009] 者+(見命)【宋】【元】【明】【宮】
[0116010] 行=法【宋】【元】【明】【宮】
[0116011] 〔者〕-【宋】【元】【明】【宮】
[0117001] 邪徑=所經【宋】【元】【明】【宮】
[0117002] 隨=墮【宋】【元】【明】【宮】
[0117003] 時=已【宋】【元】【明】【宮】
[0117004] 此=比【宋】

[0117005] 彩＝綵【宋】【元】【明】【宮】
[0117006] 猗＝倚【宋】【元】【明】【宮】下同
[0117007] 則＝亦【明】
[0118001] 如是乃至尸羅二句宋元明宮四本俱作長行
[0118002] 生＝相【宋】【元】【明】【宮】
[0118003] 無＝有【宋】【元】【明】【宮】
[0118004] 自＝生【宋】【元】【明】【宮】
[0118005] 如＋（是）【宋】【元】【明】【宮】
[0118006] 者＝是【宋】【元】【明】【宮】
[0118007] （行）＋者【宋】【元】【明】【宮】
[0119001] 求＝淨【宋】【元】【明】【宮】
[0119002] 〔求〕－【宋】【元】【明】【宮】
[0119003] 明註曰戒南藏作滅
[0119004] （有沙門）＋具【宋】【元】【明】【宮】
[0119005] 明註曰八南藏作入
[0119006] （但）＋於【宋】【元】【明】【宮】
[0119007] 人＝會【宋】【元】【明】【宮】
[0119008] 〔名〕－【宋】【元】【明】【宮】
[0119009] 樂＝隱【宋】【元】【明】【宮】
[0119010] 間＝人【宋】【元】【明】【宮】
[0120001] 任＝住【宮】
[0120002] 七＝三十四【宋】【元】【宮】，＝三十五【明】
[0120003] 〔之初〕－【宋】【元】【明】【宮】
[0120004] 得＝能【宋】【元】【明】【宮】
[0120005] 御＝禦【宋】【元】【明】【宮】
[0120006] 度＝渡【宋】【元】【明】【宮】
[0120007] 刃＝刀【宋】【元】【明】【宮】
[0120008] 凡＝尼【宋】
[0120009] 如＋（是）【宮】
[0120010] 〔人〕－【宮】
[0120011] 涅槃＝但槃【宋】
[0120012] 惱＝悔【宋】【元】【明】【宮】
[0120013] 〔所可〕－【宋】【元】【明】【宮】
[0121001] 旅＝者【宋】【元】【明】【宮】
[0121002] 沙＝好【宋】【元】【明】【宮】
[0121003] 杖＝仗【宋】【元】【明】【宮】
[0121004] 八＝三十五【宋】【元】【宮】，＝三十六【明】
[0121005] 菩薩乃至輪王二十字宋元明三本俱作五言四句偈
[0121006] 輞＝網【宋】【元】【宮】，明註曰輞南藏作網
[0121007] 叉＝又【明】

Variant Readings in Other Editions

[0121008] 健＝捷【宋】【元】【明】【宮】
[0121009] 瓔珞＝纓絡【宋】【元】【宮】＊ [＊ 1]
[0121010] 象＝家【宋】【元】【宮】
[0121011] 王＝生【宋】【元】【明】【宮】
[0121012] 眾＝家【宋】【元】【明】【宮】
[0121013] 技＝伎【宋】【元】【明】【宮】
[0121014] 車璖馬瑙＝硨磲碼碯【宋】【元】【明】【宮】
[0121015] 頗梨＝玻[王＊梨]【宋】【元】【明】【宮】
[0121016] 嚴莊＝莊嚴【宋】【元】【明】【宮】
[0121017] 婆＝羅【宋】【元】【明】【宮】
[0121018] 且＝直【元】【明】
[0121019] 覆＝竅【宋】【元】【明】【宮】
[0121020] 珂＝軻【宋】
[0121021] 睛＝青【宋】【元】【明】【宮】
[0122001] 蝗＝橫【宋】【元】【明】【宮】
[0122002] 王＝生【元】【明】
[0122003] 技＝伎【宋】【元】【宮】
[0122004] 盛＝上【宋】【元】【宮】，＝士【明】
[0122005] （於）＋耆【宋】【元】【明】【宮】
[0122006] 能除＝與不【宋】【元】【明】【宮】
[0122007] 七＝五【明】【宮】，七＝五(亦曰十住論)【宋】【元】

Bibliography

Bodhi. (2000). *The Connected Discourses of the Buddha: A New Translation of the Saṃyutta Nikāya* ; translated from the Pāli ; original translation by Bhikkhu Bodhi. (Teachings of the Buddha). Somerville, MA: Wisdom Publications.

Bodhi. (2012). The Numerical Discourses of the Buddha: A Translation of the Aṅguttara Nikāya (Teachings of the Buddha). Boston: Wisdom Publications.

Burlingame, E., Buddhaghosa, & Lanman, Charles Rockwell. (1921). Buddhist legends (Harvard oriental series ; v. 28-30). Cambridge, Mass.: Harvard Univ. Press.

Conze, E., & Suzuki Gakujutsu Zaidan. (1967). Materials for a Dictionary of the Prajñāpāramitā Literature. Tokyo: Suzuki Research Foundation.

Dharmamitra. (2009) Nāgārjuna on the Six Perfections: An Ārya Bodhisattva Explains the Heart of the Bodhisattva Path. A translation of chapters 17-30 of Ārya Nāgārjuna's Exegesis on the Great Perfection of Wisdom Sutra. Seattle: Kalavinka Press.

Dharmamitra. (2009) Nāgārjuna's Guide to the Bodhisattva Path: Treatise on the Provisions for Enlightenment. A translation of the Bodhisaṃbhāra Śāstra by Ārya Nāgārjuna. Seattle: Kalavinka Press.

Edgerton, F. (1953). Buddhist Hybrid Sanskrit grammar and dictionary. (William Dwight Whitney linguistic series). New Haven: Yale University Press.

Hirakawa, A. (1997). Buddhist Chinese-Sanskrit Dictionary / Bukkyō Kan-Bon daijiten. Tokyo]; [Tokyo] :: Reiyūkai : Hatsubaimoto Innātorippusha; 霊友会：発売元いんなあとりっぷ社.

Malalasekera, G. (1937). Dictionary of Pāli proper names (Indian texts series). London: J. Murray.

Ñāṇamoli, & Bodhi. (1995). The Middle Length Discourses of the Buddha: A New Translation of the Majjhima Nikāya (Teachings of the Buddha). Boston: Wisdom Publications in association with the Barre Center for Buddhist Studies.

Nattier, J. (2003). A Few Good Men: The Bodhisattva Path According to the Inquiry of Ugra (Ugraparipṛcchā) (Studies in the Buddhist traditions). Honolulu: University of Hawai'i Press.

Powers, J. (2016). The Buddhist World (Routledge worlds). London ; New York: Routledge, Taylor & Francis Group.

Rahder, J. (1928). Glossary of the Sanskrit, Tibetan, Mongolian, and Chinese Versions of the Daśabhūmika-Sūtra. Compiled by J. Rahder. (Buddhica, Documents et Travaux pour l'Étude du

Bouddhisme publiés sous la direction de J. Przyluski; Deuxième Série; Documents—Tome I). Paris: Librarie Orientaliste Paul Geuthner, 1928.

Rahder, J., & Vasubandhu. (1926). Daśabhumikasutra. Leuven: J.B. Istas.

Ruegg, D. (1981). The Literature of the Madhyamaka school of Philosophy in India (History of Indian literature ; v. 7, fasc. 1). Wiesbaden: Harrassowitz.

Stefania Travagnin (2013) Yinshun's Recovery of ShizhuPiposha Lun 十住毗婆沙論: a Madhyamaka-based Pure Land Practice In Twentieth-Century Taiwan, Contemporary Buddhism, 14:2, 320-343, DOI: 10.1080/14639947.2013.832497 To link to this article: https://doi.org/10.1080/14639947.2013.832497

Takakusu, J., & Watanabe, Kaigyoku. (1924). Taishō shinshū Daizōkyō. Tōkyō; 東京 :: Taishō Issaikyō Kankōkai; 大正一切經刊行會.

Vaidya, P. L., ed. Daśabhūmikasūtram. Darbhanga: The Mithila Institute of Post-Graduate Studies and Research in Sanskrit Learning, 1969.

Williams, M. Monier, Sir. (n.d.). A Sanskrit-English Dictionary. Delhi: Sri Satguru.

Zhonghua dian zi fo dian xie hui. (2004). CBETA dian zi fo dian ji cheng = CBETA Chinese electronic Tripitaka collection (Version 2004. ed.). Taibei; 台北 :: Zhonghua dian zi fo dian xie hui; 中華電子佛典協會.

Glossary

A

Abhidharma: A category of Buddhist texts devoted to detailed scholastic analyses of the teachings contained in the sutras.

afflictions: Otherwise known as "the three poisons" (*triviṣa*) these are: 1) greed (including lust and desire in general); 2) hatred (including all of the permutations of aversion such as irritation, anger, and rage); and 3) delusion or ignorance. There are many subcategories of afflictions (*kleśa*) listed in the various dharma schemas. For example, in the Sarvāstivāda school, there are six root afflictions and ten subsidiary afflictions.

aggregates: See "five aggregates."

anāgamin: The *anāgamin* or "nonreturner" is one who has gained the third of the four fruits of the individual-liberation path of the śrāvaka disciple.

anuttarasamyaksaṃbodhi: "Anuttarasamyaksaṃbodhi" refers to "the utmost, right, and perfect enlightenment" of a buddha.

arhat: An arhat is one who, having put an end to all of the afflictions, fetters, and contaminants and having put an end to rebirth, has gained the fourth and final fruit on the individual-liberation path of the śrāvaka disciple.

ārya: One who has realized one of the fruits of the path from which they can never fall away. This includes any one of the eight fruits of the arhat path, or any of the irreversible stations on the bodhisattva path to Buddhahood.

asaṃkhya, asaṃkhyeya: In Sanskrit, this is an incalculably and infinitely large number.

asura: As one of the paths of rebirth, this refers to a demi-god or titan. More loosely, this refers to beings much characterized by anger, hatred, jealousy, and contentiousness who may also appear as humans, animals, hungry ghosts (*pretas*), or hell-dwellers.

avadāna stories: Stories of the previous lives of a buddha.

avaivartika: one who has become irreversible on either the individual liberation path of the arhats or on the universal-liberation path of the bodhisattvas and buddhas. Throughout this text, "stage of certainty" (必定, 必定地) is most likely a translation of *avaivartika*.

B

bases of psychic powers: The four bases of psychic power (*catvāra ṛddhi-pāda*) are: zeal (*chanda*); vigor (*vīrya*); [concentration of] mind/

thought (*citta*); and reflective or investigative consideration, examination, or imagination (*mīmāṃsā*).

Bhagavat: "Bhagavat" is one of the titles of a Buddha. It may be translated as "Blessed One," "Lord," or, as rendered in Chinese Buddhist texts, "World Honored One," *shizun* (世尊).

bhikshu: A fully ordained celibate Buddhist monk within one of the traditional schools of Buddhism.

bhikshuni: A fully ordained celibate Buddhist nun within one of the traditional schools of Buddhism.

bhūta ghost: According to MW, one of the many meanings of *bhūta* is: "a spirit (good or evil), the ghost of a deceased person, a demon, imp, goblin." PDB: "A class of harm-inflicting and formless obstructing spirits (i.e. 'elemental spirits')…"; "…sometimes equivalent to *preta* (hungry ghosts)…."; "Because they obstruct rainfall, the *bhūta* are propitiated by rituals to cause precipitation."

bodhi: "Enlightenment" or "awakening." In its most exalted form this refers exclusively to the utmost, right, and perfect enlightenment (*anuttarasamyaksaṃbodhi*) of a buddha.

bodhimaṇḍa: A *bodhimaṇḍa* is the "site of enlightenment" wherein enlightenment is cultivated and fully realized. It may be used as a general reference to Buddhist temples, though it often refers specifically to the site beneath the bodhi tree where a buddha gains complete realization of the utmost, right, and perfect enlightenment.

bodhisattva: A bodhisattva is a being who, in his pursuit of the utmost, right, and perfect enlightenment of buddhahood, is equally dedicated to achieving buddhahood for himself while also facilitating all other beings' achievement of buddhahood. His primary practice is classically described as focusing on the six (or ten) "perfections" (*pāramitā*): giving, moral virtue, patience, vigor, meditative skill (*dhyāna*), and world-transcending wisdom (*prajñā*).

bodhi tree: The tree in Bodhgaya in the Indian state of Bihar under which the Buddha reached enlightenment approximately 2600 years ago.

Brahmā: Per PDB: "An Indian divinity who was adopted into the Buddhist pantheon as a protector of the teachings and king of the Brahmaloka ['Brahma world'] (in the narrow sense of that term)." "Brahmaloka" here refers to the first three heavens of the form realm.

brahmacārin: Per MW, "A young Brahman who is a student of the veda (under a preceptor) or who practises chastity, a young Brahman before marriage (in the first period of his life)."

brahmacarya: Celibacy.

brahman: Someone who belongs to the highest caste in Hinduism; a member of the Hindu priestly caste.

buddha: Anyone who has achieved the utmost, right, and perfect enlightenment (*anuttarasamyaksaṃbodhi*), whether we speak of the Buddha of the present era in this world, Shakyamuni Buddha, any of the seven buddhas of antiquity, or, in Mahāyāna cosmology, any of the countless buddhas of the ten directions and three periods of time.

C

clear knowledges: "Clear knowledges" refers to the "three knowledges" (*trividyā*): 1) The remembrance of previous lives (*pūrvavanivāsānusmṛti*); 2) Knowledge of beings' rebirth destinies (*cyutyupapattijñāna*); and 3) Knowledge of the destruction of the defiling contaminants or "taints" (*āsravakṣaya*).

contaminants: "Contaminants" (āsrava) are usually defined as either threefold or fourfold: 1) sensual desire (*kāma*); 2) [craving for] becoming (*bhāva*), i.e. the craving for continued existence; 3) ignorance (*avidyā*), i.e. delusion; 4) views (*dṛṣṭi*) This fourth types is not included in some listings. Often-encountered alternate translations include "taints" and "outflows" and, less commonly "influxes" and "fluxes."

D

dāna pāramitā: The perfection of giving

deva: Devas are divinities residing in the heavens that collectively constitute the highest of the six rebirth destinies within the realm of *saṃsāra*. There are 27 categories of devas and their heavens in the desire realm, form realm, and formless realm. Although the life spans of the devas in these various heavens may be immensely long, when their karmic merit runs out, they are all still destined to eventually fall back into the other five paths of rebirth wherein they are reborn in accordance with their residual karma from previous lifetimes.

dhāraṇī: Dhāraṇīs are of many types, but the two main types are mantra-like spells that serve the purpose of protection from negative spiritual forces such as ghosts and demons and formulae that aid the retention even for countless lifetimes of the Dharma teachings one has acquired in this and previous lives.

Dharma: The teachings of the Buddha

dharmas: 1) Fundamental constituent aspects, elements, or factors of mental and physical existence, as for instance, "the 100 dharmas" with which Vasubandhu analytically catalogued all that exists. In this sense, dharmas are somewhat analogous to the elements of the periodic table in chemistry; 2) Any individual teaching, as for instance in "the dharma of conditioned origination."

Dharma realm: As a Buddhist technical term, "Dharma realm" or "dharma realm," *dharma-dhātu*, has at least several levels of meaning:

1) At the most granular level, "dharma realm" refers to one of the eighteen sense realms, dharmas as "objects of mind" (*dharma-āyatana*);

2) In the most cosmically and metaphysically vast sense, "Dharma realm" refers in aggregate to all conventionally-existent phenomena and the universally pervasive noumenal "true suchness" (*tathatā*) that underlies and characterizes all of those phenomena. In this sense, it is identical with the "Dharma body" (*dharma-kāya*);

3) As a classifying term, "dharma realm" is used to distinguish realms of existence (as in the ten dharma realms consisting of the realms of buddhas, bodhisattvas, śrāvaka disciples, *pratyekabuddhas*, devas, *asuras*, humans, animals, hungry ghosts, hell-dwellers) or metaphysical modes of existence (as in the "four dharma realms" of the Huayan hermeneutic tradition that speaks of: a] the dharma realm of the "noumenal" [synonymous with emptiness or śūnyatā]; b] the dharma realm of the "phenomenal"; c] the dharma realm of the unimpeded interpenetration of the phenomenal and the noumenal; and d] the dharma realm of the unimpeded interpenetration of all phenomena with all other phenomena in a manner that resonates somewhat with quantum entanglement and non-locality).

Dharma wheel: The "wheel of Dharma" or "Dharma wheel" (*dharma-cakra*) refers to the eight-spoked wheel emblematic of the Buddha's teaching of the eightfold path of the Āryas or "Noble Ones" consisting of right views, right volition or intentional thought, right speech, right physical action, right livelihood, right effort, right mindfulness, and right meditative concentration. This term is also synonymous with the three turnings of the four truths as initially taught by the Buddha to his original five disciples.

dhūta, dhūtaṅga, or *dhūtaguṇa* austerities: In contrast to the non-beneficial ascetic practices of non-Buddhists (lying on a bed of nails, etc.), these are austerities beneficial to progress on the path such as wearing only patchwork robes sewn from discarded cloth, eating only food obtained on the alms round, eating only a single meal each day, always sitting and never lying down, dwelling at the base of a tree, or residing in a charnel field where one observes the stages of the body's decomposition.

dhyāna: "Dhyāna" is a general term broadly corresponding to all forms of Buddhist meditative skill. The Chinese *"ch'an"* or *"chan"* (禪) and the Japanese term *"zen"* are transliterations of the same Sanskrit word *"dhyāna."* All forms of Buddhist "calming" and "insight" meditation are subcategories of *"dhyāna."*

dhyāna pāramitā: The perfection of meditative skill.

E

eight difficulties: Birth in the hells, birth as a hungry ghost, birth as an animal, birth as a long-lived deva, birth in a border region (where there is no Buddha Dharma), birth as someone who is blind, deaf, mute, or otherwise possessed of impaired physical or mental faculties, birth as someone who is possessed of merely worldly knowledge and intelligence (and hence who uses his cleverness to deny the truth of the Dharma); and birth at a time before or long after a buddha appears in the world.

eight precepts: Eight vows involving abstaining from: 1) killing; 2) taking what is not given; 3) sexual misconduct; 4) false speech; 5) intoxicants; 6) use of perfumes, jewelry, other personal adornments, dancing, singing, or watching such performances; 7) sleeping on high or wide beds; and 8) eating after midday.

eighteen sense realms: These consist of the six sense faculties (eye, ear, nose, tongue, body, and mind), the six sense objects (visual forms, sounds, smells, tastes, touchables, and ideas, etc. as objects of mind), and the six sense consciousnesses (visual, auditory, olfactory, gustatory, tactile, and mental).

F

fetters: The fetters (*saṃyojana*) are ten mental characteristics of unenlightened existence that bind beings to uncontrolled rebirths in the six destinies of rebirth. They are: 1) "Truly existent self view," the wrong view that believes in the existence of an eternally existent self in association with the five aggregates; 2) "Skeptical doubt" about the truth of the Dharma and the path to enlightenment; 3) "Clinging to [the observance of] rules and rituals" in and of themselves as constituting the path to spiritual liberation; 4) Sensual desire; 5) Ill will; 6) Desire for rebirth in the form realm [heavens]; 7) Desire for rebirth in the formless realm [heavens]; 8) "Conceit," i.e. the belief that "I" exist; 9) "Agitation" or "restlessness" that prevents deep concentration; and 10) "Ignorance."

five aggregates: 1) form; 2) feelings (i.e. sensations as received through eye, ear, nose, tongue, body, or mind); 3) perceptions; 4) karmic formative factors (such as volitions); and 5) consciousness (visual, auditory, olfactory, gustatory, tactile, and mental).
five desires: Wealth, sex, fame, flavors, and leisure or, alternatively, the objects of the five basic sense faculties (visual forms, sounds, smells, tastes, and touchables).
five faculties: faith; vigor; mindfulness; concentration; wisdom.
five powers: faith; vigor; mindfulness; concentration; wisdom.
five precepts: Five vows involving abstaining from killing, stealing, sexual misconduct, false speech, and intoxicants.
four bases of meritorious qualities: truth, relinquishment, quiescence, and wisdom. (Per VB, the Sanskrit correlates of the Pali *saccādhitthāna, cāgādhitthāna, upasamādhitthāna* (= base of peace), and *paññādhitthāna* would be *satyādhiṣṭhāna, tyāgādhiṣṭhāna, upaśamādhiṣṭhāna,* and *prajñādhiṣṭhāna*.)
four bases of supernatural power: Zeal; vigor; mind; investigation.
four great elements: earth, water, fire, wind.
four right efforts: Causing already arisen evil to cease; causing not yet arisen evil to not arise; causing already arisen goodness to increase; causing not yet arisen goodness to arise.
four requisites: Food obtained on the alms round; robes; residences; medicines.
four stations of mindfulness: Mindfulness of the body; mindfulness of feelings or sensations (experienced via the eye, ear, nose, tongue, body, and mind consciousnesses); mindfulness of thoughts or mind states; mindfulness of dharmas.
four truths / four truths of the Āryas: Suffering; its origination; its cessation; the path to its cessation.

G

gandharva: *Gandharvas* are a type of celestial music spirit that is said to rely on fragrances as their means of survival.
garuḍa: *Garuḍas* are a type of spirit that manifests as an immense golden-winged bird that feeds on young dragons.
ground, grounds: These are levels or planes of spiritual development through which a practitioner proceeds on the way to complete enlightenment.

H

hindrances: "Hindrances" usually refers to "the five hindrances" which are desire, ill will, lethargy-and-sleepiness, excitedness-and-regretfulness, and afflicted doubtfulness. These five hindrances must be overcome in order to successfully enter deep states of meditation.

I

inverted views: The four inverted views (*viparyāsa-catuṣka*) consist of imputing permanence to the impermanent, pleasure to what cannot deliver it, self to what is devoid of any inherently existent self, and purity to what does not actually possess that quality. Standard objects of such upside-down perception are: thought, or mind states, the six categories of "feeling" manifesting in association with the six sense faculties, dharmas (as components of the falsely imputed "self"), and the body.

K

kalaviṅka bird: The Himalayan cuckoo bird that sings with an incomparably beautiful sound even before it breaks out of its shell.

kalpa: The Sanskrit "*kalpa*" roughly corresponds to the English term "eon" with the primary distinction being that, in Buddhist and Hindu cosmology, kalpas occur in various relatively precisely designated immensely long durations.

kāṣāya robe: The robes of an fully ordained bhikshu or bhikshuni.

kinnara: Kinnaras (skt. *kiṃnara*) are a type of celestial music spirit with the body of a human and the head of a horse.

kumbhāṇḍa: According to MW: "Having testicles shaped like a *kumbha* [a winter melon]," a class of demons (at whose head stands Rudra). PDB: "In Sanskrit, a type of evil spirit, and typically listed along with especially *rākṣasa*, but also *piśāca*, *yakṣa*, and *bhūta* spirits. Virūḍhaka, one of the four world-guardians, who protects the southern cardinal direction, is usually said to be their overlord, although some texts give Rudra this role instead. The *kumbhāṇḍa* are also sometimes listed among the minions of Māra, evil personified.

koṭī: A *koṭī* is a number that is defined in the Flower Adornment Sutra Chapter Thirty as the product of multiplying a *lakṣa* (100,000) by a *lakṣa*. Hence it equals 10,000,000, i.e. ten million.

kṣaṇa: A *kṣaṇa*, corresponds to a micro-moment. This is variously defined, one traditional definition being "a ninetieth of a finger-snap." Elsewhere in the text, this may be referred to as "a single thought," "a mind-moment," or "a thought-moment" as approximate translations of the term.

kṣānti pāramitā: The perfection of patience.

kṣatriya: The second of the four castes of traditional Indian culture consisting primarily of the warrior and royalty class.

kṣetra: The Sanskrit word *kṣetra* refers to a land or realm or field and in Buddhist texts it may refer specifically to a "buddha land."

M

mahāsattva: A *mahāsattva* is a great bodhisattva, one who has cultivated the bodhisattva path for countless kalpas.

mātṛkā: *Mātṛkās* are "matrices" consisting of lists of dharmas, technical terms, and concepts discussed in the sutras. They served as the basis for the Abhidharma.

Māra, *māras*: In Buddhism, Māra is generally regarded as the personification of evil and death who is also a particular deity dwelling in one of the desire realm heavens who delights in interfering with spiritual liberation from perpetual rebirths in *saṃsāra*. More specifically, there are said to be four kinds of *māras*: 1) the *māra* of the five mental and physical aggregates in association with which all beings wander endlessly in *saṃsāra*; 2) the *māra* of the afflictions consisting of the three poisons of greed, hatred, and delusion and all of their subcategories; 3) the *māra* of death; and, as mentioned above, 3) the deity known as Māra as well as all of his *devaputra* minions. Additionally, there are also "ghost and spirit" *māras* who may manifest in countless ways to interfere with a practitioner's cultivation of the path.

mind-moment: See *kṣaṇa*.

mahorāga: *Mahorāgas* are a type of serpent spirit often portrayed as having the upper body of a human and the lower body of a snake.

N

nayuta: A very large number, usually defined as a one hundred billion.

nirvāṇa: Nirvāṇa is the ultimate goal of the path of Buddhist spiritual cultivation that corresponds to the elimination of the three poisons (covetousness, aversion, delusion) and the ending of compulsory and random rebirth in *saṃsāra*, the cycle of existences in the deva realm, the demigod realm, the human realm, the animal realm, the hungry ghost realm, and the hell realms.

In the case of the individual liberation path practitioner exemplified by arhats and *pratyekabuddhas*, all future existence ends for them with the acquisition of nirvāṇa.

In the case of the universal liberation practitioners exemplified by bodhisattvas and buddhas, they achieve the direct cognition of the emptiness of all beings and phenomena and realize an ongoing realization of a nirvana-like state even as, by force of vow, they continue to take on intentional rebirths within *saṃsāra* in order to facilitate the spiritual liberation of all beings.

nirvāṇa without residue: The final nirvāṇa realized at death by fully awakened beings whether they be arhats, *pratyekabuddhas*, or buddhas.

nivāsana robe: The *nivāsana* is the monastic's skirt-like inner robe.

O

once-returner: See *sākṛdāgāmin*.

P

pāramitā: One of the six (or ten) "perfections" cultivated and perfected by the bodhisattva on the path to buddhahood.

Paranirmita Vaśavartin Heaven: The Paranirmita Vaśavartin Heaven is the sixth of the six desire realm heavens. PDB: "The heaven of the gods who have power over the creations of others, or the gods who partake of the pleasures created in other heavens."

piśāca: PDB: "In Sanskrit, "flesh-eater," a class of ogres or goblins, similar to rākṣasa and yakṣa, who eat human flesh." The female is called *piśācī*.

prajñā: Prajnā is the world-transcending wisdom that cognizes and understands all phenomena associated with "self," others, and the world as they truly are and in accordance with ultimate reality.

prajñā pāramitā: The perfection of wisdom.

pratyekabuddha: One who, in the absence of a buddha or his Dharma, achieves a level of enlightenment comparable to that of an arhat, doing so on his own through the contemplation of the cycle of dependent origination (*pratītyasamutpāda*). Mahāyāna literature attributes this ability to awaken in the absence of a buddha or his Dharma to direct exposure to the Dharma in previous lives, the seeds of which enable enlightenment in the present life.

pratyutpanna samādhi: The *pratyutpanna* samādhi is a samādhi wherein one becomes able to see the buddhas of the present and listen to them teach the Dharma.

provisions (for enlightenment): The provisions for enlightenment (*bodhisaṃbhāra*) are the spiritual prerequisites for enlightenment that must be accumulated in order to fully realize the path to buddhahood. These are usually considered to be merit (*puṇya*) and knowledge (*jñāna*).

pūtana: Per PDB: "Stinking hungry demons."

R

rākṣasa: A swift flying malignant flesh-eating demon which changes its form to seduce humans and eat them.

S

sakṛdāgāmin: The *sakṛdāgāmin* or "once-returner" is one who has gained the third of the four fruits of the individual-liberation path of the śrāvaka disciple.

samādhi: Samādhi refers both to any single instance of one-pointed concentration and also, more usually, to enduring states of persistently maintained one-pointed concentration.

saṃghāṭī robe: The *saṃghāṭī* is the monastic's outer robe.

saṃkakṣikā robe: The *saṃkakṣikā* is the monastic's robe that is worn over the left shoulder and under the right arm.

saṃsāra: Saṃsāra, for which the usual Sino-Buddhist rendering is "births-and-deaths," *shengsi* (生死), refers to the endless cycle of rebirths in the six realms of rebirth: devas (gods), *asuras* ("demi-gods" or "titans"), humans, animals, hungry ghosts (*preta*), and hell-dwellers.

Sangha: A community of at least ten fully ordained bhikshus in Buddhist countries or at least five fully ordained bhikshus in countries where Buddhism is only just being established for the first time. As the third object of refuge in "the Three Refuges" or "the Three Jewels," this refers exclusively to those persons who have already acquired one of the fruits of the path from which they can never fall away, whether on the individual-liberation paths of the arhats or *pratyekabuddhas*, or on the bodhisattva path.

śarīra: Śarīra are the remains or "relics" of eminent monks, bodhisattvas, or buddhas that are contained in their cremation ashes.

seven enlightenment factors: assessment or skillful selection of dharmas; vigor; joy; mental pliancy; concentration; equanimity with respect to the saṃskāra (karmic formative factors) aggregate.

śīla pāramitā: The perfection of moral virtue.

six rebirth destinies: gods (*deva*), demi-gods or titans (*asura*), humans, hungry ghosts (*pretas*), animals, and hell-dwellers.

skandha: See "aggregates."

skillful means: "Skillful means" (*upāya*) are individually tailored skillful techniques adopted by the bodhisattva in teaching the various kinds of beings. These various techniques are adopted precisely because all beings are possessed of different capacities, karmic obstacles and predilections due to which they respond best to individually tailored teachings.

spiritual superknowledges: The usual Sanskrit antecedent for "spiritual superknowledges" is *abhijñā* ("superknowledges") or *rddhi* ("supernatural powers"). This includes such abilities as "the six superknowledges" (the spiritual powers, the heavenly eye, the heavenly ear, the cognition of others' thoughts, past life recall for both self and others, and complete elimination of all "defiling contaminants" or "taints" [*āsrava*]).

śramaṇa: More generally, a *śramaṇa* is a mendicant, one who has left the home life and relies on alms for sustenance. In the Buddhist context, this refers specifically to a bhikshu, i.e. a Buddhist monk.

śrāvaka, *śrāvaka* disciple: A follower of the individual-liberation path to arhatship.

stream enterer: The stream enterer (*srota-āpanna*) is one who has gained the first of the four fruits of the path to arhatship.

śūdra: A member of the fourth and lowest caste of traditional Indian culture consisting primarily of servants and such.

sutra: A scripture attributed to the Buddha.

T

tathatā: "Suchness," i.e. the true nature of the ultimate reality of any and all things as it really is.

Tathāgata: *"Tathāgata"* ("Thus Come One") is one of the ten primary titles by which all buddhas are known.

Ten directions: North, south, east, west, the four midpoints, the zenith, and the nadir.

Thirty-seven wings of enlightenment / thirty-seven enlightenment factors: These consist of: the four stations of mindfulness; the four right efforts; the four bases of supernatural powers; the five faculties; the five powers; the seven enlightenment factors; and the eightfold path of the Āryas.

Three Jewels: The Buddha, the Dharma, and the Ārya Sangha.

Three periods of time: Past, present, and future.

Three Refuges: The Buddha, the Dharma, and the Ārya Sangha, the Three Jewels in which one "takes the refuges" to become a Buddhist disciple and upon which one must rely to advance on the Buddhist path.

Three Vehicles: The Śrāvaka-disciple Vehicle, the Pratyekabuddha Vehicle, and the Great Vehicle (Mahāyāna) the endpoints of which are arhatship, pratyekabuddhahood, and Buddhahood.

three wretched destinies: The three wretched destinies are rebirth as either an animal, a hungry ghost (*preta*), or a hell dweller.

trichiliocosm: A world system consisting of countless worlds.

tripiṭaka: The three divisions of the three-fold Buddhist canon, otherwise known as "the Tripiṭaka": the sutras (scriptures attributed to the Buddha or disciples authorized by the Buddha), the commentarial treatises (śāstra), and the moral codes (vinaya).

tripiṭaka master: A "tripiṭaka master" is someone who has completely mastered the three divisions of the three-fold Buddhist canon.

twelve sense bases: the six sense faculties (eye, ear, nose, tongue, body, and mind) and their respective sense objects (visual forms, sounds, smells, tastes, touchables, and ideas, etc. as objects of mind).

Two Vehicles: The two individual liberation vehicles taught by the Buddha, the Śrāvaka-disciple Vehicle leading to arhatship and the Pratyekabuddha Vehicle leading to pratyekabuddhahood.

V

vaiśya: A member of the third caste in traditional Indian culture comprised primarily of the merchant and agricultural classes.

vajra: An indestructible substance equated with the diamond. A symbol of indestructibility. Also, a pestle shaped sceptre or "thunderbolt" weapon held by Dharma protectors and deities.

vibhāṣā: A *vibhāṣā* is an extensively detailed explanatory treatise.

vinaya: The Buddhist moral codes.

vīrya pāramitā: The perfection of vigor.

W

wheel-turning king: In Buddhism, a "wheel-turning king" (*cakravartin*) is a universal monarch.

worthy: In Mahāyāna literature, a "worthy" (*bhadra*) is a bodhisattva practitioner who has brought forth the bodhisattva vow but who is still cultivating the preparatory stages and thus has not yet reached the ten bodhisattva grounds and has not yet become an ārya.

Y

yakṣa: Yakṣas are a kind of either good or evil spirit possessed of supernatural powers that may either serve as a guardian or a demon.

yojana: A measure of distance in ancient India usually defined as being the distance that an ox cart would travel in a day without unharnessing (somewhat less than ten miles).

About the Translator

Bhikshu Dharmamitra (ordination name "Heng Shou" – 釋恆授) is a Chinese-tradition translator-monk and one of the earliest American disciples (since 1968) of the late Guiyang Ch'an patriarch, Dharma teacher, and pioneer of Buddhism in the West, the Venerable Master Hsuan Hua (宣化上人). He has a total of 33 years in robes during two periods as a monastic (1969–1975 & 1991 to the present).

Dharmamitra's principal educational foundations as a translator of Sino-Buddhist Classical Chinese lie in four years of intensive monastic training and Chinese-language study of classic Mahāyāna texts in a small-group setting under Master Hsuan Hua (1968–1972), undergraduate Chinese language study at Portland State University, a year of intensive one-on-one Classical Chinese study at the Fu Jen University Language Center near Taipei, two years of course work at the University of Washington's Department of Asian Languages and Literature (1988–90), and an additional three years of auditing graduate courses and seminars in Classical Chinese readings, again at UW's Department of Asian Languages and Literature.

Since taking robes again under Master Hua in 1991, Dharmamitra has devoted his energies primarily to study and translation of classic Mahāyāna texts with a special interest in works by Ārya Nāgārjuna and related authors. To date, he has translated more than fifteen important texts comprising approximately 150 fascicles, including most recently the 80-fascicle *Avataṃsaka Sūtra* (the "Flower Adornment Sutra"), Nāgārjuna's 17-fascicle *Daśabhūmika Vibhāśa* ("Treatise on the Ten Grounds"), and the *Daśabhūmika Sūtra* (the "Ten Grounds Sutra"), all of which are current or upcoming Kalavinka Press publications.

Kalavinka Buddhist Classics
(http: www.kalavinka.org)
Fall, 2019 Title List

Meditation Instruction Texts

The Essentials of Buddhist Meditation
A marvelously complete classic *śamathā-vipaśyanā* (calming-and-insight) meditation manual. By Tiantai Śramaṇa Zhiyi (538–597).

Six Gates to the Sublime
The early Indian Buddhist meditation method involving six practices used in calming-and-insight meditation. By Śramaṇa Zhiyi

Bodhisattva Path Texts

On Generating the Resolve to Become a Buddha
On the Resolve to Become a Buddha by Ārya Nāgārjuna
Exhortation to Resolve on Buddhahood by Patriarch Sheng'an Shixian
Exhortation to Resolve on Buddhahood by the Tang Literatus, Peixiu

Letter from a Friend - The Three Earliest Editions
The earliest extant editions of Ārya Nāgārjuna's *Suhṛlekkha*:
  Translated by Tripiṭaka Master Guṇavarman (ca 425 CE)
  Translated by Tripiṭaka Master Saṅghavarman (ca 450 CE)
  Translated by Tripiṭaka Master Yijing (ca 675 CE).

Marvelous Stories from the Perfection of Wisdom
130 Stories from Ārya Nāgārjuna's *Mahāprājñāpāramitā Upadeśa*.

Nāgārjuna's Guide to the Bodhisattva Path
The *Bodhisaṃbhāra Treatise* with abridged Vaśitva commentary.

The Bodhisaṃbhāra Treatise Commentary
The complete exegesis by the Indian Bhikshu Vaśitva (ca 300–500).

Nāgārjuna on Mindfulness of the Buddha
Ch. 9 and Chs. 20–25 of Nāgārjuna's *Daśabhūmika Vibhāṣā*
Ch. 1, Subchapter 36a of Nāgārjuna's *Mahāprājñāpāramitā Upadeśa*.

Nāgārjuna on the Six Perfections
Chapters 17–30 of Ārya Nāgārjuna's *Mahāprājñāpāramitā Upadeśa*.

A Strand of Dharma Jewels (Ārya Nāgārjuna's *Ratnāvalī*)
The earliest extant edition, translated by Paramārtha: ca 550 CE

The Ten Bodhisattva Grounds
Śikṣānanda's translation of The Flower Adornment Sutra, Ch. 26

Nāgārjuna's Treatise on theThe Ten Bodhisattva Grounds
Nāgārjuna's 35-chapter *Daśabhūmika Vibhāṣā*

The Ten Grounds Sutra
Kumārajīva's translation of the *Daśabhūmika Sūtra*

Vasubandhu's Treatise on the Bodhisattva Vow
By Vasubandhu Bodhisattva (*ca* 300 CE)

www.ingramcontent.com/pod-product-compliance
Lightning Source LLC
Chambersburg PA
CBHW031609160426
43196CB00006B/71